1989

Yearbook
of Science
and the
Future

1989

Yearbook
of Science
and the
Future

Encyclopædia

Britannica, Inc.

Chicago
Auckland
Geneva
London
Manila
Paris
Rome
Seoul
Sydney
Tokyo
Toronto

1989

Yearbook of Science and the Future

Editor
David Calhoun

Associate Editor
Charles Cegielski

Editorial Staff
Daphne Daume, Karen Justin, Arthur Latham

Art Director
Cynthia Peterson

Planning Analyst
Marsha Check

Senior Picture Editor
Kathy Nakamura

Picture Editor
La Bravia Jenkins

Layout Artist
Dale Horn

Illustrators
Anne H. Becker, John L. Draves, Curtis E. Hardy

Art Production
Richard A. Roiniotis

Art Staff
Amy B. Brown, Amy I. Brown, Daniel M. Delgado, Patricia A. Henle, Paul Rios

Director, Yearbook Production and Control
J. Thomas Beatty

Manager, Copy Department
Anita Wolff

Senior Copy Editors
Julian Ronning, Barbara Whitney

Copy Staff
Elizabeth A. Blowers, Madolynn Cronk, Ellen Finkelstein, Anthony L. Green, Patrick Joyce, Elizabeth Laskey

Manager, Copy Control
Mary C. Srodon

Copy Control Staff
Marilyn L. Barton, Lisa A. Hatfield

Manager, Composition and Page Makeup
Melvin Stagner

Coordinator, Composition and Page Makeup
Philip Rehmer

Composition Staff
Duangnetra Debhavalya, Morna Freund, John Krom, Jr., Thomas Mulligan, Gwen Rosenberg, Tammy Tsou

Encyclopædia Britannica, Inc.

Contents

Encyclopædia Britannica Science Update

The Science Year in Review

A Science Classic

Institutions of Science

The Scientific Tradition in

ART

by Jeannette Murray

Artists today are enlisting elements of science to open creative vistas and reach for novel understandings of our world. Yet the idea itself is not new; it springs from a rich tradition of science in painting and sculpture.

James Turrell, an American artist in his mid-40s, has a volcanic vision—literally. Not content to create within the limits of a canvas or even within the three-dimensional world afforded by sculpture, Turrell convinced a wealthy U.S.-based art foundation in 1977 to purchase a piece of Arizona landscape for his own private use. Today he flies out to Arizona and takes an all-terrain vehicle to the site, which is located between the sands of the Painted Desert and the San Francisco Volcanic Field. Called Roden Crater, it is the remnant of a dormant volcano, rising almost 6,000 feet above sea level. (One foot is about 0.305 meters.) Once there, he oversees the shaping of the crater into a perfect circle, the smoothing of the inner walls, and the building of ramps, tunnels, and chambers at its base.

If his funding holds out for the next five or ten years, Turrell will have created a unique environment: on a clear night a visitor lying in a kind of bathtub in one of the chambers at the base of the volcano will actually hear the sounds of the stars visible overhead. The artist intends to convert their radio energy into acoustic vibrations, which will resonate in the bathwater. Or a person might stand at the end of a thousand-foot tunnel the artist is carving out of the crater bottom and see the Moon exactly fill the entire mouth of the tunnel. Being there on the right day is important, however, since the event will occur only once every 18.61 years. Alternatively, a person might view a "star painting." One chamber in the crater will double as a celestial observatory, oriented in such a way that someone standing within it can watch the natural colors of actual stars play across the walls.

But what exactly is Turrell making? Is it art? Architecture? Science? Or is it all these things? Turrell certainly sees it as art, an elaborate—and, he feels, ingenious and moving—example of the kind of contemporary effort known as an earthwork. Artists worldwide have been building

JEANNETTE MURRAY, an artist and writer, is Art Adviser to the American Association for the Advancement of Science.

(Overleaf) "Phenomenon of Anti-Gravity," oil on canvas by Remedios Varo, 1963; 75.64 × 49.68 cm; private collection. Painting, courtesy of Walter Gruen; photo, courtesy, Unexpected Journeys by Janet Kaplan, Abbeville Press

10

earthworks for well over a decade. Their intent is to evoke an emotional response based on what they contend is a primal human need for orientation with one's natural environment, a need to feel a part of, and connected to, one's surroundings. So, in one form or another, "earth-artists" shape a landscape and thus make art.

Turrell brings to this pursuit a lifelong fascination with several sciences. At Roden Crater the most obvious science is astronomy. Working with the advice of an astrophysicist, he is literally bringing in the cosmos as a collaborator—the stars to paint his sculpted walls with color and the Sun and Moon periodically to accept roles as elements in a celestial canvas framed by his sculptured chambers and tunnels. However, he also wants to force the Earth itself, his shaped crater, to create visual effects for human observers. For this purpose he turns to another branch of science that has absorbed him for a quarter century: perception theory. As an observer walks down Roden's carefully shaped inner slope, heading from the crater rim to the bottom of the bowl, the sky appears to lower like a giant lid, descending into the crater until it seems almost within reach. The explanation is a trick of the eye (an earthwork trompe l'oeil) called the homogeneous field effect.

It was Turrell's manipulation of the homogeneous field that first brought him prominence in the art world. In 1980, at the invitation of New York City's Whitney Museum of American Art, he constructed a series of chambers, most the size of small rooms, and filled them with light, usually of a single shade. Throughout his career he has used a variety of light ranging from the natural—moonlight as well as sunlight—to the artificial—argon, quartz halogen, tungsten, and fluorescent. By manipulating the dimensions of the chambers and the illumination, he created what are called "light mists." The fields of view inside the chambers would appear alternately transparent and opaque to the eye of someone inside. Viewers sometimes experienced an illusion of solidity so powerful

Aerial view (opposite page) looks north over Roden Crater, a dormant volcano near Flagstaff, Arizona. Artist James Turrell is reshaping the natural feature into an elaborate earthwork imbued with concepts and technology drawn from astronomy, archaeology, and perception theory. (Below) "Wedgework III," a chamber whose inner space is partitioned and modified by light, offers an example of Turrell's longtime fascination with the power of illumination and space to create visual effects for the observer.

(Opposite page) By courtesy of the Skystone Foundation; photo, James Turrell; (below) installation view of "Wedgework III" by James Turrell, 1969, from the exhibition James Turrell: Light & Space at the Whitney Museum of American Art; photo, Jon Cliett, New York City

that they tried to lean on nonexistent walls. In fact, three visitors to the
exhibition filed suits when they fell after trying to support themselves on
a light mist. At Roden Crater, Turrell is exploiting the greatest natural
homogeneous field of all, the sky. Framed by the artificial horizon of
the crater rim, the sky seen from the bottom of the crater appears to
hang just overhead.

The key to Turrell's success has been his ability to yoke science to
art. While in college, he had learned about early 20th-century work on
the homogeneous field, the visual equivalent of white noise. These fields
are featureless "undifferentiated surrounds" of the kind occasionally experienced by pilots flying over the Antarctic or by travelers engulfed in
a blinding snowstorm. Called whiteouts, these natural effects can totally
disorient the portion of the human brain that distinguishes direction and
calculates distance. The Gestalt psychologists of the 1930s had hoped
that study of the phenomenon would reveal something of the nature
of the visual experience. Experimental work continued into the 1950s,
when a typical technique used to generate the fields was to tape split
table-tennis balls over the eyes of a subject and project light onto them.
Because psychologists found it hard to measure and categorize their
subjects' reactions, however, this line of research languished. Turrell
rediscovered it as a college student. In 1968 he entered into collaboration with physiological psychologist Ed Wortz and artist Robert Irwin to
explore what could be made of homogeneous fields. Thus, the science
already existed, but it took the artist to devise ways to bring that science
into the experience of the observer.

The process of making science work hand in glove with artistic creativity seems to have suddenly blossomed in an extraordinary variety of
forms. Across the globe artists are blending theories of art and science
and achieving both public approbation and critical acclaim. Many work

12

in more traditional media and on a more conventional scale than Turrell. Others have struck out in different directions, using traditional materials to express abstract scientific theory or to portray the unobservable—the fourth dimension, for example—as if in homage to their medieval forebears who had been commissioned to render for their patrons the unobservable affairs of heaven. Placed in the context of the 20,000-year-old tradition of art, such efforts are neither radical nor isolated statements. Rather they are part of a surprisingly rich and consistent tradition of science in art.

In the beginning: science, art, and magic

From earliest times art has been the servant of knowledge, ever on hand to express fresh and profound understandings. In the contemporary world, where science is generally accepted as the epitome of human knowledge, it is relatively easy to see the way in which art both reflects and employs current scientific principles either explicitly or implicitly. For much of human history, however, science was an often distrusted, even vilified, element of the human belief structure, forced to hide below the surface of codified religion or, before that, of magical constructs. Still, science has always been at the call of the artist. To perceive science in early artworks—ones inevitably expressing magical or religious themes—one need only look past their content to the inescapable sciences of tools, materials, techniques, and observation. Even thousands of years before the modern scientific method was developed, artists had no choice but to apply their sensory experiences and empirical investigations of the natural world to humanity's very first artistic expressions. It is in those expressions that can be discovered many elements of the tradition upon which today's artists stand.

Perhaps the first instance of the interweaving of art and science occurs in the spectacular and moving images of animals and occasionally of humans and weapons applied to smoky cave walls in ice-age Europe 10,000–15,000 years ago. According to paleoanthropologists, the people of these artistic cultures believed that they could ensure abundant prey and future hunting success by depicting their quarry—in some instances even the moment of the kill—on the walls of a sacred cave. In this case art was being used to support magic, but the magic nevertheless subsumed the early human's scientific knowledge. The artists had to observe their subjects carefully, because without a certain verisimilitude in the depictions, the spirits might ignore or reject them. For much the same reason, they had to use their knowledge of pigments and their application, hard won by trial and error, to work their art successfully. The modern observer cannot but marvel over the discovery by Stone Age artists that painting on natural rock projections would turn their two-dimensional depictions of animals into reliefs that seem to leap from the surface.

The Greeks and Romans, more than any other pre-Christian civilization, were able to rise above superstition and openly employ scientific principles in their art. Their mastery of observational knowledge is clearly demonstrated in their frescoes, mosaics, and sculptures, which

Wall tilings from the Alhambra, a palace-fortress built by the Moorish rulers of Granada in the 13th and 14th centuries, display patterns now known to correspond to types of symmetry found in the atomic arrangements of crystalline materials.

Photos, Haeseler Art Publishers/Art Resource

13

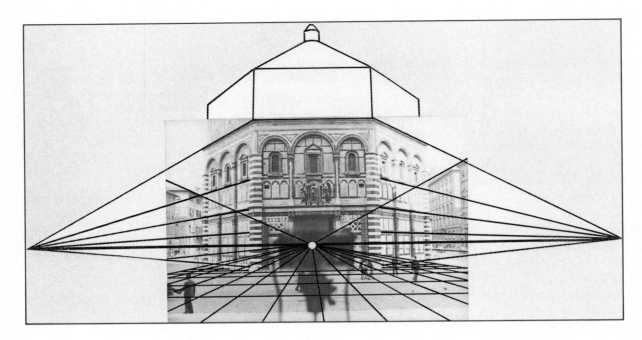

often approach high realism as well as achieving aesthetic beauty. Yet the classical writings that exist today contain little to indicate that Greek and Roman artists understood the scientific principles of optics and perspective. While there is evidence that Ptolemy and other classical scientists knew about geometric perspective, they apparently applied it only to mapmaking and stage design. What elegant use of perspective exists in classical art may well have been unconscious.

Except for such occasional flowering of humanism and scientific inquiry, art and science remained bound to magic and religion until the Renaissance. The Islamic world, for example, produced some highly sophisticated scientific thinkers but in a culture religiously driven and artistically hamstrung. Interestingly, although the Arab mosaicists who decorated mosques to the glory of Allah were barred from naturalistic images, they turned to intricate patterns that are now recognized as implicit in every known variety of symmetrical crystalline structure. It was only in the 19th century that scientists identified the various types of symmetry in crystals, and much more time passed before anyone noticed their correspondences in Islamic art. Meanwhile, the great thinkers of medieval Europe were busily studying both magic and science within a religious context, and once again artists were feverishly serving religion. It took the experimentalist spirit of such people as Roger Bacon, in the 13th century, to begin moving magical thought toward applied knowledge, proposing naturalistic explanations for previously unexplained phenomena. All the while, however, medieval artists remained so obsessed with the supernatural that they could scarcely match the scientific sophistication of their cave-painting ancestors.

The rise of science

With the coming of the Renaissance, the transition to modern science began, and the wall separating natural from supernatural phenomena was removed, brick by brick. Both artist and scientist were now able to

study the world with new eyes, unencumbered by superstition and the restraints of the past. As the search for knowledge and enlightenment became supreme, art and science commingled with increasing success. One obvious example was the rediscovery of linear perspective and its conscious application to art. Art scholars take the word of Renaissance painter and art historian Giorgio Vasari that the event occurred in 1425, when Filippo Brunelleschi painted Florence's exquisite baptistry from a viewing point located inside a doorway of the adjacent Duomo, the city's main cathedral. Brunelleschi would not have called himself a painter. In fact, he was a model of the early Renaissance "artisan-engineer" and the designer of the magnificent dome of the Cathedral of Santa Maria del Fiore, the most advanced feat of architectural engineering of its time. One day, as an exercise, he carried an easel, a small wooden panel, a miniaturist's paintbrush, and some small flat mirrors into the Duomo. Standing with his back to the baptistry and framing its reflection in a mirror positioned next to the wooden panel, he produced a small painting on wood that demonstrated the way realistic perspectives could be achieved by observation of nature's geometry. The original panel unfortunately has been lost, and Brunelleschi did not himself capitalize on this discovery. His demonstration had an extensive influence on the future of Western art, science, and technology, however, for he passed it on to his friends, the painters Masaccio and Masolino and the sculptor Donatello. From that time on, every competent Renaissance painter came to use perspective almost as second nature.

Another aspect of the "legitimization" of the interdependence of art and science is based indirectly on the rediscovery of the artworks of classical Greece. Whereas a medieval artist interested in observing nature would be suspect, Renaissance appreciation of classical objets d'art made clear the great value of careful observation of nature by an accomplished man of culture. This idea, for which Leonardo da Vinci has come to be the embodiment, was reflected with unparalleled brilliance not merely

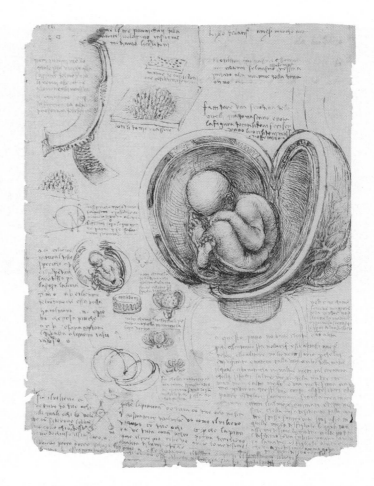

in his paintings but also in his extraordinary achievements in such fields as engineering, botany, geology, biology, and meteorology. The pages of his sketchbooks, which record his investigations of everything from human anatomy to the nature of flight, are both works of art and scientific documents.

If there was ever a single time and place in which scientific inquiry became so all-pervasive that science and art were inseparable, however, that time was the 17th century, and the place was Holland. The Dutch artists of that period pursued artistic concerns in the everyday, observable world and beyond into heretofore unknown worlds being revealed by explorers and scientists. The Dutch were practically inclined, dependent on the navigational sciences—astronomy, geometry, cartography, and the like—to maintain their thriving global trade. The map is, in fact, a recurrent image in 17th-century Dutch painting. Furthermore, as the Dutch charted routes to such lands as the West Indies and Brazil, they commissioned maps embellished with astronomy, city views, costumes, and flora and fauna—works that blurred the distinction between the ends of cartography and art.

One development of the Renaissance that had a strong effect on the worlds of Dutch art and science was the application of lenses and mirrors

to astronomy, microscopy, and optical phenomena. Aspects of nature formerly unobservable because of immense distance or minute size could now be studied with the telescope and Antonie van Leeuwenhoek's remarkable magnifying lenses. Lenses, mirrors, and prisms were employed by Christiaan Huygens and others as laboratory tools for probing the nature of light. Concurrently, the artists of northern Europe became fascinated with lenses and reflecting surfaces—mirrors, glass vials, jewels, and eyeglasses—and took great delight in capturing on canvas the power of these objects to create and distort images.

The paintings of the extraordinary Jan Vermeer have been said to express a scientist's knowledge of the observable. Each work seems a scientific treatise, a visual summary of results and conclusions from analytic experiments with light and microscopic observations of matter. Their perspectives suggest those seen in modern photographs taken with wide-angle and telephoto lenses. (Leeuwenhoek was executor of Vermeer's will, a relation that suggests a friendship of the two men and a familiarity of Vermeer with the lens maker's discoveries.) Vermeer also portrayed the scientific setting with great care. In "The Astronomer" (1668) Vermeer includes a globe of the heavens that was painted directly from a globe produced by Jodocus Hondius in 1600. On the table lie an astrolabe and a pair of dividers. In the painting of a geographer that forms a pair with this work, there appears the terrestrial mate to the celestial globe (the two were produced as a set), accompanied by charts and cartographic instruments.

Scientific objects were more than a subject for painters; some found their way into the artist's toolbox. As an aid to his preliminary drawings, Vermeer used a camera obscura, which by the 17th century had taken

Detail of a map of Brazil is from Kleucke Atlas, *a Dutch atlas published in 1647. As Dutch geographers of the 17th century charted the new worlds being revealed by exploration, they commissioned maps whose exquisite artistry blurred the distinction between the purposes of cartography and art.*

17

the form of a darkened box or chamber fitted with an arrangement of lenses and mirrors. The device projected a reduced image of its field of view onto a flat surface, on which an artist could trace a precise and detailed drawing. Cartographers of the 16th and 17th centuries also used projected images in their work.

In the mid-19th century a new science entered the world of art, one that was to have a profound influence on early modernist painting. The development of scientific psychology created a framework for the rigorous artistic study of the elements of light and color. This research made its appearance in many canvases. The French Impressionist painter Camille Pissarro states, "Surely it is clear that we could not pursue our studies of light with much assurance if we did not have as a guide the discoveries of Chevreul and other scientists." Michel-Eugène Chevreul's great contribution to art was a systematic study of the perceptual effects of adjacent colors. In the work of Neo-Impressionist Georges Seurat, this research was a cornerstone of his pointillist theory. Seurat was a serious student of contemporary visual science. The surfaces of such paintings as "Sunday Afternoon on the Island of La Grande Jatte" (1884–86) were conceived of as abstract screens composed of tiny, discrete color cells that radiated light like the array of phosphor dots in the picture tubes of modern color television sets. Seurat may well have been influenced by primitive color photographs of the day. The use of dots of the three primary colors to create color halftones had, in fact, been invented in France in 1869.

Modern times: the return of the unseen

The 20th century ought to go down in art history as unique in its pluralism. In just one form, painting, art has moved from Cubism through

Futurism and Surrealism to abstraction (with its absorption with the surface of painting) and Abstract Expressionism, thence to Op and Pop art (with their obsession with images), and finally back to realism, albeit Neo-Realist Expressionism. If there is one truth, it is that every tradition in art has been fair game to be tried, rebelled against, and tried again. Many see Cubism as a direct rebellion against the Renaissance portrayal of the world in geometric perspective. For 500 years artists had been captive to the concept of painting as an imitation of visual reality. Finally they began to ask: What is illusion and what is reality? In painting, for example, is reality the image depicted on the canvas and formed in the mind of the spectator, or is it simply the surface of the canvas, the very brushstrokes themselves?

To express these radical questions, Cubists dismantled three-dimensional forms into flat planes deliberately to emphasize the surface reality of painting. The result left much to the observer's intuition and, for the first time in half a millennium, reintroduced the idea of the unseen and the abstract into art. This time, however, the concept of an unobservable reality was no longer antiscience or beyond science, for science itself had proposed it.

The Cubists lived in the age of Einstein and quantum theory. Although they may not have wholly comprehended or been consciously interested in the convention-shattering changes taking place in understanding the "reality" of time, space, and matter, they—like all good artists—were sensitive to their environment. In the new physics, time and space were

Vermeer's careful portrayals of the scientific setting of his time include (above left) "The Astronomer," painted in 1668, and (above) "The Geographer," done a year later.

wedded in a geometry having seen and unseen dimensions. Apparently "straight" lines and "flat" space curved invisibly under the influence of gravitational fields. Two different people observing the same event might measure different times and distances. Even matter was ambiguous, acting like particles in some circumstances and like waves in others. In an age where twisting objects into Möbius strips and Klein bottles could change the number of their surfaces and the dimensional space they occupied, a painting that transformed three-dimensional objects to two and glorified its own two-dimensionality could hardly be called antiscientific.

The scientific basis of the Cubist approach to painting can also be seen more directly in Pablo Picasso's and Georges Braque's intuitive mastery of aspects of the new understanding of perception, for example, those expressed in theories of figure-ground ambiguity. Even as these artists were breaking with the past, Danish psychologist Edgard Rubin established between 1912 and 1920 that ordinary visual experience has two primary parts, the figure and the ground. The figure is seen as an object surrounded by a contour, and the ground is seen as an undifferentiated field behind the figure. This scientific principle, among others, lies at the very core of Cubism.

Not all early 20th-century giants turned to scientific principles in a purely intuitive way, however, and not all wanted to probe beneath the surface of the world that science was revealing. For example, in the 1920s the machine was seen as a symbol of all that was positive and exciting in the modern age, and one group of artists, the Precisionists, turned toward technology to discover a new visual language. In the work of Charles Sheeler, for example, the machine is transformed into a glorious, elegant icon. His factory scenes, reduced to their sparsest elements, are admiring symbols of the expanding world of industry.

Nineteenth-century research in visual science became a cornerstone of Georges Seurat's pointillist painting technique. In such works as "Sunday Afternoon on the Island of La Grande Jatte" (above), he applied pigment to the canvas in discreet dots of contrasting colors that were designed to blend from a distance into solid color fields while radiating a brilliant, vibrating light.

"Sunday Afternoon on the Island of La Grande Jatte," oil on canvas by Georges Seurat, 1884–86, 207.6 X 308 cm; Helen Birch Bartlett Memorial Collection, © 1987 The Art Institute of Chicago

Meanwhile, other artists of the period consciously looked to science to help them see truths beneath the surface of technology all around them. In 1920 Paul Klee published his "Creative Credo" wherein he tried to express the nature of underlying perceptual processes: "Art does not reproduce the visible, rather it makes visible. . . . We reveal the reality behind visible things." In that year he joined the Bauhaus school, a group of influential artists who were powerfully affected by current developments in visual science. The stated purpose of the Bauhaus movement, which had been started in Germany by architect Walter Gropius, was to combine art and technology. Painter Wassily Kandinsky, another member, focused on mathematics and the relationship of straight and curved lines in space, themes that at the time were in the avant-garde of scientific thought. He sought mathematical formulations to describe analogous structures in nature and art, and in his later work he raided the biologic sciences for microscopic images. His painting "Environment," for example, is strongly suggestive of a living cell.

Still other modern painters refocused their artistic vision to include more than just the scientifically unseen. In so doing they recast, for their own uses, positively medieval concerns, once again permitting the supernatural to join the perceptually unobservable on the canvas.

In Picasso's "Ambroise Vollard" (above left) and Braque's "Young Girl with a Guitar" (above), three-dimensional forms are dismantled into flat planes to emphasize the two-dimensionality of the painting surface. The Cubists' reintroduction of unseen realities into the art of the early 20th century parallels the changes in the scientific understanding of reality that were being wrought by Einstein and the founders of quantum theory.

(Left) "Ambroise Vollard" by Pablo Picasso, 1909-10; in the collection of the Pushkin Museum, Moscow; photo, Kavaler/Art Resource, copyright ARS N.Y./ SPADEM, 1988; (right) "Young Girl with Guitar" by Georges Braque, 1913; photo, Musée National d'Art Moderne, Centre Georges Pompidou, Paris, copyright ARS N.Y./ADAGP, 1988

Nevertheless, their work did not reject science and in many cases welcomed it, creating a wholly new blend of magic (in the mystical sense), art, and science.

One such artist, who recently enjoyed a posthumous rediscovery with exhibits at the New York Academy of Sciences and the National Academy of Sciences, Washington, D.C., is Remedios Varo. Born in Spain in 1908, Varo lived in a family that embodied the commingling seen in her art. Her father was an engineer and atheist, her mother a devout Catholic who believed in the devil and sent her to a convent school. From her father came lifelong interests in astronomy, physics, mathematics, engineering, biology, and psychoanalysis. From convent life and her mother's spiritual fervor came an absorption in the metaphysical world, mysticism, alchemy, and reincarnation. All this became source material for her painting after she fled the convent for a Madrid art school, and it continued to be central to her work through successive flights from the Spanish Civil War and Nazi-occupied France to Mexico, where she lived until her death in 1963.

Varo's theme in many paintings seems to be the human's relationship to the cosmos. Everywhere are objects scientific in appearance but magical in operation—cogs, wheels, spheres, bottles, and retorts that evoke a world both rational and supernatural. In "Phenomenon of Anti-Gravity" she pictures a scientist and a globe—images reminiscent of Vermeer but involved in a very different experience. The alarmed man finds his globe being drawn to the open window by a mysterious floating object. The

Painted by Wassily Kandinsky in 1923, ''Composition 8'' (above) probes the relationship of straight and curved lines in space and their underlying mathematics—topics that at the time were in the forefront of scientific thought. Kandinsky's amoeba-like ''Environment'' (right), from 1936, seems to reflect on the microscopic world of, and within, the living cell.

Earth has shifted its axis, and he is left straddling two dimensions. The setting, as in much of Varo's other work, is not so much post-Renaissance as medieval in architecture, clothing, and style of representation. Perhaps the concerns are likewise more medieval than rational, for this is a world of alchemy and astrology, science embracing the sacred.

Varo has great respect for science but cannot cede to it the sole power of governing the universe. ''Fabric of Space-Time'' once again contains her weird blend: two medieval figures appear out of the crisscrossed threads of the universe. The only straight line in the fabric, the axis of time, passes through a cuckoo clock. The other threads bend in arcs reflecting the curvature of space. In her late work ''Still Life Reviving,'' which is surely one of her most striking accomplishments, she expresses her concern with the coexistence of the mythic and the scientific. It was painted after she had read a book by British astronomer Fred Hoyle on the nature of the expanding universe. According to Hoyle's so-called steady-state theory, the universe is a constantly growing entity with no beginning and no end. In contrast to earlier predictions of the big-bang theorists, the universe will not perish in a massive gravitational collapse, nor will it die a thermodynamic ''heat death,'' running out of usable

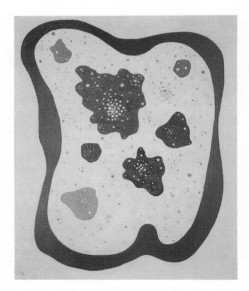

(Top) ''Composition 8,'' oil on canvas by Wassily Kandinsky, July 1923, 141.3 X 202.9 cm; (bottom) ''Environment,'' oil on canvas by Wassily Kandinsky, October 1936, 100.6 X 82.05 cm; both paintings in the collection of the Solomon R. Guggenheim Museum, New York; photos, David Heald

energy. Varo uses revolving fruits as symbols of the solar system, or more broadly, of the cosmos. As if first conceding to the fate predicted by the big-bang supporters, some fruits swerve out of orbit and shatter, but they drop their seeds to the ground. In response to Hoyle's suggestion of continual regeneration and immortality for the universe, the seeds sprout, promising new fruit. "Dead nature," the literal meaning of the Spanish term for "still life," has come back to life.

Remedios Varo, though comparatively little known, is as fine an embodiment as any 20th-century painter of the modern artist's need to look beneath the observable world that had ruled painting for so long. Throughout her career she tried, as she once described one of her own characters in a painting, "to encounter the invisible thread that unites all things." In so doing, she poignantly illustrated the changing concepts of time and space from the Middle Ages to modern times, from the mechanistic, clockwork view of the universe to Einstein's theories of relativity.

Some contemporary concerns

It is on the shoulders of such visionaries—be they world famous or only now being appreciated—that contemporary artists are forging new and

Two paintings by Remedios Varo, "Fabric of Space-Time" (above) and "Still Life Reviving" (above right), explore mankind's relationship to the cosmos in a blend of science and magic.

(Left) "Fabric of Space-Time," oil on canvas by Remedios Varo, 1956, 66.35 × 54.80 cm; private collection; (right) "Still Life Reviving," oil on canvas by Remedios Varo, 1963, 113.46 × 80.45 cm; Beatriz Varo de Cano, Valencia, Spain. Paintings, courtesy of Walter Gruen; photos, courtesy, *Unexpected Journeys* by Janet Kaplan, Abbeville Press

24

expanding relationships between science and art. While no single article can encompass the sweeping range of expression of these relationships, a selection of recently acclaimed artists can be discussed.

One painter who has been exploring scientific concerns with conventional media is Lewandowski Lois. Born in Syracuse, New York, Lois has been fascinated with machines ever since she noticed that the papers under the celluloid on the keys of her old typewriter had altered their shade of yellow depending on how often human fingers had hit the keys. The lesson—that machines are changed by human use—inspired her to probe the human-machine relationship in her paintings.

She began with that typewriter, "Underwood Typewriter 1898," and moved on to cars, aircraft, and other products of technology. Working in the tradition of such early modern movements as the Precisionists, Lois has pursued her subject matter even when it has meant spending many hours in Boeing 727 cockpits and under automobile engines. She endows her machines with significant symbolism and animates these creations of "man-made to serve man" with a human quality. In this sense her paintings are true portraits, revealing the character of the subjects through the careful study of their function.

In "Mechanical Man," one of the most intense expressions of her humanistic views of machinery, Lois creates a human being wholly of artificial body parts available from modern medicine. She studied these devices in Veterans Administration hospitals and factories that manufacture prosthetics. Her surreal image is in reality a positive statement about the way machines extend human life and improve its quality.

Like Lois, Pat Adams, a Californian who now teaches in Vermont, uses nothing more than a framed canvas to investigate the worlds of science and painting. However, Adams is an abstract painter whose work, in

An aspect of the human-machine relationship—that machines change with human use—inspired Lewandowski Lois to paint "Underwood Typewriter 1898" (below left). A more intimate form of that relationship appears in her "Mechanical Man" (below), an affirmation of the way machines extend human life and improve its quality.

(Left) "Underwood Typewriter 1898," oil on canvas by Lewandowski Lois, 1958, 79.5 X 133.3 cm; (right) "Mechanical Man," oil on canvas by Lewandowski Lois, 1986, 123.1 X 184.6 cm; both courtesy of the Richard Green Gallery, New York City; reproduced by permission of the artist

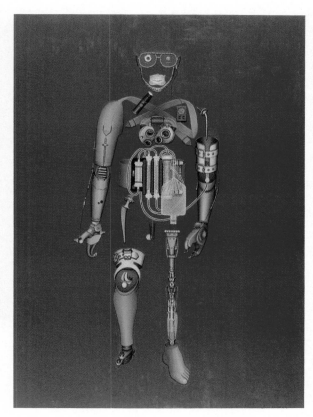

the tradition of Kandinsky's late work, can suggest cellular structure or elements of the solar system. In each Adams work the expressive ambiguities of abstraction are fully exploited. A correspondence is established between the large and small and the internal and external. Her circular forms are capable of appearing remote and immediate or biologic and astronomical at the same time. A large pink circle might be an object from the farthest reaches of the galaxy or the nucleus of a cell, while two small circles may suggest the growth of bacteria. Giorgio Celli, a curator for the Art and Science exhibition of the 42nd International Venice Biennale of Art, has suggested that abstract artists like Adams are indeed realists, naturalists of the invisible, enchanted by visions from the microscope and the cosmos.

Adams does not claim to be metaphoric or illustrative. She merely wishes to recognize the parallels between natural and aesthetic phenomena. Her works reveal her attraction to such physical processes as the effects of forces upon surfaces and within substances. They can suggest, for example, the influence of pressure and heat or the effect of cooling on the formation of crystals or the layering of sediment, or they may stimulate thoughts of the gravitational tugs that make the tides, the magnetic fields that guide the hot gases of a solar flare, or the vastness of space.

If Lois and Adams represent the painterly approach to the expression of scientific concerns, Tony Robbin must stand in for those who work in three dimensions. In the late 1970s the Washington, D.C.-born artist was painting boldly colored geometric patterns on two-dimensional surfaces and adding projecting constructions of painted metal rods. Gradually he eliminated the painted canvas background and moved his constructions directly onto the wall.

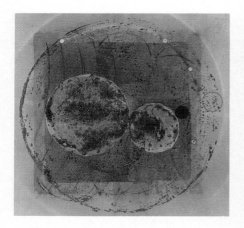

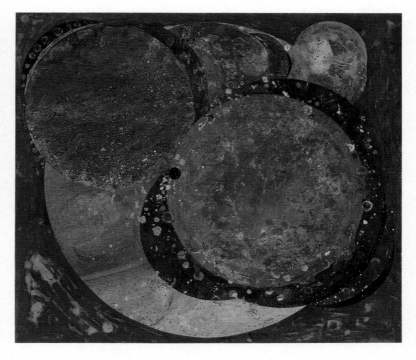

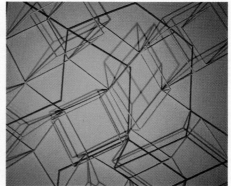

Jacob Bronowski, a mathematician noted for his exploration of the humanistic aspects of science, observed, "What lies below the visible world is always imaginary. . . . There is a new architecture there, a way that things are put together which we cannot know: we only try to picture it by analogy, through the act of imagination." This idea—that an act of imagination could express the way the unobservable framework of the universe works—so absorbed Robbin that he hired a tutor to help him study physics. Eventually the concept he settled on pursuing in art was nothing less than the fourth dimension, an effort that has occupied the last ten years.

Robbin's constructions challenge the observer to leave behind the familiar guidelines of Euclidean geometry and linear perspective, the traditional rules of picture making. Even this departure with convention is part of a tradition, however, one that coincides with the popularization of relativity theory. Beginning in the first decade of the 20th century, the Cubists and Italian Futurists looked for an unseen reality based on the revolutionary concepts of the fourth dimension, while as early as 1909 *Scientific American* magazine sponsored an essay contest for the best popular explanation of the fourth dimension. Robbin's own quest began with the four-dimensional geometry used to describe a space-time continuum for relativity theory. Whereas Einstein had taken a geometry of four spatial dimensions and appropriated one to represent time, a Robbin work returns the original spatial sense to the fourth dimension and asks the observer to experience it.

To create such works, Robbin used a computer to generate rotating sections of what physicists call a hypercube, a cube extended into an extra spatial dimension. He then translated this information into a painted canvas-and-rod construction that approximates the experience of four-dimensional vision. His "Lobofour" (named to pay homage to Russian mathematician N. I. Lobachevsky, whose non-Euclidean geometry is key to Robbin's work) starts with a canvas stretched over panels and painted

In "Lobofour" (detail, above left), a framework of welded rods extending from a painted canvas, Tony Robbin offers the observer an opportunity to experience a spatial sense of the fourth dimension. The offer is renewed in his "Project Four" (detail, above), comprising painted rods laid against a white wall and lighted with colored lights. The latter work is intended to be viewed with 3-D glasses.

(Left) Detail from "Lobofour," acrylic on canvas and welded steel rods by Tony Robbin, 1982, 246.2 X 369.2 X 46.15 cm; (right) detail from "Project Four," welded steel, triangular rods, and ellipsoidal lights by Tony Robbin, 1985, 215.4 X 379.5 X 276.92 cm; both courtesy of the Tibor de Nagy Gallery, New York City; reproduced by permission of the artist

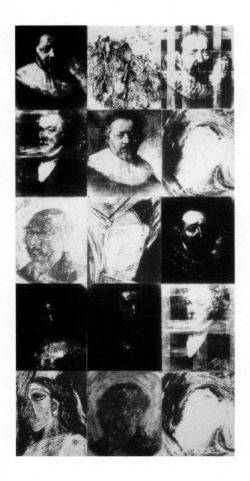

in acrylics, yielding a base field of geometric forms. From the corners of these forms emerge thin metal rods, also painted in colors, that give the canvas forms complex volumes that at first appear three-dimensional. As the viewer moves past the canvas, however, their orientations with respect to one another seem to shift in some odd way, hinting at something more. Robbin would hope that "something more" is the fourth dimension.

In a more recent work, "Project Four," Robbin eliminates the element of painted canvas altogether, the ground being simply a bare white wall. The painted rods are lit by pairs of blue, red, and yellow lights. As in the earlier work, the viewer must move past the piece to experience fully the spatial complexity. The shadows cast by the rods on the white wall create a vivid and ever changing display. When the piece is viewed with provided 3-D glasses, the forms project dynamically into the observer's space and achieve a new degree of solidity. In this novel manipulation of the process of perception, Robbin offers his audience another opportunity to experience an unseen dimension through art.

Turrell, Lois, Adams, and Robbin, in their distinct way, all have found their muse in a particular aspect of science and then have adapted it to the artistic style they were pursuing. Agnes Denes, by contrast, voraciously digests huge chunks of science and reconstitutes them in an enormous variety of artistic forms. Based in New York City, Denes produces drawings, paintings, prints, photos, projections, and even site works. In her oeuvre are X-ray and documentary photographs, graphic condensations, map projections, and numerical sequences, and all are distinguished by an abiding interest in science. If Denes is driven, a hint of the compulsion that drives her may be found in a statement she made when asked her view of modern science: "Once we abandon Newtonian static physics and accept Einstein's four-dimensional principles of relativity, we question reality and know that even the laws of nature may undergo evolutionary changes."

One of Denes's efforts to picture the process of evolutionary change takes the form of a 17-foot-long monoprint, "Introspection I: Evolution." Surely among her most ambitious pronouncements, it gives visual form to the journey of man from his separation from the ape to the beginnings of knowledge and art. A tour of the monoprint reveals material condensed from comparative anatomy, physics, biology, cytology, and genetics. Interspersed among the images, which have been drawn with extraordinary craft and sensitivity, are scientific data. Even Denes's technique is state-of-the-art, her prints being made by a direct surface printing technique of her own invention.

In "Introspection III: Aesthetics," a series of X-ray studies, Denes reveals the underlayers of famous paintings. Using the X-ray, a tool of science, she literally travels beneath the surface of the works of such masters as Rembrandt, van Gogh, and Picasso to expose working habits and painting techniques—and at the same time makes them into works of art of her own devising. In "Kingdom Series" she applies the same technique to objects of the natural world. Here she has created aesthetic

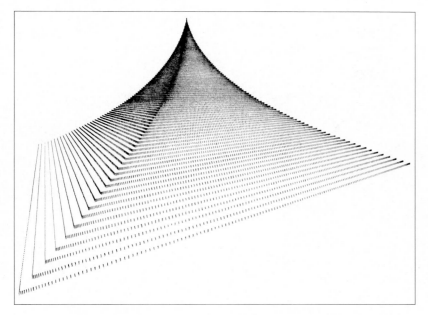

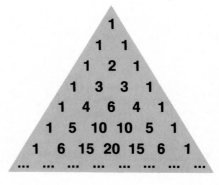

images of irises and stingrays, among other organisms, by altering in some mysterious way the X-rays of the original forms. The result is unique and haunting.

In yet another series, the "Pyramid Project," Denes investigates two themes. One is the pyramid as symbol, a bridge between ancient civilizations and contemporary society. The other is her visualization of Pascal's triangle, a special group of numbers—the binomial coefficients—ordered in a triangular array such that the sum of two adjacent numbers in a row equals the number directly below them in the next row. In subsequent pyramid pieces, the structure of numbers is replaced by stones and individualized human figures.

While working on pyramids and triangles she also turned her attention to topology. The resulting series of map projections, "Isometric Systems in Isotropic Space," is a group of superbly executed works in which the map of the world is transformed from a sphere into various other solids. She used a computer to produce topologically correct distortions of the continents and seas, as if the world had been molded onto these odd forms, and then drew up the final images by hand.

In the words of art critic Donald Kuspit: "Denes seems to straddle science and art in a way reminiscent of Leonardo—the effort to totalize nature in a single system and to take the visible as a sign of the invisible to be comprehended." In extending her ambitious reach, Denes has encompassed many of the themes expressed in the long tradition of commingled art and science. And like the great artists before her, she continues to grasp for a still greater purchase on the total knowledge of humanity. It is this bold purpose that sets the true artist apart—to express something of the unique vision of humankind. For Denes and the kindred artists who preceded her and who are at work today, science affords a toehold on comprehension.

The works of Agnes Denes span a broad range of artistic forms and themes. "Introspection III: Aesthetics" (opposite page, top) comprises an array of X-ray images of paintings of famous artists. A map projection from her series "Isometric Systems in Isotropic Space" (opposite page, bottom) transforms the spherical Earth into an egg-shaped world with topologically correct distortions of surface features. In "Pascal's Perfect Probability Pyramid & the People Paradox: The Predicament" (above left), Denes combines investigation of the pyramid as symbol with that of a special group of numbers known as Pascal's triangle. A detail of the work (above), near the apex of the pyramid, reveals the structure to be made of individual human figures. Also illustrated are the first few rows of numbers of Pascal's triangle (top).

(Opposite page, top) "Introspection III: Aesthetics," monoprint by Agnes Denes, 1972; 109 × 220.5 cm; (opposite page, bottom) "Isometric Systems in Isotropic Space—Map Projections: The Egg," ink and charcoal on graph paper by Agnes Denes, 1974, 76.92 × 61.54 cm; (this page, top and detail) "Pascal's Perfect Probability Pyramid & The People Paradox: The Predicament," ink on silk vellum by Agnes Denes, 1980, 82.05 × 110.3 cm; all works reproduced by permission of the artist

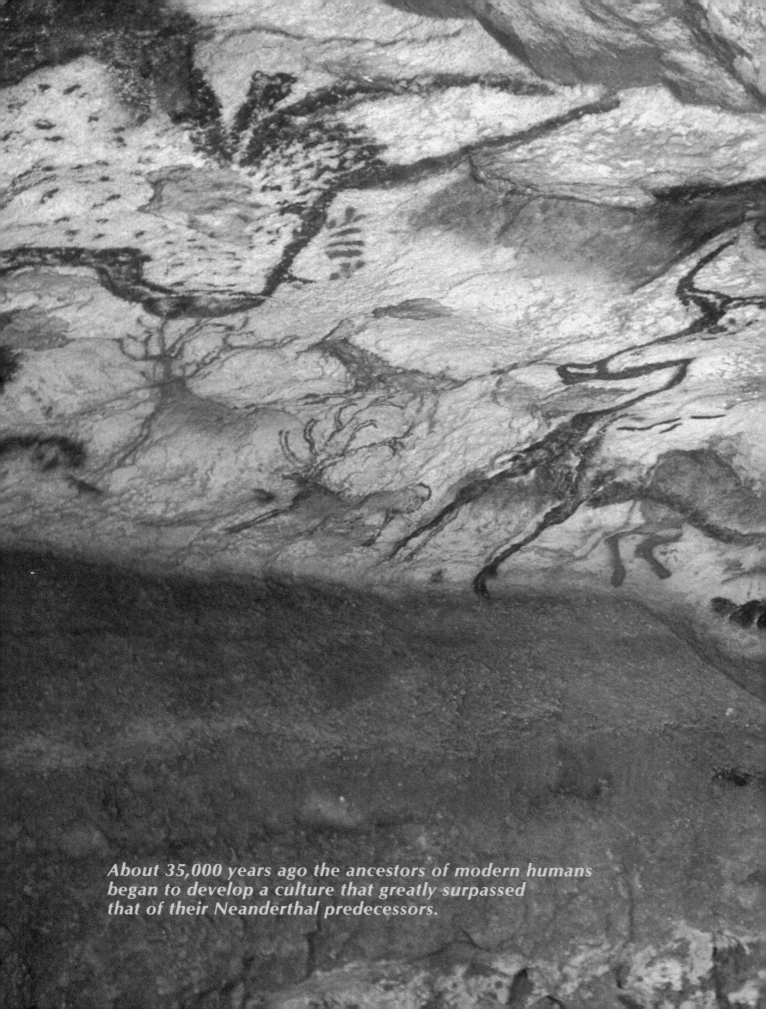

About 35,000 years ago the ancestors of modern humans
began to develop a culture that greatly surpassed
that of their Neanderthal predecessors.

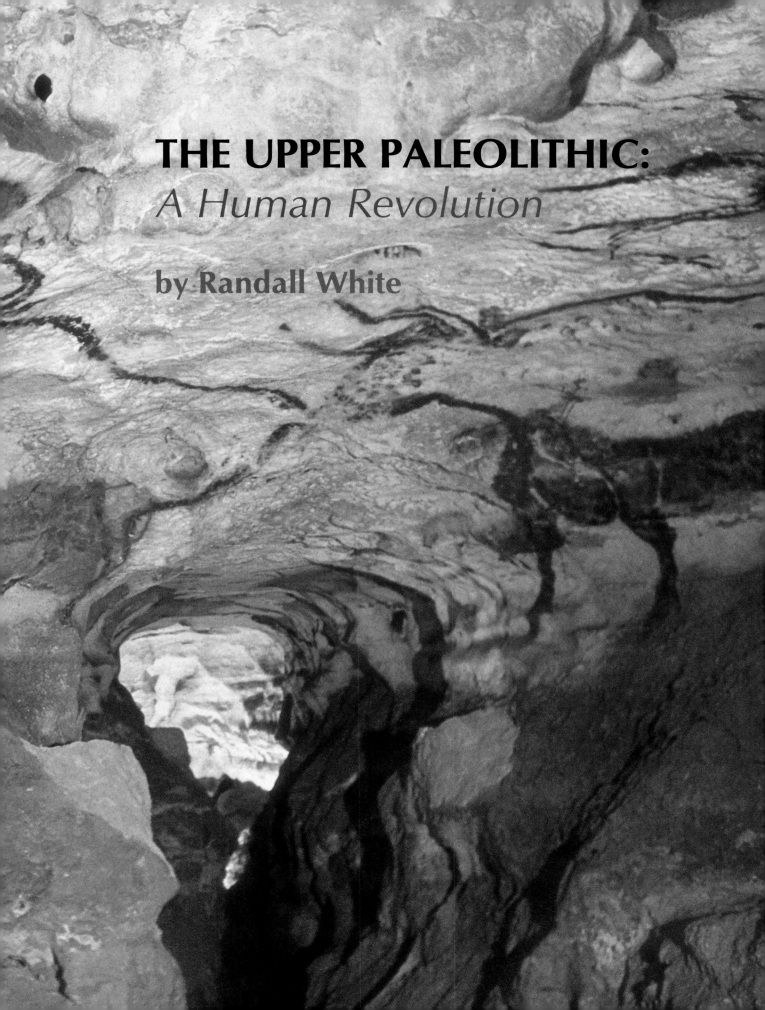

THE UPPER PALEOLITHIC:
A Human Revolution

by Randall White

RANDALL WHITE is an Associate Professor of Anthropology at New York University, New York City.

(Overleaf) Photograph, Rene Burri— Magnum

The Upper Paleolithic, or late Ice Age (from 35,000 to 12,000 years ago), witnessed the remarkable accomplishments of the first anatomically and culturally modern humans in Europe. The record that has been found of their life there provides one of the most exciting stories of new ideas and practical advances in the whole span of the human past. This revolutionary period of human achievement contrasts sharply with the preceding period, beginning about 100,000 years ago, when the Neanderthals lived scattered over many of the same areas.

By at least 100,000 years ago, a physical type known as Neanderthals (*Homo sapiens neanderthalensis*) occupied Europe. In general, Neanderthals were considerably more robust than modern humans (the term modern humans is preferable to the much-abused Cro-Magnon, which refers only to populations from a restricted region of southwestern France during the early part of the Upper Paleolithic). They were much more muscular, especially in the neck and shoulder region, than all but the most massive of modern humans. The walls of their bones were very thick. One of their most obvious traits was a bony ridge above the eyes, which, combined with a protruding lower face, gave them a very robust appearance.

An intriguing observation by anthropologist Erik Trinkaus is that Neanderthals used their teeth as tools, producing an odd wearing down of their incisors. The precise activity that produced this wear remains to be explained, but it implies to some anthropologists that they solved fewer problems with technology than did the forebears of modern humans.

The material record left by Neanderthals between 100,000 and 35,000 years ago is known as the Mousterian period. The record for the Mousterian contrasts sharply with that of the modern humans that followed. While the Neanderthals made a variety of tools in stone, some of them quite complicated, the lack of innovation over more than 50,000 years is surprising from a modern perspective. For example, not a single tool form existed 40,000 years ago that had not already been present 100,000 years ago. In the words of the French prehistorian François Bordes, "They made beautiful tools stupidly." He simply meant that there was an almost mechanical redundancy to Mousterian tools that makes them seem the result of more programmed behavior than that of later people.

Also surprising is the similarity of Mousterian stone tools from region to region. In form and relative numbers, they are often virtually identical across vast distances; collections from sites in France often cannot be distinguished from those found in the Middle East, for example.

From the beginning of the Upper Paleolithic in Europe, modern humans used a wide variety of materials to manufacture tools and other objects. The Mousterians did not. Only a few examples of objects in bone, antler, and ivory have been discovered in Mousterian sites, and even these are hotly disputed by specialists. However, wood, if used as a raw material, would not be preserved.

Neanderthals made tools from stone that almost always came from the immediate vicinity of their campsites. This pattern led archaeologist Lewis Binford to argue that their tool manufacture and use was expedient; that is, they did not make long-term plans and thus, for example, did not carry tools as they moved about but instead discarded them immediately after use. This idea of limited planning is perhaps supported by the Neanderthals' apparent failure to profit by cyclical patterning in the environment. For example, migratory fish, which provide a rich resource at the same time each year, were not exploited. Nor did Neanderthals seem to have taken advantage of the highly predictable migrations of reindeer, which became very important for the early modern humans.

If Mousterians lacked certain universal characteristics of modern humans, others were clearly present. Notably, it is in the Mousterian (but probably only after about 60,000–50,000 years ago) that we find the first purposeful and ritualized burial of the dead. Graves frequently include animal parts that have often been interpreted by archaeologists as offerings for use in life after death. In addition, this burial activity indicates a conventionalized set of ways for dealing with death. The very fact of establishing a convention suggests a cultural coding and externalizing of emotional responses and a shared body of ideas.

It is becoming clear from other regions, such as Africa, the Middle East, and central and eastern Europe, that fully modern humans did not appear at the same time everywhere. For example, anatomically modern humans were present significantly earlier in eastern Europe and the Middle East than in western Europe. Also, there is considerable evidence emerging from Africa, and even Australia, for anatomically modern humans prior to any in Europe.

Europe is the focus of this discussion, but it is important to emphasize that it had no monopoly on important evolutionary trends. Exciting evidence, both cultural and biologic, is being sought and found in virtually every part of the world.

During much of the late Ice Age in hilly to mountainous terrain, such as that of southwestern France, southern Germany, and Czechoslovakia, many kinds of large herbivores coexisted; they included mountain goats, reindeer, bison, and horses. The prehistoric human occupants shared these landscapes with as many as a dozen species of large-bodied animals, a situation unknown in these latitudes in the modern world. Far from being impoverished, these environments supported more animals than any occupied by hunting and gathering peoples today.

Because animal bones are well preserved for thousands of years and plant remains are not, archaeologists tend to underestimate the potential contribution of plant foods to the Ice Age diet. In fact, the pollen grains recovered from late Ice Age sites in Europe include those of a number of edible species of tubers, nuts, and berries.

New technologies

The pattern that began 35,000 years ago was one of frequent, if not continual, change in human behavior. The succeeding 25,000 years are subdivided into cultural periods, each with its own style of technology and each characterized by a set of innovations. Many of these new ways of doing things were undoubtedly stimulated by practical needs in the

face of constantly changing environmental conditions. In many respects, however, the evidence gives the impression of change for the sake of change. After hundreds of thousands of years during which there was little or no change in technology or subsistence strategies, the Upper Paleolithic represents a technological revolution.

Upper Paleolithic toolmakers no longer produced stone tools mostly on amorphous flakes but used pieces of rock similar in form and sharpness to a modern knife blade. This allowed Upper Paleolithic craftspeople to obtain ten times more usable "cutting edge" than could their Neanderthal predecessors from the same amount of flint.

These stone blades, used as cutting, scraping, chiseling, and perforating implements, were probably not self-contained tools. There is now quite early evidence for the process of hafting, whereby stone blades were attached to a handle or socket made from organic material. Thus, the tools may have been suitable for a number of tasks, depending upon how they were mounted in their hafts.

One of the most distinctive inventions of the late Ice Age was a diverse bone/antler spear-point technology. By about 20,000 years ago, Upper Paleolithic people had invented a deadly device for launching their spears with improved accuracy and velocity. This device, the spear thrower, was less than a meter long and had a handle on one end and a hook on the other that fitted into the blunt end of the spear. This arrangement extended the throwing arc of the hunter. By about 15,000 years ago, spear throwers were elaborately decorated with animal forms.

Many items of technology may well have existed that did not survive for archaeologists to discover. However, soon after the discovery of the

Stone hand ax (above) was made by a Neanderthal craftsman, who chose to leave a gold band of color along one edge. The Neanderthals almost always used stone for their tools and other objects. Spear point fragments decorated with incised designs (above center) and a harpoon (above right) were carved from reindeer antlers by ancestors of modern humans about 14,000 years ago. The carving was done with stone tools that resembled a modern knife blade in shape and sharpness.

Photos, Randall White

34

painted cave of Lascaux in France in 1940, excavations produced the earliest known fragment of rope or cord. Made of three braided plant fibers, now turned to humus, this rope has profound implications. Cordage must have been technologically important and probably served a variety of tasks. People who know how to make cord can easily produce nets and snares, which increase hunting and fishing efficiency enormously.

Lamps were most often small slabs of limestone hollowed in the center to hold the fuel, probably animal fat with a moss wick. Hundreds of these lamps have been discovered from sites throughout Europe. Some lamps were carefully prepared from special kinds of stone obtained from distant regions. These special lamps, which seem especially prevalent in painted caves, were often decorated with abstract or animal forms.

For warmth, people relied primarily on cobble-lined fireplaces. These take a surprising number of different forms that vary from period to period and from region to region. Wood and animal bones served as the primary fuels. Cooking included techniques for boiling. Often, pits are found in Upper Paleolithic sites that are full of cobbles fractured by temperature change. People simply took red-hot cobbles from a fire and dropped them into a skin-lined pit full of water.

Upper Paleolithic people developed strategies for reducing their fuel requirements. For example, in southwestern France as well as in the Ukraine, 75% of known Upper Paleolithic sites are located on south-facing slopes and at the bases of south-facing cliffs. Such locations absorb heat from the Sun during the day and yield it slowly at night.

The places where Upper Paleolithic people chose to live were important reflections of strategies for survival and often reveal something about how they obtained necessary resources. Often sites were so well situated that they were occupied, at least on a seasonal basis, for thousands of years. The thickness of deposits rich in artifacts at these sites can exceed 5 meters (16.4 feet).

Proximity to reliable sources of water was one of the most important criteria in choosing a place to live. More than 90% of all camps were located near springs or on the banks of rivers and streams. Many sites seem to have been chosen because they provided a good view of the surrounding area. Such vantage points would have been important for observing game animals and perhaps other humans.

One thing is clear. People could live where they chose, on the basis of decisions about availability of necessary resources. Frequently they chose caves and rock-shelters—but only if the shelters were suitably located. Many of the most important sites recently discovered are in open-air locations, often miles from any cave or rock-shelter.

In open-air sites researchers have found rich evidence for a variety of architectural features. Frequently these include pavements made of river cobbles carried from some distance away. Such pavements, often square or rectangular, were probably the foundations for shelters made from skins and wood or animal bones. It seems that the builders heated the cobbles in a fire and then arranged them on frozen ground to form a secure platform.

Lamp was made during the Upper Paleolithic from a small slab of limestone. Fat that was burned in the lamp caused its reddish color.

Randall White

Sometimes open-air sites reveal spectacular and unexpectedly complex architectural features. These are especially noteworthy at recently discovered sites in the Ukraine, where the primary building material was the bones of woolly mammoths; in one case, bones of 95 of these 4,550-kilogram (10,000-pound) animals were used to make just one dwelling. At Mezirich, the site of this structure, there were four more such dwellings composing a 15,000-year-old village. Each dwelling had a different arrangement of the giant bones, which came not from hunted animals but from the skeletons of long-dead ones that the occupants of the site had retrieved from the surrounding area.

A fact of life for Ice Age hunter-gatherers was the changing availability and quality of resources from season to season. Plant foods would have been available only in spring, summer, and fall. Some animals migrated and therefore came and went seasonally. Upper Paleolithic people had to schedule their activities accordingly. They occupied sites for only a portion of the year before moving on to other places and other resources. They regularly returned to the same locations each year to hunt the same animals and gather the same plants.

The clothing that late Ice Age people wore has not been preserved. However, many indirect forms of evidence allow us to draw inferences. One of the important innovations of the Upper Paleolithic was the eyed sewing needle, which first appeared about 23,000 years ago. The needles were most frequently made of ivory or bone, and many were as small as large modern examples. They had a tiny eye made by a very fine pointed flint drill or perforator. The "thread" was probably animal sinew or plant fiber. The appearance of the needles suggests that Upper Paleolithic people had tailored clothing, probably made from animal skins like those of modern Eskimo and some American Indians.

One of the most remarkable bodies of evidence concerning clothing comes from the 24,000-year-old site of Sungir, one of the most northerly sites on the Russian Plain, where three burials were found. The skeletons

were covered with thousands of beads that had apparently been sewn onto a skin garment worn by the dead person. The outline of the beads suggests that the clothing consisted of a tunic pulled on over the head and a one-piece pants/boots combination.

Social organization

Clearly, the people of Upper Paleolithic Europe had at their command a body of technological knowledge as sophisticated as that of many modern hunting and gathering peoples. This knowledge was passed down through hundreds of generations, who added to it and improved upon it. Such continuity and intergenerational communication cannot exist, however, without means of organizing people and production so as to ensure both social and biologic reproduction.

There are many gaps in the knowledge of the ways in which Upper Paleolithic societies were organized. Social anthropologists studying modern people can make direct observations about such social institutions as marriage and kinship relations. Because archaeologists are restricted to the study of material objects left behind and the ways such objects are patterned in space, they have great difficulty drawing inferences about social organization. Therefore, knowledge of Upper Paleolithic societies is of a general nature.

Estimates of surface areas of Upper Paleolithic sites reveal that there is a wide variety of site sizes for any given period. This finding seems to indicate that there were different kinds and sizes of social units. Group size probably fluctuated seasonally, with at least one period during the year when large numbers of people aggregated around some abundant resource. Such aggregations could not be sustained, however, because the environment could not support such dense concentrations of consumers for long and because hunting and gathering societies seldom have the so-

Gypsy woman in 1925 photograph (opposite page, top) makes use of a rock-shelter in France that had been occupied during the Upper Paleolithic. Another rock-shelter in France (opposite page, bottom) was occupied about 12,000 years ago. Because it is unusually small, the shelter probably was only used for short periods such as overnight stays. A third French rock-shelter from the same era (above) had by the 1920s been emptied of all of its deposits.

(Opposite page, top) Alonzo W. Pond; (opposite page, bottom and this page) Randall White

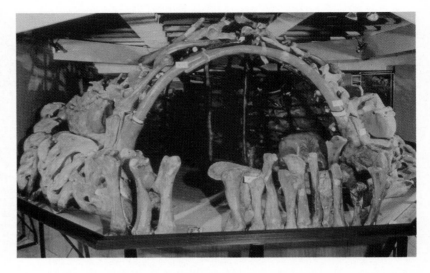

cial institutions for resolving the conflicts that occur when many humans come together. It can therefore be hypothesized that the many small and few large sites of the European Upper Paleolithic reflect a social pattern of fluctuation between small and large social units.

Many of the largest sites appear to be located at places suitable for efficient exploitation of seasonally abundant resources, such as migrating reindeer or fish. The largest sites, even when only a small area within them has been excavated, commonly yield many more art objects than do the smaller ones, suggesting that much of the artistic endeavor took place within the socially charged context of seasonal aggregation. The analysis of human activities in many of the small sites indicates the presence of only one socioeconomic unit rather than a clustering of several self-sufficient units, as is usually found when large numbers of hunter-gatherers come together. The occupants often divided the rock-shelter into complementary work areas for butchering, cooking, bone boiling, marrow extraction, and dumping of garbage. This seems to be the work of a single household that organized itself according to available space.

Another important social question is the area over which social ties were developed and extended. The answer is surprising to those who conceive of Upper Paleolithic societies as small, self-contained units. Certain Upper Paleolithic sites in the Ukraine contain seashells found only in the Mediterranean. Amber from northern Europe near the Baltic Sea has been found in sites in southern Europe. Sites in inland France and Spain contain shells from the Mediterranean, the Atlantic, the English Channel, and fossil shell beds hundreds of kilometers distant. Late Upper Paleolithic sites in Poland contain flint from several hundred kilometers away. It is most reasonable to suppose that these goods moved in hand-to-hand exchange, as has been observed in many modern hunting and gathering peoples.

Exchange or trade operates as a vehicle of social obligation in most small-scale societies. The acts of giving and receiving set up a never-ending series of obligations much like the exchange of gifts at Christmas.

Obligations are social bonds capable of tying together different social groups. It is perhaps in this context that shells and flint moved across the ancient European landscape.

Even the least hierarchical societies known to anthropologists are subdivided along lines of age, gender, and personal achievement. In archaeology, information about this internal subdivision is most frequently recovered from burials. The European Upper Paleolithic reveals a wide diversity of burial treatment within given regions. There is much variation in such features as the position of the body, ritual treatment of the corpse, nature and quantity of grave goods accompanying the corpse, structures associated with the burial, number of corpses interred in the same grave, and the way in which the body was clothed or decorated. Observed differences in the way the dead are treated within the same society can reasonably be assumed to reflect different statuses or roles filled in life by the dead persons.

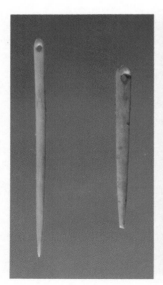

An abundance of art

It is safe to say that the most widely known but least understood aspect
of Upper Paleolithic life is the extraordinary art produced during the
period. Nearly 200 caves bearing wall paintings and engravings have
been discovered in southwestern Europe, especially France and Spain. In
addition, perhaps 10,000 sculpted and engraved objects are known from
other parts of Europe, Siberia, and several locations in Africa. Upper
Paleolithic people mastered a wide range of artistic media, including
stone, bone, antler, ivory, wood, paint, and clay. The visual representation ranges from naturalistic to abstract but encompasses relatively
few themes. Animal images are clearly the most important of these;
plants and landscape features appear less often. Contrary to a common
misconception, humans or humanlike forms (including painted human
handprints) are numerous, with approximately 1,000 examples known. A
wide variety of nonrepresentational signs also exist. These cannot be interpreted because they undoubtedly comprise a body of arbitrary symbols.

One of the defining characteristics of modern members of *Homo sapiens sapiens* is that they experience their world through complex conceptual frameworks that are often mutually unintelligible between cultures.
While art is regarded as evocative, that which is evoked is heavily reliant
upon participation in a mutually understood system of meaning; that is,
a shared body of ideas, conceptions, and experience. The fact that Ice
Age humans, using visual media, were conveying ideas so complicated
as to totally confound present-day researchers indicates that the nature
of the human adaptation had begun to change. In a very real way these
people produced their own world, a symbolic one that included imaginary
creatures and deities.

While one can demonstrate long-term continuity in art styles and certain organizational attributes, there are also major differences through
time in location, media employed, subject matter, and form in Upper
Paleolithic graphic representation. Part of the complexity of human
symbolic systems lies in the fact that the same image can carry several
meanings, either at once or at different points in time. One must avoid
the assumption that an engraved horse in the Gravettian (30,000 to

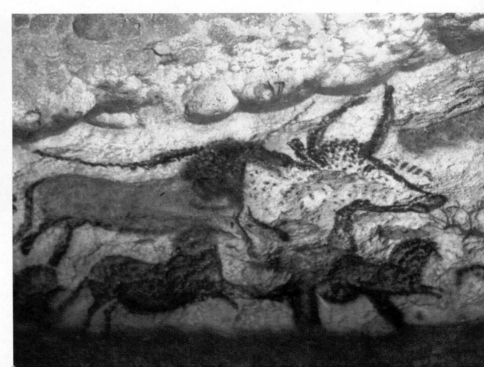

22,000 years ago) is the symbolic equivalent of an engraved horse in the Magdalenian (18,000 to 11,000 years ago) or that a barbed sign in Spain meant the same thing that it did in the Dordogne or Italy.

Several attempts have been made to create relative chronologies for the art on the basis of stylistic similarities and differences in the paintings, engravings, and sculptures themselves. The most recent was that of the French anthropologist André Leroi-Gourhan, whose work in the 1960s quickly replaced the earlier framework of the Abbé Henri Breuil, a pioneer in examining, documenting, and analyzing Ice Age art. Leroi-Gourhan used the small sample of dated portable art objects as a basis for describing the evolution of art styles. He then dated images painted or engraved on cave walls according to their stylistic similarity to the dated portable objects. There is controversy over the accuracy of this approach, and perhaps even more over Leroi-Gourhan's basic conclusion: that Upper Paleolithic art underwent a continuous development over a 25,000-year period, a development in many ways independent of technological evolution. In other words, he concluded that there is an underlying artistic and symbolic continuity behind major changes in material culture.

The earliest objects showing a clear aesthetic sense were made by Neanderthals more than 35,000 years ago. In some instances a glimmering of artistic sensitivity is evident in nothing more complicated than an interest in curious forms or the imposition of symmetry in the manufacture of tools. The site of La Ferrassie in France has yielded small blocks of limestone with depressions pecked out of them. However, these examples indicate the limit of artistic expression before the Upper Paleolithic. There are no representations of animals and few, if any, markings on bone. Artistic production became slightly more complicated in the earliest phase of the Upper Paleolithic, known in western Europe as the Châtelperronian. Among the findings were a sandstone plaquette (small plaque) bearing an uninterpretable engraving and a small number of bone objects bearing parallel incisions. Leroi-Gourhan regarded the incisions as perhaps the earliest evidence for rhythmic arrangements and an interval scale that was the prototype for the ruler, the calendar, and even the musical scale.

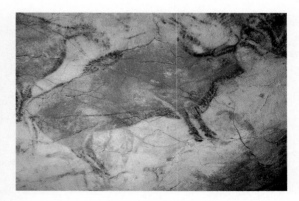

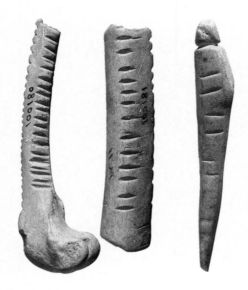

The Aurignacians (34,000 to 30,000 years ago) produced the first unmistakably human and animal figures. They fashioned a surprising diversity of graphic forms, including fragments of bird bone with carefully spaced incisions, engravings and sculptures in the form of sexual organs, limestone blocks engraved with simple animal forms, and ivory plaques inscribed with series of dots. There are even examples of painting in red, black, and yellow. Some of the earliest surviving art objects are tiny three-dimensional animal sculptures and bas-reliefs in ivory from mammoth tusks.

The Gravettian period, which follows the Aurignacian, was marked by an increase in the complexity of art forms. In Czechoslovakia, at the sites of Predmost and Dolni Vestonice, numerous fired-clay figurines in the form of humans and animals are perhaps the earliest evidence for ceramic art. Recently at Dolni Vestonice, a firing kiln was identified, indicating that the first complex ceramic technology had nothing to do with the fabrication of practical containers, as is usually supposed.

Wall paintings exist in the Gravettian, and many have probably not survived. Often at rock-shelter sites, blocks that have apparently fallen from the ceiling bear traces of red and black coloring. An important theme at some Gravettian sites is the negative human handprint, produced by brushing or blowing pigment around a hand that was held flat against a rock surface. The most impressive site featuring such prints is the cave of Gargas in the French Pyrenees, where there are more than 150 handprints. One of the most puzzling characteristics of the Gargas hands is that all except ten have missing fingers. Many have hypothesized that this was a result of ritual mutilation, a practice known from modern societies. However, Leroi-Gourhan suggested that the fingers only appeared to be missing, having been held back against the palm of the hand. He went so far as to propose that a kind of gestural language or code was involved.

Incised bird bones (above, left and center) were found in France and are believed to be 32,000 years old. Each bone bears the same number of incisions on three sides, and anthropologists believe that such carvings were used for counting or tallying. A human figure carved from the tusk of a woolly mammoth (above right) is of approximately the same age. (Right) Carved in a limestone slab about 12,000 years ago, a horse is given many pairs of legs to indicate motion.

Photos, Randall White

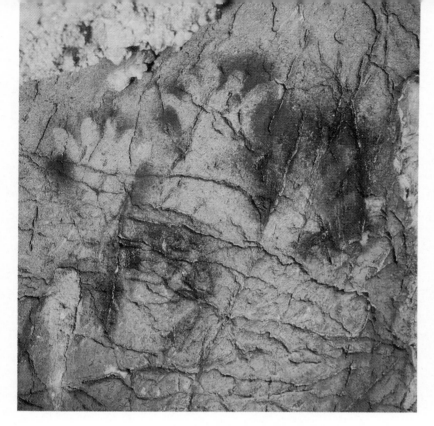

Human handprints decorate the cave of Gargas in the French Pyrenees. An important component of the art of the Gravettian period (about 30,000 to 22,000 years ago), the prints were formed by brushing or blowing pigment around a hand that was held flat against a rock surface.

Toward the end of the Gravettian, deeply incised engravings are common and are found in habitation sites rather than deep underground. For Leroi-Gourhan these represent the prototype for the subsequent emergence of large-scale bas-relief sculpture. An excellent example of such a figure was found in the rock-shelter of Labattut in southwestern France on a large block that had fallen from the ceiling of the shelter. The form of a highly stylized horse engraved in broad and deep lines on the block's surface may have been made after the block fell. The back of the horse conforms almost perfectly to the line of fracture, as if the fracture line had suggested the back of an animal to the artist.

By far the most distinctive art objects in the Gravettian are the carved and engraved female figures. These are found throughout Europe, often showing regional differences. They are made from a variety of materials, including limestone, ivory, steatite, and calcite. The figures range in style from those that are highly exaggerated anatomically, such as the magnificent Venus of Lespugue, to more moderately proportioned examples, such as the Venuses of Brassempouy. Some appear pregnant; many do not. Facial features are seldom represented, nor are lower legs, which most often end in points. Breasts are most often large and pendulous, and buttocks are generally pronounced.

It must be kept in mind that evidence does not exist to confirm or refute the notion that the female figures are Venuses. In any case, the idea that these females were part of a fertility cult pervades the literature. However, all known hunters and gatherers today are much more concerned with limiting population than with increasing it. It is difficult to imagine circumstances in which hunting and gathering peoples would purposely seek to increase population density. A look at current world

43

population problems strongly suggests, however, that people do not always strive to match their numbers to available resources.

Perhaps the most unexpected objects surviving from the Gravettian are wind instruments, frequently described as flutes. One from the Vezere Valley of southwestern France has six holes, two on the top and four on the underside. The complexity of its sound capability makes it clear that this instrument was not just a whistle or animal call. The flutes indicate clearly that music was part of the artistic and symbolic environment that people had created for themselves.

During the Solutrean, 22,000 to 18,000 years ago, a new and dramatic art form, with roots in the deeply incised and occasional bas-relief forms of the Gravettian, became dominant. These are large-scale bas-reliefs located in the midst of or immediately adjacent to living areas. Two sites in southwestern France have yielded friezes composed of these bas-reliefs. The most spectacular is the site of Roc de Sers in the Charente region, in which a series of massive sculpted limestone blocks lined the back wall of a rock-shelter and more were found on the slope in front of the shelter. The blocks were decorated with horses, bison, reindeer, mountain goats, and at least one human figure, all executed in relief that exceeded 15 centimeters (6 inches) in some instances. These magnificent works adorned the place where people slept, ate, and cooked.

Many other engraved and sculpted blocks are known from Solutrean sites, most of them done on a smaller scale than those described above. In some areas the practice of deep cave painting seems to have been significant. The cave of Tête du Lion in the Ardèche region of France is one of the few painted caves positively dated to this period. Along with some traces of red paint, it yielded a group of animals painted in red: a deer, an aurochs, and the heads of two ibex associated with a series of yellow dots. Careful excavations by Jean Combier at the base of the paintings yielded four smears of red pigment and a number of fragments of charcoal, apparently from a torch used by the painters to light their way. No stone tools or animal bones were found, indicating clearly that Solutrean people did not live in the cave but merely visited it.

At least 80% of all the known Upper Paleolithic graphic representations date to the Magdalenian period, beginning about 18,000 years ago. The Magdalenian exhibits a richness and diversity of art forms, and there seems to have been much change during the period in the media employed and the locations chosen for artistic production.

The early phases of the Magdalenian witnessed some of the most remarkable deep cave painting, most notably that of Lascaux Cave, painted some 17,000 or more years ago. Curiously, the people responsible for the spectacular paintings of Lascaux seem not to have produced much in the way of portable art. In the early Magdalenian there are a few engravings on stone slabs and bone plaquettes, but for the most part decoration is restricted to functional implements, particularly spear points, and is most often nonanimal in subject matter.

There is more to Lascaux than meets the eye. Pamela Vandiver of the Smithsonian Institution, Washington, D.C., recently demonstrated that the colors used to paint the cave resulted from the heating of ochers to extreme temperatures, in the range of 500° C (932° F). This provides further evidence for symbolic needs rather than practical ones as the motivation for technological complexity and innovation.

The middle phases of the Magdalenian period, beginning about 15,000 years ago, saw a continuation of deep cave paintings. Indeed, it is during this period, especially in the French Pyrenees, that painters achieved their deepest penetration underground. There is also strong evidence for the reemergence of the large-scale bas-reliefs that were common at

Large-scale bas-relief of a horse and mountain goat adorned living quarters in a rock-shelter in France during the Solutrean period, 22,000 to 18,000 years ago. Such bas-reliefs became a dominant form of art in the Solutrean.

the end of the Solutrean. For example, the rock-shelter of Cap-Blanc in the Dordogne is decorated with a frieze of deeply sculpted animals along its entire 15-meter (49-foot) length. Like the Solutrean bas-reliefs at Fourneau-du-Diable, this remarkable work seems to have adorned the scene of everyday activities.

Middle Magdalenian people also created a rich and spectacular body of small portable art objects. Especially noteworthy are the finely incised limestone slabs and the bone and antler objects sculpted both in bas-relief and in the round. This period witnessed the reemergence of abundant female images, which are virtually unknown in the Solutrean and Early Magdalenian. They are usually engraved, although bas-relief has been found. Surprisingly, many of these female images have some of the same defining characteristics as their Gravettian counterparts some 8,000–10,000 years earlier.

Elaborately decorated spear throwers date from this period, as well as finely sculpted horse-head pendants from a number of sites. These horse heads, as well as horses' legs, were carved from throat bones, usually those of horses, and were most often perforated for suspension.

The final phases of the Magdalenian, after about 13,000 years ago, seem to indicate the abandonment of deep caves as centers for artistic activity. As Leroi-Gourhan has documented, most of the Late Magdalenian art is found at cave entrances and in rock-shelters and open sites, always in areas illuminated by daylight. Moreover, this late art, mostly in the form of engraved slabs and cave walls, has the appearance of what Leroi-Gourhan calls "hyper-realism." In contrast to this apparent realism with respect to animal art, the very end of the Magdalenian is marked by a highly conventionalized, even schematicized, treatment of the female form consisting of a very few outlines of generally headless, footless women.

Different animals were apparently considered appropriate in different contexts. Bison, for example, are often found on stone plaquettes and cave walls but are nearly absent on other media. Commonly, combinations of forms and animals repeat themselves on batons made from pierced antlers, phallus/fish and horse/reindeer being the most common. The horse/bison combination never exists on the batons, even though it is the most common combination on cave walls. Reindeer, the most frequent food animal, is most commonly seen on engraved limestone slabs but is rarely painted. This patterning appears to reflect a rich body of shared knowledge, beliefs, myths, and stories.

In examining these graphic representations, it is easy to overlook the fact that they are highly conventionalized (not to be confused with simplified). These conventions are repetitious and consistent for any given period and indicate a well-defined set of standards, artistic norms, subject matters, and media that had to be met if an artistic representation was to be acceptable and understandable.

The natural contours of a rock wall or a piece of bone or ivory often provided the basis for the animal chosen to be represented by the artist. This approach applies equally to cave art, where protuberances

and stalagmites often bound or help to define the painted or engraved image, and to portable art, where the form of a tool suggests that of the animal represented.

Leroi-Gourhan's best known search for patterning in the art led him to examine 50 of the painted caves in what is now part of southern France and northern Spain. A similar but independent search was conducted simultaneously by Annette Laming. The goal in both cases was to determine whether the painted caves were structured with respect to the distribution and location of different animals and signs. Were the different caves organized in similar ways? Both Leroi-Gourhan and Laming arrived at the same conclusion: that the distribution of animals and signs in the caves was not random and that certain animals/signs were consistently associated with other animals/signs. Often they could actually predict that a certain image would be in a certain location before they arrived there. Although there are certainly disagreements over the specifics and statistical significance of Leroi-Gourhan's results, most prehistorians today accept his argument that the caves were organized according to some preconceived plan and were not simply the sites of multiple random painting/engraving events.

Recently there have been powerful confirmations of Leroi-Gourhan's and Laming's work. French archaeologist Denis Vialou, in the context of a broader study of Pyrenean cave art, analyzed in detail the magnificent painted cave of Niaux. The relationship between such variables as paint color, type of sign, species of animal, and location within the cave is so strong and predictable that Vialou refers to Niaux as a "symbolic construction."

Conclusions

For the early researchers in the 1860s who were finding portable art objects in Upper Paleolithic sites, the only motivation that they believed

47

necessary for the production of such works was an aesthetic one. For anthropologists this is the most unsatisfying of all explanations for Ice Age art. In no society, including contemporary society, is art motivated purely by aesthetic pleasure. Moreover, aesthetics is culturally relative and is always imbedded with social, political, economic, and religious meanings.

By the beginning of the 20th century, when cave paintings were first accepted as authentic, a new realization had emerged, largely because anthropologists were learning more about the context of art in non-Western societies. The notion of totemism, or a special, even magical relationship between animals and humans, was being developed. This concept led Salomon Reinach to argue in 1903 that the art of the Upper Paleolithic reflected a set of magical beliefs embodied in the notion of "sympathetic magic." Through art, Reinach proposed, Upper Paleolithic people sought to increase the numbers of game animals and to ensure hunting success. His view seemed to be supported by the observation that most of the cave art concerned food animals and that it appeared deep underground in places difficult to reach—and, therefore, not decorated for purely aesthetic reasons.

Henri Breuil, who dominated the study of Upper Paleolithic art for nearly 60 years, willingly inherited Reinach's "sympathetic magic" framework. Until Breuil's death in 1961, this framework was widely accepted. According to Breuil's version, Upper Paleolithic people had penetrated deep underground to perform rituals for increasing game and ensuring hunting success. Thus, they exercised ritual control over predators. These ceremonies were one of the contexts in which adolescents were initiated into adulthood. The artists ritually killed their painted animals by drawing spears or wounds on their sides. Certain abstract forms were interpreted as traps and nets, drawn to capture the painted animals ritually.

There is considerable empirical basis for at least a general version of this view. About 15% of painted and engraved animals bear markings that can be interpreted as spears or wounds. Moreover, the startling discoveries in the Pyrenean cave of Montespan in the 1920s seemed a perfect confirmation of the "sympathetic magic" interpretation. At Montespan several animals, including clay models, appear to have been pierced or stabbed ritually.

If Leroi-Gourhan has succeeded in convincing his scientific colleagues that the art caves were carefully laid out according to a preconceived plan, he has been much less successful in persuading them to accept his ideas as to the meaning of the patterning. Although he has modified his position somewhat, he originally attributed sexual significance to the paired associations of different signs and animals in the caves. He suggested that the Upper Paleolithic cosmology was one that divided the world into things that exhibited maleness and things that exhibited femaleness.

Recently John Pfeiffer, a science journalist, proposed another way of understanding the deep cave art that may complement Leroi-Gourhan's structuralist approach. Pfeiffer concentrated on the effect that the cave environment has on the senses and on the psyche. He suggested that the

Two 15,000-year-old bison sculpted in clay stand in Le Tuc d'Audoubert, a deep cave in the French Pyrenees. Anthropologists have suggested that this may be a mating scene that played a role in the ceremonies initiating boys and girls into adulthood.

© Jean Vertut

experience of visiting caves was much different for Upper Paleolithic people, who had only the unsteady and flickering light of burning torches and lamps. With that kind of light, Pfeiffer concluded, the animals would appear to move and breathe. In a situation of, at one and the same time, sensory deprivation and heightened sensory stimulation, the impact of multicolored bison emerging from the darkness must have been awe-inspiring and dramatic.

It is often suggested that at least some of the decorated caves were places where boys and girls were initiated into adulthood. In particular at Le Tuc d'Audoubert, a deep cave in the French Pyrenees, footprints of supposed young people have been interpreted to suggest dancing in a small chamber off the main corridor, about one kilometer (0.62 mile) from the cave entrance. Deeper in the cave, past this side chamber, stand two spectacular bison sculpted in clay, dating to about 15,000 years ago. At the time of discovery, a third sculpted figure, often interpreted as a young bison, was present but in a very poor state of preservation. Although the sexes of the two larger bison are not explicitly shown, this may well be a mating scene constructed for ritual purposes associated with initiation ceremonies.

In seeking to understand the motives for Upper Paleolithic art, one must also steer away from a tendency for explanations that rely on single causes. After all, these were complicated humans, perfectly capable of integrating a number of cosmological, magical, or functional goals within the same image.

Finally, one of the most recent realizations is that "art" cannot be understood as a separate category of human endeavor, as one tends to do in modern Western society. In the Ice Age symbolic and aesthetic pursuits were not practiced only when people had free time but, in fact, motivated and made possible much of the technological innovation so evident in the Upper Paleolithic. Thus, it is no coincidence that a burst of symbolic endeavor should accompany one of the greatest periods of technological and social innovation in all of human history.

by David H. Clark

Giant stellar explosions are thought to be the
progenitors of some of the most exotic celestial objects known,
black holes, neutron stars, and spectacular nebulas among them.
Recently astronomers were able to study one in their own "back yard."

DAVID H. CLARK *is Head of the Science Division, Science and Engineering Research Council, Swindon, England. His books include* Superstars, The Quest for SS433, The Historical Supernovae, *and* The Cosmos from Space.

(Overleaf) Illustration by Jane Meredith

Tycho Brahe (below right) marvels at the "certain strange star" of 1572, as depicted in an illustration from a 19th-century astronomy text. A drawing (below) from Tycho's account De Nova Stella (1573) locates the supernova, labeled I, above the W shape of the constellation Cassiopeia.

Photos, Ann Ronan Picture Library

I was returning to the house, and during my walk contemplating the sky here and there since the clearer sky seemed to be just what could be wished for in order to continue observations after dinner; behold, directly overhead, a certain strange star was suddenly seen, flashing its light with a radiant gleam and it struck my eyes. Amazed, and as if astonished and stupefied, I stood still, gazing for a certain length of time with my eyes fixed intently upon it. When I had satisfied myself that no star of that kind had ever shone forth before, I was led into such perplexity by the unbelievability of the thing that I began to doubt the faith of my own eyes.

With these words the Danish Renaissance astronomer Tycho Brahe recorded his sense of wonder and awe at the sudden appearance in 1572 of a brilliant star in the sky. Nevertheless, what Tycho had witnessed was not the birth of a new star but the death of a very old star. Today, four centuries later, scientists have a fair understanding of the phenomenon whereby stars in their death throes blow themselves apart, shining forth brilliantly for months or years before fading from view. Knowledge of how certain stars die in what are known as supernova explosions has been obtained in two ways: from the study of the historical records of events such as that witnessed by Tycho (and that witnessed by his pupil Johannes Kepler in 1604) and, more recently and more importantly, from telescopic observations of the faint outbursts from supernovas occurring in distant galaxies. In the realm of supernovas one rapidly runs out of superlatives—suffice it to say that they are by far the most energetic stellar events known and are responsible for some of the most exotic objects in the universe.

Although supernovas are believed to occur once every few decades among the 100 billion stars of our own Galaxy, the Milky Way, the light of all but the closest is obscured from view on Earth by intervening

Telescopic photographs of galaxy NGC 4725 in the constellation Coma Berenices taken in May 1940 (far left) and January 1941 (left) reveal the position of a "new" star above and to the left of the galaxy's central region. For a short time the light from a supernova may rival the combined brightness of all other stars in the parent galaxy. No supernova in our Galaxy has been seen distinctly with the naked eye since the early 1600s.

Photos, copyright California Institute of Technology

interstellar dust. No supernova in the Milky Way has been witnessed since the advent of the telescope for astronomical research in the early 1600s. Looking out of the plane of the Milky Way, however, into the dust-free depths of intergalactic space, astronomers can use telescopes to detect supernovas in even distant galaxies. At its brightest a supernova might for a short time outshine the combined light of all other stars in its parent galaxy.

The last supernova bright enough to be seen distinctly with the naked eye was that witnessed by Kepler 383 years ago—until February 24, 1987. On that date what generations of astronomers had been hoping to witness finally happened.

Discovery

The young Canadian astronomer Ian Shelton had been given permission to use a small, 0.25-meter (10-inch) telescope at the Las Campanas Observatory in northern Chile to photograph the Large Magellanic Cloud (LMC) in a search for variable stars—stars whose brightness varies with time, often in a regular manner. At a distance of some 160,000 light-years, the LMC is one of the Milky Way's companion galaxies and its nearest galactic neighbor. (A light-year, the distance light travels in one year, is roughly ten trillion kilometers, or 6.2 trillion miles.) Modern observatories are sited on remote mountaintops (Las Campanas is at an altitude of more than 2,440 meters, or 8,000 feet), far from sources of light contamination and in less disturbed air than at sea level. The night of February 23–24 was just the second of Shelton's planned variable star survey of the LMC.

At about 2:40 AM local time, Shelton determined that his night's observing was complete, but he decided to develop the last photographic plate before getting to bed. Lifting the developed plate from the fixing bath, he looked in disbelief at what appeared to be a brilliant star adjacent to the Tarantula Nebula, one of the LMC's well-known beauty spots. There had been no sign of such a star on a plate taken the previous night,

53

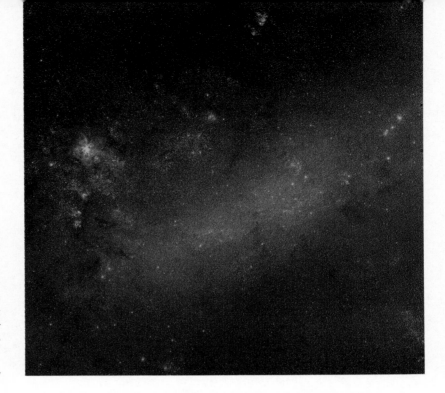

The Large Magellanic Cloud (LMC), at a distance of 160,000 light-years, is the nearest galaxy to the Milky Way. It contains perhaps ten billion stars, a tenth that of the Milky Way, and is easily seen with the naked eye from the Earth's Southern Hemisphere. The prominent pink spot on the left just above center is the Tarantula Nebula, a massive gas cloud.

European Southern Observatory

Ian Shelton (below) of the University of Toronto first noticed the supernova in the LMC during the early morning of February 24, 1987, on a photographic plate exposed earlier that night. His discovery photo (far right) is compared with a photo made by Shelton the previous night (right) only hours before the progenitor star exploded. The Tarantula Nebula lies to the left of the supernova.

Photos, © University of Toronto

his first of the new survey. Shelton's initial reaction of incredulity must have been similar to that of Tycho Brahe long ago. Shelton suspected that there was a flaw in the photographic plate, but on the chance that the image was real he rushed outside and gazed southward, thus becoming the first person in almost four centuries to view a supernova without the aid of a telescope.

In doubt no longer, Shelton quickly alerted other observers on the mountain, who were able to confirm his interpretation that at the observed brightness the star had to be a supernova. In Nelson, New Zealand, amateur sky watcher Albert Jones independently discovered the supernova later that morning. Undoubtedly, many others looked at the LMC on that night and noticed something unusual. In fact, the new supernova unknowingly had been photographed before Shelton's discovery. At the Siding Spring Observatory in New South Wales, Australia, astronomer

Robert McNaught had, like Shelton, been photographing the LMC in search of variable stars. His film record of the nights of February 22–24 had not been checked before word of Shelton's find arrived. McNaught's photograph of February 23 reveals the brightening supernova some 18 hours before Shelton's plate was made.

The astronomical world is alerted to new discoveries via a system of telegrams and airmail circulars emanating from the International Astronomical Union's (IAU's) clearinghouse in Cambridge, Massachusetts. Shelton made sure the IAU telegram service was informed as soon as possible about his discovery, and Service Director Brian Marsden alerted some 150 astronomical institutions worldwide. Marsden acknowledges that Shelton was the first to get the message through to Cambridge (his repeated attempts to alert Marsden by telephone from the mountaintop had failed, necessitating a trip down the mountain to send a telex) but also that Jones should be recognized as codiscoverer since he got word through to Cambridge a short time later.

Within 24 hours of Shelton's first sighting, telescopes around the world were being trained toward the Tarantula's new mate, which had been given the name Supernova (SN) 1987A. Instruments on spacecraft, able to detect radiation such as X-rays and ultraviolet waves that cannot penetrate the Earth's atmosphere, were commanded to point at the new supernova. For astronomers with access to advanced instrumentation, a new era had dawned: at last a supernova had been discovered that was bright enough to be studied in great detail with the extensions to the human senses provided by advanced technology. Its study would dominate the use of the world's most advanced telescopes and lead to some interesting innovations in the use of instrumentation. The dustcovers were removed from equipment not touched for decades. New instruments optimized to analyze the bright light of the supernova were hurriedly constructed. The most powerful stellar spectrograph ever deployed was put together within weeks by scientists at the Anglo-Australian Observatory using homemade components mounted in a wooden frame. After more than a decade, the Woomera rocket range in Australia was reopened to

Amateur astronomer Robert McNaught (above) poses with the camera with which he photographed the February supernova 18 hours before Shelton's discovery plate was made. A photo of the LMC that McNaught took on February 22 (below left) is compared with one he made on the following night (below), when the supernova was only a few hours old.

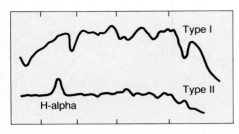

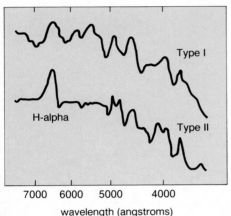

7000 6000 5000 4000

wavelength (angstroms)

Early searches for supernovas uncovered two different kinds—now known as Type I and Type II—that can be distinguished by spectroscopic analyses of their light. In the sample spectra above, the two types are compared near their maximum brightness (top) and one month later (bottom). Type II supernovas show distinct features associated with hydrogen—the H-alpha peak, for example—while Type I's do not. Another difference is apparent in the way the brightnesses of the two types vary with time; see the light-curve plot on page 63.

From *Superstars*, by David H. Clark, McGraw-Hill Book Company, New York, 1984, reproduced by permission.

civilian rocket launches to study the supernova. Observational astronomy had never before witnessed such a frenzy.

Searching for supernovas

The father of modern supernova research was Fritz Zwicky, who instigated the first systematic survey for supernovas in 1934 by using a rooftop camera at the California Institute of Technology. At the time, the true nature of supernovas was not understood. Zwicky and his collaborator, Walter Baade, argued that they were explosions of a star's outer envelope of matter, brought on by exhaustion of the star's internal supply of energy and consequent implosion, or violent collapse, of its central core. The Zwicky-Baade thesis was not widely accepted when first postulated but has subsequently been shown to be valid in large measure. Zwicky's initial survey failed to make any discoveries, and a new 0.45-meter (18-inch) telescope at Mount Palomar, California, was assigned to the task. Within months Zwicky was discovering supernovas in abundance.

Zwicky initially thought that supernovas were all of the same kind since the first 12 detected—now known as Type I supernovas—seemed to be so similar. However, the next two discovered—now classified as Type II supernovas—were entirely different. The differences are most pronounced in a spectroscopic analysis, in which the supernova's light is spread out into its component colors. Type I are devoid of wavelengths associated with hydrogen (the most abundant element in the cosmos), while Type II develop distinct hydrogen features. Another important difference is in the way the brightness of the two types varies with time—depicted by their so-called light curves. Both types usually brighten spectacularly over just a few days before fading gradually, but the declining brightness of a Type I supernova is more uniform and protracted than that of a Type II. Type I supernovas seem to be remarkably consistent in their properties (although two subclasses of Type I are recognized), while Type II appear highly individualistic.

Techniques for finding supernovas vary. In the most successful surveys, selected fields of the sky are monitored month by month and the photographic plates compared for the appearance of new stars. Automated surveys have not so far realized their promise, and there is to date no better supernova detector than the human eye, laboriously scanning photographic images of distant galaxies. Supernova surveys are also an exercise the diligent amateur astronomer can perform with reasonable chance of success, as evidenced by Albert Jones's codiscovery of SN 1987A. (The most successful amateur supernova sleuth has been Robert Evans, a Uniting Church minister from New South Wales. Of 18 supernovas detected by amateur astronomers in this century, Evans can lay claim to 15. Sadly, on the night of February 23 his telescope was clouded out. Just four days later, by way of compensation, Evans discovered SN 1987B, a very much fainter and more distant supernova.)

Once a discovery has been confirmed, the IAU designates the event with the year plus a letter indicating discovery order. For example, SN 1961E was the fifth supernova discovered in 1961. Almost 600 supernovas have been discovered since Zwicky's pioneering survey, but all at much greater distances and consequently thousands or even millions of times fainter than SN 1987A. Previously astronomers could only guess at the intricacies of the supernova phenomenon. SN 1987A would allow the full power of modern astronomical research to be unleashed.

The road to superstardom

Astronomers have a reasonable understanding of how certain stars evolve toward their eventual demise in supernova explosions. A star produces its energy in a central core at temperatures so extreme (hundreds of millions of degrees) that certain nuclear burning processes, called fusion reactions, can occur. For the bulk of a star's life, hydrogen nuclei are fused to form helium nuclei, with the release of vast quantities of energy that sustain the stellar structure against the inward pull of gravity. The eventual fate of a star—and whether it ends in explosive death—depends on its mass.

Consider first the case of a star of about 20 solar masses; *i.e.*, having a mass about 20 times that of the Sun. When all the core hydrogen in such a star has been expended, after some ten million years, the core contracts and increases in temperature under the action of gravity, precipitating the burning of the helium "ash" left over from the earlier hydrogen transmutation. Helium nuclei now fuse to form the heavier nuclei of carbon and oxygen. The outer envelope of the star expands and cools, and the star becomes what is known as a red supergiant, a rather unstable phase in a massive star's evolution. After all the helium in the core has in turn been expended, later stages of nuclear burning follow rapidly; successively heavier nuclei fuse to create elements all the way to iron. Still heavier elements cannot be made in energy-releasing reactions; instead, their production requires an input of energy. Thus, with no new energy release to sustain the star's structure, the central core collapses under the action of gravity. The core crunches together in a fraction of a second to a state of extreme density.

The blink-of-an-eye collapse initiates some of the most exotic phenomena known. The atomic material making up the core is compressed to densities found in atomic nuclei, forming what is called a neutron star. Individual protons and electrons fuse together to form neutrons; this reaction releases strange will-o'-the-wisp particles called neutrinos, which have zero or negligible mass and travel at or very near the speed of light. The sudden perturbation of space from the massive collapse is believed to generate an outwardly propagating gravitational wave. For particularly massive stars, core collapse is thought to continue beyond nuclear densities to create a black hole, an object having a gravitational field so intense that even light itself cannot escape from it.

In collapsing, the core of a star initially overshoots neutron-star density and then bounces back, producing an expanding shock wave. Having lost the supporting core, the outer envelope of the star collapses behind it. Before meeting the newly formed neutron star, however, it encounters the outwardly moving shock wave, which blasts the envelope into space

Astronomers looking for new supernovas adjust an automated-search telescope operated by the University of California at Berkeley. A computer moves the 0.76-meter (30-inch) reflector, which is equipped with a highly light-sensitive charge-coupled-device (CCD) camera, from one galaxy to the next and automatically records the images for comparison with reference images. Electronic methods of image comparison have been tried in conjunction with automated search but have not yet proved the equal of the human eye.

matter transfer

b

Type II supernovas (opposite page) occur in stars of perhaps 15–20 solar masses that have exhausted their nuclear fuel. The interior of such a star resembles an onion (a), comprising layers of successively heavier elements—from hydrogen to iron—that have been formed during a lifetime of nuclear burning. With the formation of iron, the chain of energy-releasing reactions comes to an end. Energy output no longer sustains the star's structure, and its core suddenly begins to crush together (b). In collapsing, the core first overshoots its final density (c) and then rebounds (d). The resulting shock wave encounters the star's outer envelope, which now also has begun to collapse, and blasts it into space in a violent explosion (e–f).

a

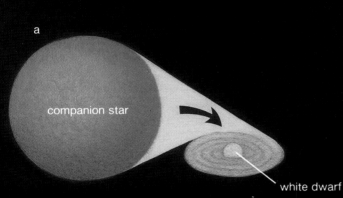

companion star

white dwarf

c

Type I supernovas, though not well understood, are thought to occur in close binary systems in which one star is a compact white dwarf (a). Under the action of gravity, matter is transferred from the larger, more normal companion to the white dwarf (b) until enough mass accumulates to trigger an explosive nuclear reaction, which destroys the smaller star (c).

Illustration by Jane Meredith

at speeds of thousands of kilometers per second. In this way the bulk of the mass of the dying star is ejected like shrapnel from a bomb—an act of stellar suicide that is witnessed on Earth as a Type II supernova.

The energy released in a supernova, equivalent to that from the simultaneous explosion of a hundred billion billion billion hydrogen bombs, defies comprehension. Only a minute fraction of the energy appears in the optical outburst; most resides in the enormous flux of neutrinos, with the balance being in the exploding debris. For centuries and millennia after the explosion, the expanding debris can be seen flying away from the site of the holocaust. The expanding shock wave sweeps up surrounding interstellar material like a snowplow. Some of the most spectacular nebulosities in the heavens, such as the Crab Nebula, are the remnants of past supernova explosions.

The likely explanation for Type I supernovas is less certain. Stars about the mass of the Sun or a few times larger do not burn as quickly

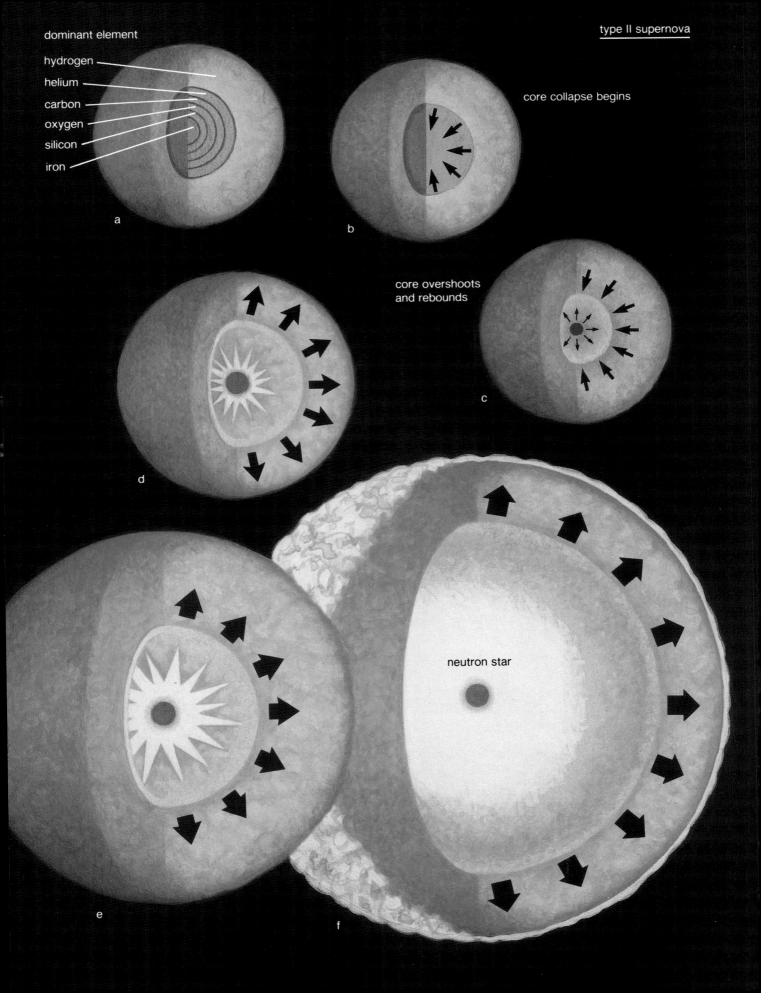

dominant element

hydrogen
helium
carbon
oxygen
silicon
iron

a

b

core collapse begins

core overshoots
and rebounds

c

d

e

neutron star

f

or die as catastrophically as more massive stars but evolve comparatively sedately over billions of years to become white dwarfs, burned-out receptacles of nuclear garbage. Stars often occur in pairs, each star orbiting the other and forming a binary system. In some of these systems the two stars are near enough for matter to be transferred from one to the other under the action of gravity. Any such close binary system in which one of the stars has already evolved to become a white dwarf is a potential Type I supernova candidate. Transfer of material from the normal star to the white dwarf is believed in certain situations to trigger an explosive nuclear reaction, which completely destroys the white dwarf in a Type I supernova.

Supernovas have had a major influence on the chemical evolution of the universe. The primordial universe that resulted from the epoch of creation known as the big bang was almost entirely hydrogen and helium. Only after stars formed were heavier elements up to iron fused into existence in the centers of stars and then blasted into interstellar space in supernova explosions. Indeed, it is in the particularly energetic conditions of supernovas themselves that many of the rarer, heavier elements above iron have been created. From such enriched matter fed to the interstellar medium in supernova events have come new generations of stars, planetary systems, and Earthly life.

It is even likely that supernovas have played more direct roles in the destiny of planet Earth. First, there is circumstantial evidence that the collapse of the protosolar cloud from which the Sun and its planetary system formed was precipitated by a nearby supernova. Second, because supernovas within a few light-years of the solar system can be expected as frequently as every 100 million years on the average, the Earth probably received several doses of radiation intense enough to have had profound effects on its biologic and climatic evolution.

60

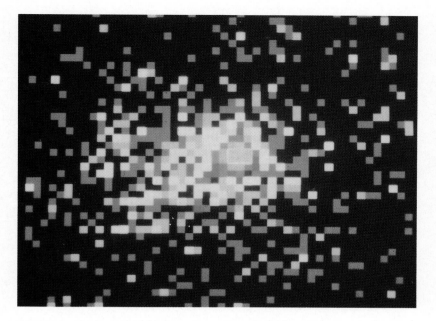

Computerized, color-coded image of SN 1987A was obtained by a visible-light acquisition camera aboard the International Ultraviolet Explorer (IUE) prior to observation with the spacecraft's ultraviolet detectors. Red represents the brightest regions of the supernova, followed by green, blue, white, gray, and black. IUE's apparent detection of ultraviolet radiation from Sanduleak −69 202 after the explosion seemed at first to eliminate the star as the progenitor, but later IUE data showed that the ultraviolet was from nearby objects and that the star had disappeared.

NASA

What ever happened to Sanduleak −69 202?

Early spectral observation of SN 1987A quickly identified it as a Type II supernova, but it soon became obvious that this dying star was neither an ordinary Type II nor about to part docilely with its secrets. Robert McNaught was the first to realize that the position of the supernova coincided (to better than a few hundredths of a second of arc) with that of a star previously catalogued as Sanduleak −69 202. By its position this star was a prime suspect as the progenitor of SN 1987A, but it had one glaring deficiency: it was not a red supergiant. In fact, Sanduleak −69 202 was a bright, massive star of a type known as a blue supergiant, previously showing no indication of unstable behavior and thought to be far too young and compact for premature demise.

The confusion seemed to lift for a time after a satellite designed to measure ultraviolet radiation, the International Ultraviolet Explorer (IUE), appeared to detect radiation still emanating from Sanduleak −69 202. Thus, it was argued, the actual star that exploded must have been a much fainter star lying close to, and perhaps masked by, the blue supergiant. IUE also initially detected comparatively strong ultraviolet emission from the supernova itself, but the emission rapidly faded, indicating that SN 1987A was cooling more quickly than expected.

Ginga, a Japanese satellite launched just three weeks before the supernova outburst, made an initially fruitless search for X-rays from the supernova, although they had been detected by October as the expanding envelope of the supernova became translucent to X-rays. Ground-based radio telescopes picked up emission from the supernova, although at a much fainter level than that observed from previous Type II's. (On the other hand, maximum radio brightness is not expected to follow until months or years after the explosion.) Theoretical modeling suggested that the progenitor star had a mass about 15 to 20 times that of the Sun.

61

Later in the year, as the ultraviolet emission from the supernova rapidly faded, IUE observations finally settled the debate about the progenitor—but not in the way many supernova pundits had expected. The residual ultraviolet was shown conclusively to be coming from nearby objects and not from Sanduleak −69 202, which was nowhere to be found. The blue supergiant and the theory that linked Type II supernovas exclusively with red supergiants had both been exploded.

A very peculiar light curve

Supernova 1987A refused to follow the established rules. The one characteristic of an exploding star that theorists thought they could explain with reasonable confidence was the way its brightness varied with time. Both types were known to brighten rapidly (within a few days) before fading over varying time scales. The light curve for a Type I supernova shows a particularly rapid rise that peaks typically at an absolute magnitude of −19. (See Sidebar.) After an initial drop of about three magnitudes in 20–30 days, the light curve falls about one magnitude in each successive interval of 50 days. The rather slow decline in the brightness of Type I supernovas has been ascribed to continued injection of energy from the decay of radioactive nickel (to cobalt and subsequently to iron) that was created in the extreme conditions of the Type I outburst. By comparison, Type II supernovas typically reach an absolute magnitude of −17, decline to a short-lived plateau, and then fade rapidly, although, as mentioned above, there is no such thing as "typical" Type II behavior.

The light curve of SN 1987A, however, proved to be much more than individualistic. It was positively bizarre. After increasing in brightness by about eight magnitudes over a few tens of hours to its discovery magnitude of +4.5, SN 1987A eschewed the usual peak and subsequent decline. Instead it remained almost uniformly bright for months, indeed slowly increasing to a magnitude of +2.9 in late May before returning to its discovery magnitude by late July. Only one previous supernova studied, SN 1961V, had displayed such a peculiar light curve. Even at its maximum of magnitude +2.9, however, SN 1987A was a fainter-than-typical Type II; at the distance of the LMC its brightness corresponded to an absolute magnitude of −15 rather than the expected −17. The low luminosity and peculiar light curve are believed to result in some way from the progenitor star's being a blue (rather than red) supergiant, this in turn being due to the deficiency of heavy elements in the LMC interstellar material, from which the star was originally formed.

What powered the slow postdiscovery increase in brightness? One plausible suggestion is the radioactive decay of almost a tenth of a solar mass of nickel created in the outburst, first to cobalt and subsequently to iron. This mechanism is the same as that invoked to explain the slow decline in the light curve of Type I supernovas, although in the latter case nearly a full solar mass of nickel is required. Supporting evidence has come from a NASA satellite known as Solar Max, whose primary task has been the study of the Sun. Solar Max detected an emission identified with cobalt, the radioactive decay product of nickel.

A likely continuing influence on the evolving remnant of SN 1987A is the activity associated with the newly formed neutron star. The pre-supernova star probably had been rotating with a rather sedate period of a few weeks. The collapsing core, however, must have spun itself up like a pirouetting ice skater such that it now rotates tens or even hundreds of times per second. Such rapidly spinning neutron stars can behave like radio beacons, emitting a directional beam of emission that sweeps over the Earth with each turn of the star. Such objects, called radio pulsars, have been discovered at the sites of supernova explosions; the Crab Nebula, for example, has a pulsar flashing 30 times each second at its center. It is possible that a nascent, as yet undetected pulsar rotating some 200 times per second may have contributed to the unusual light curve of SN 1987A and will influence the evolution of the supernova's remnant.

Supernova 1987A is the brightest extragalactic stellar source ever available to astronomers for studying the intervening intergalactic and interstellar medium. The space between the stars is not a perfect vacuum but is pervaded by a tenuous gas, usually concentrated into vast clouds. Likewise, the space between galaxies also contains gas, but of even lower density. A bright background source of light such as a supernova can be used to probe the distribution and composition of the interstellar and intergalactic medium. Observations of SN 1987A have revealed at least 40 gas clouds along the line of sight to the supernova: 6 in the outer reaches of the Milky Way, 12 in the LMC itself, and the remainder in a tenuous bridge of gas linking the two galaxies. Never before has it been possible for astronomers to study the ethereal intergalactic medium in such detail.

Another first for the superstar

Despite its vagaries, SN 1987A did make the theoreticians happy in one regard—it produced a detectable flux of the mysterious neutrinos. The explosion was sufficiently close that instruments on Earth for the

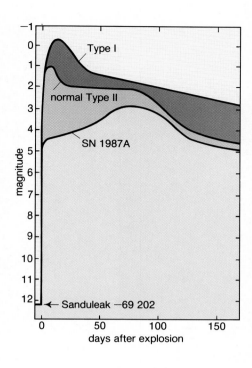

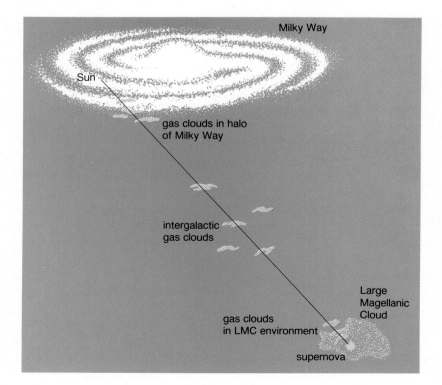

Light curves for Type I and normal Type II supernovas and SN 1987A are compared (above). The vertical scale, calibrated in apparent magnitudes, depicts all three events as they would look from the same 160,000-light-year distance of the LMC. Before the explosion Sanduleak −69 202 shone with a magnitude of about +12. (Left) Observations making use of the bright background light provided by SN 1987A have revealed at least 40 gas clouds along the line of sight to the supernova. Some of the clouds exist near the edge of the Milky Way or in the LMC, while others lie in a tenuous bridge of gas between the two galaxies.

(Above) adapted from *New Scientist*, vol. 116, no. 1585. This first appeared in *New Scientist*, London, the weekly review of science and technology

first time actually recorded the neutrino burst long predicted to occur during the violent seconds of a stellar core collapse. In that instant SN 1987A gave birth to a new branch of astronomy—neutrino astronomy. Detectors built to spot neutrinos had previously been used to study the Sun, since the nuclear processes occurring deep within it are expected to produce measurable fluxes of neutrinos (although in the case of solar neutrinos there remains a yawning gap between theoretical expectations and experimental reality).

The most compelling evidence for neutrinos from SN 1987A actually came from experiments designed for a completely different purpose, to investigate the possible decay of protons. To avoid contamination from background cosmic rays, these experiments are conducted in deep underground mines. Large tanks of highly purified water are used to "trap" the ethereal neutrinos, which pass through material with little chance of interacting—hence the penetration of neutrinos from the supernova through the Earth's crust to the deep mine experiments. Yet within the enormous volume of water in the tanks, some few neutrinos do interact, resulting in a flash of deep blue light called Cherenkov radiation. This light is then detected by a submerged array of photoelectric cells.

Researcher inspects rows of photomultiplier tubes near the tank bottom of the Kamiokande II detector in Japan. During operation the tank is filled with 3,000 tons of highly purified water to provide a medium for particle interaction. In February 1987 the detector registered a burst of 12 neutrinos whose time and direction of arrival showed them unequivocably to be from SN 1987A.

Courtesy of Kamiokande-II Collaboration

The first reported neutrino detection came from Japan by way of an experiment called Kamiokande II, located 910 meters (3,000 feet) underground in a mine of the Kamioka Mining and Smelting Co. in Gifu. The time of the detection and the calculated direction of arrival left no doubt that the neutrinos were from SN 1987A. Neutrinos from the supernova were also detected by a U.S. experiment under the shore of Lake Erie in Ohio. The detection levels were remarkably close to those predicted from the collapse of a stellar core to form a 1.5 solar-mass neutron star. In other words, here was the first genuine observational evidence

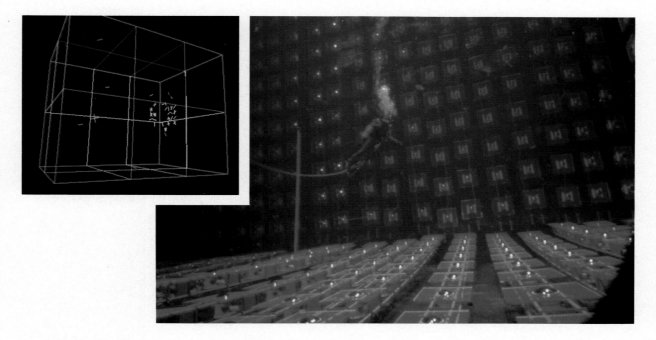

confirming that gravitational energy was the driving force behind Type II supernovas. In addition, the duration of the neutrino event confirmed that the supernova left a neutron star, rather than a black hole, as its stellar remnant. If a black hole had formed, it would have trapped the latter portion of the neutrino pulse, resulting in a sharp cutoff.

The detection of neutrinos from SN 1987A also reveals much about the nature of the mysterious particles themselves. First, they are clearly comparatively long-lived, having survived the 160,000-year journey from the LMC. One explanation for the lower-than-expected level of solar neutrinos, now disproved by the supernova results, had been that they had decayed on their eight-minute journey from the Sun. Second, the time that neutrinos from the supernova were detected on Earth fits well with the assumption that they traveled at the speed of light. This places a very tight upper limit on a possible mass for neutrinos because relativity theory forbids objects with mass to achieve light speed. Whereas neutrinos have generally been regarded as massless, some contradictory evidence gathered in the past decade has prompted speculation about the consequences of a nonzero neutrino mass. Even if the mass of a single neutrino was a minute fraction of that of an electron, neutrinos collectively might make a significant contribution to the mass required for binding galaxies in clusters and even for allowing the eventual contraction of the presently expanding universe. By any measure, the advent of neutrino astronomy will greatly influence astronomy and physics.

Tycho's supernova of 1572 deeply affected Renaissance science and the post-Ptolemaic view of a perfect and immutable universe. The power of modern observational astronomy will ensure that the effect of Superstar 1987 on modern scientific thought will be just as profound.

See also Feature Article: A NEW UNDERSTANDING OF OUR SUN.

Eight neutrinos from the February supernova were also detected by an experiment in Ohio comprising an underground tank of 7,000 tons of purified water monitored by some 2,000 photomultiplier tubes (above). Computer-generated display (inset on left) reconstructs one of the detection events as seen from the direction of the supernova. Faces of the tank are outlined in various colors. The cluster of yellow crosses in the far corner of the tank represents photomultiplier tubes that recorded light signals arising from interaction of the neutrino with a proton in the water.

Photos, The IMB Collaboration

A New Understanding of Our Sun

by Jay M. Pasachoff

"What is that big ball of light in the sky?" The old cloudy-weather joke remains the central question for solar astronomers, who continue to make fascinating discoveries about our nearest stellar neighbor.

The bright, shining surface of the Sun is the astronomical object people see most often. When it is in the sky, its bright light turns the sky blue, blocking our view of the distant stars and rest of the universe. Nevertheless, astronomers who study the Sun are far from discontent with their solitary daytime object of interest. They are learning not only about the properties of a particular, average star but also much about the details of processes that must take place in most stars. Moreover, insights gained from studying the Sun provide important clues about the nature and behavior of matter and energy.

JAY M. PASACHOFF is Field Memorial Professor of Astronomy and Director of the Hopkins Observatory, Williams College, Williamstown, Massachusetts.

Photograph © Jay M. Pasachoff

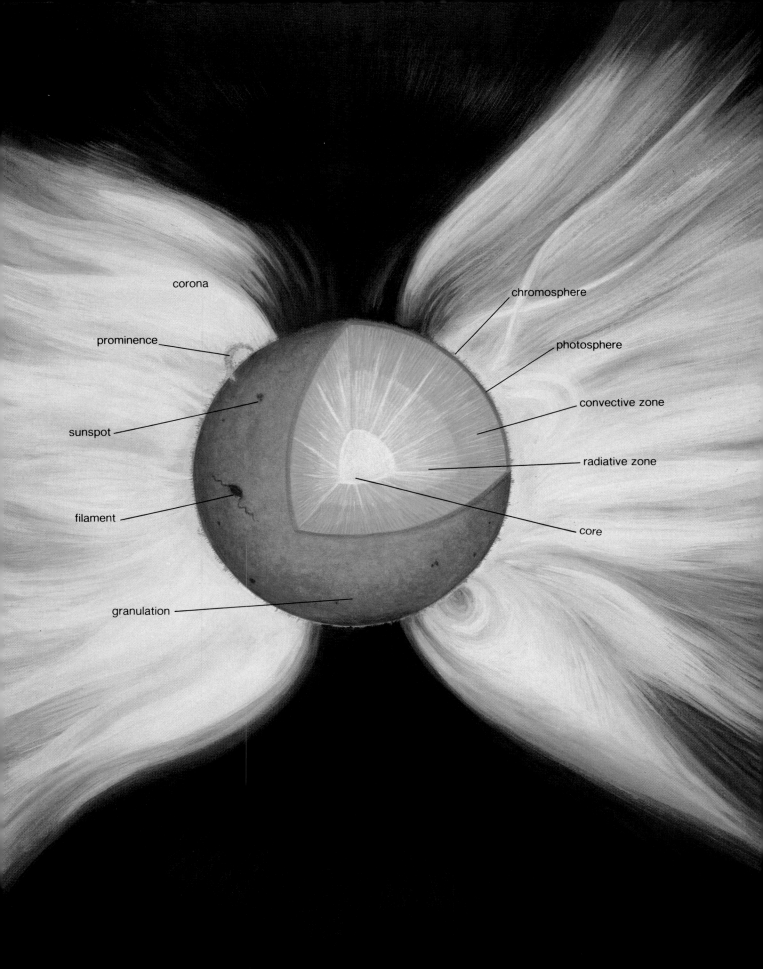

The solar surface

The bright visible surface of the Sun is called the photosphere, from the Greek words for "sphere of light." The photosphere is only one layer of the Sun, actually the lowest layer of its atmosphere. Beneath the photosphere is the solar interior—denser than the atmosphere but still gaseous—at the center of which is the core, where all of the Sun's energy is generated. Energy from the core travels gradually outward through a thick radiative zone and a thinner convective zone before reaching the photosphere. Above the photosphere lie two tenuous upper layers of atmosphere: a comparatively thin, spiky-looking, reddish layer called the chromosphere ("sphere of color") and, above that, a white, ghostly halo called the corona ("crown"), which extends many millions of kilometers into space.

The smallest regions on the photosphere that can be seen with a telescope are a salt-and-pepper effect known as granulation. The new solar observatory in the Canary Islands has provided especially good images of the constituent granules, which are only about 700 kilometers across. (One kilometer is about 0.62 miles.) The granulation is no larger in angular size in the sky than the finest regions the Earth's atmosphere allows observers to see. The granulation is a boiling effect, caused by convection as hotter regions of gas are buoyed upward in the solar atmosphere.

Turbulence in the Earth's atmosphere has kept earthbound astronomers from studying well how the granulation changes with time. Each granule appears to last only about 15 minutes. The Solar Optical Universal Polarimeter (SOUP), an instrument carried into orbit with the Spacelab module on a U.S. space shuttle flight in 1985, was able to make a series

The parts of the Sun's atmosphere and interior are shown in the cutaway diagram on the opposite page. Energy released in thermonuclear reactions in the core is gradually transported by radiation and convection to the visible surface, or photosphere, and then into the chromosphere and corona.

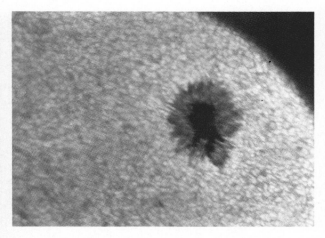

Especially sharp image of a sunspot and surrounding granulation (above) was made with the new Vacuum Tower Telescope of the Kiepenheuer Institute for Solar Physics in the Canary Islands (left).

(Left) NASA; (right) Lockheed Research Laboratory, Lockheed Solar Physics Group

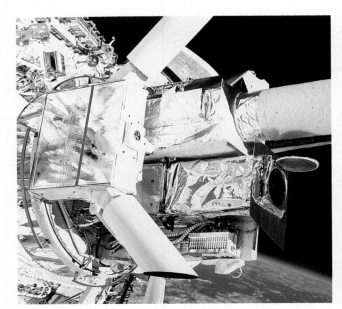
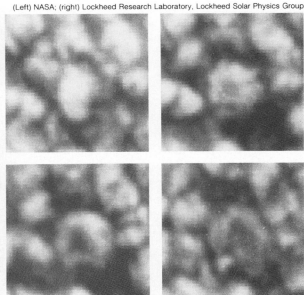

The Solar Optical Universal Polarimeter (SOUP), carried into orbit on a U.S. space shuttle mission in 1985, appears in the photo above as the rectangular, open-lidded box near the center. Its pictures of granulation include long sequences showing individual granules in the process of exploding. In the series of images from SOUP at the top right, taken three to four minutes apart, a granule gradually disperses its material outward along the solar surface.

of images of granulation many hours long. The pictures showed that many granules seem to explode, diffusing their material outward along the solar surface as they end their lives.

While earlier observations of the Sun from space had extended astronomers' view beyond visible light into other regions of the spectrum, they had not equaled the highest resolution obtained from ground-based observatories. The Spacelab results thus represented a new phase in high-resolution solar observations. Unfortunately, the explosion of the shuttle *Challenger* has postponed further Spacelab flights for many years. Another space observatory, the Solar Optical Telescope, which had been designed to send back observations ten times more precise than the Spacelab images, was first simplified to the High Resolution Solar Observatory and now has been held up indefinitely. Consequently, solar scientists in the United States have been looking for a solar mission that NASA will take forward.

Luckily for solar astronomy, Earth-orbiting satellites are commonly designed with solar panels that automatically face the Sun. Taking advantage of this feature, scientists have succeeded in arranging for the series of National Oceanic and Atmospheric Administration spacecraft that will be launched starting in the early 1990s to carry solar telescopes. Mounted on the panel structures, the telescopes will constantly track the Sun. The first ones, at least, will be devoted to studying solar X-rays, which come from active regions on the Sun where intense concentrations of magnetic fields lead to sunspots and violently eruptive flares. Data will be radioed back to Earth as they are taken, as often as once a minute.

Solar active regions

The number of active regions on the Sun rises and falls in a well-known cycle that is about 11 years long. The last maximum in the cycle

70

Photos, Mukul R. Kundu, University of Maryland, College Park

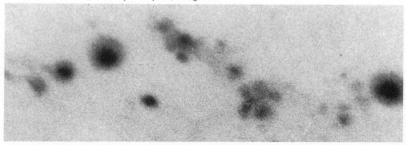

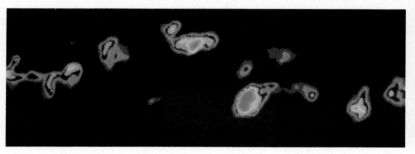

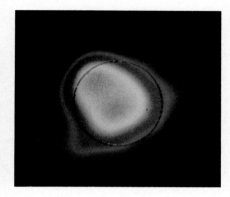

took place in late 1979, and the next will occur in 1991. A peak in the number of sunspots—dark, comparatively cool regions on the solar surface—is the most obvious manifestation of the maximum. Other solar phenomena peak as well; for example, the number of solar flares is higher than it is at solar minimum. The cause of flares—which are hot, particle- and radiation-spewing storms lasting minutes to several hours—is not yet known, though clearly flares are connected with the storage of energy in the Sun's magnetic field. Observations made by the Solar Maximum Mission spacecraft (Solar Max) in the visible and X-ray parts of the Sun's spectrum and from telescopes on the ground have together helped astronomers better understand the order of processes that a solar flare comprises.

Solar Max was launched in February 1980 just after the last maximum of the sunspot cycle, largely to study flares and other phenomena of the Sun at its most magnetically active. Nine months later the system that controlled the pointing of the spacecraft failed. After years of planning and rehearsal, space-shuttle astronauts brought the spacecraft to the shuttle's cargo bay and repaired it in April 1984, the first satellite ever to be repaired in orbit. Just two weeks later instruments aboard Solar Max observed the most intense flare of the cycle.

Temperatures in solar flares can rise above 10 million kelvins (K), making them strong emitters of X-rays and gamma rays. (At the high temperatures of the Sun, the kelvin and Celsius scales are virtually identical; to convert kelvins approximately to Fahrenheit, multiply by 1.8.) Interpretation of Solar Maximum Mission data has helped investigators understand this emission process during the brief, violent phase of a flare known as the impulsive phase. The impulsive phase lasts from a few seconds to ten minutes and is followed by a gradual phase, which can go on for hours. It apparently occurs when an expanding loop of

White-light image of a solar active region (left, top) is compared with an image made with the Very Large Array radio telescope in New Mexico (left, bottom). A radio image of the whole Sun (above), with a tracing of the solar disk superimposed in black, was recorded with the Clark Lake radio telescope in California. Recent ground-based radio-wave studies have contributed to a better understanding of sunspots, flares, and other phenomena of the active Sun. (Below) U.S. space shuttle astronauts make in-orbit repairs on the Solar Maximum Mission satellite in April 1984.

NASA

Images of a solar active region in X-ray wavelengths (top left) and white light (top right) were obtained by Solar Max on April 25, 1984, just two weeks after it was repaired in space. Before the spacecraft's pointing system failed in 1980, an on-board ultraviolet telescope made observations of arches and loops associated with flare activity on the edge, or limb, of the Sun (bottom left and right).

magnetic force lines on the Sun runs into a second loop and "shorts out," perhaps reaching temperatures of 100 million K in the process. An X-ray telescope aboard Solar Max showed that X-rays come from the footpoints of the loops where they intersect the chromosphere and photosphere. Beams of high-energy charged particles, especially electrons, flow along these magnetic loops; when they reach denser material and are stopped abruptly, their kinetic energy is changed into X-rays and gamma rays. Since the pulses of X-rays and gamma rays are received nearly simultaneously, the particles in the beams must be decelerated within a very small region near the solar surface, perhaps in the chromosphere. An ultraviolet telescope on board Solar Max showed that the small regions brighten in ultraviolet emission simultaneously with the impulsive X-ray emission. After the flare deposits energy at low altitudes in the solar atmosphere, the material there explodes upward at hundreds of kilometers per second to become coronal loops. Some of the loops are detectable for hours afterward from the X-rays they radiate.

Since X-rays normally penetrate any surface they hit head on, including mirrors intended to collect and focus them, X-ray telescopes until recently were designed to be used at grazing incidence. Just as a rock can skip off a lake surface if thrown at a low angle, an X-ray can reflect off a surface if it hits at a low angle. When seen at a low angle, however, a surface has a small projected area for reflection. Thus, to observe faint sources of X-rays, grazing-incidence telescopes need very large reflective surfaces. A new type of X-ray telescope circumvents this limitation by making use of a mirror with special thin coatings that reflect head-

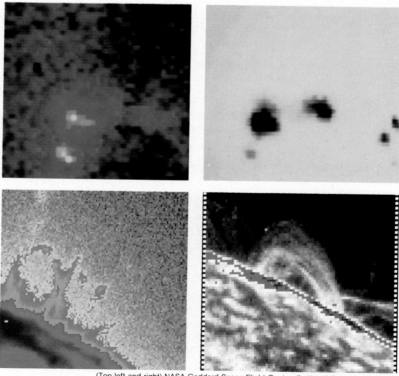

(Top left and right) NASA Goddard Space Flight Center; (bottom left and right) NASA Marshall Space Flight Center

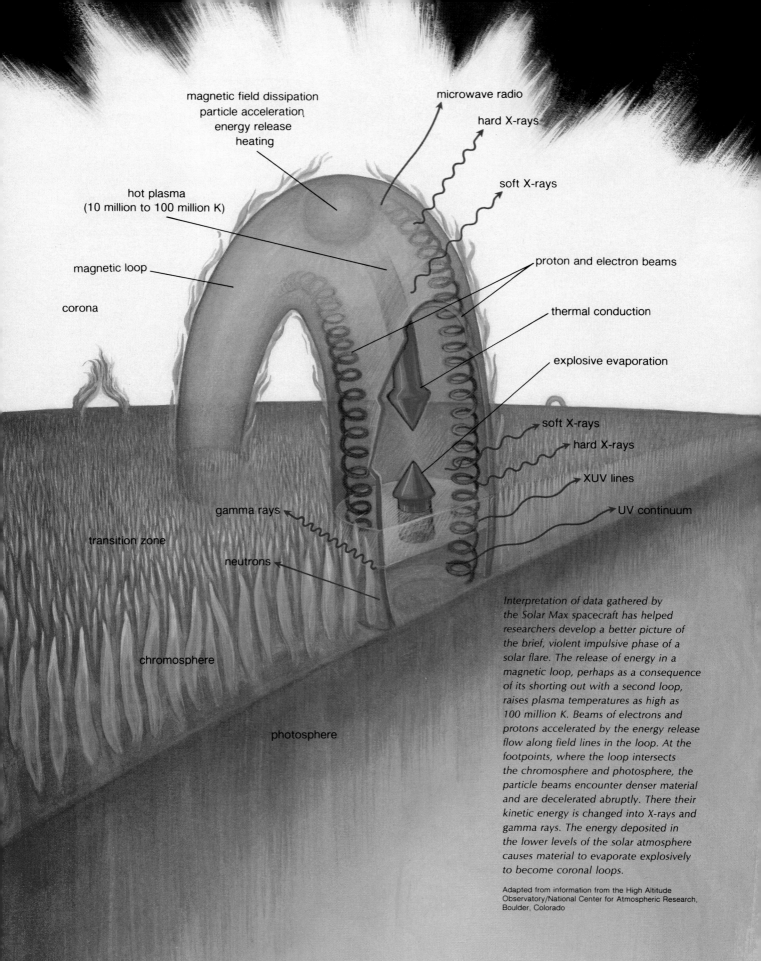

magnetic field dissipation
particle acceleration
energy release
heating

microwave radio

hard X-rays

soft X-rays

hot plasma
(10 million to 100 million K)

proton and electron beams

magnetic loop

thermal conduction

corona

explosive evaporation

soft X-rays

hard X-rays

XUV lines

UV continuum

gamma rays

transition zone

neutrons

chromosphere

photosphere

Interpretation of data gathered by
the Solar Max spacecraft has helped
researchers develop a better picture of
the brief, violent impulsive phase of a
solar flare. The release of energy in a
magnetic loop, perhaps as a consequence
of its shorting out with a second loop,
raises plasma temperatures as high as
100 million K. Beams of electrons and
protons accelerated by the energy release
flow along field lines in the loop. At the
footpoints, where the loop intersects
the chromosphere and photosphere, the
particle beams encounter denser material
and are decelerated abruptly. There their
kinetic energy is changed into X-rays and
gamma rays. The energy deposited in
the lower levels of the solar atmosphere
causes material to evaporate explosively
to become coronal loops.

Adapted from information from the High Altitude
Observatory/National Center for Atmospheric Research,
Boulder, Colorado

(Top) Lockheed Palo Alto Research Laboratory, Palo Alto, CA/Lawrence Berkeley Laboratory, Berkeley, CA; (bottom) NASA Goddard Space Flight Center

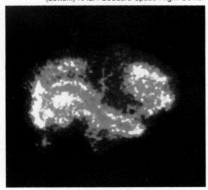

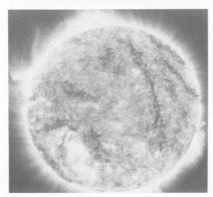

New telescopes making use of mirrors with special X-ray–reflective coatings obtained X-ray photographs of a solar active region (top) and the full solar disk (above). In both cases the telescopes were carried above the Earth's atmosphere aboard sounding rockets.

on X-rays. Such a telescope was recently carried by a sounding rocket to a height of 290 kilometers, where it obtained X-ray images of a solar active region.

Sunspots

That the number of sunspots goes through a cycle has been known since before the 1860s. At the turn of the century, British astronomer E. Walter Maunder plotted the latitudes of sunspots on the Sun and found that they seem to appear closer and closer to the solar equator as the solar cycle wears on. When the spots are plotted cumulatively, they form a "butterfly diagram" that clearly shows the 11-year cycle. The diagram also reveals that spots from the next cycle appear at high latitude at the same time that those from the current cycle are appearing nearest the equator.

Sunspots are regions of high magnetic field, about a thousand times the average magnetic field of the Sun or the Earth. The magnetic field in a sunspot holds down activity and makes the sunspot about 1,000 K cooler than the surrounding photosphere, thus accounting for its darkness against the hotter background. How is the magnetic field generated? It seems likely that it is a result of the Sun's differential rotation—the Sun rotates at different rates at different latitudes (fastest at the equator and increasingly more slowly toward the poles) and also at different distances out from the center to the surface. Nevertheless, the details of the way sunspots are generated and why they have an 11-year cycle are not yet understood. In the standard model the differential rotation stretches out lines of magnetic force and wraps them around the Sun just under the photosphere. Where they kink and push through the solar surface, there appears a pair of sunspots having opposite magnetic polarities, one where the kink leaves and the other where it enters. According to this model, the magnetic field is broken up as sunspots disperse, and the remnant field from the old cycle goes into making the new cycle. Succeeding cycles occur with north and south polarities reversed.

New ground-based observations have challenged this model. Studies of surface features, made at Mt. Wilson Observatory in California, show that

Sunspots plotted cumulatively by latitude and time form a "butterfly diagram" (bottom plot) that reveals the 11-year cycle. Spots from the next cycle begin appearing at high latitude at the same time that spots from the current cycle are forming nearest the equator. At the peak of the cycle 0.25–0.50% of the solar surface may be covered by sunspots (top plot).

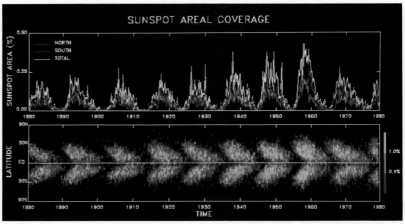

David Hathaway, NASA Marshall Space Flight Center

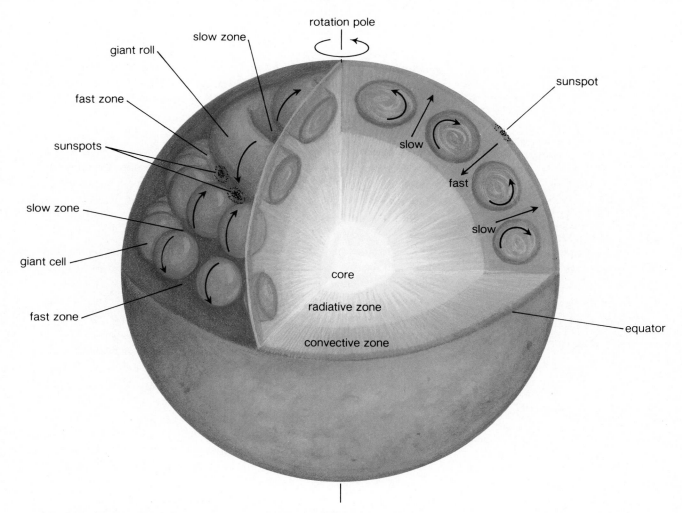

different bands around the Sun appear to move slightly more rapidly or more slowly than average for their latitudes. These bands migrate closer to the equator over an 18–22-year period, longer than the 11 years of the observed sunspot cycle. Studies at the National Solar Observatory's site at Sacramento Peak, New Mexico, show a similar phenomenon, but with features in the corona. Taken together, the observations indicate that signs of the new 11-year solar cycle appear at least half a dozen years before the current cycle is over. If these findings are verified, then the magnetic field from the old cycle may not be available to form the new cycle.

A new interpretation proposes that the bands are formed by giant rolls of gas lying just under the solar surface. The rolls are large, perhaps as thick as the one-third of the solar radius covered by the Sun's convection zone. The gas in the rolls moves north or south along the solar surface and circles back in the opposite direction beneath the surface. On the average there are four such rolls in each hemisphere. Solar activity originates near one of the low-latitude regions where adjacent rolls meet. The final consensus is not in as to whether the east-west circulation pattern is a major cause of the sunspots or whether it is a result of the sunspot-causing configuration of magnetic field under the solar surface. It may seem strange that such a basic phenomenon as the sunspot cycle remains

Ground-based observations have revealed the existence of a number of bands or zones around the Sun that appear to move more quickly or more slowly than average for their latitudes and that migrate toward the equator over an 18–22-year period. A new model of the solar interior proposes that the zones are formed by giant, doughnut-shaped rolls of gas lying just under the surface and rotating in opposite directions. At low latitudes the rolls break up into separate cells. Solar activity originates near one of the low-latitude regions where adjacent rolls meet.

Adapted from information obtained from Peter R. Wilson, California Institute of Technology

Eight years of measurements taken by the Active Cavity Radiometer Irradiance Monitor aboard the Solar Maximum Mission spacecraft show both short-term and long-term changes in the solar constant. The briefer fluctuations are much more pronounced during the active part of the solar cycle; all of the prominent dips are due to large sunspot groups moving across the Sun's surface. The long-term decline measured in the solar constant between 1980 and 1985 first seemed to part of a steady decrease. More recently, however, it leveled off and began to rise, suggesting a cyclical variation (traced by dashed curve) linked to the sunspot cycle.

Adapted from information obtained from Richard C. Willson, Jet Propulsion Laboratory

unexplained. Part of the reason may be the abundance of detailed information astronomers must fit into an acceptable theory. The Sun might seem simpler and more understandable if it were light-years distant like the other stars instead of only eight light-minutes away.

The solar constant

Only in recent years have scientists been able to monitor precisely the amount of energy the Earth gets from the Sun. A device known as ACRIM (Active Cavity Radiometer Irradiance Monitor) aboard the Solar Max satellite has watched the solar constant—the amount of solar radiation falling each second on a given area at the top of the Earth's atmosphere. With its unprecedented accuracy and ability to measure the Sun's ultraviolet and infrared radiation as well as its visible light, ACRIM has been able to detect variations as small as tenths of a percent. It showed that the presence of a giant sunspot on the Sun's surface can lower the solar constant as much as 0.25%. The information has been confirmed by measurements from the scientific satellite Nimbus-7.

In addition to the fluctuations, a slow drop in the solar constant has been noted, 0.02% per year during 1980–85. Though small, the decline is sufficiently large that it would have produced noticeable changes in the Earth's climate had it been going on for long. Over the course of centuries such a decline could bring on an ice age, but in 1986, near the minimum in the sunspot cycle, the decline seemed to level off, inviting speculation that it is linked with the cycle. Indeed, by early 1988 the solar constant seemed to be rising. Presumably its variations match the sunspot cycle.

The overall decline has been linked with a variation in the brightness of small areas of the solar photosphere scattered over the solar surface, rather than merely in sunspot regions. The small areas in turn seem to be related to small-scale variations in the Sun's magnetic field. These recent discoveries suggest an interesting new interpretation for a period

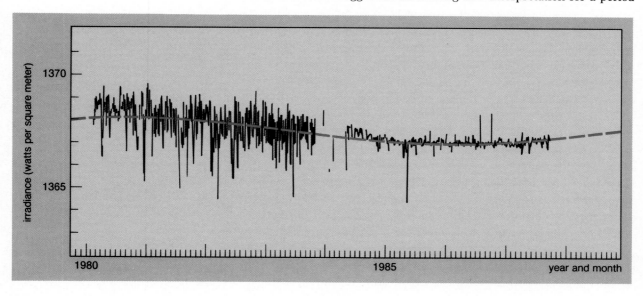

Photos, High Altitude Observatory/National Center for Atmospheric Research, Boulder, Colorado. The National Center for Atmospheric Research is sponsored by the National Science Foundation. Solar Maximum Mission operations are funded by the National Aeronautics and Space Administration

between AD 1645 and 1715 called the Maunder Minimum, during which sunspot activity was negligible and Europe and North America experienced a prolonged stretch of severely cold weather. If the overall solar magnetic field was diminished during the Maunder Minimum, the Sun may well have been slightly darker, thus leading to a cooling on the Earth.

Above the solar surface

Although the Moon is 400 times smaller than the Sun, it is also 400 times closer to the Earth. Thus, when the Moon passes in front of the Sun in the sky, it can mask the larger body almost exactly. It does so about every 18 months, producing a total solar eclipse. During such an event, just as the Moon completely covers the Sun, a reddish region appears around the Sun's edge, or limb, for a few seconds. This is the chromosphere, a layer of gas at a temperature of 7,000–15,000 K that glows largely in the light of hydrogen gas. Detailed views of the chromosphere show that it is made out of small spikes called spicules, each about 1,000 kilometers across and 10,000 kilometers high.

A person can view the chromosphere without the assistance of a solar eclipse by looking through a filter that passes only hydrogen light or the light of ionized calcium. Gas at a temperature similar to that of the chromosphere is sometimes suspended high in the solar atmosphere by the Sun's magnetic field. When the gas is seen on the limb of the Sun against the dark background of space, it appears bright and is called a prominence. On the other hand, when it is is seen straight on against the photosphere, it looks dark and is called a filament. The chromosphere is a region where energy is being injected into the solar atmosphere. This energy seems to come from below the solar surface.

As a solar eclipse progresses, covering both the chromosphere and prominences, the faint white solar corona can be seen around the dark lunar disk. The corona is gas at a temperature of about 2 million K. It looks white because electrons in the inner corona scatter sunlight to

Sequence of views of the Sun's atmosphere follows the progression of a loop-shaped mass ejection through the corona over an approximately 20-minute period. Each view is actually a montage of images derived from three different instruments making nearly simultaneous measurements. The innermost image, in the lower left corner, was made with a prominence monitor at the Mauna Loa Solar Observatory in Hawaii. The solid black circle is the occulting disk used to block direct light from the photosphere. The red light comes from cool hydrogen gas that forms the chromosphere; in one place the gas has been ejected up into the lower corona as a solar prominence. The intermediate part of the image, showing the white light scattered by electrons in the lower corona, came from a coronagraph at Mauna Loa. A coronagraph/polarimeter aboard Solar Max made the outermost image, which reveals the dim, outer corona.

the Earth. Although the corona does give off some light of its own, this radiation is only a minor fraction of the total and is measurable only within a small fraction of a solar radius above the solar limb. The visible corona extends five solar radii or more above the limb. It is irregular in shape, its gas held in place by the Sun's magnetic field.

A coronagraph is a special telescope that uses an occulting (blocking) disk to make an artificial eclipse of the Sun within the instrument under certain conditions. In visible light even the best coronagraphs can study only the innermost, brightest portion of the corona. A coronagraph on Mauna Loa, a high volcano in Hawaii, exploits the fact that the Sun's coronal light is polarized (whereas the blue sky near the Sun is not) to make images of the lower corona almost every day. A coronagraph aboard the Solar Maximum Mission has made many images of the dim, outer solar corona. The device, known as the coronagraph/polarimeter since it can measure the polarization of coronal light, also failed in orbit in 1980 and was repaired by shuttle astronauts when they fixed the spacecraft's pointing system. Every few hours a giant eruption passes through the corona, rapidly carrying matter out into the solar system. Since disruption of the magnetic field near the Earth by these ejections may cause magnetic storms on the planet, scientists are particularly interested in them. The difference between the ejection rates at sunspot maximum and minimum, however, has been found to be less than expected. Solar Max observations revealed that some of the coronal mass ejections occurred along with only a small burst of X-rays and were already under way when a flare erupted. Thus, these ejections were not caused by the flare but rather may have been the cause.

It may be many years before a coronagraph is made that can eclipse the Sun as well as the Moon does. A key requirement is that both the disk that occults the solar photosphere and the image of the Sun must be in focus at the same time. An occulting disk suspended in front of the telescope will be blurred when the focus is set on a distant object. Current coronagraphs succeed by having the disk within the telescope body, but the price is overoccultation. The one on the Solar Maximum Mission hides 1.75 solar radii and then has diffraction rings that mask even more. Thus, natural eclipses remain important for studying the middle region of the corona. Furthermore, eclipses allow researchers to use state-of-the-art equipment with much less advance time and much less cost than any mission launched into space.

Though a total eclipse is visible somewhere on the Earth about every 18 months, some are trivially short and others are visible only very low in the sky or in regions where the weather is perennially bad. Only every second or third eclipse is a favorable one. One such eclipse occurred on June 11, 1983, prompting a U.S. expedition, funded by the National Science Foundation, to go to Java. The dozen universities, colleges, and observatories represented performed a variety of observations on the photosphere, chromosphere, and corona during the five minutes of totality.

One of the expedition's instruments took a series of observations of the Sun through various filters, including a filter that was especially

Natural eclipses continue to provide excellent opportunities for studying the solar atmosphere. For the June 1983 eclipse (far left, shown in partial phase) U.S. astronomers set up a variety of instruments on the north coast of Java (left) to make observations of the photosphere, chromosphere, and corona during totality. A special filter that grows decreasingly dense outward from the center allowed investigators to view and photograph detailed structure in a wide range of the corona (below).

dense around the solar limb and decreasingly dense outward. This filter flattened the intensity gradient of the solar light and enabled astronomers to view structure in a wide range of the solar corona. Other experiments mapped the density and temperature structure of the corona and studied the velocities of various parts of the corona.

An experiment conducted by my own group and cosponsored by the National Geographic Society was devoted to studying why the corona is so hot. It had been thought until a decade ago that the solar corona is heated by acoustic waves—sound waves that originate under the solar photosphere and travel up to dissipate their energy in the corona. Theories had been worked on for years to explain the acoustic heating of the corona, although just why the energy should be deposited in the lower corona had never been clear. Then, in 1977, an instrument aboard the 8th Orbiting Solar Observatory (OSO) found that the energy was not passing through the chromosphere, ruling out acoustic heating of the corona. New theories that were advanced took advantage both of the OSO data and of X-ray views of the corona that had been obtained in the early 1970s by the Skylab Apollo Telescope Mount. These images had made it clear that the corona was heated especially over active regions, thus implicating the Sun's magnetic or electric fields in the process. They also showed that the corona was entirely composed of magnetic loops of every size. There was no "average" corona.

One of the new theories was based on the idea of magnetic waves, known as Alfvén waves, traveling over the solar surface. When they hit the footpoints of coronal loops, the loops would start to vibrate. Loops of a suitable size would vibrate with a period of about a second. My group made observations to test this prediction. A telescope made an image of the Sun, from which fiber-optic strands picked out small regions of the corona. We could adjust the positions of the strands during the eclipse by

79

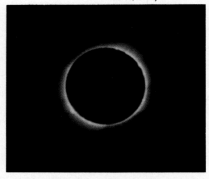

Although the November 1984 solar eclipse in Papua New Guinea (top) lasted only 42 seconds, it was put to good use in studies of coronal irregularities typical of the phase of the solar-activity cycle at that time. Local children (above) conduct their own observations of the eclipse using pinholes to project the solar image on makeshift screens.

looking at their silhouettes. The light that went down the optical fibers passed through a filter that transmitted only light being generated by hot gas in the corona. The light was detected by photomultipliers kept cool with dry ice and was digitized and recorded. Although such a train of apparatus may not be odd in a university laboratory, transporting it and making it work in an isolated region on the north coast of Java was a challenge. Indeed, a replacement instrumental tape recorder had to be located in the U.S. and hand carried to Java, arriving only 25 hours before totality. Analysis of the data showed that oscillations were taking place in the observed coronal loops with a period of about two seconds, in good agreement with the prediction.

The next total solar eclipse occurred on Nov. 23, 1984, in Papua New Guinea. Since totality was to last only 42 seconds, few astronomers attended this eclipse—although weather conditions proved far superior to those of the longer 1983 eclipse. Since many eclipse observations involve only the beginning or the end of totality, or take only a few seconds during totality, even short eclipses can be put to good use. Studies of the shape of the corona during the 1984 eclipse showed clearly the irregularities typical of this phase of the solar-activity cycle. By contrast, the 1980 eclipse was close to solar maximum, a time when so many coronal streamers exist that the corona appears relatively round.

The March 18, 1988, total eclipse crossed over Sumatra and Borneo in Indonesia, Malaysian parts of Borneo, and the island of Mindanao in the Philippines. Because of widespread clouds and fog not all the observers, myself included, succeeded in seeing the eclipse. Particularly successful on the ground were a British experiment to time totality and an observation of coronal structure by the U.S. National Center for Atmospheric Research through a radial density filter. High aloft, NASA's Kuiper Airborne Observatory, a specially instrumented aircraft, allowed scientists from the University of Hawaii and the National Optical Astronomy Observatories to study the solar atmosphere in the far infrared, which is inaccessible from the ground. Earlier on eclipse day a rocket had taken an X-ray picture of the corona for comparison with eclipse results.

The solar interior

The fundamental part of the Sun, including the core where thermonuclear fusion generates energy, is hidden from view by the bright surface. Still, new methods of investigation are allowing astronomers to probe the solar interior.

No form of electromagnetic radiation carries information directly from below the solar surface, but processes inside the Sun do affect the surface. The first clue came 25 years ago, when small surface regions were discovered to be oscillating up and down with a period of five minutes. For a number of years these oscillations were studied as if they were isolated in location and in period. Only recently have astronomers realized that the Sun has a whole set of oscillatory periods that range as high as 160 minutes. The Sun is ringing like a bell. The actual patterns observed on the solar surface are caused by interference of many of the simple oscillation patterns. By studying the periods and deciding which are fundamental and which are overtones, astronomers can now deduce something about conditions deep inside the Sun. The effort is called helioseismology by analogy with the seismic studies earth scientists have long conducted to elucidate the terrestrial interior.

When the measured frequencies of the Sun's oscillations are plotted, they align to form a distinctive, sweeping pattern of lines. Theoretical models of the distribution of temperature and density inside the Sun can be made that explain the pattern. The models depend on calculations of the depth within the Sun at which trapped acoustic waves would be bent or bounced back when passing through regions of differing temperature and density, just as light waves are refracted or reflected at interfaces between differing materials such as glass and air. Waves of different periods penetrate the Sun to different distances.

Each oscillatory mode of the Sun can be analyzed independently. The simplest are easiest to picture. In the real Sun the modes at all levels of complexity are superimposed. So that they can be interpreted, measurements must be made of the brightness of the whole Sun and how it varies with time second by second. (Since the technique involves gathering data from an entire celestial object, it can be applied as well to more distant stars, although, of course, much less light is available.) Because some of the periods are hours long, lengthy stretches of uninterrupted observation are needed; otherwise, the Sun's daily rising and setting introduce false signals. The problem can be ameliorated by two ground-based approaches (though a space mission for the purpose should eventually be launched).

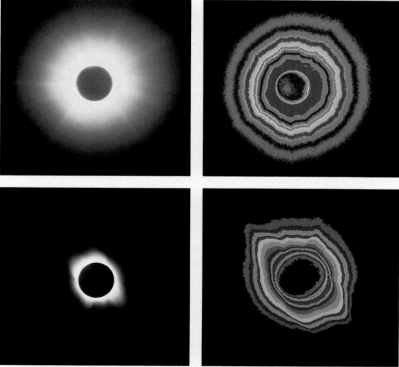

Photos, © Jay M. Pasachoff

Photos compare the solar coronas at totality during the 1980 eclipse in India (far left, top) and the 1984 eclipse in Papua New Guinea (far left, bottom). Isophote images of the coronas (left, top and bottom), in which zones of roughly equal light intensity have been assigned false colors, highlight the differences in shape. The 1980 eclipse occurred close to a solar maximum, when numerous coronal streamers make the corona appear round. By contrast, the corona during the 1984 eclipse shows much irregularity.

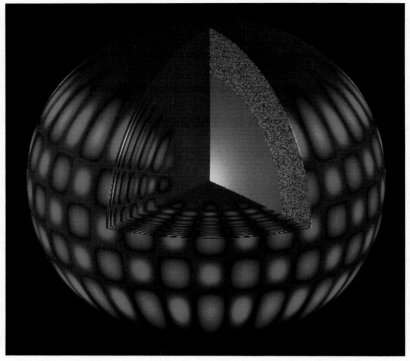

A computer representation depicts one of millions of oscillation modes discovered in the Sun. Receding regions are shown in red, approaching regions in blue. By studying many such modes, astronomers are learning much about the structure and dynamics of the solar interior.

One is to observe from some place on the Earth where the Sun is visible for dozens of hours at a time. After initial trials in Greenland, such observations have been made in Antarctica. The alternative is to station telescopes around the world so that one or another instrument is always watching the Sun.

Getting a long run of solar observations is so important that it has gained the long-term cooperation of solar astronomers around the world in a program called the Global Oscillation Network Group (GONG). Prototype telescopes have been set up in several locations, and the network is expected to start operations in 1991. Observations will be made into the mid-1990s to compile enough solar data to produce an accurate plot of the distribution of periods. Scientists hope for at least three consecutive years of nearly unbroken observations. So much data will be accumulated that computing is to be a major activity of the program.

Another way of tackling the structure of the solar interior is to watch the solar limb. Is the Sun round? That question, asked by physicist Robert Dicke of Princeton University and colleagues a dozen years ago, started a long-term controversy. They made a series of brightness measurements of a ring-shaped region around the Sun that included the solar limb, looking for deviations from a perfect circle. From their results they concluded that the Sun was out of round by a difference of about 35 kilometers out of the solar radius of 700,000 kilometers. Such a distortion, it was held, could be explained by a solar core rotating every 4 days, instead of the 25 days or so of the surface. The rapid rotation, however, would upset one of the greatest triumphs of Einstein's general theory of relativity—

its precise accounting for the excess 43 seconds of arc per century that had been observed in the advance around the Sun of the planet Mercury's perihelion (its point of closest approach to the Sun). A solar core with a four-day period would have explained four seconds of arc of the excess, destroying general relativity's precise agreement. Could the effect found by Dicke and collaborators be ascribed to some other cause? The variation of faculae, relatively bright regions on the solar surface, was suggested as a way of explaining the observed distortion without requiring a real distortion. No agreement was ever reached between the two opposing camps on the issue.

In the early 1980s Kenneth Libbrecht, working with Dicke at Princeton, remeasured the Sun and found no deviation from roundness. According to the two investigators, there could have been an error in either the prior or the current set of observations; on the other hand, the Sun's roundness may vary, perhaps with the solar cycle. In any case, the more recent measurement does not suggest a rapidly rotating solar core, although helioseismological studies indicate that the core does turn more rapidly than the surface.

Solar neutrinos

Energy generated at the Sun's core takes ten million years in the form of photons of electromagnetic radiation to perambulate up to the solar surface, from which it is radiated into space. Only one type of particle emerges directly from the core: the neutrino. Neutrinos interact so weakly with other matter that they come straight out through the Sun, reaching the Earth about eight minutes after they are made in the solar furnace. Unfortunately, the same weakness of interaction that gets them so promptly to Earth makes them difficult to observe.

Since the late 1960s Raymond Davis of the University of Pennsylvania, formerly at Brookhaven National Laboratory, Upton, New York, has used a large underground tank holding 400,000 liters (about 100,000 gallons) of a chlorine-containing molecule to detect solar neutrinos. The chlorine is sensitive only to relatively high-energy neutrinos formed in a minor branch of the chain of fusion reactions that is thought to give the Sun its energy. The underground siting takes advantage of overlying soil and rock to screen out other cosmic particles whose interactions would confuse neutrino observations. In two decades of observation Davis has consistently found about one neutrino detection per three days.

Most of the theoretical work on solar neutrinos has been carried out by John N. Bahcall of the Institute for Advanced Study at Princeton. Over the years he has refined his predictions of the rate at which neutrinos should be emitted from the Sun, accounting for more and more effects such as solar rotation. Still, the lowest value Bahcall has been able to predict is about one detection per day. Thus, Davis's result is one-third the theoretical minimum.

Bahcall's predictions are sensitive to the temperature at the solar core. If the Sun's center were slightly cooler than the 15 million K believed, fewer neutrinos would be emitted. One proposal that may not be as

Astronomer checks a solar monitoring telescope in Antarctica (below) where the 24 hours of daylight during the summer months afford lengthy stretches of observation time for helioseismology studies. Another technique for long-term uninterrupted solar observations is to station telescopes around the world so that at least one is always watching the Sun. One such telescope, a prototype being tested for the Global Oscillation Network Group (GONG) program, is installed at the Udaipur Solar Observatory in India (bottom).

(Top) National Optical Astronomy Observatories; (bottom) Arvind Bhatnagar, Udaipur Solar Observatory

farfetched as it first seems is that a hypothetical elementary particle, dubbed a cosmion, collects near the solar center. These weakly interacting massive particles, or WIMPs, would conduct energy out of the core, lowering the temperature and decreasing the neutrino flux.

Theoretical physicist Hans Bethe of Cornell University, Ithaca, New York, recently elaborated on a suggestion of two Soviet scientists that may well solve the solar-neutrino problem. Although physicists know of at least three different types of neutrinos—electron, muon, and tau neutrinos—Davis's apparatus is sensitive only to electron neutrinos, the primary type emitted by the Sun. If something induced neutrinos to transform from one type to another such that they became distributed among the three types, then the predicted number of electron neutrinos reaching Earth could be cut by a factor of three, allowing theory to agree with experiment. Bethe pointed out that, from what was known of neutrino-matter interactions, the passage of electron neutrinos through regions of very high density near the solar center could indeed cause them to transform to other types.

A major difficulty with this idea, however, is that it requires neutrinos to have a small but finite mass. In general, neutrinos have been thought to have zero rest mass, which allows them to travel at the speed of light. The transformation among neutrino types can take place only if neutrinos have some mass, but then they would travel slightly slower than the speed of light. A variety of experimental attempts on Earth to determine neutrino masses has sometimes found a small mass and sometimes not. There is still no consensus.

In 1987 a low upper limit for the neutrino mass was set by detections from an unexpected source—the supernova that appeared in the Large Magellanic Cloud on the night of February 23–24. This explosion, which signaled the violent death of a massive star, was the brightest since the year 1604. Davis's apparatus was predicted to be insensitive to the expected neutrino flux from the supernova, and indeed no extra neutrino signals were detected, but two sets of apparatus originally built to search for proton decay were sensitive to the supernova's neutrinos. The day before astronomers first noticed the light from the supernova, the Irvine-Michigan-Brookhaven device in an Ohio mine detected 8 neutrinos in a 6-second interval, while the Kamiokande device in a mine in Japan detected 11 neutrinos in a 13-second interval. Presumably these numbered among the 10^{58} neutrinos that supernova models predicted would be released during the collapse and rebound of the core of the dying star. The small spread in arrival time indicated that the neutrino mass could not be more than about 20 electron volts, which is 25,000 times smaller than the mass of an electron. Still, if this were the actual neutrino mass, not only would the solar-neutrino problem be resolved but there would also be enough added mass in the universe in the form of neutrinos to have major consequences for the structure and fate of the cosmos; for example, perhaps enough gravitational attraction to make the universe eventually stop expanding and fall back on itself. Thus, basic problems about the Sun and basic problems of cosmology are fundamentally linked.

Raymond Davis's neutrino detector, located deep in a gold mine in South Dakota, consists mainly of a tank holding 400,000 liters of perchloroethylene, a chlorine-containing organic compound. In operation the tank is covered with water to help shield it from unwanted cosmic particles. Currently the experiment is being modified to see if a difference in the neutrino detection rate exists between daytime, when solar neutrinos come directly from space, and nighttime, when they must first pass through almost the whole Earth.

Brookhaven National Laboratory

Scientists at the European Laboratory for Particle Physics (CERN) in Geneva prepare to test a prototype liquid-argon chamber for a neutrino detector to be installed in the Gran Sasso Tunnel in Italy. Within a few years this detector and others being built or contemplated should provide a better picture of conditions and events at the Sun's core.

Scientists cannot count on another supernova soon, but they can improve their observations of neutrinos from the Sun. Several types of detectors are expected to be more sensitive than the chlorine detector now running. One type uses a few dozen tons of gallium, a metallic element that interacts with neutrinos of much lower energy than chlorine can detect. In the late 1980s gallium detectors were under construction in several places, including a 30-ton device by a West German-French-Italian-Israeli collaboration in the Gran Sasso Tunnel in Italy and a 50-ton device by a Soviet group in a tunnel under a mountain in the Caucasus. Gallium detectors should detect neutrinos at a much higher rate than the chlorine experiment. Other future experiments, such as a liquid-argon detector at Gran Sasso, could also detect some solar neutrinos. The chlorine experiment itself is being modified to see if a difference can be detected between nighttime, when neutrinos have to penetrate almost the whole Earth to reach the detector, and daytime. Within a few years scientists expect to have a much better understanding of conditions and events at the Sun's core.

As the Sun becomes better understood, so too do fundamental processes in the distant stars. Astronomers have observed coronas in other stars from their X-rays and chromospheres in other stars from their ultraviolet radiation. They have begun to study the surface oscillations of other stars and use the results to interpret stellar interiors. As it has been for centuries, the Sun remains an important key for unlocking the secrets of the universe.

See also Feature Article: SUPERSTAR 1987.

85

CIRCLES OF STONE

Striking geometric patterns of rocks, soil, and ice develop spontaneously in
Arctic and alpine soils where the temperature fluctuates about the freezing point.

by Bernard Hallet

A vast barren plain on the Arctic island of West Spitsbergen stretches for kilometers. It is marked by countless lakes nested between ancient beach ridges. In many of the low-lying areas, the monotony of the featureless ground surface is broken by conspicuous arrays of geometric forms that range from circles to contorted polygons; these forms typically range from three to six meters (one meter = 3.28 feet) in diameter. They consist of domains of fine-grained soil encircled by curving ridges of pebbles and cobbles. These intriguing forms are exceptional examples of patterned ground, a term used for a variety of soil patterns best developed in areas where the earth is frozen. The patterns vary considerably in size, geometry, composition, and geographic distribution.

One of the most common soil patterns in the North American Arctic is a mosaic of polygons of uniform size and shape defined by intersecting vertical cracks filled with ice. These ice-wedge polygons, which are characteristic of permafrost terrains, typically stretch ten meters from side to side and vary in form from squares to hexagons. Patterned ground also occurs in alpine areas, usually as stone stripes trending downslope and defined by a systematic alternation of stripes of rock fragments of contrasting sizes. Where they are best developed, as on the slopes of the Hawaiian volcano Haleakala, they exhibit a striking regularity reminiscent of meticulously raked stone gardens.

Several types of patterned ground have been recognized for more than a century, but, despite the obvious curiosity and interest they have instilled among casual observers as well as scientists, little is actually known about how they form. A number of schemes, many rather ingenious, have been proposed to explain the development of such features. Nearly 20 hypotheses for the genesis of patterned ground are included, for example, in comprehensive reviews by geomorphologist A. L. Washburn. However, none has been clearly verified through direct field measurement and observation. Furthermore, with the possible exception of ice-wedge polygons, there is no current consensus about the genesis of patterned ground.

BERNARD HALLET is Professor of
Geological Sciences and Director
of the Periglacial Laboratory at the
Quaternary Research Center, University of
Washington, Seattle.

This article describes an effort to define the processes that are
presently active in stone circles in the hope of better understanding the
origins and dynamics of these and other enigmatic soil patterns. On the
basis of the results of field observations and electronic measurements,
the dynamics of these features can be analyzed, and instructive analo-
gies can be drawn between sorted circle dynamics, fluid convection, and
plate tectonics.

Physical features

Stone circles and polygons form largely in Arctic and alpine areas
of permafrost, where the soil, described as periglacial, is permanently
frozen except for the "active layer"—an approximately one-meter-thick
upper soil stratum that thaws each summer. The orderly geometry of
these figures and the distinct segregation of material according to grain
size within them both represent a degree of self-organization that is
striking, given that they generally originate from a featureless mixture
of mineral material.

A survey of the literature indicated that exceptionally well-developed
stone patterns occur in West Spitsbergen. During a reconnaissance of
the area by a team of researchers, a study site was selected on Kvade-
huksletta, a broad plain with spectacular sorted circles. It is located at
latitude 79° N, longitude 12° E on the southwestern shore of Kings Ford,
approximately eight kilometers (five miles) northwest of Ny-Ålesund,
where the Norwegian Polar Research Institute maintains an active research station throughout the year. The institute's generous and competent logistical support has proved invaluable for field studies. Given the
high latitude of the plain, the climate is relatively mild, with the mean
annual temperature and precipitation averaging about −5° C (23° F) and
37 centimeters.

The most distinctive soil patterns in the study area generally comprised equidimensional domains of essentially unvegetated, fine-grained
soil bordered by broad curvilinear ridges of gravel. Although these figures only rarely approach a true circular form, scientists refer to them
as "stone circles" (or "sorted circles" because of the distinct sorting

of material according to size). Whereas certain neighboring areas are completely covered with polygonal arrays of coalescing stone circles that share common borders, adjacent circles in the study sites are generally separated by lower areas that lack the textural contrasts characteristic of stone circles. In extreme cases individual stone circles may be separated from all others.

The size of stone circles varies considerably from one area to another. Within a single network, however, they tend to be rather uniform in size. Aerial photographs of the study area indicate that the outside diameters of stone circles, including the one-half-meter to one-meter-wide stone ridges, range from three to six meters.

Typically the surfaces of fine-grained soil domains are smooth and upwardly convex. The highest point is near the center of the circle and is 50 to 200 millimeters higher than the edges. The transition between the fine-grained domain and the ridges is abrupt, in terms of both texture and slope. The surface of the fine-grained domain and the interior surface of the ridge each dip toward this sharply defined boundary. The surface marking this boundary commonly dips about 20° radially outward directly below the surface and steepens to an almost vertical drop below about 20 centimeters. The border height varies considerably from area to area, ranging from a few millimeters to 50 centimeters.

Study method

Nearly all field studies of patterns in periglacial soils have consisted largely of qualitative observations made during the summer. During other seasons the patterns are generally hidden from view by snow, and the inhospitable weather renders field studies difficult. It is apparent that the lack of systematic quantitative measurements of the principal physical parameters and of their year-round variation in space and time has hampered precise understanding of the phenomena. To improve this situation, Bernard Hallet and a team of graduate students initiated a long-term study of periglacial sorted patterns that focused on the underlying processes and involved tightly coordinated field, laboratory, and theoretical work.

A variety of patterns of soil and rock are found in mountainous and Arctic regions. Ice-wedge polygons in Alaska (opposite page) are defined by intersecting vertical cracks filled with ice; they typically extend ten meters from side to side and occur in permafrost terrains. Patterned ground in mountainous areas often takes the form of stone stripes trending downslope, as seen in the summit region of Haleakala Volcano in Hawaii (far left). Hexagonal stone polygons are found in West Spitsbergen (left).

(Opposite page) U.S. Army/Cold Regions Research and Engineering Laboratory, Corps of Engineers, Hanover, N.H.; (this page, left) Stephen Porter, Quaternary Research Center, University of Washington, Seattle; (right) Bernard Hallet

Much effort was directed at the development and installation of automated data-acquisition systems capable of periodically monitoring the many sensors imbedded in stone circles throughout the seasons. Several modern portable computers were suited to controlling acquisition of field data in remote areas and then to storing the information. These battery-operated computers could be programmed to adjust both the sampling interval and the series of sensors being monitored in response to readings that reflected certain key physical changes. For example, a researcher might wish to sample soil displacements much more closely once the soil thawed. This can be done by means of a computer programmed to decrease its sampling interval after a particular temperature sensor indicated temperatures that were above freezing. Modern electronics have also greatly facilitated the production of instruments capable of precisely monitoring all important physical properties of the soil. Hallet's research team monitored more than 130 sensors to define the variations of temperature, moisture content, displacement, tilt, and pressure of the soil under stone circles. These measurements promise to play an important role in defining the complicated dynamics of stone circles.

In addition to this instrumentation effort, the research team established extensive marker arrays that permitted precise definition of complicated displacement patterns at the soil surface. These complemented the electronic measurements; whereas the electronic instruments provided precise and essentially continuous but local data from each sensor, the many surface markers supplied related information over a broad area but did so only sporadically, when observers visited the site.

Displacements

Considerable upward and downward motion due to freezing and thawing has long been recognized near the surface of sorted circles, notably by periglacial geomorphologist Alfred Jahn, who conducted extensive studies in West Spitsbergen. Observations by the research team yielded similar

results, with maximum surface heaves due to seasonal cooling measuring approximately ten centimeters, roughly 10% of the thickness of the active layer. Summer thawing of the soil starts shortly before the surface is exposed by melting of the snow. The surface first settles quickly at rates up to 20 millimeters per week, particularly in fine-grained domains. After a few weeks settling slows to very low rates, and it eventually yields again to heaving as air temperature returns to the freezing point, usually in the late summer.

In all the sorted circles that were monitored, horizontal displacements of individual surface markers were as great as millimeters; they averaged a few millimeters during the thawing season. The rate and direction of these displacements during successive time intervals are complicated, but by the end of the thaw season markers on the fine-grained domains had moved outward toward the stone ridges and those on the ridges had moved inward. Negligible net motion was recorded in intercircle areas.

The study team then raised the question as to how much of these relatively well-documented thaw-season displacements are reversed during the freezing period. The answer was not known, and yet it is pivotal in understanding the long-term dynamics of sorted circles. The few sets of data that span more than a single seasonal cycle revealed considerable cumulative motion. Most notable were the net systematic divergences of surface markers across stone ridges as well as fine-grained soil domains, and their net convergences across fine/coarse boundaries.

Dynamic maintenance of the microrelief

The bulbous ridges of coarse material and the sharp troughs that separate them from the domed domains of fine-grained soil are prominent stone circle characteristics that appear to vary only slowly over periods on the order of 1,000 to 10,000 years. This broad time estimate is based on the age of the surface being studied, which is in excess of 40,000 years, and also on the observation that sorted circles on terraces formed as recently

Isolated stone circle is found in West Spitsbergen (opposite page). Such circles may coalesce to form polygonal networks when new ones arise between those that are already established. The boundary between the fine-grained and coarse-grained material in a circle is sharply defined and marked by a pronounced trough (left). The fine-grained domains are domed upward. The shadows cast by the horizontal aluminum rod and the box of film aid researchers in measuring various aspects of the circle.

Photos, Bernard Hallet

as 9,000 years ago are similar to those in the study area. The vertical relief of individual stone circles is particularly striking in view of the numerous processes that tend to reduce such relief. These include frost-induced soil movement, erosion by raindrops, and surface disturbances produced by living organisms, all of which result in downslope transfer of material. Because relatively steep slopes converge to form the troughs at the boundaries between the fine-grained and coarse-grained soils, the troughs would be expected to fill particularly quickly; yet they persist. A simple model suggests that, in the absence of processes that actively maintain the relief, it would disappear in decades or, at most, centuries. Thus, in order for the vertical relief to persist for much longer periods, degradational processes filling in the troughs must be offset by downward soil motion.

Similarly, given the expected and measured lateral divergence of material from topographic high points, these domains can remain in their raised positions only through the upward motion of underlying soil relative to adjacent areas. Thus, the convex upward profiles of both the fine-grained domains and the stone ridges reflect long-term upwelling of soil in those areas. The horizontal displacements measured at the surface and the inferred vertical surface displacements require a specific pattern of subsurface motion so that cavities do not form and soil does not pile up; this is needed to satisfy the rule of conservation of material. However, the actual soil motions are likely to be much more complicated because they reflect large fluctuating displacements associated primarily with seasonal freezing and thawing; nevertheless, measurements by the study team indicated that the pattern of net motion over a number of years can be inferred with confidence.

Interpretation of lateral motion

As noted above, measured patterns of relative horizontal displacements on the soil surface reflect motion at depth and can be used for estimating

92

rates of vertical motion. A convergence of soil markers on a particular soil domain would, for example, reflect a net addition of soil to that domain. If possible compaction is ignored, this extra soil would elevate the soil surface over the domain unless the soil actually moved downward at an appropriate rate. Since the microrelief of the studied circles appears not to change appreciably with time, local elevations are essentially constant over a time scale of decades or longer. Thus, in view of the large measured lateral displacements, the microrelief can be maintained only if upwelling occurs in areas of soil divergence and downwelling occurs in areas of convergence.

If the reasonable assumption can be made that subsurface soil movements are largely restricted to vertical planes radiating from pattern centers, the rate of vertical motion is simply the product of the rate of horizontal convergence per unit length and the thickness of soil undergoing that motion. This thickness can be inferred to be a small fraction of the thickness of the active layer because, if the motion resembles fluid convection, the horizontal velocity at the top of a convecting roll diminishes to zero near the center of the convecting layer and reverses sign below that. An array of relative horizontal displacements spanning a full year yields a clear pattern of widespread upwelling and spreading in both the fine-grained domains and the coarse borders. Marked downwelling and convergence are localized close to the periphery of the fine-grained domains. Deep-seated return flows are required for the observed long-term surface displacements to be maintained. These surface motions offer strong independent support for the pattern of motion inferred from surface relief.

Radial motion and the tilts of dowels that were initially inserted vertically in the fine-grained domains of sorted circles were measured by several researchers, notably by Jahn in the Hornsund area of Spitsbergen and by Washburn at Resolute, North West Territories. The dowels generally moved and tilted outward in accordance with the inferred convective motion of the fine-grained soil. Maximal rates of long-term lateral motion were approximately ten millimeters per year. Diverse geologic evidence also led geomorphologists J. R. Mackay and F. H. Nicholson, among others, to hypothesize similar circulatory motion in other types of patterned ground. However, no previous measurements had led the researchers to suspect that stone ridges were the sites of considerable activity.

Several aspects of the sparse vegetation cover also support the inferred long-term convective motion. First, at the periphery of the fine-grained domains, the vegetation mat and the underlying soil commonly form small folds with axes that parallel the boundary between the fine- and coarse-grained domains. These folds probably result from radial compressive stresses arising from the load of the coarse-grained soil border and from the rapid convergence. That they are generally localized within about ten centimeters of the coarse-grained border is consistent with the displacement records; horizontal divergence in a radial direction measured in the fine-grained material during the thaw period switches abruptly to radial convergence at the periphery of the fine-grained do-

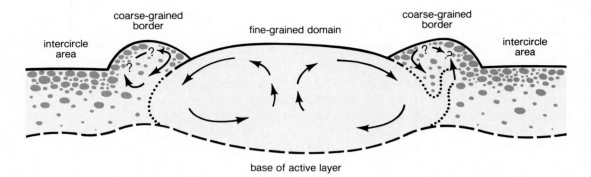

coarse-grained border   fine-grained domain   coarse-grained border

intercircle area   intercircle area

base of active layer

mains. The folded nature of the vegetation mat further indicates that at least a portion of the convergence recorded during the thaw period near the fine-coarse boundary persists in the long term.

Second, downwelling at the periphery of the fine-grained domains (which can be inferred from the microrelief, the horizontal surface displacements, and the extension of fine-grained material under the coarse-grained ridge) is expected to transport organic material from the surface of the ground into the active layer. Along with previous researchers, Hallet's study team found that organic carbon content does not necessarily decrease with depth, as would be expected in a static soil. Instead, throughout the active layer the organic carbon content of the soil at the periphery of a fine-grained domain is considerably higher than it is in the center. Because material that has not been at the surface recently will presumably be depleted of its content of organic carbon, the very low amounts of this material in the central portions of the fine-grained domains throughout the entire sampled depth probably reflect upward motion there. The fact that the vegetation cover is often discontinuous or absent in those areas, whereas it is thickest at the periphery of the fine domains, also reflects the expected increase in time available at the fringe areas for biotic colonization and growth. These observations all support the inferred pattern of soil motion.

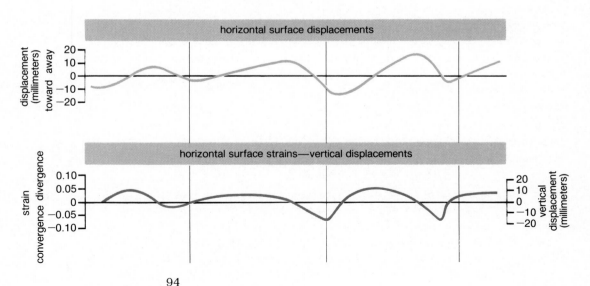

horizontal surface displacements

displacement (millimeters) toward away

horizontal surface strains—vertical displacements

strain convergence divergence

vertical displacement (millimeters)

94

Additional geologic data gathered by a number of researchers further support the hypothesis of long-term convective soil motion. Upward flow of material in circle centers is compatible with the recognized upward migration to the surface of stones and fossils, which in places form islands of coarse material near the centers of fine domains. Furthermore, the radial flow pattern characteristic of hexagonal convection cells is in accord with the preferred alignment in a radial direction of elongated rock fragments in sorted patterns reported by J. H. Schmertmann and R. S. Taylor in their comprehensive study of sorted patterns in Alaska.

Driving mechanism for soil convection

In view of the fact that the early work on free convection dealt with fluid motion driven by temperature-induced density differences, it is natural that considerations of soil convection first focused on temperature gradients as a mechanism that would generate buoyancy forces to drive such motion. It was soon recognized that the density of water, which is greatest at 4° C (39° F), could be expected to decrease with depth during the thaw season because near the surface it would tend to be a few degrees above 0° C (32 ° F) while the ground below remains frozen. Simple calculations show, however, that the maximum variation in bulk density of the soil that could result from varying the water temperature from 0° to 4° C is insufficient to induce soil convection. Moreover, such small bulk density differences, on the order of one part in 10,000, are likely to be completely overshadowed by the natural variability of the soil bulk density arising from realistic variations in soil moisture or texture.

It became apparent that differences in soil moisture may actually produce vertical gradients in soil bulk density that could provide the driving mechanism for convective motion of the soil, but no precise mechanism emerged to account for the requisite decrease in soil bulk density with depth. The work of Hallet's research team, however, points to a possible solution based on a more explicit consideration of active-layer processes. Records showing that the soil surface heaves upward on the order of ten centimeters during each seasonal freeze period indicate that the soil in a one-meter-thick active layer expands on the average by about 10% seasonally. Because this expansion is due primarily to water intake and subsequent ice growth, the average soil bulk density at the end of the freezing season, which is about twice that of water, must be about 5% lower than it is at the onset of freezing. The expansion of the active layer will be relatively large in fine-grained soils in areas of abundant moisture because they provide particularly favored sites for ice growth. It follows, therefore, that the average soil bulk density increases throughout the thaw season by about 5% as excess water is pressed out of the pore space in the soil. This is more than 500 times the maximum soil bulk density difference that would result from cooling pore water from 4° to 0° C. Soil densification starts near the surface, where soil thaws first, and it progresses downward at a rate determined by the rate of water percolation (passage of the water through the soil) above the thaw front. Near-surface consolidation may give rise to denser thawed material

The diagrams on the opposite page illustrate the simplest pattern of soil motion that can be inferred for isolated stone circles based on surface relief, measured displacements of surface soil, and indications of upward motion of fine-grained material under the ridge lines of stone ridges. Necessary conditions for the motion include soil convection in the fine-grained domain, downwelling of fine-grained material at the fine/coarse boundaries, and a rolling motion of the material within the borders of the circle.

there than that found at greater depths, where water migration has been limited owing to the relatively short thaw period. Measurements of soil bulk density in sorted circles show that in certain cases the density does decrease with depth under parts of a sorted circle, but more data must be obtained for this to be substantiated.

One can gain useful insights into the postulated convective motion of periglacial soils by regarding fine-grained soil as a very viscous fluid and considering whether the buoyancy forces that would drive the motion are sufficient to overcome the viscous forces that would resist it. This consideration suggests that soil convection is plausible in very fine-grained soils with low effective viscosities and permeability. The latter property is of importance because water percolation dictates the rate at which the soil can consolidate once it has thawed.

An explanation now emerges for the contrast between the abundance of stone circles in wet lowlands rich in fine material and their absence from adjacent beach ridges. Convection would be strongly favored in fine-grained materials because they would tend to have relatively low effective viscosities and low permeability. Moreover, the moist fine-grained soils are likely to contain considerable ice, leading to low bulk density and a high capacity for consolidation at the onset of the thaw period. On the beach ridges, in contrast, the very coarse-grained soils, the relatively low soil moisture, and the thinner snow cover are all unfavorable for soil expansion resulting from ice growth.

On a broader geographic scale, West Spitsbergen appears particularly well suited for the development of sorted patterns because the relatively mild Arctic climate results in soil temperatures only slightly below 0° C for nearly nine months each year. This prolonged near-freezing thermal state is conducive to frost heaving because considerable unfrozen water persists in fine-grained soils at slight subfreezing temperatures and, therefore, can continue to migrate toward freezing centers near the cold soil surface throughout much of the year. In addition, because the mean annual temperature is close to 0° C, the seasonal thaw propagates deeply into the soil, giving rise to a thick active layer that is highly favorable for convection.

Free convection of water in the active layer

Although the expected decrease in the density of water resulting from a decrease in temperature with depth in the active layer is incapable of causing soil convection, chemical engineer William B. Krantz, geomorphologist Nelson Caine, and co-workers at the University of Colorado recently recognized that this density gradient could induce percolative convection of water through the soil. Moreover, they proposed that such water convection could affect the pattern of melting at the bottom of the active layer. The resulting uneven base of the active layer is then assumed to dictate the initial development of certain patterned ground.

Much as is the case for soil convection, pore water convection is an attractive mechanism because it is in accord with the regularity, shape, and size of stone circles. However, this novel and ingenious mechanism only addresses a factor that may influence the geometry of incipient patterns; the pattern of sorting, the development and maintenance of the features with distinct microrelief, and the measured surface displacements of the soil are not accounted for directly. Moreover, whether percolative convection of water can actually take place and be sufficiently vigorous to affect heat transport significantly in fine-grained soil typical of sorted circles is questionable.

Mini plate tectonics in stone circles

The measured radial and vertical displacements in stone circles reveal striking parallels with displacement patterns characteristic of plate tectonic phenomena. Areas of localized convergence and downwelling at fine/coarse boundaries correspond to convergent plate boundaries and subduction zones. Indeed, fine-grained and organic rich material commonly extend under the stone ridge or under an "accretionary wedge" of stones. The radial divergence across the stone ridge, which is in close proximity to the zone of radial convergence on the inner portion of the ridge, resembles the north–south extension recently reported within the Himalayas, a region of known plate tectonic convergence. The apparent rolling motion of the stone ridges seems unique to sorted circles and may be possible only because of the cohesionless nature of this coarse material. This motion does, however, share geometric similarities with the circulatory motion of material entrained into subduction zones and subsequently returned to the Earth's surface.

Another characteristic common to both stone circles and plate tectonics is the difficulty in pinpointing the driving mechanism for the motions. The relative motions themselves are readily documented, but the details of the driving mechanisms remain elusive. Plate tectonics is ultimately driven by thermal energy liberated from the Earth's interior, but the relative importance of mantle convection, spreading at the oceanic ridges, sliding downslope, and pulling at subduction zones remains poorly understood. Similarly, whereas the seasonal freezing and thawing driven by solar energy are clearly responsible for the stone circles, the mechanisms that produce the observed motions remain a source of controversy.

Conclusions

The size, geometry, topography, surface soil displacements, vegetation cover, and subsurface distribution of organic carbon of the stone circles that were studied are all compatible with a simple pattern of long-term soil convection. Theoretical considerations of convection and of active-layer processes suggest that intermittent free convection is plausible in thawed fine-grained soil and that the requisite decreases of bulk density with depth arise naturally during the thawing and consolidation of ice-rich soil. The ongoing, automated instrument monitoring of stone circles promises to yield considerable additional data about sorted circle dynamics and about more general processes in the active layer. This should permit further assessment of the ideas discussed above and, therefore, improved understanding of stone circles and similar patterns.

ENERGY
from the
OCEAN:
A RESOURCE FOR THE FUTURE
by Terry R. Penney and Thomas H. Daniel

By harnessing the tides, waves, and currents of the ocean and exploiting the differences in the temperature and salt content of the water, scientists and engineers can develop an almost limitless and pollution-free source of energy.

Exploitation of the oceans has brought humanity a wealth of treasures for centuries. Even so, it can confidently be forecast that the ocean will be far more important to future generations than it has ever been in the past. Although many researchers endeavor to explore outer space, the ocean holds the crucial elements for maintaining a growing industrialized population in search of raw materials, food, fresh water, and energy.

Futurists from Japan and the U.S. have unveiled plans for self-sustaining floating ocean cities designed to take full advantage of the ocean's resources. Humans, however, cannot afford to ravage the ocean as they did the land. They must choose their options so that the ecosystem is not endangered. This requires careful study and selection of innovations that will provide future generations with an unlimited renewable and pollution-free energy source with advantageous side benefits. Perhaps ocean energy will provide this choice.

Ocean energy options

Ocean energy technologies specifically developed to generate electricity can be classified as tidal, ocean thermal, wave, current, and salinity gradient. The most developed is tidal, which uses the rise and fall of tidal waters to provide a source of power. As of 1988, operating tidal units included a 240-megawatt plant in Rance, France, and several smaller installations such as the 18-megawatt unit at Annapolis Royal in Nova Scotia. Relatively few sites are suitable for harnessing tidal energy, however.

The most researched technology has been ocean thermal energy conversion (OTEC), which uses differences in water temperatures to produce power in a conventional heat engine. During the past few years, visions for OTEC have focused on units delivering 5–50 megawatts of electricity. Experiments with a limited output of less than 100 kilowatts have proved that the concept is feasible. Larger sizes have not been built, however, because of the high initial capital costs and uncertain life expectancy of the required long seawater pipelines.

TERRY R. PENNEY is Section Manager, Thermal Applications Research, at the Solar Energy Research Institute in Golden, Colorado. He also serves as Chairman of the Ocean Energy Technical Committee of the Solar Energy Division of the American Society of Mechanical Engineers.
THOMAS H. DANIEL is Laboratory Director of The Natural Energy Laboratory of Hawaii at Kailua-Kona.

(Overleaf) Illustration by Paul R. Alexander

La Rance hydroelectric plant at Saint-Malo, France, harnesses ocean tides to generate electricity. During high tides the dam (below) is opened to allow water to fill the artificial basin behind it. At low tides, when the water level in the ocean drops below that of the basin, water is allowed through the dam in the opposite direction. Water flowing in either direction is used to drive turbines (below right).

Literally hundreds of wave energy devices have been conceived to take advantage of the power of the ocean's endless waves. Wave energy systems of low power levels (less than 500 kilowatts) have been operated as experimental demonstrations by the British, Norwegian, Japanese, and, to a limited degree, U.S. governments. However, large-scale commercial efforts have been hindered by the difficulty of maintaining stations during stormy seas and by the costly power conditioning equipment required for providing steady outputs under varying wave conditions. Devices tapping ocean currents and salinity gradient devices, which depend on differences in the salt content of the water, have on a laboratory scale demonstrated power production at outputs of less than ten kilowatts.

The present high financial risk in developing any ocean energy devices is due to a lack of proven large-scale prototypes and unresolved problems with the conversion machinery. The concept of combining OTEC with other possible benefits that can be derived from the resource of cold, nutrient-rich seawater appears to be the vision most likely to gain worldwide attention. Although the other ocean-energy technologies are maturing, this article will deal only with the progress of OTEC and recent advances in associated technologies.

The OTEC resource

OTEC development requires a suitable thermal resource and the equipment necessary to convert this thermal energy into electrical power. The thermal resource consists of temperature differences between the ocean's warm surface waters, heated by solar radiation, and the deeper colder water. It is characteristic of many tropical ocean regions that the upper layer of perhaps 100 meters (one meter is about 3.28 feet) in depth is consistently warm, well above 25° C (77° F). With increasing

Photos, Michelangelo Durazzo—Magnum

(Left) AeroViroment Inc.; (right) courtesy of Dr. Stephen H. Salter, University of Edinburgh

depth there is a sharp transition to colder temperatures, reaching 4° C (39° F) at a depth of 500 to 1,000 meters, depending on the location. This temperature difference presents an energy source that can be used to produce power. It is generally accepted that a temperature difference of at least 20° C (36° F) is a prerequisite for a viable OTEC operation.

In some coastal areas, such as those in Florida, the shallow near-shore bottom waters may not be cold enough to achieve sufficient temperature gradients, even with very warm surface waters. When an adequately low temperature is reached, it may be at such a great distance from shore that it will warm up while it flows to the plant. The maximum offshore distance for a viable OTEC plant will vary from site to site, depending in part on the cost of alternate energy sources, but probably will not exceed 25 kilometers (one kilometer is about 0.62 mile) from shore for the near future.

Near some islands the slope of the coastal seafloor is very steep, and so the thermal resource can be reached relatively close to shore. This allows OTEC power plants to be constructed onshore or on platforms in the near-shore areas. OTEC power plants that are moored or floating in the open ocean and would use conventional techniques of the offshore drilling platform technology have also been studied.

Artist's conception reveals the design of a device that would capture the energy of ocean currents (above left). Currents off the coasts of Florida, for example, could generate thousands of megawatts of power. Salter's Duck (above), a device for harnessing the energy of waves, is tested at Loch Ness in Scotland.

Map reveals the differences in water temperatures in the world's oceans. These variations can be exploited to produce energy.

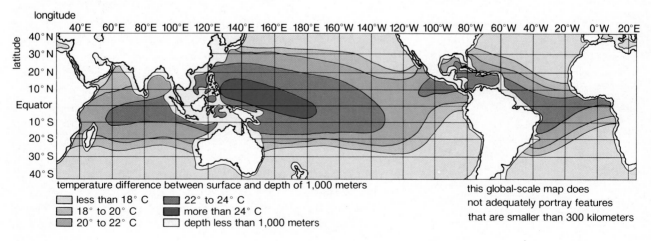

temperature difference between surface and depth of 1,000 meters

- less than 18° C
- 18° to 20° C
- 20° to 22° C
- 22° to 24° C
- more than 24° C
- depth less than 1,000 meters

this global-scale map does not adequately portray features that are smaller than 300 kilometers

Country/area	Temperature difference (°C) of water between 0–1,000 m	Distance from resource to shore (km)
Africa		
Benin	22–24	25
Gabon	20–22	15
Ghana	22–24	25
Kenya	20–21	25
Mozambique	18–21	25
São Tomé and Príncipe	22	1–10
Somalia	18–20	25
Tanzania	20–22	25
Latin America and the Caribbean		
Bahamas, The	20–22	15
Barbados	22	1–10
Cuba	22–24	1
Dominica	22	1–10
Dominican Republic	21–24	1
Grenada	27	1–10
Haiti	21–24	1
Jamaica	22	1–10
Saint Lucia	22	1–10
Saint Vincent and the Grenadines	22	1–10
Trinidad and Tobago	22–24	10
U.S. Virgin Islands	21–24	1
Indian and Pacific oceans		
Comoros	20–25	1–10
Cook Islands	21–22	1–10
Fiji	22–23	1–10
Guam	24	1
Kiribati	23–24	1–10
Maldives	22	1–10
Mauritius	20–21	1–10
New Caledonia	20–21	1–10
Pacific Islands Trust Territory	22–24	1
Philippines	22–24	1
Samoa	22–23	1–10
Seychelles	21–22	1
Solomon Islands	23–24	1–10
Vanuatu	22–23	1–10

Many less developed countries have access to energy obtained through exploitation of the differences in water temperatures. They must be within 25 kilometers (15.5 miles) of an ocean region where there is a temperature difference of about 20° C (36° F) in the first 1,000 meters (3,280 feet) below the surface.

Since 71% of the Earth's surface is covered by oceans, the Sun never sets on the ocean thermal resource. Although the ocean thermal resource is thus quite stable on a daily basis, it has a seasonal variation that increases with distance from the Equator. The global region of interest thus comprises a band from latitudes of about 25° south to 32° north of the Equator. A simple calculation shows that these tropical seas each day absorb solar radiation equivalent in heat content to that of about 170 billion barrels of oil. Further calculations show that the heat equivalent of seven billion barrels of oil could be removed per day without changing the ocean's temperature significantly. This would allow the generation of approximately ten million megawatts of electricity from the OTEC resource on a continuous, renewable basis.

A United Nations report from the Department of International Economic and Social Affairs pointed out that many islands and less developed countries have convenient access to the OTEC resource. The World Bank indicated that less developed countries account for 15% of global energy consumption. Of this amount 60% is supplied by petroleum, 80% of which is imported. This dependence on oil imports affects the balance of payments of these nations and reduces the resources available for basic human needs as well as for economic development.

Closed and open OTEC cycles

Jacques-Arsène d'Arsonval, a French engineer, first proposed the concept of OTEC in 1881. His ideas for a closed-cycle system, which are still employed today, utilize a secondary working fluid such as freon or ammonia. Heat transferred from the warm surface seawater vaporizes the working fluid through a heat exchanger (the evaporator). The vapor expands under moderate pressures, turning a turbine attached to a generator and thus producing electricity. Cold seawater pumped from the depths of the ocean to another heat exchanger (the condenser) provides a cold surface to reliquefy the vapor. The working fluid remains within the closed system, continuously vaporizing and recondensing it.

Georges Claude, Arsonval's student, first proposed open-cycle OTEC in the late 1920s. Claude's cycle uses water vapor as the working fluid. Warm surface seawater partially vaporizes when it is injected into a near vacuum. This relatively low-temperature steam (25° C [or 77° F]) is expanded through a low-pressure (1,400 pascals) steam turbogenerator, thus producing electricity. The steam is then condensed in "direct contact" with cold seawater. A vacuum pump maintains the required system pressure in this continuous process. Less than 0.5% of the incoming warm water is turned into steam. Typically 7,000 kilograms per second of warm and 3,000 kilograms per second of cold seawater are required for producing one megawatt of net power from an OTEC cycle.

A recent innovation, the "Mist Lift" process, also takes advantage of the open-cycle system. Warm seawater is injected into a vacuum through small holes, creating a mist of droplets. Steam is created around the droplets during the evaporation process at a pressure of 1,400 pascals. It flows to the lower-pressure top of the column with sufficient coupling

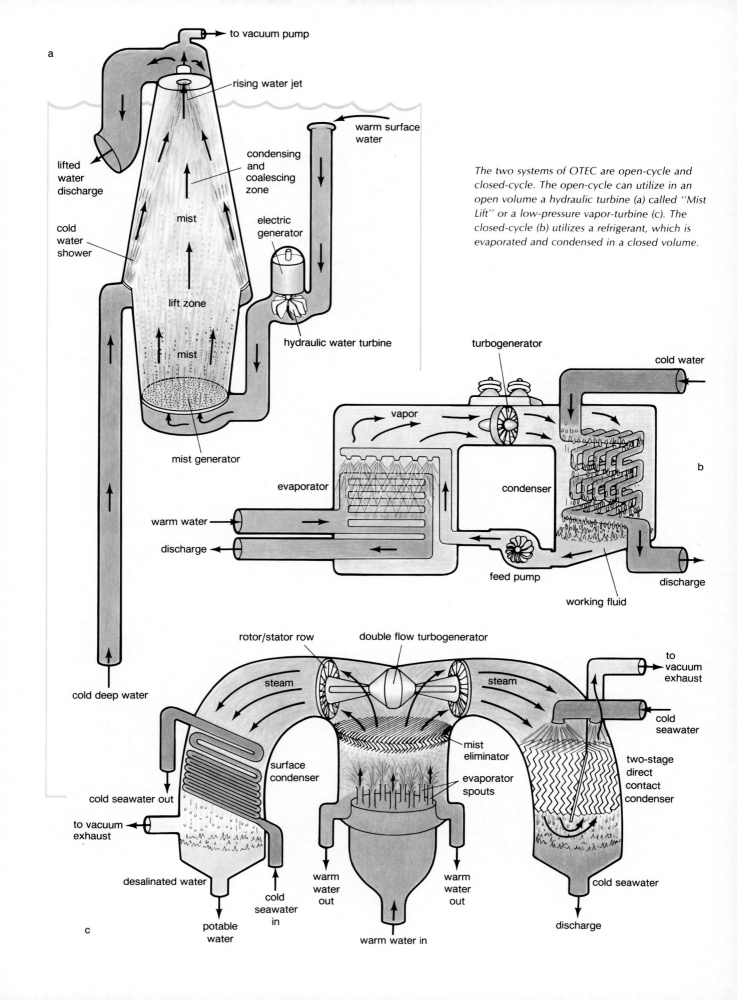

a

to vacuum pump

rising water jet

lifted water discharge

condensing and coalescing zone

cold water shower

mist

electric generator

lift zone

warm surface water

mist

hydraulic water turbine

mist generator

cold deep water

The two systems of OTEC are open-cycle and closed-cycle. The open-cycle can utilize in an open volume a hydraulic turbine (a) called "Mist Lift" or a low-pressure vapor-turbine (c). The closed-cycle (b) utilizes a refrigerant, which is evaporated and condensed in a closed volume.

turbogenerator

cold water

vapor

evaporator

condenser

warm water

discharge

feed pump

working fluid

discharge

b

rotor/stator row

double flow turbogenerator

to vacuum exhaust

steam

steam

cold seawater

mist eliminator

surface condenser

evaporator spouts

two-stage direct contact condenser

cold seawater out

to vacuum exhaust

desalinated water

cold seawater in

warm water out

warm water out

cold seawater

potable water

warm water in

discharge

c

Operating on a modified U.S. Navy barge off the coast of Hawaii (top), the Mini-OTEC (ocean thermal energy conversion) project became in 1979 the first to generate usable levels of power by tapping the temperature diffferences of ocean water. Below, a huge steel tube is launched into Matanzas Bay, Cuba, in 1930. Designed by French scientist Georges Claude (below right), the tube was submerged and used to pump cold water from the bay's lower levels. It was part of a system that exploited temperature diffferences of the water to generate 22 kilowatts of gross power.

(between the steam and droplet) to create a "negative rainstorm," lifting the stream of droplets up a column. A spray of cold seawater acts as a direct-contact condenser near the top of the lift tube and reliquefies the steam at a lower pressure of about 700 pascals. The energy obtained from lifting the water can be extracted by means of a conventional hydraulic turbine such as those used in hydroelectric plants.

By 1988 closed-cycle OTEC systems were close to achieving efficient power generation and ultimate commercialization. However, both the technical risks associated with unproven technologies and the capital investment required for OTEC cycles remained.

Experimental OTEC systems

Although Arsonval envisioned a closed-cycle system in 1881, he never tested it. It was not until 1926 that Claude—already well known for inventing the neon sign—became obsessed with making OTEC a reality. He designed an open-cycle system, which he tested at Matanzas Bay

Photos, Global Marine Development Inc.

in northern Cuba in 1930. The turbine generated 22 kilowatts of gross power, but the system needed more than that to function. (Gross power is the power produced by the turbine, while net power is the power left after other system components such as power to run the pumps is subtracted from the gross.) If Claude had traveled to southern Cuba, and set up a test at Santiago, he might well have generated two megawatts of net power. Exploiting the greater temperature difference (24° C [74° F]) there, pumping water at greater speed through his cold-water pipe (1.6 meters in diameter by 2 kilometers long), and using a larger turbine could have yielded that result. In any case, the experiment did demonstrate that cold water could be brought up from a depth of more than 700 meters with low frictional losses in the pipe. On July 2, 1935, Claude was granted a patent for his process for conversion of ocean thermal gradients to power with an open-cycle OTEC method.

Claude's next major effort was a floating open-cycle plant. Installed on a cargo vessel moored off the coast of Brazil, the experimental effort failed because waves destroyed the cold-water pipe as it was being deployed. Claude, who had helped fund these projects with his own money, died virtually bankrupt and never achieved his goal of generating net power with an open-cycle system.

Influenced by Claude's work, the French government continued research on open-cycle systems for several years. In 1956 a French team designed a three-megawatt plant to be built at Abidjan, on the west coast of Africa, where a 20° C temperature difference between surface and deep ocean waters is available. For various reasons, including difficulty in positioning a long cold-water pipe, the plant was not built.

The energy crisis of the 1970s triggered by the Arab oil embargo stimulated the U.S. and several other countries to seriously consider the OTEC system as a viable energy source. In 1979 the state of Hawaii funded the Lockheed Aircraft Corp., with technical support from the Dillingham Corp., to build Mini-OTEC, the first OTEC plant to yield net electrical power. It was a closed-cycle system mounted on a barge moored about two kilometers off Keahole Point on the island of Hawaii. The plant operated for up to ten days at a time over a span of four months, generating 50 kilowatts of gross power and 18 kilowatts of net power.

On a converted U.S. Navy tanker renamed OTEC-1 (above left), the U.S. Department of Energy tested closed-cycle heat exchangers and a bundle of three cold-water pipes, each 1.2 meters (3.9 feet) in diameter. The tests validated the heat-exchanger designs and proved that an OTEC plant could operate by moving at low speed through tropical waters. A cold-water pipe (above) is the lifeline of an OTEC system. In order to transport nutrient-rich, cold, clean water, the pipe must be strong enough to survive powerful ocean forces. Such pipes are usually made of nonmetallic materials.

105

Photos, The Tokyo Electric Power Co., Inc.

During the same years, the U.S. Department of Energy funded and directed the construction of OTEC-1, an experimental system installed on board a converted U.S. Navy tanker. The system, designed to test closed-cycle heat exchangers of commercial scale as well as a bundle of three cold-water pipes (each 1.2 meters in diameter), showed the validity of the heat-exchanger designs and proved that an OTEC plant can operate by "grazing"—moving at low speed through tropical waters.

Somewhat later the Tokyo Electric Power Co. and the Toshiba Corp. built a closed-cycle plant on the Pacific island republic of Nauru. With freon as the working fluid, the plant generated 100 kilowatts of power (35 kilowatts net) during intermittent operation from October 1981 to September 1982. All of these pilot plants were designed to test OTEC systems; they were not expected to achieve the 70% ratio of net-to-gross power that would be a commercial target for OTEC plants.

As of the spring of 1988 the Nauru operation was the last field test of a complete OTEC system, but work on OTEC components continues. In the United States, research on closed-cycle systems has focused on improving heat exchangers, which are expected to account for at least 20% of a closed-cycle plant's cost. The work includes efforts aimed at reducing corrosion of the apparatus by seawater and fouling by marine organisms.

A conventional heat exchanger for a closed-cycle system has what is generally called a shell-and-tube configuration. As seawater flows through the tubes, the working fluid evaporates or condenses around them within an outer shell. For increased efficiency a more advanced plate-fin design utilizes an array of parallel plates. The plates are arranged so that one carries seawater, the next carries working fluid, and so on throughout the apparatus. Fins between the plates help transfer heat.

Because of its resistance to corrosion by seawater, titanium was originally chosen as the material for closed-cycle heat exchangers. It is a costly choice for a closed-cycle plant, however, because of the quantity required. For that reason, the Argonne National Laboratory recently investigated modified brazed aluminum heat exchangers, commonly found in refrigerators. Tests suggest that they will last more than 30 years in the warm seawater characteristic of the OTEC environment. Aluminum heat exchangers should cost about a third as much as those made of titanium.

This closed-cycle OTEC plant was built by Tokyo Electric Power Co. and the Toshiba Corp. on the Pacific island of Nauru. During intermittent operation from October 1981 to September 1982, the plant generated 100 kilowatts of gross power (35 kilowatts net).

106

The Argonne workers discovered that fouling will not be a problem for the parts of a plant exposed only to cold seawater, an environment in which chemical and biologic reactions are slow. For controlling fouling in warm seawater, intermittent chlorination totaling one hour per day has been shown to be effective. The resulting chlorine levels would be well below U.S. Environmental Protection Agency standards.

As of 1988 these findings had yet to be applied to a closed-cycle pilot plant. Designs and plans were under way for such plants as a U.S. installation in Hawaii, a French plant on Tahiti, an Indonesian operation on Bali (aided by the Dutch), and a floating British plant. Financing has been a problem in each case, however. Various sources in the U.S. estimate that a 50-megawatt plant would cost $200 million–$550 million, depending on site and components. These costs translate to a cost of $4,000–$11,000 per kilowatt of installed capacity and delivered costs of 5–14 cents per kilowatt-hour. In contrast, a generating station fueled by oil at $20 per barrel delivers electricity at 5.6 cents per kilowatt-hour. The capital cost of an OTEC plant is significantly higher than that of a conventional steam plant, and investment at present is not easily obtained.

Research and development activities

Scientists in recent years have gone to The Natural Energy Laboratory of Hawaii (NELH), located at Keahole Point on the Kona coast of the island of Hawaii, to find new ways to produce food, fresh water, and energy from the ocean's resources. Since its formation NELH has developed into the world's foremost laboratory and test facility in support of OTEC research and cold seawater aquaculture. It has installed a cold seawater pipeline 30 centimeters (1 foot) in diameter that extends to a depth of 600 meters (2,000 feet). Submersible pumps near the shore

The Natural Energy Laboratory of Hawaii, on the Kona coast of the island of Hawaii, is the world's leading test facility for OTEC research and cold seawater aquaculture. Submersible pumps near the shore draw up large volumes of cold water through a pipeline, while surface pumps furnish comparable quantities of warm water.

107

Direct-contact condenser (above) was tested for use in open-cycle OTEC systems. The open-cycle test chamber at The Natural Energy Laboratory of Hawaii (above center) produced the first desalinated water at an OTEC facility in late 1987. Vertical spout evaporator (above right) transfers heat 70 times more efficiently than conventional shell-and-tube evaporators.

continuously pull up large volumes of the cold seawater (below 10° C [50° F]) for distribution to various projects. Additional surface pipelines provide continuous large volumes of warm seawater (about 25° C [77° F]) for projects that use it either alone or mixed with the cold water to achieve wide-range water temperature control.

Since 1978 the U.S. Solar Energy Research Institute (SERI) has been conducting research on the open-cycle OTEC concept. The major focus initially was to concentrate on lowering cost and improving the performance of the massive heat exchangers required for an open-cycle plant. In 1984 SERI won an Industrial Research and Development award for its OTEC vertical spout evaporator. A modification of a French invention used in an experimental OTEC plant at Abidjan, Ivory Coast, the evaporator was tested in fresh water and proved to be more than 70 times more efficient than the conventional shell-and-tube heat exchanger.

Using fresh water, SERI also developed and tested direct-contact condensers for open-cycle OTEC. To verify these freshwater heat exchanger results, testing began at NELH with seawater. SERI, in collaboration with Argonne National Laboratory, began seawater testing of vertical spout evaporators and surface and direct-contact condensers. Surface condensers have the added benefit of producing desalinated water by means of condensing low-density steam on their metal surfaces. During August 1987 fresh water was produced from seawater with this facility under prototypical open-cycle OTEC conditions. Although no turbine is now in place between the evaporator and condenser, within five years the U.S. Department of Energy plans to develop a turbine to be used in phased experiments in an OTEC system experiment. These results have stimulated renewed interest in OTEC on island markets in need of electricity and fresh water. For example, during 1986 the Pacific

International Center for High Technology Research (PICHTR) initiated OTEC projects ranging from technical studies to market assessments.

These result-oriented activities concerning OTEC and its by-products are encouraging. As the technologies mature from the research phase to commercial viability, it seems likely that OTEC will emerge as a major alternative energy source.

By-products of OTEC

Three properties of the cold seawater available at NELH make it particularly useful for aquaculture: (1) coldness—not only does the cold water permit the culture of plants and animals that could not otherwise tolerate tropical temperatures but it also provides a simple, accurate, and cost-effective means of year-round temperature control throughout a culturing system; (2) nutrients—the high nutrient levels of the cold, deep water provide the opportunity for rapid growth rates in marine plants either for plant production itself or as food for desirable animals; (3) purity—since the deep water comes from well below the zone penetrated by light rays, viable plant cells are scarce, allowing the culture of pure strains of algae without costly filtration. Bacteria and other pathogen levels in the deep water are also extremely low, permitting culture of very sensitive animal larval stages.

Both research and commercial aquaculture projects have been conducted with the use of cold seawater. Animals such as abalone, salmon, Maine lobster, and oysters grow well as do such plants as nori (the seaweed used for wrapping Japanese sushi). These opportunities may prove profitable in conjunction with an OTEC plant, enough to improve significantly the near-term economic viability of the OTEC process. Some projects use such small amounts of water that they can produce commercial amounts of food in conjunction with current experimental-scale OTEC operations, while in others the value of the product is high enough so that the installation costs of deep-ocean pipeline are economically recoverable by industry standards.

Giant kelp (below) are grown in two tanks of nutrient-rich cold seawater (below left) at The Natural Energy Laboratory of Hawaii. In the tank at the left, the kelp are just beginning to grow; in the tank at the right, they are ready to be harvested. The kelp provide food for the abalone raised at the laboratory as part of its aquaculture program.

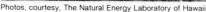
Photos, courtesy, The Natural Energy Laboratory of Hawaii

Photos, courtesy,
The Natural Energy Laboratory of Hawaii

Not yet exploited to its full potential is the opportunity to mine the ocean water for its 57 elements dissolved in solution. In the past, most economic analyses showed that mining the ocean for trace elements dissolved in solution would be unprofitable owing to the energy required for pumping the large volume of water needed and the processing costs required for separating the mineral from seawater. However, because OTEC plants will already be pumping the water economically, the only problem to solve is the extraction process. Also, the Japanese recently began investigating the concept of combining the extraction of uranium dissolved in seawater with wave-energy technology. They found that developments in other technologies (especially materials sciences) were improving the viability of mineral extraction processes that employ ocean energy.

Soil temperatures on many tropical islands are too warm for growing certain types of cool-weather plants, including flowers and vegetables. An array of cold-water pipes of small diameter can be buried in the ground to exchange their temperature with that of the surrounding soil. Varying the flow rate of cold seawater allows control of a plant's root temperature, providing the possibility of rapid seasonal cycling for increased fruit production. In another possible use of cold seawater pipes, since most islands have moderate ambient humidity levels, the condensation of water from the atmosphere on exposed cold pipes could provide natural drip irrigation. Using these ideas, University of Hawaii investigators conducted experiments with strawberry plants. To their surprise they found that strawberries grown with these techniques consistently had about five times the sugar content of control plants watered with tap water.

Millions of dollars are spent each day on electricity to produce chilled water for industrial processes, the cooling of buildings, and refrigeration for food storage. The 5° C (41° F) seawater could be sold at a competitive price to resorts for air conditioning. Cooling to nearby industries needing refrigeration provides another possible use for the water. The

Courtesy, The Natural Energy Laboratory of Hawaii

concept was tested successfully by the use of the deep seawater for space conditioning in a laboratory building at NELH. Because the cold seawater is highly corrosive, adequate maintenance and selection of hardware is essential. New advances in low-cost materials, particularly treated plastics, have reduced the need for and cost of maintenance.

Looking ahead: the year 2035

On June 15, 2035, you electronically scan your personalized Sunday morning newspaper. In the travel section you notice a number of vacation options: "Journey aboard *Starfetch VII.* "Enjoy three days on the planet Alicia. Board the *Starfetch VII,* a new, composite interplanetary spacecraft designed with a cruise speed of 7,300 miles per hour to minimize jet lag. At a cost of $1.3 million you can. . . ." No, you think. Although reasonably priced, most of the interplanetary voyages nowadays are like the travel that existed 100 years ago in the U.S. Just not what you are looking for. "Maglev 16-Earth core revisited. Aboard the *Maglev 16,* let a magnetically levitated train using superconductors move you and your family to the Lava Lauren picnic site. Travel at speeds up to 800 miles per hour through the Earth-core Tunnel. See the prehistoric fish as you pass through the hydrosphere. Departures from New York City at the base of the historic Empire State Building and from Perth, Australia, on a daily basis. Book reservations 18 months in advance. Priced at only $130 per seat mile."

That sounds interesting but a bit expensive for a family vacation. What about an old-fashioned vacation at a clean beach? Let's see . . . there're several here. "Akua Kelby Kai. The first floating city, completed in the fall of 2010 about 70 miles off the Kona coast of the Big Island of Hawaii. National headquarters for McIslands, the international chain of pollution-free resorts. Specializing in Lotta-Bingos that pay for your stay!"

This sounds perhaps a little plastic; let us see the detailed background. "The original resort was financed speculatively on the theory that ocean thermal energy could be utilized to run low-pressure steam turbines coupled to generators. Today, one-half million gallons of fresh water are converted for every megawatt of electricity produced daily. Self-sufficient island economy provides for its 100,000 inhabitants. Annual shell and fin fish production totals 150 million pounds. Exporter of every major fruit and vegetable to non-OTEC neighboring islands. A regular stop for tankers loading fuel (hydrogen and methanol) produced by excess electrical power generated from the renewable energy power plant. Visit the Craven Museum of Ocean History to see historic notes and film clips of the attempts of early pioneers who fostered the Ocean Energy vision."

"The price?," you inquire. A mere $15,000. A 15-minute plane trip from the new San Andreas Airport. The thought of returning to the rebuilt Los Angeles airport intrigues you. Dreams of the fresh food, water, and long-gone healthy life-style of fun and sun on the beach convince you.

Your terminal queries, "Do you wish to purchase a family ticket?" "Yes," you type. Quickly the printer responds, "One round-trip ticket to Akua Kelby Kai. Depart June 17, 2035; return June 23, 2035."

Lettuce plants (opposite page, top) were grown near buried pipes containing cold seawater. Giant clams (opposite page, center) thrive in the cold seawater provided at OTEC facilities. Large raceways at The Natural Energy Laboratory of Hawaii (opposite page, bottom) contain cold seawater in which microalgae that have high concentrations of beta-carotene—a substance believed to prevent or slow the progress of certain types of cancer—are grown.

111

CREATING
with
EXPLOSIVES

by William C. Davis and Per-Anders Persson

Best known for its violence and destruction, the power
of high explosives also serves our constructive
aspirations—from rock blasting and metal welding
to the creation of diamonds and objects of art.

Most people regard the power of high explosives with the awe and respect
due a dramatic, terrifying, almost magical force. The suddenness of the blast,
the flash, and the frightful noise combine to erase all thought from the
mind, returning humans to the animal world of instinct. The violence and the
sight of change occurring faster than senses can follow lead to a feeling of
loss—loss of control over one's circumstances and loss of one's model of an
orderly universe.

Yet everywhere are things produced with the help of explosives. The extensive use of steel and other metals; concrete and macadam; coal, oil, and
electric power; and an efficient transportation system are all characteristic
and fundamental for industrially developed civilization. The supply of these
necessities depends more than most people realize on high explosives and
advanced techniques for their use. High explosives are essential for extracting ores and coal from mines; for producing limestone, crushed rock, and
macadam in quarries; for building roads, railroads, city subway systems, airports, canals, and harbors; for constructing hydroelectric plants with their
dams, underground generator halls, and outlet tunnels; and for numerous
other human endeavors.

The special states of high pressure and high velocity that can be attained
in explosions have led to marvelous technical and scientific advances. Metals
can be formed and welded, diamonds made from graphite, ordinary rocks
compressed to the condition in which they exist deep in the Earth, stones
blasted inside the bladder of a living person, and enormous magnetic field
strengths reached.

While such productive applications of explosives usually take place out of
sight, military applications make more of an impression, particularly in this
day of battlefield television coverage. Military high explosives are used to take
lives and destroy property or as a threat to do so in an extension of diplomacy
for securing the goals of nations.

Whether one feels gratitude for the practical applications of explosives and
horror at their use in weaponry, or perhaps horror at the efficiency with which
explosives can devastate the environment and gratitude for the way the threat
of weapons keeps the world at peace, there is no question that the phenomena

WILLIAM C. DAVIS *is a Fellow at the Los Alamos (New Mexico) National Laboratory.*
PER-ANDERS PERSSON *is Director of the Center for Explosives Technology Research and the Research Center for Energetic Materials and Professor of Mining Engineering, New Mexico Institute of Mining and Technology, Socorro.*

(Overleaf) Print of Alfred Nobel, by Swedish artist Verner Molin, was made from an explosively formed copper plate. Molin painted the image on the plate and then used a thin layer of explosive to engrave the pattern into the metal surface. Photograph by Jake Garcia, courtesy of Per-Anders Persson

Illustrations by Pawel Bodytko

of explosions are very different from ordinary events. This departure from the ordinary demands a creative jump from those who apply explosives, whether for industry or threat of war.

What is an explosive?

The basic principles that describe the actions of explosives are the same whatever their intended use. In order to appreciate some of the more creative applications, it will help to look briefly at the theory of explosives, itself a considerable creative jump.

One may begin by considering a closed container filled with a liquid explosive like nitroglycerin. When the substance is exploded, the liquid becomes gas. Since gas usually occupies much more space than liquid of the same weight, the gas in the container is at high pressure. For example, nitroglycerin has the chemical formula $C_3H_5(ONO_2)_3$. When it explodes, it turns into water, carbon dioxide, nitrogen, and oxygen, according to the formula $2C_3H_5(ONO_2)_3 \rightarrow 5H_2O + 6CO_2 + 3N_2 + \frac{1}{2}O_2$. At normal atmospheric pressure and at 200° C (392° F), a temperature at which the water exists as steam, the gaseous products would occupy about 2,000 times the volume of the original liquid explosive. Confined to their original volume, however, the pressure of the products is about 100,000 atmospheres—a pressure that puts stresses into the vessel walls many times the strength of any known material. Moreover, the temperature of the explosion is quite high, perhaps 4,000° C (7,232° F). The expansion of the gases, as they drive the vessel walls before them, does work to accelerate the vessel material.

A good explosive, then, has high initial density so that as much material as possible fits into the given space, and it turns into products that have the largest possible number of gas molecules. In addition, the chemical energy liberated in the chemical reactions must be large to make the temperature and pressure high.

However, high energy and much gas are not sufficient for a good explosive. The propellant in a shotgun cartridge has these properties, but it does not reach the high pressures needed for the shattering action of an explosive. The difference is that propellants and low explosives react by burning, a relatively slow process, whereas high explosives detonate. Det-

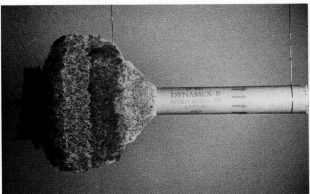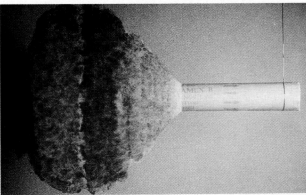

onation is a very special combustion process that proceeds with extreme rapidity. It goes so fast that the pressure is confined by the explosive itself, its own mass holding it together while the reaction goes on. The effect is called inertial confinement. In an inertially confined detonation, the chemical reaction takes place within a wave motion that travels through the explosive at great speed. In typical explosives the wave speed is from 3,500 meters per second to as much as 9,000 meters per second (two to five miles per second). Liberation of the stored chemical energy at this rate translates into extraordinarily high power densities and leads to the attainment of shattering pressures and high velocities.

Propellants and some other combustible materials have most of the properties of high explosives, but they avoid detonation because their chemical reactions have been made slow enough that inertially confined reaction cannot occur in pieces as small as those that will be used. This can be accomplished with a mix of fuel and oxidizer (a material that supports fuel combustion, often by supplying oxygen), each of sufficiently large grain size, rather than a molecular explosive such as nitroglycerin (where the oxygen and "fuel" are close together in the same molecule). Care must be taken at every stage of their production to ensure that the quantities are always too small to detonate.

Many materials, perhaps 20,000 or more, are known to be explosives. Only a small fraction, 100–200, have been studied sufficiently to make them practical for production and use. Still, there are plenty with well-known properties from which to choose.

Influence of wartime development

When Roger Bacon described black powder in the middle of the 13th century, he made the point that explosives, really firecrackers, made such a flash and bang that soldiers could be frightened off without any lasting injury. He was sure that war would no longer be practical. This dream of weapons so demoralizing, or so terrible, that war could no longer be considered a reasonable extension of diplomacy has followed explosives through the centuries as they have been exploited for war. For the past 40 years nuclear explosives, which have power densities many times greater than those of chemical explosives, have been considered

Sequence of high-speed photographs reveals the progress of a chemical reaction wave traveling through a detonating dynamite stick. Exposure time for each photo is one ten-millionth of a second (0.1 microsecond); the time between exposures is about seven-millionths of a second (seven microseconds). The light from explosively shocked argon gas provided the intense illumination needed for such short exposures.

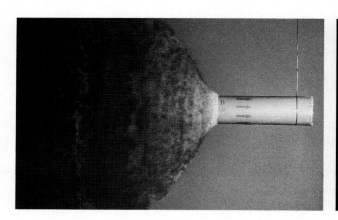

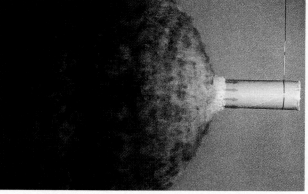

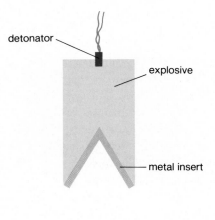

detonator

explosive

metal insert

jet charge

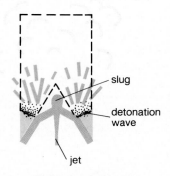

slug

detonation wave

jet

formation of jet during detonation

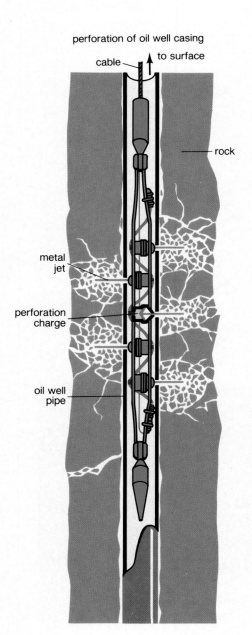

perforation of oil well casing

to surface

cable

rock

metal jet

perforation charge

oil well pipe

the ultimate weapons. Perhaps with these, all-out war has finally become too devastating to risk. The construction of the atomic bomb, carried out during World War II, required a great creative leap, one that has influenced the peacetime use of explosives ever since.

Consider a mass of fissionable matter in the form of a sphere. If a neutron enters this matter from outside, there is a certain probability that it will be captured by a nucleus, which in turn may fission, turning into two lighter nuclei and releasing some neutrons. These neutrons may in turn be captured by other nuclei and cause more neutrons to be made; on the other hand, they may escape from the sphere to the outside and be lost. The probability for capture depends on the mass of material, and the probability of escape depends on the surface area of the sphere. If more neutrons are captured than escape, a runaway nuclear reaction will proceed. If more escape than are captured, the reaction will decay until no more neutrons are present in the material. If one starts with a sphere that is below the critical mass for a runaway reaction and then compresses it with high explosive, the mass of material remains the same, but the surface area decreases. Thus, a subcritical mass becomes a supercritical mass. If a neutron is sent into the material, more new neutrons are produced than can escape, and a nuclear explosion follows.

When the idea for explosive compression of fissionable material was first suggested in 1943, conventional explosives had never been used for precision work. In the atomic bomb the explosive was to be used to compress the rarest and most expensive materials ever produced: plutonium or specially separated uranium. With brilliant ideas and hard work, scientists and engineers achieved the necessary precision and in the process laid the foundation for an explosives technology that would be able to meet the demands of the modern world for precision, reproducibility, adaptability, and long shelf life.

Explosive piercing, cutting, and welding

War-driven research into explosives has also made more direct contributions to modern peaceful applications. One of the most useful, called

116

a jet or shaped charge, was developed for piercing the armor plate of World War II tanks. In its original military form, it consists of a solid cylindrical piece of explosive, perhaps the size of a small drinking glass, with a thin metal cone inserted point first into the explosive at one end and a detonator at the center of the other end. As the reaction wave initiated by the detonator spreads through the explosive, it first contacts the apex of the inserted metal, accelerating it to high velocity. The wave then continues to advance along the insert, progressively accelerating the rest of the metal. Pressure is highest where the wave first contacts the insert because that region is surrounded by the most explosive. As the wave moves along the insert, there is less and less surrounding explosive to confine the reaction; consequently, the pressure grows ever weaker toward the mouth of the cone. The metal at the center of the explosive thus receives a longer and harder push than metal nearer the end and winds up going faster.

After the explosive is consumed, all the metal is in motion, but the metal that had been at the center of the explosive is traveling faster than the metal that originated closer to the end. This velocity difference makes the metal stretch. The strength of the metal holds it together, and the end result is a long strand or jet of metal, still stretching, flying through the air at high speed, typically ten kilometers (six miles) per second at the forward tip. When this jet strikes armor, concrete, or other solid material, the impact creates pressures much higher than the strength of the hardest steel and drives a hole through the target. Under the best conditions, a charge ten centimeters (four inches) long may make a metal jet 75 centimeters (30 inches) long that will penetrate a meter (3.3 feet) of steel, making a smooth hole about 1¼ centimeters (½ inch) in diameter.

The trick to maximizing the penetrating power of jet charges is to ensure that the jet of metal comes out perfectly straight. If it does not, the later parts will not enter and deepen the hole made by the earlier parts but will move off line to start a new hole. Achieving perfection

The basic jet, or shaped, charge consists of a small piece of solid explosive having a cone of thin metal inserted at one end and a detonator at the other end (opposite page, top left). During detonation, as the reaction wave passes through the explosive (opposite page, top right), the cone is crushed into a high-velocity jet of metal that can penetrate steel plate, rock, concrete, or other hard material. Some of the metal, called a slug, is also launched in the reverse direction. Jet charges are commonly used to perforate oil well pipe and fracture some surrounding rock after the well has penetrated oil-bearing strata (opposite page, bottom). Water spouts from a shallow-water rock-blasting operation (below left), another application of jet charges. A bridge in Louisiana (below) is demolished by means of numerous linear-shaped charges, which create blade-shaped metal jets that can slice through steel beams.

(Left) Center for Explosives Technology Research, New Mexico Institute of Mining and Technology; (right) courtesy, Dykon, Inc., Tulsa, Oklahoma

requires that the explosive be uniform in composition and density, that the metal insert be uniform in density and thickness, and that the initiation and propagation of the detonation wave be flawless. Even though real charges are less than perfect, they must be made precisely enough to work as expected. Born in war, jet charges have since been employed widely in industry. Thousands of small inexpensive jet charges are used every year to puncture oil well casings and some surrounding rock.

A variation called a linear-shaped charge, comprising an elongated piece of explosive into which is inserted a V-shaped metal channel, creates a long, blade-shaped metal jet that can make flat cuts through steel beams or concrete walls. Linear-shaped charges are employed extensively in demolition work; for example, for dismantling old oil platforms at sea and bringing down steel-beam buildings and bridges. Smaller, precision charges employing the same cutting principle are installed in military aircraft and space launchers to facilitate parts separation; for example, quickly removing the canopy of a fighter plane to allow the pilot to eject in an emergency, or separating burned-out rocket stages from the payload.

Surprisingly, the same action that forms the jet in the above applications is the key to the process of explosive welding, or cladding. In that process, a sheet of metal covered with a layer of explosive is positioned a short distance above another, thicker metal plate. By careful selection of the explosive's thickness and detonation velocity, the upper metal sheet can be made to collide progressively over its whole surface with the lower plate. Under these conditions, a jet is formed that removes the oxidized surface layers of the two mating metals, forging them together to form a strong, intermetallic bond. Although some local melting can take place at the interface as a result of heating in the jet-formation process, explosive welding is essentially a low-temperature process, which consequently avoids many of the disadvantages of large-scale melting inherent in conventional welding.

Explosive welding is employed extensively to bond dissimilar metals, particularly those that are difficult or impossible to weld conventionally. The chemical industry depends on pressure vessels made from high-strength steel explosively clad on one side with stainless steel or titanium. In shipbuilding, extensive use has been made of aluminum-to-steel transition joints to avoid the very difficult conventional welding of aluminum to steel. The transition joint is formed by cutting strips out of blanks of explosively bonded aluminum on steel. Wherever an aluminum structure is to be joined with the steel, a strip is inserted so that conventional aluminum-to-aluminum and steel-to-steel welding can be applied.

Rock blasting and building demolition

The application that consumes the largest quantities of explosives per year is rock blasting. In the U.S. alone more than 1⅓ billion kilograms (three billion pounds) of explosives were used in 1985 for this purpose, compared with a total of 2¼ billion kilograms (five billion pounds) of military explosives during the whole of the war in Vietnam. With only

118

minor deviations reflecting the ups and downs of the economy, the trend has been one of steady, exponential growth in keeping with the expanding population and the demands for building materials, metals, coal, and excavations for roads, tunnels, and building foundations.

The reason explosives have been so attractive as a means for rock fragmentation since long before the days of Alfred Nobel and dynamite is that they are such a convenient and reliable source of concentrated energy. Rock, like all brittle materials, is much weaker in tension than in compression; *i.e.*, it can be pulled apart much more easily than it can be squeezed. Thus, when an explosive is made to exert its high pressures in a drill hole bored in a rock formation, the rock easily fractures.

Rock-blasting operations thus start with the drilling of the holes. These vary in size, from thumb-width holes for in-city controlled blasting near vibration-sensitive structures or small in-city cable-trench building to holes about a third of a meter (12–15 inches) in diameter and 21 meters (70 feet) deep for large open-pit mining of iron ore, copper, or coal. For small-diameter holes, cartridged explosives wrapped in waxed paper are used. Some of these explosives are similar in composition to the dynamites invented by Nobel in the late 1800s, having nitroglycerin as the most sensitive ingredient. Others, which are later developments, use an intermolecular mixture, often in the form of emulsions. These consist of microscopically small droplets of an oxidizer, mostly ammonium nitrate dissolved in a small quantity of water, dispersed in a small amount of fuel oil. Such explosives, although still able to detonate just like a cartridge of dynamite, are safer to manufacture and use because they are less

In explosive welding or cladding, a sheet of metal covered with a layer of explosive is positioned above and at an angle to, or often parallel with, a thicker metal base plate. The explosive is detonated at one end, and the traveling detonation wave drives the upper sheet progressively against the lower plate. The collision creates a metallic jet that removes the oxidized surface layers of the two metals, allowing them to unite in a strong bond. Seen in microscopic cross section (inset), the weld has a characteristic wavy appearance.

(Inset) Courtesy, A. S. Bahrani, the Queen's University of Belfast, Northern Ireland

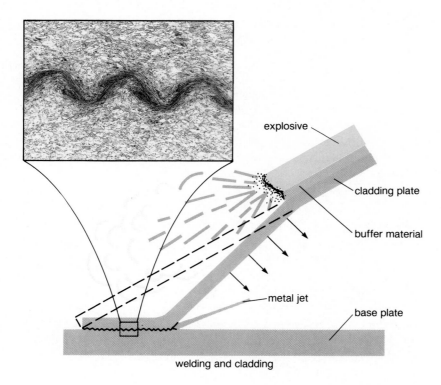

explosive

cladding plate

buffer material

metal jet

base plate

welding and cladding

prone to explode by friction or low-velocity impact. In small-diameter drill holes, the cartridges are most often loaded by hand, with the use of a wooden tamping pole.

For larger blasts the explosive is delivered into the drill hole in bulk form by being pumped from a tank truck at rates exceeding 450 kilograms (1,000 pounds) per minute. To ensure safe transportation, the explosive is often taken to the blasting site in a combined mix-pump truck, which has been loaded at the supply point with the nonexplosive oxidizer and the nonexplosive fuel components in separate tanks. The materials become an explosive (or blasting agent, as it is called in the U.S. if it cannot be initiated by a single blasting cap) only when they are combined in an in-line mixer directly connected to the loading pump. All blasting agents require a primer or booster charge to be placed in contact with the detonator for reliable initiation of the main charge.

The most frequently used blasting agent for large-scale rock blasting is ANFO, an oxygen-balanced mixture of ammonium nitrate (AN) in the form of small free-flowing pellets (prills) and fuel oil (FO). In a sufficiently large drill hole, the mixture can be made to detonate by means of a large primer charge. ANFO's disadvantage of being water soluble and therefore difficult to use in wet holes is offset by its low price. Mixed with an emulsion blasting agent, ANFO can be used reliably in wet holes.

Bulk explosive is pumped into large-diameter drill holes from a tank truck (above). For safety reasons, the fuel and oxidizer components of the explosive are often loaded on the truck in separate tanks and then mixed at the site during pumping. Diver (bottom left) places a charge of bulk explosive into a disused underwater oil well pipe exposed above the seafloor. After the pipe is severed, the debris is brought to the surface (bottom right).

The ANFO and the emulsion are delivered separately on a tank-mix truck and mixed in transit or as the material is loaded into drill holes.

In large blasting operations each drill hole can contain several tons of blasting agent, and blasts of several hundred drill holes are not uncommon. The ground vibrations resulting from such large blasts, if all the explosive were initiated simultaneously, would be similar in building-damage potential to a small earthquake. In order to control ground vibrations, detonators with individual, different time delays are used in all industrial rock blasting. Each detonator carries a small pyrotechnic charge in a tube inserted between the electrically initiated fuse head and the primary explosive charge. The pyrotechnic charge burns at a well-defined rate of a fraction of an inch per second. Through selection of the length of pyrotechnic inserted, detonators can be given time delays ranging from a few thousandths of a second to several seconds. With a detonator having a different time delay in each drill hole, arranged in a pattern so that the rock mass is gradually removed in slices as row after row of drill holes detonate, the ground vibration can be reduced by a factor of a thousand or more. Even large-scale mining operations can be conducted safely and without disturbances within a few miles of urban areas.

A special application of the same principles used in rock blasting is building demolition. The high tempo of urban area development increasingly demands that existing large buildings that have served their purpose be removed to make room for new construction. Conventional demolition is a hazardous, time-consuming process. By drilling a large number of holes in the lower walls of the building to be demolished and charging them with carefully selected amounts of explosive, the whole building can be made to collapse gently on its own foundation, creating perhaps a cloud of dust but no damage to the surrounding structures. The entire process is over in a few seconds with much less disturbance to the neighborhood than the subsequent removal of the rubble.

Lightning, radio transmissions, and other electrical disturbances can cause sudden, unexpected heating of the fine metallic resistance wire, called the bridge or bridge wire, that is the trigger for the fuse head of

Photo sequence follows the explosive demolition of a hotel in Houston, Texas. In contrast to the hazardous, time-consuming process of conventional demolition, carefully placed explosive charges can bring down an entire structure gently on its own foundation in a matter of seconds, with no damage to nearby buildings.

Courtesy, Dykon, Inc., Tulsa, Oklahoma

121

Photos, Center for Explosives Technology Research,
New Mexico Institute of Mining and Technology

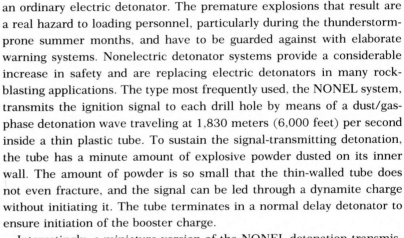

A detonation wave traveling at 1,830 meters (6,000 feet) per second inside a thin plastic tube (above) is the key to the NONEL nonelectric detonator system for rock-blasting applications. The wave, which transmits the ignition signal to each explosive charge, is sustained by a light dusting of explosive powder on the inner wall of the tube. An explosives worker (above right) hooks up multiple NONEL transmission lines for a large tunnel blast. Semiconductor bridge detonator (below) measures 1.5 millimeters (0.06 inch) on a side. When the chip receives the proper electrical signal, the middle of the H-shaped pattern turns into a plasma, triggering an explosive charge 1,000 times faster than a conventional bridge-wire detonator.

Sandia National Laboratories

an ordinary electric detonator. The premature explosions that result are a real hazard to loading personnel, particularly during the thunderstorm-prone summer months, and have to be guarded against with elaborate warning systems. Nonelectric detonator systems provide a considerable increase in safety and are replacing electric detonators in many rock-blasting applications. The type most frequently used, the NONEL system, transmits the ignition signal to each drill hole by means of a dust/gas-phase detonation wave traveling at 1,830 meters (6,000 feet) per second inside a thin plastic tube. To sustain the signal-transmitting detonation, the tube has a minute amount of explosive powder dusted on its inner wall. The amount of powder is so small that the thin-walled tube does not even fracture, and the signal can be led through a dynamite charge without initiating it. The tube terminates in a normal delay detonator to ensure initiation of the booster charge.

Interestingly, a miniature version of the NONEL detonation transmission line has found experimental use in medicine to initiate a milligram-scale explosion to fragment kidney stones in the human body. The special tubing, with an outer diameter no greater than an injection needle, has at its end a charge of lead azide (PbN_6), a sensitive primary explosive, weighing a few milligrams. The charge is brought into contact with the kidney stone using the tubing as a catheter. Although the explosion fragments the stone, the technique has not found widespread use because of the greater convenience of ultrasonic methods now in routine use.

Recent developments in electric detonator technology include the use of semiconductor microchips. The bridge wire is replaced by a microscopic bridge etched out of a micrometer-size layer of doped silicon on the surface of the chip, which also can have circuitry for effecting the required time delay. Built-in microelectronics can even give the detonator the ability to distinguish a coded initiating signal, without which no initiation can take place. It is interesting to compare the size of the solid-state bridge, its thickness measured in millionths of a centimeter, with the tree-trunk-size charge it will ultimately initiate. There is indeed a great deal of sophistication in modern explosives technology.

Creating for industry and art

As long ago as Nobel's time, explosive power was used to form metal sheet into complex shapes. The procedure began with the placement of the sheet against a concave, cast-iron form of the desired shape. The rim of the plate was sealed to the form with wax, and the whole was placed under water. A small dynamite charge was detonated in the water above the plate. The sudden expansion of the gaseous reaction products set the water in motion, pushing the metal plate into the form to take on its minutest detail.

Today explosive forming is used commercially for many shapes either too large or too complicated for conventional pressing. An example is the nose cone of a rocket, the warts, recesses, and holes of which make pressing a very complicated task. Enormous hemispheric end plates for thick-walled steel reactor tanks have been explosively formed, as have the bulbs installed at the bows of large tankers to reduce wave resistance.

Explosive forming recently has become an artist's tool, helping to create works whose attraction comes as much from the way they are made as from the artistic visions they express. In Sweden the late mystic artist Verner Molin used a thin layer of explosive to engrave a painted pattern into the surface of a thin copper plate. He then employed the plate like an ordinary etching plate in a press to imprint on paper with ink. His works, inhabited by a multitude of fanciful creatures of the dark winter night, were created, as he put it, in a hundred millionths of a second.

Socorro, New Mexico, is not far from Trinity Site, the testing grounds that mark the beginning of the age of nuclear explosives. There, in comparative peace, two artists—Evelyn Rosenberg and Alice Warder Seely, working sometimes together and sometimes separately—have created spectacular metal bas reliefs by a combination of explosive forming and etching that Rosenberg calls detonography. Rosenberg first makes a large

Industrial metal forming is usually carried out in a tank filled with water, a more efficient medium than air for transmitting shock waves. A sheet of the metal to be formed is placed and sealed against a die of the desired shape, after which the air between them is evacuated with a vacuum pump. An explosive charge is then detonated in the water above the plate. The sudden expansion of the gaseous reaction products sets the water in motion, driving the plate into the die.

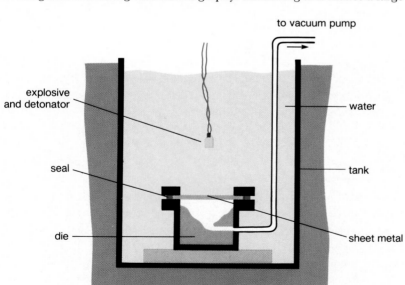

forming

(Bottom) Susan Contreras; (others) Ovak Arslanian

plaster mold that contains all of the details to be transferred to the final sculpture. She then takes it to a firing range operated by the New Mexico Institute of Mining and Technology, where the mold is set on the ground and covered with a properly sized sheet of stainless steel, brass, or other metal. On top of this is laid a thin sheet of explosive, separated from the metal only by a rubber film. When the explosive is detonated, the metal sheet is thrown with high velocity against the mold, which survives the impact just long enough to lend its form and detail to the metal.

Another application of explosive force that creates new objects, rather than takes them apart, is explosive powder compaction. The technique, which is just beginning to find industrial applications, offers exciting possibilities for the future. In its simplest form, a steel tube is filled with a metal powder, perhaps a mixture of alloying metals, and surrounded by an explosive charge. When the explosive is detonated, the shock wave generated in the powder by the inward motion of the tube wall compacts the powder into a solid metal cylinder. In the process of deforming and rubbing against each other, the powder particles partially melt and resolidify, all within a fraction of a microsecond, creating new alloys free of segregation, crystal growth, and other adverse effects of conventional melt alloying.

In an interesting recent development, powdered ingredients that react chemically with each other have been compressed explosively to synthesize new solids having useful properties. One example is the semiconductor gallium arsenide, which can be made by mixing and shock synthesizing the two elements gallium and arsenic in powder form. Titanium and aluminum, which normally resist alloying from melts, react as powders under explosive shock to yield new alloys of interest to the aerospace industry. Researchers also have employed shock synthesis to make some of the new high-temperature superconducting ceramics from metal oxide ingredients.

Experiments have shown that powders of substances as hard as diamond and cubic boron nitride (the two hardest materials known) fuse and bond chemically when compacted by explosive action. Large polycrystalline diamonds, suitable for use in tool bits or electronic devices, have been made in this way. Unfortunately, the release of pressure converts some of the diamond to graphite, turning the mass black. Even if they could be made translucent, their polycrystalline nature would keep them from having the fiery sparkle of natural single-crystal diamonds.

Generating electricity with explosives

A conventional electric generator converts mechanical energy into electricity by the motion of a conductor through a magnetic field. As the conductor moves across the field, eddy currents appear in the conductor, causing electricity to flow and producing magnetic forces that resist the motion. This phenomenon is called electromagnetic induction. Usually the energy for moving the conductor comes from a steam turbine, a water-driven turbine, a diesel engine, or another source of mechanical energy, but it can also come from the detonation of high explosives.

Explosive generators produce short electrical pulses, lasting only as long as it takes the explosive to detonate, but they are pulses of extraordinarily high power.

As with other applications of explosives, special circumstances must exist to make an explosive-driven generator a practical solution to a requirement. The generator must be used only once for a short period of time, for it destroys itself as it operates. Given this limitation, it has many attractive features: it occupies little space for the power it provides; it has none of the usual moving parts and mechanisms; and it needs no maintenance, preparation for starting, or attention from an operator. Shelf life can be extremely long. The disadvantages are those of all explosive devices.

In any generator the conductors meet resistance as they are pushed through the magnetic field. They become electromagnets whose fields resist penetration by the original field. If a magnetic field is set up within a container made of a conducting metal and then the volume of the container is reduced by compression with explosive, eddy currents are induced in the moving walls of the container. The currents produce magnetic fields that oppose the original field and trap it inside the container. As the volume of the container shrinks, the strength of the trapped field rises in inverse proportion. Simultaneously, the increasing field strength causes the currents in the conducting walls to rise. If the walls have been connected into an electric circuit, electricity will flow as an enormous pulse. Because of the way these devices operate, they are often called explosive magnetic-flux-compression generators.

Explosive-driven generators use external power sources, usually capacitor banks, to produce the initial magnetic field. Explosive energy then compresses the field and moves conductors through it, producing a large electrical pulse. The ratio of the energy in the output pulse to that of the input pulse from the capacitor bank is called the energy multiplication ratio. In typical practical systems, the ratio may be between 10 and 100. Because they are used only once and for a short time, explosive-driven generators usually employ the same conductors to produce the initial magnetic field and then to move through the field and generate the output pulse.

In the form of explosive-driven generator known as a plate generator, explosive blocks are detonated simultaneously over the outer surfaces of two parallel conducting plates. As the plates move toward each other, they compress a magnetic field set up by the flow of electricity through the plates from a capacitor bank. The pulse of electricity induced in the moving plates is fed through a load coil, which may be the primary windings of a transformer that will couple the energy output to another load. A variation called a strip generator produces a longer pulse than a plate generator. It consists of two conducting plates set at an angle to each other and an explosive strip laid along one of the plates. The explosive is detonated at one end rather than simultaneously over a surface, and the detonation wave propagates along the contacting metal plate, forcing it progressively from one end to the other toward the second plate. In

125

(Opposite page) The explosive transformation of artist Evelyn Rosenberg's ideas into metal bas reliefs begins with large plaster molds—created by various techniques—that contain all of the details to be transferred to the metal (top). Trucked to a New Mexico firing range, the molds are set on the ground, covered with the metal sheets that will bear the final images, and then topped with thin layers of explosive (second from top). After the detonation sculpts the molded forms in metal (second from bottom), Rosenberg works the sheets with grinding and polishing tools and coloring solutions into such finely detailed artworks as "Forest Floor" (bottom).

Photomicrograph of a mixture of two metal oxides after explosive compression to about 220,000 atmospheres (22 gigapascals) reveals large, round particles of ferric oxide (Fe_2O_3) with particles of softer zinc oxide (ZnO) squeezed into the spaces between them. The experiment, which attempted the shock synthesis of $ZnFe_2O_4$, produced an example of the way brittle, ceramiclike materials can flow plastically under sudden high pressure.

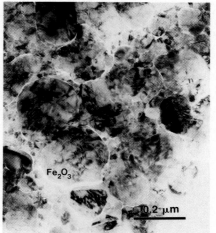

Fe$_2$O$_3$

0.2 μm

M. J. Carr and R. A. Graham, Sandia National Laboratories

Schematic diagrams on the opposite page illustrate the operating principles of plate, strip, and helical explosive-driven generators. Each variation is discussed on pages 125–126.

yet another variation, the helical type, the explosive contained in a metal tube expands the tube progressively along its length to short out successive turns of a surrounding helical conductor, pushing the magnetic field ahead of the traveling contact point between tube and helix. Helical generators can produce very large voltages.

Numerous experiments in which plasmas (hot ionized gases) were ejected from rockets to study the Earth's magnetic field at high altitude have used explosive-driven generators as lightweight, compact sources of electrical power for the plasma guns. Explosive flux compression has also been used in experiments with railguns—devices that exploit a traveling electromagnetic field to propel projectiles to high velocity—and in the creation of X-ray–emitting plasmas for radiography and radiation studies.

Shock waves in gases

High explosives drive shock waves in gases at high velocity, an effect that has practical applications. In certain cases the shocked gas can become extremely hot, making it useful as a specialized source of light.

The amount of energy per unit mass of a shocked gas depends very little on the choice of gas. The temperature reached, however, depends on the specific heat of the gas—in other words, on the quantity of heat energy it takes to raise the temperature of a unit mass of the gas by a certain amount. The smaller the specific heat, the greater the temperature that can be reached with a given energy input. Xenon is the best gas for reaching high temperatures, krypton is next best, and argon is appreciably poorer. On the other hand, xenon and krypton are expensive, whereas argon, present to about 1% in air, is inexpensive. Most experiments to date have been done with argon.

In argon the temperature at the shock wave driven by a good solid high explosive is above 25,000 kelvins (K), and in xenon above 36,000 K. (At such high temperatures the kelvin and Celsius scales can be regarded as identical; to convert kelvins approximately to Fahrenheit, multiply by 1.8.) The shocked gas emits light nearly as a perfect radiator; the pressure and density are so high that the usual atomic line structure is broadened such that the lines merge and the spectrum is continuous. An argon shock wave is about 60 times brighter than the Sun, and a xenon shock wave about 100 times brighter.

These intense light sources serve well as illumination for the photography of explosive experiments. The Sun provides adequate illumination for making photographic exposures as short as a few thousandths of a second. In photographing an explosion, such an exposure time would be unacceptably long and give only a blur. To capture explosives in the process of detonating, exposure time must be less than a millionth of a second, and in some cases only a few billionths of a second. For these brief shots the argon shock wave has become the standard light source.

While illumination for explosive photography puts the visible spectrum of a shocked gas to use, the ultraviolet region also has advantages. Optically pumped lasers, for example, require illumination of the laser material with high-intensity light in a certain frequency range. For some

A load coil for an explosive-driven generator and a complete plate generator are pictured below. In use the generator carries explosive blocks mounted between the two upturned edges of each plate. The load coil is made massive to keep the high magnetic pressure developed within the hollow of the coil from tearing the coil apart before the generator has finished its task.

Los Alamos National Laboratory

plate generator

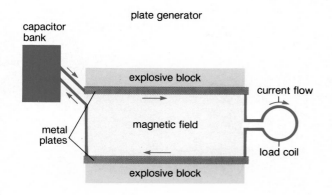

capacitor bank

explosive block

metal plates

magnetic field

current flow

load coil

explosive block

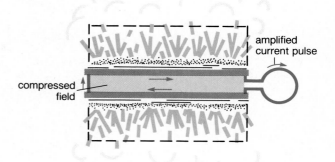

compressed field

amplified current pulse

strip generator

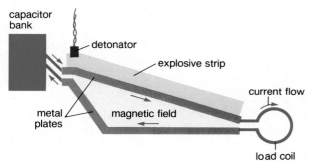

capacitor bank

detonator

explosive strip

current flow

metal plates

magnetic field

load coil

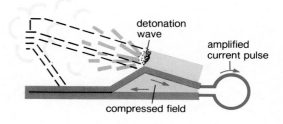

detonation wave

amplified current pulse

compressed field

helical generator

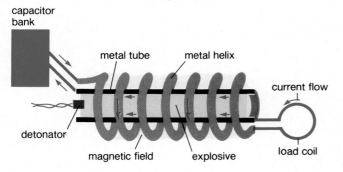

capacitor bank

metal tube

metal helix

current flow

detonator

magnetic field

explosive

load coil

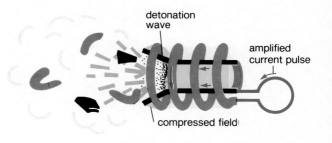

detonation wave

amplified current pulse

compressed field

lasers this so-called pump light lies in the ultraviolet, and argon and xenon light sources have been used to pump them.

Shock waves in liquids and solids

The initial phase of an explosive shock-compression event proceeds through an orderly, precise, understandable sequence of events. The sequence takes place very rapidly, however. The shock rises to full pressure in a space the length of a few molecules, and it is over in a millionth of a second or less. Afterward, on a human time scale, all is chaos, and it becomes impossible to understand the end of the event in the same way as its beginning. Nevertheless, the first, orderly part of an explosion has become a valuable experimental tool for studying materials.

Explosively generated shock waves in liquids and solids attain pressures much beyond those reached in ordinary laboratory experiments. Scientists use these waves to probe the properties of matter at high pressure and temperature. The need to know how much the fissionable metal in an atomic bomb could be explosively compressed gave the first impetus for an extensive mapping, by means of shock-wave experiments, of the densities of metals at high pressures, but knowledge of high-pressure behavior now serves many other purposes.

For example, the pressure inside the Earth rises with depth such that materials at the planet's center experience a pressure of about four million atmospheres. Shock-wave experiments can subject a sample of material to similar pressures while measurements are made of the speed of sound in the sample and the density. Through detailed comparison of the properties of materials under simulated deep-Earth conditions with actual seismological measurements, geologists can develop improved models of the Earth's structure. Measurements of the properties of matter at high temperature and pressure also help scientists to understand the way meteorite impacts form craters on the Earth and other bodies of the solar system and to anticipate the destructive effect on spacecraft of

Crisscrossed pattern of dislocations is visible in a photomicrograph of a sample of stainless steel submitted to an explosive shock of 100,000 atmospheres (ten gigapascals). The compression altered the atomic spacing within the crystalline solid, leading to an ordered rearrangement of the atoms along specific planes. The study of such explosively created dislocations has improved scientists' understanding of materials and their strength.

C. R. Hills, Sandia National Laboratories, from his master's thesis at New Mexico Institute of Mining and Technology

128

collisions with microscopic meteorites, which can have impact velocities of many tens of thousands of meters per second.

Even when matter is not subjected to the extreme pressures of the Earth's core, it is valuable to perform experiments that exceed the range of interest to be sure that nothing remarkable happens at just slightly more extreme conditions. Remarkable things do happen at high pressures. When metals are compressed they often change the arrangement of their atoms; such solid-solid phase changes yield materials with new properties. One example is the high-pressure transformation of the more common graphite form of carbon into diamond, a metastable form in which the carbon atoms are closely bound in a very different crystalline structure. This transformation occurs naturally under geologic pressures. It can also be attained by shock compression to make artificial diamonds.

The compression of crystalline solids in a shock wave first pushes the layers of atoms closer together in one direction, the direction of wave travel, making the atomic distance less in that direction than in others. The imbalance of distances leads to an imbalance of forces, and the atoms must move to adjust. The adjustments do not occur by disorganized motion of the atoms but along lines and surfaces that resemble zippers with the teeth offset one space. These zippers, called dislocations, allow an ordered rearrangement of the crystalline solids. In this way the crystal adjusts the atomic spacings from the unbalanced form produced by a directional shock-wave compression to a balanced form wherein pressure is equal in every direction. The study of the creation and motion of the dislocations has contributed greatly to the understanding of materials and their strength.

The readjustment by means of dislocations behind a shock wave leads to other new effects in shocked matter. Along the dislocations, where matter moves, more work is done, and the local temperature rises above what would be produced by a symmetrical compression. Thus, a shock wave leaves hot spots in its wake. Chemical and physical changes take place at these local hot spots, and they are often ones that cannot be found in experiments in which shock waves do not occur.

Guiding the touch of a giant

The mind-boggling violence of an explosion seems to contradict the idea that it could ever be used for precision purposes. Yet in its early stages the explosive process is orderly and controlled; chaos comes only after everything important has been accomplished. High explosives offer a source of concentrated, pulsed power for numerous endeavors. They achieve pressures and velocities beyond the range attainable with other techniques. In addition, in situations where high power concentrations are needed, the safety and reliability of explosives are unmatched. Moreover, as artists like Rosenberg and Seeley have shown, even blasts that shake the desert landscape like a giant fist slamming the Earth can be tamed and directed to imbue metal with textures as delicate as the veining in a leaf. If such things are possible, can anyone deny that even more remarkable uses for explosives lie ahead?

Explosive-driven laser (opposite page, top) contains a gas-filled laser tube running through the center of the box. Explosive disks set into the box walls are initiated by special plane-wave explosive lenses (brown cones). In operation the box is filled with argon gas. Detonation drives a strong shock wave into the gas, heating it and causing it to radiate a large amount of ultraviolet light. This so-called pump light is absorbed by the lasing gas in the tube and its energy reradiated as a laser beam.

The New
SUPERCONDUCTORS
A Scientific Breakthrough

by Praveen Chaudhari

Within two years physicists have
found materials that are superconductors
of electricity at temperatures far higher
than most scientists had ever believed possible.

Metals are good conductors of electricity; that is, they tend to have low values of resistivity. Their resistivity does, however, vary over a wide range and, normally, only as the temperature of a metal approaches absolute zero will the resistivity approach zero.

In a metal some of the electrons are free to move, and their average drift velocity constitutes an electrical current. When a voltage from a battery is applied across the ends of a wire, these free electrons are accelerated. In a hypothetical perfect metal this acceleration would continue until a tremendous current flowed through the wire. In a real metal the acceleration is quickly interrupted by the scattering of the electrons. That is, the direction and magnitude of their velocity are suddenly changed as they encounter the various imperfections in the metal.

In the scattering process the energy given to the electrons by the battery appears as an increase in the random motion of the atoms of the metal, and the result is heat. This heat must be removed from any electrical device, whether it is a huge electrical generator or a tiny computer chip. Otherwise the temperature will continually increase until it destroys the device.

There is one exception to this otherwise inevitable generation of heat by electrical currents. It was discovered by Heike Kamerlingh Onnes. In 1908 he succeeded in liquefying helium gas by using techniques pioneered by Sir James Dewar. Dewar had succeeded in liquefying oxygen in 1878 and hydrogen in 1898. Only helium has a lower boiling point than hydrogen. Dewar tried in vain to complete his conquest of all the elements by liquefying helium, which boils at 4.2 K. (Kelvin, or K, is the absolute scale of temperature, 0 K being the lowest possible temperature, the point at which virtually all the random motions of atoms and molecules cease. It corresponds to $-273°$ C.) In 1911 Onnes found that the resistance of several metals vanished when they were immersed in liquid helium and that this transition occurred sharply at a very definite temperature as the temperature of the metal was continuously lowered. He had discovered the phenomenon of superconductivity.

PRAVEEN CHAUDHARI is Vice-President, Science, and Director of Physical Sciences, IBM Research, Yorktown Heights, New York.

(Overleaf) Illustration by John Craig

A small magnet levitates above a high-temperature superconductor in a demonstration of the Meissner effect. The magnet is repelled by the superconductor until the repulsive force is balanced by the attractive force of gravity.

Properties of superconductors

The complete vanishing of electrical resistivity is just one of the unique properties of superconducting materials. Another was found by Walther Meissner and R. Ochsenfeld in 1933. They found that when an object is cooled through its superconducting transition temperature in the presence of a magnetic field, the field is expelled from the interior of the object. (The field will be completely expelled only if the object is a needle or sheet with its length in the direction of the field much greater than its dimensions perpendicular to the field. These geometric complications will be ignored in the remainder of this article.) This property has interesting consequences. For example, if a piece of iron is brought close to the pole of a magnet, it is attracted to it. In contrast, a superconductor is repelled by the magnet. Thus, iron is ferromagnetic, while a superconductor is diamagnetic. The accompanying illustration shows a more dramatic version of the diamagnetic effect. The superconductor is placed on a table, and the magnet is above it. The magnet is repelled by the superconductor until this repulsive force is just balanced by the attractive force of gravity. Thus, levitation in this case is accomplished by the combination of magnetism and superconductivity.

Superconductors may be divided into two classes, depending upon their response to a magnetic field. In the case of a Type I superconductor, a magnetic field penetrates the material for only a certain characteristic distance, called the penetration depth. If the field is increased to a value called the critical field, it suddenly penetrates the entire object and quenches the object's superconductivity completely. In contrast, a Type II superconductor will allow the penetration of a magnetic field when it is increased above its lower critical field. In this case, however, the field penetrates the material in a finely divided pattern that consists of a large number of parallel threads called flux lines. At the center of each

132

flux line, described as the "normal region," the magnetic field has its maximum value and the material is not superconducting; however, the material between the flux line continues to be superconducting. As the external magnetic field is increased, the number of flux lines increases. Finally, at the upper critical field the normal regions completely cover the material, and, therefore, no superconductivity remains. Researchers discovered that the upper critical field of a Type II superconductor may be of an order of magnitude larger than the critical field of a Type I superconductor.

From its discovery by Onnes in 1911 until the publication of a paper by John Bardeen, Leon N. Cooper, and John Robert Schrieffer in 1957, the electronic structure of a material in a superconducting condition was a mystery. Normally, because of their electrical charges two electrons repel each other. Cooper showed, however, that even an arbitrarily small attraction can cause two electrons in a solid to form a bound pair. In their paper Bardeen, Cooper, and Schrieffer showed that the interaction of the electrons with the atoms of a metal can generate an attractive force between electrons and that this attraction can result in the formation of the peculiar electronic state of superconductivity, which is characterized by the formation of bound pairs of the free electrons of the material. This BCS (Bardeen, Cooper, and Schrieffer) theory became the foundation of all superconducting theory until the 1980s.

Very briefly the BCS picture of the superconducting state can be visualized as follows. In forming a metal, the originally neutral atoms give up some of their negatively charged electrons to form the sea of free electrons that conduct electrical currents as discussed above. The atoms of a metal are, therefore, left with a positive charge and become positive ions. As an electron moves, the positive ions are attracted and move slightly toward the electron as it approaches and then relax back to their original position as it recedes. A second electron whose path happens nearly to intersect the path of the first electron will detect a higher density of positive ions in the vicinity of the path of the first electron and therefore be attracted toward that electron. Thus, there is an attractive interaction between the two electrons that arises from the

Figure 1. A free electron attracts and thereby displaces ions in a superconducting metal; a second free electron is then drawn toward the first one when it is attracted to the displaced ions. The two electrons form a bound pair—named a Cooper pair after one of the scientists who discovered the phenomenon. The formation of such pairs is an essential characteristic of the state of superconductivity.

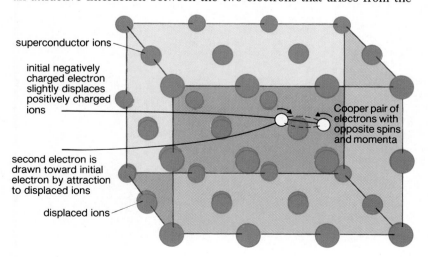

superconductor ions

initial negatively charged electron slightly displaces positively charged ions

Cooper pair of electrons with opposite spins and momenta

second electron is drawn toward initial electron by attraction to displaced ions

displaced ions

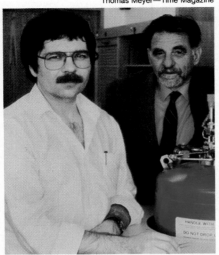

Johannes Georg Bednorz (left) and Karl Alex Müller won the Nobel Prize for Physics in 1987 for their discovery in 1986 of a class of copper oxides that become superconductors at temperatures of over 30 K.

motion of the ions (Figure 1). Cooper's argument can then be applied to this interaction to conclude that bound pairs of electrons will form at temperatures that are low enough so that their attraction to one another will not be offset by thermal energy. The BCS theory then predicts that all the free electrons will participate in the pairing, that the scattering of electrons will not occur, and that a current may flow without resistance.

Physicists call the interaction of electrons arising from the motion of the positive ions of a metal a phonon interaction. A phonon in a solid is to sound waves in the solid as photons are to radio or light waves in free space. That is, the motion of the sound waves or the electromagnetic fields in space can be represented as the superposition of waves of different frequencies and different wave lengths. In terms of quantum mechanics these waves become collections of particles called phonons or photons, respectively.

High-temperature superconductors

In January 1986 Johannes Georg Bednorz and Karl Alex Müller performed experiments on a class of copper oxides that showed that the superconducting transition temperatures of those materials was over 30 K. Their result was confirmed in December 1986 by groups in Japan and the United States. For their discovery Bednorz and Müller were awarded the Nobel Prize for Physics in 1987.

By the end of January 1987 materials had been prepared with superconducting transition temperatures in the neighborhood of 95 K. The first announcement of such a material was made by a team headed by Ching-Wu Chu. Since then researchers in Japan and the United States increased the temperature even higher, to 125 K.

It took 75 years for researchers to find materials with a superconducting transition temperature that was four times that of the very early materials, but it required barely a year for achievement of another factor of four in the copper oxide superconductors, now commonly called the high-

Figure 2 reveals that it took scientists 75 years to find materials with superconducting transition temperatures that were four times those of the very early materials but only one year to raise these temperatures by another factor of four. The temperatures are on the Kelvin (K) scale, where 0 K equals −273° C.

evolution of superconductive critical temperatures

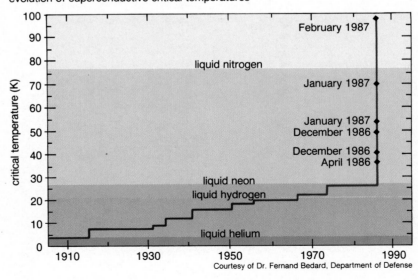

Courtesy of Dr. Fernand Bedard, Department of Defense

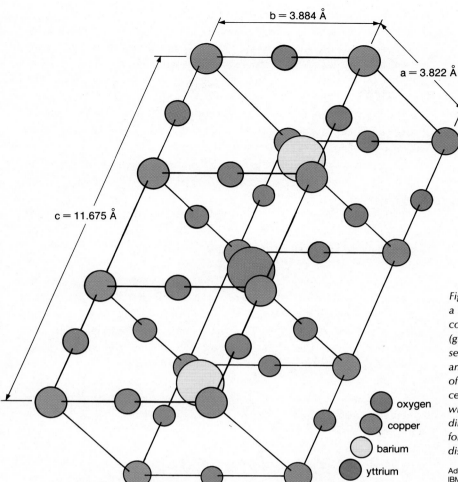

b = 3.884 Å

a = 3.822 Å

c = 11.675 Å

oxygen

copper

barium

yttrium

Figure 3. The atomic arrangement of a high-temperature superconducting compound reveals layers of copper (green) and oxygen (blue) atoms separated by those of barium (yellow) and yttrium (red). This is the outline of a unit cell of this compound; a unit cell is the smallest array of atoms that, when repeated many times in the three directions indicated in the drawing, will form a crystal of the compound. For a full discussion of this figure, see text.

Adapted from information courtesy of William Krakow, IBM Research

temperature superconductors (Figure 2). Another factor-of-four increase would make superconducting phenomena possible at room temperature. This rapid and unexpected increase in the transition temperature and the anticipated increase in the usefulness of superconducting devices has generated great excitement in the scientific and technological community. In the rest of this section these materials and their properties will be described, along with the technological issues that need to be resolved so that they can be brought into practical application.

A typical superconductor whose critical temperature is near 95 K contains the elements yttrium (Y), barium (Ba), copper (Cu), and oxygen (O). This compound has the chemical formula $Y_1Ba_2Cu_3O_{7-x}$, where x is a number between zero and one, a typical value being around 0.2. Although yttrium and barium may be replaced by other elements having similar electronic properties, there is no confirmed example to date of a superconducting material with the copper or oxygen completely substituted by another element.

In $Y_1Ba_2Cu_3O_{7-x}$ the atoms lie in layers, with those of copper and oxygen separated by those of yttrium and barium (Figure 3). In one of the copper oxide layers the atoms lie in chains that are separated by rows in which some of the oxygen atoms are missing. For further understanding of the atomic arrangement, three mutually perpendicular axes are drawn in Figure 3. The c-axis is special because it is perpendicular to the layers, while the a- and b-axes lie in the plane of the layers. The a- and b-axes are, respectively, parallel and perpendicular to the chains and therefore are also special. A material whose structure has special directions is called anisotropic. In an anisotropic material some physical properties will vary with direction. This is indeed the case in these materials; both the electrical conductivity in the normal state and the critical fields in the superconducting state vary with the direction of the current or the magnetic field.

Figure 3 also shows the outline of what is known as the unit cell of $Y_1Ba_2Cu_3O_{7-x}$. A unit cell is the smallest array of atoms that when repeated many times in all three directions will form the crystal in question. Although the three axes of this crystal are mutually perpendicular, none of the three dimensions of the unit cell are equal. Such a crystal structure is said to be orthorhombic. A picture of a sample of $Y_1Ba_2Cu_3O_{7-x}$ made with a transmission electron microscope is shown in Figure 4.

As mentioned above, the physical properties of these materials are known to be anisotropic. It is currently believed that the superconductivity is associated with the layers. The upper critical field is five times greater if the field is applied parallel to the copper oxide layers. In either direction the critical field has the largest value ever reported for a superconductor. At very low temperatures it is extrapolated to be substantially more than 100 Tesla, which is more than one million times the Earth's magnetic field.

Why do these materials, so different from the pure metals and alloys that had been the dominant superconductors until the 1980s, have such remarkable properties? Scientists have shown experimentally that the basic idea of electron pairing is still valid for the high-temperature superconductors. However, most believe that the force that leads to this pairing is not the phonon coupling of the BCS theory discussed above. It is not a strong enough attractive force to overcome the thermal energy associated with the higher temperatures. Many new mechanisms have been proposed, but so far none has gained wide acceptance by the scientific community.

Applications for high-temperature superconductors

Much of the excitement generated by the discovery of the high-temperature superconductors was in anticipation of a great increase in the use of superconducting materials. Helium is an expensive gas, and apparatus to liquefy it is also costly. Therefore, superconductors that must be cooled by liquid helium have limited application. The rise of critical temperatures to the 100-K range, however, allows the superconductor to be cooled by liquid nitrogen; nitrogen is the least expensive of all the gases and is liquefied at 77 K.

Almost all applications require that the superconductor have a high critical current density. (The critical current density is the maximum

Figure 4. Atoms of a high-temperature superconducting compound are revealed in a transmission electron micrograph. The yttrium atoms are black; those of barium are yellow; and the copper atoms are red. Oxygen atoms are not seen because of oxygen's low atomic number.

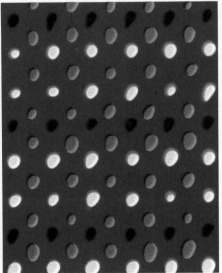

Micrograph courtesy of William Krakow and Thomas M. Shaw, IBM Research

current that a superconductor can carry without showing a measurable resistance to flow.) As originally prepared, the high-temperature materials had low critical current densities. It was not known whether these values were characteristic of the materials or if they were merely due to the methods of preparation. This question was settled by scientists at the IBM Thomas J. Watson Research Center at Yorktown Heights, New York. They made samples with critical currents that exceeded one million amperes per square centimeter at very low temperatures and were more than 100,000 at liquid nitrogen temperatures. These values were later confirmed and exceeded by other groups in the United States and Japan. They are large enough for almost all conceivable applications.

As of 1988 the fabrication of actual wire, coils, or other objects with the desired superconducting properties had not been accomplished. Wires and tapes are first prepared as ceramic powders and then processed into final form. Oxides of yttrium, barium, and copper are mixed together and heated in an oxygen atmosphere to temperatures in the range of 900° C (1,652° F), causing them to react and form $Y_1Ba_2Cu_3O_{7-x}$. The resulting product is cooled, ground into a fine powder, compressed into the desired form, and heated to sinter the grains to a solid mass. Materials prepared in this manner, however, have low critical currents and poor mechanical strength. Materials produced by first alloying the metals and then oxidizing the alloy suffer from the same shortcomings.

High-temperature materials have also been prepared by the laying down of thin film on various substrates by means of a number of differ-

Scientist dips a sample of superconducting material into a flask containing liquid nitrogen (above left). One of the great advantages of the new superconducting materials is that they can be cooled by liquid nitrogen, which is the least expensive of all gases and can be easily liquefied. (Above) Scientists measure the resistance of a superconducting thin film. The graph on the upper monitor reveals a sudden drop in the resistance of the film while its temperature is being lowered by immersion in liquid nitrogen.

137

Scientists use the technique of plasma spraying to coat a wide variety of objects—including spirals, a flat panel, and spherical vessels—with high-temperature superconducting material (above). A view into the port of an electron-beam vapor-deposition system shows sources of yttrium, barium, and copper glowing as a result of heating by electron beams (above right). This vaporized material is then deposited on a substrate as a thin superconducting film.

ent processes. These include evaporation, sputtering, laser ablation, and plasma spraying. The mechanical strength of the superconducting thin film is not an issue since it is supported by the substrate. However, only on very special substrates, such as single-crystal strontium titanate, does the superconductor develop the desired high critical current density. Such a substrate determines the orientation of the superconductor crystals. In these so-called epitaxial films laid down on strontium titanate, high critical current densities were first demonstrated. When laid down on most substrates, superconductors become composed of small crystalline grains having random orientations. The boundaries between these grains cannot support large critical current densities and, therefore, the critical current densities of films on ordinary substrates are low. An example of the microstructure of a material with grains boundaries is shown in Figure 5. Control of this type of microstructure is an essential step in producing materials that can carry large currents.

Electrical-power generation, transmission, and storage are considered to be promising areas for the use of superconductors. Magnetic fields in conventional generators are limited by the necessity of removing the heat produced by the currents passing through their coils. The use of superconducting coils would improve the efficiency of generators and allow the design of more compact models.

Materials at high temperatures can absorb more heat than they can at low temperatures. This may be crucial in fusion reactors that operate in a pulsed mode. The hot plasma produced during a pulse will heat the superconducting coils. High-temperature superconductors can absorb much more heat than those operating only at low temperatures and still remain superconducting.

It is estimated that from 3 to 10% of electrical power is lost as heat during transmission. This loss may be greatly reduced by the use of superconducting wires, although there is an obvious increase in capital expense and in maintenance of lines that must be refrigerated. Energy must be saved to compensate for the increased cost of such lines. The desirability of placing nuclear reactors far from the centers of population may make the economical transmission of electrical power more important in the future than it is at present. Still farther in the future, the advent of fusion reactors that may generate large amounts of power at a single site will require very long transmission lines.

The energy demands of large urban centers vary considerably according to the time of day and the season. The ability to store energy even for a few hours can reduce the amount of production capacity required for times of high consumption. Large coils of superconductors can, in principle, store energy in the form of magnetic fields. The design of such coils would require the development of superconducting materials and support structures able to withstand the large pressures of the fields.

The magnetic fields in high-energy particle accelerators are generated by the use of superconducting coils. The effort to achieve higher energies and fluxes of particles in these sophisticated machines will encourage early tests of the usefulness of the high-temperature materials as sources of large magnetic fields.

Laboratory instrumentation is another area in which superconductors have already found application and in which the use of high-temperature superconductors can provide added convenience and simplicity. Many of

IBM Research

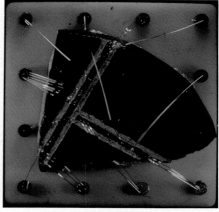

A thin film of high-temperature superconducting material is grown on a substrate of single-crystal strontium titanate to demonstrate that a critical current density of more than 100,000 amperes per square centimeter can be achieved. This is accomplished because the substrate determines the orientation of the superconductor crystals rather than allowing them to be random.

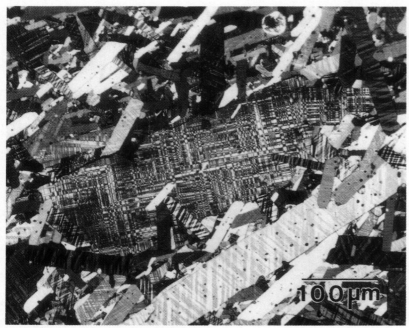

Micrograph courtesy of Thomas M. Shaw, IBM Research

Figure 5. An optical micrograph reveals the structure of a polycrystalline superconducting compound consisting of yttrium, barium, copper, and oxygen. The line on the scale has a length of one ten-thousandth of a meter.

these devices depend upon phenomena predicted by Brian Josephson in 1962 and called the direct current (DC) and alternating current (AC) Josephson effects. The DC effect is the passage of a current through a Josephson junction, which consists of two superconductors separated by a very narrow insulating or empty space. The current passes by means of a quantum mechanical effect called tunneling. The AC effect takes place in the same device and consists of an alternating-current signal that is generated when a constant voltage is maintained between the two superconductors. This latter effect is used for establishing high-precision voltage standards by measurement of the frequency of the produced signal.

A wide variety of sensitive measurements are made by SQUIDS (superconducting quantum interference devices), which consist essentially of two Josephson junctions connected in a loop. A very small magnetic field in the loop causes the generation of an oscillating current. SQUIDS have already been made from high-temperature materials and may claim to be their first application.

The development of superconductors for computer circuitry has often been attempted, but as of early 1988 none was in use in any commer-

Magnified more than 500 times is the first thin-film, high-temperature superconducting electronic device— a SQUID, or superconducting quantum interference device (below). Only one one-hundredth the thickness of a human hair, it can be used to measure extremely small magnetic fields, such as those associated with the tiny electrical currents in the human brain. Below right, a patient undergoes a noninvasive brain scan by a machine that contains such a device.

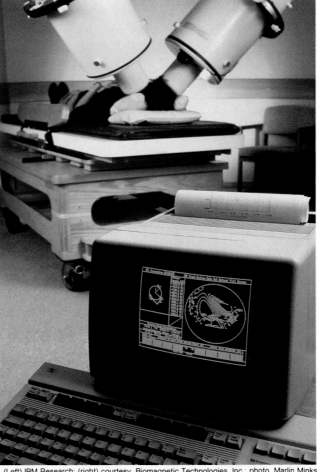

(Left) IBM Research; (right) courtesy, Biomagnetic Technologies, Inc.; photo, Marlin Minks

cial product. There was, however, considerable anticipation that high-temperature superconductors might be combined with semiconductors to produce a hybrid technology consisting of semiconductor transistors connected by superconductor transmission lines. Such a technology would be advantageous in those cases in which the time to propagate a signal between transistors is determined by the resistance of the line. This application requires very high critical currents because silicon technology uses current densities in transmission lines in excess of a million amperes per square centimeter.

Summary and future prospects

In the middle 1980s superconducting materials were discovered with transition temperatures in the neighborhood of 100 K. These materials are crystals containing oxygen, copper, and at least two other elements. The structure of these materials is quite complex, and the theoretical reason for their high transition temperatures remains unknown. They are capable of conducting electrical currents of high density in the presence of high magnetic fields.

These properties give promise of a number of important applications, but considerable further development of the materials is required. Many of these applications will depend on the fabrication of large, strong magnetic coils and thin films.

A power transmission test facility (top) demonstrates that niobium-tin superconducting cables (in the long white pipe at the upper left) can provide a cost-effective means of transmitting large amounts of electrical power underground. A train in Japan (above) employs superconducting magnets that allow it to be levitated about ten centimeters (four inches) and ride on a cushion of air.

141

VOYAGER

In December 1986 a "flying gas tank" carried a crew of two nonstop around the Earth without refueling. The achievement was simultaneously a triumph of individualism and a spectacularly successful demonstration of innovation in aircraft design.

"Okay, you are cleared, Edwards-to-Edwards, flight-plan route, maintain 8,000 feet."

Those were the words from the control tower at Edwards Air Force Base in California that sent the aircraft *Voyager* off on a flight to circle the Earth. Nine days later, without a single stop for fuel, that same aircraft soared out of the morning mist and flew over the crowd that had come to greet its pilots, then touched down for a landing. The craft had flown 24,987 miles—the official distance recognized by the International Aeronautical Federation in Paris—on a single load of gas. (One mile is about 1.61 kilometers.)

It was more than a pathbreaking achievement in aviation; it was a triumph of the human spirit. It was the work of a handful of individuals in an age of mass organizations, contrasting sharply with such accomplishments as the Apollo flights to the Moon, in which the astronauts had been backed by 300,000 people working on the ground. *Voyager's* flight thus would rank with such triumphs as the first four-minute mile, the ascent of Mt. Everest, and the descent to the oceans' ultimate depths.

Moreover, it was an achievement of a surprising and unexpected character. Everest, the Moon, the ocean's depths—all had been predicted decades in advance, by Jules Verne and other writers, and had been pursued extensively over long periods of time. Nonstop flight around the world, by contrast, lay almost entirely outside the realm of the imaginable. No Verne or similar writer had foreseen it; only a satirical 1931 short story by James Thurber, "The Greatest Man in the World," hinted of the possibility. And this possibility became a serious prospect only when *Voyager's* crew was actively preparing for the flight.

That flight, in turn, offered an astonishingly lengthy list of ways in which *Voyager* might have failed catastrophically. Most of them stemmed from the eggshell-like fragility of the craft. There were 17 fuel tanks in the wings and body, for instance, and if anyone had tried to fill them by pumping in the gas the way one fills up a car, the resulting weight would have broken the aircraft. It took 15 hours to fill the tanks, in a meticulous procedure that added a few gallons at a time to each one in a calculated sequence until a total of 1,200 gallons was aboard. (One gallon is about 3.8 liters.)

THE   PLANE   FLOWN   . .

Prior to its round-the-world flight, the plane had never been completely fueled and tested at full weight, not even in its ability to taxi on the runway. Such a fully loaded condition was considered so dangerous that only one occasion justified it—the flight itself. When the craft was fully fueled, the wings dragged on the runway, and the resulting abrasion caused part of the right wing to tear loose. If a tire had blown during the takeoff run, the resulting strain would have snapped the landing gear, pitching *Voyager* into a fiery crash. And although the tires held, the plane accelerated so slowly that it used all but 700 feet of its 15,000-foot runway before reaching flying speed. (One foot is about 0.3 meter.)

. . 'ROUND THE WORLD

by T. A. Heppenheimer

T. A. HEPPENHEIMER is a free-lance writer with a Ph.D. in aerospace engineering.

(Overleaf) © Jeffrey Vock—Visions

Map summarizes Voyager's *nonstop, unrefueled, Earth-circling flight of Dec. 14–23, 1986.*

The record flight

Takeoff occurred on Dec. 14, 1986, just after 8 AM. At that hour the air was close to a dead calm. This was important, for *Voyager* was in danger from anything stronger than a light breeze. It did not climb quickly but gained altitude at only 50 feet per minute. It thus was quite vulnerable to any downdraft, and as it flew over California's coastal mountains, there was danger from turbulence. Had the aircraft been buffeted with an acceleration of only 1½ times that of gravity, its wings would have broken. Moreover, once it was under way, it could not go back. *Voyager* had no ability to dump fuel in an emergency and was far too heavy to land safely.

Two pilots were aboard: 48-year-old Dick Rutan, who had flown jet fighters in Vietnam, and 34-year-old Jeana Yeager, holder of several world aviation records. Rutan, the more experienced, spent 55 of the first 60 hours at the controls. Near the end of the second day, the two encountered a typhoon over the western Pacific, and Rutan maneuvered close to its northern edge to pick up its powerful tailwinds. The following day, crossing the South China Sea, he had to steer between thunderheads to the south and the hostile coast of Vietnam to the north. The U.S. State Department had informed *Voyager*'s pilots that they could not overfly Vietnam except to make an emergency landing.

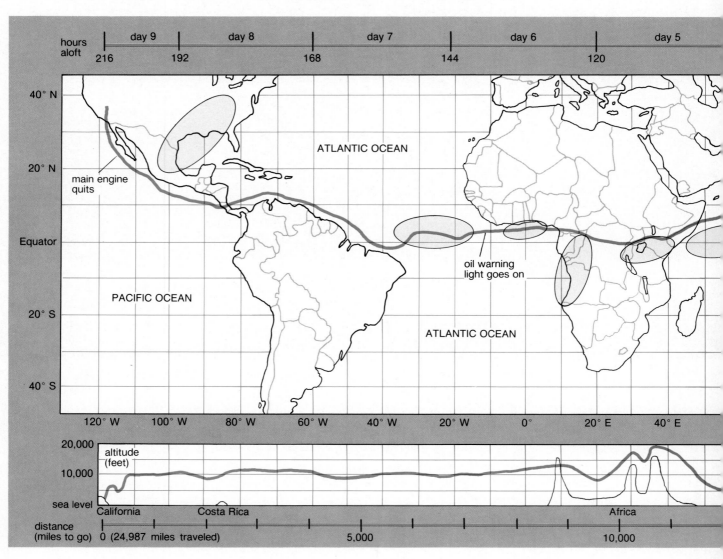

Voyager's fuel-laden wings scrape the runway during takeoff for the record flight attempt. Both wingtips suffered severe abrasion damage and were discarded shortly after the plane left the ground.

AP/Wide World

The passage over Africa, on the fifth day, was harrowing. A line of thunderstorms lay athwart the path, and *Voyager* climbed to 20,000 feet to surmount them. Even so, the plane was battered about quite badly. There also was concern that its maneuvering had cost more fuel than it could spare to get home. Consequently, a light plane flew up from Nairobi, Kenya, to observe *Voyager* while Rutan pitched the aircraft, making its nose bob up and down. Because the sluggishness of these

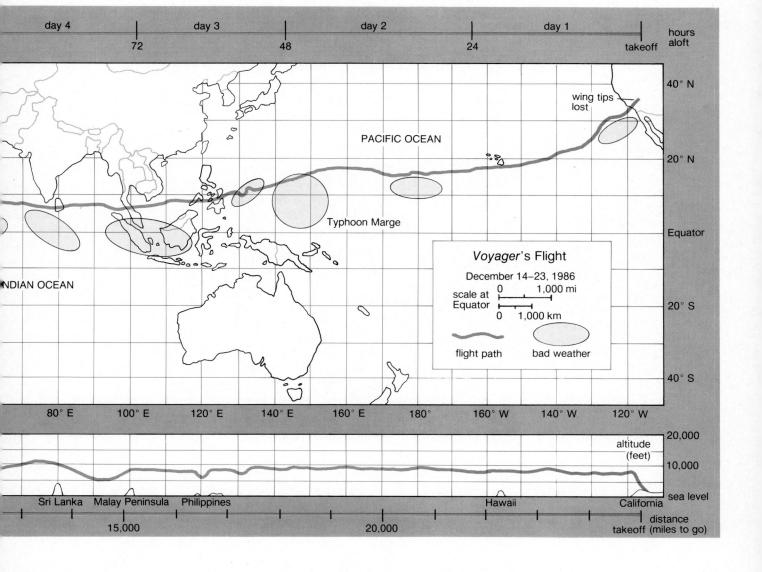

motions was related to the amount of fuel the plane carried, the test amounted to "weighing" the craft in flight and disclosed that there was indeed enough fuel.

Nevertheless, *Voyager* nearly ran into trouble for lack of oil. Its main engine began overheating because the weary pilots, preoccupied with the turbulence over Africa, had neglected to replenish the supply. Fortunately, putting in fresh oil solved the problem, and the temporary lack proved not to have caused damage. As they headed out over the Atlantic, Rutan radioed, "I'm tired. I want to go to bed in California."

Rutan and Yeager proceeded to cross the Atlantic near the Equator, then hugged the north coast of South America as they entered the Caribbean. Eight days into the flight, they crossed Costa Rica and once again were over the Pacific. This was their last full day in the air, and they cruised northwestward off the Mexican coast.

Then, with only a few hours to go, the craft came close to a new disaster. In the pitch-dark early hours of the last morning, it developed a fuel-pump problem. *Voyager* relied on pumps to transfer fuel from its scattered tanks into a feed tank close to its two engines, but one pump had failed. Since the engines sucked fuel directly from this feed tank, Rutan and Yeager tried to use this suction to bypass the failed pump by allowing the main engine, at the rear, to draw fuel directly from a more remote tank. The effort demanded too much suction, however; the engine drew in air rather than fuel and shut down.

"We were a glider for five minutes," Rutan later remarked. They needed that one engine to stay up, and if they could not restart it, they would have to ditch at sea in total darkness. Rutan held the nose up to get fuel to flow back toward the engine. After several attempts, while the plane was losing altitude minute by minute and its pilots were struggling to restart the front, auxiliary engine as well, the rear motor finally caught and they were once again under power. That was the last bad moment. To head off more trouble, *Voyager* completed the flight with both motors running. In the cool of the early morning, nine days almost to the minute from takeoff, Rutan brought the plane in to the Edwards Air Force Base runway and gently eased it down. Yet as *Voyager* landed, it still had gas for more. About 18 gallons remained, enough to take it hundreds of miles farther.

(Above) Affirming the decision in 1982 to build Voyager *are Burt Rutan (left), its pilots-to-be, Jeana Yeager (second from right) and Dick Rutan (right), and two Rutan employees, Sally and Mike Melvill. (Opposite page)* Voyager's *design was largely the work of Burt (top), whose inventive home-builder concepts and fiberglass-on-foam construction technique had led earlier to such aircraft as (bottom, clockwise from bottom) the Grizzly, Vari Eze, Vari-Viggen, Defiant, and Long EZ.*

(Above) Visions; (opposite page) Visions; (top) © Mark Greenberg; (bottom) Pat Storch

146

Background to *Voyager*

This remarkable aircraft was largely the work of Dick Rutan's brother, aircraft designer Burt. He had made his name during the 1970s as an engineer of pathbreaking inventiveness. Much of his early work had been aimed at home builders, hobbyists who construct full-size piloted aircraft from kits or sets of instructions. Burt Rutan introduced techniques whereby wings and fuselage structures could be cut from large blocks of lightweight polystyrene-foam plastic, then stiffened by being covered with multiple layers of fiberglass. One such design, the Vari Eze, could top 200 miles per hour and was widely regarded among home builders as an aeronautical hot rod. Some 6,000 such craft were built. Then Rutan introduced a larger and more convenient model, the Long EZ, which quickly outsold its predecessor.

The true significance of this fiberglass-on-foam building technique was that it permitted rapid, inexpensive construction of piloted aircraft on a one-of-a-kind basis. Such custom aircraft had hitherto been highly expensive, for the aircraft industry was set up for mass production of standardized designs. The U.S. Air Force and National Aeronautics and Space Administration thus became steady customers of Burt Rutan, commissioning numerous such one-of-a-kind aircraft. This gave him a great deal of design experience and allowed him to gain familiarity with a wide range of approaches.

Then in 1981, as Dick and Jeana were beginning to plan a new aviation company together, Burt joined them one day for lunch and made a radical suggestion—that it now was possible to build an aircraft that could circle the globe with a single load of fuel. He proceeded to sketch such a plane on a napkin. That first design concept was not *Voyager,* however; there would be many more napkins, and other paper drawings, before its eventual design emerged. For Burt was proposing to build a

craft with a range twice the world's distance record, three and a half times the longest scheduled commercial-airliner nonstop routes.

Everything about the design would revolve around the fuel supply. A standard mathematical formula, the Breguet range equation, could show how much gas such a flight would need, but Burt soon found himself up against a vicious cycle: fuel represents weight, and it takes more to carry more. Each additional gallon demanded tankage, an enlarged wing to hold the load, then still more fuel to carry the resulting extra weight—around and around in a spiral. In the end each extra pound of weight carried at takeoff would demand six additional pounds of fuel to go the distance.

Burt's design studies showed that such a craft would demand long, heavy auxiliary tanks riding on the wings. Those tanks would be hard to accommodate within a lightweight design. Then he had his first flash of insight: he could turn this difficulty into an advantage. Make the tanks still longer, to the point where they would become twin fuselages, each carrying landing gear. The wings themselves then would act as structural beams, joining the tanks in a cross-braced frame that would be light but strong. The central fuselage, for its part, would shrink to become a cockpit and cabin for the pilots, together with arrangements for mounting two engines and supplying them with fuel.

Mounting the engines was another problem. In any other airplane it would be taken for granted that the motors would run continuously from start to finish, but this conflicted with the fact that *Voyager* would be five times heavier at takeoff than at landing. For the flight to succeed, both low drag and high engine efficiency were needed. To reduce drag, the plane would have to cruise at low speed, 110 miles per hour on the average. To keep the speed from increasing as the plane burned fuel and became lighter, it would be necessary to cut the engine power. Aircraft engines are not efficient over a wide range of throttle settings, however; at low power the efficiency would fall off markedly. How, then, could Burt have both good efficiency and low speed?

Burt and Dick Rutan and Jeana Yeager (above) ponder one of many construction problems that had to be overcome for Voyager to succeed. Accommodating the necessary fuel while minimizing takeoff weight became the guiding principle around which the plane took shape. Details of design are illustrated on the opposite page.

148

The answer lay in an unusual engine-installation arrangement, one Burt himself had used earlier in an aircraft design called the Defiant. It called for two engines mounted at the front and back of the craft—one pulling, the other pushing. At takeoff both engines would run for maximum power. As the flight progressed, power would be cut back, but only to a degree. When the plane grew sufficiently light, one engine would be shut off, and the flight would proceed entirely on the power of the second. This approach not only would preserve the engines' efficiency but also would add a measure of safety, since the turned-off engine could be used in an emergency. Furthermore, both engines would have "centerline thrust," with the direction of their thrust passing through the plane's center of gravity. This arrangement was a great improvement over conventional twin-engine designs, in which the shutdown of one engine would tend to make the plane veer to the side.

Another innovation lay in the use of computers in design. Although Burt's design experience was invaluable, a round-the-world flight would press an aircraft to its limit, making it essential to predict its performance with high accuracy. Aircraft manufacturers have long relied on wind-tunnel tests for needed data, but Rutan had no access to a wind tunnel. Manufacturers in recent years have also predicted performance by means of lengthy calculations conducted by supercomputers, but Rutan had no supercomputers. He did, however, have ordinary desktop computers and the insight that, at the low flight speeds being contemplated, these machines could work successfully using highly simplified mathematical representations of the airflow, known as vortex-lattice calculations. While

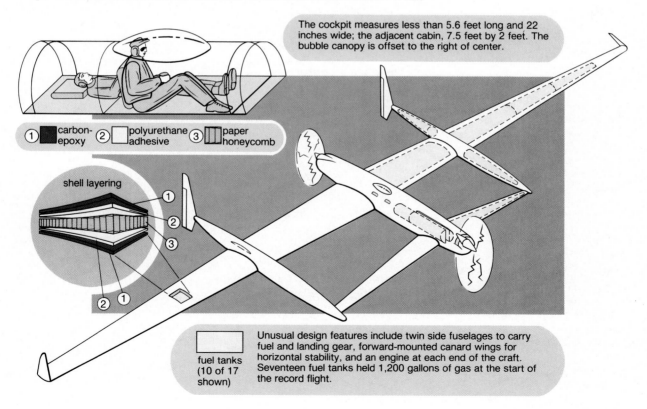

The cockpit measures less than 5.6 feet long and 22 inches wide; the adjacent cabin, 7.5 feet by 2 feet. The bubble canopy is offset to the right of center.

① carbon-epoxy ② polyurethane adhesive ③ paper honeycomb

shell layering

fuel tanks (10 of 17 shown)

Unusual design features include twin side fuselages to carry fuel and landing gear, forward-mounted canard wings for horizontal stability, and an engine at each end of the craft. Seventeen fuel tanks held 1,200 gallons of gas at the start of the record flight.

such computations were far too simple to deal with the high speeds of commercial jets, they would suit *Voyager* just fine.

The canard design

An unusual design feature of the plane was its use of small wings placed near the nose, ahead of the main wings. The wing is called a canard, the French word for duck, and gives *Voyager* the ducklike appearance of flying backward. The canard acts as a horizontal stabilizer, working in tandem with the vertical fins at the rear of the twin fuselages. Such an arrangement—canards in front, vertical fins in back—was the basis for the original Wright brothers' aircraft of 1903. It fell out of favor early in aviation history as designers turned to the conventional arrangement of forward-placed wings and a tail consisting of both vertical and horizontal stabilizers. Burt Rutan had long favored canard designs and had made them a hallmark of his aircraft.

To understand the canard's significance, it is necessary to appreciate some of the thinking that imbues aircraft design. An aircraft has a center of gravity, at which its weight is balanced. It also has an aerodynamic center, which amounts to a pivot point. The airplane rocks up and down about this point when it pitches in flight. These two points, the aerodynamic center and center of gravity, must be well separated. If they are too close together, the airplane will be hard to control and will tend to sustain an up-and-down motion while in flight.

Not only must these points be well apart but the center of gravity also must be forward of the aerodynamic center; *i.e.*, the plane must be nose-heavy. If the center of gravity is to the rear, the plane will be unstable, and any pitching motion will tend to increase without limit. An upward bob of the nose, for example, would flip the plane on its back.

By mid-1984 Voyager *begins to take shape (above). Black surfaces are carbon-epoxy composite laminated on paper honeycomb. Lighter surfaces are made of aramid-fiberglass sandwich, used in selected areas for increased toughness or transparency to radio waves. (Opposite page)* Voyager's *wingspan stretches almost 111 feet (one foot = 0.3 meter), although each wing is only two feet wide at its roots and a foot wide at the tip. To save weight, only the upper wing surfaces were painted.*

On the other hand, a nose-heavy aircraft will tend to point downward, so a second set of wings is needed on the craft. These wings generate a counterbalancing force to prevent nosing down.

In most aircraft the additional wings take the form of horizontal stabilizers at the plane's rear. There they develop a downward force, a negative lift that pulls the tail down and keeps the nose from drawing the plane downward. In a canard design the extra wings are mounted at the front, where they generate an upward force, a positive lift that raises the heavy nose and permits stable flight.

Canards and horizontal rear-mounted stabilizers, despite their identical purposes, lead to different consequences. It is a principle of aerodynamics that when an aircraft falls off in speed, the forward wings lose lift before the rear ones. In a conventional design a slowdown can lead to a stall, in which the main wings lose lift and the plane falls out of the sky. In a canard design, however, only the canards at the front lose lift. The plane, being nose-heavy, noses downward and recovers flying speed. This effect offers a safety advantage to inexperienced pilots like the home builders who bought so many of Burt Rutan's designs.

There are further differences. In a conventional design the main wings must be made large enough to carry both the airplane's weight and the weightlike downward force from the rear stabilizers. In a canard design the main wings actually can be made smaller since both they and the canards generate lift. They thus share between them the load of the plane's weight. In *Voyager,* where every pound counted, this feature of canards brought a welcome reduction in the total weight of the aircraft.

The above comparisons are not meant to imply that canards offer advantages for most aircraft. In airliners, for example, the ability to stall is actually an advantage. Relying on flying skill, the pilot keeps the plane just above stall speed while landing, thus losing altitude in a controlled fashion and touching down at the lowest possible speed. If a canard-design craft were to fly this way, its nose would pitch downward and the plane could crash. Canards thus demand higher landing speeds and longer runways. Canards are also at a disadvantage in making steep climb-turns at takeoff, which reduce aircraft noise over the surrounding community. For *Voyager,* however, in which lightness was of overriding concern, canards excelled. This factor, together with Burt Rutan's use of canards virtually as his personal trademark, sealed their incorporation in *Voyager*'s design.

Use of composite materials

Another innovative feature of *Voyager* was its reliance on composite materials in construction—materials that owe their existence largely to the demands of the aerospace industry for substances combining low density and high strength. Conventional aircraft aluminum alloys, for instance, can have strengths as high as 70,000 pounds per square inch while weighing only 0.1 pound per cubic inch (2.7 grams per cubic centimeter). Such alloys have the strength of steel plate at one-third the density.

Nevertheless, some fibrous materials do far better. Certain glass fibers

151

Yeager (above) cuts carbon-epoxy fabric for a structural component of Voyager. *With the aid of a heat gun, Rutan employee Bruce Evans and Yeager (top) lay down paper honeycomb material on a wing form. Much of the aircraft was built by the pilots themselves, who wanted no doubts about the integrity of a machine to which they would be entrusting their lives.*

Photos, Visions

offer the density of aircraft aluminum plus a strength as high as 700,000 pounds per square inch. Carbon fibers give nearly the same strength but are only two-thirds as dense. Aramid, a synthetic fiber marketed by Du Pont as Kevlar, offers strength and density similar to carbon. None of these fibers, however, can stand alone as structural material. They must be embedded in a matrix, a surrounding substance that holds them together. Fiberglass, for instance, comprises glass fibers in a matrix of plastic. Materials of this general type, called composites, do not achieve the full strength of their fibers, for the matrix materials usually are considerably weaker than the carbon, glass, or aramid. Nevertheless, they often are substantially lighter and stronger than aluminum.

Carbon composites are the basic structural material of *Voyager*. Their existence is a testimonial to the value of fundamental research, for they came out of the same research community that discovered the molecular structure of DNA, the genetic material. That discovery was made by James Watson and Francis Crick at the University of Cambridge in 1953. In their work Watson and Crick relied on X-ray diffraction images of the DNA molecule made by Rosalind Franklin, a crystallographer working at King's College in London. Before she had gone to King's, Franklin had worked in Paris on the molecular structures of carbon, laying the foundation for carbon fiber as a structural material.

The carbon fiber used in composites begins as polymer compound, typically polyacrylonitrile (PAN). When PAN fiber is heated in the absence of oxygen, it gives off gases and turns to carbon fiber, much as wood turns to charcoal under similar conditions. The fibers are gathered into flat bundles and woven into a thick, flexible, matlike fabric. The manufacturer then impregnates the fabric with epoxy adhesive—not the common household form, which cures at room temperature when mixed with a catalyst, but an industrial type that cures when heated in an oven.

Uncured carbon composite is sold in wide rolls, like garment makers' fabrics. It is shiny and black, dry rather than sticky to the touch. In building *Voyager*, Rutan used it as a lamination on panels of paper honeycomb. This latter material, a quarter-inch thick, closely resembles the honeycomb of a beehive but is made of treated paper. Its density is only 1.8 pounds per cubic foot (28.8 kilograms per cubic meter), less than half that of polystyrene foam. It has no useful strength on its own; in *Voyager* it served as the filler for a "sandwich" having carbon-epoxy lamination on each side. After being cured in an oven, this sandwich formed strong, stiff panels weighing only four ounces per square foot. The carbon-epoxy provided the strength; the honeycomb filler gave stiffness, for the carbon composite would have proven excessively flexible if bonded together directly.

Voyager's wings were built around a spar, or long beam, made entirely of cured carbon-epoxy. To form the wings to the proper shape, the builders prepared templates, or molds, and laid uncured panels of the carbon-honeycomb sandwich within these molds, using air pressure to force the panels against the forms for a true fit. These then went into the oven. When the cured wing panels emerged, they were fitted to the spar, top and bottom, and secured with industrial adhesives. Body panels, used for building the fuselages, were fashioned with the aid of templates in the same way. There were a few bulkheads, or walls, within the fuselage and wings for extra strength, but mostly the plane relied on the inherent stiffness of the carbon-honeycomb sandwich. Moreover, these bulkhead-strengthened enclosures were sufficiently leakproof to serve as the fuel tanks. Near the wing roots, where the wing and fuselages join, the builders used fiberglass and aramid sandwiches. These materials gave greater toughness than carbon while allowing the structure to stretch slightly as needed.

Voyager carried no structural metal; if its shell had been run through a metal detector, only a few rivetlike fasteners would have registered. Its wingspan was almost 111 feet, longer than that of a Boeing 727 airliner. The wings themselves, only two feet wide at their roots and half that at the tips, were expected to flex as much as nine feet during rough weather. Bare, *Voyager* weighed only 939 pounds. The addition of engines nearly doubled this, to 1,858 pounds, and the eventual fuel load at takeoff came to 7,011.5 pounds. Voyager was virtually a flying gas tank, carrying nearly seven and a half times its weight in fuel.

Engines and flight instruments

Voyager's builders turned to Teledyne Continental of Mobile, Alabama, for the engines. The front motor was a standard air-cooled design of 130 horsepower, which had been in production from 1962 to 1980. It thus was well understood and known to be reliable, with all its bugs long since worked out. It served as the auxiliary engine during takeoff, climb, and the first 80 hours of the cruising flight while furnishing additional power when *Voyager* had to climb over storms.

The main engine in the rear, however, was a still experimental, high-compression, liquid-cooled model. Liquid-cooled designs are heavy and thus are rarely used, but they offered *Voyager* a tempting gain in power and efficiency. The reason lies in the ability of such an engine to maintain closely the tolerances, or gaps between moving parts, specified by the designer.

For best performance, for example, an engine might need 0.0005 inch of clearance between the piston rings and the cylinder walls, no more and no less. (One inch is about 2.54 centimeters.) If the gap is 0.0006 inch, these parts may allow high-pressure gases to leak past, reducing performance and leading to excessive wear. If the clearance is 0.0004 inch, then there may be inadequate lubrication, again leading to increased wear. Such tolerances, in turn, depend on the engine's maintaining a specified temperature. Metal parts expand and contract as their temperature changes, leading to changes in clearances, and a liquid-cooled engine can maintain a design temperature far more precisely than an air-cooled design, which depends on the somewhat variable cooling provided by the airstream rushing past.

Improved fit of the engine parts meant that *Voyager*'s liquid-cooled motor could achieve a higher compression ratio of 11.4 to 1, compared with the 7 or 8 to 1 of air-cooled engines. Indeed, when the pistons were at maximum compression, they approached within 0.04 inch of the cylinder head. Within this confined space injected fuel and air swirled in turbulent eddies, thoroughly mixing and ensuring better combustion. The result was a 20% gain in fuel economy, with the engine's overall efficiency coming to 36%, compared with 25% or less for ordinary auto engines. Although this liquid-cooled motor was heavier than an air-cooled design of equal power, the gain in fuel economy made up for the extra weight during the first half-day of flight. The engine developed 110 horsepower and ran continuously for the full 216 hours of the flight, except for five minutes on the last morning when it was starved for fuel.

Flight instruments, or avionics, also demanded unusual care. They came from King Radio Corp. of Olathe, Kansas, whose chairman ap-

Voyager was powered by two Teledyne Continental engines: a liquid-cooled main engine mounted at the rear (below) and a standard air-cooled auxiliary engine at the front (bottom). The main motor, which ran for all but five minutes of the record nine-day flight, was heavy, but its high fuel efficiency made up for the extra weight in the first half-day airborne. The auxiliary motor, of a well-seasoned design, was run during takeoff, climb, and the first part of the cruising flight, as well as during climbs over storms.

Photos, © Mark Greenberg—Visions

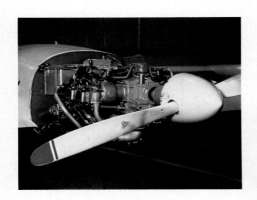

The instrument panel in Voyager's cockpit (top) was fitted with an avionics package that included (left stack, top to bottom) four-color weather radar, VHF communications and navigation system, autopilot, and long-range navigation system. A gyrostabilized compass (panel center) and a long-range high-frequency communications system (bottom center, showing red numerical display) were also carried. (Bottom) Maze of gas lines and valves in the cockpit allowed the pilots to shift fuel among the storage tanks, feed tank, and engines. (Below) In the hours before the world flight, Voyager's 17 tanks were carefully filled in a calculated sequence that added a few gallons at a time to each tank.

proached the Rutans and Yeager and offered to "open the catalogue" for them, supplying whatever they needed. Particularly important was the autopilot, which was regarded as "mission critical" because it would take over much of the routine and wearying task of maintaining speed, course, and altitude. Without an autopilot Rutan and Yeager would have had to put much more physical and mental effort into flying the aircraft, particularly in heavy weather.

Conventional small-aircraft autopilots control the plane by automatically moving the ailerons on the wings. This system works well for most such planes, which are maneuverable and responsive. *Voyager*, by contrast, was sluggish in responding to its controls, hard to maneuver, and prone to bend or oscillate in highly uncomfortable ways. To deal with these characteristics, King Radio engineers modified the autopilot

to turn *Voyager* by moving its right rudder rather than its ailerons. They also incorporated a circuit to vary the speed of the autopilot's response, thus compensating for the aircraft's large change in weight as its fuel burned off.

There also were instruments for navigation and communication. To set their course the pilots steered by a worldwide network of 17 ground stations, each broadcasting navigational signals by radio. The onboard instruments received the signals and used them to calculate the shortest route between any two points in the flight plan. They also displayed the aircraft's course and position, direction and distance to navigational checkpoints, true speed over the ground, and the speed and direction of the winds aloft. For communication *Voyager* relied on a high-frequency radio whose signals would bounce off the ionosphere—a rarefied region of electrically charged gases high in the atmosphere—and reflect back to Earth, to be received by a distant station.

Like Magellan and Columbus, *Voyager*'s pilots carried a compass. It was gyrostabilized, however, to keep it from bouncing around wildly in turbulent air. It also was linked electronically to the autopilot to provide information about course. The pilots had an onboard radar as well; equipped with a four-color video monitor, it could show thunderstorms up to 200 miles ahead while displaying coastlines and the shapes of islands.

The human element

"It's not going to be anything like fun," said Dick Rutan prior to the flight. "Just being inside this flailing carbon structure a long way from home, listening to engines and hoping they keep running." He knew very well how his mind could wander in such circumstances, for he had experienced hallucinations while on a record-breaking flight in 1979, which had kept him continually in the air for less than a day and a half. "There were no lights, nobody to talk to, nothing but the stars," he recalled of that earlier experience. "All alone with the drone of the

Yeager inspects food, emergency equipment, and personal supplies before packing the aircraft for the world flight. To reduce weight, objects were stripped of unnecessary materials. Parachutes, for example, had no rip cords or pilot chutes, and even the camera to be taken aboard lost its leather exterior.

engine, flat nothing to do. And time stopped. You know how long it takes a minute to go by when there's a steam engine sitting on your toe? A horrible experience. All these mystical hallucinations. A little guy sitting on the canard, talking to me. We had a very lucid conversation.''

Rutan and Yeager spent the nine-day *Voyager* flight cooped up within a cabin and cockpit. The cabin, where the off-duty pilot could try to sleep, was 7.5 feet long and 2 feet wide. The cockpit was 5.6 feet by 22 inches. Headroom was only 40 inches. The central fuselage where the pilots lived has been aptly described as a pair of joined-together megaphones with an engine at each end. The pilots had special noise-canceling earphones, but they proved to be of limited help.

They consulted with astronauts who had flown two-week missions in highly cramped quarters and applied this experience in preparing for the flight. Food would be supplied in prepackaged pouches, with the flight plan calling for one full meal a day along with snacks the rest of the time. Human waste would be collected in plastic bags, astronaut-style. Survival gear included parachutes, a U.S. Navy life raft with two radio beacons, and inflatable life jackets. To save weight, the parachutes had particularly small canopies, which the user would pull out by hand without benefit of a rip cord or pilot chute. Also aboard were flares, signalling mirror, flashlight, knife, money, passports—and MasterCards.

In preparation for the round-the-world try, Rutan and Yeager took *Voyager* on a 4½-day mission in July 1986, covering 11,587 miles as they looped back and forth over California. Dick, a macho test pilot, wondered if he could trust fragile Jeana with the responsibility of steering the aircraft. He watched her closely during the first two days, losing considerable sleep. When he decided she could do it, he relaxed and then overslept. All this put stress on Yeager. She failed to eat or drink enough, losing 6 pounds of her total of 97.

This experience showed them what would have to be done to achieve success in their round-the-world effort. An important task was to monitor

A bristly Dick Rutan, in the pilot's seat, is observed by weary-looking Jeana Yeager on the fifth day of the flight, over Africa (above). The climb over high mountains necessitated their use of oxygen, supplied by plastic nose tubes. (Top) Voyager, followed by a chase plane, passes over clouds near Los Angeles on the last leg of the journey.

food and water intake and to drink according to a schedule so as to prevent dehydration. The July flight also showed the need for soundproofing within the cabin. After this modification and several fixes to mechanical problems that cropped up during that mission, Rutan and Yeager were prepared to go for the big record. They were well aware that they might not succeed, that it might take more than one try, but they carried it off on the first attempt.

Beyond *Voyager*

The unrefueled transatlantic solo of Charles Lindbergh's *Spirit of St. Louis* in 1927 pointed to a new era in long-range aviation. Can anything remotely comparable be expected from *Voyager*?

Aircraft designers have long made use of wind tunnels, wherein often highly sophisticated models of aircraft costing $200,000 to $2 million are put through simulated flight conditions. Tunnel tests yield measurements of lift, drag, pitching and yawing moments, dynamic loads, side forces, pressure distributions, and coefficients that define the aircraft's ability to steady itself after a disturbance. On the other hand, an actual flying prototype adds much more information: handling qualities, stall characteristics, maneuvering loads, oscillation and bending of wings and fuselage in flight, engine noise, fuel economy, speed as a function of power, and tests of structural strength. A prototype, however, typically is far more costly than a wind-tunnel model. Moreover, by the time an aircraft maker has reached the prototype stage, an engineering change to one system of the aircraft not only can lead to alterations in other systems but also can force expensive changes in production tooling.

One-of-a-kind planes like *Voyager,* which cost $2 million to build, represent a reasonable alternative for developing and testing new aircraft. Such design characteristics as aerodynamics, distribution of stiffness, engines and their method of installation, and total weight can all be incorporated into an all-composite aircraft of simplified design, even if the final version is to be of conventional aluminum. Data taken with the experimental craft then can be extrapolated to apply to production models. This kind of approach offers the low cost of wind-tunnel testing along with the highly detailed data of prototype flights. Demonstrator aircraft, as they are called, can be built early enough during a development program for the test results to offer a valuable guide to the changes that will be needed for a successful final design.

Voyager itself could lead to a class of lightweight and highly efficient aircraft capable of serving both civil and military purposes. They could fly at high altitude, cruising for days or weeks on modest quantities of fuel or even staying aloft on solar power and electric motors. Because their composite materials are transparent to radar, they would be difficult to detect and thus could serve for reconnaissance. Similar craft, carrying television relay equipment, could broadcast across regions hundreds of miles wide; *e.g.,* California, the U.S. Northeast, or the nations of Western Europe or Japan. An airborne system would improve on the present practice of placing broadcast antennas atop mountains or tall buildings.

158

A triumphant Voyager *comes home to an expectant crowd at Edwards Air Force Base.*

(Left) © Mark Greenberg—Visions; (below) © Rick Rickman—Black Star

Eventually, low-cost aircraft might take on some tasks presently performed at much greater expense by orbiting satellites.

For the more distant future there is the possibility of commercial airliners built largely or wholly of composites. Such materials exist in current airliners but in limited quantities. Finished parts of composite cost some $250 per pound, compared with $3.50 to $4 per pound for aluminum parts. The only way an airline can recoup this outlay is by massive fuel savings due to the lighter weight of a composite design. Today, in a time of moderate fuel costs, such savings are not in store. Someday, however, rising oil prices could make all-composite designs more attractive. If such airliners indeed are built and enter service, passengers with long memories may remember that one of the first aircraft constructed in this fashion was the famous circumnavigator called *Voyager*.

The Changing Practice of Dentistry

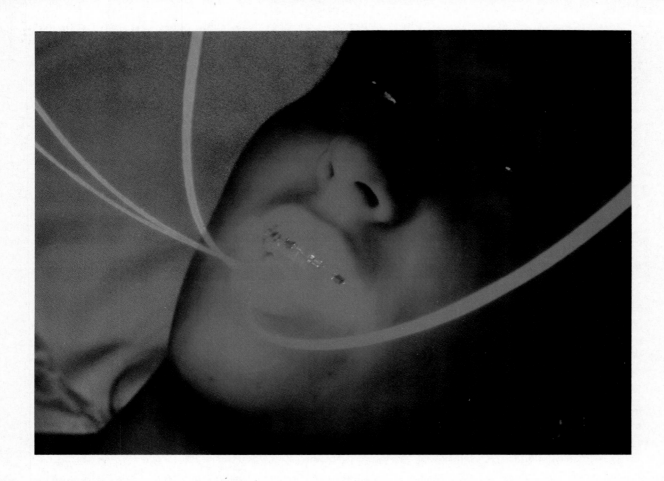

*Thanks to recent advances in science and technology, dentistry has undergone
a tremendous shift in emphasis from the mechanical correction of existing
oral problems to disease prevention and the health of the entire patient.*

Scientific discoveries, advances in technology, and new insights into the causes, treatment, and prevention of oral diseases in recent years have had a profound effect on the way dentistry is practiced in the 1980s. Gone are the days when dental care was largely mechanical, consisting primarily of pain and pull and drill and fill. Instead, the emphasis today is on prevention of disease and on the well-being of the whole patient. The greatest changes occurred after World War II, when dental research on the two most common dental diseases—tooth decay and periodontal (gum) disease—produced some long-sought solutions. These developments, coupled with the changing needs of society, have altered dental practice dramatically. Dentists are devoting more time to preventive and aesthetic dentistry and to the control of oral diseases. Concurrently, they are addressing the problems of patients' anxieties and pain and increasingly are serving the dental needs of a growing population of persons aged 65 or older.

Tooth decay and its prevention

The tormenting pain of tooth decay, or dental caries, has plagued humans throughout the ages. References to caries, the Latin word for decay, appear in the writings of the Roman physician Celsus in the 1st century AD. Around the turn of the last century, research disclosed that cavities were caused by acids, but the exact mechanism remained unclear. After scientists in the 1950s and 1960s unraveled the mysteries of the disease, each link in the chain of events leading to tooth decay became a target in the fight against this ancient scourge.

The chain starts with plaque, a sticky, colorless film that forms in the mouth constantly and is laden with bacteria. When some of these microorganisms, primarily *Streptococcus mutans*, act on sugars and starches in food, acids are produced. In time the acids, by dissolving the minerals in hard tooth tissue, make the tooth structure porous, leading to cavities.

by L. Anne Hirschel

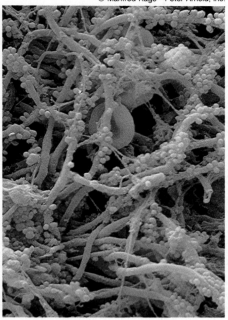

Plaque is a colorless, bacteria-laden film present on all but the most freshly cleaned teeth. Under magnification it is seen to be a complex community of microorganisms (above), comprising long filamentous bacteria covered with spherical bacteria called cocci. One coccal bacterium, Streptococcus mutans, is the primary cause of tooth decay.

The permanent teeth in the lower jaw (right) include four incisors, two canines, four premolars, and six molars. They are matched by counterparts in the upper jaw. The exposed part of each tooth is covered by a hard layer of enamel. Beneath lies a somewhat softer, bonelike material called dentin. The dentin is nourished by the innermost pulp, which consists of a mass of cells, blood vessels, and a nerve enclosed in a chamber. The root of each tooth is embedded in a socket in the jawbone and is held in place by a layer of fibrous connective tissue called the periodontal membrane. The temporomandibular joints hinge the lower jawbone to the skull.

Even before the offending bacteria were identified, dental scientists had discovered that the element fluorine in the form of the fluoride ion, which is naturally present in varying concentrations in water throughout the world, protects teeth from demineralization. Studies confirmed these findings in 1954 when caries incidence in children living all their lives in areas supplied with naturally fluoridated water was compared with the incidence in children drinking nonfluoridated water. Children in the former group had a startling caries reduction of 50% or more. Later, in the early 1970s, researchers learned that the fluoride ion actually enters the crystalline structure of tooth enamel, changing it to a form much more resistant to acid attack.

As soon as the advantages of drinking water containing an optimum fluoride concentration of one part per million were verified, dentists endorsed the artificial fluoridation of municipal water supplies. By the late 1980s approximately 7,000 U.S. communities as well as communities all over the world fluoridated their drinking water. In the U.S. the dental health of young patients—37% of whom were cavity-free in 1980, compared with 28% just nine years earlier—reflects the enormous benefits of this public health measure.

Fluoride dietary supplements are often prescribed for children living in areas where drinking water is not fluoridated. Fluoride solutions and gels applied to the teeth topically either by health-care professionals or by the children themselves further increase resistance to caries; so do fluoride toothpastes and mouth rinses that have become available over the counter. Other fluoride-delivery methods under development—such as a pellet that can be easily affixed by a dentist to a back tooth, where it slowly releases fluoride for months—will expand the options for treatment. The incidence of caries, which had been rising continuously in industrialized countries worldwide into the 1960s, is now declining, much of the drop having been attributed to the use of fluorides.

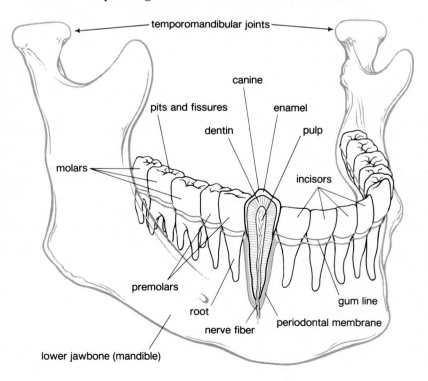

Almost 85% of cavities in school-aged children develop on the fissured chewing surfaces of back teeth, where fluoride protection is least effective. Today dentists can protect these areas with adhesive resins known as pit-and-fissure sealants. Used successfully since the early 1970s, sealants form a barrier that prevents bacteria and their acids from reaching the tooth enamel. The teeth are first "acid etched," or roughened with a mild acid, to improve adhesion. A colorless or lightly colored liquid plastic is then painted onto the biting surfaces, rather like nail polish. It hardens chemically or, more commonly, after being exposed to a special light. Sealants have been shown to last several years, and small cavities trapped underneath the resin coatings do not enlarge but actually tend to remineralize. Because long-term exposure to fluorides aids in the remineralization or repair of early cavities, dental researchers are investigating fluoride-releasing sealants.

Fluorides and sealants, a low-sugar diet, the practice of scrupulous oral hygiene, and regular professional dental care—these are today's major weapons in the fight against tooth decay. Although dental caries remains prevalent worldwide, dentistry is definitely closing in on cavities.

Periodontal disease

While tooth decay is declining, especially in young patients, periodontal disease continues to be a major threat to oral health. The disease insidiously ravages the gums and bone that anchor teeth in the jaw. It starts, often unbeknownst to the victim, as an inflammation of the gums adjacent to the teeth (gingivitis). The first signs may be bleeding or tender gums and a reddening and swelling of the tissues. As the disease progresses, gums begin to pull away from the teeth, and pockets that trap bacteria and debris form between teeth and gums. Eventually it may destroy the supporting structures of the teeth, including the bone. Symptoms of more advanced disease (periodontitis) may include loose and shifting teeth, presence of pus when the gums are pressed, pain, mouth odors, a bad taste, and, finally, tooth loss. Although with insight gained in recent years it is largely preventable or controllable, periodontal disease continues to afflict 75% of the U.S. population over age 35 and accounts for 70% of all teeth lost in adults. It can strike at any age; a particularly virulent form, juvenile periodontitis, is seen in children.

Research in the last 30 years has yielded more information about gum disease than had been learned in the preceding 300, making eventual control of the disease a real possibility. The breakthrough began in the 1950s when U.S. and European scientists verified that bacteria in plaque play a crucial role in the development of periodontal disease. Consequently, dentists' preventive efforts focus on mechanical plaque control—an endeavor that, to be successful, demands meticulous oral hygiene from the patient as well as regular dental checkups. Although this concept continues to be the cornerstone of prevention for all dental diseases, the recent introduction of plaque-controlling mouthwashes and toothpastes offers the possibility that some plaque buildup may be preventable chemically. Antibiotics and surgery have proved successful in

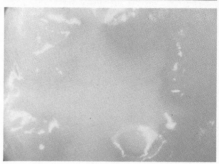

Dentists protect the chewing surfaces of children's back teeth with adhesive resins known as pit-and-fissure sealants, which form a physical barrier to decay bacteria and their acids. In the top photo, a tooth surface is ready for sealing after having been lightly etched with acid to improve adhesion. In the bottom photo, a light-colored sealant has been applied and hardened with a special light.

L. ANNE HIRSCHEL, a retired dentist, writes on medical subjects.

(Page 160) Photograph, Tsiaras—Medichrome/The Stock Shop

A healthy mouth (top left) is compared with teeth and gums in various stages of periodontal disease. The disease starts as gingivitis (top right), an inflammation of the gums that may take the form of reddened, swollen tissues. Later, as it progresses to periodontitis (bottom left), gums pull away from the teeth and pockets of bacteria and debris form between teeth and gums. In advanced periodontitis (bottom right) there is pain, mouth odor, pus in the gums, loose and shifting teeth, destruction of the periodontal membrane and jawbone, and eventually tooth loss.

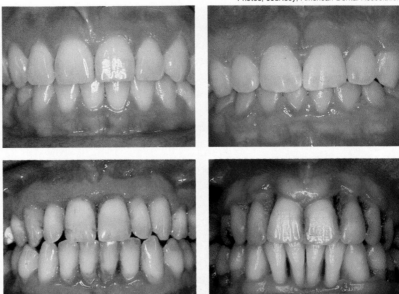

treating more advanced cases of periodontal disease. Current investigations are directed toward developing better diagnostic tools, identifying contributing factors and specific causative organisms more precisely, and creating more effective techniques in preventing and treating the disease.

Bonding

While looking for suitable pit-and-fissure sealants for back teeth, researchers in the 1950s laid the groundwork for the development of modern tooth-colored restorative materials known as composite resins or, simply, composites. Today composites are employed in a revolutionary restorative technique called bonding for repairing chipped or broken teeth, camouflaging stained or discolored teeth, hiding tooth defects, anchoring fixed bridges and orthodontic appliances, and closing unsightly spaces. Composites have become the filling of choice for small cavities in front teeth and, although they still lack the strength of metal fillings, their use in back teeth is increasing. Until recently, successful bonding was confined to the enamel, the outermost layer of the tooth. The development of new materials has now allowed bonding to dentin, the hard

Teeth and gums of a victim of periodontitis are shown before treatment (right) and after treatment (far right). Although antibiotics and surgery have proved successful in dealing with more advanced cases of periodontal disease, the cornerstone of prevention remains the mechanical control of plaque through good oral hygiene and regular dental checkups.

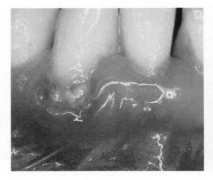
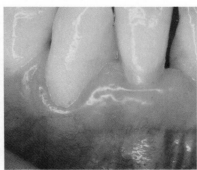

tissue between the enamel and the pulp that is exposed in large cavities, and thus constitutes a significant breakthrough.

Bonding achieves aesthetically pleasing results painlessly, quickly, and relatively inexpensively. The procedure is reversible, and normally there is no drilling or sacrifice of tooth tissue (filling of cavities being the major exception). The technique for bonding is similar to the placing of sealants. After the tooth surface to be bonded is etched with acid, it is coated with a liquid resin that serves as an adhesive. Then a puttylike composite containing resin and an inert filler of glass or quartz particles is pressed into place, shaped, hardened, and polished. A relatively new technique for camouflaging unsightly defects or discolorations makes use of porcelain or acrylic veneers resembling artificial fingernails bonded to the fronts of teeth.

Orthodontics

Orthodontists can now give their patients orthodontic appliances that are much more comfortable to wear and cosmetically pleasing than in the past. Partly as a result the number of adult Americans seeking orthodontic treatment has more than doubled since 1970, while 27% of patients having their teeth straightened and their bites corrected are now over 18 years of age. Although an adult with braces is no longer an unusual sight, some people are wearing orthodontic appliances that are virtually invisible. Transparent or tooth-colored brackets made of plastic and bonded directly to the teeth have replaced many of the traditional conspicuous metal bands. In selected cases brackets can be bonded to the backs of teeth, out of sight.

A very elastic type of metal wire, nitinol, containing nickel and titanium was invented in the early 1960s. In orthodontic use since 1972, the wire has the advantage of requiring fewer visits for wire adjustments than traditional stainless steel wires, saving patients time and discomfort. The potential orthodontic applications for nitinol's extraordinary property of shape memory, returning to its original manufactured shape when it is heated through a specific temperature range, are under investigation.

Special dental problems of the elderly and the sick

As advances in medical treatment and health care are allowing more and more people to live longer, dentistry is becoming increasingly involved in finding solutions to the specific oral problems of the elderly. The incidence of periodontal disease rises with age. Consequently, tooth roots, exposed as a result of the receding gums that accompany this disease, become susceptible to caries. As more people keep more teeth for a longer time, dentists are finding and treating an increasing number of root cavities. In addition, older teeth become brittle and prone to fracture, and edentulous jaws (jaws without natural teeth) shrink, causing problems for denture wearers. The elderly are often plagued by dry mouth, burning tongue, and disturbances of the sense of taste. Moreover, older persons in frail health may be taking multiple prescription medications, some or all of which may have oral side effects.

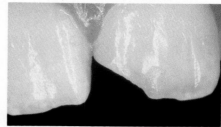

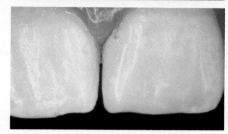

The aesthetically pleasing results of bonding are apparent in the virtually invisible repair of a chipped tooth. Bonding makes use of natural-looking composite resins as restorative, camouflaging, and anchoring materials.

165

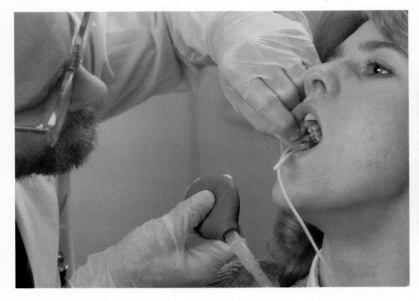

A dentist engaged in dry-mouth studies places a saliva collection device in a patient's mouth (above). The saliva then drains into a container packed in ice (above right). Insufficient salivary flow is a common problem both of the elderly and of cancer patients whose salivary glands have been damaged by radiation therapy.

It is in treating an increasing number of dental patients—young and old alike—who have other medical problems that today's dentists may face their greatest challenge. Oral diseases that are easily controlled in a healthy person can become virulent, even life-threatening, because of a specific systemic disease or the therapy used to treat it. Diabetes is an example of the intimate link that exists between general and oral health. Not only may patients with uncontrolled diabetes have an aggravation or increased incidence of periodontal disease, but also the presence of periodontal infection may make it more difficult to control the patient's diabetes. Dentists' roles as health-care professionals are expanding as practitioners become increasingly cognizant of this profound interplay between systemic problems and oral health.

Every year in the U.S. an estimated 965,000 persons learn that they have cancer. For the approximately 40% or more who will receive chemotherapy, the oral side effects may include inflamed and bleeding gums, mouth ulcers, pain, and oral infections that have the potential to rage out of control; furthermore, preexisting mild periodontal disease tends to exacerbate. Additional problems face many of the 30,000 Americans diagnosed with head and neck cancer annually whose disease is treated with radiotherapy. Salivary glands in the path of radiation can be damaged permanently. Deprived of the cleansing, neutralizing, lubricating, and remineralizing properties of saliva, patients may experience a dry, painful mouth, difficulties with wearing dentures comfortably, and rampant caries. Irradiated bone may lose its vitality and heal poorly after surgery.

Fortunately, consultation between the dentist and members of the patient's medical team, close dental supervision before and during therapy, and a careful oral-hygiene program help limit many potentially devastating oral side effects of cancer treatment. Ideally, and time permitting, all existing dental problems are corrected or controlled before therapy is

166

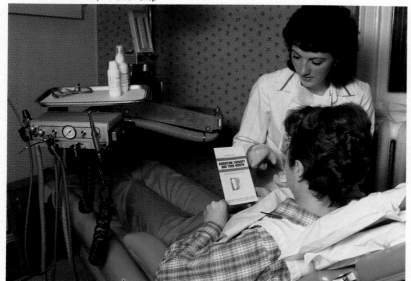

Dental hygienist instructs a patient on the oral side effects of radiation treatment for cancer. Close dental supervision before and after therapy, a careful dental hygiene program, and consultation between the dentist and the patient's doctors can help control many of the oral problems associated with radiotherapy.

started. Because radiation damage tends to be permanent, patients given radiotherapy are monitored closely for the rest of their lives, while daily home fluoride treatments are prescribed for preventing tooth decay.

Persons suffering from some forms of arthritis or related rheumatic diseases constitute another high-risk group of dental patients. Like cancer patients, these individuals can now be protected from overwhelming oral complications by good preventive dental care. In addition to occasional direct involvement of the temporomandibular joint (or TMJ, the joint connecting the lower jaw and the skull), some rheumatic diseases have oral symptoms; for example, the dry mouth and rampant caries that may accompany Sjögren's syndrome and the gum ulcerations seen in patients with systemic lupus erythematosus. A further complication is that most medications used to treat rheumatic diseases have oral side effects, which range from bleeding of the gums to a susceptibility to infections.

Other systemic conditions, including certain infections, stress, and a weakened immune system, produce symptoms that may be revealed in the course of a dental examination. Such examinations take on additional importance when they happen to be the patient's only regular contact with a health-care professional. AIDS (acquired immune deficiency syndrome) is perhaps the latest, and certainly the most publicized, disease that may first be noticed in the oral cavity. For instance, a dental scientist studying homosexual men recently confirmed that hairy leukoplakia, characterized by unusual white lesions on the side of the tongue, is clearly a clinical marker for later development of AIDS in many patients. Bulimia, a serious eating disorder accompanied by furtive forced vomiting, is another disease that provides the examining dentist with oral clues to a medical problem. Frequent regurgitation of stomach acids causes telltale erosion of the tooth enamel. Similar erosion may be detected in cases of hiatal hernia and acid reflux associated with excess intake of carbonated beverages.

167

Pain and anxiety control

Ancient myths and superstitions, vividly documented in the world's literature and in old cartoons and caricatures, have long perpetuated the notion that dentistry and pain are synonymous. For millions of people this belief is still very real. An estimated 35 million Americans experience dental anxiety; they make each dental appointment reluctantly and face it with dread. Another 12 million are classified as dental phobics—individuals so terrified they avoid dental treatment altogether. Increasingly sensitive to this dilemma, dentists are now addressing it successfully. To do so, they have at their disposal a host of pharmacological agents and behavioral techniques that not only make dental treatment virtually painless but also can allay their patients' worst fears. Although commonly used drugs have a good safety record, all drugs carry a potential risk and are not appropriate in every case. The choice of drug, just as the choice of other forms of treatment, therefore must always rest with the dentist.

Traditionally, dentists have relied on local and general anesthetics, analgesics, and antianxiety drugs for controlling pain and reducing fear. Today, as researchers gain new insights into the perception of pain and develop new families of drugs and new technology, these medications are being employed in more effective combinations and delivered by means of new techniques.

Much dental fear has centered on the needle. In truth, modern use of fine, sharp, disposable needles and, when necessary, a preliminary dab of topical anesthetic on the injection site have minimized discomfort for most people. A relatively new local anesthetic technique, intraliga-

French-language cartoon stresses the fear associated with dentistry in years past. The belief that pain and dentistry are synonymous still exists, even though today's anesthetics and behavioral techniques make dental treatment virtually painless.

National Institute of Dental Research

mental injection, provides limited anesthesia speedily with a minimum of discomfort. With a very fine needle, a small amount of anesthetic solution is injected into the ligament surrounding the tooth. Because only a small area of the mouth—possibly just one tooth—is anesthetized and because the effects wear off promptly, the technique is not appropriate for lengthy or complex procedures. Needleless jet syringes deliver anesthetic solution through a fine orifice at high pressure, causing the solution to penetrate the superficial layers of the gums. They are ineffective, however, when deep-lying nerves must be anesthetized. For complex procedures that are likely to cause pain for some time after the office visit, oral surgeons are turning to injections of long-acting local anesthetics capable of controlling postoperative discomfort for up to 12 hours. Use of these agents reduces the need for strong oral medications for pain, which may have unwanted side effects.

Another option being tested clinically for pain relief is transcutaneous electrical nerve stimulation (TENS). This process relies on the pain control that can be achieved when a mild electric current is applied to nerve endings near the skin surface close to the site of the pain. TENS devices, which are compact, battery-powered stimulators resembling personal headphone radios, have been used by physical therapists for some years to relieve chronic joint and muscle pain. For dental pain control, an electrode is placed in the patient's mouth and a headset adjusted on the head. In the majority of dental patients tested, TENS controlled pain associated with several kinds of dental procedures, including tooth extractions.

Narcotic and nonnarcotic analgesics such as codeine and aspirin have long served, singly or in combination, to control dental pain. Recently introduced nonsteroidal anti-inflammatory drugs such as ibuprofen have proved as effective as aspirin-with-codeine combinations but without the latter's mood-altering effects. They not only reduce postsurgical pain significantly when given before oral surgery but also promote the secretion of a natural substance, beta-endorphin, believed to be involved in pain reduction.

Nitrous oxide, or laughing gas, was used by dentist Horace Wells when he helped introduce general anesthesia to the world in the mid-1800s. In recent years nitrous oxide has regained popularity for conscious sedation—the patient's level of consciousness is depressed sufficiently to tolerate treatment, but he or she remains awake and able to communicate. Conscious sedation is intended primarily to calm patients; local anesthetics are employed in conjunction to control pain. Other chemical antianxiety and sedative agents available for calming nervous patients before or during dental treatment include barbiturates, narcotics, and tranquilizers.

General anesthetics produce a pain-free state of unconsciousness. In dentistry they are usually reserved for complex oral surgery or for patients who cannot tolerate treatment satisfactorily any other way, including very young children or physically or mentally disabled persons.

Increasingly, dentists are turning to nonchemical methods to allay anxiety. Techniques learned from behavioral scientists, when successful,

Courtesy, Norman L. Corah, University of New York at Buffalo

Dental patient plays a video game as work is done on her teeth. Both video games and television comedy programs have been shown to provide the distraction and relaxation necessary to reduce dental anxiety and perception of pain during treatment.

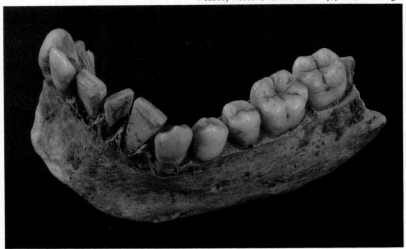

Replacing missing natural teeth with artificial substitutes is an old idea. A fragment of lower jawbone found in Honduras and dating from about AD 600 contains three tooth-shaped pieces of shell that had been inserted in empty tooth sockets.

have a more positive long-term effect than do drugs. Such new approaches include desensitization (gradually exposing the patient to dreaded dental procedures until they no longer appear threatening), distraction (for example, allowing the patient to play video games or listen to music), conscious relaxation (teaching the patient ways to reduce anxiety, possibly with the help of biofeedback machines that monitor heart rate, breathing rate, or temperature), and hypnosis. About 20% of American dentists have had training in dental hypnosis.

Dental implants and bone replacement

For many people the recent advances in prevention of dental disease have come too late. Most adults are missing one or more natural teeth, and one-third of the population of the Western world are edentulous. An estimated one out of three individuals who could benefit from partial or full dentures experience serious difficulties wearing them or are psy-

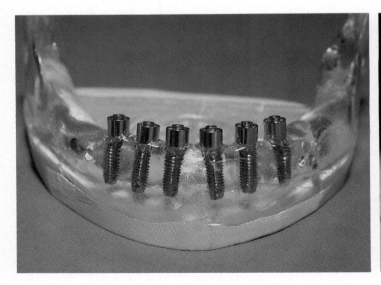

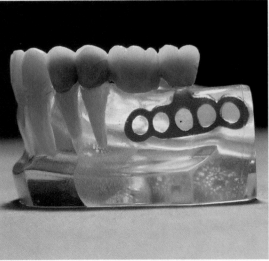

chologically unable to accept them. Dental implants now offer many of these people an alternative.

The dream of replacing missing natural teeth with artificial substitutes anchored in the jaw is not new. A jaw fragment dating from about AD 600 and now in the Peabody Museum at Harvard University contains tooth-shaped pieces of shell that had been placed into empty tooth sockets. Modern oral implantology got its start in the late 1940s, but it has been mainly since the late 1970s that great gains have been made and that the procedure has gained wider acceptance.

Available in many shapes and sizes, implants are made of various materials, for example, titanium or cobalt chrome alloys, that are chosen for their strength and compatibility with living tissue. Depending on the type, they are placed surgically either underneath the gum but on top of the bone or into or through the bone. Implants rooted in the bone may have special coatings to encourage surrounding bone growth and a permanent bond to the jaw. By means of metal posts that protrude through the gum, the implants can support a single tooth, a few teeth, or a whole arch. A somewhat different approach to anchoring dentures calls for the addition of mushroomlike protrusions to the underside of the denture. These protrusions fit into depressions surgically created in the gums to achieve better denture stability.

Dental implants are not appropriate for every patient, nor is every dentist trained to perform the procedure. Careful patient selection is critical to success. Most implantologists agree that candidates for implants should be in good general health and be prepared to practice excellent oral hygiene. Also, patients must recognize that even the most successful implant cannot function as well as a natural tooth.

After a person has worn dentures for many years, the edentulous bony areas of the jaws tend to shrink. Consequently, many people are left with a bony ridge inadequate for supporting dentures comfortably. Advanced periodontal disease is another cause of bone loss. Rebuilding lost bone

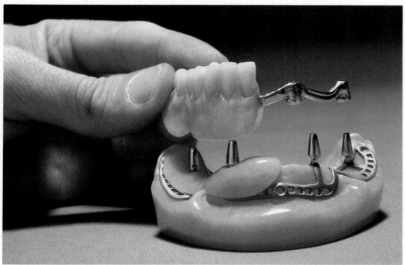

Bruce Flynn—Picture Group

Three types of dental implants that serve as anchors for artificial teeth are compared. (Opposite page, left) Titanium screws are inserted into holes drilled in the jawbone; the protruding screw heads are later covered with tooth caps. (Opposite page, right) A metal blade implanted in the jawbone supports three to six teeth cemented to a protruding post. (Left) For a badly deteriorated jaw that cannot withstand drilling, a metal frame that grips the bone can be placed under the gum.

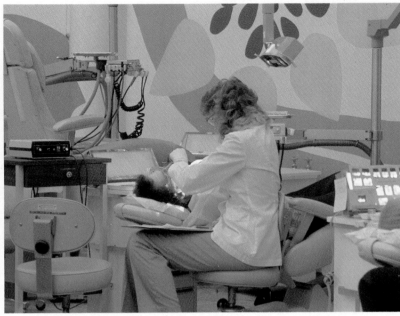

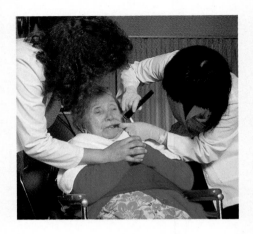

The recent changes in dental practice have been paced by changes in the setting and decor of the dental office. Dentists now see patients in nursing homes (above), shopping malls, and hospitals, while many dentists maintain cheerfully decorated treatment rooms containing furnishings that are comfortable and functional for the both the patient and the dental team (above right).

with a substitute, hydroxylapatite (HA), a mineral-like substance that resembles natural bone very closely and apparently bonds with it, is now a viable option. HA became available in the U.S. in 1982, and in the two succeeding years alone it was used to build up the bony ridge in more than 20,000 patients. The procedure is simpler than grafting bone from the patient's own body and has the advantage that HA does not shrink with time. Implantologists occasionally employ the technique in conjunction with implants, and some oral surgeons are placing HA in empty sockets after tooth extractions to guard against future bone shrinkage.

New looks, new tools

Not only are dental offices springing up in such nontraditional settings as shopping malls, hospitals, and nursing homes but, as dental practice has changed, so have the looks and furnishings of the treatment room, or operatory. Patients recline on sleek chairs while dentist and assistant sit comfortably on either side, practicing "four-handed dentistry." This efficient team concept, wherein an assistant handles suction equipment and other instruments, has gained popularity within the past three decades. The dental hygienist is another increasingly familiar figure on the dental health team. These licensed dental auxiliaries are trained to clean teeth, give fluoride treatments, and advise patients on dental hygiene and oral health. In the late 1980s, about 32% of U.S. independent dental practitioners employed at least one full-time dental hygienist and 34% used a hygienist part-time.

Concerned about the spread of AIDS, hepatitis, and other infections, dentists are donning rubber gloves, face masks, and eye protectors, and the "wet-fingered dentist" of the past is fast disappearing. Vanishing, too, is the old arm-suspended, belt-driven handpiece, generating clatter,

172

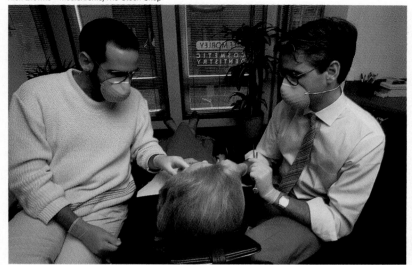

Growing concern about the spread of AIDS, hepatitis, and other infections has encouraged dental workers to wear rubber gloves, face masks, and eye protection.

vibration, and heat as it drills and polishes. Replacing it is a lightweight, air-driven, hand-held device capable of speeds in excess of 400,000 revolutions per minute. Equipped with a built-in fiber-optic light and spurting water on the tooth as it runs, it operates coolly and smoothly albeit not altogether quietly.

While use of the revolving bur for removing decay is not yet obsolete, equipment that dissolves decayed tooth tissue chemically and without anesthetics is already a reality suitable for some cavity preparations. Called Caridex, the system employs a small handpiece to spray a warm, pulsating stream of a chemical solution onto the decayed area of the tooth. Chemical action softens the decay sufficiently for it to be scraped away but leaves sound tooth tissue, the nerve, and surrounding soft tissues unaffected. In most cases some drilling is still needed for reaching deep areas of decay and preparing the cavity for filling.

The application of medical-imaging technology to dentistry has made great strides since panoramic X-ray machines, capable of surveying jaws and surrounding structures on one large piece of film, were introduced after World War II. More sensitive films and other technological improvements have significantly reduced patients' exposure to radiation during all dental X-ray examinations. Computed tomography (CT) scanning, in which a series of digitally recorded X-rays of the tissue of interest is reconstructed by computer into cross-sectional and three-dimensional video images, has been put to good use in implantology. Until recently, for example, placing implants that rest on top of the jawbone—*i.e.*, subperiosteal implants—required two separate surgical procedures, the first to make an impression of the bone and the second to implant the custom-made device. Now a subperiosteal implant can be constructed by means of information gained from a CT scan, sparing the patient the preliminary invasive procedure. CT scans are also being explored for making three-dimensional images of the jawbone as an aid in diagnosing periodontal disease and certain TMJ disorders.

173

Scientists are applying computer-aided design (CAD) and computer-aided manufacturing (CAM) to automate the manufacture of dental crowns, which are replacements for all or part of the tooth above the gum line. Ordinarily, the dentist makes an impression of the prepared tooth and its neighbors for the dental laboratory, which then uses the mold to make a customized crown of cast gold or ceramic material; meanwhile, the patient wears a temporary crown. In one envisioned version of a CAD/CAM system, the dentist scans the prepared tooth and its environment with a laser/camera device. A computer then uses the digitized images to create a three-dimensional model of the crown—both its external shape and the internal cavity that will be mated to the natural tooth. From this model the computer instructs a small milling machine to produce the crown from a block of precast material like ceramic or stainless steel. Dental practices that wished to invest in the entire system would be able to make their own crowns on the spot, eliminating the need for patients' return visits. Alternately, dentists might opt for the scanning equipment alone and send the digitized data to a laboratory equipped to machine the crowns.

The computer is also being used in conjunction with a newly devised "artificial mouth" to test the equivalent of years of wear on dental materials in just a few weeks. Named ART (artificial resynthesis technology), the mouth contains freshly extracted human teeth, simulates human chewing movements, and mimics the warm, moist environment of a living mouth. ART's effects are monitored by a specially designed computer system capable of measuring minute changes in tooth or restoration anatomy, which are then displayed as three-dimensional graphs.

Dental researcher (above) uses a computer and video displays to measure tiny changes in teeth and supporting tissues not detectable in conventional dental X-rays. The equipment is a prototype of a system currently under development. Three-dimensional model of an artificial tooth (below) was produced from digitized images by means of a computer-aided design and manufacturing system for automating the making of dental crowns.

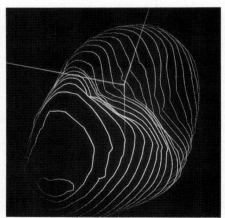

University of Minnesota, School of Dentistry and Productivity Center

An artificial mouth that simulates the motions of chewing can test the equivalent of years of wear on dental materials in a few weeks. Various combinations of teeth mounted in a flexible base are bathed in a synthetic saliva and moved against each other with hydraulic pistons.

Ultrasonic technology has several dental applications. Dentists remove tartar (calculus) from patients' teeth with water-cooled ultrasonic scalers having a tip that vibrates at a frequency of about 25,000 hertz (cycles per second). Ultrasonic instrument-cleaning devices are found in many dental offices. When the nerve inside a tooth dies as a result of dental disease or injury, root-canal, or endodontic, treatment can save the tooth. The object of root-canal work is to remove dead pulp tissue consisting of nerve, blood vessels, and lymphatic vessels from the pulp canal and to replace it with a filling. Its success depends on the correct shaping, disinfecting, and sealing of the canals. Endosonics, the application of ultrasonic energy for this purpose, was introduced in 1976, and its use has increased since then.

The intense energy concentrated in laser beams is currently being tested for its usefulness in sterilizing and sealing root canals that are difficult to treat with conventional techniques. Lasers are also under investigation for smoothing out the fissured and pitted chewing surfaces of teeth where decay-causing bacteria tend to cling, for vaporizing decay material from cavities prior to filling, and for their ability to detect the slight changes in enamel that accompany the beginnings of decay. Laser

Laser beams are being investigated for their ability to detect the beginnings of tooth decay (below). In the future, lasers may also be used to remove decay material from cavities before filling and to smooth out the decay-prone pits and fissures of back teeth.

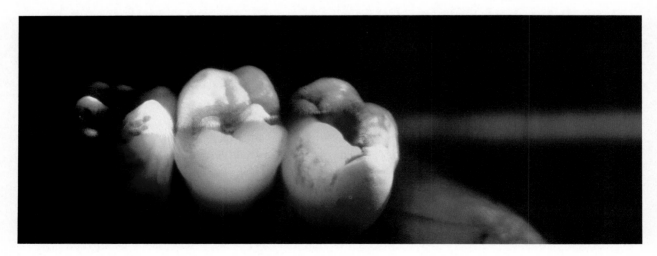

surgery units for removing oral lesions have been developed and are now on the market.

Vaccines and broader concerns

For 15 years investigators in several countries have been working to develop a safe, effective vaccine against tooth decay and gum disease. Cavities are not a life-threatening illness like AIDS or malaria. Consequently, before gaining regulatory approval for its use, an anticaries vaccine must prove totally safe and show no potential side effects. Many approaches have been attempted, and some have been abandoned. Vaccines against an infectious organism usually contain either weakened or killed forms of the organism or constituents of it that, when introduced into the body, stimulate antibody production and thus confer immunity. Some anticaries vaccines currently under investigation are based on killed *S. mutans,* while others exploit internal structures or surface proteins of the bacterium. Efforts are also being directed toward ways to encourage antibody production in the secretory immune system rather than the bloodstream so that high levels of antibodies concentrate in the mucous membranes, including those of the mouth.

Another approach targeted against *S. mutans* attempts to oust decay-producing strains from their ecological niche in the mouth with harmless mutant strains. As a competitive advantage, the mutants could be equipped genetically with the ability to secrete an antibacterial substance against the disease-causing bacteria.

Genetic engineering researchers are exploring the possibility of cloning human tooth enamel for fillings and other restoration work. In addition to mineral-like material, tooth enamel contains several proteins encoded by their own genes. By means of modern recombinant DNA technology, the genes can be isolated and inserted into microorganisms, which will manufacture the proteins in quantity. In theory, a paste made from one or more enamel proteins would be used to fill prepared cavities, where the remineralization properties of saliva would act on the proteins to form new enamel virtually indistinguishable from natural tooth material.

A recently introduced diagnostic technique, which records sounds picked up by sensitive microphones placed over a patient's jaw joints, promises more accurate discrimination among major conditions responsible for pains associated with TMJ disorders. Afflicting about one person out of every five, TMJ disorders may cause headaches, tender jaw muscles, ringing in the ears, hearing loss, dizziness, limited jaw opening, clicking noises, sinus pain, or aching around the ear. For 40 years the disorders were all attributed to muscle spasms caused by malocclusion (faulty bite). Now that additional underlying causes—*e.g.,* degenerative diseases such as arthritis or a displaced or slipped disk—have been identified, more precise diagnostic techniques will help the dentist choose the most appropriate treatment. Therapy may include muscle-relaxing techniques or the wearing of a bite plate to reposition the jaw or to reduce the damage caused by tooth grinding and clenching.

In the search for ever better dental materials, scientists are developing

176

efficient ways of synthesizing the natural glue that allows marine mussels to adhere to underwater structures. Potential applications for this "superglue," which quickly forms strong bonds in wet, saline environments, include uses as filling and bonding material and as an aid in periodontal surgery for bonding teeth and gum tissue.

"Supersaliva" mouth rinses are being tested clinically to help arrest caries and to remineralize tiny demineralized areas of enamel before they can enlarge. Containing varying amounts of calcium, phosphorus, and fluoride, they are intended to better natural saliva in replacing the chemicals that are lost when teeth decay. High on the list of potential candidates for supersaliva are victims of xerostomia, or dry mouth. At increased risk for caries, this group includes persons receiving medications that reduce natural salivary flow and cancer patients whose salivary glands have been damaged by radiotherapy. Supersaliva has also been shown to benefit the acid-ravaged teeth of bulimics.

As new solutions are found to old dental problems, dentistry can focus on other oral health needs, including the correction and repair of congenital abnormalities and facial deformities caused by disease or trauma. An example is a new approach to correcting cleft lip and cleft palate that gives children born with an abnormal opening between the mouth and nose a functional palate for eating and speaking 18 months earlier than was formerly possible. At six weeks of age, the infant is fitted with a small prosthesis that is fastened with pins and anchored to the bone in the roof of the mouth. At six months the lip and nonbony parts of the palate are completely repaired. Final closing of the bony hard palate is delayed until age six, when the upper jaw is fully grown. Traditionally, hard and soft palate repairs have been performed at age two. The new technique allows for undisturbed bone growth while eliminating some of the eating problems formerly encountered in the first two years.

The preliminary results of a yearlong nationwide survey of the dental health of nearly 21,000 American adults were announced in March 1987. The data, gathered between 1985 and 1986, show a remarkable improvement in oral health in the U.S. compared with a generation ago. Similar surveys in other Western industrialized countries would doubtlessly reflect comparable gains. In the short span of the last 40 years, dentistry has catapulted from relative ignorance to real knowledge, and dental practice has changed in ways undreamed of only a generation or two ago.

FOR ADDITIONAL READING

Challenges for the Eighties (National Institute of Dental Research, 1984).

Guide to Dental Health (American Dental Association, 1987).

J. U. Hyman *et al., Your Mouth Is Your Business: The Dentist's Guide to Better Health* (Appleton-Century-Crofts, 1980).

Robert M. Rubin, *Your Dental Health* (Eastern Printing Company, 1984).

S. Sigmund Stahl, *What Dentists Do: A Patient's Guide to Modern Dentistry* (Appleton-Century-Crofts, 1980).

Sheldon B. Sydney, *Ignore Your Teeth—And They'll Go Away* (Devida Publications, 1982).

Science and the Thoroughbred Horse
by George W. Pratt, Jr.

Racing records confirm that horses have been running in ever faster times. Are "superhorses" like Secretariat part of the trend, or animals apart? What makes the great horse? Can racing performance be predicted? Science is finding at least some of the answers.

The world of Thoroughbred horse racing experienced a vast change starting in the late 1960s and early 1970s. Millions of spectators either at the track or watching television were treated to a series of outstanding, record-breaking champions. Beginning in 1973, after a gap of 25 years, the U.S. Triple Crown (Kentucky Derby, Preakness, and Belmont Stakes) was claimed three times in the space of six years. In 1970 the English Triple Crown (Epsom Derby, St. Leger, and Two Thousand Guineas) was won for the first time in 35 years. Wealthy buyers, particularly from the Middle East, became attracted to the glamour, the magic, and the notoriety of a sport whose heroes could bear their name and their colors. They willingly pumped huge sums into the yearling market, which then fed on its own momentum.

By the late 1980s individual, untried stallion prospects were being marketed at more than $3.6 million each. The average price of select yearlings stood at a level 15 times above that of a decade and a half earlier, while over 170 yearlings were bought for more than $1 million apiece, with one individual going for $13.3 million. At the same time, annual attendance levels in North America rose to more than 55 million, and stakes races emerged with purses above $1 million. Fans in 1984 saw the inauguration of the Breeders' Cup, which consists of seven consecutive races in one day at one track that offer a total purse of $10 million.

These spectacular developments in Thoroughbred racing raise many questions for fans, owners, and trainers alike. Where have such amazing animals come from and, more generally, what makes a great winner? Will records continue to fall, or are racehorses finally reaching their speed and endurance limits? How much of a great horse is breeding, how much training, and how much luck? And, what can science and technology contribute to understanding, recognizing, and encouraging superior animals?

Magic of the greats

Racing, like all other sports, is elevated from the routine to the level of fantasy and legend by its champions. For the Thoroughbred two closely related paths lead to fame: the racetrack and the breeding shed. The phenomenal growth of the industry in the past 25 years can be traced to a handful of stars of each type.

Certainly no horse has been more influential than Northern Dancer. This small-sized animal (15.2 hands, or 60.8 inches, from the ground to the highest

GEORGE W. PRATT, JR., is Professor of Electrical Engineering and Computer Science at the Massachusetts Institute of Technology, Cambridge.
Illustration by Leon Bishop

Horses leave the starting gate for the third race of the 1987 Breeders' Cup, a seven-race event that offers a total purse of more than $10 million. Huge prize winnings, an inflated yearling market, and record annual attendance levels reflect the vast change in Thoroughbred racing that has taken place in the past 25 years.

Mike Powell—All-Sport

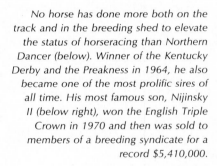

No horse has done more both on the track and in the breeding shed to elevate the status of horseracing than Northern Dancer (below). Winner of the Kentucky Derby and the Preakness in 1964, he also became one of the most prolific sires of all time. His most famous son, Nijinsky II (below right), won the English Triple Crown in 1970 and then was sold to members of a breeding syndicate for a record $5,410,000.

(Left) Courtesy, Keeneland Association;
(right) UPI/Bettmann Newsphotos

point of the withers), who could not bring a bid of $25,000 as a yearling, in 1964 won the Kentucky Derby in a record two minutes flat, took the Preakness in near-record time, and was third in the Belmont. He went on to become one of the most prolific sires of all time, 22% of his offspring becoming stakes winners, 12% graded-stakes winners, three Epsom Derby winners, and 23 Champions. (A graded-stakes race is a particularly prestigious contest with a major portion of the purse payable to the winner.) His stud fee ran close to $1 million near the end of his career. Of the top 50 active sires in 1987, 11 were his sons.

Northern Dancer's most famous son, Nijinsky II, won the English Triple Crown in 1970. This horse, bred in Canada, was picked out of an auction of several hundred horses by the legendary Irish trainer Vincent O'Brien for the American industrialist Charles W. Engelhard, who purchased him for $84,000, a record price at the time. Less than two years later, ownership in the horse was split into 40 shares, which were sold to members of a breeding syndicate for a world record $5,410,000.

Engelhard's success in these prestigious races coupled with a lavish financial return set an example for both American and European owners. He had shown that buying at the top of the yearling market could be an excellent investment. Moreover, the brilliance of such other American-

bred classic colts and fillies as Sir Ivor, Dahlia, Allez France, Nonoalco, Mill Reef, and Thatch in European racing suggested to the English racing establishment as early as 1973 the possibility of foreign domination of their sport. This threat, or perhaps opportunity, was to attract incredible levels of investment in American bloodstock.

Nijinsky II was followed by a U.S. Triple Crown winner, Secretariat. His sire was Bold Ruler, whose offspring in eight separate breeding seasons won more money than those of any other stallion; *i.e.*, he was "leading sire" eight times. (Bold Ruler shares a common ancestry with Northern Dancer, both being grandsons of Nearco bred by Frederico Tesio, the "genius of Dormello," who from a small farm in Italy produced an amazing succession of great horses, including the unbeaten Champion Ribot.) The first two-year-old ever to be chosen Horse of the Year, Secretariat was syndicated in February 1973 before his first start as a three-year-old for a new record of $190,000 a share and a total $6,080,000.

He rewarded his backers by winning the Kentucky Derby, Preakness, and Belmont in the most spectacular fashion seen in the history of racing. His Derby set a new record at 1 minute 59⅖ seconds for the 1¼ miles, every quarter mile being run faster than the preceding segment. (One mile equals about 1.61 kilometers.) He covered the final two furlongs (eighths of a mile) in 23 seconds, an unprecedented feat for a Derby horse. In the Preakness the official timing mechanism was erratic, but a television film analysis showed that he had broken the record for that 1³⁄₁₆-mile race at 1 minute 53⅖ seconds (although he remains a second slower in the official record book). The Belmont Stakes at 1½ miles was perhaps the greatest race ever run by any horse anywhere. Secretariat's winning margin of 31 lengths capped a race run in 2 minutes 24 seconds, without urging by his jockey, Ron Turcotte. He lowered the American dirt-track record for 1½ miles by 2⅕ seconds. On his way to the wire, he broke the track record for 1¼ miles by two seconds and the record for 1⅜ miles by three seconds. While being pulled up to a stop, he broke the world record for 1⅝ miles by covering the distance in 2 minutes 37⅗ seconds, a full second faster than the previous mark. An almost otherworldly aura enveloped this great horse, which, with his charismatic owner, Helen Chenery, became a major media star. Particularly through television they dramatically elevated public perception of the sport and helped set the stage for the first million-dollar yearling.

A genetic trend to faster times

Secretariat's remarkable performance raises questions about its origins. Was it an aberration or related to a possible underlying evolutionary trend toward faster horses? The winning times for the Kentucky Derby from 1900 to 1987 are shown in Figure 1 on page 182. If the results are regressed (*i.e.*, the best possible straight-line fit made to the data) over the period, the times are seen to have decreased at the rate of 0.114 second per year. The fit turns out to be quite accurate, and the trend toward shorter times is confirmed at a high level of statistical significance. This trend is already clearly established in the years 1910–40, well before the

Jockey Ron Turcotte looks in vain for the field as he rides Secretariat to a 31-length win in the 1973 Belmont Stakes (above). Secretariat and his owner Helen Chenery (below) dramatically enhanced the glamour and magic of racing, particularly through television, and helped push individual yearling sales over the million-dollar mark.

(Top) UPI/Bettmann Newsphotos; (bottom) Neil Leifer—Sports Illustrated

explosion in livestock prices and the consequent ballooning of the foal crop after 1970. It also predates recent technological developments in equine exercise physiology and modern racetrack-surface management. A similar trend appears in the Belmont record book starting in 1929, when it was first run at 1½ miles; winning times decrease at a rate of 0.05 second per year. Regressing the Jockey Club Gold Cup, a two-mile race, from 1921 to 1975 produces a 0.056-second decrease per year. At a shorter distance, regression of the Metropolitan Mile from 1916 to 1986 reveals a decrease of 0.079 second per year, while the world record for the mile is decreasing at a rate of 0.091 second per year.

Like the trend for the dirt-track races mentioned above, a decrease is also observed on the turf. The Two Thousand Guineas has been run over the Rowley Mile grass course in Newmarket, England, since 1809, while times have been continuously recorded since 1880. Regressing these data to 1986 shows a yearly decrease of 0.069 second. Similar regressions for the Epsom Derby and the St. Leger reveal annual decreases of 0.09 and 0.12 second per year. In the United States, times for the United Nations Handicap are shortening by 0.073 second annually.

Thus, in every major race in which there are sufficient data, horses have been improving their times at a constant rate for periods exceeding a half century. Moreover, the same trend is seen on both dirt and turf in Europe and North America. Taken together, these observations suggest that the mechanism behind the improvement is of a fundamental physiological nature. It seems unlikely that dietary improvements, different shoeing techniques, or other environmental factors can explain the constancy of the change. A genetic basis for the improvement is supported by the fact that almost all stallions that have been highly successful as sires also have been outstanding racehorses.

Human runners are lowering the world record for the mile at a rate of 0.42 second per year, or 4.6 times the rate of improvement of the horse (*see* Figure 2). The comparatively slow progress of horses has been attributed to a diminished genetic pool on which to draw due to the

Kentucky Derby 1900–1987
winning times: actual and regressed

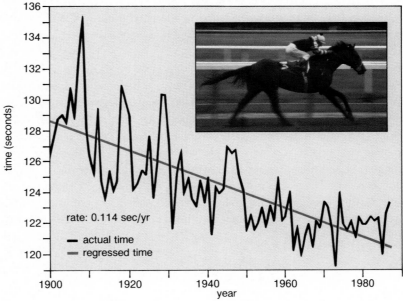

rate: 0.114 sec/yr

■ actual time
■ regressed time

origin of the Thoroughbred from only three or four foundation sires three centuries ago. This often-quoted explanation may be simplistic because, as discussed below, the speed of the horse is limited by structural considerations not faced by humans. To support the increased stresses that come with increased speed, the horse needs to develop stronger tissue and bone. This requirement seems to be the bottleneck to progress.

The physiology of quality

The 1970s saw the appearance of other great names, including Forego, Ruffian, Seattle Slew, Affirmed, and Spectacular Bid in the U.S. A top stallion could be worth more than $80 million, and his stud fees could approach $30 million a year. The great boom in yearling prices naturally focused attention on the selection process and the management of these animals during their competitive careers. Thus, the question "What makes a good horse?" became one of multimillion-dollar significance.

The quality of a racehorse has always been gauged in terms of courage or the will to win. Underlying and subtly connected to this romantic measure are four interconnected physiological systems: cardiovascular, respiratory, musculoskeletal, and locomotive. In recent years sophisticated new tools have been put into the hands of veterinary researchers, enabling them to improve their understanding of these factors.

In animals the basic source of energy at the muscular level is the conversion of the energy-rich molecule ATP (adenosine triphosphate) in muscle cells to ADP (adenosine diphosphate). A mere 25% of the energy produced in this process is available for mechanical work, the balance being released as heat. The ATP stored in the muscles can produce only two or three contractions and therefore must be rapidly regenerated. This is accomplished by reverse conversion of ADP to ATP by means of either aerobic metabolism or a nonoxidative anaerobic process.

The aerobic (oxygen-requiring) source of muscular power falls far short of meeting the demands of the race. It depends upon gas exchange of blood in the lungs, where carbon dioxide, a waste product, is given

Figure 2. Between 1923 and 1981, human runners lowered the world record for the mile at a rate of 0.42 second per year, or 4.6 times the rate of improvement of the horse (0.091 second per year). British miler Steve Ovett (inset) set world records in 1980 and 1981.

(Inset) Tony Duffy—All-Sport

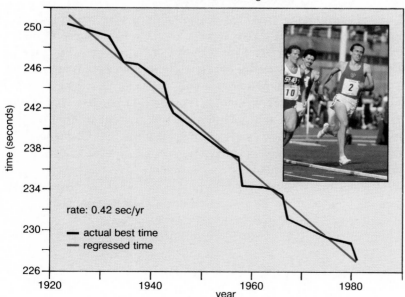

World Records for Human-run Mile 1923–1981
times: actual and regressed

rate: 0.42 sec/yr
— actual best time
— regressed time

off and oxygen, a fuel component, is absorbed by the red blood cells. This process is followed by a reverse exchange in the muscle tissues, oxygen being delivered and carbon dioxide taken away. Once absorbed by tissue cells, the oxygen goes on to participate in reactions in which fuel molecules like glucose are oxidized. The energy released from these reactions is used to drive the regeneration of ATP from ADP.

The cardiovascular system provides the transport mechanism whereby energy-producing nutrients are supplied to the muscle and waste products removed. At racing speed, 1,000 meters/minute (55 feet/second), the heart rate of the horse has jumped from a resting rate of 24–34 beats per minute to a plateau value of 220–240 beats per minute. There is a 70-fold increase in blood flow, compared with a 15-fold increase for a human being. Cardiac output can rise to 550 milliliters per kilogram of body weight per minute (ml/kg-min), or 4.125 liters/second for a 450-kilogram (990-pound) horse. (A liter is about 1.06 quarts.) At 240 beats per minute, the heart puts out between 1.0 and 1.1 liters of blood per beat. This stroke volume of blood spends only a fourth of a second in the lungs. Important performance factors for a horse are peak heart rate, stroke volume, and the fraction of red blood cells in the blood. In Thoroughbreds the value of this last factor ranges from 32 to 46% at rest. At maximum physical effort the contraction of the spleen, where additional red blood cells are stored, can raise the figure to more than 65%.

The next step in the oxidative process, after oxygen transport to the tissues, hinges on the capacity to consume oxygen, which is usually expressed as VO_2 in milliliters of oxygen per kilogram of body weight per minute, or in liters per minute for the entire animal. In the great human milers the maximum value lies in the neighborhood of 74 ml/kg-min. In the horse oxidative capacity has been measured and found to vary linearly with speed up to the rather modest value of 500 meters/minute (27.3 feet/second), at which it reaches 93 ml/kg-min. If this linear behavior were to continue up to racing speeds, oxygen consumption would rise near 200 ml/kg-min. This almost certainly cannot take place, however, owing to a key factor unique to the horse.

At the gallop the horse's breathing is synchronized to its gait such that one inhale-exhale cycle is completed in every stride. Furthermore, the horse increases its speed most importantly by lengthening its stride, not by taking more strides per second. Over the whole range of racing speeds, the stride time for most Thoroughbreds remains very close to 0.42 second, which means that the rate of ventilation flattens out at about 2.4 breaths per second. Moreover, at this high rate, breathing becomes more inefficient owing to greater air resistance, incomplete emptying of the lungs and airways with each breath, and probably a less complete exchange of carbon dioxide and oxygen in the lungs. The total pulmonary ventilation achieved in one minute has been measured at 1,600 liters of air per minute at a speed of 650 meters/minute (35.5 feet/second). This corresponds to 11.2 liters per breath, at which level the lungs process about 27 liters of air per second. From this 27 liters a maximum of 1.26 liters of oxygen can be extracted by the red blood cells.

184

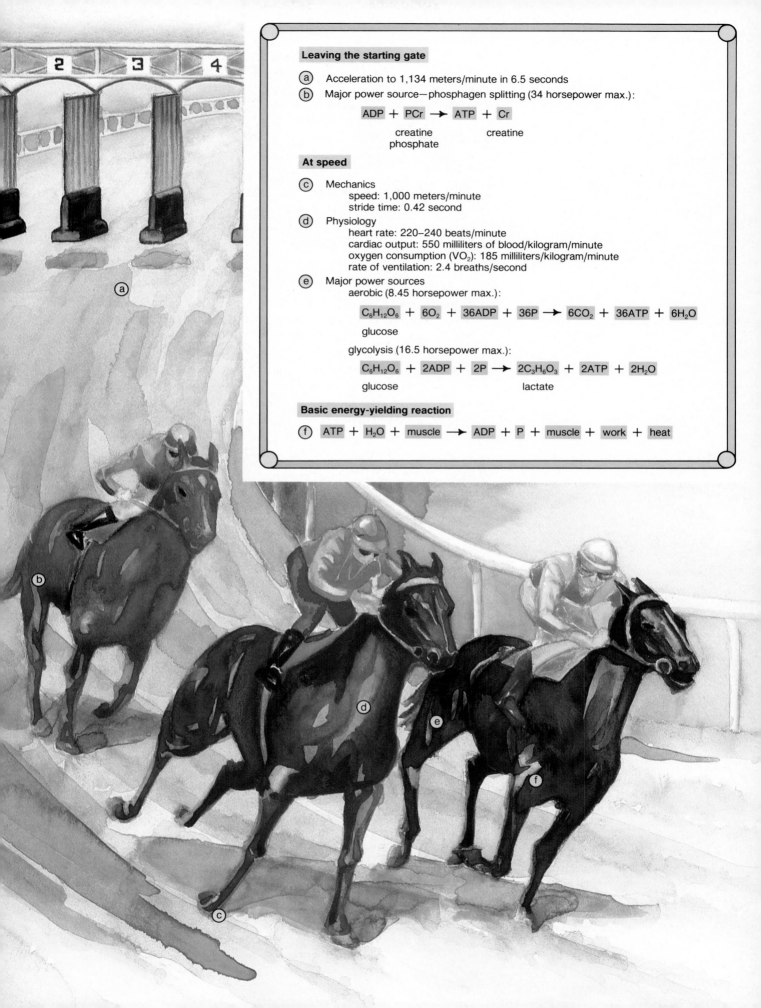

Leaving the starting gate

(a) Acceleration to 1,134 meters/minute in 6.5 seconds

(b) Major power source—phosphagen splitting (34 horsepower max.):

$$ADP + PCr \rightarrow ATP + Cr$$

creatine phosphate   creatine

At speed

(c) Mechanics
    speed: 1,000 meters/minute
    stride time: 0.42 second

(d) Physiology
    heart rate: 220–240 beats/minute
    cardiac output: 550 milliliters of blood/kilogram/minute
    oxygen consumption (VO_2): 185 milliliters/kilogram/minute
    rate of ventilation: 2.4 breaths/second

(e) Major power sources
    aerobic (8.45 horsepower max.):

$$C_6H_{12}O_6 + 6O_2 + 36ADP + 36P \rightarrow 6CO_2 + 36ATP + 6H_2O$$

glucose

    glycolysis (16.5 horsepower max.):

$$C_6H_{12}O_6 + 2ADP + 2P \rightarrow 2C_3H_6O_3 + 2ATP + 2H_2O$$

glucose   lactate

Basic energy-yielding reaction

(f) $$ATP + H_2O + muscle \rightarrow ADP + P + muscle + work + heat$$

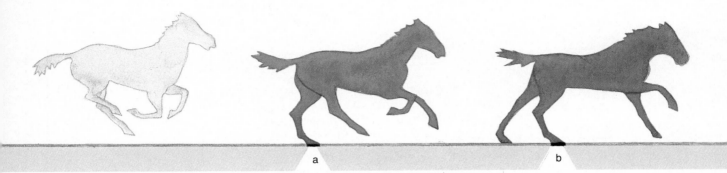

a   b

The surface area of the lung tissue is so large and the capillary network so extensive that the entire volume of blood from each heartbeat can be spread out into a layer a single red blood cell in thickness. Each red blood cell in its one-fourth-second residency has one chance to exchange carbon dioxide for oxygen. In spite of this, blood-gas analyses of horses running in treadmill tests show that as the intensity of effort increases to a level still well below that required for racing, the partial pressure of oxygen in the blood decreases; in other words, even below racing speeds the cardiovascular system begins failing to meet the demands of the muscles for oxygen. This means that the limiting factor in aerobic power production is the ability to saturate the blood with oxygen. Anything that impedes respiratory efficiency, *e.g.*, bleeding in the lungs, seriously limits performance potential.

Bioenergetics

Biochemists have shown that the metabolic reactions in muscle cells can liberate 20 kilojoules of energy from each liter of absorbed oxygen. (For comparison, 4.2 kilojoules roughly equals one food calorie.) Therefore, the oxidative metabolic pathway is capable of generating about 25.2 kilowatts of power. If 25% is available for mechanical work, the aerobic power available to move the horse is 6.3 kilowatts, or 8.45 horsepower. High-speed-film analysis, however, shows that a racehorse breaking from the starting gate typically accelerates in 6.5 seconds to 1,134 meters/minute (62 feet/second). An 8½-horsepower motor could hardly perform that well on a 500-kilogram (1,100-pound) animal equivalent to horse and rider. In fact, the burst of energy that accelerates the horse from the gate requires a peak power output near 42 horsepower.

This extra energy comes from a special anaerobic process known as phosphagen splitting whereby compounds called phosphagens, which are stored in so-called fast-twitch muscle cells, produce the energy necessary for brief, high-intensity activity. This short-lived source, of about six-seconds' duration, reconverts ADP to ATP and can produce as much as 25 kilowatts, or 34 horsepower. Once depleted, phosphagen levels need to be replenished, a process that takes several hours for horses, compared with minutes for humans. A second, more sustained anaerobic process, glycolysis, breaks down glucose into lactic acid while producing ATP from ADP and yields a maximum attainable power of 12.3 kilowatts, or

The stride of a galloping racehorse is a four-beat gait in that the hooves strike the ground in four successive impacts. Beginning with the impact of the first rear hoof to come down (a), the progression is second impact from the second rear hoof (b), third impact from the first front hoof (c), and fourth impact from the second (lead) front (d). There follows an airborne phase, after which the pattern repeats.

Illustration by Leon Bishop

186

c   d

16.5 horsepower. Unfortunately, lactic acid builds up in the muscle cells and inhibits the further production of ATP, resulting in fatigue. Thus, once the horse gets up to speed, it is essential that it derive as much power as possible from the aerobic oxidative pathway.

If the linear regressions for oxygen consumption that are so well obeyed at moderate speeds are extrapolated to 1,000 meters/minute (55 feet/second), one finds that at racing speed the horse would consume more than 100 liters of oxygen per minute, derived from an oxygen uptake of 460 milliliters per heartbeat (the so-called oxygen pulse), and each breath would take in a gigantic tidal volume of more than 15 liters. As mentioned above, the corresponding VO_2 would be approximately 200 ml/kg-min. These are impossible numbers; the ordinary horse is forced to supplement its aerobic source of power with glycolysis, which must contribute power at a level in the neighborhood of 11.6 kilowatts, or 15.6 horsepower. Nevertheless, Secretariat's Belmont, a race for the ages, when analyzed by means of a theoretical model of the bioenergetics of running that has been experimentally verified for humans, pegs his VO_2 at 192.5 ml/kg-min. Moreover, if the regression for the winning time of the Belmont is applied, it predicts that Secretariat's 2 minutes 24 seconds could not have been expected to occur until the year 2064. These figures all point to an evolutionary leap—a horse far ahead of its time.

Gait analysis

Another interesting aspect of Secretariat's greatness is the amazing mechanical efficiency of his stride; *i.e.*, his "way of going." At the gallop the stride is a four-beat gait in that the hooves come down in four successive impacts. Starting with the beat of the first rear hoof to come down, the progression is second beat from the second rear, third beat from the first front, and fourth beat from the second, or lead, front. Next there is an airborne phase (all hooves off), after which the pattern repeats. Except for the lead foreleg, before any leg leaves the ground, the next leg in the sequence makes contact so that there is an overlap period when both legs are down. Actually, the legs would work most efficiently if they behaved like the spokes of a wheel, in which case there would be no duplication or overlap and the horse would derive the maximum forward progress per step. The most inefficient coordination of the legs would have them all move in unison like a four-legged pogo stick. Thus,

The four beats of the gallop appear clearly in an oscilloscope trace of the sounds from a racing horse as picked up by a high-performance microphone. The long stretch to the right of the fourth peak represents the airborne phase, which is followed by the first beat in the next stride.

George W. Pratt, Jr.

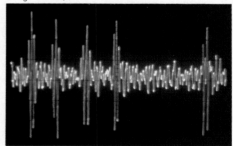

187

Secretariat (foreground) is photographed on the verge of passing Riva Ridge in the 1973 Marlboro Cup, in which both horses broke the world record for 1⅛ miles. A gait analysis of the two animals, based on a high-speed-film record of this point in the race, is summarized in the table. Stance is the time of hoof ground contact averaged over the four legs. Swing is the average off-the-ground time per leg. Stride time is the sum of stance and swing times.

a key to efficiency is to minimize the overlap periods in the stride. In the language of dressage, this translates to the development of extension.

In the photograph above, Secretariat (in the foreground) and Riva Ridge are shown racing in the 1973 Marlboro Cup, in which both horses broke the world record for 1⅛ miles. Secretariat is just at the point of passing his opponent. Both horses are at exactly the same point in their stride: first foreleg on the track and the leading foreleg about to come down. Clearly Secretariat approaches the spokes-of-the-wheel ideal of maximum extension more closely as his first foreleg is nearer the completion of its step than that of Riva Ridge. Moreover, both of Secretariat's rear hooves are off, while the second rear of Riva Ridge is just coming off. A high-speed-film analysis of the strides of these horses at this point in the race produces the comparisons shown in the table.

Experiments have shown that the coordinated timing of an animal's stride is controlled by a "gait program," which resides in spinal nerve centers. By electrically stimulating the brain stem of totally paralyzed cats, for example, it has been possible to generate coordinated stepping. Increasing the intensity of the stimulation has produced in succession the trot, canter, and gallop (which are natural gaits of cats as well as horses).

Each limb is moved by flexor or extensor muscle groups. The flexors take over at the completion of one step to swing the leg forward for the next step. At the completion of the forward motion, the extensors bring the leg down to ground contact and produce the forward propulsion during the step. The principal means of increasing speed is to lengthen the stride, primarily by decreasing the on-the-ground overlap between the second hind leg and first foreleg. At the canter they move as a diagonal pair with complete overlap. As speed increases from an easy to a fast gallop, stance, swing, and airborne times quicken only slightly, but overlap time drops by more than a factor of two. In passing it should be noted that stride length is the product of speed and stride time. Therefore, such traditional statements as "Man O' War had a 27-foot stride" are meaningless unless the speed is known.

The gait program is affected by feedback signals generated by pain or fatigue. As the horse tires because its cardiovascular and respiratory systems cannot keep up with its energy demands, it attempts to inhale more air. The inhale-exhale cycle, however, is locked onto the stride, which the horse is now forced to modify. Inspiration starts at that point in the stride when the airborne phase begins. It ends when the first foreleg comes down in the next stride. Expiration takes place from that point until the second (lead) foreleg leaves the ground in that stride. To get more air, the laboring horse attempts to prolong its airborne period, which increases the work it must do against gravity. Horsemen call this effort climbing. Additionally, the overlap in the stride increases. Therefore, as fatigue sets in, the efficiency of the stride goes to pieces. The analysis of Secretariat's gait summarized in the table was made from a point in the Marlboro Cup just before the horse completed one mile, which he reached in a track record-breaking time of 1 minute 33 seconds. At only 18.6% overlap, there is no sign of his beginning to tire.

The superior horse must be endowed not only with highly efficient cardiovascular, respiratory, and musculoskeletal systems but also with a a gait program to match. In the all-out gallop the horse does not, nor does it have time to, think about such issues as how high the knee should be raised. Instead it obeys a preprogrammed set of instructions. The stride of a champion shows no wasted motion. This efficiency cannot be trained into a horse; thus, the addage "Great horses are born, not made." This fact reemphasizes the challenge of recognizing ability in the horse as a yearling. The study of high-speed films has produced a set of stride characteristics that correlate well with performance potential. At a given speed the length of the stride, the percentage of time spent off the ground, the swing time of the legs, and other characteristics are used to produce a profile of the gait, which when treated statistically can make a very meaningful prediction about the quality of the horse. Even though it is possible to identify a potentially superior horse before it ever races, finding the great horse is still a needle-in-the-haystack proposition because they are so rare.

Figure 3. A boom in yearling prices began in 1976, when the first offspring of Secretariat came on the market. In 1984 the average price per horse at the Keeneland Select Yearling Sale peaked at more than $610,000. During the July 1981 sale a bay colt (inset) sired by Northern Dancer went for almost $3 million.

(Inset) Courtesy, Keeneland Association

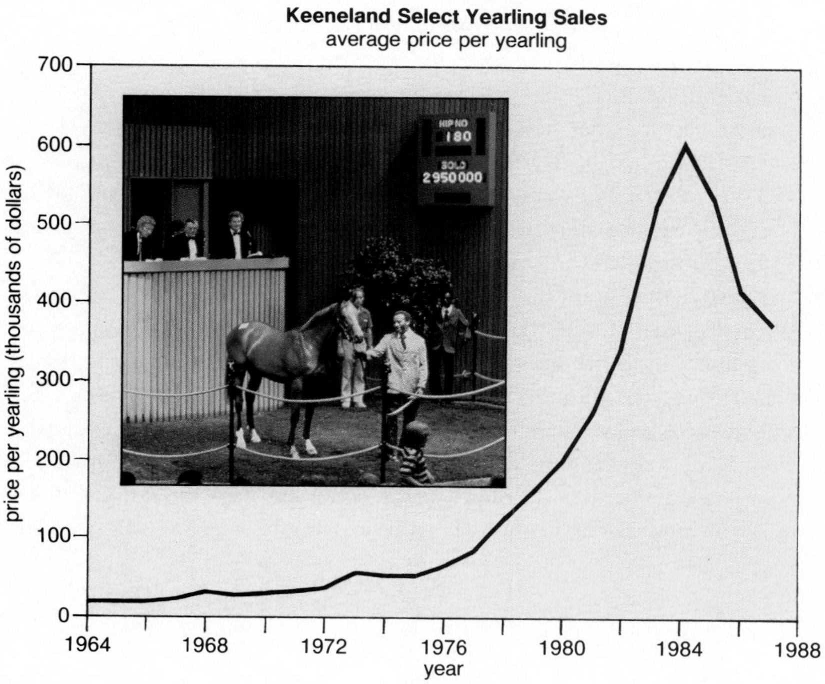

Keeneland Select Yearling Sales
average price per yearling

The largest investors in the yearling market in the 1980s were D. Wayne Lucas (top left), Vincent O'Brien (bottom left) and partner Robert Sangster (top right), and Sheikh Muhammad ibn Rashid al-Maktoum (bottom right) and brothers.

Still an art

A fabulous boom in yearling prices, as shown in Figure 3 on page 189, began in 1976, when the first offspring of Secretariat came on the market. His mating to Charming Alibi, the dam (mother) of Dahlia (who was Horse of the Year in the U.S. at ages three and four and Champion in England at age five while winning $1.2 million in purses), resulted in a colt named Canadian Bound. When the bidding was over, this offspring had brought the spectacular price of $1.5 million. Lightning did not strike twice, however. With total lifetime earnings of $4,781 gathered in three years of trying, he now stands at stud for a fee of $1,000.

In this vein it is indicative of the level of uncertainty in picking winners to look at the record of the three largest investors in the yearling market in the 1980s, when the market peaked and the price per horse at the 1984 Keeneland Select Yearling Sale in Lexington, Kentucky, averaged $610,467. The huge influx of foreign money at that sale alone accounted for 98 yearlings at an average price of $1,031,326. The biggest European buyers in the early 1980s were trainer Vincent O'Brien, with his partner, Robert Sangster, and the Maktoum brothers from the Persian Gulf emirate of Dubai, whose racing is based in England. The largest American buyer was trainer D. Wayne Lukas, representing a domestic group.

Between 1980 and 1984 the Maktoums bought 136 yearlings at an average of $912,000 and a total of $124,015,000 at the annual Keeneland Select Sale alone. An analysis by the magazine *Thoroughbred Record* reveals that of these horses, 4.4% became Group I Grade stakes winners, compared with a 2.1% average for all horses in those sales. The total earnings averaged over the Maktoum purchases came to $36,679 per horse. In estimating the value of these horses in 1987, the analysis showed that the original $124 million investment was worth between $59.6 million and $106.9 million. The same analysis showed that the O'Brien-Sangster total investment of $67.7 million for 52 yearlings at an average of $1,302,000 per horse produced average earnings of $39,-440 per horse and 5.8% Group I Grade stakes winners. In 1987 their original investment was worth between $38.2 million and $75.7 million. On the other hand, Lukas and partners were found to have spent only $17.9 million for 37 horses, averaging $482,000 per horse. They had average earnings per horse of $164,000, while their original investment was estimated to be worth between $5.6 million and $23.6 million in 1987. If the training expenses are deducted from the purse earnings, the operating budgets show losses for both European groups and a surplus of $3.9 million for the Lukas horses.

These figures point up how few of even the best bred, best conformed (most well-structured) horses, carefully screened from a large number for admission to the select sales, win an important race. For the 86,022 North American runners in 1986, for example, there were 406 graded-stakes races won by 265 horses, or 0.3% of the group. They further show that at present the selection of yearlings is an art form and by no means a science. Seattle Slew, which could not pass the admission test to Keeneland, brought only $17,500 at a minor yearling sale in 1975.

He won the U.S. Triple Crown in 1977, never having lost a race in his career. His winnings totaled $717,720, and two single breeding rights to him were sold at auction in 1984 for $710,000 each. John Henry was a $1,100 yearling; in two years he had six owners, one of whom, an experienced horseman, owned him twice and in the process had him gelded. He became the greatest money winner ever ($6,597,947) and Horse of the Year twice, in 1981 and 1984. At the 1981 Keeneland Summer Sale a striking-looking son of Northern Dancer attracted the attention of the experts, who had been scouring the farms before the sale, studying pedigrees and using X-rays, endoscopes, bone measurement, and every other available measure of quality on the select group of youngsters intended for sale. This colt set a world-record yearling price for the time of $3.5 million and was sent to Vincent O'Brien for training in Ireland. In four starts he won a single minor race, was quickly retired from the scene, and now stands in Oklahoma. The disappointed underbidder paid $3.3 million for his second choice, Shareef Dancer, who became the champion three-year-old in England and Ireland and was later syndicated for $40 million. To cap it off, there is no statistical correlation between the ranking of horses in the Experimental Handicap (a rating system that orders horses by proven ability) and their auction price.

Training and its limits

If the great horses are born and not made, what of the role of the trainer? The key to the trainer's success is the ability to divine the needs of the horse in terms of work, rest, and racing. Curing soreness and preserving soundness is the continual struggle. Moreover, the trainer has to have a deep understanding of each horse so as to create the individually tailored routine that brings out the best effort from that animal. The human runner typically trains 60 miles per week and the cyclist rides 400 miles weekly. The horse simply cannot tolerate such levels of activity.

The horses of U.S. trainer Woody Stephens have won the Belmont five consecutive times. Using a traditional training schedule to prepare his horses for that event, Stephens raced Caveat a total of only 11.4 miles and had workouts totaling 15 miles over a five-month period, just a bit

The trainer's success resides in divining the needs of the horse in terms of work, rest, and racing (above). Horses cannot tolerate the same high level of activity accepted by human athletes in training. In preparing for the 1982 Belmont Stakes, trainer Woody Stephens raced Conquistador Cielo (both below) only 6.2 miles and had workouts totaling 11 miles over a five-month period, a traditional training schedule.

(Top) All–Sport; (bottom) Al Messerschmidt—Focus on Sports

191

over one mile per week at speed. Over the same period, his previous Belmont winner, Conquistador Cielo, raced only 6.2 miles and trained 11 miles. Attempts have been made at interval training, in which the horse is given very large workloads broken down into a series of work periods separated by rest intervals. Although this technique has been successful to the point of becoming a necessity for training the human athlete, it has not had much effect on training the racehorse. As pointed out above, if the world record by humans for the mile is regressed from 1923 to the present, the rate of improvement is found to be about 4.6 times that seen for the horse. Very likely the reason for this difference is the ability of the human to withstand much higher levels of stress than the horse can accept.

The comparison between human and horse is interesting in terms of their maximum ability to consume oxygen; *i.e.*, their VO_2. The ratio of the speed at which the horse runs the mile (1,000 meters/minute, or 55 feet/second) to that of the human (400 meters/minute, or 22 feet/second) is 2.5 to 1. This ratio is exactly the same as that of their maximum rates of oxygen consumption. The horse, however, is six times as heavy as the human. While stroke volume of the heart does scale as the

The vital role of the jockey is borne out by the consistent appearance of the same few names in the yearly list of outstanding riders. Laffit Pincay (right) jockeyed three consecutive Belmont winners (1982–84). Willie Shoemaker (far right) has won several hundred stakes races and more money than any other rider in racing history. Still, some great horses seem to make their own winning decisions. In the 1981 Jockey Club Gold Cup John Henry (opposite page, leading) beat Peat Moss by changing leads in the final stride before the wire.

ratio of weights (6 to 1), respiratory capacity does not. If the maximum VO_2 for the horse, about 180 ml/kg-min, were scaled down by a factor of six to fit the human, the human would run the mile in just under ten minutes. If the VO_2 for the human were scaled up by a factor of six to fit the horse, the horse would run at 90 miles/hour, far too fast for its legs to survive the stress.

As the horse evolves, developing ever higher oxygen-metabolism rates, it has to develop the skeletal strength to carry the increased speed, but without paying too high a price in increased bone mass. The best horses are now on the verge of tearing themselves to pieces. Ruffian, the great mare who was so fast that no horse ever got in front of her at any point in any race, paid the price of blinding speed with shattered sesamoid bones. Bone fracture has been the common lot of many outstanding horses. Thus, the trainer of the horse is working with an athlete on the very edge of self-destruction.

The jockey

Racing records clearly establish the vital role of the jockey. The same few names appear consistently in the annual list of outstanding riders. The jockey has to be an expert judge of pace. It is suicidal to go too fast too soon since the consequence is lactic acid buildup, which effectively stops the horse. It is equally fatal, however, to spot a front-runner too large a lead in hopes that the horse will burn out. Some horses will stop if hit with a whip, and some who like to run on another's shoulder have to be tricked into winning.

Nevertheless, many jockeys have said that on the truly great horses they were merely passengers. An excellent example is John Henry, who apparently set his own strategy. He beat Peat Moss in the Jockey Club Gold Cup in 1981 by changing leads in the final stride before the wire. A change of lead, in which the gait completely reverses to the opposite hooves, produces a stride about six inches longer than normal, and with

(Opposite page, top) Ruffian drops behind Foolish Pleasure after shattering the sesamoid bones in her right foreleg during a match race at Belmont Park in July 1975. As racehorses evolve toward ever faster animals, they are having difficulty developing sufficient skeletal strength to carry the increased speed.

Neil Leifer—Sports Illustrated

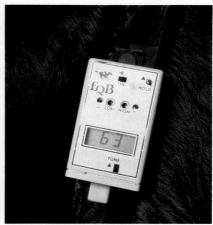

A horse exercising on an indoor treadmill (above) is monitored for heart rate, oxygen consumption, and other physiological indicators of health and fitness. The heart-rate meter (above right) has proved itself one of the most practical, noninvasive tools for training. Devised for studies of blood chemistry, radio-controlled device (below) draws blood samples through an inserted catheter as the horse is given an on-track workout.

this jump he won the race. His style was one of gritty determination and lofty superiority. He celebrated each win with Napoleonic behavior in the winner's circle. In his last race he was uncharacteristically far behind, eighth after three-fourths of a mile. His jockey, Chris McCarron, wondered what the nine-year-old veteran had in mind. He found out with five-eighths of a mile to go. John Henry picked up the pace, ran down the seven horses ahead of him, went to the front in mid-stretch, and won by nearly three lengths, equaling the track record.

New instrumentation

Significant recent advances in equine exercise physiology are having effects on training methods. The treadmill, for example, has become an important research tool for evaluating competitive potential. The horse is made to trot or gallop on a moving belt, which can be inclined to simulate going uphill to increase the stress level. With this device the performance of the respiratory and cardiovascular systems can be measured directly. Hence, VO_2, the work level at which blood lactate starts to increase (*i.e.*, the lactic acid threshold), and any other factor that describes the exercising horse can be evaluated.

From such research a very useful, catch-all training parameter has emerged: the speed of the horse when the heart rate reaches 200 beats per minute, or V200. Almost all of the key elements that affect performance have been found to be related to V200, which can be measured in actual training by use of an onboard heart-rate meter. Consequently, it is possible to accurately follow progress in conditioning, to detect the overtrained situation, and to compare the capabilities of different horses.

The heart-rate meter has proved itself one of the most practical, noninvasive training devices. Electrodes leading from the meter are attached to the chest wall, and the electrocardiogram, *i.e.*, the electrical signal generated by the heart muscle during its rhythmic contractions, is recorded. From this record the heart rate can be determined under racing

194

conditions, and V200, the peak heart rate, and the speed of recovery to the unstressed rate can be derived.

Blood chemistry of the running horse can be studied both on the treadmill and during training by means of sampling catheters inserted in blood vessels in the neck. For on-the-track studies, blood samples are drawn by remote control at various times during the workout.

Ultrasound (sound above the range of human hearing) is being used to image tendons, internal organs, and other soft-tissue structures. This technique, which has become a common tool of diagnostic medicine for human beings, is based on detection of the reflected waves that always arise when a beam of sound strikes a boundary between two different tissue types. In particular, ultrasound is being used to test for pregnancy in the mare, a crucial matter when the breeding fee can be hundreds of thousands of dollars. It is also used to probe the mechanical structure of the heart, *e.g.*, to measure chamber size and wall thicknesses, to assist in predicting performance potential. Another application of ultrasound has been the evaluation of the loading capacity of bone. The velocity of sound through bone depends on its elastic modulus and density. Both of these factors are directly related to bone strength. While still in the research stage, the technique may prove important in identifying horses having a high risk of fracture.

A device called an electronic force plate is helping to identify and measure weight-bearing lameness in the leg. If a person were to stand on a scale with a stone in his or her shoe, the dial registering the weight would jump about owing to the person's attempts to cope with the discomfort. These body movements can actually be very subtle. The force plate is simply an electronic scale that can be read thousands of times during the brief attention span of the horse. One leg is placed on the plate, and the time-dependent force fluctuations are measured. From these values a computer constructs a graph called a histogram that shows how many times during the measurement period the force on the leg fell

Investigators take an ultrasound measurement of a horse's metacarpal bone (above left), while an oscilloscope displays the reflected signal as a peak (above). Still in the research stage, ultrasound evaluation of bone may become an important technique for identifying horses having a high risk of fracture. (Below) Horse stands on an electronic force plate, which can detect and measure weight-bearing distress in the legs.

Photos, George W. Pratt, Jr.

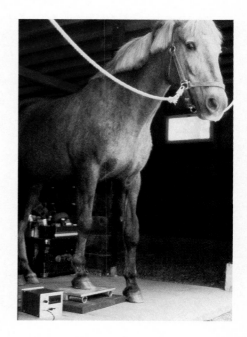

within a certain range. The histogram takes the form of a bell-shaped curve centered on the average force on the leg. The width of the curve is a measure of the weight-bearing distress. This technique has been very successful not only in locating the problem leg but also in quantifying the level of distress and monitoring the response to treatment.

Ahead: improving the racing environment

In the future more advances in biomedical engineering and exercise physiology should find their way into racehorse-training techniques. Consequently, better care, fewer injuries, and better average performance are anticipated. On the other hand, because the final outcome of any race depends not only on the quality of the horses but also on where they run, *i.e.*, the track, the air they pass through, and other extrinsic factors, one can also expect increasingly more attention to be paid to the racing environment.

The traditional racing surfaces, turf and dirt, both have serious drawbacks. Turf can withstand only limited use and cannot be run on in very wet weather without being destroyed. Dirt tracks are very dependent on sand and clay content and on the moisture level. For optimum performance moisture must be kept within a rather narrow range, usually 7 to 11%. Water binds soil together by surface-tension attraction between moisture-jacketed particles. Too little moisture creates a running surface of inadequate shear strength that is difficult to run on and that tends to produce tendon damage. Too much moisture produces a sloppy track that gives the horse little support; the hoof penetrates the dirt cushion and contacts the track base, which has a hardness similar to concrete. In many locations a soil composition that works in winter weather must be replaced with another blend for summer racing because of different temperature and rainfall conditions.

Equitrack, the brand name for a racing surface comprising sand particles coated with a water-repelling polymer, resists monsoon rain at a dirt track in Hong Kong (above). On a conventional dirt track (above right) too much moisture produces a sloppy surface that gives the horse little support, allowing the hoof to penetrate to the concrete-hard track base.

(Left) Courtesy, En–tout–cas (USA), Inc.; (right) © Paul Fusco—Magnum

196

Some of the limitations of dirt tracks have recently been circumvented with a racing surface comprising sand particles coated with a hydrophobic (water-repelling) polymer that is also slightly sticky. Thus, water runs through the racing cushion without wetting it, while the weak cohesion of the particles provides shear strength. The new surface, which has passed extensive tests in both summer and winter conditions, appears to have great potential and should stimulate the search for other ways to improve track quality.

Another advance awaiting implementation and exploitation is the reduction of aerodynamic drag. Riding equipment and techniques have so far paid little attention to this important factor. In bicycle racing, in which 90% of the rider's energy at speeds above 20 miles per hour goes into overcoming air resistance, skintight suits and teardrop helmets have become standard equipment. The power required to overcome drag varies as the product of the frontal area and the cube of the speed. The racing Thoroughbred runs typically at 1,000 meters/minute (55 feet/second), whereas a racing cyclist pedals at roughly 660 meters/minute (36 feet/second). If one assumes that a horse and rider present a frontal area about twice that of the cyclist (a 2-to-1 ratio), then the power consumed to overcome drag by a horse and rider is seven times that of the cyclist. If the frontal area of horse and rider is taken as six square feet, then at racing speed the horse is using close to two horsepower just to move through the air—almost 25% of its maximum aerobic power output. Every square foot of area reduction saves almost 0.5 horsepower, or about 6% of the aerobic power, yet it is not uncommon to see saddlecloths flapping and the wind billowing out the jockey's shirt. Instead of a streamlined helmet, the rider often has a decorative pom-pom on his riding hat. In today's high-spending world of the Thoroughbred, it seems only a matter of time until the horse catches up technologically with the bicycle.

Thoroughbred racing has thus far paid little attention to the very real effects of air resistance. Billowing jockey shirts and flapping saddlecloths, both common sights at the track (below left), contrast markedly with the skintight suit and teardrop helmet of the modern bicycle racer (below right).

(Left) Harold Roth—Black Star;
(right) © David Madison—Bruce Coleman Inc.

"MICROLIVESTOCK"

When Smaller Is Better

by Noel D. Vietmeyer

In many parts of the world, farmers do not have enough land
and resources to raise such large livestock as cattle,
sheep, and hogs. An answer to their problem might be
the use of much smaller animals.

In less developed nations most villagers subsist exclusively on the products from their homes or tiny farms: store-bought meat, milk, and eggs
are beyond their meager budgets. However, because houses and crops
are taking over the land, fewer and fewer of these farmers have much
pasture left. In scores of countries millions of poor farmers cannot support even a single large cow.

In seeking animals that such farmers can use, researchers have begun looking beyond normal-sized cattle to tiny, pint-sized species. Like
computers, they say, livestock should be getting smaller and becoming
more "personal." "Mainframes," such as conventional cattle, require too
much space and expense for the world's poorest people. "Miniframes,"
such as sheep and goats, will be increasingly important, but user-friendly
"microlivestock" seem to be the most promising in the long run.

A 1988 report from the U.S. National Research Council described
more than 40 of these miniature species. It pointed out that livestock research usually overlooks small animals, and it proposed that international
attention be focused on microlivestock and that they be promoted for
use by third world farmers. For example, a farmer unable to raise cattle
could raise a dozen rabbits in cages beside the house. Moreover, he would
have little financial risk, gain a quick return on his investment, and have
a flexible source of ready cash. In addition, a family can consume the
meat in a rabbit-sized animal before it spoils, which is vitally important
in areas where there are no refrigerators.

Even if poverty were to get no worse, the less developed countries
need to produce more livestock. Throughout Latin America, Asia, and
Africa, poor people eat almost no meat, milk, or eggs. In Mexico an
estimated 25 million persons cannot afford meat. The consequent lack
of animal protein contributes to malnutrition, particularly in children.

The microlivestock that could help solve this problem are of two types. One consists of extremely small breeds of conventional livestock— miniature cattle, sheep, goats, and pigs, for example. The other comprises species that are inherently small—poultry, rabbits, and rodents, for example. Among both, there are animals with outstanding promise for helping the world's most destitute people.

Microbreeds

Small breeds of cattle, sheep, goats, and pigs are common in less developed countries, but most of them are raised for family use rather than for market and thus are often left out of national statistics and research programs. Also, because they look puny compared with giant imported bulls, rams, bucks, or hogs, they tend to be brushed off as second-rate.

Many of these "microbreeds" have remarkable qualities, however, and are appropriately sized for local requirements. Unlike their imported brethren, they—and their ancestors before them—have contended with hostile climates, ravaging pestilence, and poor diets throughout their lives. Only the most robust could survive, and many microlivestock are therefore adapted to extreme stresses.

The Navajo sheep is an example in North America's own backyard. Perhaps the oldest breed of sheep in the United States, it may have been introduced to North America in 1540 by the Spanish explorer Francisco Vázquez de Coronado, who was seeking the mythical Seven Golden Cities of Cíbola in the region that is now Arizona and New Mexico. Hardly bigger than many dogs, the Navajo sheep weighs only 30 kilograms (70 pounds), but it became a major part of the culture of the Southwest. Though the Navajos and other local Indians had never seen sheep before, they soon became shepherds and weavers, and their rugs became famous.

NOEL D. VIETMEYER was staff officer for a 1988 report on small livestock published for the benefit of less developed countries by the National Research Council in Washington, D.C.

(Overleaf) Karl Weidmann— Animals Animals

200

Navajo sheep have white or brown wool that hangs in ringlets around their bodies. The fleece is a double coat: long, coarse guard hairs on the outside and short wool on the inside. Consequently, warm, waterproof, and long-lasting products are made from this wool. Many of the sheep have four horns because the Indians believed that this trait was sacred, and they favored four-horned rams for breeding purposes.

In modern times there has been so little commercial and scientific interest in this "microsheep" that by the 1970s only a handful of purebred specimens remained. Since the late 1970s, however, Utah State University professor Lyle McNeal has been working to save it from extinction. By 1988 he had a burgeoning flock at the university and was learning that this supposedly obsolete dwarf is amazingly useful.

The breed originated in the arid south of Spain (where it is called the churro), and it thrives in hot, dry climates. Unlike normal breeds, Navajo sheep can exist in the desert without supplementary food and with little water. As McNeal has pointed out, any sheep that can survive and raise a lamb in the aridity and searing heat of the American Southwest has to be superior. He has found that the ewes have a strong maternal instinct, which is vital for protecting lambs against the coyotes that are common in the region.

Thanks to the efforts of McNeal and his colleagues, Indians are beginning to use Navajo sheep again; by 1988 there were more than 400 on the Navajo reservation. The tough little sheep could prove valuable not only for American Indians but for poor people in many other dry regions as well. The National Research Council report recommends that similar efforts be made with dozens of the world's neglected breeds of tiny sheep. They too should be preserved from extinction.

Navajo sheep (opposite page) weigh only 30 kilograms (70 pounds) when fully grown. Adapted to hot, dry climates, they have a double coat of fleece that can be made into warm, waterproof, and durable woolen clothing. An adult miniature Brahman cow and her calf stand next to a Brahman of normal size, below. Though only one-fifth as heavy as the normal cow, a miniature Brahman provides two-thirds as much milk each day.

Sergio Dorantes—Sygma

Adult miniature pig weighs about 23 kilograms (50 pounds). Developed at Colorado State University by selectively breeding swine from Mexico's Yucatan Peninsula, the pigs are exceptionally docile and have proved useful in biomedical research.

Linda Panepinto

Promising microlivestock can also be found among other species. In Mexico, for example, researchers are creating "microcattle." In 1970 Juan Manuel Berruecos Villalobos, former director of the Veterinary Medicine School at the National Autonomous University of Mexico, became director of this enterprise. Berruecos and his colleagues deliberately miniaturized cows by selecting the smallest specimens out of a herd of humped Brahman cattle and breeding them with one another, generation after generation. After five generations the cows are only 60 centimeters (2 feet) tall and weigh just 140 kilograms (300 pounds). These animals—only one-fifth the weight of normal cattle—are shorter than the turkeys that share the barnyard with them and are so small that they get lost in the grassy pastures.

Berruecos believes that up to ten of the tiny cows can survive on the land needed to support one normal cow. He reports that they are giving remarkable amounts of milk: up to four liters (one gallon) a day, compared with six liters (1.5 gallons) from their full-sized counterparts. This program thus seems to have yielded a productive animal that can be cheaply and easily maintained in a small space.

Research on several varieties of Mexico's tiny pigs was also under way. Linda Panepinto of Colorado State University in 1977 began selectively breeding a miniature pig from the hot, arid Yucatan Peninsula, reducing the mature weight from 75 kilograms (165 pounds) to about 30 kilograms (66 pounds) in current generations. Her ultimate goal is a pig that gets no bigger than 20 kilograms (44 pounds). Its main use would be in laboratories, where its small size would make it cheaper and easier to maintain, but it has potential far beyond that. Panepinto reported that the miniature pig is intelligent, resistant to disease, odorless, and exceptionally docile. Even old boars and sows with piglets—which are fierce and unpredictable in normal-sized breeds—are as tame as household pets. For use in the third world, where women and children are often the keepers of the family animals, such pigs could be extremely valuable.

Guinea pigs

Miniature sheep, cattle, and pigs represent one aspect of microlivestock. There are also, however, dozens of other animals that never grow large and might also prove useful. Many people cannot conceive of them as farm animals, and the idea of eating them may seem repulsive. In parts of the world that do not have the traditions and prejudices of the West, however, they are, or could be, important resources. Guinea pigs are one example.

Some 7,000 years ago Indians of the high Andes Mountains in South America adopted wild cavies and found that these rodents (which are more closely related to porcupines than to rats or mice) were easy to raise, produced many offspring, and could be fed with table scraps and vegetable peelings. By the time the Spaniards arrived in the 1500s, the animal was a major food source from Argentina to the Caribbean. The invaders were impressed, and they introduced the "guinea pig" to Europe, where the little animals also were considered a suppertime delicacy. Within a century guinea pigs had begun appearing on tables throughout the Spanish Empire. Elsewhere they became house pets and laboratory animals. Even today in the Andes most Indians still eat guinea pigs. To celebrate special occasions they enjoy them fried like chicken or barbecued on wooden skewers. Peruvians alone eat an estimated 70 million guinea pigs each year.

Livestock scientists began studying guinea pigs when meat shortages became serious in Peru. In 1972, a time when beef was available only 15 days a month, researchers at the National Agrarian University near Lima began a guinea-pig-improvement project. They scoured the Peruvian countryside, gathering different kinds of guinea pigs—short-haired, long-haired, black, white, brown, and even purple. They bred together the biggest, meatiest ones, and the results were outstanding. The original animals averaged 750 grams (1.65 pounds) at maturity, but those resulting from the program weighed almost 2 kilograms (4.4 pounds). By the late 1980s these "super guinea pigs" were receiving international recognition. They are a new food animal with promise for the poor in much of the third world.

Other rodents

Guinea pigs are just one example of dozens of rodents that are commonly eaten. In many countries bush rats, squirrels, and porcupines are among the most eagerly sought and expensive meats. In colonial days in the United States squirrel meat was considered a treat. Thomas Jefferson enjoyed it, and Brunswick stew, the most famous dish to emerge from the cabins of colonial America, was originally made of it. Even today, squirrel is widely hunted for food in the United States.

Russell Kyle

Guinea pigs are raised on a ranch in Peru (above). When meat shortages became serious in Peru in the early 1970s, livestock scientists began a breeding program that increased the average size of an adult guinea pig from 750 grams (1.65 pounds) to almost 2 kilograms (4.4 pounds). Such "super guinea pigs" have become an important source of food in many parts of South America.

Victor Englebert

Photos, Oxford Scientific Films: (left) M. J. Coe; (right) © Partridge Films Ltd.; (bottom) © David Macdonald

Rodents are adaptable animals, and it seems probable that many would make suitable microlivestock. Some types reproduce prolifically, grow fast, learn quickly, and are precocious from birth. Most are not vermin and never live in filth. Like guinea pigs or rabbits, they live on grass and leaves and digest some fiber even though they have simple stomachs, like the human's. Among possible microlivestock candidates are the grasscutter, the paca, and the capybara.

The grasscutter is found in tropical savannas throughout sub-Saharan Africa. Except for its ratlike tail it looks somewhat like a beaver, and it feeds mostly on coarse, canelike grasses. It weighs up to 9 kilograms (20 pounds), and its meat is extremely popular. In a single year one local market in Ghana's capital city of Accra sold more than 15,000 animals—

Small animals that show promise as microlivestock include the grasscutter (above), a native of sub-Saharan Africa, and the paca (above right) from tropical forests in Central and South America. The meat of both tastes like pork. Capybaras (right), which can weigh as much as 50 kilograms (110 pounds), are raised for food in the hot, humid regions of South America, where cattle do not grow well.

representing 73 tons of meat. The deep red flesh is usually smoked before it is eaten and is said to resemble suckling pig. In West Africa it costs far more than beef, pork, or lamb. In Ghana, for example, an animal weighing four kilograms (nine pounds) can cost the equivalent of $75.

Although it is able to produce all the cereal grains its population needs, Ghana cannot satisfy its citizens' demand for meat. The government, therefore, is encouraging farmers to raise grasscutters in captivity. It provides breeding stock and information, and it maintains a central office for keeping records. Reportedly, the grasscutter is proving amenable to domestication. Researchers in countries near Ghana as well as in South Africa were also reporting early success in attempts to tame it.

The grasscutter is just one of the possibly domesticable field rodents that might help reduce the third world's chronic malnutrition. Throughout the tropics there are others. A Latin-American example is the paca, which is considered such a delicacy that in October 1985 it was served to Queen Elizabeth when she visited the Central American country of Belize.

Pacas live in dense forests throughout Central America and northern South America. They are the size of a large domestic cat, and their furry brown bodies have white streaks and spots. They weigh up to about 11 kilograms (24 pounds). People eagerly seek them because the white, tender meat tastes like pork. Selling for a higher price than beef, it is a special treat served in restaurants as well as at weddings and other celebrations.

The high esteem in which its meat is held has made the paca an endangered species in countries such as Costa Rica and Panama. Scientists are now trying to rebuild the population by learning how to raise pacas in captivity. If treated gently, young pacas quickly become tame; they undergo "imprinting," which is characteristic of most species that have been successfully domesticated. A paca that is imprinted to accept humans and captivity seeks people's company and voluntarily returns to its cage.

Zoologist Yolanda Matamoros of the National University in Heredia, Costa Rica, spent more than ten years studying paca husbandry. By 1988 under her supervision 50 farmers were maintaining pacas in small enclosures on their farms. Also, biologist Nicholas Smythe of the Smithsonian Institution, Washington, D.C., was studying the biology of pacas in Panama. If they could be domesticated successfully, Smythe said, pacas could produce as much protein in the wet tropics as do cattle.

Another gentle South American species, the capybara, has also been an object of domestication research. Weighing up to 50 kilograms (110 pounds), it is the world's largest rodent and looks like a giant guinea pig. Throughout much of the Americas its populations have been destroyed because people have prized it as food. One particular reason for this is that centuries ago Latin Americans petitioned the pope for special dispensation to eat capybara on the religious calendar's meatless days. Because the animal is semiaquatic (like a beaver), the pope allowed it to be ecclesiastically classified as a fish. Since that time it has been an

Mass production of rabbits is widespread in France, where in the late 1980s each person consumed an average of about 3 kilograms (6.6 pounds) of rabbit meat per year. Many less developed countries in Africa, Asia, and Latin America were beginning similar projects to produce rabbits on a large scale.

The blue duiker, a variety of antelope not much larger than a hare, is nearing extinction in parts of its native central and southern Africa because of its popularity as food for humans. Scientists are finding, however, that this animal is easy to raise and thus might prove to be an important source of meat in hot and humid regions.

© Leonard Lee Rue III—Animals Animals

important food. In Venezuela, for example, more than 400 tons of it are sold each year during the Easter period.

Living along the banks of rivers such as the Amazon and Orinoco, the capybara feeds on grasses and reeds that grow near water. A peaceable creature, it spends its days quietly resting on its haunches or lazily wallowing in muddy pools. When tame, it becomes so docile that in Suriname a blind man once used one as a guide "dog."

Attempts to domesticate the capybara are being made, particularly in Venezuela. In the 1970s researchers at the Central University in Maracay, for instance, started a breeding program using 20 females and 5 males. Through selection and management, they improved the rate of reproduction and hoped to obtain 16 offspring per year from each female. Venezuelan farmers already are "ranching" the hundreds of thousands of wild capybaras that are found on their lands. With the combination of the ranchers' practical management and the researchers' basic science, the animal seems on its way to becoming a domesticated species for use in the hot, humid regions of South America, where cattle grow poorly.

Rabbits

Domesticating a new species is extremely difficult, but in the last 100 years there have been successes with laboratory rats and mice, hamsters, gerbils, and chinchillas. Before that, the rabbit was the last major farm animal to be converted from the wild state.

The rabbit was domesticated in about AD 600, when the pope declared that rabbit embryos were "not meat." Within a few years monks in northern France had tamed the wild rabbit and were raising it inside their monasteries for use on holy days, when meat was prohibited. Later, commercial rabbit raising became well established throughout Europe. In the late 1980s the French were eating approximately 3 kilograms (6.6 pounds) of rabbit meat per person annually, and among barnyard animals France's rabbits provided half as much revenue as did chickens, ducks, and other poultry.

If such widespread rabbit production could be created in less developed nations, millions of malnourished people would eat well. By 1988 attempts to accomplish this were under way. The domestic rabbit, originally a native of Spain and Portugal, is inherently adapted to temperate climates. However, it is proving useful in the tropics, where most of the less developed countries are found. Indeed, in the late 1980s national rabbit programs had begun in many nations of Africa, Asia, and Latin America. For those where information was available, rabbit production almost doubled between the 1960s and the 1980s.

Ghana provides an example. In a response to the nation's meat shortage, the government organized "Operation Feed Yourself" in the 1970s. As part of this project, farmers were provided breeding stock and practical information on raising rabbits. Schools began teaching rabbit breeding and serving rabbit meat in school lunches. The government supported advertising campaigns, complete with jingles: "Grow rabbits— grow children!" and "Get into the rabbit habit!"

Other countries have mounted similar programs. In Mexico, for example, teachers train students to raise rabbits in rural schools, government officials breed rabbits in their homes, and army units raise rabbits as mess-hall substitutes for costly beef and pork. In Nigeria farmers buy rabbits from 18 government rabbit-breeding centers, which distribute thousands of animals each year.

Antelope and deer

Among undomesticated hoofed mammals, possible candidates for micro-livestock are various dwarf species of antelope and deer. The blue duiker is an example. Hardly bigger than a hare, this tiny creature is plummeting toward extinction in some areas of central and southern Africa because people like to eat it. If duikers can be raised successfully, both food and a way to rescue the animal from extinction would be provided.

Researchers in several countries have had good luck in raising duikers. The experiences of nutritionist Robert Cowan in his laboratories at Pennsylvania State University suggest that these animals are easy to maintain, produce well, and do not seem fussy about environmental conditions. In fact, they seem to enjoy living in cages—perhaps because they normally live in thick, thorny bush.

Few people know much about these tiny ruminants, which, even when fully grown, stand only about 36 centimeters (14 inches) high and weigh only 4 kilograms (9 pounds). Reportedly, they are nervous, shy, and nocturnal, but Cowan found that specimens raised by hand are tame and playful; he has even kept some indoors as house pets.

Blue duikers have a digestion efficiency similar to that of sheep, and Cowan and his colleagues began using them in digestion trials. Because the duikers are so small, a trial needs only 5 kilograms (11 pounds) of feed, whereas sheep would require 150 kilograms (330 pounds) and much larger facilities. This makes it cheaper and easier to perform experiments, and the research could result in a new species with widespread benefit to farmers in the duiker's native habitat, Africa's hot and humid heart.

The blue duiker is only one of Africa's dwarf antelope species. Suni, dikdik, royal antelope, and pygmy antelope might prove similarly adaptable, and in central Asia from Siberia to India, there is a similar-sized deer with notable promise. The musk deer is so small that a fully grown specimen reaches only a height of 50–60 centimeters (20–24 inches). Despite this small size, males produce one of the most valuable materials in the animal kingdom. Called musk, it is a thick oil secretion that is an ingredient in oriental medicines as well as in expensive European perfumes. In recent years it has sold for up to three times the price of gold.

To support this industry more than 20,000 male musk deer are slaughtered in the Himalayas each year. Unfortunately, thousands of females and fawns are also killed. (The sexes look alike from a distance, and the hunters kill both and sort out the males later.) This devastates the population. Females and fawns yield no musk, and their destruction is bringing the musk deer to the brink of extinction in several countries.

The musk deer, a native of central Asia, reaches a height when full grown of only 50–60 centimeters (20–24 inches). Because the male produces musk, an important ingredient in perfumes and medicines, many deer are slaughtered each year, and the breed is nearing extinction in many countries. To forestall this, farmers in China have begun to raise musk deer, and other countries are planning similar efforts.

207

Green iguanas, inhabitants of hot lowland forests from the southern United States to South America, are becoming endangered because people in those areas have prized their eggs (above) and meat. On a recently developed iguana farm in Panama, a captive-born iguana hatchling poses on the back of a captive-grown yearling (above right).

International bans on the sale of musk have done little to slow the trade. However, this diminutive animal might be saved if its husbandry can be perfected. Musk would then be obtained from formal farming operations and a regularized trade. Already the animal is being raised in a small way in China, where techniques for scooping out the musk without harming the animals have been developed. So far, the success has been modest because many specimens have not adapted to captivity. However, the experiments are continuing, and they have given cause for hope. Researchers in India, Nepal, and the United States are also beginning musk-deer research. Given an expanded international effort, these researchers think, the musk deer not only might be saved but could become one of the most valuable resources in the animal kingdom.

Iguanas

Microlivestock are by no means restricted to mammals. The large leaf-eating lizards called green iguanas are likely candidates, too. Throughout much of Latin America, for instance, they are a popular food. To fill the demand, they are hunted by rifle, slingshot, trap, and noose; they are even run down by trained dogs. Because of this human appetite for both the animal and its forest habitat, the green iguana population is disappearing. Twenty years ago some city markets stocked them by the hundreds; by 1988 they had few or none.

Weighing up to about 2 kilograms (4.4 pounds), these lizards have a greenish, scaly, dragonlike skin, as well as claws, spines, crests on the tail, and frills around the throat. They inhabit hot lowland forests from the southern United States to South America. Many Hispanic Americans willingly pay more for iguana meat than for fish, poultry, pork, or beef. It tastes somewhat like chicken and typically is cooked in spicy stews.

208

Iguana eggs are also prized. Small and leathery-shelled, they are said to cure various ailments.

In Panama, Smithsonian Tropical Research Institute biologist Dagmar Werner, in cooperation with the Panamanian government, demonstrated how to produce large numbers of these alert, curious, and social reptiles. Her research farm near the Panama Canal looks more like a poultry run than a cattle ranch. The whole facility covers roughly the area of a suburban residential lot. It contains pens made of bamboo and corrugated roofing iron (constructed in ways that can easily be duplicated by third world farmers). Inside the pens short lengths of bamboo are piled up to form "apartments," in which the lizards sleep. The whole is shaded by trees with thick branches, where the animals indulge in their favorite pastime—sunning.

Iguanas normally scamper up and down trees to feed on tender shoots in the treetops that few other herbivores can reach. In the wild nine out of ten iguanas are eaten by hawks and other predators before they are one year old, but on the farm almost all survive. They also grow well, more than doubling in length in six months. They are fed a "smorgasbord" of fresh-cut leaves and flowers.

Fortunately, despite their endangered status, iguanas reproduce well. Each female lays 30 or more eggs a year, and most of the eggs hatch. Thus, if the young ones are protected from predators during their first year, iguana populations can increase rapidly. After that they have no natural enemies, other than humans, and so their numbers can remain high.

In its most fundamental aspect the iguana-farming project demonstrates a way to keep the tropical forests standing and still providing their human inhabitants with an income. By farming an animal that lives in trees, people can benefit without cutting the forests down. It is an alternative to the current destruction of the jungle to create fields for crops or pastures for cattle.

Chickens forage in a farmyard in Costa Rica. Because they are comparatively small and easy to manage, chickens are among the most important sources of food in Asia, Africa, and Latin America.

David Thompson—Oxford Scientific Films

Poultry

Travelers in rural areas of the third world often see poultry scavenging around the villages. The widespread use of these birds shows how important small, easily managed household livestock can be to poor people. It confirms the importance of the microlivestock concept.

Small size, the ability to forage for themselves, and a natural inclination to stay around the house cause chickens to be among the most vital food resources of rural Asia, Africa, and Latin America. Scratching a living out of dirt, dust, ditches, and debris, these often scrawny creatures are a resource of huge importance. For the poorest of the poor, a bony bird may be the only type of meat eaten throughout a lifetime.

The chicken, however, is just one type of bird that researchers are considering as microlivestock for poor people. Others include pigeons and quail. To most people pigeons seem like pests, but in former times these hardy birds were mainstays of the human diet in Europe and Asia. They are still widely kept for food in North Africa and the Middle East. Most farmed pigeons are of the size commonly seen in cities, but a few large breeds weigh up to 1.4 kilograms (3 pounds), which is almost the size of chickens. Farmed pigeons are housed in towering dovecotes erected on roofs or in backyards. They forage widely, often ranging over many square kilometers to find seeds and edible scraps, yet they return home each night.

Pigeons produce squab (young pigeon), one of the tastiest of all meats. It is finely textured, is easily digested, and could be a major food source for many parts of the world. Donald Huss of the United Nations Food and Agriculture Organization in Santiago, Chile, is fostering pigeon-raising programs throughout Latin America.

Quail, too, are small and efficient and are suited to home rearing. Native to Asia and Europe, the domestic quail has been farmed since ancient times, especially in the Far East. This sparrow-sized bird can lay

210

Long raised commercially in Japan for their eggs (opposite page and left) and considered a delicacy for their meat in Europe, quail are now being introduced into less developed countries. Projects to grow the birds were begun in Mexico, India, and the Dominican Republic.

eggs when it is hardly more than five weeks old, and it may produce 400 or more eggs over the following two years. It is said that about 20 of these "lively little protein factories" are sufficient to keep an average family in eggs throughout a year. In a few countries quail are raised commercially in large numbers. In Japan, for example, quail eggs are a well-known food; stores offer them canned, pickled, or packed in plastic cases. Quail meat is also a delicacy in Europe, where more than 500 million of the tiny birds are consumed annually.

Sam Varghese of Michigan State University began a program to introduce quail to less developed countries. He started by getting children in 600 Michigan schools to raise the birds and has since begun projects in the Dominican Republic, Mexico, and India. In addition, a large corporation has been opened in Greensboro, Georgia, to provide 50,000 quail a day to U.S. supermarkets and restaurants. With such attention yet another microlivestock is being "rediscovered."

Conclusion

Scientists are beginning to open up a new agricultural frontier of lilliputian animals. Microlivestock may seem exotic, colorful, and, in some cases, repulsive, but in the future they could become important resources for third world nations. Because these animals are practical for production in areas where people are generally undernourished, they could eventually make a huge impact.

Microlivestock specialists see a bright future resulting from their work. Raising "mainframe" livestock, such as cattle, on open pastures will never get meat to the poorest people as effectively as raising small "personal" animals, such as guinea pigs, on weeds and table scraps in boxes under the bed. For millions of poor people the choice is not between large and small livestock but between microlivestock and no livestock at all.

211

The Self-destructing Book

Books throughout the world are decaying at an alarming rate,
placing in jeopardy much of the accumulation of human knowledge.

by John F. Dean

The invention of writing is possibly humankind's most significant
achievement, and the book has served as memory, becoming a vital
part of the building of knowledge, theories, and ideas disseminated over
space and time. It is difficult to conceive of a time when this steady
accumulation of knowledge could be interrupted, but there is clear evidence that our collective memory is being gradually destroyed and will,
like the dying of brain cells, render us incomplete. The materials on
which our writings are recorded are decaying at an alarming rate, and
the institutions charged with the preservation of the sum total of human
knowledge, libraries and archives, are waging a losing battle to prevent
it. Every day, irreplaceable books disappear. The Library of Congress
of the United States estimates that 25% of its collections are in brittle,
possibly unusable, condition and that many more are highly acidic, with
approximately 77,000 of them becoming brittle every year.

When paper becomes brittle, usually defined as the inability to withstand a single or double corner fold, the next use of a book may result
in its destruction. Libraries throughout the United States report the same
or worse rates of deterioration. Both Yale University and the University of Michigan have concluded that half of their Western European
literature collections are brittle. The situation in other countries is similarly discouraging.

Papyrus, parchment, and paper

The book as a portable, permanent container of information and knowledge appeared on clay tablets produced in Mesopotamia about 3000 BC.
About the same time, papyrus rolls began to be produced in Egypt. Papyrus provided a light, flexible writing material, consisting of thin strips
of the pithy center of the plant stalk laid into cross-plyed layers pressed
into sheets. At first, papyrus sheets were glued at the edge and made into
rolls for works of any length, but when the codex (the book form) was
developed in about the second century AD, papyrus was used in that form.

The limitations of strength of papyrus became more apparent as the
codex became more popular, and parchment gradually replaced it for
both rolls and codices. Parchment is made from the skins of calves,

sheep, and goats and has considerably more strength and durability than papyrus. One could write on both sides of the parchment, make erasures and corrections on it, and stitch it together in greater bulk than papyrus. Because of its long-term stability and permanence, scholars and librarians soon began to use parchment almost exclusively, and St. Jerome recorded that the damaged papyrus volumes in the library of Pamphilus of Caesarea were all replaced by parchment copies.

Parchment proved its worth over hundreds of years in the scriptorium, where manuscripts were laboriously copied, and it is not surprising that when paper was introduced into Europe in the early 12th century, it was regarded as a much inferior material. In 1494, some time after the invention of printing, Trithemius, abbot of a Benedictine monastery, noted somewhat scornfully: "If writing is inscribed on parchment it will last for a thousand years. But if on paper, how long will it last? Two hundred years would be a lot."

Paper is made by forming a felted mat of intertwining fibers, which is achieved by passing a liquid suspension of the fibers through a screen. When the water drains away, the sheet is removed from the screen and allowed to dry. The fibers are mainly cellulose (the basic structural component of plant cell walls), and the interaction of them with water creates the strength and flexibility characteristic of paper. The first paper was made from macerated tree bark, plants, and grass by the Chinese in AD 105, and sizing, a process of filling the paper surface to reduce the spread of ink, had been developed in China by AD 700. The Chinese first used gypsum as a size and then later rice starch and lichen glue, smoothing and polishing the surface of the paper with smooth stones to produce a stable finish.

Because of chemical degradation, the paper of the book shown above has deteriorated so much that merely turning the pages causes it to disintegrate. Books in this condition cannot withstand a single use.

JOHN F. DEAN is Conservation Librarian at the Cornell University Libraries, Ithaca, New York.

(Overleaf) Illustration by John Zielinski

214

The art of papermaking traveled from China to Korea and Japan and then to the Arab world, where rags were first used as the raw material for the fibers. An apparatus called the stamper began to be used to more effectively macerate the fibers to a pulp. Introduced into Spain by the Moors, papermaking then spread to Italy, and the first European watermark was used at Fabriano in 1282. By 1495 papermaking was practiced in France, Germany, Flanders, Poland, and England. Gelatin size was first used in 1337 and was produced as animal glue from hides, horns, and hooves. The finished paper sheet was dipped into the hot gelatin solution to impart a smooth and stable finish.

Effect of printing

The introduction of paper as an alternative to parchment does not seem to have had any significant effect on the number of books produced by hand. However, the invention of modern printing by Johannes Gutenberg about 1450 both promoted and was promoted by the more easily available paper. Although paper was still regarded with suspicion and distaste by many, the increased book production made possible by the printing press demanded that paper be used for printing. At first, the quality of paper was superb; the combination of linen rags, the absence of chemicals, the minimum of mechanical processing, and the abundance of clean water produced thousands of books still preserved in excellent condition. As the demand for more books increased, however, the quality of paper began to decrease, owing mostly to shortages of pure raw materials, advances in technology, and the increasing use of chemicals to speed up the manufacturing process. The rate of quality deterioration was quite slow at first but then began to accelerate, culminating in a final disastrous drop in the mid-19th century with the use of unpurified wood fiber.

Mechanical innovation was, at first, modest. Variations in stamper design did not significantly reduce fiber length, but sometime between 1630 and 1655 a machine known as the Hollander beater was developed

Engraving reveals the method of printing books in the mid-1500s. At that time the production of books was increasing rapidly.

to speed up the fiber-maceration process. The Hollander was a machine that circulated the fiber and water from a tub through a beater roller and grooved bedplate, chopping and macerating the rag into a pulp much more quickly. Although the Hollander performed the necessary pulping much faster than did the stamper, it resulted in shorter fiber length, which reduced paper strength; also, some versions of the machine used iron parts that released minute metal particles into the paper.

As noted, gelatin was the principal material used for sizing. About the middle of the 17th century, alum (aluminum potassium sulfate) was described in the literature as an additive to gelatin. There is evidence that alum had been used somewhat earlier. England's first papermaker, John Tate (active after 1496), may have used alum, as his watermark bears a striking resemblance to the Greek symbols for that substance. William Barrow, a pioneer researcher into the cause and prevention of paper deterioration, noted that almost 25% of the 16th-century books tested by him contained alum.

Long used in dyeing textiles, alum was added to gelatin size to make it less viscous, to inhibit the putrification of the gelatin in the tub, and to harden the size and thereby improve the gelatin's resistance to blurring by ink when it is used on the paper. Alum is a type of double salt, usually consisting of aluminum sulfate, water of hydration, and the sulfate of another element. Aluminum potassium sulfate is water soluble and acidic when dissolved. For many papermakers alum became a cure-all, despite evidence that excessive amounts of it caused high acidity that led to serious paper deterioration. Alum can react with chlorides to form aluminum chloride, which, in combination with elevated levels of heat and moisture, will form hydrochloric acid, one of the acids most damaging to cellulose. Barrow's studies indicated that papers produced in the second half of the 17th century were 16 times more acidic than those produced in the first half and that the paper strength (determined by fold endurance) had diminished by two-thirds. He attributed this drastic increase in acidity to the increased presence of alum, and the reduction of strength possibly to the introduction of the Hollander beater. An additional factor was the decreasing level of carbonates in the paper. Carbonates are alkaline substances that tend to counteract acids. The water sources used by early papermakers frequently contributed dissolved limestone, a form of calcium carbonate; also, lime and milk that were used to ferment rags prior to beating also contributed calcium. Barrow found that 24% of 16th-century papers tested contained carbonates, while only 7% of 17th-century papers showed traces of them.

During the 18th century the Hollander beater was being used throughout Europe, and its greater efficiency at reducing rag to pulp suggests that the fermentation process, which incorporated the use of lime, was probably much reduced or even eliminated. Greatly increased demand for rags resulted in scarcity, and in England the Burying in Woollen Act, in force from 1666 to 1814, prohibited the use of any material but wool to be used for burial shrouds. Although the act was originally intended to help the woolen trade, it has been estimated that its effect

was to save 113,500 kilograms (250,000 pounds) of rag per year. In 1800 England used 11 million kilograms (24 million pounds) of rags for papermaking, 2.8 million kilograms (6.3 million pounds) of which were imported from Europe.

Various methods of bleaching were attempted to make the use of colored rags possible, and for a time sulfuric acid was used, with disastrous consequences. When chlorine was discovered by Carl Wilhelm Scheele in 1774, it proved an effective bleach and, although criticized for weakening paper, became a standard treatment. Early use of chlorine seems to have been experimental and crude. Thomas Hansard reported that early in the 19th century it "was not at all an uncommon occurrence for a parcel of paper to become so completely perished from the circumstances of its not having been thoroughly washed after bleaching, that an entire ream, composed of 480 sheets, might be readily snapped asunder as a piece of rotten wood."

In the early years of the 19th century Henry and Sealey Fourdrinier built the first practical papermaking machine at Frogmore, England; it increased the speed of paper production tenfold. In 1814 the first powered printing press produced *The Times* newspaper with an increase in impression rate from 250 sheets per hour on the old hand press to 1,100 sheets per hour on the new steam press.

The enormous increase in print production and literacy in the early 1800s led to a surge in demand for books, which resulted in a continued decline in paper quality, and by 1823 the Fourdrinier machine had been joined by 34 others like it in England alone. The machine-made paper could be made with shorter, weaker fibers than could the handmade, and many of the laborious hand processes for drying had become impractical. Although alum had contributed to the degradation of gelatin size, gelatin was still basically sound and stable.

Early in the 19th century Moritz Illig developed a size composed of rosin and alum that, because of its low cost and ease of use, virtually replaced gelatin sizing. The size was made by dissolving rosin (an organic acid obtained from wood) in an alkali, mixing it with the paper fibers in a tub (engine sizing), and precipitating it by the addition of alum, creating aluminum rosinate. The process became widely accepted by papermakers and is still the most widely used size today. However, the method creates an extremely acidic environment in the paper, and Barrow noted that it "contributed more to the deterioration of paper than any other development in papermaking of the 19th century." The size was further degraded by the substitution of "papermaker's alum" for aluminum potassium sulfate in order to reduce cost. Papermaker's alum, or aluminum sulfate, is made by treating bauxite with sulfuric acid; the resultant "alum" tends to contain residual sulfuric acid, increasing the acid components even more.

The search for alternative fibers received a boost in 1851 with the invention of the soda process, which uses caustic soda to help separate cellulose fibers from wood. About 20 years later the sulfite process, which uses calcium bisulfide, and the sulfate process, which uses sodium sulfide, were developed. The practical use of wood as a papermaking fiber brought about a dramatic change in manufacturing processes and fathered the present industry. Although chemical wood pulp represented a sharp decline in fiber strength, it was to decline much more with the development in the 1860s of groundwood, or mechanical, pulp. Groundwood pulp does not rely on chemical processing in its initial stages, as it is made by grinding wooden billets against a wheel to produce an extremely short-fibered pulp containing lignin, a natural substance occurring in plants that oxidizes readily. Although lignin is largely eliminated in the chemical pulp process, it remains in the groundwood process and further contributes to the degradation of the paper. Mechanical wood pulp is today commonly used to produce newsprint, but it has often been used to produce works of more lasting value, particularly in third world countries.

Cartoon from the War of 1812 (right) was restored (opposite page) by treatment with a dilute sodium borohydride solution. Great care must be taken with such solutions, however, because of their tendency to cause soluble inks to bleed.

Early investigations

As previously noted, disintegrating paper had been remarked upon soon after the introduction of chlorine bleaching and alum and alum-rosin sizing. However, most early scientific investigation tended to minimize the role of acidity as the chief culprit, possibly because the new sizing methods had become so firmly entrenched in the industry. Because the worst paper was produced after 1850, most of the investigations and reports tended to consider rag substitutes and industrial pollution as the main causes of the problem rather than as contributory factors. An early researcher into the chemical deterioration of paper was John Murray, a lecturer in chemistry. In his *Practical Remarks on Modern Paper*, published in 1829, Murray noted that his 13-year-old Bible, which was "crumbling literally into dust," contained chloride and the alum size. Murray used a tincture of litmus as an aid to the detection of chlorine.

After Murray a number of committees and commissioned researchers studied the problem, and an important breakthrough occurred in 1925 when a new method was developed for determining the acidity of paper. In 1928 Royal Rasch reported to the U.S. Bureau of Standards that, because alpha cellulose is present in rag and chemical wood pulp, purified wood pulp could be equal to rag in long-term stability. In 1901 Edwin Sutermeister recommended that paper be made with an alkaline filler, calcium carbonate, to neutralize the acidity and provide long-term stability. William Barrow's investigations, beginning in the 1930s, took the work of Sutermeister and others further, particularly in applying their research to the restoration of paper. Barrow developed a deacidification system to neutralize acidity and to add an alkaline reserve to buffer the paper against future acid absorption. A further benefit of Barrow's work was the development, in the 1960s, of his specifications for an inexpensive permanent/durable paper made from purified wood pulp. Both Barrow's deacidification system and his permanent/durable paper have provided the foundation for modern conservation/preservation practice.

Photos, Charles Harrington, Conservation Department, Cornell University

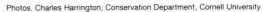

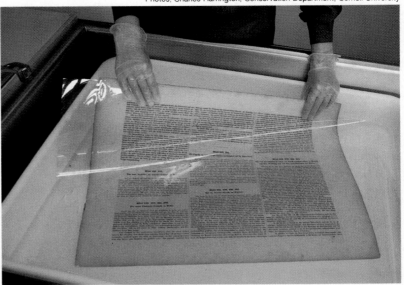

Addressing the problem

As may be gathered from the foregoing remarks, the problem of deteriorating paper is complex, massive, and apparently growing. In a general sense the solution lies in three main areas: the promotion of permanent/durable paper at competitive cost and willingness by publishers to use it; the further development of conservation as both an art and a science to carry on the work of restoration with increased speed and rigor; and the replacement by reformatting of the millions of brittle works.

During the last several years various attempts have been made by interested organizations to persuade the publishing trade and papermaking industry to produce books on permanent/durable paper. Although some companies were by 1988 producing such paper and some publishers were using it (notably university presses), the percentage of alkaline papers produced in the United States remained lamentably small—15%, as compared with Europe's 50%. Although alkaline paper costs no more to produce than acid paper, it would require paper manufacturers to spend considerable amounts of money to retool their plants and, in an industry that produced only 2% of its output for books, there seemed little economic incentive to do so. Ultimately, only the consumer has the power to effect change in the industry, and thus far there seemed to be little public concern.

The conservation of books and documents is based on ancient craft traditions concerned largely with immediate practicability rather than on long-term stability. Since the late 1960s, however, the art and craft of document repair and bookbinding have become greatly influenced by a more scientific and judicious approach. The instability of previous treatments has given way to methods that are much more stable. Basic to most treatments is stabilization of the paper by deacidification or alkalization. When practical, most conservators prefer aqueous treatments—thoroughly washing the paper to remove soluble acids and then

An old sheet of printed paper undergoes washing and alkalization (deacidification) in a solution. As soil and water-soluble acids are washed out of the paper, the water becomes discolored.

220

stabilizing it with an alkaline solution. The original Barrow "two-step" method involves immersion in a calcium hydroxide solution followed by a calcium bicarbonate bath, but many conservators in the United States today seem to prefer a single magnesium bicarbonate solution. In Europe a single bath of calcium hydroxide is used by many conservators, who maintain that magnesium bicarbonate both weakens and yellows the paper; however, some conservators are uncomfortable with the high level of alkalinity and possible ink-fading effects of calcium hydroxide.

Other nonaqueous processes were developed with varying degrees of success. Both Barrow and A. D. Baynes-Cope of the British Museum Research Laboratory worked on processes involving ammonia and volatile amines before discovering that the deacidifying effects were only temporary. Similarly, the development by W. H. Langwell of a chemically impregnated tissue paper based on cyclohexyl amine carbonate was found to be temporary in its effect. A breakthrough came with the development of Richard Smith's magnesium methoxide solution and George Kelly and John Williams's methyl magnesium carbonate solution. The Smith process was successfully commercialized.

No matter what solution is used, it should be remembered that deacidification serves only to stabilize the paper chemically. Thus, if the paper is brittle and weak before treatment, it will remain so afterward. In the past, various techniques for strengthening brittle paper were used; they generally consisted of adhering various materials to the paper. For many years a fine silk was pasted onto the paper, but this gradually gave way to cellulose acetate lamination applied by a heated press. Barrow devised a heated rotary press and incorporated thin transparent tissue paper both to speed up the process and to further support the paper. Many conservators today prefer to use polyester encapsulation, which involves sandwiching the document between sheets of thin polyester film and sealing the resultant package only around the edge, thus rendering the process completely reversible. These techniques, however, have been

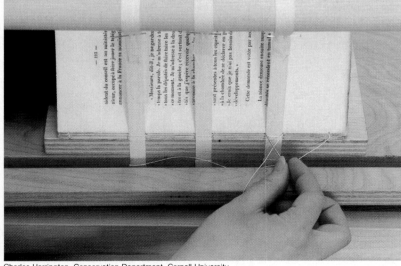

Charles Harrington, Conservation Department, Cornell University

After washing, deacidification, and any other necessary repairs, books are hand sewn onto linen tapes prior to rebinding. This process cannot be performed when paper is fragile.

An ultrasonic polyester welder is used to encapsulate deteriorated manuscripts (above). The manuscripts are first stabilized by deacidification and then are sandwiched between sheets of polyester. Such encapsulated manuscripts (above right) may be safely handled without damage; the process is completely reversible because the polyester is welded only around the edges.

developed for single items of high value, and they seem irrelevant to the main problem, which is the mass treatment of large numbers of bound volumes.

To deal with these bound volumes, mass deacidification has been discussed by conservators, librarians, archivists, and scientists since the 1960s. Most have agreed that, to be fully acceptable, mass deacidification must chemically stabilize book paper without damage to the book's components, be capable of processing large numbers of books in a short time cycle, have a low unit cost, and be safe to operate and environmentally sound. A number of processes for achieving these ends were developed, with varying degrees of success. In the late 1950s and early 1960s in the Soviet Union some success with ammonia gas was reported, but information on the methods is sparse. A promising process was that developed at the Barrow Research Laboratory between 1970 and 1977. It employed morpholine (an organic liquid commonly used as a solvent in cleaning solutions) in combination with water vapor in a vacuum chamber. Although the morpholine process seemed to satisfy some of the criteria, books treated in this way reverted to an acid state in the presence of high relative humidity.

A process that has been operating successfully since 1981 is Smith's magnesium methoxide system, installed in the records conservation department of Canada's Public Archives and National Library. The process involves drying books in a vacuum dryer, deacidifying them with the solvent solution in a process tank, and vacuum drying to remove the solvent. A drawback is the need to presort books prior to treatment to avoid processing those with soluble inks, dyes, and bookcloths. In 1976 Kelly and Williams of the U.S. Library of Congress designed a vapor-phase process employing diethyl zinc (DEZ). An organometallic compound, DEZ successfully deacidifies the paper, leaving in it an alkaline reserve of zinc oxide. Treatment must be carried out in an atmosphere from which all air and moisture have been excluded, as DEZ ignites on contact with air and explodes on contact with moisture. This inherent instability has retarded full development of the process. After some experiments at General Electric's Space Center in Valley Forge, Pennsylvania, 5,000 books were treated at the Goddard Space Flight Center in Maryland. Although the treatments yielded mixed results, a pilot plant was developed. Unfortunately, a fire broke out during the first dry run in the pilot plant, followed by another fire when the process was restarted. A new pilot plant at Houston, Texas, was scheduled to begin operations soon under the direction of Texas Alkyls Corp., and a full-scale plant was to be built at Frederick, Maryland.

Some investigations into the mass strengthening of paper were also under way. Bruce Humphries of the Nova Tran Corp. successfully employed parylene, a coating used for protecting electronic equipment from moisture. It permeates the paper and substantially improves fold endurance, but the high cost of parylene treatment makes the process impractical on a large scale. The British Library began constructing a plant to strengthen paper by a graft copolymerization process, a method that seemed promising.

At the present time the most effective way to preserve information is to replace brittle books with microfilm. Microfilming programs have been under way for many years, and the experience that libraries have gained has led to stringent processing and storage standards. Because microfilming lends itself to a cooperative preservation approach among

Microfilm is inspected for quality and durability. At present the most effective method of preserving information is to replace brittle books with microfilm. Because brittle materials are often destroyed as a result of the filming, it is important that the microfilm last as long as posssible.

Courtesy of the Johns Hopkins University

libraries, various library groups have developed programs designed to reduce duplicative effort and establish national priorities. The Council on Library Resources, under the direction of Warren J. Haas, was particularly active in alerting the nation to the preservation crisis, and Haas's efforts led to the establishment of the Commission on Preservation and Access. The commission was charged with encouraging the development of a national preservation program and with helping to generate the necessary funding. New technologies, such as the optical disc, seemed to offer some promise for the future, but until fully developed and proved stable, their use as preservation tools would be largely experimental.

Role of environment

Much of the early investigations of paper deterioration placed a great deal of blame on the environment, particularly on the use of coal gas for illumination. In 1919 J. A. Chapman demonstrated the rapid deterioration of books stored in the hot and humid regions of India as compared with other copies of the same works stored in northern India and England. Other studies confirmed Chapman's findings, and there is little doubt that high temperatures, high levels of relative humidity, and air pollution greatly accelerate the degradation of books. There is strong evidence that the atmosphere in a badly polluted city can lower the fold endurance of paper by as much as 15% in ten days, chiefly because of concentrations of sulfur dioxide.

The most damaging substances are either acidic or oxidizing; thus, sulfur dioxide, the oxides of nitrogen, and ozone are foremost in their harmful effects. Such gases are absorbed by library materials and accelerate deterioration. For example, sulfur dioxide interacts with impurities in paper to oxidize as sulfur trioxide, which, combined with moisture, produces sulfuric acid. Particulate matter, such as ash, soot, dust, and pollen, soils book and shelf surfaces and, if relative humidity is high, provides nutrients for mold growth.

Exposure to high temperatures, even for a short period, can cause most papers to yellow and become brittle, and exposure to moderate heat for a long period has the same effect. For every increase of 6° C (11° F), the life of paper is halved; thus, a book produced on wood pulp paper that would last 100 years if maintained at 20° C (68° F) would be too brittle for normal use in 25 years if kept at 31° C (88° F). Inconsistent or cycling levels of temperature and relative humidity are also damaging. For example, if the temperature in a library varies drastically over a 24-hour period, the books will be at a higher or lower temperature than the room; thus, the "object" humidity (the relative humidity of the air immediately surrounding the books) can be considerably higher than the measured ambient relative humidity.

Light, too, can be quite damaging, mainly because of ultraviolet radiation. Too much exposure causes fading and yellowing and further weakens fibers. The optimum environment for a library in which readers interact with books would be 20°–21° C (68°–70° F), 45–50% relative humidity, an air-conditioning system capable of filtering gaseous substances, screened or filtered windows, and ultraviolet-filtered lights.

Future prospects

Although the prospects for preservation seem bleak, much progress has been made since the late 1960s. More is known about the causes of deterioration and the scope of the problem. In the United States in particular, cooperation among the major research libraries has grown into a nationwide effort. More of everything will be needed if the loss of knowledge is to be arrested, however—more cooperation, particularly on an international level; more central funding in recognition that the problem is indeed universal; more research to produce alternative preservation technologies; more preservation/conservation specialists; and more public awareness that the memory of humankind is at risk.

FOR ADDITIONAL READING

B. L. Browning. "The Nature of Paper," *Library Quarterly* (January 1970, pp. 18–38).

J. Shahani Chandru and William K. Wilson, "Preservation of Libraries and Archives." *American Scientist* (May–June 1987, pp. 240–251).

Verner W. Clapp, "The Story of Permanent/Durable Book Paper 1115–1970," *Restaurator* (1972, pp. 1–51).

George Martin Cunha and Dorothy Grant Cunha, *Library and Archives Conservation: 1980s and Beyond*, vol. 1 and 2 (1983).

Carl J. Wessel, "Environmental Factors Affecting the Permanence of Library Materials," *Library Quarterly* (January 1970, pp. 39–84).

John C. Williams, "A Review of Paper Quality and Paper Chemistry," *Library Trends* (Fall 1981, pp. 203–224).

Volunteers for Science

by Theodore L. Reid

Every year members of the public eagerly pay for the chance
to spend their summer vacations participating in field research.
In return they experience adventure, a sense of accomplishment,
and a unique appreciation for scientists and their work.

The idea that members of the public could help scientists with field
research had its start in Great Britain during the late 19th century. It
was at that time, in the early period of the Darwinian revolution, that
excitement and debate raged concerning evolution and its implications
for beliefs then held in both science and religion. In the late 1940s, as
the new state of Israel was being established, a similar public interest in
a better understanding of the history of that biblical region encouraged
volunteers to participate in field research there. In the U.S., particularly
within the past 15 years, the idea of nonscientist participation in field
research has grown such that a number of opportunities in a broad spectrum of scientific disciplines now exists. For the most part, participants
pay their own transportation costs plus a fee that covers a proportionate
amount of the overall costs of the field activities. In return, they become
active members of the research team—in excavation, sample collection,
observation of animal behavior, or whatever tasks constitute the research
program. In this manner members of the public engage in interesting
and worthwhile scientific endeavors while at the same time providing
financial support for them.

Two organizations in particular have developed extensive networks
of field-research support based on this model: Earthwatch, located in
Watertown, Massachusetts, near Boston, and the University Research
Expeditions Program (UREP), headquartered at the University of California at Berkeley. Both serve research at field sites throughout the U.S.
and worldwide. The extensive spectrum of disciplines covers all of the
sciences that lend themselves to fieldwork, together with many of the
social sciences and humanities. Earthwatch project leaders come from
research institutions throughout the country; their projects are selected
for Earthwatch support by a system of peer review. UREP projects are
similarly chosen, with the project leaders being drawn from institutions
in the University of California system. Opportunities for volunteers to
participate, together with descriptions of the various projects, are ad-
vertised nationwide by both organizations. Most projects are conducted
during the summer months and are usually for a two-week period. Fees
range from several hundred to several thousand dollars per person. On a

THEODORE L. REID is Associate Program
Director, Office of Undergraduate
Science, Engineering, and Mathematics
Education, National Science Foundation,
Washington, D.C.

(Opposite page) An orphaned orangutan
is given a drink by one of the 100
volunteers who participate yearly in a
project supported by Earthwatch and
the Indonesian government to observe
orangutan behavior patterns. Infant
orangutans are usually cared for by their
mothers for the first six years of life.
Photo, Earthwatch

226

smaller scale, many colleges and universities throughout the U.S. operate their own field stations, where research is conducted on a regular basis and where public participation is sometimes possible.

Giving and receiving

What kinds of people are moved to become scientific volunteers? All of them share certain characteristics: an interest in travel; experience in "roughing it," or at least a willingness to do so, since many of the sites are remote; a natural curiosity; and the ability to work productively as a member of a team. A background in science, although helpful, is not a necessary prerequisite.

Other characteristics are more varied. In an analysis provided by UREP of the participants in its 1987 program, about one-third were male and two-thirds female. Age distribution included all segments from under 25 to over 65, with the segments between 36 and 65 being somewhat larger, although the fraction above 65 was not insignificant. Educational background ranged from high school to advanced degrees, with those holding the baccalaureate or master's degree making up the largest groups. Occupations of the participants ranged broadly and included education, the professions, management and business, medicine, technical and clerical fields, and the arts. A significant number of participants were retired.

For volunteer-dependent field expeditions to succeed, there must be an appropriate symbiosis between the scientific objectives of the projects and the needs and desires of the participants. On the one hand, the experience in some way should be "worthwhile" for the participants, although a poll asking "Was it worthwhile, and why?" would probably elicit nearly as many answers as the number polled. In a more specific sense the experience should be educationally broadening, and a large majority of exit interviews indicate that it has been. On the other hand, interviews with project leaders document that volunteers generally perform effectively in the pursuit of science, functioning not just as another pair of hands but as true members of the research team.

Earthwatch volunteers (above) measure a female sea turtle during egg laying as part of an award-winning project to save the endangered reptiles in the Caribbean Sea. Sea turtle eggs are carefully excavated from the nest built by the mother (opposite page, left). Because the females sometimes plant their eggs directly in the path of beach erosion, volunteers replant the eggs in a safer spot on the beach to improve the hatchlings' chances of survival. Volunteer (opposite page, right) examines a new member of the species her team is working to rescue.

Education and more

To expand on the educational aspects of being field-research volunteers, both UREP and Earthwatch in recent years have solicited financial support from a variety of sources—for example, the U.S. National Science Foundation, other government agencies, business and industry, and private foundations—to allow high school teachers and, to some extent, high school students to participate in these projects. It was felt that such opportunities, which most teachers and students could not afford from their own resources, would benefit science education in a unique way. The effort has proved successful. Many projects now include several teachers or students, whose contributions to field research equal and sometimes surpass those of the regular participants. One of the expected benefits to participating teachers is improvement in their own teaching. To that end teachers are encouraged to develop local field activities for their students, to meet periodically to share ideas, and eventually to produce improved teaching materials. Preliminary information suggests that these objectives are being met.

That these projects have the potential to benefit much more than research is readily illustrated. Earthwatch received the U.S. Department of the Interior's 1987 Conservation Service Award for its extensive, long-term fieldwork in support of efforts to save endangered sea turtles on the Caribbean islands of Saint Croix and Culebra. A noteworthy example from UREP's experience is its effort to develop expeditions known by the acronym SHARE, or Science to Serve Humanity and Research for the Environment. SHARE projects, which are developed in cooperation with

229

UREP team members test well water in northern Kenya in a project aimed at developing new water resources for an arid environment. Local desertification being caused in part by herders and their animals camping semipermanently near existing sources of water might be halted or even reversed if a more extensive network of low-cost wells could be established.

scientists of the host country, emphasize research that can be applied to improving people's lives and preserving the Earth's resources. In the description of UREP's 1988 projects, seven SHARE projects are listed.

Personal experiences

In the summer of 1986 I participated personally in two UREP expeditions in East Africa. One, located in the arid regions of northern Kenya, was directed by Robert Matthews of the University of California at Davis and involved a study of water resources, focusing particularly on the distribution and source of native wells. The other project, in central Tanzania, was designed to document the life-style of a culture in transition—that of the Barabaig, traditional pastoralists who are distantly related to the Masai. Both projects included teachers as volunteers.

Trained as a chemist and with 20 years' government service, I was interested in broadening my experience—a desire that was certainly fulfilled. In Kenya, in addition to receiving practical education in hydrology and geology, I had the opportunity to interact with the local people, the nomadic Rendille. Still following a traditional life-style, the Rendille depend on their herds of goats, sheep, and camels for most of the necessities of existence. Desertification is becoming a serious problem in the region as a consequence of overgrazing brought about, in part, by the Rendille and their herds camping semipermanently near sources of water. If a more extensive network of low-cost, native-built and native-maintained wells could be established, local desertification might be halted or even reversed. Our project was involved in a preliminary collection of data to be used toward those ends. Language was not a serious problem; we were assisted by Simon Karaba, a Rendille whose job in that region is the equivalent of that of a county commissioner in the U.S. A blend of the modern and the traditional, Karaba served as guide, interpreter, and focus for entry into Rendille society. A highlight of my time there was a goat feast organized by Karaba at which the Rendille acted as host.

The expedition in Tanzania, which emphasized sociology and anthropology, is an example of a SHARE project. The coleaders were Jean Colvin, director of UREP, and Vedasto Mbanga, senior curator of the National Museums of Tanzania in Dar es Salaam. In its transition from a pastoral society to one in which some farming is involved, the traditional life-style of the Barabaig is undergoing change, and the skills needed for producing many of their traditional artifacts are no longer as necessary as they once were. Our task was to document these changes by means of interviews and inventories of household effects. To record and save examples of their traditional artifacts, which include intricate beadwork on leather, pottery and gourd containers, copper and brass jewelry, and spearheads and knives, we made museum collections, often by barter, for the National Museums of Tanzania and for a museum at the University of California at Los Angeles.

The opportunities that these activities gave me to interact on a personal basis with the Barabaig were enlightening. Although farming is becoming an important part of their life, real "wealth" is still measured in numbers of cattle and goats. Their farming practices are quite sophisticated, involving irrigation from a nearby river. Crops include beans, sweet potatoes, corn, and onions, with onions the important cash crop. As in the Kenya project, language problems were minimal, since Mbanga was, of course, fluent in Swahili, which most of the younger Barabaig spoke. A local Lutheran minister, the Rev. Samuel Slaa, who is a native of the region and fluent in Barabaig, agreed to be an adviser to

Jean Heilbron—UREP

Traditional metalworking techniques of the Barabaig of Tanzania are documented by a UREP volunteer participating in a SHARE project to record the changes taking place in a people undergoing a transition in life-style.

the project and functioned as interpreter for the older people who spoke only their native tongue.

One other UREP project, which seems fascinating although I was not a participant, involved a study of carnivals in several cultural milieus. The parades, masquerades, pageants, and other forms of revelry that accompany these traditional festivals have their roots in ancient pagan rites that celebrated life's springtime renewal and are deeply ingrained with the superstitions and folklore of pre-Christian times. What is now a pre-Lenten celebration prior to a solemn season of fasting has been studied in several places by UREP so the effect of the local culture on the nature of the celebration can be examined. To date, research has included carnival in Rio de Janeiro, Brazil, where the culture is a blend of African and Portuguese; carnival in Goa, India, where the culture combines Portuguese and Indian influences; and carnival in the Spanish Canary Islands.

Alan McClellan, who recently joined the National Science Foundation after a long career with the Du Pont Co., provided the following examples of his Earthwatch project experiences.

On a study of the species diversity of coral reefs off the island of Carriacou in the Caribbean, the expedition leader, marine biologist Mel Goodwin, first spent two days instructing his volunteers on the identification of the 35 varieties of hard coral found there. The balance of the two weeks was devoted to wading, snorkeling, and scuba diving on reefs, collecting information on the distribution of species.

Another Earthwatch project, part of a larger study directed by Louis Herman of the University of Hawaii, involved identification of individual humpback whales in the inner passage of Alaska to allow scientists to determine migration and behavior patterns of the species. The white

Earthwatch divers scout the underwater area surrounding the world's second largest coral reef, off the coast of Carriebow Cay, Belize. The aim of the project is to catalog the numerous types of algae growing on the reef.

Earthwatch

markings on the bottom of the tail flukes constitute a unique "finger-print" for each individual. The task of the group was to follow the whales in small boats as they dived for food, photograph their tails, and record their actions. The photographs were added to a master file serving whale biologists throughout the northern Pacific Ocean, allowing estimates of the number of whales and their migration routes.

A third project, under the direction of Jefferson MacKinnon of the University of Wisconsin, involved archaeological excavations in Belize of Mayan village sites on the shore and on offshore islands. This work has since helped clarify the role of sea-oriented Mayan populations, which had received little previous attention primarily because they did not construct large stone ceremonial buildings at the shore sites. Earthwatch projects, however, located a previously unknown ceremonial site 29 kilo-meters (18 miles) in from the coast, the closest to the sea of any known ceremonial site from the Mayan Classic period or earlier. Excavations of that site currently under way should further integrate the shore people into the total picture of Mayan civilization.

Upcoming projects
Brief descriptions of a selection of projects for 1988, abstracted from UREP and Earthwatch publications, offer further insight into their vari-ety and geographic distribution.

UREP volunteers will study Patagonian wildlife in the Lihue Calel National Park in Argentina, making observations of bird and mammal habitats. Changes since the previous year in the population of viscacha, a rabbit-sized cousin of the chinchilla, will be determined. Volunteers will help map and survey viscacha habitats and capture and mark animals to determine changes in colony membership and the status of the popula-

Earthwatch volunteers working off the Alaskan coast wait for the opportunity to photograph the tail flukes of a humpback whale as it dives for food. The white markings on the bottom of the flukes serve as a unique "fingerprint" for each individual, thereby allowing estimates to be made of whale numbers and migration routes.

Larry Kolczak—Earthwatch

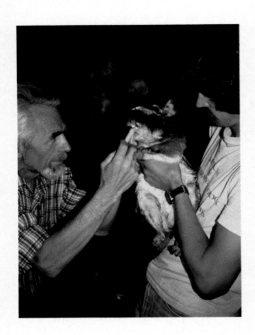

UREP participants (above) examine a viscacha, a relative of the chinchilla, in an ongoing study of the rodent's colony populations and habitats in Lihue Calel National Park, Argentina. (Below) In another multiyear UREP project, a volunteer observes mother-pup interactions of sea lions on Kangaroo Island, Australia.

(Top) Lyn Branch—UREP; (bottom) Leslie Higgins—UREP

tion. Viscachas are nocturnal, so much of the work with them will occur at night, while surveys of other animals will take place during the day.

Another UREP team will continue behavioral studies of the Australian sea lion, particularly mother-pup interactions, begun by a UREP team in 1987. In addition, the current team will investigate male territoriality and breeding behavior. Among questions the fieldwork will address are the kind and amount of maternal investment; the amount of time females spend on land, at sea, and with pups; and the pups' growth rates. Team volunteers will assist in marking and then observing and documenting selected mothers and pups in their various daily activities. Radio transmitters will be attached to certain animals as a means of tracking female attendance patterns with the pups.

The ancient rock art of Hawaii will be documented by a UREP team at sites on the island of Lanai, an unspoiled remnant of the "old Hawaii." The fieldwork will complement a five-year study of Easter Island rock art as a comparative investigation of common origins and religious concepts in Polynesia. Volunteers will assist in locating and mapping sites, making scale drawings of all art found, measuring and noting the orientation of all designs, and then photographing them.

Pursuing a more contemporary aspect of culture, a UREP team will investigate jazz music in Puerto Rico, in response to increasing evidence that the seeds of innovative jazz styles, different from those in the U.S., are blossoming in Puerto Rico (and elsewhere in the world), being shaped by the people and cultures unique to each region. Participants will document the blending of jazz with other musical forms and the innovative approaches to jazz performance as it moves from place to place. They will help conduct interviews with musicians, academicians, and students; document performances by means of photography and video and audio recordings; and search libraries for books on jazz and printed jazz music.

A UREP SHARE project in Morocco will study sheep flocks in various parts of that country. Team members will record data on flock numbers

and breed characteristics and will weigh and grade fleece in order to provide information on wool production of breeds of sheep in different areas. In addition, blood samples will be collected from sheep in order to help map selenium deficiency in various regions.

In another SHARE project, a UREP team will provide medical and dental care to inhabitants along the Amazon River in isolated regions of the forest. Participants will observe and note health-related behavior, including dietary patterns, oral health habits, and traditional treatments. In addition, they will investigate the influence of environmental factors and changes in diet on the blood pressure of village inhabitants. Patients from the villages will receive dental exams and care and participate in the blood pressure study on a voluntary basis. UREP volunteers will be trained in instrument-sterilization techniques, the recording of information about patients, and basic screening techniques. Licensed medical professionals, including doctors, dentists, dental hygienists, and nurses, will have an opportunity to participate in clinical activities.

As a final example of a SHARE project, a team will continue the reconnaissance work of earlier UREP teams in contributing to the eventual designation of the region known as Lomas Barbudal as a wildlife reserve in Costa Rica. Participants will observe and record behavior and habitat locations of bird and bee populations as part of an overall effort to assess the park's wildlife resources. In exploring new techniques for protecting habitats from fire, teams will also construct firebreaks of fast-growing species, measure their growth, and investigate new water-delivery systems.

Entering its 13th year, an Earthwatch project studying the interactions of moose, timber wolves, and their environment in Isle Royale National Park, Michigan, will continue investigations of the effect of vegetation fluctuations, which seem to occur over a 30–40-year cycle, on moose

Members of a UREP team make scale drawings of designs engraved on boulders by early inhabitants of Easter Island. Their findings will be combined with those from similar studies of Hawaiian rock art in an investigation of common origins and religious concepts in Polynesia.

235

and wolf populations. Numbers of moose appear to peak with vegetation, those of wolves about a decade later. The team will collect moose skeletons, from which the age and condition of the animals at death can be determined, and wolf scat, an analysis of which will indicate the diet of the wolves. Populations of such other animals as the snowshoe hare will also be recorded.

About 26,000 years ago an estimated 100 Ice Age mammoths were lured to their death in a steep-sided pond from which they could not escape, located near the present site of Hot Springs, South Dakota. Other mammoths and occasional carnivores followed until the pond filled in, so preserving the New World's largest natural deposit of mammoth remains. To date, excavators have unearthed the bones of 41 Columbian mammoths—the slightly larger, hairless cousin of the wooly mammoth—and the first wolf and great short-faced bear fossils found in the north-central plains. Standing 3.4 meters (11 feet) high, the short-faced bear was probably one of the most ferocious predators of the Ice Age. Because of the site's educational and scientific value, it has earned the status of National Natural Landmark. Field research there has received support from both Earthwatch and the National Geographic Society. In 1988 Earthwatch volunteers wielding trowels and dental picks will dig, map, record, preserve bones, and, in particular, search for more bear fossils.

While exploring rain forest canopy life in Peru since 1984, Earthwatch expeditions have found more than 3,000 insect species, most of which were previously unknown. For a collection to be made, an area of canopy

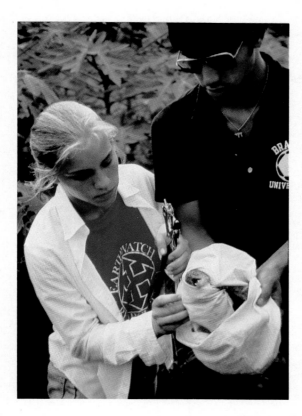

Members of an Earthwatch team restrain a small but feisty mongoose for close examination. A joint program conducted by Earthwatch and the U.S. Fish and Wildlife Service has focused on studies of the population and adaptive behavior of the animals at the Sandy Point National Wildlife Refuge on Saint Croix in the U.S. Virgin Islands.

Russ Schleipman—Earthwatch

is sprayed with an organic insecticide and the resulting "insect rain" is caught in trays. From this work it has been estimated that the rain forests of the world harbor untold numbers of unknown insects and that the total number of insect species worldwide may be closer to 30 million than to the traditional figure of 10 million. Rain forests are tremendously complex environments. An insect species may be endemic to only one species of tree rather than to a forest type, and it may appear in that tree regardless of the surrounding trees. To get a realistic picture of how many insects there are and how they fit into the rain forest ecology, the 1988 Earthwatch expedition had planned to spray one tree at a time in order to study the relationships between tree defenses and insect foraging, insect defenses and the predators that threaten them, and the degree to which insects are exclusive in their choice of habitats. Sadly, a tree poacher with a chain saw entered one of the research plots, destroying three years' work and causing the expedition to be canceled.

Scattered across the Red Sea's sandy bottom, aggregates of coral heads and rocks covered with sponges, mollusks, and other invertebrates offer shelter to millions of brilliantly colored reef fish. It has been noted that members of one species, *Anthias squamipinnis*, live in groups spread out evenly over a reef, with much unoccupied space between. How are such patterns created? Do juvenile fish, after starting life as floating eggs in the open sea, stay on a reef where they settle? Do they settle among adults, or do they set up their own colonies? Earthwatch volunteers will dive in pairs to 12.5 meters (41 feet) to locate, measure, and map all

237

existing groups of *A. squamipinnis,* using tape measures and underwater slates to record the location of fish. The identification of newly settled juveniles will determine where and how often new groups form and new juveniles join established groups.

Indonesians once believed that orangutans could talk but chose not to for fear of being put to work. Today orangutans face a much greater threat: extinction. Habitat destruction, hunting, and the pet market have drastically reduced the numbers of these magnificent primates. Fifteen years ago the first long-term study ever undertaken of orangutans in the wild was begun. This work has centered on both a general study of orangutan biology and an attempt to rehabilitate ex-captive animals so they can live in the forest. Orangutans are primarily arboreal. Large older males frequently travel on the ground, but the rest spend almost all their time in the trees, traveling several kilometers a day through the treetops searching for ripe fruit and making beds for themselves each evening high in the branches of the rain forest. Unlike gorillas and chimpanzees, orangutans live solitary lives. The females live alone with their young offspring, associating with males only for a brief mating period. In 1988 Earthwatch volunteers will collect long-term data on mother-infant relations and monitor the impact of orangutan feeding patterns on the forest. Under the guidance of native park assistants, they will track and observe the apes and their social behavior.

In the 1830s, when Charles Darwin visited Tierra del Fuego on the HMS *Beagle,* he met several tribes of native Americans. Their state shocked him: "These poor wretches were stunted in their growth, their hideous faces bedaubed with white paint, their skins filthy and greasy, their hair entangled, their voices discordant and their gestures violent." Darwin could scarcely believe "that they are fellow-creatures and inhabitants of the same world." Recent investigations, however, have found evidence that some of these people were more sophisticated, especially as fishermen, than Darwin's descriptions and existing chronicles would suggest. Did the Indians of the Beagle Channel learn to make complex hunting tools, including boats? Did they become sedentary and undergo a rapid rise in population? What happened after their first encounters with Europeans? Did they return to simpler ways? To shed light on these questions, Earthwatch volunteers will make contour maps, note surface features, and trench through depressions and mounds to identify them as dwelling sites in use before European contact. They will study animal and cultural remains in column samples to determine how the use and size of a site changed over several seasons.

In 1982 Earthwatch joined the effort begun earlier by the Tunisian government in launching the International Campaign to Save Carthage. Earthwatch volunteers first excavated the huge Roman circus, then constructed Carthage's first Musée Romain et Paleochrétien ("Roman and Paleo-Christian Museum") to house finds and explain the tangle of excavations, and finally excavated a Vandal housing development to explore how later Carthaginians adopted the ancient Roman city grid. The 1988 expedition will focus on the individual lives of Romans buried in graves that have been uncovered at a late-Roman cemetery north of the city. Each grave's occupant will help reveal the wealth and position that separated the city's social classes as well as the common rituals that bound them together. In addition, a study of bones will provide information about Carthaginian life expectancy, possible causes of death, and dietary deficiencies.

A team of volunteers at the end of a field expedition begin the return to their scattered communities and varied jobs. Most likely they will be bringing back a memory of exciting experiences, a deep sense of satisfaction, and a much improved appreciation of science and scientists.

Earthwatch

Improving public understanding of science

Scientific volunteers clearly play a significant role in furthering field research and in improving science education in the traditional sense. In a broader sense, they play an educational role in the public understanding of science. There is wide agreement that the U.S. has been facing a crisis in science and science education. Too few people are entering scientific and technological careers. Public understanding of the crucial role of science and technology in daily life is at best indifferent, at worst hostile. The perception of science as unrelated to practical concerns—of scientists as ivory-tower types in white coats who spend their lives in dingy laboratories working on projects of no consequence to anyone but themselves—is widely held. These misperceptions often extend to government leaders, very few of whom have backgrounds in science or the experience of living and working with scientists that being a field-research volunteer provides.

Projections of the number of scientifically trained personnel needed for the scientific work force of the U.S., after account is taken of the decreasing pool of college-age students over time (the baby boom has passed), show that by the start of the 21st century, given a continuation of the current rate of production of scientists, there will be a shortfall of as much as 600,000 in the pool. This deficit, which will be represented in all segments of the population, will be particularly severe for women, minorities, and the disabled.

Better appreciation is needed of the fact that all domains of science, even those that seem highly esoteric, thrive on a blend of theory and practice. Also needed is a concerted effort, beginning in the early grades, to nurture, encourage, motivate, and provide the proper educational background for students so that when they reach college age, careers in science and technology will represent viable options. The effort cannot begin too soon, since the children entering elementary school now will be in college at the turn of the century. Children begin life with a sense of curiosity—"Why is the sky blue?"—and it is vital that curiosity remain with them throughout their lives. What better way to encourage curiosity than by introducing children to the process and excitement of science by means of local field trips, focusing on scientific principles appropriate to their age level and conducted by teachers (and others) who themselves have been inspired firsthand by science?

Expanded participation in field expeditions, in which the blend of theory and practice is obvious, can play a significant role in the total picture. Increased efforts to publicize the opportunities and advantages of public involvement in field research would do much to improve public understanding of science and scientists. Nothing can change the perception of what scientists do, and what they are really like, quite so quickly as assisting them with research projects or camp chores, watching their struggle to fix a broken-down piece of essential equipment, or listening to their often hair-raising anecdotes of meeting an unexpected aspect of nature face-to-face in the field.

Encyclopædia

Britannica

Science Update

Major Revisions from the 1988 *Macropædia*

The purpose of this section is to introduce to continuing *Yearbook of Science and the Future* subscribers selected *Macropædia* articles or portions of them that have been completely revised or written anew. It is intended to update the *Macropædia* in ways that cannot be accomplished fully by reviewing the year's events or by revising statistics annually, because the *Macropædia* texts themselves—written from a longer perspective than any yearly revision—supply authoritative interpretation and analysis as well as narrative and description.

Two articles have been chosen from the 1988 printing: SUBATOMIC PARTICLES and VOLCANISM. Each is the work of distinguished scholars, and each represents the continuing dedication of the *Encyclopædia Britannica* to bringing such works to the general reader. New bibliographies accompany the articles for readers who wish to pursue certain topics.

Subatomic Particles

Subatomic particles are, literally, particles that are smaller than atoms. The physical study of such particles became possible only during the 20th century, with the development of increasingly sophisticated apparatus to probe matter at scales of 10^{-15} metre and less; yet the basic philosophy of the subject now known as subatomic particle physics dates to at least 500 BC when the Greek philosopher Leucippus and his pupil Democritus put forward the notion that matter consists of invisibly small, indivisible particles, which they called atoms. For more than 2,000 years, however, the idea of atoms lay largely neglected, while the opposing view that matter consists of four elements—earth, fire, air, and water—held sway.

It was in the early years of the 19th century that the atomic theory of matter returned to favour, strengthened in particular by the work of John Dalton, an English chemist, whose studies suggested that each chemical element consists of its own unique kind of atom. As such, Dalton's atoms are still the atoms of modern physics. By the close of the century, however, the first indications began to emerge that atoms are not indivisible, as Leucippus and Democritus had imagined, but that they instead contain smaller subatomic particles.

In 1896 the French physicist Henri Becquerel discovered radioactivity, and in the following year J.J. Thomson, a professor of physics at Cambridge University, England, demonstrated the existence of tiny particles much smaller in mass than hydrogen, the lightest atom. Thomson had discovered the first subatomic particle, the electron. Six years later, Ernest Rutherford and Frederick Soddy, working at McGill University in Montreal, found that radioactivity occurs when atoms of one type transmute into those of another kind. The idea of atoms as immutable, indivisible objects had become completely untenable.

The basic structure of the atom became apparent in 1911, when Rutherford, who had moved to Manchester University, showed that most of the mass of an atom lies concentrated at its centre, in a tiny nucleus. Rutherford postulated that the atom resembled a miniature solar system, with light, negatively charged electrons orbiting around the dense, positively charged nucleus, just as the planets orbit around the Sun. The Danish theorist Niels Bohr soon refined this model by incorporating the new ideas of quantization that had been developed by the German physicist Max Planck at the turn of the century. Planck had theorized that electromagnetic radiation, such as light, occurs in discrete bundles, or "quanta," of energy known as photons. By 1913, Bohr's theory of the atom already incorporated some of the basic elements of modern ideas about subatomic particles.

This article discusses the further development of subatomic particle theory, the various classes of subatomic particles, and current areas of research. See also the articles ATOMS; PHYSICAL PRINCIPLES AND CONCEPTS; MECHANICS; and RADIATION for additional information on the interactions of subatomic particles and on their role in the structure of matter. For specific details on the detection and measurement of subatomic particles, see PARTICLE ACCELERATORS and ANALYSIS AND MEASUREMENT, PHYSICAL AND CHEMICAL.

For coverage of related topics in the *Macropædia* and *Micropædia,* see the *Propædia,* section 112.

The article is divided into the following sections:

BASIC CONCEPTS

Subatomic particles play two vital roles in the structure of matter. They are both the basic building blocks of the universe and the mortar that binds the blocks together. Although the particles that fulfill these different roles are of two distinct types, they do share some common characteristics, foremost of which is size.

Subatomic particles are very small. The particles that inhabit the nucleus, for example, are called nucleons. Nucleons can be either positively charged protons or electrically neutral neutrons. A single nucleon has a diameter of about 10^{-15} metre (a distance known as a fermi in honour of the Italian physicist Enrico Fermi, who did much experimental and theoretical work on understanding the nature of the nucleus and its contents). In comparison an atom is typically 10^{-10} metre across, and the distance across an atomic nucleus of average size is roughly $1/10,000$ the diameter of an atom, or 10^{-14} metre.

The sizes of atoms, nuclei, and nucleons are measured by firing a beam of electrons at an appropriate target. The higher the energy of the electrons, the farther they penetrate before being deflected by the electric charges within the atom. A beam with an energy of a few hundred electron volts (eV), for example, scatters from the electrons in an atom. The way in which the beam is scattered can then be studied to determine the general distribution of the atomic electrons.

At energies of a few hundred megaelectron volts (MeV; 10^6 eV), electrons in the beam are little affected by atomic electrons; they penetrate the atom and are scattered by the positive nucleus. Therefore, if such a beam is fired at liquid hydrogen, whose atoms contain only single protons in their nuclei, the pattern of scattered electrons reveals the size of the proton. At energies greater than a gigaelectron volt (GeV; 10^9 eV), the electrons penetrate within the protons and neutrons, and their scattering patterns indicate an inner structure. Thus, protons and neutrons are no more indivisible than atoms are; instead, they contain still smaller particles, which are called quarks.

Elementary particles. Quarks are as small as or smaller than physicists can measure. In experiments at very high energies, equivalent to accelerating electrons to nearly 1,000 GeV, quarks appear to behave as points in space, with no measurable size; they must therefore be smaller than 10^{-18} metre, or less than one-thousandth the size of the individual nucleons they form. Similar experiments show that electrons, too, are smaller than it is possible to measure.

Electrons and quarks contain no discernible structure; they cannot be reduced or separated into smaller components. It is therefore reasonable to call them "elementary" particles, a name that in the past was mistakenly given to particles such as the proton, which is in fact a complex particle that contains quarks. The term subatomic particle refers both to the true elementary particles, such as quarks and electrons, and to the larger particles that quarks form.

Although both are elementary particles, electrons and quarks differ in some respects. Whereas quarks together form nucleons within the atomic nucleus, the electrons generally circulate toward the periphery of atoms. Indeed, electrons are regarded as distinct from quarks and are classified in a separate group of elementary particles called leptons. There are several types of lepton, just as there are several types of quark (see below). Only two types of quark are contained within protons and neutrons, however, and these together with the electron and one other elementary particle are all the "blocks" that are necessary to build the everyday world. The last block required is an electrically neutral particle called the neutrino.

Neutrinos   Neutrinos do not exist within atoms in the sense that electrons do, but they play a crucial role in certain types of radioactive decay. In the basic process of one type of radioactivity, known as beta decay, a neutron changes into a proton. In making this change, the neutron increases its electric charge by one unit. To keep the overall charge constant, and thereby conform to the fundamental physical law of charge conservation, the neutron must emit a negatively charged electron. In addition, according to the fundamental law of energy conservation, the sum of the energies of the final particles must equal the energy of the initial particle. The combined energy of the electron and proton is less than the energy of the neutron, however, because the neutron emits not only an electron but also a neutrino, which has little or no mass but does have energy. Beta decays are important in the transitions that occur when unstable atomic nuclei change to become more stable, and for this reason neutrinos are a necessary component in establishing the nature of matter.

The neutrino, like the electron, is classified as a lepton. Thus it seems, at first sight, that only four kinds of elementary particles—two quarks and two leptons—should exist. In the 1930s, however, long before the concept of quarks was established, it became clear that matter is more complicated.

Spin.   The success of Bohr's model of the atom and its implementation of quantization led during the 1920s to the development of quantum mechanics, which appeared to provide physicists with the correct method of calculating the structure of the atom. In his model, Bohr had taken Planck's ideas of quantization a step further by postulating that the electrons in the atom move only in orbits in which the angular momentum (angular velocity multiplied by mass) has certain fixed values. Each of these allowed values is characterized by a quantum number that can have only integer values. In the full quantum mechanical treatment, developed in the 1920s, three quantum numbers relating to angular momentum arise because there are three independent variable parameters in the equation describing the motion of atomic electrons.

In 1925, however, two Dutch physicists, Samuel Goudsmit and George Uhlenbeck, realized that in order to explain fully the spectra of light emitted by the atoms of alkali metals, such as sodium, which have one outer electron beyond the main "core," there must be a fourth quantum number that can take only two values, $-\frac{1}{2}$ and $+\frac{1}{2}$. Goudsmit and Uhlenbeck proposed that this quantum number refers to an internal angular momentum, or spin, that the electrons possess. This implies that the electrons, in effect, behave like spinning electric charges. Each therefore creates a magnetic field and has its own magnetic moment. The internal magnet of an atomic electron orients itself in one of two directions with respect to the magnetic field due to the rest of the atom. It is either parallel or antiparallel; hence, there are two quantized states—and two possible values of the associated spin quantum number.

Antiparticles.   Two years after the work of Goudsmit

and Uhlenbeck, the English theorist P.A.M. Dirac provided a sound theoretical background for the concept of electron spin when he introduced the German physicist Albert Einstein's special theory of relativity into quantum mechanics in order to describe the behaviour of an electron in an electromagnetic field. Dirac's relativistic theory showed that the electron must have spin and a magnetic moment, but it also made what seemed a strange prediction. The basic equation describing the allowed energies for an electron would admit two solutions, one positive and one negative. The positive solution apparently described normal electrons. The negative solution was more of a mystery; it seemed to describe electrons with positive, rather than negative, charge.

The mystery was resolved in 1932, when Carl Anderson, an American physicist, discovered the particle called the positron. Positrons are very much like electrons: they   **The** have the same mass and the same spin but opposite   **positron** electric charge. Positrons, then, are the particles predicted by Dirac's theory, and they were the first example of the so-called antiparticles to be discovered. Dirac's theory, in fact, applies to any subatomic particle with spin $\frac{1}{2}$; therefore all spin-$\frac{1}{2}$ particles should have corresponding antiparticles. Matter cannot be built from both particles and antiparticles, however. When a particle meets an appropriate antiparticle, the two disappear in an act of mutual destruction known as annihilation. Atoms can exist only because there is an excess of electrons and protons in the everyday world, with no corresponding positrons and antiprotons.

Positrons do occur naturally, however, which is how Anderson discovered their existence. High-energy subatomic particles—cosmic rays—rain down on the Earth's atmosphere from outer space, colliding with atomic nuclei to generate showers of particles that cascade toward the ground. In these showers, the enormous energy of the incoming cosmic ray is converted to matter, in accordance with Einstein's special theory of relativity, which states that $E = mc^2$, where E is energy, m is mass, and c is the velocity of light. Among the particles created are pairs of electrons and positrons (see Figure 1). The positrons survive until they come close enough to electrons to annihilate. The total mass of each electron-positron pair is then converted to energy, in the form of a gamma-ray photon.

Using particle accelerators, physicists can mimic the ac-

Figure 1: Electrons and positrons produced simultaneously from individual gamma rays curl in opposite directions in the magnetic field of a bubble chamber. In the top example, the gamma ray has lost some energy to an atomic electron, which leaves the long track, curling left. The gamma rays do not leave tracks in the chamber, as they have no electric charge.

tion of cosmic rays, creating collisions at high energy. In 1955 a team led by the Italian scientist Emilio Segrè and the American Owen Chamberlain found the first evidence for the existence of antiprotons in the collisions of high-energy protons produced by the Bevatron, an accelerator at what is now the Lawrence Berkeley Laboratory, in California. Shortly afterward, a different team working on the same accelerator discovered the antineutron.

THE PRESENT STATE OF SUBATOMIC PARTICLE THEORY

Since the 1950s physicists have discovered that protons and neutrons consist of quarks with spin $1/2$ and that antiprotons and antineutrons consist of antiquarks. Neutrinos, too, have spin $1/2$ and corresponding antineutrinos. Indeed, it is an antineutrino, rather than a neutrino, that emerges when a neutron changes by beta decay into a proton. This reflects a basic law of nature regarding the production and decay of quarks and leptons: in any interaction the total number of quarks and leptons must

Conservation of quarks and leptons

separately remain constant. Thus, the appearance of a lepton—the electron—in the decay of a neutron must be balanced by the simultaneous appearance of an antilepton, in this case the antineutrino.

In addition to such familiar particles as the nucleons and the electron, studies have slowly revealed the existence of more than 200 other subatomic particles. These "extra" particles do not appear in the low-energy environment of everyday human experience; they emerge only at the higher energies found in cosmic rays or particle accelerators. Moreover, they soon decay to the more familiar particles after brief lifetimes of only fractions of a second. The variety and behaviour of these extra particles initially bewildered scientists but have since come to be understood in terms of the quarks and leptons. In fact, only six quarks, six leptons, and their corresponding antiparticles seem to be necessary to explain the variety and behaviour of all the subatomic particles, including those that form normal atomic matter.

These quarks and leptons are the building blocks of matter, but they require some sort of mortar to bind themselves together into more complex forms, whether on a nuclear or a universal scale. The particles that provide this mortar are associated with four basic forces.

On the largest scales, the dominant force is gravity, which governs the aggregation of matter to form stars and galaxies and which influences the way that the universe is evolving from its initial big bang. The best understood force, however, is the electromagnetic force, which underlies the related phenomena of electricity and magnetism. The electromagnetic force binds negatively charged electrons to positively charged atomic nuclei and gives rise to the bonding between atoms to form matter in bulk.

Both gravity and electromagnetism are well known at the macroscopic level. The other two forces act only on subatomic scales, indeed on subnuclear scales. The strong nuclear force keeps quarks bound together within protons, neutrons, and other subatomic particles; and rather as the electromagnetic force is ultimately responsible for holding bulk matter together, so the strong nuclear force keeps protons and neutrons together within atomic nuclei. The fourth force is the weak nuclear force. Unlike the strong force, which acts only between quarks, the weak force acts on both quarks and leptons. This is the force that is responsible for the beta decay of a neutron into a proton and for the nuclear reactions that fuel the Sun and other stars.

Since the 1930s physicists have recognized that they can use field theory for all the four basic forces. In mathematical terms, a field describes something that varies continuously through space and time. A familiar example is the field that surrounds a piece of magnetized iron. The magnetic field maps the way that the force varies in strength and direction around the magnet. The appropriate fields for the four basic forces appear to have an important property in common: they all exhibit what is known as gauge symmetry. Put simply, this means that certain changes can be made that do not affect the basic structure of the field. It also implies that the relevant physical laws are the same in different regions of space and time.

At a subatomic, quantum level, these field theories dis-

play a significant feature. They describe the action of a force in terms of subatomic particles, called gauge bosons, which in a sense carry the force. These particles differ from the building blocks—the quarks and leptons—by having integer values of the spin quantum number, rather than a value of $1/2$. The most familiar gauge boson is the photon, which transmits the electromagnetic force between electrically charged objects, such as the electrons and protons within the atom. The photon acts as a private, invisible messenger between these particles, influencing their behaviour with the information it conveys, rather as a ball influences the actions of children playing catch. Other gauge bosons, with varying properties, are involved with the other basic forces.

Gauge bosons

In developing a gauge theory for the weak nuclear force in the 1960s, physicists discovered that the best theory, which would always yield sensible answers, must also incorporate the electromagnetic force. The result was what is now called electroweak theory. It was the first workable example of a unified theory linking forces that manifest themselves differently in the everyday world. The unified theory reveals the outwardly diverse forces as separate facets of a single underlying force. The search for a unified theory of everything, which incorporates all four fundamental forces, is one of the major goals of particle physics. It is leading theorists to an exciting area of study that involves not only subatomic particle physics but also cosmology and astrophysics.

THE BASIC FORCES AND THEIR MESSENGER PARTICLES

Gravity. The weakest, and yet the most pervasive, of the four basic forces is gravity. It acts on all forms of mass and energy and thus acts on all subatomic particles, including the gauge bosons that carry the forces. The 17th-century English scientist Isaac Newton was the first to develop a quantitative description of the force of gravity. He argued that the force which binds the Moon in orbit around the Earth is the same force which makes apples and other objects fall to the ground, and he proposed a universal law of gravitation.

According to Newton's law, all bodies are attracted to each other by a force that depends directly on the mass of each body and inversely on the square of the distance between them. For a pair of masses, m_1 and m_2, a distance r apart, the strength of the force, F, is given by $F = Gm_1m_2/r^2$. G is called the constant of gravitation and is equal to 6.67×10^{-11} newton-metre^2-kilogram^{-2}.

The constant G gives a measure of the strength of the gravitational force, and its smallness indicates that gravity is weak. Indeed, on the scale of atoms the effects of gravity are negligible compared with the other forces at work. To compare the strengths of the different forces, physicists prefer to use constants that have no dimensions. For gravity, the appropriate pure number is given by the product of G and the square of the mass of the proton, divided by two other fundamental constants of nature, the velocity of light and Planck's constant. The result is about 5×10^{-39}, a very small number that reflects the relative weakness of the gravitational force on the atomic scale.

Although the gravitational force is weak, its effects can be extremely long-ranging. Newton's law shows that at some distance the gravitational force between two bodies becomes negligible but that this distance depends on the masses involved. Thus, the gravitational effects of large, massive objects can be considerable, even at distances far outside the range of the other forces. The gravitational force of the Earth, for example, keeps the Moon in orbit some 384,400 kilometres distant.

The range of the gravitational force

Newton's theory of gravity proves adequate for many applications. In 1915, however, Einstein developed the general theory of relativity, which incorporates the concept of gauge symmetry and yields subtle corrections to Newtonian gravity. Despite its importance, Einstein's general relativity remains a classical theory in the sense that it does not incorporate the ideas of quantum mechanics. In a quantum theory of gravity, the gravitational force must be carried by a suitable messenger particle, or gauge boson. No workable quantum theory of gravity has yet been developed, but general relativity determines some of

Table 1: The Four Basic Forces						
name	acts on:	particles of exchange	range	strength	examples	
					stable systems	reaction induced by force
Gravity	all particles*	proposed graviton, g	long; $i.e.$, $F \propto 1/r^2$	$\sim 10^{-39}$	solar system	object falling
Weak nuclear force	all particles except γ	weak bosons, W and Z	$<10^{-17}$ m	10^{-5}	none	neutron beta decay
Electromagnetism	particles with electric charge	photon, γ	long; $i.e.$, $F \propto 1/r^2$	1/137	atoms, rocks	chemical reactions
Strong nuclear force	quarks and gluons	gluons, g	10^{-15} m	1	hadrons, nuclei	nuclear reactions

*Because all particles have energy or rest mass.

the properties of the graviton, the hypothesized particle of gravity. In particular, it must have a spin quantum number of 2 and no mass, only energy.

Electromagnetism. The first proper understanding of the electromagnetic force dates to the 18th century, when a French physicist, Charles Coulomb, showed that the electrostatic force between electrically charged objects follows a law similar to Newton's law of gravitation. Coulomb found that the force F between one charge q_1 and a second charge q_2 is equal to the product of the charges divided by the square of the distance r between them, or $F = q_1q_2/r^2$. The force can be either attractive or repulsive, because the source of the force, electric charge, exists in two varieties, positive and negative. The force between opposite charges is attractive, whereas bodies with the same kind of charge experience a repulsive force. Coulomb also showed that the force between magnetized bodies varies inversely as the square of the distance between them. Again, the force can be attractive (opposite poles) or repulsive (like poles).

Magnetism and electricity are not separate phenomena; they are the related manifestations of an underlying electromagnetic force. Experiments in the early 19th century by, among others, Hans Ørsted (in Denmark), André-Marie Ampère (in France), and Michael Faraday (in England) revealed the intimate connection between electricity and magnetism and how the one can give rise to the other. The results of these experiments were synthesized in the 1850s by the Scottish physicist James Clerk Maxwell in his electromagnetic theory. Maxwell's theory predicted the existence of electromagnetic waves—undulations in intertwined electric and magnetic fields, traveling with the velocity of light.

Maxwell's electromagnetic theory

Planck's work at the turn of the century, in which he explained the spectrum of radiation from a perfect emitter, led to the concept of quantization and photons. In the quantum picture, electromagnetic radiation has a dual nature, existing both as Maxwell's waves and as streams of particles called photons. The quantum nature of electromagnetic radiation is encapsulated in quantum electrodynamics, the quantum field theory of the electromagnetic force. Both Maxwell's classical theory and the quantized version contain gauge symmetry, which now appears to be a basic feature of the fundamental forces.

The pure number that characterizes the strength of the electromagnetic force is given by $e^2/\hbar c$, where e is the electric charge of the electron (or proton), $\hbar$ is Planck's constant divided by 2π, and c is the velocity of light. The result, known as the fine structure constant because of its relationship to certain effects in atomic spectra, is approximately $1/137$. It shows that the electromagnetic force is intrinsically much stronger than the gravitational force—some 10^{36} times as strong. At an atomic level the electromagnetic force is almost completely in control; gravity dominates on a large scale only because matter as a whole is electrically neutral.

The gauge boson of electromagnetism is the photon, which has zero mass and a spin quantum number of 1. Photons are exchanged whenever electrically charged subatomic particles interact. The photon has no electric charge, so it does not experience the electromagnetic force itself—in other words, photons cannot interact with one another. Photons do carry energy and momentum, however, and in transmitting these properties between particles they produce the effects known as electromagnetism.

In these processes, energy and momentum are conserved overall (the totals remain the same in accordance with the basic laws of physics); but at the instant one particle emits a photon and another particle absorbs it, energy is not conserved. Quantum mechanics allows this imbalance provided that the photon fulfills the conditions of Heisenberg's uncertainty principle. This rule, described in 1927 by the German scientist Werner Heisenberg, states that it is in principle not possible to know all the details about a particular quantum system. For example, if the exact position of an electron is identified, it is impossible to be certain of the electron's momentum. This fundamental uncertainty allows a discrepancy in energy, ΔE, to exist for a time, Δt, provided that the product of ΔE and Δt is very small—less than the value of Planck's constant $(6.6 \times 10^{-34}$ joule seconds) divided by 2π, or 1.05×10^{-34} joule seconds. The energy of the messenger can thus be thought of as "borrowed," within the limits of the uncertainty principle ($i.e.$, the more energy borrowed, the shorter the time of the loan). Such borrowed photons are called virtual photons to distinguish them from the real photons, which constitute electromagnetic radiation and can in principle exist forever. This concept of virtual particles in processes that fulfill the conditions of the uncertainty principle applies to the exchange of other gauge bosons as well.

Virtual particles

The weak nuclear force. Since the 1930s physicists have been aware of a force within the atomic nucleus that is responsible for certain types of radioactivity which are classed together as beta decay. A typical example of beta decay occurs when a neutron transmutes into a proton. The force that underlies this process is known as the weak nuclear force to distinguish it from the strong nuclear force that binds quarks together (see below).

The correct gauge field theory for the weak nuclear force incorporates the quantum field theory of electromagnetism (quantum electrodynamics) and is called electroweak theory. It treats the weak nuclear and electromagnetic forces on an equal footing by regarding them as different manifestations of a more fundamental electroweak force, rather as electricity and magnetism appear as different aspects of the electromagnetic force.

The electroweak theory requires four gauge bosons. One of these is the photon of electromagnetism; the other three are involved in reactions that occur via the weak force. These weak gauge bosons include two electrically charged versions, called W^+ and W^-, where the signs indicate the type of charge, and a neutral variety called Z^0, where the zero indicates zero charge. Like the photon, the W and Z particles have a spin quantum number of 1; unlike the

Table 2: Gauge Bosons					
symbol	spin	mass (GeV)	mean life (s)	typical decays	name
γ	1	0	stable	—	photon
$W^\pm$	1	81,800	10^{-25}	$\rightarrow ev,$	W
Z^0	1	92,600	10^{-25}	$\rightarrow e^+e^-$	Z
g	1	0	stable	—	gluon
g	2*	0	stable	—	graviton

*Deduced from general relativity; there is no direct evidence for the graviton.

photon, they are very massive. The W particles weigh 81.8 GeV, while the mass of the Z^0 is about 92.6 GeV. By comparison, the mass of the proton is 0.94 GeV, or one-hundredth that of the Z particle.

The charged W particles are responsible for processes, such as beta decay, in which the charge of the participating particles changes hands. For example, when a neutron transmutes into a proton, it emits a W^-; thus the overall charge remains zero before and after the decay process. The W particle involved in this process is a virtual particle. Because its mass is far greater than that of the neutron, the only way that it can be emitted by the lightweight neutron is for its existence to be fleetingly short, within the requirements of the uncertainty principle. Indeed, the W^- immediately transforms into an electron and an antineutrino, the particles that are observed in the laboratory as the products of neutron beta decay. Z particles are exchanged in similar reactions that involve no change in charge.

In the everyday world, the weak nuclear force is weaker than the electromagnetic force but stronger than the gravitational force. Its range, however, is very short. Because of the large amounts of energy needed to create the large masses of the W and Z particles, the uncertainty principle ensures that a weak gauge boson cannot be borrowed for long, which limits the range of the force to distances less than 10^{-17} metre. In terms of a pure number, the weak nuclear force couples to protons with a strength of about $^1/_{100,000}$ or 10^{-5}. As the electroweak theory reveals and as experiments confirm, however, this weak nuclear force becomes slowly stronger as the energies of the participating particles increase. When the energies reach 100 GeV or so—roughly the energy equivalent to the mass of the W and Z particles—the strength of the weak nuclear force becomes comparable to that of the electromagnetic force. This means that reactions that involve the exchange of a Z^0 become as common as those in which a photon is exchanged. It also means that real W and Z particles, as opposed to virtual ones, can be created in high-energy reactions.

Unlike the photon, which is stable and can in principle live forever, the heavy weak gauge bosons decay to lighter particles within an extremely brief lifetime of about 10^{-24} second. This is roughly a million million times shorter than experiments can measure, but physicists can detect the particles into which the W and Z particles decay and so can infer their existence (see Figure 2).

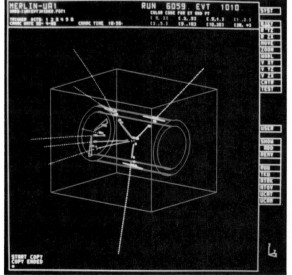

Figure 2: Tracks emerging from a proton-antiproton collision at the centre of the UA1 detector at CERN include those of an energetic electron (straight down) and a positron (upper right). These two particles have come from the decay of a Z^0; when their energies are added together the total is equal to the Z^0's mass.

The strong nuclear force. Although the aptly named strong nuclear force is the strongest of all the fundamental forces, it, like the weak nuclear force, is short-ranged and is ineffective much beyond nuclear distances of 10^{-15} metre or so. Within the nucleus and, more specifically, within the protons and other particles that are built from quarks, however, the strong nuclear force rules supreme; it is typically 100 times stronger than the electromagnetic force, and its strength is characterized by a pure number with the value 1.

During the 1970s physicists developed a theory for the strong nuclear force that is similar in structure to quantum electrodynamics. In this theory, quarks are bound together by exchanging gauge bosons called gluons. The quarks carry a property called colour that is analogous to electric charge. Just as electrically charged particles experience the electromagnetic force and exchange photons, so colour-charged, or coloured, particles feel the strong nuclear force and exchange gluons. This property of colour gives rise in part to the name of the theory of the strong nuclear force: quantum chromodynamics.

 Gluons

Gluons are massless and have a spin quantum number of 1. In this respect they are much like photons, but they differ from photons in one crucial way. Whereas photons do not interact among themselves—because they are not electrically charged—gluons do carry colour charge. This means that gluons can interact together, which has an important effect in limiting the range of gluons and in confining quarks within protons and other particles.

The three types of colour charge are called red, green, and blue, although there is no connection between the colour charge of quarks and gluons and colour in the usual sense. Quarks each carry a single colour charge, while gluons carry both a colour and an anticolour charge.

The strong nuclear force acts in such a way that quarks of different colour are attracted to one another; thus, red attracts green, blue attracts red, and so on. Quarks of the same colour, on the other hand, repel each other. The quarks can combine only in ways that give a net colour charge of zero. In particles, such as protons, that contain three quarks, this is achieved by adding red, blue, and green. An alternative, observed in particles called mesons (see below), is for a quark to couple with an antiquark of the same basic colour. In this case, the colour of the quark and the anticolour of the antiquark cancel each other out. These combinations of three quarks (or antiquarks) and quark-antiquark pairs are the only combinations that the strong nuclear force seems to allow.

The constraint that only colourless objects can appear in nature seems to limit attempts to observe single quarks and free gluons. Although a quark can radiate a real gluon just as an electron can radiate a real photon, the gluon never emerges on its own into the surrounding environment. Instead, it somehow creates additional gluons, quarks, and antiquarks from its own energy and materializes as normal particles built from quarks (see Figure 3). Similarly, it appears that the strong nuclear force keeps quarks permanently confined within larger particles. Attempts to knock quarks out of protons by, for example, knocking protons together at high energies only succeed in creating more particles—that is, in releasing new quarks and antiquarks that are bound together and are themselves confined by the strong nuclear force.

LEPTONS AND ANTILEPTONS

The electron is the component of atoms that makes interatomic bonding and chemical reactions—and hence life—possible. Probably the most familiar subatomic particle, the electron was also the first to be discovered. Its negative charge of 1.6×10^{-19} coulomb seems to be the basic unit of electric charge, although theorists have a poor understanding of what determines this particular size.

Physicists classify the electron as a type of lepton. Leptons are a group of subatomic particles that do not experience the strong nuclear force. They do, however, feel the weak nuclear force and the gravitational force; and electrically charged leptons interact via the electromagnetic force.

The electron, with a mass of 0.511 MeV, is the lightest of the charged leptons. The next heaviest charged lepton

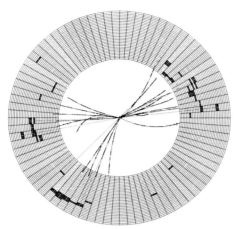

Figure 3: Three "jets" of particles streaming out from an electron-positron collision at the centre of the JADE detector at the DESY laboratory, Hamburg. Two of the jets come from a quark and an antiquark formed in the electron-positron annihilation; the third jet comes from a gluon, radiated by either the quark or the antiquark.

By courtesy of the JADE collaboration

The muon is the muon. It has a mass of 105 MeV, which is some 200 times greater than the electron's mass but is significantly less than the proton's mass of 938 MeV. Unlike the electron, which appears to be completely stable, the muon decays after an average lifetime of 2.2 microseconds into an electron, a neutrino, and an antineutrino. This process, like the beta decay of a neutron into a proton, an electron, and an antineutrino, occurs via the weak nuclear force. Experiments have shown that the intrinsic strength of the underlying reaction is the same in both kinds of decay, thus revealing that the weak nuclear force acts equally upon leptons (electrons, muons, neutrinos) and quarks (which form neutrons and protons).

Unlike the charged leptons, the neutral neutrinos do not come under the influence of the electromagnetic force. They experience only the weakest two of nature's forces, the weak nuclear force and gravity. For this reason, neutrinos react extremely weakly with matter. They can, for example, pass through the Earth without interacting, which makes it difficult to detect neutrinos and to measure their properties. Thus, even though one experiment has indicated that the neutrino's mass may be around 40 eV, or less than $1/10,000$ the mass of an electron, the results are questioned by other researchers. Theory does not require the neutrino's mass to be any specific amount, and in the past it was assumed to be zero.

Table 3: Leptons

symbol	spin	mass (MeV)	mean life (s)	typical decays	name
ν_e, ν_μ, ν_τ	1/2	0?*	stable	—	neutrino
e^-	1/2	0.5	stable	—	electron
μ^-	1/2	106	2×10^{-6}	$\rightarrow e\nu_\mu\bar{\nu}_e$	muon
τ^-	1/2	1,784	3×10^{-13}	$\rightarrow$ hadrons $+ \nu_\tau$	tau

*There is uncertainty as to the precise mass, if any, of the three types of neutrino.

Although electrically neutral, the neutrinos seem to carry an identifying property that associates them specifically with one type of charged lepton. In the example of the muon's decay, the antineutrino produced is not simply the antiparticle of the neutrino. The neutrino carries a muon-type hallmark, while the antineutrino, like the antineutrino emitted when a neutron decays, is always an electron-antineutrino. In interactions with matter, such electron-neutrinos and antineutrinos never produce muons, only electrons. Likewise, muon-neutrinos only give rise to muons, and never to electrons.

The tau There is a third, heavier type of charged lepton, called the tau. The tau, with a mass of 1,784 MeV, is even heavier than the proton and has a very short lifetime of about 10^{-13} second. Like the electron and the muon, the tau has its associated neutrino.

The tau can decay into a muon, plus a tau-neutrino and a muon-antineutrino; or it can decay directly into an electron, plus a tau-neutrino and an electron-antineutrino. Because the tau is heavy, it can also decay into particles containing quarks. In one example, the tau decays into particles called pi-mesons (see below), which are accompanied by a tau-neutrino.

In summary, there are three types of charged lepton and three types of neutral lepton, together with six related antileptons (see Table 3). In all three cases, the charged lepton has a negative charge while its antiparticle is positively charged. Physicists coined the name lepton from the Greek word for "slender" because, before the discovery of the tau in 1975, it seemed that the leptons were the lightest particles. Although the name is no longer appropriate, it has been retained to describe all spin-$1/2$ particles that do not feel the strong nuclear force.

HADRONS

The proton and the neutron are the most common examples of the class of subatomic particles known as hadrons. The name hadron comes from the Greek word for "strong"; it refers to all those particles that are built from quarks and therefore experience the strong nuclear force.

Experiments have revealed a large number of hadrons, of which only the proton appears to be stable. Indeed, even if the proton is not absolutely stable, experiments show that its lifetime is at least in excess of 10^{32} years. In contrast, a single neutron, free from the forces at work within the nucleus, lives an average of 15 minutes before decaying. Within a nucleus, however—even the simple nucleus of deuterium, which consists of one proton and one neutron—the balance of forces is sufficient to prolong the neutron's lifetime so that many nuclei are stable and a large variety of chemical elements exist.

Some hadrons typically exist only 10^{-10} to 10^{-8} second. Fortunately for experimentalists, these particles are usually born in such high-energy collisions that they are moving at velocities close to the speed of light. Their time-scale is therefore "stretched" or "slowed down" so that in the high-speed particle's frame of reference, its lifetime is 10^{-10} second, but in a stationary observer's frame of reference, the particle lives much longer. This effect, known as time dilation in the special theory of relativity, allows stationary particle detectors to record the tracks left by these short-lived particles. These hadrons, which number around a dozen (see Table 4), are usually referred to as stable to distinguish them from still shorter-lived hadrons with lifetimes typically in the region of a mere 10^{-23} second. | Stable hadrons

The stable hadrons usually decay via the weak nuclear force. In some cases they decay by the electromagnetic force, which results in somewhat shorter lifetimes because the electromagnetic force is stronger than the weak nuclear force. The very short-lived hadrons, however, which number 200 or more, decay via the strong nuclear force. This force is so strong that it allows the particles to live only for the amount of time it takes light to cross the particle; the particles decay almost as soon as they are created.

These very short-lived particles are called resonances because they are observed as a resonance phenomenon; they are too short-lived to be observed in any other way (see Figure 4). Resonance occurs when a system absorbs more energy than usual because the energy is being supplied at the system's own natural frequency. For example, soldiers break step when they cross a bridge because their rhythmic marching could make the bridge resonate—set it vibrating at its own natural frequency—so that it absorbs enough energy to cause damage. | Unstable resonances

Subatomic particle resonances occur when the net energy of colliding particles is just sufficient to create the rest mass of the new particle, which the strong nuclear force then breaks apart within 10^{-23} second. The absorption of energy, or its subsequent emission in the form of particles as the resonance decays, is revealed as the energy of the colliding particles is varied.

The hadrons, whether stable or resonant states, fall into

Table 4: Stable Hadrons

symbol	spin	mass (MeV)	mean life (s)	typical decays	name
Mesons					
(Baryon number $B = 0$)					
$\pi^{\pm}$		140	3×10^{-8}	$\rightarrow \mu^{\pm} \, v_{\mu}$ $\Big\}$	pion
π^0		135	1×10^{-16}	$\rightarrow \gamma\gamma$	
$K^{\pm}$		494	1×10^{-8}	$\rightarrow \mu^{\pm} \, v_{\mu}$	kaon
K^0	0	498	$\begin{cases} 1 \times 10^{-10} \\ 5 \times 10^{-8} \end{cases}$	$\begin{array}{l} K_S \rightarrow 2\pi^* \\ K_L \rightarrow 3\pi^* \end{array}$ $\Big\}$	
$D^{\pm}$		1,869	9×10^{-13}	$\rightarrow K^0 + \ldots$ $\Big\}$	D
D^0		1,865	4×10^{-13}	$\rightarrow K^0 + \ldots$	
$D_S{}^+$		1,971	3×10^{-13}	$\rightarrow \varphi\pi$	D_S
$B^{\pm}$		5,271	1×10^{-12}	$\rightarrow D^0\pi^+$ $\Big\}$	B
B^0		5,275	1×10^{-12}	$\rightarrow D^0\pi^+\pi^-$	
Baryons					
(Baryon number $B = 1$)					
p		938	stable†		proton
n		940	1×10^3	$\rightarrow pe^-\bar{v}_e$	neutron
Λ		1,116	3×10^{-10}	$\rightarrow p\pi^-$	lambda
Σ^+		1,189	8×10^{-11}	$\rightarrow p\pi^0$	
Σ^0	1/2	1,193	6×10^{-20}	$\rightarrow \Lambda\gamma$ $\Big\}$	sigma
Σ^-		1,197	1×10^{-10}	$\rightarrow n\pi^-$	
Ξ^0		1,315	3×10^{-10}	$\rightarrow \Lambda\pi^0$ $\Big\}$	xi, or cascade
Ξ^-		1,321	2×10^{-10}	$\rightarrow \Lambda\pi^-$	
Ω^-	3/2	1,672	1×10^{-10}	$\rightarrow \Lambda K^-$	omega-minus
$\Lambda_c{}^+$	1/2	2,281	2×10^{-13}	$\rightarrow \Lambda + \ldots$	lambda-c

*The K^0 and its antiparticle $\bar{K}^0$ mix quantum mechanically to form two physical states, K_L and K_S. †Could be unstable according to grand unified theories, but experiments show that its lifetime is at least 10^{32} years.

two classes: baryons and mesons. Originally the names referred to the relative masses of the two groups of particles. The baryons (from the Greek word for "heavy") included the proton and heavier particles; the mesons (from the Greek word for "between") were particles with masses between that of the electron and the proton. Now, however, the name baryon refers to any particle built from three quarks, such as the proton and the neutron. Mesons, on the other hand, are particles built from a quark combined with an antiquark. As described above, these are the only two combinations of quarks and antiquarks that the strong nuclear force apparently allows.

The baryons are characterized by a baryon number, B, of 1; antibaryons have a baryon number of −1; and the baryon number of the mesons, leptons, and messenger particles is 0. Baryon numbers are additive; thus, an atom

containing one proton and one neutron (each with a baryon number of 1) has a baryon number of 2. Quarks therefore must have a baryon number of $^1/_3$, and the antiquarks a baryon number of $-^1/_3$, in order to give the correct values of 1 or 0 when they combine to form baryons and mesons.

The empirical law of baryon conservation states that in any reaction the total number of baryons must remain constant. If any baryons are created then so must be an equal number of antibaryons, which in principle negate the baryons. Conservation of baryon number explains the apparent stability of the proton. The proton does not decay into lighter positive particles, such as the positron or the mesons, because those particles have a baryon number of 0. Neutrons and other heavy baryons can decay into the lighter protons, however, because the total number of baryons present does not change.

At a more detailed level, baryons and mesons are distinguishable in terms of their spin. The basic quarks have a spin of 1/2 (which may be oriented in either of two directions). When three quarks combine to form a baryon, their spins can only add up to half-integer values; but when quarks and antiquarks combine to form mesons, their spins always add up to integer values. Table 4 lists the stable baryons and mesons and indicates their spins, as well as some of their other properties.

Conservation of baryon number

QUARKS AND ANTIQUARKS

The baryons and mesons are complex subatomic particles that are built from more elementary objects, the quarks. To account for all the hadrons that experiments have revealed, at least five and probably six types of quark are necessary, together with their corresponding antiquarks. The six varieties of quark have acquired unusual names: up, down, charm, strange, top, and bottom. (The top quark is the one whose existence is uncertain.) The meaning of these names is not in itself important; they have arisen for a number of reasons. What is more important is the way that the quarks contribute to matter at different levels and the properties that they bear.

The quarks are unusual in that they carry electric charges that are smaller in magnitude than e, the size of the charge of the electron (1.6×10^{-19} coulomb). This is necessary for the quarks to combine together to form, in particular, the proton. Only two types of quark are necessary to build protons and neutrons, the constituents of atomic

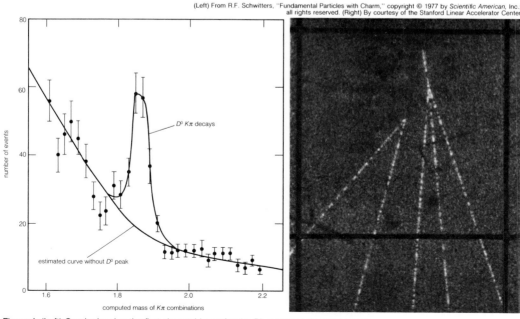

Figure 4: (Left) Graph showing the first clear evidence for the D^0, a neutral charmed meson with a lifetime (4×10^{-13}s) so short that it could at first be detected only as a resonance, here in the total mass-energy of pion-kaon pairs. (Right) The "footprint" of the D^0 in a bubble chamber sensitive enough to reveal its brief life. Because it is neutral, the D^0 leaves no track and is seen as a short gap before it decays into the two charged particles whose tracks form the V on the left.

nuclei. These are the up quark, with a charge of $+^2/_3e$, and the down quark, which has a charge of $-^1/_3e$. The proton consists of two up quarks and one down quark, giving it a total charge of $+e$. (The positive charge of the proton exactly balances the electron's negative charge, so that matter is neutral overall.) The neutron, on the other hand, is built from one up quark and two down quarks, so that it has a net charge of zero. The other properties of the up and down quarks also add together to give the measured values for the proton and neutron. For example, the quarks have spins of $^1/_2$. In order to form a proton or a neutron, which also have spin $^1/_2$, the quarks must align in such a way that two of the three spins cancel each other, leaving a net value of $^1/_2$.

Up and down quarks can combine to form other particles. For example, the spins of the three quarks can be arranged so that they do not cancel. In this case they form short-lived resonance states, which have been given the name delta, or Δ. The deltas have spins of $^3/_2$, and the up and down quarks combine in four possible configurations—*uuu, uud, udd,* and *ddd*—where *u* and *d* stand for up and down. The charges of these Δ states are $+2e$, $+e$, 0, and $-e$, respectively.

The up and down quarks can also combine with their antiquarks to form mesons. The pi-meson, or pion, which is the lightest meson and an important component of cosmic rays, exists in three forms: with charge e (or 1), with charge 0, and with charge $-e$ (or -1). In the positive state, an up quark combines with a down antiquark; a down quark together with an up antiquark compose the negative pion; and the neutral pion is a quantum mechanical mixture of two states—$u\bar{u}$ and $d\bar{d}$, where the bar over the top of the letter indicates the antiquark.

Up and down are the lightest varieties of quarks. Somewhat heavier are a second pair of quarks, charm (*c*) and strange (*s*), with charges of $+^2/_3$ and $-^1/_3$, respectively. There also is a still heavier quark, called bottom (or beauty, *b*), with charge $-^1/_3$. Because the up and down quarks, and the charmed and strange quarks, are pairs, physicists are confident that the bottom quark must also have a partner, with a charge of $+^2/_3$, and they have named this quark top (or truth, *t*). These heavier quarks and their antiquarks combine with up and down quarks and with each other to produce a range of hadrons, each of which is heavier than the basic proton and pion, which represent the lightest varieties of baryon and meson. There is, however, still no convincing evidence that any hadrons contain a top quark.

THE DEVELOPMENT OF MODERN THEORY

Quantum electrodynamics. The year of the birth of particle physics is often cited as 1932. Near the beginning of that year James Chadwick, working in England at the Cavendish Laboratory in Cambridge, discovered the existence of the neutron. This discovery seemed to complete the picture of atomic structure that had begun with Rutherford's work in 1911. The elementary particles seemed firmly established as the proton, neutron, and electron. By the end of 1932, however, Carl Anderson in the United States had discovered the first antiparticle: the positron, or antielectron. Moreover, Patrick Blackett and Giuseppi Occhialini, working, like Chadwick, at the Cavendish Laboratory, had revealed how positrons and electrons are created in pairs when cosmic rays pass through dense matter. It was becoming apparent that the simple pictures provided by electrons, protons, and neutrons were incomplete and that a new theory was needed to explain fully the phenomena of subatomic particles.

Dirac had provided the foundations for such a theory in 1927 when he wrote his quantum theory of the electromagnetic field. Dirac's theory treated the electromagnetic field as a "gas" of photons (the quanta of light) and it yielded a correct description of the absorption and emission of radiation by electrons in atoms. It was the first quantum field theory.

A year later, Dirac published his relativistic electron theory, which took correct account of Einstein's special theory of relativity. Dirac's theory showed that the electron must have a spin quantum number of $^1/_2$ and a magnetic

moment. It also predicted the existence of the positron, although Dirac did not at first realize that this was a new particle, believing instead that it was a proton. Only with Anderson's discovery of the positron did the picture become clear: radiation—a photon—can produce electrons and positrons in pairs, provided the energy of the photon is greater than about 1 MeV, the total mass-energy of the two particles.

Dirac's quantum field theory was a beginning, but it explained only one aspect of the electromagnetic interactions between radiation and matter. During the following years other theorists began to extend Dirac's ideas to form a comprehensive theory of quantum electrodynamics (QED) that accounts fully for the interactions of charged particles not only with radiation but also with one another. One important step was to describe the electrons in terms of fields, in analogy to the electromagnetic field of the photons. This enabled theorists to describe everything in terms of quantum field theory. It also helped to cast light on Dirac's positrons.

According to QED, the vacuum is filled with electron-positron fields. Real electron-positron pairs are created when photons, represented by the electromagnetic field, interact with these fields. Virtual electron-positron pairs, however, can also exist for minute durations, as dictated by Heisenberg's uncertainty principle, and this at first led to fundamental difficulties with QED.

During the 1930s it became clear that, as it stood, QED gave the wrong answers for quite simple problems. For example, the theory said that the emission and reabsorption of the same photon would occur with an infinite probability. This led in turn to infinities occurring in many situations; even the mass of a single electron was infinite according to QED because, on the time scales of the uncertainty principle, the electron could continuously emit and absorb virtual photons.

It was not until the late 1940s that a number of theorists working independently resolved the problems with QED. Julian Schwinger and Richard Feynman in the United States and Tomonaga Shin'ichirō in Japan proved that they could rid the theory of its embarrassing infinities by a process known as renormalization. Basically, renormalization acknowledges all possible infinities and then allows the positive infinities to cancel the negative ones; the mass and charge of the electron, which are infinite in theory, are then defined to be their measured values.

Once these steps are taken, QED works beautifully. It is the most accurate quantum field theory scientists have at their disposal. In recognition of their achievement, Feynman, Schwinger, and Tomonaga were awarded the Nobel Prize for Physics for 1965; Dirac had been similarly honoured in 1933.

Quantum chromodynamics. As early as 1920, when Rutherford named the proton and accepted it as a fundamental particle, it was clear that the electromagnetic force is not the only force at work within the atom. Something stronger must be responsible for binding the positively charged protons together, thereby overcoming their natural electrical repulsion. The discovery in 1932 of the neutron showed that there are (at least) two kinds of particle subject to the same force. Later in the same year, Heisenberg made one of the first attempts to develop a quantum field theory that was analogous to QED but appropriate to the nuclear binding force.

According to quantum field theory, particles can be held together by a "charge-exchange" force, which is carried by charged intermediary particles. Heisenberg's application of this theory gave birth to the idea that the proton and neutron were charged and neutral versions of the same particle—an idea that seemed to be supported by the fact that the two particles have almost equal masses. Heisenberg proposed that a proton, for example, could emit a positively charged particle that was then absorbed by a neutron; the proton thus became a neutron, and vice versa. The nucleus was no longer viewed as a collection of two kinds of immutable billiard balls but rather as a collection of continuously changing protons and neutrons that were bound together by the exchange particles flitting between them.

Heisenberg believed that the exchange particle involved was an electron (he did not have many particles from which to choose). This electron had to have some rather odd characteristics, however, such as no spin and no magnetic moment, and this made Heisenberg's theory ultimately unacceptable. Quantum field theory did not seem applicable to the nuclear binding force. Then, in 1935, a Japanese theorist, Yukawa Hideki, took a bold step: he invented a new particle as the carrier of the nuclear binding force.

The Yukawa meson

The size of a nucleus shows that the binding force must be short-ranged, confining protons and neutrons within distances of about 10^{-14} metre. Yukawa argued that to give this limited range, the force must involve the exchange of particles with mass, unlike the massless photons of QED. According to the uncertainty principle, exchanging a particle with mass sets a limit on the time allowed for the exchange and therefore restricts the range of the resulting force. Yukawa calculated a mass of about 200 times the electron's mass, or 100 MeV, for the new intermediary. Because the predicted mass of the new particle was between those of the electron and the proton, the particle was named meson.

Yukawa's work was little known outside Japan until 1937, when Carl Anderson and his colleague Seth Neddermeyer announced that, five years after Anderson's discovery of the positron, they had found a second new particle in the cosmic radiation. The new particle seemed to have exactly the mass Yukawa had prescribed and thus was seen as confirmation of Yukawa's theory by the Americans J. Robert Oppenheimer and Robert Serber, who made Yukawa's work more widely known in the West.

In the following years, however, it became clear that there were difficulties in reconciling the properties expected for Yukawa's intermediary particle with those of the new cosmic ray particle. In particular, as a group of Italian physicists succeeded in demonstrating (while hiding from the occupying German forces during World War II), the cosmic ray particles penetrate matter far too easily to be related to the nuclear binding force. To resolve this apparent paradox, theorists both in Japan and in the United States had begun to think that there might be two mesons. The two-meson theory proposed that Yukawa's nuclear meson decays into the penetrating meson observed in the cosmic rays.

The two-meson theory

In 1947, scientists at Bristol University in England found the first experimental evidence of two mesons in cosmic rays high on the Pic du Midi in France. Using detectors equipped with special photographic emulsion that can record the tracks of charged particles, the physicists at Bristol found the decay of a heavier meson into a lighter one. They called the heavier particle π, and it has since become known as the π-meson or pion. The lighter particle was dubbed μ and is now known simply as the muon. (According to the modern definition of a meson as a particle consisting of a quark bound with an antiquark, the muon is not actually a meson. It is classified as a lepton—a relation of the electron.)

Studies of pions produced in cosmic radiation and in the first particle accelerators showed that the pion behaves precisely as expected for Yukawa's particle. Moreover, experiments confirmed that positive, negative, and neutral varieties of pions exist, as predicted by Nicholas Kemmer in England in 1938. Kemmer regarded the nuclear binding force as symmetric with respect to the charge of the particles involved. He proposed that the nuclear force between protons and protons, or neutrons and neutrons, is the same as the one between protons and neutrons. This symmetry required the existence of a neutral intermediary that did not figure in Yukawa's original theory. It also established the concept of a new "internal" property of subatomic particles, called isospin.

Kemmer's work followed to some extent the trail Heisenberg had begun in 1932. Close similarities between nuclei containing the same total number of protons and neutrons, but in different combinations, suggest that protons can be exchanged for neutrons and vice versa without altering the net effect of the nuclear binding force. In other words, the force recognizes no difference between protons and neutrons—it is symmetrical under the interchange of protons and neutrons, rather as a square is symmetrical under rotations through 90°, 180°, and so on.

To introduce this symmetry into the theory of the nuclear force, it proved useful to adopt the mathematics describing the spin of particles. In this respect, the proton and neutron are seen as different states of a single basic nucleon. These states are differentiated by an internal property that can have two values, $+\frac{1}{2}$ and $-\frac{1}{2}$, in analogy with the spin of a particle like the electron. This new property is called isotopic spin, or isospin for short, and the nuclear binding force is said to exhibit isospin symmetry.

Isospin

Symmetries are important in physics because they simplify the theories needed to describe a range of observations. For example, as far as physicists can tell, all physical laws exhibit translational symmetry. This means that the results of an experiment performed at one location in space and time can be used to predict correctly the outcome of the same experiment in another part of space and time. This symmetry is reflected in the conservation of momentum—the fact that the total momentum of a system remains constant, unless it is acted upon by an external force.

Isospin symmetry is an important symmetry in particle physics, although it occurs only in the action of the nuclear binding force—or, in modern terminology, the strong nuclear force. The symmetry leads to the conservation of isospin in nuclear interactions that occur via the strong force, thereby determining which reactions can occur.

The discovery of the pion in 1947 seemed to restore order to the study of particle physics, but this order did not last long. Later in the year Clifford Butler and George Rochester, two British physicists studying cosmic rays, discovered the first examples of yet another type of new particle. The new particles were heavier than the pion or muon but lighter than the proton, with a mass of about 800 times the electron's mass. Within the next few years, researchers found copious examples of these particles, as well as other new particles that were heavier than even the proton. The evidence seemed to indicate that these particles were created in strong interactions in nuclear matter, yet the particles lived for a relatively long time without themselves interacting strongly with matter. This strange behaviour in some ways echoed the earlier problem with Yukawa's supposed meson, but the solution for the new "strange" particles proved to be different.

By 1953 at least four different kinds of strange particles had been observed. In an attempt to bring order into this increasing number of subatomic particles, Murray Gell-Mann in the United States and Nishijima Kazuhiko in Japan independently suggested a new conservation law. They argued that the strange particles must possess some new property, called "strangeness," that is conserved in the strong nuclear reactions in which the particles are created. In the decays of the particles, however, a different force is at work, and this weak nuclear force does not conserve strangeness—as with isospin symmetry, which is respected only by the strong nuclear force.

Conservation of strangeness

According to this proposal, particles are assigned a strangeness quantum number, S, which can have only integer values. The pion, proton, and neutron have $S = 0$. Because the strong nuclear force conserves strangeness, it can produce strange particles only in pairs, in which the net value of strangeness is zero. This phenomenon, whose importance was recognized by both Nishijima and the American physicist Abraham Pais in 1952, is known as associated production.

With the introduction of strangeness, physicists had several properties with which they could label the various subatomic particles. In particular, values of mass, electric charge, spin, isospin, and strangeness gave physicists a means of classifying the strongly interacting particles—or hadrons—and of establishing a hierarchy of relationships between them. In 1962 Gell-Mann and Yuval Ne'eman, an Israeli scientist, independently showed that a particular kind of mathematical symmetry provides the kind of grouping of hadrons that is observed in nature. The name of the mathematical symmetry is SU(3), which stands for "special unitary group in three dimensions."

SU(3) symmetry

SU(3) contains subgroups of objects that are related to each other by symmetric transformations, rather as a group describing the rotations of a square through 90° contains the four symmetric positions of the square. Gell-Mann and Ne'eman both realized that the basic subgroups of SU(3) contain either eight or 10 members and that the observed hadrons can be grouped together in eights or 10s in the same way. For example, the proton, neutron, and their relations with spin ½ fall into one group of eight, while the pion and its relations with spin 0 fit into another group of eight (see Figure 5). A group of nine very short-lived resonance particles with spin 3/2 could be seen to fit into a group of 10, although at the time the 10th member of the group, the particle known as the Ω^-, had not yet been observed. Its discovery early in 1964, at the Brookhaven National Laboratory in New York, was confirmation of the validity of the SU(3) symmetry of the hadrons.

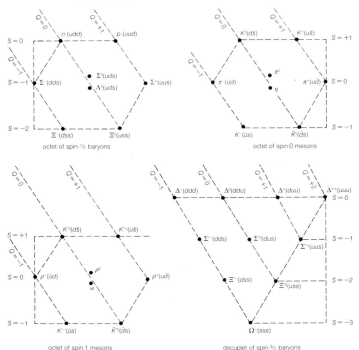

Figure 5: Combinations of the quarks *u*, *d*, and *s* and the corresponding antiquarks to form hadrons. The octets (hexagons) and the decuplet arise when particles are grouped according to strangeness, *S*, and charge, *Q*.

The beauty of the SU(3) symmetry does not, however, explain why it holds true. Gell-Mann and another American physicist, George Zweig, independently decided in 1964 that the answer to that question lies in the fundamental nature of the hadrons. The most basic subgroup of SU(3) contains only three objects, from which the groups of eight and 10 can be built. The two theorists made the bold suggestion that the hadrons observed at the time were not simple structures but were instead built from three basic particles. Gell-Mann called these particles quarks—the name that remains in use today.

By the time Gell-Mann and Zweig put forward their ideas, the list of known subatomic particles had grown from the three of 1932—electron, proton, and neutron—to include most of the "stable" hadrons (see Table 4) and a growing number of short-lived resonances, as well as the muon and two types of neutrino. That the seemingly ever-increasing number of hadrons could be understood in terms of only three basic building blocks was remarkable indeed. For this to be possible, however, those building blocks—the quarks—had to have some unusual properties.

These properties were so odd that for a number of years it was not clear as to whether quarks actually existed or were simply a useful mathematical fiction. For example, quarks must have charges of $+^2/_3 e$ or $-^1/_3 e$, which should be very easy to spot in certain kinds of detectors; but intensive

searches, both in cosmic rays and at particle accelerators, have never revealed any convincing evidence for fractional charge of this kind. By the early 1970s, however, 10 years after quarks were first proposed, scientists had compiled a mass of evidence which showed that quarks do exist but are locked within the individual hadrons in such a way that they can never escape one at a time.

This evidence resulted from experiments in which beams of electrons, muons, or neutrinos were fired at the protons and neutrons in such target materials as hydrogen (protons only), deuterium, carbon, and aluminum. The incident particles used were all leptons, particles that do not feel the strong nuclear binding force and that were known, even then, to be much smaller than the nuclei they were probing. The scattering of the beam particles caused by interactions within the target clearly demonstrated that protons and neutrons are complex structures that contain structureless, pointlike objects—the quarks.

Gell-Mann and Zweig required only three quarks to build the particles known in 1964. These quarks are the ones known as up (*u*), down (*d*), and strange (*s*). Since then, experiments have revealed a number of heavy hadrons—both mesons and baryons—which show that there are more than three quarks. Indeed, the SU(3) symmetry is part of a larger mathematical symmetry that incorporates quarks of several "flavours"—the term used to distinguish the different quarks. In addition to the up, down, and strange quarks, there are quarks known as charm and bottom (or beauty), and there is great theoretical prejudice, though scant experimental evidence, for a sixth quark, called top (or truth). These flavours are all conserved during reactions that occur through the strong nuclear force; in other words, charm must be created in association with anticharm, bottom with antibottom, and so on. This implies that the quarks can change from one flavour to another only by way of the weak nuclear force responsible for the decays of particles. Table 5 lists the characteristics of the six quarks.

The up and down quarks are distinguished only by their differing electric charges, while the heavier quarks each carry a unique quantum number related to their flavour. The strange quark has strangeness, $S=-1$, the charm quark has charm, $C=+1$, and so on. Thus, three strange quarks together give a particle with an electric charge of $-e$ and a strangeness of -3—just as is required for the Ω^- particle; and the neutral strange particle known as the lambda contains *uds*, giving the correct total charge of zero and strangeness of -1. Using this system, the lambda can be viewed as a neutron with one down quark changed to a strange quark; charge and spin remain the same, but the strange quark makes the lambda heavier than the neutron. Thus the quark model reveals that nature is not arbitrary when it produces particles but is in some sense repeating itself on a more massive scale.

The realization, in the late 1960s, that protons, neutrons, and even Yukawa's pions are all built from quarks changed the direction of thinking about the nuclear binding force. Although at the level of nuclei Yukawa's picture remained valid, at the more minute quark level, it could not satisfactorily explain what held the quarks together within the protons and pions, or what prevented the quarks from escaping one at a time.

The answer to questions like these seems to lie in the

Conservation of quark flavour

Table 5: Quarks*							
quark type	baryon number	charge	strangeness†	charm†	bottom†	top†	mass (MeV)
Down (*d*)	1/3	$-^1/_3 e$	0	0	0	0	7
Up (*u*)	1/3	$+^2/_3 e$	0	0	0	0	5
Strange (*s*)	1/3	$-^1/_3 e$	−1	0	0	0	150
Charm (*c*)	1/3	$+^2/_3 e$	0	1	0	0	1,400
Bottom (*b*)	1/3	$-^1/_3 e$	0	0	−1	0	4,800
Top (*t*)‡	1/3	$+^2/_3 e$	0	0	0	1	?

*Note that antiquarks exist for all flavours of quark and have opposite values for all the quantum numbers listed here. †These are quantum numbers that must be assigned to the quarks to differentiate the various flavours. ‡There is no convincing experimental evidence for the top quark, but its mass must certainly be greater than about 23,000 MeV, otherwise its bound state, toponium, would have been found.

The quark property of colour

property called colour. Colour was originally introduced to solve a problem raised by the exclusion principle that was formulated by the Austrian physicist Wolfgang Pauli in 1925. This rule does not allow particles with spin $1/2$, such as quarks, to occupy the same quantum state; therefore particles containing three quarks of the same flavour, such as the Ω^-, which consists of sss, should not exist. The Ω^- can contain one s spinning in one direction and a second s spinning in the opposite direction, but because there is no third direction, the third s should not be allowed.

To resolve this paradox, in 1964–65 Oscar Greenberg in the United States and Yoichiro Nambu and colleagues in Japan proposed the existence of a new property with three possible states. In analogy to the three primary colours of light, the new property became known as colour and the three varieties as red, green, and blue.

The three colour states are comparable to the two possible states of electric charge (positive and negative), and hadrons are analogous to atoms. Just as atoms contain electrically charged constituents whose charges balance overall to give a neutral atom, hadrons consist of coloured quarks that balance to give a particle with no net colour. Moreover, nuclei can be built from colourless protons and neutrons, rather as molecules form from electrically neutral atoms. Even Yukawa's pion exchange can be compared to exchange models of chemical bonding.

This analogy between electric charge and colour led to the idea that colour could be the source of the force between quarks, just as charge is the source of the electromagnetic force between charged particles. The force was seen to be working not between nucleons, as in Yukawa's theory, but between quarks. In the late 1960s and early 1970s, theorists turned to developing a quantum field theory based on coloured quarks. In such a theory, colour would take the role of charge in QED.

It was obvious that the field theory for coloured quarks had to be fundamentally different from QED because there are three kinds of colour as opposed to two kinds of electric charge. To cancel each other and give neutral objects, the two kinds of electric charge must be equal in magnitude but opposite in sign. With colour, three different charges must add together to give zero, so that the colours cannot be equal in the way that electric charges are. In addition, because SU(3) symmetry (the same type of mathematical symmetry that Gell-Mann and Ne'eman used for three flavours) applies to the three colours, quarks of one colour must be able to transform into another colour. This implies that a quark can emit something—the quantum of the field due to colour—that itself carries colour. And if the field quanta are coloured, then they can interact between themselves, unlike the photons of QED, which are electrically neutral.

Despite these differences, the basic framework for a field theory based on colour already existed by the late 1960s, due in large part to the work of theorists, particularly Chen Ning Yang and Robert Mills in the United States, who had studied similar theories in the 1950s. The new theory of the strong nuclear force was called quantum chromodynamics, or QCD, in analogy to quantum electrodynamics, or QED. In QCD the source of the field is the property of colour, and the field quanta are called gluons. Eight gluons are necessary in all to make the changes between the coloured quarks according to the rules of SU(3).

In the early 1970s several theorists working independently discovered that the strong nuclear force between quarks becomes stronger as quarks move apart, preventing the separation of an individual quark, but that it becomes weaker at smaller distances—unlike the behaviour of the electromagnetic force. The quarks have been compared to prisoners on a chain gang. When they are close together, they can move freely and do not notice the chains binding them. If one quark/prisoner tries to move away, however, the strength of the chains is felt and escape is prevented.

Asymptotic freedom

This effect, known as asymptotic freedom, has been attributed to the fact that the virtual gluons that flit between the quarks within a hadron are not neutral but carry mixtures of colour and anticolour (the colour of antiquarks). The farther away a quark moves, the more gluons appear, each contributing to the net force. When the quarks are close together, they exchange fewer gluons and the force is weaker. Only at infinitely close distances are quarks free.

The strong coupling between the quarks and gluons makes QCD a difficult theory to study. Mathematical procedures that work in QED cannot be used in QCD. The theory has nevertheless had a number of successes in describing the observed behaviour of particles in experiments, and theorists are confident that it is the right theory to use for describing the strong nuclear force.

Electroweak theory. The strong force binds particles together: by binding quarks within protons and neutrons, it indirectly binds protons and neutrons together to form nuclei. Nuclei can, however, break apart, or decay, naturally in the process known as radioactivity. One type of radioactivity, called beta decay, in which a nucleus emits an electron, thereby increasing its net positive charge by 1 unit, has been known since the late 1890s; but it was only with the discovery of the neutron in 1932 that physicists could begin to understand correctly what happens in the radioactive process.

The most basic form of beta decay involves the transmutation of a neutron into a proton, accompanied by the emission of an electron to keep the balance of electric charge. In addition, as Pauli realized in 1930, the neutron emits a neutral particle that shares the energy released by the decay. This neutral particle has little or no mass and is known as the neutrino. On its own, a neutron will decay in this way after an average lifetime of 15 minutes; only within the confines of certain nuclei does the balance of forces prevent neutrons from decaying and thereby keep the entire nucleus stable.

The rates of nuclear decay indicate that any force involved in beta decay must be much weaker than the force that binds nuclei together. It may seem counterintuitive to think of a nuclear force that can disrupt the nucleus; however, the transformation of a neutron into a proton that occurs in neutron decay is comparable to the transformations by the exchange of pions that Yukawa suggested to explain the nuclear binding force. Indeed, Yukawa's theory originally tried to explain both kinds of phenomena—weak decays and strong binding—with the exchange of a single type of particle. To give the different strengths, he proposed that the exchange particle couples strongly to the heavy neutrons and protons and weakly to the light electrons and neutrinos.

Yukawa was foreshadowing future developments in unifying the two nuclear forces in this way; however, as is explained below, he had chosen the wrong two forces. He was also bold in incorporating two "new" particles in his theory—the necessary exchange particle and the neutrino predicted by Pauli only five years previously.

Pauli had been hesitant in suggesting that a second particle must be emitted in beta decay, even though that would explain why the electron could leave with a range of energies. Such was the prejudice against the prediction of new particles that theorists as eminent as Bohr in Copenhagen preferred to suggest that the law of conservation of energy might break down at subnuclear distances.

By 1935, however, Pauli's new particle had found a champion in Enrico Fermi. Fermi named the particle the neutrino and incorporated it into his theory for beta decay, published in 1934. Like Yukawa, Fermi drew on an analogy with QED; but Fermi regarded the emission of the neutrino and electron by the neutron as the direct analogue of the emission of a photon by a charged particle, and he did not invoke a new exchange particle.

Fermi's theory, rather than Yukawa's, proved highly successful in describing nuclear beta decay, and it received added support in the late 1940s with the discovery of the pion and its relationship with the muon (see above). In particular, it became clear that the muon decays to an electron and two neutrinos in a process that has exactly the same basic strength as the neutron's decay to a proton. The idea of a "universal" weak interaction that, unlike the strong nuclear force, acts equally upon light and heavy particles (or leptons and hadrons) was born.

The nature of the weak force began to be revealed in 1956, as the result of work by two Chinese-American theorists, Tsung-Dao Lee and Chen Ning Yang. Lee and

Yang were trying to resolve some puzzles in the decays of the strange particles. They discovered that they could solve the mystery, provided that the weak nuclear force does not respect the symmetry known as parity.

The parity operation is like reflecting something in a mirror; it involves changing the coordinates (x, y, z) of each point to the "mirror" coordinates ($-x$, $-y$, $-z$). Physicists had always assumed that such an operation would make no difference to the laws of physics. Lee and Yang, however, proposed that the weak nuclear force is exceptional in this respect, and they suggested ways that parity violation might be observed in weak interactions. Early in 1957, just a few months after Lee and Yang's theory was published, experiments involving the decays of neutrons, pions, and muons showed that the weak nuclear force does indeed violate parity symmetry. Later that year, Lee and Yang were awarded the Nobel Prize for their work.

Parity violation and the concept of a universal form of weak interaction were combined in one theory in 1958 by the American physicists Murray Gell-Mann and Richard Feynman. They established the mathematical structure of the weak interaction in what is known as V-A, or vector minus axial vector, theory. This theory proved highly successful experimentally, at least at the relatively low energies accessible to particle physicists in the 1960s. It was clear that the theory had the correct kind of mathematical structure to account for parity violation and related effects, but there were strong indications that in describing particle interactions at higher energies than experiments could at the time access the theory began to go badly wrong.

The problems with V-A theory were related to a basic requirement of quantum field theory—the existence of a gauge boson, or messenger particle, to carry the force. Yukawa had attempted to describe the weak nuclear force in terms of the same intermediary that is responsible for the strong nuclear binding force, but this approach did not work. A few years after Yukawa had published his theory, a Swedish theorist, Oskar Klein, proposed a slightly different kind of carrier for the weak force.

In contrast to Yukawa's particle, which had spin 0, Klein's intermediary had spin 1 and therefore would give the correct spins for the neutrino and electron emitted in the beta decay of the neutron. Moreover, within the framework of Klein's concept, the known strength of the weak force in beta decay showed that the mass of the particle must be approximately 100 times the proton's mass, although the theory could not predict this value. All attempts to introduce such a particle into V-A theory, however, encountered severe difficulties, similar to those that had beset quantum electrodynamics during the 1930s and early '40s. The theory gave infinite probabilities to various interactions, and it defied the renormalization process that had been the salvation of QED.

Throughout the 1950s, theorists tried to construct field theories for the nuclear forces that would exhibit the same kind of gauge symmetry inherent in Maxwell's theory of electrodynamics and in QED. There were two major problems, which were in fact related. One concerned the infinities and the difficulty in renormalizing these theories; the other concerned the mass of the intermediaries. Straightforward gauge theory requires particles of zero mass as carriers, such as the photon of QED; but Klein had shown that the short-ranged weak nuclear force requires massive carriers.

In short, physicists had to discover the correct mathematical symmetry group for describing the transformations between different subatomic particles and then identify for the known forces the messenger particles required by fields with the chosen symmetry. Early in the 1960s Sheldon Glashow in the United States and Abdus Salam and John Ward in England decided to work with a combination of two symmetry groups, namely, SU(2) × U(1). Such a symmetry requires four spin-1 messenger particles, two electrically neutral and two charged. One of the neutral particles could be identified with the photon, while the two charged particles could be the messengers responsible for beta decay, in which charge changes hands, as when the neutron decays into a proton. The fourth messenger, a second neutral particle, seemed at the time to have no

obvious role: it apparently would permit weak interactions with no change of charge—so-called neutral current interactions—which had not yet been observed.

This theory, however, still required the messengers to be massless, which was all right for the photon but not for the messengers of the weak force. Toward the end of the 1960s, Salam and Steven Weinberg, an American theorist, independently realized how to introduce massive messenger particles into the theory while at the same time preserving its basic gauge symmetry properties. The answer lay in the work of Peter Higgs, an English theorist, who had discovered the concept of symmetry breaking, or, more descriptively, hidden symmetry.

A physical field can be intrinsically symmetrical, although this may not be apparent in the state of the universe in which experiments are conducted. On Earth, for example, gravity seems asymmetrical—it always pulls down. From a distance, however, the symmetry of the gravitational field around the Earth becomes apparent. At a more fundamental level, the fields associated with the electromagnetic and weak nuclear forces are not overtly symmetrical, as is demonstrated by the widely differing strengths of weak and electromagnetic interactions at low energies. Yet, according to Higgs's ideas, these forces can have an underlying symmetry. It is as if the universe lies at the bottom of a wine bottle. The symmetry of the bottle's base is clear from the top of the dimple in the centre, but it is hidden from any point in the valley surrounding the central dimple.

Higgs's mechanism for symmetry breaking provided Salam and Weinberg with a means of explaining the masses of the carriers of the weak force. Their theory, however, also predicted the existence of one or more new "Higgs" particles, which would carry additional fields needed for the symmetry breaking and have zero spin. With this sole proviso, the future of the electroweak theory began to look more promising. In 1971 a young Dutch theorist, Gerard 't Hooft, proved that the theory is renormalizable (in other words, that all the infinities cancel out), and many particle physicists became convinced that the electroweak theory was, at last, an acceptable theory for the weak force.

In addition to the Higgs particle, or particles, electroweak theory also predicts the existence of an electrically neutral carrier for the weak force. This neutral carrier, called the Z^0, should mediate the neutral current interactions, weak interactions in which electric charge is not transferred between particles. The search for evidence of such reactions, and thus further confirmation of the validity of the electroweak theory, began in earnest in the early 1970s.

The first signs of neutral currents came in 1973 from experiments at the European Organization for Nuclear Research (CERN) near Geneva. A team of more than 50 physicists from a variety of countries had diligently searched through the photographs taken of tracks produced when a large bubble chamber called Gargamelle was exposed to a beam of muon-antineutrinos. In a neutral current reaction, an antineutrino would simply scatter from an electron in the liquid contents of the bubble chamber. The incoming antineutrino, being neutral, would leave no track; nor would it leave a track as it left the chamber after being scattered off an electron. But the effect of the neutral current—the passage of a virtual Z^0 between the antineutrino and the electron—would set the electron in motion, and, being electrically charged, the electron would leave a track, which would appear as if from nowhere. Examining approximately 1.4 million pictures, the researchers found three examples of such a neutral current reaction. Although the reactions occurred only rarely, there were enough to set hopes high for the validity of electroweak theory.

In 1979 Glashow, Salam, and Weinberg, the theorists who had done much of the work in developing electroweak theory in the 1960s, were awarded the Nobel Prize. By that time enough information on charged and neutral current interactions had been compiled to predict that the masses of the weak messengers required by electroweak theory should be about 80 GeV for the charged W^+ and W^- particles and 90 GeV for the Z^0. There was, however, still no sign of the direct production of the weak messengers, because no accelerator was yet capable of producing collisions energetic enough to create real particles of such large masses (nearly 100 times as massive as the proton).

A scheme to find the W and Z particles was under way at CERN, however. The plan was to accelerate protons in one direction around CERN's largest proton synchrotron (a circular accelerator) and antiprotons in the opposite direction. At an appropriate energy (initially 270 GeV per beam) the two sets of particles would be made to collide head-on. The total energy of the collision would be far greater than anything that could be achieved by directing a single beam at a stationary target, and physicists hoped it would be sufficient to produce a small but significant number of W and Z particles.

Discovery of W and Z particles

In 1983 the researchers at CERN, working on two experiments code-named UA1 and UA2, were rewarded with the discovery of the particles they sought. The Ws and Zs that were produced did not live long enough to leave tracks in the detectors, but they decayed to particles that did leave tracks. The total energy of those decay particles, moreover, equaled the energy corresponding to the masses of the transient W and Z particles, just as predicted by electroweak theory (see Figure 2). It was a triumph both for CERN and for electroweak theory. Hundreds of physicists and engineers were involved in the project, and in 1984 the Italian physicist Carlo Rubbia and Simon van der Meer, a Dutch engineer, received the Nobel Prize for their leading roles in making the discovery of the W and Z particles possible.

CURRENT RESEARCH

Experiments. Electroweak theory, which describes the electromagnetic and weak nuclear forces, and quantum chromodynamics, the gauge theory of the strong nuclear force, together give what theorists call the "standard model." Although the model works well, as far as can be measured using present technology, a few points still await experimental verification.

The Higgs particle

Current research is focused on the Higgs particle, the particle associated with the mechanism that allows the symmetry of the electroweak force to be broken, or hidden, at low energies and that requires the W and Z particles, the carriers of the weak force, to have mass. The particle is necessary to electroweak theory because the Higgs mechanism requires a new field to break the symmetry, and according to quantum field theory all fields have particles associated with them. Researchers know that the Higgs particle must have spin 0, but that is virtually all that can be definitely predicted. Theory provides a poor guide as to the particle's mass or even the number of different varieties of Higgs particles involved.

Good experimental evidence for the top quark is also required. There is strong theoretical prejudice for such a quark because it would complete a set of three pairs of quarks. The quarks are linked together by weak interactions that change one flavour of quark to another, as when a down quark converts into an up quark in the beta decay of the neutron. To change into an up quark, the down quark emits a virtual W^- particle, which materializes as an electron and an electron-antineutrino. In an equivalent reaction, an electron-neutrino and a down quark can interact through the exchange of a W^- particle: the W^- flits from the quark to the lepton, creating an electron and an up quark. It is clear that the weak force, through the agency of the W^-, changes not only the flavour of the quark but also the nature of the lepton. Thus, the electron and its neutrino can be thought of as leptons of different flavour. The charm and strange quarks are similarly related, and the muon and tau pair up with their own brands of neutrino to form leptonic "flavour doublets." There are three lepton doublets, so it seems logical that there should be three quark doublets. Scientists therefore hope to find the sixth flavour of quark, top, which would pair with the bottom quark.

Theory shows that the top quark must be heavier than any of the other quarks but does not provide an estimate for the particle's mass. Experimentalists therefore are not certain at what energies they should look for the top quark. They do know, however, that one of the easiest

ways to observe the top quark would be in the production of "toponium," a particle consisting of a top quark bound with a top antiquark. The charm and bottom quarks were discovered in this manner in, respectively, charmonium and bottomonium.

Toponium

In an "onium" state, the quark and antiquark orbit each other until they annihilate either through the strong nuclear force into gluons or through the electromagnetic force into a photon. The strong force, being stronger, dominates, but for technical reasons to do with colour, the decay must involve more than one gluon and the process is slowed down. The quark-antiquark state is thus relatively long-lived, lasting 1,000 times longer than "ordinary" resonance particles, which also decay by the strong nuclear force but live for only 10^{-23} second.

Charmonium and bottomonium are relatively easily produced in the collisions of electrons and positrons. They show up as unusually narrow resonance spikes among the mass of particles produced when the total energy of the electron and positron equals the total energy—or equivalently the mass—of the quark-antiquark state (see Figure 6). Physicists hope to detect toponium in a similar way, using an electron-positron collider. Existing machines have failed to reveal toponium, so it is clear that the particle's mass must be greater than about 45 GeV. There has been speculation that top particles (particles containing a top quark, or antiquark, in combination with a lighter antiquark, or quark, specifically of bottom flavour) have been produced in proton-antiproton collisions at CERN. Certainly, these collisions could produce toponium with a mass of up to 100 GeV or so, but the decay would be extremely difficult to detect amid the debris of the proton-antiproton collisions.

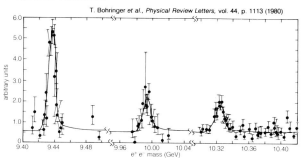

T. Bohringer et al., *Physical Review Letters*, vol. 44, p. 1113 (1980)

Figure 6: Resonance bumps reveal three members of the bottomonium family, particles built from a bottom quark orbiting a bottom antiquark in different energy states.

Some experimentalists continue to search for signs of free quarks, even though quantum chromodynamics seems to provide an explanation for why quarks appear only in clusters, as baryons and mesons. With an electric charge either $\frac{1}{3}$ or $\frac{2}{3}$ the size of the standard unit of charge, a single quark would have a distinctive "signature." This is important experimentally because charged particles are detected when they lose energy ionizing, or knocking electrons from, atoms in the material they travel through. The energy lost in this way depends on the square of the charge: a quark with a charge of $\frac{2}{3}$ produces $\frac{4}{9}$, or just under half, the ionization of an ordinary particle, while a quark with a charge of $\frac{1}{3}$ produces only $\frac{1}{9}$ the ionization. No convincing evidence for particles with fractions of charge has yet been found, but until it has been proved that single quarks cannot exist, researchers conducting high-energy experiments will continue to keep a close watch to see if quarks are liberated.

Theory. The standard model combining electroweak theory and quantum chromodynamics provides a satisfactory way of understanding most experimental results in particle physics, yet it is far from satisfying as a theory. In addition to the missing Higgs particle and top quark, many problems and gaps in the model have been explained in a rather ad hoc manner. Values for such basic properties as the fractional charges of quarks or the masses of quarks and leptons must be inserted "by hand" into the model; that is, they are determined by experiment and observation rather than by theoretical predictions.

Many theorists working in particle physics are therefore looking beyond the standard model in an attempt to find a more comprehensive theory. One important approach has been the development of grand unified theories, or GUTs, which seek to unify the strong, weak, and electromagnetic forces in the way that electroweak theory does for two of these forces. General arguments indicate that the intrinsic strengths of the electroweak and strong forces become equal at extremely high energies of about 10^{15} GeV, or 10 million million times the energies at which the electromagnetic and weak forces merge into the electroweak force. These energies are far beyond the reach of modern particle accelerators, but GUTs do make predictions that can be tested at more accessible low energies.

Any gauge field theory that contains QCD and electroweak theory, in other words, any GUT, must use a mathematical symmetry group that contains the symmetries of both QCD and electroweak theory. There are various possibilities, one of the simplest and among the first to be studied being a theory based on the group SU(5). The idea is that above the grand unification energy of 10^{15} GeV, the larger SU(5) group describes the symmetry of the unified field theory. At lower energies, this grand symmetry breaks down into the symmetries of QCD and electroweak theory.

A theory that links strong and electroweak interactions in this way must link the quarks with the leptons so that the main distinction between the two groups of particles appears only when the grand unification is broken and leptons, which do not feel the strong force, "decouple" from quarks. Indeed, grand unified theories tend to bring the quarks and leptons together into one family. This implies that a quark can convert into a lepton (or vice versa), which in turn leads to the conclusion that protons are not stable but decay into leptons. Protons must be manifestly stable, however, at least on time scales of 10^{17} years, otherwise all matter would be radioactive.

The key to resolving this seeming contradiction can be found in the gauge bosons of the grand unified theories. These gauge bosons include not only the photon, Z^0, W^+, W^-, and the gluons of the standard model but also new bosons, named X, that mediate the transitions between quarks and leptons. The X bosons must be very massive; indeed, their masses must be comparable to the energy scale of grand unification and therefore at least 10^{15} GeV. This tremendous mass means that proton decay occurs only rarely, and, in fact, the lifetime of the proton is calculated to be at least 10^{30} years.

It might seem impossible to verify experimentally such a lifetime. Particle lifetimes, or strictly half-lives, are only averages, however. Given a large enough collection of protons, there is a chance that a few may decay within an observable time. This has encouraged physicists to set up a number of proton decay experiments in which large quantities of inexpensive material, usually water, iron, or concrete, are surrounded by detectors that can spot the particles produced if a proton decays. So far, there is no clear evidence that protons decay, and this rules out some of the simplest possible GUTs.

Grand unified theories automatically resolve some of the problems with the standard model. For example, they correctly predict the charges of the quarks and leptons, as well as the relationship between the strengths of the different forces. They are, however, inadequate in many respects. They give no explanation, for example, for the number of pairs of quarks and leptons; they even raise the question of why such an enormous gap exists between the masses of the W and Z bosons of the electroweak force and the X bosons of lepton-quark interactions. Most importantly, they do not include the fourth force, gravity.

The dream of theorists is to find a totally unified theory—a theory of everything, or TOE. Attempts to derive a quantum field theory containing gravity always ran aground, however, until a remarkable development in 1984 first hinted that a quantum theory that includes gravity might be possible. The new development, which is known as superstring theory, contains two important ingredients. First, it regards subatomic particles—quarks, leptons, and bosons—not as points in space, as in conventional field theories, but as extended objects, or "strings." String theories were originally developed in the early 1970s by Yoichiro Nambu at the University of Chicago in an attempt to find a theory for the strong nuclear force. Quantum chromodynamics is now accepted as providing the correct description of strong interactions, but in 1976 the French physicist Joël Scherk and his colleagues found they could rid string theories of certain inconsistencies if they introduced the concept of "supersymmetry."

Supersymmetry provides a means of linking the quarks and leptons, which have spin $^1/_2$ and are collectively called fermions, with the bosons of the gauge fields, which have spins of 1 or 2 (see Table 2), and the Higgs particle, which has spin 0. Although this has great appeal to many physicists because it helps to unite the otherwise different kinds of particles, it generally leads to a doubling of the number of fundamental particles by introducing photinos, winos, zinos, gluinos, and gravitinos, which have spins of $^1/_2$ or $^3/_2$ and are supersymmetric counterparts for the bosons, and sleptons and squarks, fermion counterparts with integer values of spin.

The incorporation of supersymmetry into string theory is known as superstring theory. Its importance was not recognized until an English theorist, Michael Green, and an American, John Schwarz, showed that in two specific cases the superstring theory is entirely self-consistent. All potential problems cancel out, despite the fact that the theory automatically contains a quantum description of gravity. The two cases correspond to superstrings described by two unusually large mathematical symmetry groups—SO(32) and the "exceptional" group $E_8 \times E_8$. The E_8 symmetry group contains the smaller group E_6, one of the symmetry groups favoured by theorists studying possible GUTs. E_6 contains within it the symmetries of QCD and electroweak theory—the theories known to work at low energies. For the first time, a theory, rather than observation, has determined which symmetry group to use and, as far as physicists can tell, has done so accurately.

The superstring theory seems to operate in a 10-dimensional space—that is, in six dimensions over and above the three dimensions of space and one of time that are perceived in the everyday world. Although this idea seems daunting at first, it does not necessarily pose a problem. Fifty years before the advent of superstrings, the Polish physicist Theodor Kaluza and Oskar Klein considered a unified theory of gravity and electromagnetism based on five dimensions. They argued that the fifth dimension "curls up" to be very small, thus leaving only the four familiar dimensions of space and time. The effects of the fifth dimension would be perceived as electromagnetism when viewed from the restricted perspective of four dimensions. The Kaluza-Klein theory may not have been the ultimate TOE, but it indicated to theorists in the 1980s one possible way to deal with the 10 dimensions of superstrings. The six unwanted dimensions can be considered to be curled up, leaving the physics observed in the low-energy world, where the superstrings, which have miniscule dimensions of 10^{-35} metre, appear as points, with QCD and electroweak theory as workable approximations of the effects of the extra dimensions. It remains to be seen whether superstring theory is the much-desired theory of everything.

Grand unified theories

Stability of the proton

Superstring theory

BIBLIOGRAPHY. Nonspecialist introductions to particle physics that give a broad outline of the subject include FRANK CLOSE, MICHAEL MARTEN, and CHRISTINE SUTTON, *The Particle Explosion* (1987); YUVAL NE'EMAN and YORAM KIRSH, *The Particle Hunters* (1986; originally published in Hebrew, 1983); PETER WATKINS, *Story of the W and Z* (1986); Y. NAMBU, *Quarks: Frontiers in Elementary Particle Physics* (1985); CHRISTINE SUTTON, *The Particle Connection: The Most Exciting Scientific Chase Since DNA and the Double Helix* (1984, reissued 1985); PAUL DAVIES, *Superforce: The Search for a Grand Unified Theory of Nature* (1984, reprinted 1985); FRANK CLOSE, *The Cosmic Onion: Quarks and the Nature of the Universe* (1983, reissued 1986); HARALD FRITZSCH, *Quarks: The Stuff of Matter* (1983, reissued 1984; originally published in German, 1981); and J.H. MULVEY (ed.), *The Nature of Matter* (1981). More detailed historical accounts can be found in ABRAHAM PAIS, *Inward Bound: Of Matter and Forces in the Physical World* (1986); LAURIE M. BROWN and LILLIAN HODDESON (eds.), *The Birth of Particle*

Physics (1983); and STEVEN WEINBERG, *The Discovery of Subatomic Particles* (1983). More technical introductory texts are DONALD H. PERKINS, *Introduction to High Energy Physics,* 3rd ed. (1987); B.G. DUFF, *Fundamental Particles: An Introduction to Quarks and Leptons* (1986); L.B. OKUN, *Particle Physics: The Quest for the Substance of Substance,* trans. from Russian (1985); IAN J.R. AITCHISON and ANTHONY J.G. HEY, *Gauge Theories in Particle Physics: A Practical Introduction* (1982, reprinted 1984); and GRAHAM G. ROSS, *Grand Unified Theories* (1984). An interesting collection of important papers on electroweak theory is contained in C.H. LAI (ed.), *Selected Papers on Gauge Theory of Weak and Electromagnetic Interactions* (1981). For more recent developments, as well as useful past references, see, for example: SIMON ANTHONY, "Superstrings: A Theory of Everything?" *New Scientist,* 107(1471):34–36 (Aug. 29, 1985); GERARD 'T HOOFT, "Gauge Theories of the Forces Between Elementary Particles," *Scientific American,* 242(6):104–138 (June 1980); P.Q. HUNG and C. QUIGG, "Intermediate Bosons: Weak Interaction Couriers," *Science,* 210(4475):1205–11 (Dec. 12, 1980); and "Anomaly Cancellation Launches Superstring Bandwagon," *Physics Today,* 38(7):17–20 (July 1985). Many of the articles published in *New Scientist* are collected in CHRISTINE SUTTON (ed.), *Building the Universe* (1985).

(Christine Sutton)

Volcanism

Volcanoes figure prominently in the mythology of many peoples who have learned to live with eruptions, but science was late in recognizing the important role of volcanism in the evolution of the Earth. One major 18th-century school of thought held that molten rock and volcanoes were simply accidents caused by burning coal seams. Geologists today agree that volcanism is a profound process resulting from the thermal evolution of planetary bodies. Heat does not easily escape from large bodies by conduction or radiation. Instead, partial melting and buoyant rise of magma are major contributors to the process of heat flux from the Earth's interior. Volcanoes are the surface manifestation of this thermal process, which has its roots deep inside the Earth and which hurls its ashes high into the atmosphere.

The term volcano can either mean the vent from which magma erupts to the surface, or it can refer to the landform created by the solidified lava and fragmental volcanic debris that accumulate near the vent. One could say, for example, that large lava flows are erupted from Kilauea Volcano in Hawaii, the word volcano here signifying a vent. By contrast, one could say that Kilauea is a gently sloping volcano of modest size as Hawaiian volcanoes go, the reference in this case being to a landform.

Broadly defined, all igneous rocks are the result of volcanism. If igneous rocks solidify from magmas that have not reached the surface, they are called intrusive igneous rocks, and this process in a more restricted sense is termed plutonism. Igneous rocks that cool and solidify at the Earth's surface are known as extrusive igneous rocks, and these are unequivocally products of volcanism.

Volcanoes (and their products) are not the realm of any single scientific discipline. Rather, they require study by many scientists from several specialties: geophysicists and geochemists to probe the deep roots; geologists to decipher prehistoric activity; biologists to learn how life becomes established and evolves on barren volcanic islands; and meteorologists to determine the effects of volcanic dust and gases on the atmosphere, weather, and climate.

This article discusses volcanism both by topics and by examples. Under the topic of types of volcanic activity, the 1980 eruption of Mt. St. Helens in southwestern Washington is used as an example of an explosive eruption that involves ejection of pyroclastic fragments. The 1984 eruption of Mauna Loa Volcano in Hawaii serves to illustrate a "quiet" eruption involving the effusion of lava. The widely varying composition of volcanic gases from fumaroles is explained by studies at Kilauea Volcano, and Yellowstone National Park in the western United States provides classic examples of hot springs and geysers.

Volcanic landforms evolve from the cumulative effects of both constructive and destructive eruptions. Mt. Fuji exemplifies a stratovolcano and Mauna Loa typifies a shield volcano. Iceland provides fine examples of volcanic plateaus, and since it sits astride the Mid-Atlantic Ridge, it is also a logical starting place for a discussion of submarine volcanic structures.

Volcanoes are closely associated with tectonic activity. Most of them occur on either the overriding or the diverging margins of the enormous lithospheric plates that make up the Earth's surface. The volcanoes of Japan provide an excellent example of the former, while those of the Mid-Atlantic Ridge the latter. Intraplate volcanoes such as those of the Hawaiian chain occur within lithospheric plates, but they provide important evidence as to the direction and rate of plate motion.

Volcanoes affect humankind in many ways. Their destructiveness is awesome, but the risk involved can be reduced by assessing volcanic hazards and forecasting volcanic eruptions. Volcanism provides fertile soils, valuable mineral deposits, and geothermal energy. Over geologic time volcanoes recycle the Earth's hydrosphere and atmosphere, and explosive eruptions can affect climate.

For coverage of related topics in the *Macropædia* and *Micropædia,* see the *Propædia,* sections 212 and 231.

This article is divided into the following sections:

Types of volcanic activity

VOLCANOES

Basis for classification

Volcanoes can be classified by their eruptive habits and are generally arranged by progressive increases in the explosiveness of their eruptions. The type of volcanic eruption also plays an important role in the evolution of a volcanic landform, thus forming a significant link between eruptive habit and volcanic structure.

Less explosive eruptions involve the effusive outpouring of basaltic magma that is relatively low in viscosity and in gas content. (The term lava is applied to molten magma after it has erupted to the surface.) More explosive eruptions generally involve magma that is more viscous and has a higher gas content. Such magma is shattered into pyroclastic fragments by explosive boiling during an eruption.

Types of eruptions. In classification schemes based on character of eruption, volcanic activity and volcanic areas are commonly divided into six major types in order of increasing degree of explosiveness: (1) Icelandic, (2) Hawaiian, (3) Strombolian, (4) Vulcanian, (5) Pelean, and (6) Plinian.

Fissure eruptions

The Icelandic type is characterized by effusions of molten basaltic lava that flow from long parallel fissures. Such outpourings often build lava plateaus.

The Hawaiian type is similar to the Icelandic variety. In this case, however, fluid lava flows from summit and radial fissures to form shield volcanoes.

The Strombolian type involves moderate bursts of expanding gases that eject clots of incandescent lava in cyclical or nearly continuous small eruptions. Because of such small intermittent outbursts, Stromboli Volcano (off the west coast of Italy) has been called the "lighthouse of the Mediterranean."

The Vulcanian type, named for the island of Vulcano that neighbours Stromboli, generally involves moderate explosions of gas laden with volcanic ash (*i.e.,* fine volcanic particles). This mixture forms dark, turbulent eruption clouds that rapidly ascend and expand in convoluted shapes.

Explosive eruptions

The Pelean type is associated with explosive outbursts that generate dense mixtures of hot volcanic fragments and gas. It is named for the destructive eruption of Mt. Pelée in Martinique in 1902. The fluidized slurries produced by Pelean-type eruptions are heavier than air but are of low viscosity and pour down valleys and slopes at velocities exceeding 100 kilometres per hour (60 miles per hour). Variously called *nuées ardentes,* glowing avalanches, ash flows, or pyroclastic flows, such hot fluidized flows of volcanic gases and fragments are extremely destructive.

The Plinian type is an intensely violent kind of volcanic eruption exemplified by the outburst of Mt. Vesuvius in AD 79 that killed the famous Roman scholar Pliny the Elder, from whom the name is taken. In this type, gases boiling out of gas-rich magma generate enormous, nearly continuous jetting blasts that rip apart and core out the magma column. The uprushing gases and volcanic fragments appear like a gigantic rocket blast directed vertically upward. Plinian eruption clouds can rise into the stratosphere and are sometimes sustained for several hours.

Figure 1 features schematic diagrams of these eruption types. There are, however, many gradations among—and exceptions to—such idealized types, and it is not unusual for an eruption sequence to involve more than one type of activity. For example, the eruptions of Mt. St. Helens from 1980 to 1986, in sequence, consisted of small Vulcanian-type explosions, large Pelean and Plinian explosions, and extrusions of viscous lava into a lava dome that caps the vent. The different types of volcanic activity can best be described by comparing specific eruptions.

Some notable examples. *Mt. St. Helens, Washington, 1980–86.* Prior to 1980 Mt. St. Helens was a steep, conical volcanic peak rising to 2,950 metres (9,680 feet). Its summit was capped by snowfields and small glaciers. It had erupted during at least 20 intervals over the past 4,500 years, with the last active period between 1831 and 1857. Dwight Crandell and Donal Mullineaux of the U.S. Geological Survey studied the volcanic deposits in the vicinity of Mt. St. Helens and noted in their 1978

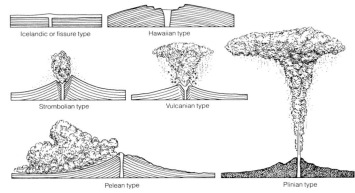

Figure 1: The major types of volcanic eruptions.
From A. Holmes, *Principles of Physical Geology*; reproduced with permission of Van Nostrand Reinhold (UK) Ltd, Wokingham Berkshire UK

report that the volcano would probably erupt violently and intermittently, just as it had in the recent geologic past, "within the next 100 years, and perhaps even before the end of this century." Two years later these prophetic words became reality.

Pre-eruption earthquake swarm

On March 20, 1980, an earthquake swarm began near Mt. St. Helens. By March 25 the swarm increased to its maximum energy release with 47 earthquakes of magnitude 3 or greater on the Richter scale within a 12-hour period. Seismographs located the source of the earthquake swarm at shallow depth beneath the north flank of the mountain (Figure 2).

An eruption was expected, and it soon began. The first small explosions on March 27 excavated a crater about 70 metres wide on the ice-covered summit. Several such small Vulcanian-type eruptions occurred daily. They ejected dark, turbulent clouds of volcanic ash that blackened the downwind snowfields. No new magma appeared in the ash, however; only old volcanic debris was thrown out. These small explosive eruptions apparently resulted from groundwater in the volcanic cone being heated above its subsurface boiling point and flashing into steam. The crater was enlarged by the small explosive eruptions to an oval basin 500 by 300 metres wide and 200 metres deep.

At the peak of seismic energy release on March 25, large east–west cracks formed across the summit of Mt. St. Helens. Soon after this, people familiar with the mountain noticed changes in its shape and in ice fracture patterns on

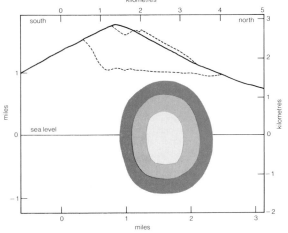

Figure 2: *Topographic profiles of Mt. St. Helens and location of the pre-eruption earthquake swarm.*
The solid line represents the profile before March 20, 1980; the upper line depicts the profile of May 17, 1980, just before the main eruption; and the lower line indicates the profile immediately after the eruption of May 18. The shaded area represents the region in which the earthquake swarm of March 20–May 18 occurred. The darker the shading, the higher the density of earthquake locations.

the high north face of the volcano. Geodetic surveys and aerial photographs in April and early May 1980 confirmed that a growing bulge nearly two kilometres (1.2 miles) in diameter on the high north slope was moving upward and outward by as much as one to two metres per day.

Most of the scientists studying the mountain at this time agreed that an intrusion of magma was being injected at a shallow depth beneath the north side of the volcano. Whether this intrusion would erupt at the surface—and if so, when—were unanswered questions.

On the morning of May 18, Mt. St. Helens was shaken by an earthquake of about 5 Richter magnitude, and ice falls occurred within the crater. The entire north side of the summit then began to move as one huge mass. This giant landslide, composed of more than two cubic kilometres (0.48 cubic mile) of rock and ice, was immediately followed by an enormous explosion of expanding steam and volcanic gases. Fluidized by the expanding gases, the avalanche reached velocities as high as 250 kilometres per hour. One lobe swept into Spirit Lake, but the main body of the debris avalanche roared 21 kilometres down the valley of the Toutle River, forming a hummocky deposit one to two kilometres wide and up to 150 metres deep.

As the great avalanche suddenly released the pressure inside the volcanic cone, superheated groundwater flashed into steam, and gases dissolved in the magma boiled out with explosive violence. These expanding gases formed a lateral blast of hot, dense, debris-filled clouds that surged northward along the ground at high speed. The blast devastated 550 square kilometres (210 square miles) of mountain terrain to the northeast, north, and northwest of Mt. St. Helens. The ground-hugging black clouds of steam and hot rock fragments rolled over four major ridges and valleys as far as 28 kilometres from the volcano's summit.

The destruction was awesome. For the first few kilometres everything was obliterated. Great conifer trees up to three metres in diameter were uprooted and blown away. Beyond this was a blowdown zone where virgin Douglas firs were snapped off like matchsticks. The U.S. Forest Service estimated that 10,000,000 trees were felled by the blast. At the limits of the blast cloud, trees were still standing but their needles were scorched beyond recovery. About 55 to 60 people were killed by the avalanche and blast.

As the ground-hugging blast clouds raced northward, a Plinian eruption began to jet upward from the exposed-magma column. This vertical eruption cloud mushroomed to more than 20 kilometres in altitude and was sustained most of the day by the escaping gases as they cored out the gas-rich magma. Northeast and east winds blew ash from the Plinian cloud in a wide swath over Washington, Idaho, and Montana. At Ritzville, Wash., 330 kilometres east-northeast of Mt. St. Helens, volcanic ash that appeared "like gray talcum powder" was seven centimetres (nearly three inches) thick. The weight of the measured ashfall equaled 0.15 cubic kilometre of magma, and the fine ash and gases dispersed into the stratosphere were estimated to equal another 0.1 cubic kilometre of magma.

During the afternoon of May 18, pyroclastic flows of fine ash and pumice blocks began rushing down the north slope of Mt. St. Helens through the deep breach in the north face of the mountain. These fluidized emulsions of hot rock fragments mixed with hot volcanic gases were denser than the ascending ash cloud, and they issued from the crater beneath the uprushing cloud. In effect, both Plinian- and Pelean-type eruptions occurred at the same time.

Floods and mudflows consisting of slurries of volcanic ash and fine rock particles mixed with water poured down the rivers draining Mt. St. Helens. The largest mudflow occurred in the north fork of the Toutle River where it exceeded historic flood levels by nine metres.

The May 18 eruption displaced 2.7 cubic kilometres of volcanic rock, including 0.5 cubic kilometre of new magma, and destroyed the summit of Mt. St. Helens. Before the eruption the peak was 2,950 metres high (Figure 3). This was replaced by a horseshoe-shaped crater two kilometres across and roughly 750 metres deep, whose rim has an elevation of 2,400–2,550 metres—400 metres below the old summit elevation. Overall, Mt. St. Helens

lost about 1,100 metres of elevation from the old peak to the new crater floor.

Following the great eruption of May 18, Mt. St. Helens produced five smaller explosive eruptions during the summer and fall of 1980. After 1980 a dome of lava grew intermittently in the crater. This lava is so viscous that it does not flow away; instead it piles up into a steep mound or dome over the vent. By 1986 the dome measured about 250 metres high and 1,000 metres wide, and it contained some 75,000,000 cubic metres of dacitic lava (see below *Determinants of size and shape*; see also Figure 4).

Explosive eruptions of fragmental volcanic rocks vary greatly in scale. Measured by the volume of new magma involved, the May 18 eruption of Mt. St. Helens was only a moderate eruption. The explosive eruption of Tambora Volcano in Indonesia in 1815 is estimated to have expelled from 50 to 100 cubic kilometres of magma, and the 1883 eruption of Krakatoa spelled Krakatau in Bahasa Indonesia), another Indonesian volcano, about 18 cubic kilometres. Fortunately, as the eruptive magnitude increases, the frequency of eruptions greatly decreases. Civilizations have never been tested by a cataclysm on the scale of the eruption at Yellowstone about 2,000,000 years ago; that eruption involved nearly 3,000 cubic kilometres of explosively boiling magma.

Mauna Loa, Hawaii, 1984. The May 18, 1980, eruption of Mt. St. Helens is a classic example of explosive volcanism. The 1984 eruption of the great shield volcano Mauna Loa, by contrast, is illustrative of effusive volcanism.

Every three to four years, on average, Mauna Loa erupts with fountains and streams of incandescent lava. The summit of the volcano is 4,170 metres above sea level and more than 9,000 metres above the seafloor that surrounds the Hawaiian Ridge. Its volume above the seafloor, estimated to be about 40,000 cubic kilometres, qualifies it as the world's largest volcano.

Following a year of increased seismicity, Mauna Loa began erupting at 1:25 AM on March 25, 1984. The outbreak began along a fissure that split the long axis of the summit caldera, a cliff-bounded basin with a three-by-five-kilometre diameter that had been formed by prehistoric subsidence. Lava fountains along the fissure formed a curtain of fire that illuminated the clouds and volcanic fume into a red glow backlighting the black profile of the volcano's huge but gently sloping summit. Lava from the summit fissure ponded in the caldera, and the first observers in the air reported that much of the caldera floor was covered by a lake of orange-red molten rock, which quickly cooled to a black crust with zigzag, still incandescent fractures.

At dawn the summit fissure began to propagate down the northeast rift zone, and a new line of lava fountains formed at an elevation of 3,800 metres (Figure 5). Two hours later the fracture broke an additional six kilometres down the northeast rift, forming another curtain of fire about two kilometres long and 50 metres high at an elevation of 3,450 metres. As new vents opened at lower elevations, the higher vents stopped erupting.

The vents at 3,450 metres continued to erupt throughout the early afternoon, sending a small lava flow down the high southeast flank of Mauna Loa. At about 4:00 PM the lava fountains dwindled, and a swarm of new earthquakes indicated that the fissure was breaking even farther down the rift. The new and final vents opened at 4:40 PM at an elevation of 2,900 metres, some seven kilometres down the ridge from the 3,450-metre vents.

The output of lava from these vents was vigorous. Although the fountains were only about 20 metres high, the volume of lava amounted to approximately 500,000 cubic metres per hour (about 17,600,000 cubic feet per hour). In 24 hours the river of lava flowed 12 kilometres northeast toward the city of Hilo. The temperature of the erupting lava was 1,140° C (2,084° F) and its viscosity about 10^3 poise (roughly the same as liquid honey at 20° C).

The fissure did not break any farther down the northeast rift zone of Mauna Loa, and the vents at 2,900 metres remained in steady eruption for the next 10 days. Even though the eruption rate remained high, the advance of the front of the lava flow slowed—six kilometres the second

Margin notes

Massive landslide of rock and ice

Plinian cloud

Formation of a lava dome

Fiery lava fountains

day, four kilometres the third day, and three kilometres the fourth day. This progressive slowing of the lava-flow front was caused by several factors: slow widening of flows at higher elevations; thickening of flows at higher elevations by overplating (*i.e.,* accumulation of new layers on top of layers only a few hours or days old); thickening and widening of flows at lower elevations where the slope of the land is more gradual; and branching of the flows upstream into new lobes that robbed the lower flows of their lava supply. A household analogue of a Hawaiian lava flow in miniature is the slow and erratic advance of molten wax as it adds new lobes to a pile of candle drippings.

By April 5 the output from the vents at 2,900 metres began to wane, and by April 15 the eruption was over. The longest flows traveled 27 kilometres, stopping at an elevation of 900 metres—10 kilometres from the outskirts of Hilo. The total volume of the eruption was 220,000,-000 cubic metres, and new lava flows covered 48 square kilometres. No one was hurt, and the only significant damage was the cutting of power lines and the blocking of a few jeep roads.

Controlling factors in eruptions

Why are some volcanic eruptions so explosive while others are so spectacular but relatively harmless? The answer involves at least three factors: the amount of gas dissolved in the magma, the viscosity of the magma, and the rate of decompression of the magma as it rises toward the surface. Volcanoes related to converging plate margins (see below) generally have a high gas content and their magma is very viscous. This is an explosive combination because the gases cannot easily boil out; rather, they remain pent up until they reach the pressure at which they blow the viscous magma into fragments. The rate at which pressure is reduced also controls the explosiveness. If magma moves slowly toward the surface its dissolved gases are released slowly. At Mt. St. Helens the avalanche that initiated the eruption caused very rapid decompression of the shallow intrusion, resulting in violent and explosive boiling of the trapped gases (Figure 6).

OTHER MANIFESTATIONS OF VOLCANIC ACTIVITY

Volcanic gases. The most common volcanic gases are carbon dioxide, water, sulfur dioxide, and hydrogen sulfide. Small quantities of other volatile elements and compounds also are present; *e.g.,* hydrogen, helium, nitrogen, hydrogen chloride, hydrogen fluoride, and mercury. The specific gaseous compounds released from magma depend on temperature, pressure, and overall composition of the volatile elements present. The amount of available oxygen is of critical importance. When oxygen is lacking, methane, hydrogen, and hydrogen sulfide are stable, but when hot volcanic gases mix with atmospheric gases, carbon dioxide, water, and sulfur dioxide are stable.

Some volcanic gases are less soluble in magma than others and separate at higher pressures. Studies at Kilauea Volcano indicate that carbon dioxide begins to separate from its parent magma at depths of about 40 kilometres, whereas most of the sulfur gases and water are not released until the magma has nearly reached the surface. Fumaroles (volcanic gas vents) near Halemaumau Crater at Kilauea's summit are rich in carbon dioxide that leaks from the magma chamber located at three to four kilometres beneath the surface. Fumaroles on the rift zones of Kilauea, however, are richer in water and sulfur because much of the carbon dioxide leaks away at the summit before the

magma is intruded laterally into the rift zones (Figure 8).

Hot springs and geysers

Hydrothermal features. Hot springs and geysers also are manifestations of volcanic activity. They result from the interaction of groundwater with magma or with solidified but still hot igneous rocks at shallow depths.

Yellowstone National Park is one of the most famous areas of hot springs and geysers in the world. The total heat flux from these thermal features is estimated to be 300 megawatts. The last great eruption at Yellowstone occurred about 600,000 years ago when some 1,000 cubic kilometres of rhyolite magma were ejected in huge ash flows and resulted in the formation of a caldera approximately 45 by 75 kilometres in size. (A caldera is a large circular or oval depression caused by surface collapse into the subsurface region from which magma had been removed.) Yellowstone Lake now occupies part of this giant caldera. Since that last great outburst, about 1,200 cubic kilometres of rhyolite lava flows and domes have erupted in numerous smaller events. The cooling roots of such past eruptions, or possibly new intrusions of magma at shallow depth, are the apparent sources of heat for the Yellowstone hot springs and geysers.

Geysers are actually hot springs that intermittently spout a column of hot water and steam into the air. This action is caused by the water in deep conduits beneath a geyser approaching or reaching the boiling point. At 100 metres below the surface, the boiling point of water increases to approximately 150° C because of the increased pressure of the overlying hot water. As bubbles of steam or dissolved gas begin to form and hot water spills from the vent of a geyser, the pressure is lowered on the water column below. Water at depth then momentarily exceeds its boiling point and more water flashes into steam. This chain reaction continues until the geyser exhausts its supply of boiling water.

After a geyser stops spouting, the conduits at depth refill with groundwater and reheating to near the boiling point begins again. In geysers such as Yellowstone's Old Faithful, the spouting and recharge period is quite regular. This famous geyser has gushed to heights of 35–50 metres about every 40–80 minutes for more than 100 years (Figure 9). Other geysers have much more erratic recharge times.

Volcanic landforms

DETERMINANTS OF SIZE AND SHAPE

The common mental image of a volcano is that of a steep symmetrical cone sweeping upward in a concave curve to a sharp summit peak. Mt. Fuji in Japan is the archetypal volcanic landform, but only a few volcanoes attain this ideal shape.

Fundamental variables

The shape and size of a volcano are controlled by several factors. These include (1) the volume of volcanic products, (2) the composition of volcanic products, (3) the sequence of eruption (*e.g.,* many small eruptions with short repose times between eruptions, or a few large eruptions with long repose times), (4) the variety of volcanic eruption types, (5) the geometry of the vent, and (6) the environment into which the volcanic products are erupted.

Volumes released in any one eruption can vary enormously from a few cubic metres of magma to as much as 3,000 cubic kilometres. Small volumes tend to build up mounds close to the vent, whereas very large eruptions create plateaus of lava or ash flows. Eruptions of large

name	silica (SiO$_2$) content (percent)	major minerals	colour	approximate density with no voids (g/cm^3)
Basalt	45–53	Ca feldspar, pyroxene, olivine	dark gray	3.0
Andesite	53–62	CaNa feldspar, pyroxene, amphibole	medium gray	2.9
Dacite	62–70	Na feldspar, amphibole, biotite, quartz	light gray* to tan	2.8
Rhyolite	70–78	K, Na feldspars, quartz, biotite	light gray* to pink	2.7

Table 1: Common Types of Volcanic Rock

*Obsidian glass can be dark gray to black.

ash-flow plateaus almost always form a caldera several kilometres in diameter over the eruption site.

The chemical composition of magma affects its physical properties, which in turn have a major influence on the landform built by a volcanic eruption. Four common volcanic rock types are shown in Table 1: basalt, andesite, dacite, and rhyolite. As the silica content increases, these rock types generally become more viscous; and as the magmatic gas content increases, they become more explosive. Effusive eruptions form lava plateaus or gently sloping shield volcanoes; moderately explosive eruptions form stratovolcanoes; and giant explosive eruptions form ash-flow plateaus. Naturally, since many other factors are involved in determining volcanic landforms, there are exceptions to these rules.

A series of small eruptions usually build up their products near their vents, whereas a large-volume eruption tends to disperse its products over a greater distance. Lava flows that erupt at high-volume rates usually travel greater distances from their vents. Other physical properties are, however, important in determining the character of lava flows. Hot basaltic lava forms pahoehoe flows (smooth to ropy surfaces), which, other conditions being equal, will flow farther than the cooler aa flows of the same composition (rough, broken surfaces; Figure 10).

Relation of volcanic landform to eruptive habit

If a volcano has consistent eruption habits, its landform will reflect that character. The shape of the huge but gently sloping shield volcano Mauna Loa, for example, indicates a long record of eruption of fluid lava flows from the summit and two persistent rift zones. It is these rift zones that give Mauna Loa its elongate shape.

The beautiful symmetrical shape of the stratovolcano Mt. Fuji indicates a long record of moderately explosive eruptions from its summit, the eruptions generally consisting of explosions of fragments followed by thick viscous lava flows. Such alternating layers of ash and lava make up the strata denoted by the name stratovolcano. They are not layers in a blanketlike sense, however, but are overlapping lobes or tongues of ash and lava. For this reason, many geologists refer to stratovolcanoes as composite volcanoes.

In contrast to simple shield and stratovolcanoes, many volcanoes change their eruptive habits—both in eruption type and in the location of their vents—over time. This results in a mixture of volcanic landforms called a complex volcano.

The geometry of the vent or vents also exerts profound control on volcanic landforms. In Iceland the volcanic vents often are long fissures parallel to the rift zone. Renewed eruptions generally occur from new parallel fractures offset by a few hundred to thousands of metres from the earlier fissures. This distribution of vents and voluminous eruptions of fluid basaltic lava usually build up a thick lava plateau rather than a single volcanic edifice. Hekla Volcano in Iceland is transitional between plateau-building fissure eruptions and the single-major-vent eruptions that produce a symmetrical stratovolcano. Hekla erupts from a fissure that is parallel to the Mid-Atlantic Ridge and about 20 kilometres in length. Eruptions recur from this fracture—many from its central part. The result is a volcano shaped like an overturned canoe. Viewed along the fissure, Hekla looks like a stratovolcano; perpendicular to the fissure, it appears as an elongate ridge. Multiple point-source vents that erupt only once or a few times at most form a volcanic field of dozens of small cinder cones instead of a single large volcanic edifice.

Finally, but not of least importance, is the environment into which the volcanic products are erupted. Submarine volcanoes are surprisingly similar to their counterparts on land, but their slopes are generally steeper because water cools the lavas more rapidly. Deep submarine volcanism tends to be less explosive or nonexplosive, since the pressure of the water prevents explosive boiling.

Subglacial volcanism

Subglacial volcanism is drastically different in form from subaerial volcanism. This is particularly apparent in Iceland where glaciers covered the entire island 15,000 years ago and large ice caps still cover extensive areas today. Fissure eruptions beneath the ice form steep ridges of broken lava fragments rather than lava-flow plateaus, while subglacial eruptions from point-source vents that erupt

Figure 3: The north face of Mt. St. Helens in June 1970. The summit elevation was 2,950 metres.
R.W. Decker

repeatedly form table mountains. Table mountain volcanoes have steep sides of pillow lavas that formed in deep lakes or water-filled caverns within the ice. Pillow lavas are sacklike structures that form from underwater flows of basaltic lava. These structures are capped by several tens of metres of broken lava fragments from explosive shallow-water eruptions. The broken lava fragments in turn are overlain by shield-building lava flows erupted above the glacial surface.

MAJOR TYPES OF VOLCANIC LANDFORMS

Each of the more than 1,300 potentially active volcanoes or volcanic areas listed in the Smithsonian Institution's *Volcanoes of the World* (1981) has a distinct form, but most can be generalized into nine categories (Table 2). Some of these categories were already described, but they are treated below in order of their numerical importance.

Stratovolcanoes. These are steep volcanic cones built by both pyroclastic and lava-flow eruptions. They are composed of volcanic rock types that vary from basalt to rhyolite, but their composition is generally andesite. Stratovolcanoes may erupt many thousands of times over life spans of millions of years. A typical eruption would begin with ash explosions and end with extrusion of thick viscous lava flows. The cone-shaped form begins gradually and becomes steeper (up to 35°) toward the summit, which generally contains a crater.

Shield volcanoes. Structures of this type are large, dome-shaped mountains built of lava flows (the name derives from their similarity in shape to a warrior's shield lying face up on the ground). They are usually composed of basalt. Small shield volcanoes may form rapidly from

By courtesy of the U.S. Geological Survey; photograph, Lyn Topinka

Figure 4: The lava dome of Mt. St. Helens on May 16, 1984, at which time it measured 850 metres wide and 220 metres high.

Figure 5: Curtain of fire formed by line of lava fountains along a fissure at an elevation of 3,800 metres on the northeast rift zone of Mauna Loa Volcano, Hawaii. The lava fountains are about 30–50 metres high.
Katia Krafft

almost continuous eruptions, but the larger shields are formed by hundreds of thousands of effusive eruptions of fluid lavas from their summits and rift zones over a span of about 1,000,000 years. The slopes of shield volcanoes are gentle and seldom exceed 6°. The summits are nearly flat but generally indented by cliff-walled craters or calderas.

Submarine volcanoes. These structures occur in various forms, but many are cone-shaped seamounts. Some ancient island volcanoes were eroded flat or covered with a coral cap at sea level before they sank. These flat-topped seamounts are called guyots. Most of the known active submarine volcanoes occur at shallow depths beneath the sea. They are known because their explosive eruptions can be detected and located by hydrophones. Active submarine volcanoes at depths of a few thousand metres are probably common, particularly along the mid-ocean ridges, but the water pressure at these depths prevents explosive boiling and the eruptions are undetectable. One exception to this is the submarine volcano Loihi, a seamount whose summit caldera occurs one kilometre below sea level, 30 kilometres southeast of the island of Hawaii. Although eruptions of this youngest volcano of the Hawaiian chain have not been directly observed, swarms of earthquakes at shallow depth beneath the summit of Loihi in 1971–72 and 1975 were recorded by seismographs. This is indirect evidence, but not proof, of submarine eruptions at Loihi Seamount.

Calderas. Large circular or oval depressions more than one kilometre in diameter, most calderas have formed by inward collapse. Many have steep cliffs bounding the depression, and some are filled with lakes. The terms crater

and caldera are often used synonymously, but calderas are larger than craters. A crater can occur inside a caldera, but not the other way around. Calderas are often associated with large eruptions (10 cubic kilometres or more) of dacitic or rhyolitic magma that form pyroclastic plateaus.

Calderas also occur on shield volcanoes and are thought to form when large rift eruptions or intrusions remove tremendous quantities of magma from the shallow magma chambers beneath the summit. The collapse and refilling of calderas on active Hawaiian volcanoes probably recur many times during a volcano's lifetime.

Whether a volcano is designated a caldera or shield or stratovolcano with a caldera depends on the principal landform feature. For example, Crater Lake in Oregon in the northwestern United States is designated a caldera in Table 2, but Kilauea Volcano in Hawaii is designated a shield volcano even though it has a large summit caldera.

Complex volcanoes. Such structures are mixed landforms. In most cases, they occur because of changes either in eruptive habit or in location of the principal vent area. A stratovolcano may form a large explosion crater that later becomes filled by a lava dome, or several new cones and craters may develop on a caldera's rim. One stratovolcano cone may overlap another and have multiple summits. The Three Sisters volcanic complex in Oregon is an example of a complex volcano with three summits.

Table 2: Number of Potentially Active Volcanoes of Various Landform Types*

type	number
Stratovolcanoes	577
Shield volcanoes	107
Submarine volcanoes	107
Calderas	81
Complex and compound volcanoes	76
Cinder cones	71
Volcanic fields	49
Fissure vents and crater rows	45
Lava domes	31

*Modified from *Volcanoes of the World* by T. Simkin *et al.* (1981); Smithsonian Institution.

Cinder cones. These are relatively small volcanic landforms: steep, angle-of-repose (about 30°) cones of loose pyroclastic fragments, most of which are in the cinder-size range (Table 3). Generally, the crater from which the cinder-sized fragments were ejected is located in the centre of the cone. In areas with strong prevailing winds, however, the crater may be upwind of the cone. The rock type involved in cinder cone volcanoes is generally basalt or basaltic andesite, and the eruption type is Vulcanian or high-lava-fountain Hawaiian.

Some cinder cones such as Parícutin in Mexico form during a single eruption. Parícutin is approximately 410 metres high and one kilometre wide; it formed during nearly continuous eruptions from 1943 to 1952. Cinder cones also form at some vents on shield volcanoes, but they are not included in Table 2 because they are not separate, individual volcanoes. Certain cinder cones have multiple eruptions, but if activity continues for thousands to tens of thousands of years from the same vent, they probably develop into stratovolcanoes or complex volcanoes.

Volcanic fields. Such areas have many geologically young cinder cones or other features that have not been individually identified as separate volcanoes. If the conduits through which magma ascends to the surface are scattered over a broad area, many short-lived volcanoes are formed rather than a major volcano with repeated eruptions. The area in which Parícutin formed is a volcanic field with dozens of prehistoric—but geologically young—cinder cones and lava flows. The most likely place for the birth of a new volcano is in a known volcanic field.

Fissure vents. These features constitute the surface trace of dikes (underground fractures filled with magma). Most dikes measure about one-half to two metres in width and several kilometres in length. The dikes that feed fissure vents reach the surface from depths of a few kilometres.

Fissure vents are common in Iceland and along the radial

Cone-shaped seamounts and guyots

Structures of loose pyroclastic fragments

Association with dikes

Figure 6: Explosive eruption of Mt. St. Helens on July 22, 1980, as viewed from the south.
Katia Krafft

Magnitude ≥4.5 ≥7.5	Depth (km)	Number of Earthquakes
	0-33	27,788
	34-100	17,585
	101-300	7,329
	301-700	3,167

Figure 7: *Seismicity and topography of the Earth.*
The epicentres of the larger earthquakes that occurred from 1960 to 1980 are shown as dots
in this topographic map of the continents and ocean floor. The dots sharply delineate the
boundaries of the principal tectonic plates of the Earth's surface.

rift zones of Hawaiian volcanoes. Curtain-of-fire eruptions from fissure vents produce low ramparts of basaltic spatter on both sides of the fissure. More isolated lava fountains along the fissure produce crater rows of small spatter and cinder cones. The fragments that form a spatter cone are hot and plastic enough to weld together, while the fragments that form a loose cinder cone have cooled enough during their rise and fall not to stick together.

The largest effusive eruption of lava in recorded history occurred in 1783 in Iceland from the Laki fissure. This vent produced high lava fountains, a 25-kilometre-long crater row, and 565 square kilometres of basaltic lava flows with a volume of approximately 12 cubic kilometres.

Lava domes. Landforms of this sort consist of steep domal mounds of lava so viscous that the lava piles up over its vent without flowing away. The rock types that form lava domes are generally andesites, dacites, or rhyolites. Somehow these viscous lavas have lost much of their gas content in prior eruptions or by slow rise to the surface. Even so, it is not unusual for an actively growing lava dome to have an explosive eruption that disrupts all or part of the dome. Many lava domes grow by internal intrusion of lava that causes swelling and oversteepening of the dome. Rockslides build up an apron of talus blocks around the lower sides of the dome. Lava domes can form

mounds several hundred metres high and from several hundred to more than 1,000 metres in diameter. Thick lava flows sometimes move short distances from the dome and distort its generally circular or oval shape. The dome currently forming in the explosion crater at Mt. St. Helens is a good example of a lava dome.

Other volcanic structures and features. Less common volcanic forms have also been described, and sometimes other names have been used for those cited above. Such inconsistency of nomenclature stems from the fact that no one volcanologist has examined all the world's volcanoes, and the descriptions that exist have been made by many people with diverse backgrounds. Other types and terms that may be encountered include volcanic cones, simply a descriptive term pertaining to shape with no implication of size, rock type, or genesis; explosion crater, a large circular, elongate, or horseshoe-shaped excavation with ejected debris on its rim or flanks; hydrothermal regions, fumarole fields, and solfatara fields, areas of hot springs and gas vents where magma or still-hot igneous rocks at shallow depth are leaking gases or interacting with the groundwater system; maar, a low-relief crater often filled with water and surrounded by a rim of ejected material that was probably formed by explosive interaction of magma and groundwater; tuff rings and tuff cones (Figure 11), landforms that resemble maars but that have higher rims and are not filled with water (a tuff is a compacted pyroclastic deposit that often includes some sediments); pumice cone, a structure similar to a cinder cone but made up of volcanic glass fragments so filled with gas-bubble holes that it resembles a sponge and is very lightweight; pyroclastic cone, a cone-shaped volcano composed almost entirely of pyroclastic material; scoria cone, a synonym for cinder cone (cinders or scoriae are vesicular pyroclastic fragments usually heavier than pumice); somma volcano, a caldera partially filled by a new central cone, named for Mt. Somma in Italy; and subglacial volcano, a volcanic form produced by eruptions beneath a glacier or beneath the surface of a lake within a glacier.

Taking a more distant view of volcanic landforms from space, one can see that individual volcanoes form linear to arcuate belts across the Earth's surface. It is now clear that these volcanic chains are closely related to global tectonic activity.

Table 3: Volcanic Products

form	name	characteristics (including dimensions)
Gas	fume	
Liquid	lavas	
	aa	rough, blocky surface
	pahoehoe	smooth to ropy surface
Solid	airfall fragments	
	dust	< 1/16 mm
	ash	1/16–2 mm
	cinders	2–64 mm
	blocks	> 64 mm solid
	bombs	> 64 mm plastic
	pyroclastic flows	flows fluidized by hot gases
	mudflows	flows fluidized by rainfall, melting ice and snow, or ejected crater lakes

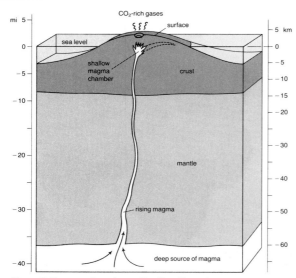

Figure 8: *Cross section of an active Hawaiian volcano.*
The vertical scale is exaggerated by a factor of three. The dotted line extending to the right from the shallow magma chamber is a rift zone that receives intermittent lateral injections of magma from the chamber. Magma rising nearly continuously from the deep source is stored in the chamber. Gases rich in CO_2 escape through fumaroles above the magma chamber.

After J.P. Eaton, U.S. Geological Survey, and T.M. Gerlach, Sandia National Laboratories

Volcanism and tectonic activity

Distribution of volcanoes

Active volcanoes are not scattered over the Earth randomly; instead, most occur in belts, especially in the island arcs and mountain ranges bordering the Pacific Ocean (Figure 12). The concept of seafloor spreading and, more broadly, the theory of plate tectonics offer a logical explanation for the location of most volcanoes.

VOLCANOES RELATED TO PLATE BOUNDARIES

Figure 7 shows the Earth's topography as well as the locations of larger earthquakes that occurred from 1960 to 1980. This map clearly indicates the boundaries of the 12 major tectonic plates. For example, the Pacific Plate

R.W. Decker

Figure 9: Old Faithful Geyser, Yellowstone National Park, Wyoming. Intermittent spouts of steam and hot water to heights of 35–50 metres occur on the average about every 60 minutes throughout the year.

is bounded by the earthquake zones of New Zealand, New Guinea, the Mariana Islands, Japan, Kamchatka, the Aleutian Islands, western North America, the East Pacific Rise, and the Pacific-Antarctic Ridge.

The Earth's plates, which move horizontally with respect to one another at a rate of a few centimetres per year, form three basic types of boundaries: convergent, divergent, and side-slipping. Japan and the Aleutian Islands are examples of convergent boundaries where the Pacific Plate is pushing beneath the adjacent continental plates—a process known as subduction. The San Andreas Fault system in California exemplifies a side-slipping boundary where the Pacific Plate is moving northwest relative to the North American Plate—a process called strike-slip, or transform, faulting. The East Pacific Rise is representative of a divergent boundary where the Pacific Plate and the Nazca Plate (west of South America) are pulling apart—a process known as rifting.

Volcanoes occur along both subduction and rift zones but are generally absent along strike-slip plate margins. Of the 1,144 volcanoes listed in Table 2, 80 percent occur along subduction zones and 15 percent along rift zones. These percentages are somewhat misleading, however, because most of the Earth's rift zones are about two to three kilometres below sea level. At those inaccessible depths active submarine volcanoes have yet to be observed, though a few hydrothermal areas have been found along submarine rift zones with deep-diving submarines.

Iceland, a rare above-water section of the Mid-Atlantic Ridge, has 70 volcanoes that have erupted during the past 10,000 years. If this is a typical number for a short section of the world rift system, it suggests that there may be several thousand potentially active volcanoes along the largely submarine world rift system that follows the crest of the mid-ocean ridges.

Most subduction-related volcanoes are explosive and build stratovolcanoes, while rift volcanoes tend to be more effusive and build shield volcanoes, though there are exceptions to both these generalities. Subduction-related volcanoes erupt basalt, andesite, dacite, and rhyolite, with andesite the predominant rock type. Rift-related volcanoes, especially on the ocean floor, erupt mainly basalt.

Subduction-related volcanoes

Figure 13 is a schematic cross section showing conceptual models of how subduction and rift volcanoes may form. As an oceanic plate (2) is subducted beneath a continental plate (3), seafloor sediments rich in water and carbon dioxide are carried beneath the overriding plate. These compounds may act as fluxes and reduce the melting temperature of magma. Frictional heating also may be important in the formation of subduction-zone magmas, but since the subducted plate is colder than the mantle rocks it is penetrating, this would counteract any frictional heating. Although the process is not clearly understood, magma apparently forms and rises by buoyancy from a depth of 100 to 200 kilometres. Subduction-zone volcanoes occur on the overriding plate and are offset inland from the actual plate boundary along the ocean trench.

The rising subduction-zone magma is probably basaltic in composition and is formed by the partial melting of mantle rocks. As the rising magma moves slowly up through the continental crust of the overriding plate, however, two things may occur to increase significantly the silica content of the magma. Crystallization of olivine and pyroxene minerals from the basalt can leave the residual melt enriched in silica and depleted in magnesium, iron, and calcium. This process is called fractional crystallization. Also, basaltic magmas have enough excess heat to partially melt the continental host rocks through which they are ascending. Because continental rocks are generally higher in silica, potassium, and sodium than are oceanic rocks, this process of assimilation and mixing can also play an important role in producing the wide range of compositions that occur in rocks from subduction volcanoes.

The additional gas content of many magma batches at subduction volcanoes (which, coupled with their often high-viscosity magma, makes them dangerously explosive) also may be explained by more than one process. Additional water and carbon dioxide may come from both subducted seafloor sediments and assimilated crustal rocks.

Figure 10: Aa lava flow (left) overlying pahoehoe lava flow on Kilauea Volcano, Hawaii. These basaltic lava flows were erupted in 1973 and were still largely barren of vegetation a decade later.
Barbara Decker

Furthermore, any fractional crystallization tends to concentrate volatile elements in the residual melt. If volcanic gases form separate fluid phases within batches of ascending magma (carbon dioxide is most likely to do this), these fluid phases may ascend more rapidly than the overall magma body and be concentrated in the upper portion. Explosive boiling of these volcanic gases at atmospheric pressure is the apparent reason for the highly explosive nature of many subduction volcanoes.

Rift volcanoes

Rift volcanoes, as shown in Figure 13, form when magma rises into the gap between diverging plates (1 and 2). They thus occur at or near actual plate boundaries. Measurements in Iceland suggest that the separation of plates is a continuous process but that the fracturing is intermittent. An analogy would be a rubber band that is slowly stretched until it snaps. Earthquake swarms and volcanic eruptions occur when the stretching exceeds the strength of the near-surface rocks, which then fracture along steeply dipping cracks parallel to the rift. Basaltic magma rising along these fractures causes Icelandic fissure eruptions.

Rift volcanoes in continental locations such as East Africa are more complex. Assimilation of continental crust apparently gives them some of the characteristics more generally associated with subduction volcanoes; *e.g.,* having a wider range of rock types and explosive habits.

To return to the example of the Pacific Plate in Figure 7, the volcanoes on the western and northern margin (New Zealand, New Guinea, Mariana Islands, Japan, Kamchatka, and the Aleutian Islands) are all subduction volcanoes. The rift volcanoes, except for a few near Baja California, are hidden along the submarine crest of the East Pacific Rise and the Pacific-Antarctic Ridge at depths of two to three kilometres below sea level. The Cascade volcanoes in the northwestern United States and the volcanoes in Mexico and Central America are subduction volcanoes related to the small Juan de Fuca and Cocos plates on the east side of the Pacific Plate. Similarly, the volcanoes of the Andes are related to the subduction of the Nazca Plate beneath the South American Plate.

INTRAPLATE VOLCANISM

A red dot representing an earthquake location in the north central Pacific in Figure 7 marks the volcanic island of Hawaii, far from any plate margin. How can it be explained in terms of plate tectonics?

The 5 percent of known world volcanoes that are not closely related to plate margins are generally regarded as hot-spot volcanoes. Hawaiian volcanoes are the best examples of this type, and though they occur near the centre of the northern portion of the Pacific Plate, they show a dramatic relationship to the past movements of that plate. Kilauea and Mauna Loa volcanoes on the island of Hawaii at the southeast end of the Hawaiian volcanic chain are two of the most active volcanoes in the world. In addition, the five volcanoes that form the island of Hawaii are all less than 1,000,000 years old.

Hot-spot volcanoes

Northwestward along the Hawaiian chain each island is progressively older. The extinct volcano that formed the island of Kauai is about 5,000,000 years old. Assuming that the hot spot that generates Hawaiian volcanoes is relatively fixed in place—and there is good evidence to support this assumption—then the movement of the Pacific Plate during the past several million years has been northwestward at a rate of about 10 centimetres per year. Figure 7 shows a major submarine continuation of the Hawaiian Ridge to the northwest of the Hawaiian Islands, and then a dogleg bend into the Emperor Seamounts, which comprise an entirely submarine ridge continuing northward to the edge of the Pacific Plate.

Ages of rocks obtained by dredging and drilling the Emperor Seamounts indicate that the Hawaiian-Emperor Ridge is a progressively older volcanic chain formed by volcanism at the Hawaiian hot spot. This major centre of volcanism in the Pacific has been active for at least 80,000,000 years, and the Pacific Plate has moved over it, first northward and later northwestward, at a rate of approximately eight to 10 centimetres per year. The bend between the Emperor Seamounts and the Hawaiian Ridge occurred about 40,000,000 years ago and indicates a significant shift in the direction of movement of the Pacific Plate.

It is not known how a volcanic hot spot maintains its position for millions of years while a plate passes over it. One concept suggests that a hot spot is a deep-mantle plume (Figure 14), which is caused by very slow convection of highly viscous mantle material. As hot but solid mantle rock moves upward, partial melting may occur from the lowering of its pressure-dependent melting temperature. Detailed seismic sounding of the mantle over the next decade or two should help to resolve this problem of the mechanism of hot spots.

Deep-mantle plumes

Small and isolated intraplate volcanoes may simply be the result of deep fractures within the plates that allow pockets of partial melt in the low-velocity layer below to leak to the surface. The low-velocity layer begins about 50 to 150 kilometres below the surface and extends to a depth of roughly 300 kilometres; it is so named because earthquake waves travel more slowly in this hot, low-strength layer than in the overlying rigid plates (Figure 13). Some studies indicate that there may be a few percent partial melt within the low-velocity layer. Once a sufficient volume of magma forms in the subsurface, it tends to rise from its own buoyancy. Any fracture system at the plate margins or within the plates will facilitate this process.

After T. Simkin *et al., Volcanoes of the World,* copyright © 1981 the Smithsonian Institution

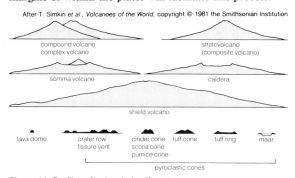

Figure 11: *Profiles of volcanic landforms.*
The shield volcano and those above it are vertically exaggerated by a factor of two. The landforms below the shield volcano are vertically exaggerated by a factor of four. Relative sizes are approximate because of large variations in size within each type.

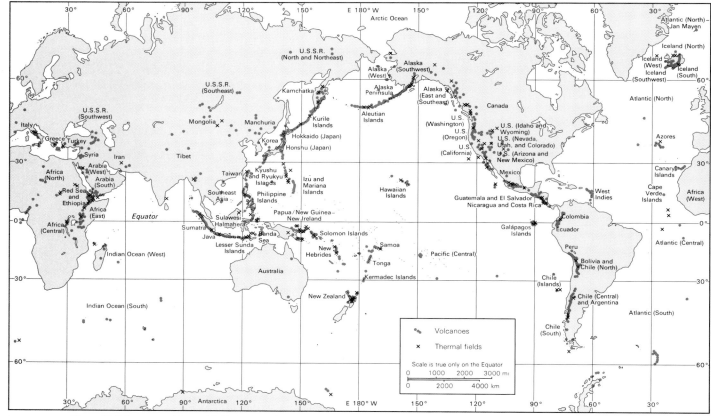

Figure 12: Volcanoes and thermal fields that have been active during the past 10,000 years.

After T. Simkin et al., *Volcanoes of the World*, copyright ©1981 the Smithsonian Institution

Impact of volcanic activity on humankind and the environment

Cata-
strophic
eruptions
of modern
times

Since the late 1700s volcanoes have caused more than 250,000 deaths. Most of these occurred during four disastrous eruptions.

The largest eruption of the four occurred at Tambora Volcano on Sumbawa Island, Indonesia, on April 10–11, 1815. Fifty cubic kilometres of magma were expelled in Plinian ash clouds and pyroclastic flows. Ash greater than one centimetre thick fell on more than 500,000 square kilometres of Indonesia and the Java Sea. Before the eruption Tambora was a 4,300-metre-high stratovolcano; following the eruption 1,400 metres of the summit cone were missing and in its place was a collapsed caldera measuring six by seven kilometres wide and one kilometre deep. About 10,000 people were killed by the explosive eruption and the tsunamis caused by massive pyroclastic flows entering the sea. Agricultural losses from the thick ash deposits resulted in famine and disease, leading to an additional 82,000 deaths.

The second largest eruption of the 19th century also occurred in Indonesia. Krakatoa (or Krakatau), a compound volcano on a small uninhabited island between Sumatra and Java, erupted explosively on Aug. 26–27, 1883. The eruption was similar to the Tambora outburst but smaller, involving only about 18 cubic kilometres of magma erupted in Plinian ash clouds and pyroclastic flows. Krakatoa was a much smaller volcano than Tambora, and when the eruption had emptied its magma chamber, it collapsed to form a caldera that was partly below sea level. Twenty-three square kilometres of the island of Krakatoa disappeared, and where a volcanic peak 450 metres high once stood was water as deep as 275 metres. The largest explosion on the morning of August 27 produced an ash cloud that was reported to have reached 80 kilometres high, and the detonation was heard in Australia, 4,800 kilometres away. A tsunami, over 30 metres high, followed the explosion and apparent caldera collapse, killing about 36,000 people on the adjacent shores of Java and Sumatra.

On May 8, 1902, there occurred a violent eruption of Mt. Pelée, a stratovolcano on the island of Martinique in the Caribbean Sea. Although less than one cubic kilometre of magma was erupted, much of it formed a high-velocity glowing avalanche of hot gases and pyroclastic fragments that swept down a steep valley to the port of St. Pierre. Within minutes the town and virtually all of its inhabitants (some 29,000 people) were incinerated.

The second worst volcanic disaster of the 20th century occurred on Nov. 13, 1985, when a relatively small eruption of Nevado del Ruiz, a stratovolcano in Colombia, killed 25,000 people. This 5,400-metre-high volcano has a glacial ice cap, and when a brief explosive eruption dumped several million cubic metres of hot pyroclastic fragments on the ice cap surrounding the summit crater, a sudden surge of meltwater sent massive mudflows down canyons on both the east and west sides of the Andean volcano. Much of the town of Armero, built on a low plain beside the Lagunilla (also spelled Lagunillas) River 50 kilometres east of and nearly five kilometres below the summit of Nevado del Ruiz, was buried by the mudflows. Twenty-two thousand of its inhabitants were killed.

About 70 percent of the people who died from volcanic eruptions in the past 200 years perished in those four outbursts. The remaining 30 percent were killed in many other less devastating eruptions. As world population increases, however, so does the risk of greater loss of life from volcanic eruptions. This was made all too clear by the tragedy at Armero. In 1845 a mudflow from Nevado del Ruiz killed approximately 1,000 people on farms near the site where the town of Armero was later built. In the 1985 mudflow, which was smaller in volume than the 1845 mudflow, more than 20 times as many people were killed.

Property damage from volcanic eruptions is difficult to estimate because of differing value systems and changes in land use. One study estimates an average of $100,000,000 per year in property damage worldwide from volcanic eruptions. As with casualties, a few eruptions cause staggering damage, while most are much less destructive. The

Mt. St. Helens eruption in 1980 did more than $1,000,-000,000 worth of damage, mainly to the timber industry.

HAZARDS FROM VARIOUS TYPES OF VOLCANIC ERUPTIONS

The list of hazards associated with volcanic eruptions is long and varied: explosions, toxic gas clouds, ash falls, pyroclastic flows, avalanches, tsunamis, mudflows, and lava flows, as well as secondary effects such as fluoride poisoning, starvation, and disease.

The sudden depressurization of a shallow hydrothermal system or gas-charged magma body or the rapid mixing of magma with groundwater can cause rapid gas expansion and massive explosions. Large blocks ejected in these explosions are sometimes hurled as far as 20 kilometres from the explosive vent. A directed blast in which one side of a volcanic cone fails, as happened at Mt. St. Helens in 1980, can cause destruction of several hundred square kilometres on the failed flank of the volcano. This is especially true if the blast cloud is heavily laden with fragmental debris and becomes a dense fluidized flow. It then takes on characteristics similar to a pyroclastic flow. Even beyond the limit of explosive destruction, the hot, ash-laden gas clouds associated with an explosive eruption can scorch vegetation and kill people by suffocation.

Toxic gas emissions and ash falls
Gas clouds from a sudden increase in fumarole emissions may also contain poisonous or suffocating gases such as hydrogen sulfide, carbon monoxide, carbon dioxide, and sulfur dioxide. At a crater lake in Cameroon, West Africa, more than 1,700 people were killed by a sudden release of carbon dioxide in August 1986.

Ash falls from continued explosive jetting of fine volcanic particles into high ash clouds generally do not cause any direct fatalities. Yet, where the ash accumulates more than a few centimetres, collapsing roofs from ash loads and failure of crops are major secondary hazards. Crop failure can occur over large areas downwind from major Plinian eruptions, and widespread famine and disease may result, especially in poorly developed countries. Lightning strikes are common close to Plinian ash clouds, adding one more element of terror to an explosive eruption.

Pyroclastic flows
Pyroclastic flows are the most dangerous and destructive aspect of explosive volcanism. They occur in many sizes and types, but their common characteristic is that they form a fluidized emulsion of volcanic particles, eruption gases, and entrapped air, resulting in a flow of low enough viscosity to be very mobile and of high enough density to hug the ground surface. A pyroclastic flow can pour over the lip of an erupting vent, or it may form when an ash cloud becomes too dense to continue rising and falls back to the ground. In major caldera collapses associated with explosive volcanoes, huge pyroclastic flows may issue from the ring fractures as the caldera block subsides.

Pyroclastic flows can move at speeds up to a few kilometres per minute and have temperatures ranging from 100° to 700° C. They sweep away and incinerate nearly everything in their path. Smaller pyroclastic flows are confined to valleys and are called *nuées ardentes*. Large pyroclastic flows may spread out as a blanket deposit across many hundreds or even thousands of square kilometres around a major caldera collapse. During the past 2,000,000 years, the Yellowstone National Park area has undergone three major caldera collapses involving pyroclastic eruptions of 300 to 3,000 cubic kilometres of rhyolitic magma.

Avalanches of rock and ice also are common on active volcanoes. They may occur with or without an eruption. Those without an eruption are often triggered by earthquakes, weakening of rock into clay by hydrothermal activity, or by heavy rainfall or snowfall. Those associated with eruptions are sometimes caused by oversteepening of a volcano's flank by intrusion of a shallow body of magma within or just beneath the volcanic cone, as happened at Mt. St. Helens.

A caldera collapse that is in part or entirely submarine usually generates a tsunami; the larger and more rapid the collapse, the larger the tsunami. Tsunamis also can be caused by avalanches or large pyroclastic flows rapidly entering the sea on the flank of a volcano.

Mudflows are common hazards associated with stratovolcanoes and can happen even without an eruption.

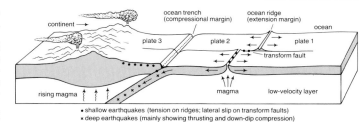

Figure 13: Cross section of plate boundaries formed by ocean ridges (rift zones), strike-slip (transform) faults, and subduction zones.

After L. Sykes *et al.*, in F. Press and R. Siever, *Earth,* second edition; copyright © 1974, 1978 W.H. Freeman and Company, used by permission

Giant mudflows
They occur whenever floods of water mixed with ash, loose soil, or rocks that have been altered to clay by hydrothermal activity sweep down the valleys draining the sides of large stratovolcanoes. The huge mudflows generated by meltwater from the ice cap of Nevado del Ruiz Volcano in 1985 are classic examples of mudflows associated with eruptions. Heavy rainfall or earthquake-induced avalanches of ice or hydrothermal clay also can cause mudflows on steep volcanoes during periods of repose.

Lava flows
A lava flow engulfs and buries the land it covers, but new soil and vegetation eventually develop again. In warm humid climates the recovery is rapid; a few decades will hide the rocky surface of flows. In desert or arctic climates recovery is slower; flows more than 1,000 years old may still retain their barren appearance.

The greatest hazard at potentially active volcanoes is human complacency. The physical hazards can be reliably estimated by studying the past eruptive activity as recorded in history or in the prehistoric deposits around a volcano. Volcano observatories can monitor the local earthquake activity and the surface deformation of a potentially active volcano and make useful, if not yet precise, forecasts of eruptions. Increased earthquake activity beneath Mauna Loa in 1983 led to a forecast of an increase in probability of an eruption for 1984 or 1985; an eruption occurred in March 1984. The major eruption of Mt. St. Helens on May 18, 1980, was much larger than anticipated, but the high level of local earthquakes and the bulge forming on the north flank of the mountain provided enough warning to encourage a partial evacuation of the surrounding area. Some lives were lost, but the toll would have been much higher if access to the area had not been restricted by the local authorities. A major problem in reducing volcanic

After G.B. Dalrymple, E.A. Silver, and E.D. Jackson, "Origin of the Hawaiian Islands," *American Scientist* (May–June 1973)

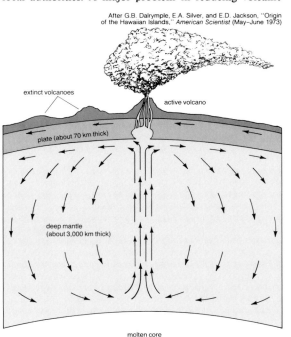

Figure 14: Hot-spot volcanoes may be formed by deep mantle plumes generated by slow convection currents.

risk is that most explosive volcanoes have such long repose periods that people living nearby consider them extinct rather than dormant.

EFFECTS OF VOLCANIC ERUPTIONS ON SOIL AND CLIMATE

Not all volcanic phenomena are destructive. The oceans, atmosphere, and continents owe their origin and evolution in large measure to volcanic processes throughout geologic time.

Soil enrichment

Volcanic ash slowly weathers to form rich loamy soils. On volcanic Java, terraced rice paddies support a dense population. Across the Java Sea is Kalimantan (part of Borneo) with a similar climate but no volcanoes. The jungles of Kalimantan provide only temporary slash-and-burn agriculture and support a much smaller population.

Climate, too, is subject to the effects of volcanic activity. High ash clouds from Plinian eruptions, especially if they are rich in sulfur dioxide, can inject much fine dust and aerosol droplets of sulfuric acid into the stratosphere. Above rain clouds, these fine particles are not washed quickly back to Earth but spread slowly into haze layers that can blanket a hemisphere or even the entire Earth.

World climate seems to have been affected by the eruptions of Krakatoa in 1883 and of Agung Volcano in Bali in 1963 in the form of a lowering of average world temperature by about 0.5° C over the few years following these eruptions. Although world temperature data was poorly recorded in the early 1800s, the eruption of Tambora in April 1815 was followed in 1816 in North America and Europe by what was called "the year without a summer." Other large volcanic eruptions such as Katmai in Alaska in 1912, however, appear to have produced no cooling effect. Records of average world temperature over the past several decades often show changes of 0.1°–0.3° C from year to year unrelated to any known volcanic eruptions, so it is difficult to establish clearly whether or not volcanic eruptions have a major impact on climate.

Direct sampling of the stratosphere has shown that the major haze-forming agent from volcanic eruptions is not fine dust but an aerosol of tiny sulfuric acid droplets. This indicates that the composition of high volcanic ash clouds may be as important as their volume in affecting climate. Atmospheric chemists are discovering that not only volcanic eruptions but also man-made aerosols of chlorofluoromethanes (commonly called Freon), exhaust from high-altitude jet aircraft, and a general increase in carbon dioxide from burning fossil fuels are perturbing the atmosphere. The Earth has many buffers that maintain its environment, but their interactions are not well understood. Questions as to how volcanic and human activity affect climate remain essentially unanswered, and they are important problems for future research and for survival.

GEOTHERMAL ENERGY

Geothermal energy is plentiful, but geothermal power is not. Temperatures increase below the Earth's surface at a rate of about 30° C per kilometre in the first 10 kilometres. This internal heat of the Earth is an immense store of energy. In the upper 10 kilometres of rock beneath the conterminous United States, it amounts to 3.3×10^{25} joules, or about 6,000 times the energy contained in the world's oil reserves. The problem in utilizing geothermal energy is extracting it.

The natural escape of the Earth's heat through its surface averages only 0.06 watt per square metre. To make geothermal power practical, some special situation must exist to concentrate the Earth's heat energy in a small area. Underground reservoirs of steam or hot water that can be funneled into a drill hole provide this special situation.

Geothermal steam wells

Some geothermal steam wells can produce six megawatts of thermal power, an amount equal to the normal heat flux from 100 square kilometres of land surface. The key to this concentration is the mass transfer of heat from deeper levels to the near surface by volcanism. Magma at temperatures close to 1,200° C moves upward to depths of only a few kilometres, where it transfers heat by conduc-

tion to groundwater. The groundwater then circulates by convection and forms large underground reservoirs of hot water and steam. Some of this thermal water may escape to the surface as hot springs or geysers.

Holes drilled into a subsurface geothermal system allow rapid mass transfer of hot water or steam to the surface. At The Geysers geothermal field north of San Francisco, superheated steam is directly tapped from porous underground reservoirs. In most other geothermal fields, however, the hot water is at or below its subsurface boiling temperature—about 300° C at a depth of one kilometre. Hot water that is near its subsurface boiling temperature partially flashes to steam at the reduced pressures in a drill hole. This mixture of steam and hot water is separated at the well head, and the steam is used to drive the turbine of an electric generator. Hot water from lower temperature geothermal reservoirs can be used for space heating. This form of geothermal power is utilized extensively in Iceland.

Hydrothermal ore deposits

Some geothermal systems act as natural distilleries in the subsurface, dissolving trace amounts of gold, silver, and other rare elements from their host rocks. These elements may then be deposited at places where changes in temperature, pressure, or composition favour precipitation. Many hydrothermal ore deposits have been formed by once active—and in a few cases still active—geothermal systems. Gold is one more legacy of volcanism.

BIBLIOGRAPHY. Because volcanoes are studied by scientists in a wide range of specialties, discussions of volcanism appear in many diverse publications. This bibliography provides only the more general sources of information on volcanism. Many of these, however, contain extensive references that can lead the reader to more specialized data.

Coverage at a nontechnical level can be found in ROBERT DECKER and BARBARA DECKER, *Volcanoes* (1981), emphasizing physical processes and the relationship of volcanoes to plate tectonics; PETER FRANCIS, *Volcanoes* (1976), concentrating on volcanic rock types; FRED M. BULLARD, *Volcanoes of the Earth*, 2nd rev. ed. (1984), describing many volcanic eruptions on a worldwide basis; and GORDON A. MACDONALD, AGATIN T. ABBOTT, and FRANK L. PETERSON, *Volcanoes in the Sea*, 2nd ed. (1983), discussing Hawaiian volcanoes and the geology of Hawaii. On a fairly high technical level are HOWELL WILLIAMS and ALEXANDER R. MCBIRNEY, *Volcanology* (1979); and GORDON A. MACDONALD, *Volcanoes* (1972), with emphasis on descriptions of eruptions and the character of volcanic rocks. R.V. FISHER and H.-U. SCHMINCKE, *Pyroclastic Rocks* (1984), is a comprehensive treatise on the origin and character of this important but diverse group of volcanic deposits. GRANT HEIKEN and KENNETH WOHLETZ, *Volcanic Ash* (1985), provides a thorough discussion of the origin and character of airfall deposits. See also T. SIMKIN et al., *Volcanoes of the World: A Regional Directory, Gazetteer, and Chronology of Volcanism During the Last 10,000 Years* (1981).

Useful popular books include HAROUN TAZIEFF, *Volcanoes*, trans. from French (1961), an account of the study of volcanoes and volcanic eruptions from Greek and Roman to modern times; *Volcano*, rev. ed. (1982), a well-illustrated account of major volcanic eruptions with a chapter on monitoring active volcanoes, prepared by the editors of Time-Life Books; and MAURICE KRAFFT and KATIA KRAFFT, *Volcano* (1975; originally published in French, 1975), a book of colour photographs of volcanoes in action and a text on the mechanism of volcanoes.

General research articles about volcanism are published in *Science* (weekly) and *Nature* (weekly); and more specialized articles in *Journal of Geophysical Research: Solid Earth and Planets* (monthly); *Bulletin of Volcanology* (bimonthly); and *Journal of Volcanology and Geothermal Research* (monthly). *SEAN Bulletin* (monthly), published by the Scientific Event Alert Network of the Smithsonian Institution, provides preliminary but up-to-date data on eruptions worldwide.

Collections of articles can be found in NATIONAL RESEARCH COUNCIL. GEOPHYSICS STUDY COMMITTEE, *Explosive Volcanism: Inception, Evolution, and Hazards* (1984); ROBERT DECKER and BARBARA DECKER, *Volcanoes and the Earth's Interior: Readings from Scientific American* (1982); PETER W. LIPMAN and DONAL R. MULLINEAUX (eds.), *The 1980 Eruptions of Mount St. Helens, Washington* (1981); and ROBERT W. DECKER, THOMAS L. WRIGHT, and PETER H. STAUFFER (eds.), *Volcanism in Hawaii*, 2 vol. (1987).

(Robert W. Decker/Barbara B. Decker)

Science
Year in
Review

Contents

The Year in Science: An Overview

by James Trefil

The progress of science is usually a slow, stately affair, and genuine surprises are few and far between. Contrary to some popular impressions, most scientific work tends to be routine and painstaking. Moments of discovery are rare indeed. Therefore, 1987 was a banner year because it produced not one but two spectacular surprises—the development of high-temperature superconductors and the appearance of a supernova in the Large Magellanic Cloud. The latter was purely fortuitous—scientists had no control whatsoever over it. The former, however, was one of those moments of serendipity in the history of science, a moment when seemingly insurmountable barriers were overcome in a blazing scientific advance.

If 1987 was a year of surprises in some fields, it was a year when long-term trends in science proceeded at their normal pace in others. Among the many such trends that could be discussed, I have chosen one to look at in some detail—the trend toward "Big Science" and away from individual work. High-energy physics, which inaugurated this movement in the 1950s, continued to lead the way with the proposal for the construction of a monumental particle accelerator known as the Superconducting Super Collider (SSC). Other fields were starting to jump on the bandwagon, however, and the most surprising of these (to me, at least) was the proposal of molecular biologists to sequence the entire human genome. This is a project that could well take a decade to complete, at a possible cost of billions of dollars. Even biology, it appears, is not immune to the allure of ambitious, large-scale undertakings.

The superconductor. When electrons flow through any material, an electrical current is said to be present. A material that carries electrical current—ordinary copper wire is a familiar example—is said to conduct electricity and therefore is called a conductor. In most materials, including copper, the moving electrons collide with atoms, thereby giving up some of their energy. This energy appears as heat. It is the effect of these collisions that causes fires in poorly wired homes; too much current is pushed through the wires, and they heat up to the point where they become a menace.

JAMES TREFIL is Clarence Robinson Professor of Physics at George Mason University, Fairfax, Va. His latest book is Meditations at Sunset.

Superconductors, on the other hand, are materials in which the electrons do not transfer energy to resident atoms; thus, a current passes through a superconductor without losing energy or generating heat. The current can flow forever—there is simply nothing to stop it. It is obvious that superconductivity would be highly prized by engineers responsible for moving electricity from one place to another and for designing devices that use electricity. To take just one example, if a suitable superconducting material were available, one could transmit all the electricity used in the United States through a wire no bigger across than a basketball!

The big surprise in 1987 was not that superconductors exist—they were discovered in The Netherlands almost 80 years ago. The surprise was that it was possible to put together materials that showed superconductivity at "high" temperatures. Until 1987 superconductivity was seen only at temperatures near absolute zero ($-273.15°$ C, or $-459.67°$ F), and many physicists would have said that the kind of superconductors discovered in 1987 simply could not exist.

One can understand why the shock was so great if I digress for a moment and describe what makes a superconductor work. As previously explained, if one tries to push electrons through an ordinary material, they will collide with the atoms found there. In the process, the electrons lose energy. In a superconductor, however, there is a way for the electrons to lock themselves into a single coherent mass that travels through the material without such loss. This process can be visualized as follows: imagine two neighboring atoms, each carrying a positive charge. Suppose an electron moves quickly between the atoms. The atoms will be attracted toward the electron by the electrical force, but being relatively ponderous they will move slowly in response to that attraction. Consequently, long after the electron has gone on its way, the two positively charged atoms will finally come close together, creating a concentration of positive charge in the solid. This concentration will, in turn, attract another electron to follow the first. By means of this mechanism, the electrons moving through the material form themselves into pairs, with the first clearing the way for the second.

The pairs of electrons, once formed, lock together. In fact, the electrons in the solid can be thought of as being analogous to a large plate of spaghetti, with each end of a spaghetti strand being an electron and the body of the strand representing the electrical forces that keep the pair together. When an electron locked into this matrix collides with an atom, it can no longer surrender energy but instead rides roughshod over anything in its way. In order to divert a single electron, an atom has to move *every* electron in the material, an impossible task. Thus, the mass of electrons moves through the solid without losing energy and the result is a superconductor.

It is not difficult to see that the delicate balance that keeps the electron pairs together could be upset if the atoms were undergoing violent vibrations in the material, as they would be if the temperature were high. It is for this reason that until very recently superconductivity was known only in materials that were maintained at very low temperatures, where the atoms move very little. In practice, "very low" meant within a few degrees of absolute zero (0 K). To maintain this temperature, superconductors were immersed in liquid helium at 4° above absolute zero (4 K).

The search for high-temperature superconductors became something of a holy grail in materials science. There are obvious practical reasons why this should be so. Having a loss-free conductor is a wonderful engineering advantage, but if one must expend considerable effort and money to keep it cold, some of the advantages disappear. One could not, for example, imagine a national grid of power transmission lines, each one in its own bath of liquid helium.

All through the 1970s and 1980s, even as helium-bath superconductors were being developed commercially, the search was on for a material that would remain a superconductor at 25–30 K. This would be warm enough that the helium could be replaced with liquid hydrogen, a much more plentiful and cheaper substance. Try as they might, however, scientists could not reach that goal. The "world champion" superconductor remained a metal alloy that "went normal" at 23 K, while the workhorse of the industry was an alloy of niobium and tin that was a superconductor at about 18 K.

My most vivid memory of this frustrating period was a speech given by the late Bernd Matthias at a meeting of the American Physical Society in Chicago. For years Matthias had been the recognized leader in the field of high-temperature superconductors; indeed, his talk was an acceptance speech for an award honoring that leadership. "In your lifetime," he told us, "you will be lucky to see a 30-degree superconductor. You will never see more than that."

It is true that Matthias (and the other speakers on the award program) had just enjoyed a lavish celebration dinner and were perhaps inclined to be a bit more expansive than they might otherwise have been. Nevertheless, he was doing no more than stating the accepted wisdom of the scientific community. We were, it seemed, doomed to a long nickel-and-dime struggle to push the critical temperatures just a few degrees higher.

One can imagine, then, the effect on university physics departments early in 1987 when rumors began to circulate that materials were being found that remained superconducting to 30 K, 40 K, and even 50 K. These materials, the rare earth compounds, seemed to push the boundaries of superconductivity to regions that physicists had visited only in their dreams. Instead of the long grind that had been anticipated, we were treated to a single blinding flash—a surprise advance that pushed the temperatures of superconducting materials not only above that of liquid hydrogen but above liquid nitrogen as well, all the way to 100 K.

This was a tremendous technological advance. Nitrogen is not only plentiful (it makes up 80% of the atmosphere) but also cheap—cheaper than milk in a supermarket, for example. In addition, building refrigerators to keep materials at 100 K is much easier than building them to keep materials at 20 K. We all settled back to watch the engineers take over and convert this marvelous discovery into thousands of practical advances, from supercomputers to computerized tomographic scanners that could be maintained in a physician's office.

The great superconducting surprise of 1987 was not over, however. Soon rumors began to trickle in that there were materials that remained superconducting at the temperature of dry ice (200 K) and then—wonder of wonders—at room temperature (about 295 K)! As of early 1988 the full story on these new materials had yet to be told, and there was

Metallurgist immerses a coil of superconducting wire in a container of liquid nitrogen. After the wire has been immersed, electricity can flow through it without encountering resistance.
Courtesy of AT&T Archives

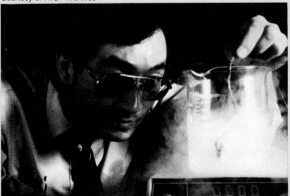

some skepticism about many of the claims. Given the developments of the past few months, it would be a very foolish person indeed who would be willing to issue a Matthias-like pronouncement. It seems quite probable that we will, in a short time, have super-conductors that need no cooling whatsoever. When this happens, one can expect to see a major boom in high-tech industries centered on these materials.

The lesson to be learned from this story was stated well by Arthur C. Clarke in another context. "When an old scientist says something can be done, he's probably right. When he says something can't be done, he is almost surely wrong." As a scientist who is, alas, moving inexorably into the age bracket Clarke talks about, and one who, moreover, agreed with Matthias at that meeting in Chicago, I can only say, "How true."

The supernova. On the night of Feb. 23–24, 1987, an extraordinary event took place. In the Large Magellanic Cloud a rather ordinary star called Sanduleak −69 202 suddenly exploded, producing what scientists call a supernova. For a few years, until it cools off and dims, there will be a new star in the southern skies.

The existence of supernovas is not, in and of itself, newsworthy. They are seen frequently in other galaxies, and they occur about once every 30 years or so in the Milky Way. They mark the death of giant stars. What is unusual about this particular event is that it is the first supernova to occur close to the Earth since astronomers greatly increased their observing power with the development of radio, X-ray, infrared, and ultraviolet telescopes in the post-World War II era. The supernova, or 1987A, as it is called by astronomers, is the first that has been studied in detail with the full panoply of "eyes" we now possess. The results have been little short of spectacular.

In ancient times the idea that sudden changes could occur in the heavens was considered unthinkable. In fact, in his *Meteorology*, Aristotle said that comets (and, one would suppose, supernovas) were conflagrations of vapors in the upper atmosphere. We now understand that supernovas are visual reminders of one of the great truths of astronomy—the fact that stars, like everything else, eventually die.

A star like the Sun exists because nuclear fires in its core consume hydrogen, producing heat and pressure that balance the inward pull of gravity. When the hydrogen fuel burns up, as it eventually must, a complex series of events occurs that leads to the death of the star. Depending on how big the star is, the process of dying can be sedate or spectacular. For a small star like the Sun, evolution takes place slowly and eventually produces a white dwarf, a compact star about the size of the Earth that slowly cools off as its energy radiates into space. For

Montage of positive and negative images of Supernova 1987A reveals the precursor star (merged with a fainter companion) as the dark negative spot at the center of the positive image of the supernova.

Anglo-Australian Telescope Board © 1987; photo by David Malin of the Anglo-Australian Observatory

very large stars, where the high mass produces huge gravitational forces, the process is more spectacular and more violent. When the star dies, it does so in a stupendous explosion that literally tears the outer covering off the star and blows it into space. This is what happened in 1987A.

From the point of view of astronomers, the most important thing about the supernova is that it allows them to test their detailed theoretical predictions about the way stars work. Since the 1930s astronomers have known that the energy of stars is produced by nuclear reactions. Unfortunately, these reactions take place deep in the core of stars, under thousands of miles of obscuring materials. From our vantage point we can see only the final product of these reactions, the outpouring of energy into space. Distant supernovas give us a tantalizing glimpse into the process by which a star tears itself apart. Until 1987, however, the supernovas that could be seen were too far away for astronomers to be able to make the observations that were needed for testing their theories. The light from most nearby supernovas, those in our own Galaxy, is blotted out by intervening dust and debris before it reaches our telescopes, so those events cannot be used either.

The observations of 1987A show one thing clearly: astronomers' notions of how stars function are pretty much on the mark. In fact, the field of supernova research before last February could well be described as a theory in search of data. Massive calculations about how heavy nuclei would be formed in these explosions had been carried out, but there had not been enough detailed observations to test their accuracy. The brightening of 1987A as the radioactive decay of those nuclei began is the most dramatic of the many confirmations of the supernova theories that have taken place during the last year.

Before leaving the supernova, I would like to point out one fact. According to the theories confirmed by 1987A, all elements heavier than lithium have been created by nuclear reactions in massive stars and returned to space by supernova explosions. There they formed the raw materials from which new stars and planetary systems were made. Thus, when the solar system condensed out of interstellar dust and gas, it incorporated atoms that had once formed part of the kind of expanding cloud now seen around 1987A. Almost every atom in your body, therefore, was once part of the kind of celestial display we are now seeing in the Large Magellanic Cloud.

Big Science, Little Science—the SSC. There is a common image of the scientist as a lonely genius working alone in a remote laboratory. I suppose there are still places where this image matches reality, but they are getting smaller and fewer every year. Big Science—science done by large groups of people on very expensive equipment—seems to be on the advance everywhere. In fact, it is becoming difficult to tell the difference between a university scientist and a corporate executive.

The field that has led all others in the rush toward bigness is elementary particle physics, the study of the basic constituents of matter. The reason for this is simple. In order to study the way that elementary particles are created and interact, it is necessary to produce beams of very energetic particles and allow them to collide with ordinary atoms. From the study of the resulting maelstrom, physicists have built our present knowledge of the way that matter is put together.

These sorts of studies require machines capable of taking ordinary particles such as protons and electrons and accelerating them to extremely high speeds. The first such machines, built just before World War II, were only a few inches across and lacked sufficient punch to knock a proton out of a nucleus in a target atom. As time went on and technological abilities increased, however, these machines became bigger as well as more powerful. During the 1960s a typical proton accelerator was a ring of magnets several hundred meters in diameter. For those machines, tearing a nucleus apart was child's play, and they produced many new and interesting particles for study.

The reason that accelerators were ring-shaped is simple. In these machines particles are constrained to move in a circular track by powerful magnets. Each time the particle passes a given point, it is given a kick; hitting the same particle many times causes very large energies to be imparted.

Because such accelerators were so large and so expensive, only a few could be built. Scientists who wished to perform experiments on them had to travel to the laboratories where the machines were located. They built their experimental apparatus at home, traveled with it to a laboratory to perform the experiments, and then went home again to analyze the data that had been obtained.

In the 1970s and 1980s still larger machines were built. At the Fermi National Accelerator Laboratory near Chicago, an accelerator was built whose main ring was 1.6 km (one mile) across, and a similar, underground ring was built at the European Organization for Nuclear Research in Geneva. The number of machines at which the frontiers of knowledge about the basic constituents of matter could be reached shrank from a few in each major country to a few in the world. The individual scientist who formerly used such a machine was eventually replaced by coalitions of scientists from many universities who collaborated on single, massive experiments. When the results of this sort of work are published, it is not at all unusual for more than 100 people to be listed as authors.

This machine was designed to fabricate the superconducting wire cable that would be used in the Superconducting Super Collider, the giant particle accelerator that has been proposed for construction in the United States.
Lawrence Berkeley Laboratory, University of California

The next step on this road to large-scale physics was taken in 1987, when U.S. Pres. Ronald Reagan announced that the SSC would be proposed to Congress. This machine would dwarf its predecessors, even as they had dwarfed theirs. The ring in which the protons are to be accelerated will be no less than 84 km (52 mi) around. When protons from the machine collide head-on with each other, the particles will be raised to temperatures never seen since the first fraction of a second in the life of the universe.

In discussing the SSC it is easy to get lost in superlatives—so many billions of dollars, so many kilometers of superconducting wire in the magnets, and so on. When I think about the machine, however, other questions occupy my mind. For example, with a machine that big and that expensive, will there be any leeway for "crazy" experiments—experiments that probably would not work but would have a huge payoff if they did? How does this centralization of facilities affect the act of individual creativity that is at the core of all good science?

I do not know the answers to these questions. I do know, however, that we are going to have an opportunity to find out. I see one field of science after another following the lead of high-energy physics. In materials research, for example, which used to be the epitome of the one-professor-and-a-couple-of-graduate-students-in-a-basement-laboratory field of physics, the move toward Big Science is on with a vengeance. For example, there is only one place, the Francis Bitter National Magnet Laboratory in Cambridge, Mass., where the responses of materials to high magnetic fields can be studied.

Sequencing the genome. Not to be outdone, biologists seem to be getting on the Big Science bandwagon as well. Their vehicle is not an accelerator but a project at once astonishing in its scope and staggering in its implications. What they propose to produce is nothing less than a detailed map of the entire human genetic makeup, the genome.

Scientists have known for some time that the genetic material that each person carries—the stuff that makes us what we are and makes us different from everyone else—consists of roughly 100,000 genes spread out along 23 pairs of chromosomes in each cell in our bodies. These genes govern the color of our eyes, our body build, our propensity to have certain diseases, and just about every other physical characteristic we possess. The information is carried in the sequence of a string of molecules known as bases along the strands of the double helix of the DNA (deoxyribonucleic acid) molecule.

The genes on an individual chromosome can be mapped—that is, we can learn in what sequence they appear—by relatively straightforward applica-

Walter Gilbert, a professor of science at Harvard University, holds a film of a DNA sequence in a human gene. Gilbert supports the proposal to map the entire human genome.
Louis Psihoyos

tions of standard, if complex, chemical procedures. To learn the arrangement of bases in an individual gene, however, it is necessary to do a lot more work. When this arrangement is determined, the gene is said to be sequenced.

From the point of view of the geneticist, everything that one wants to know about an individual is contained in the sequence of bases on all the genes in all the chromosomes. The current initiative in biology arises because for the first time scientists possess the technology for obtaining this knowledge. They can, if they want to make the effort, sequence the entire genome and learn what each segment of DNA contributes to the total human being.

Of course, the project is not trivial. Estimates of cost run into the billions of dollars, and it would take at least a decade of work by several hundred researchers to get the job done. It would involve a major portion of the money and manpower now devoted to the study of human genetics.

This move toward Big Science in biology is opposed by many prominent members of that community. They express some reservations about the project itself. For example, some wonder whether mapping would not be as useful as sequencing for medical applications. They also worry that such a project would forever change the face of their science and start them down the slippery slope traveled by the particle physicists.

For myself, I find the romance of the so-called "Genome Initiative" overwhelming. It represents nothing less than the ultimate scientific response to the Socratic dictum "Know Thyself."

See also Feature Articles: THE NEW SUPERCONDUCTORS: A SCIENTIFIC BREAKTHROUGH; SUPERSTAR 1987; PROBING THE SUBATOMIC WORLD: THE FERMI NATIONAL ACCELERATOR LABORATORY; CERN—THE EUROPEAN LABORATORY FOR PARTICLE PHYSICS.

Anthropology

Until very recently, U.S. anthropologists tended to be academically oriented. Most held a Ph.D. and taught anthropology at a college or university. This was not the case in Britain, where the need to administer a far-flung empire that included many diverse cultures led at an early date to the employment of social anthropologists specializing in the application of anthropological knowledge. If the Sun never set on the British empire, neither did it set on the anthropologists who helped keep order there. In the United States, however, applied anthropologists were comparatively rare. There was little empire to administer, and American Indians, in the popular view, did not require cultural understanding—only the education, forced if necessary, that would enable them to be submerged in the American melting pot.

One of the first U.S. anthropologists to see that anthropological insights could usefully be applied to public policy was Philleo Nash, who during his long career held a wide variety of applied and academic positions. Throughout, his concern was with people, not with bureaucratic red tape. Born Oct. 25, 1909, in Wisconsin Rapids, Wis., he was adviser to presidents, head of the Bureau of Indian Affairs, lieutenant governor of Wisconsin, an academic innovator, and founder of an elementary and secondary school. He studied violin at the Curtis Institute of Music in Philadelphia for a year before obtaining a bachelor's degree in anthropology from the University of Wisconsin in 1932. An account of his excavations at the

One of the first U.S. anthropologists to understand that anthropological insights could usefully be applied to public policy, Philleo Nash worked to end racial discrimination in all aspects of U.S. life.

Ross Lake Indian mounds, which had served as his bachelor's thesis, was published by the Milwaukee Public Museum the following year. For his doctorate, received from the University of Chicago in 1937, he made a study of the 19th-century Ghost Dance movement among American Indians, living for a time with the Klamath tribe in Oregon. Subsequently he worked for the Royal Ontario Museum, taught at the University of Toronto and the University of Wisconsin, and directed an archaeological excavation at a historic site in Canada.

In 1942, after a short period spent managing the family cranberry business, Nash was named special assistant for domestic operations in the Office of War Information. He became special consultant to the secretary of war in 1943 and, when Harry S. Truman became president, special assistant for minority affairs to the White House. He served in the last position from 1946 to 1952, becoming administrative assistant to the president in 1952 but resigning in 1953 after the Democratic defeat in the 1952 election. During this long period of government service, Nash worked to end racial discrimination in every aspect of U.S. life and government, including those that touched his private life. The Washington, D.C., schools of that period were racially segregated, and when his children reached school age, Nash founded a racially integrated school that initially had 12 students. By 1988 the school had more than 800 students and had recently moved into a new building.

During his days in the White House, Nash attracted the unwanted attention of a fellow Wisconsinite, Sen. Joseph McCarthy, then riding the crest of his anti-Communist crusade. However, Nash was defended by Truman, and the incident had so little effect on his standing with the public that he was elected lieutenant governor of Wisconsin in 1958. Upon losing his reelection bid in 1960, he returned to Washington to serve in the Kennedy administration as U.S. commissioner of Indian affairs. In that position he worked to promote economic self-sufficiency for the many tribes that still existed. His aim was not to maintain order among subservient peoples, in the manner of the earlier British anthropologists, but to preserve the identity and integrity of the distinct lifeways of Native Americans. However, he had some sharp disagreements with Stewart Udall, then secretary of the interior, and "resigned involuntarily" after a little less than five years. "I never kept a job I didn't like," he once said, "and never quit a job I did like—I always got fired."

From then until his retirement in 1977, Nash toured India for the State Department, worked as a consultant, and taught in the anthropology department of the American University in Washington, D.C., where he helped develop an academic program to train applied anthropologists and directed

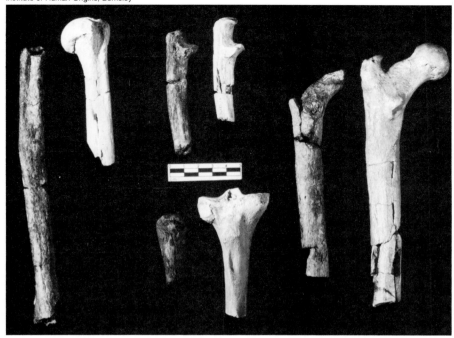

Limb bones of Homo habilis, *the earliest direct ancestor of modern humans, were discovered in Tanzania in 1986. Approximately 1.8 million years old, they are on the left of each pair; on the right are the bones of "Lucy," a three-million-year-old* Australopithecus afarensis *skeleton. Anthropologists were surprised that the two sets of bones resembled each other so closely.*

the university's Learning Center. Always an innovator, he developed techniques for using films in teaching. One of his last students was interested in archaeology and mathematics, so Nash put together a major in archaeoastronomy. He was given the Distinguished Service Award of the American Anthropological Association in 1984 and the Malinowski Award of the Society for Applied Anthropology in 1986. Nash died on Oct. 12, 1987, leaving behind a legacy of administration for the good of the people being administered.

Human evolution. The study of human evolution, in some disarray after the discoveries of unexpected human fossils in recent years, remained so in 1987, with many traditional theories under challenge. Previously, the majority view was that *Australopithecus afarensis*—or "Lucy" and the "First Family," as the fossils came to be called—dated to about 3.5 million years ago and represented the first humans. It was assumed that descendants of Lucy included *A. africanus* at perhaps 2.5 million years ago; the "robust" forms such as *A. robustus* and *A. boisei*—which were viewed as offshoots specializing in smashing seeds and nuts with their incredible teeth—at around 2 million years ago; and the roughly contemporaneous but somehow more human *Homo habilis*, so called because of its association with stone tools.

The australopithecine line became extinct by about 1.5 million years ago, while the *Homo* line evolved into *H. erectus* perhaps 100,000 years earlier. Lucy and her contemporaries were relatively short, only around one meter (3½ ft) tall; later fossils were

taller, but only about 1.6 m (5½ ft) at most, according to the accepted view. Yet a 12-year-old *H. erectus* youth found in 1984 would have been 1.8 m (6 ft) tall at maturity. A skull of a robust australopithecine with huge teeth, crested skull, and flat face was described in 1986 from Lake Turkana in northern Kenya. The shocking thing about the fossil was its age—about 2.5 million years ago—long before such forms had been dated previously. The most recently reported find was equally surprising. Donald Johanson, the discoverer of Lucy, reported in *Nature* in May 1987 that he and his colleagues had recovered a skeleton from Olduvai Gorge in Tanzania that was provisionally assigned to *H. habilis*. The bones, which dated to about 1.8 million years ago, were of an extremely short individual about the same size as the Lucy remains. To add to the confusion, archaeologists reported that stone tools, long thought to have been made only by *H. habilis*, had been found at a number of sites dating to the time period of 2 million–2.5 million years ago.

To explain these apparently contradictory findings, some have suggested the contemporaneous existence of several human and near-human lines evolving in parallel, each adapting to a slightly different environment. Others suggest that these early human populations were much more variable than scientists had previously thought, and some have even suggested that part of the variability could be accounted for by extreme sexual dimorphism, with two differing forms existing in the same population. Finally, there are those who believe it will be nec-

Rocking the anthropological world, a second "Lucy" is discovered in southern Uganda.

Archaeology

Several important developments took place in archaeology during the past year. Some of the most interesting centered on foraging, or hunting and gathering, as a long-term human adaptation. Most of the articles discussed below focus on foragers, including the earliest hominid hunter/gatherers and also those of much more recent times who maintained this life-style even after the advent of agriculture.

An exciting late-breaking development in 1987, which can be only briefly reviewed here, was the first report, published in *National Geographic*, of the world's oldest known shipwreck. It was a merchant vessel dated to the Late Bronze Age that sank off the Turkish coast about 3,400 years ago. Cargo recovered by the excavators from the Institute of Nautical Archaeology, College Station, Texas, included items representing each of the seven eastern Mediterranean civilizations in existence at the time. Thousands of artifacts, including copper and blue glass ingots, bronze weapons, ceramic storage jars, fishing nets, ivory, ostrich eggs, Mycenaean pottery,

Turkish diver cleans debris from one of the approximately 200 four-handled copper ingots retrieved from the world's oldest known shipwreck, some 3,400 years ago off the coast of Turkey.

essary to rethink the understanding of the process of evolution, including the consideration of non-Darwinian alternatives.

It should be pointed out that what is being challenged is not evolution but the understanding of it. That evolution took place is evident in the fossil record; specialists disagree only on the how and why. Classic Darwinian theory holds that evolution consists of a series of random genetic mutations. Those mutations that are harmful to the organism are lost, while those that are helpful are preserved; mutations that are neutral in terms of adaptation may or may not persist, depending on chance. In the Darwinian view, evolutionary change is very gradual and relatively constant. Punctuated equilibrium is a non-Darwinian theory of evolution that is currently gaining in popularity. It is based on the observation that actual evolution is marked by long periods of equilibrium followed (punctuated) by relatively short bursts of rapid evolutionary change. It may be that the human fossil record as it is known today fits this model better than the classic Darwinian explanation. In the long run, punctuated equilibrium may be seen as a special case of Darwinian evolution in which long periods of environmental equilibrium leading to a time of stable genetic material are followed by drastic environmental upheaval leading to rapid genetic change.

—Charles W. McNett, Jr.

Institute of Nautical Archaeology; photo, Donald Frey

and gold were found aboard the wreck. It will prove to be a valuable discovery, not only for its trove of artifacts but also for information it can provide on Late Bronze Age commerce and social organization. Writes the author, George Bass, the ship and its cargo "provide an astonishing portrait of an era symbolized by the reign of Egypt's Tutankhamun and the fall of Troy."

The earliest Americans. A series of important articles titled "The First Americans" appeared in *Natural History* magazine in 1986–87. The articles, by prominent archaeologists, commemorate the first conclusive proof in the Western Hemisphere of associations of humans with large animals of the Pleistocene Epoch (10,000 to 1.7 million years ago), discovered 60 years ago in Folsom, N.M. Each discusses an important aspect of colonization of the New World, and the series as a whole presents controversies surrounding the nature and timing of specific events. Articles discuss such topics as the Ice Age environment in Siberia and North America, the possibility that humans contributed to mass extinctions of Pleistocene animals, and human cultures in northeast Asia that may have immigrated to the New World. Others describe archaeological sites that many think contain evidence of very early Americans.

The significance of the series lies not in its presentation of new information but in its well-written and accessible discussion of a major problem in American prehistory. Rarely is the operation of archaeology, or any other field, revealed so well to a general audience. The series marks a growing cooperation between professional archaeologists and the interested public. It is a welcome trend.

The first technology. Archaeologists have known for several years that stone tool use and manufacture began sometime before two million years ago. This technology of stone flaking is the first evidence of culture, the transmission of learned behavior, in the archaeological record. Even though the artifacts have become well known, the relationship of the technology that produced them with the lifeways of early hominids is not well understood. For this reason Nicholas Toth of the University of California at Berkeley set out to understand early stone technologies by making and using tools similar to those found in the Koobi Fora region of Kenya.

Toth employed two different early technologies to create the artifacts. The first, called Oldowan, was a cobble-tool tradition between about 2.2 million and 1.5 million years ago. It was probably used by *Homo habilis* groups who inhabited southern Africa during this time. (A cobble is a somewhat rounded stone that is larger than a pebble and smaller than a boulder.) The second, the Acheulean tradition, utilized large flakes removed from boulders to make hand axes, cleavers, and picks. It began about 1.5 million years ago and was probably used by *Homo erectus.*

Toth's experiment consisted of three stages: raw material collection, tool manufacture, and animal butchering. He found that Oldowan toolmakers had learned to select for the most perfect cobbles. These early hominids seemed to reject cobbles with flaws that made them flake in unpredictable ways. Toth also tried several different flaking techniques to see which most closely matched those from the Koobi Fora sites. Not surprisingly, the simplest method, using a stone hammer to flake a cobble, was found to be the only method represented at any of the sites. Probably his most important find was the presence of wear marks on several Oldowan flakes. These suggest that sharp-edged unmodified flakes were tools of choice even at that early date. It had been thought that Oldowan hominids were using the cobble tools and discarding the flakes.

The Acheulean tradition represented a leap in development. Toth showed that these bifacially flaked tools (worked on two opposing but adjacent faces) were made with more control and with definite patterns in mind. They proved to be excellent for butchering large mammals, suggesting that the Acheulean advance was associated with the systematic butchering of large carcasses.

Research suggests that flaked stone technology emerged after a shift toward the increased exploitation of animal resources. This occurred more than two million years ago, possibly in association with major climatic shifts to much drier conditions that took place about 2.5 million years ago. Flaked stone technologies may have allowed early hominids to move into environmental niches previously dominated by carnivores and scavengers. Sharp-edged tools became the equivalent of canine and meat-cutting teeth. Heavier stones served as "bone-crunching jaws." Toth argues that once the notion of flaking had been assimilated, a learning feedback loop was created between increased tool use and an enlarging brain. This path led to modern humans and was an early step toward advanced technologies.

Gazelle hunting and farming in Stone-Age Syria. Excavations at Tell Abu Hureyra, in northern Syria, revealed unusual quantities of gazelle bones in the earliest occupation levels. These dated to the Late Mesolithic Period, between about 11,000 and 9,000 years ago. The project, reported by Anthony Legge, University of London, and Peter Rowley-Conwy, University of Cambridge, used several methods of archaeological inference to determine the nature of gazelle hunting during that time.

Because the remains represented newborns, yearlings, and adults, as shown by tooth and bone growth patterns, the authors concluded that whole herds of gazelle were represented at the site. This meant that the inhabitants of Abu Hureyra killed large numbers of these animals at a time. Hunters taking individual animals usually select only young prime specimens, which would result in a much larger proportion of yearlings and young adults in the deposits.

The same bone and tooth information also revealed that the animals had all been killed in late spring or early summer, just after the yearly calving period, as large herds of gazelle migrated northward from what is now Jordan. The animals were probably herded into large corral-like enclosures, many of which are still visible on the desert floor, and then quickly killed and processed. The meat was dried and stored at Abu Hureyra, most likely supplying the inhabitants with many months of animal protein.

Abu Hureyra was not, however, used only for seasonal gazelle processing and storing; it had been a permanent settlement since its inception. Abundant plant food remains represent species collected in the year-round foraging pattern. Probably the proximity of these different plant resources and the seasonal abundance of gazelle allowed its occupants to live more or less permanently at the site.

Ceramics and domesticated plants are found in deposits dated to about 10,000 years ago; these mark the beginning of the Neolithic Period. It is common to think that agriculture, both plant and animal domestication, brought about an end to hunter-gatherer strategies, thereby allowing a settled mode of life and the beginnings of civilization. At Abu Hureyra, however, the pattern of gazelle hunting continued for another 1,000 years, even though other sites contain evidence that domesticated sheep and goats were herded in the region throughout that time. Indeed, sheep and goats make up a small portion of the animal remains at Tell Abu Hureyra. The question then arises as to why these people adopted farming while continuing to rely on hunting wild animals for a major portion of their diet. Legge and Rowley-Conwy suggest that the answer is economic; hunting gazelles allowed a large amount of storable meat to be harvested in a few weeks each year. Large-scale herding was probably not as productive, and the proportion of gazelle remains to those of sheep, goat, and other species at the site was 80 to 20% throughout the millennium.

The pattern rapidly changed, however, about 9,000 years ago, when gazelle herds were depleted by overhunting. At that time the proportion of gazelle to sheep and goat remains was reversed, so that gazelles made up only 20% of the faunal remains at Abu Hureyra. It is only then that large-scale herding was adopted, and both plant and animal domestication became the primary subsistence strategy in northern Syria. This suggests that agriculture does not immediately take over and replace older subsistence systems. It may run parallel with highly adaptive

foraging strategies for some time, until fundamental conditions change. It also suggests that mobile pastoralism (raising of livestock), long thought to be a natural adjunct to foraging, was not always a precursor to plant agriculture and a settled lifeway. In the case of Tell Abu Hureyra, plant domestication and permanent settlement were adopted before pastoralism.

Foraging and fishing in Stone-Age Denmark. Just as hunter/gatherers established settled lifeways in northern Syria, Late Mesolithic fisher/hunter/gatherers were able to live in large semipermanent settlements in northern Europe. As in Syria, the highly adapted foraging strategy persisted well after the advent of agriculture in the region.

T. Douglas Price of the University of Wisconsin and Erik Petersen of the University of Copenhagen focused their attention on a single component site, among many larger, more complex sites, in order to determine the nature of this foraging behavior. They carefully excavated Vaenget Nord, a former island in an inlet created by rising post-Pleistocene sea levels, near Vedbaek on the Danish island of Zealand. Their technique allowed exact mapping of artifact locations over nearly the whole Mesolithic living surface of the site. This showed them that different parts of the site had been used for particular purposes. These included habitation and cooking, manufacture and repair of stone and bone tools, animal butchering, hide preparation, and woodworking.

Vaenget Nord dates to the Late Mesolithic Kongemose period, between about 7,500 and 6,500 years ago. Several environmental factors contributed to population increases during that time, including a warming climate as Ice Age glaciers receded northward, rising sea levels creating shallow inlets rich in sea life, and a general abundance and diversity of plants and animals. Hunting pressure, however, gradually eradicated large land animals, including bears, moose, and aurochs, and so there was a general shift during the period toward marine resources.

The following period, called Ertebølle, between about 6,500 and 5,000 years ago, was characterized by sophisticated marine-adapted fishing/hunting/gathering strategies and high population densities in northern Denmark. Vaenget Nord was no longer occupied at that time, as it had been inundated, but more than 40 Ertebølle sites are known from the Vedbaek area. Their inhabitants exploited whales, porpoises, fish, and shellfish, creating huge shell middens that mark the locations of large, semipermanent settlements. These settlements are associated with the formation of large cemeteries.

Agriculturalists entered the area from the south about 5,500 years ago, but Ertebølle foragers maintained their marine-based subsistence strategy for perhaps 500 more years. The introduction of ceramics, combined with lowering sea levels and a reduction in the once-abundant marine resources, helped spur the adoption of agriculture about 5,000 years ago. At that time the Neolithic Period began in Scandinavia.

These studies, among many others focusing on hunter/gatherers, have contributed to an ongoing revision in archaeologists' ideas about forager peoples. It is becoming increasingly clear that, in several places in the world, foraging groups were able to develop and maintain relatively large, affluent, and sedentary lifeways. It also seems likely that many of these groups were characterized by considerable social complexity, not usually associated with traditional views of hunters and gatherers. Not only is the view of foragers changing but so also is the notion of the relationships between those peoples and agriculturalists.

Foragers and pastoralists in the Kalahari. Archaeologists have long known that foragers similar, and possibly ancestral to, the San-speaking "Bushmen" have inhabited the Kalahari region of Botswana for several thousand years. It was assumed, however, that pastoral Bantu-speaking peoples had only recently entered the region, possibly as late as 200 years ago. Recent work reported by James Denbow of the University of Texas and Edwin Wilmsen of Boston University revealed this assumption to be wrong. Agriculturalists and foragers have coexisted, side by side, in the Kalahari for more than 2,000 years.

Archaeological studies of 34 sites in the region revealed that domesticated plant foods have been produced for the past 2,000 years. They also showed that domesticated cattle and sheep were introduced into the Kalahari from the north about 2,200 years ago. Grain cultivation, ceramic technology, and iron metallurgy followed in quick succession. Linguistic evidence supports the archaeology, showing that language diversification occurred about the time of Christ, associated with the migration of farmer/herders into the region.

Studies of geologic sediments and beach levels contribute to the picture, showing that rainfall between 2,500 and 1,500 years ago may have been significantly higher than it is at present. These more favorable conditions probably contributed to population growth, expansion, and the widespread adoption of agriculture.

At the same time, however, foragers in the Kalahari maintained their mobile lifeways, developing a long-term dynamic relationship with their farming neighbors. This relationship continued as the Iron Age economy of the Bantu speakers became much more complex, eventually leading to the establishment, about 900 years ago, of major chiefdoms along the eastern Kalahari. Long-distance trade had been established in the area 200 or 300 years ear-

lier, and chiefdoms had developed to control the flow of goods, both within the Kalahari region and with other chiefdoms in northeastern and southern Africa. The Kalahari chiefdoms collapsed about 700 years ago as they were subsumed into the Great Zimbabwe Kingdom.

Although some San speakers were reported by Europeans in the 18th century to be herders and livestock owners, the great majority did not adopt agriculture. They did, however, become part of the overall economy, with several groups exporting ivory and ostrich feathers. Copper mines and salt production were also reported to be under San control in the 19th century, indicating their widespread participation in the economy of the time.

That foragers maintained their basic subsistence strategies and at the same time participated in a larger economy suggests that production and exchange were not bounded by ethnic or linguistic divisions. This complex lattice of relations among peoples and production characterized the past 2,000 years in the Kalahari.

These developments in archaeology in 1987 show that no longer is it tenable, without thorough testing, to assume that cultural developments followed the generally accepted, ladderlike path from simple foraging to pastoralism to agriculture to civilization. Foraging, at all times in the past, appears to have been a viable and dynamic lifeway, well adapted to most conditions in which humans found themselves.

—James D. Wilde

Architecture and civil engineering

Architecture. The design of buildings during the year under review continued to be influenced by such factors as visual impact, user needs, conformity to neighborhood architecture, and—often—politics. Examples discussed below reflect some of these factors.

In response to local critics concerned about visual impact, the $4.8 billion Canary Wharf project in London was redesigned and resubmitted to the London Docklands Development Corp. for approval. The original design included three towers, each 260 m high (one meter = 3.28 feet), which exceeded the area's existing tallest building by 76 m. Most people did not want any buildings that would be higher than those already in the area. However, Olympia & York Development Ltd. of Toronto, the developer, continued to recommend one tower at the original height and two each at 210 m.

In spite of the controversy, the original area of the project remained unchanged at 930,000 sq m (10 million sq ft) of office space in the 22-building

Grande Arche monument under construction on the western edge of Paris consists of two 35-story concrete-framed towers rising from a five-story base and connected at the top by a three-story section.

complex. Participating in the project were the London Docklands Development Corp., as the planning authority; Olympia & York Development Ltd., the developer; and Skidmore, Owings & Merrill, the modifications designer, based in London.

Politics and design controversy were exemplified by the Grande Arche monument under construction in Paris, described as "monument first, building second." The controversy was between Johan Otto von

Spreckelsen, a Danish professor of architecture who designed the structure, and the project's Paris-based engineers. The engineers argued that the architect's splays at the top of piers were impractical and would not be able to be seen once the monument had been built. Von Spreckelsen argued that, though the splays would be invisible to humans, "God will see them." Because the architect's design was favored by Pres. François Mitterrand and people were reluctant to interfere with an artist, his views prevailed. However, these disagreements caused him to leave the project in 1986. He died in March 1987.

The Paris monument, nicknamed "The Cube," is 107 m wide, 112 m long, and 111 m high. It was designed to be a centerpiece among skyscrapers on the western edge of Paris. Two concrete-framed towers 35 stories high rise from a five-story base and are connected at the top by a three-story section spanning 70 m. Other materials used in the structure include white Italian marble, tinted reflective glazing on the outside of the cube, and concrete with a strength of 713.5 kg per sq cm (10,150 psi), about twice the strength of the concrete normally used in building construction. The structural elements, which were reinforced with steel, consisted of very deep concrete beams both at the bottom and in the connecting three-story section, massive columns, and structural slabs at every seventh floor.

Design and construction of this cubical monument was being accomplished in spite of significant challenges. The design and construction scheduling challenges resulted in failure to meet completion dates of various phases of the project. As of early 1988, the targeted completion date for the whole structure was July 14, 1989, to mark the 200th anniversary of the French revolution—too late for the end of François Mitterrand's term as president in the spring of 1988. Political interplay affected the original "international communications crossroads" concept of

Keehi Interchange in Honolulu, Hawaii, took 11 years to complete at a cost of $140 million. Engineers faced the challenges of building on soft clay and keeping ten lanes of traffic open at all times during construction.

Two Union Square in Seattle, Wash., required engineers to develop for the columns concrete nearly four times stronger than usual. They achieved this by making the concrete with new materials and methods.

the monument; 730,000 sq m (7.9 million sq ft) of floor space were reallocated to commercial use so that the building would be self-financing. Thus, the concept of monument first and building second was born. Once completed, the roof space was to be used for exhibitions marking the bicentennial celebration of the French Revolution; later it would be terraced to cater to about 10,000 visitors per day for a view of Paris. Along with von Spreckelsen other major contributors to the project were Société Anonyme d'Économie Mixte Nationale Tête-Défense, a state company overseeing the whole project; Bouygues SA, the company building the structure; and Coyne and Bellier, a Paris-based engineering firm that developed the structure after it had been outlined by Danish consultant Erick Reitzel.

Civil engineering. The construction function of civil engineering often confronts unforeseen natural variables. An outstanding example is the Keehi Interchange in Honolulu. The interchange is 3 km (1.9 mi) long but took 11 years to complete at a cost of $140 million. The biggest natural obstacle was the presence of a 45.7-m-deep layer of virgin, unconsolidated clay. Such clays are difficult to work in because they generally have little capacity to support loads without excessive deformation. The second hurdle was a design constraint requiring the contractor to keep ten highway lanes open at all times in order to handle 250,000 vehicles of traffic per day with minimal interference.

To overcome the natural hurdle of the soft clay layer, engineers designed 70-m concrete piles, each of which was driven into the ground in three short segments. Driving the pile sections in the clay layer generated problems such as joint breakage, random cracking, and a downward drag force. Joint breakage was overcome by the use of long, strong reinforcing bars through the joints. Limiting the maximum driving force and continually monitoring the pile response with electronic dynamic analyzers minimized random cracking, and precoating each pile section with asphalt minimized the downward drag problem. All these innovations saved an estimated $17 million. Additional site-specific problems required many more design and construction decisions. The design consultant for the interchange was Parsons, Brinkerhoff, Quade, and Douglas; and M & E Pacific was the project manager.

The creativity of civil engineers is often challenged when they must develop materials of unusual properties. Another 1987 civil engineering award-winning entry project consisted of a 58-story, 226-m-high building in Seattle, Wash. (Two Union Square). The columns of the structure consist of concrete that is nearly four times as strong as conventional concrete and is a new material for nonmilitary building structures.

The engineers obtained the high concrete strength by changing the usual method of concrete practice. These changes included maintaining a low water–cement ratio, that being the major factor in enhancing strength and abating shrinkage and creep; using the strongest available cement type; using a superplasticizer, which in the absence of large volumes of water provides workability; using a high content of cement; using hard, small, round aggregate because the round shape helps to eliminate pockets of stress concentrations; using silica lime to replace about 10% of the cement and thereby enhance concrete strength by about 25%; using design strength at 56 days of age instead of the conventional 28 days; and implementing a well-coordinated quality-assurance program. The cost of this concrete was $140 per cu yd at the ready-mix plant—nearly three times the cost of conventional concrete.

One major innovation justified the use of this expensive material; the columnar structural system lacked regular steel bars but instead was built with a permanent steel shell that was lined on the inside with short steel pieces called shear studs. This configuration, according to the designer, cost 30% less than a conventional design. Also, the high-strength concrete was designed to produce increased stiffness so that the building would not sway on windy days. Tony Tschant of the design firm Skilling Ward Magnuson Barkshire stated the firm's criterion: "Only one occupant in 100 will feel or see the sway in 10 years." A stringent quality-assurance program, which involved Weston Hester, a concrete specialist from the University of California at Berkeley, and also the Cascade Testing Laboratory ensured that the designed concrete strength was actually produced. The major contributors to this project included Skilling Ward Magnuson Barkshire (structural design firm), The NBBJ Group (architect firm), and Turner Construction Co. (general contractor).

—Badru M. Kiggundu

Astronomy

During the past year new instrumentation that will allow more efficient imaging and resolution of infrared sources was developed. The constancy of solar radiation was explored, and searches for cool companions to stars were reported. The first supernova to reach naked-eye brilliance in nearly 400 years was subjected to intense observation. New questions about our Galaxy and the structure of the universe were addressed.

Instrumentation. The use of two or more telescopes as an interferometer to improve the ability to see small angular detail has been employed by radio astronomers for many years. In recent months an infrared interferometer was constructed at the University of California at Berkeley under the direction of Charles Townes. It consists of two telescopes, each one mounted on a trailer to allow them to be placed at different distances from one another. At one kilometer, close to the maximum separation to be used, the interferometer is able to resolve angles as small as one millisecond of arc at the operating wavelength of ten micrometers.

Each telescope has two mirrors: a flat mirror, 203 cm (80 in) in diameter and movable in order to track the sky, directs light to a fixed parabolic mirror that is 165 cm (65 in) in diameter. Light focused by the paraboloid mirrors is directed through holes in the flat mirrors and mixed with a beam from a carbon dioxide laser to generate signals that can be combined to obtain interference patterns with the same flexibility available to radio astronomers. By this method astronomers will be able to determine the positions and sizes of objects with an accuracy unprecedented in infrared observations. In order to hold the separation of the optical components of the system to a small fraction of the observing wavelength, the telescopes are mounted on concrete piers during use and the optical components are positioned with a network of helium-neon laser interferometers.

Astronomers planned to use the new instrument to measure the sizes and shapes of stars forming in interstellar clouds and to obtain detailed information about the compact infrared sources observed near the galactic center. The extreme sensitivity of the interferometer to small-scale structure would provide new insights into puzzles previously uncovered by infrared observations.

A new infrared detector made at the Santa Barbara (Calif.) Research Center of the Hughes Aircraft Co. underwent tests during the year by the National Optical Astronomy Observatories, headquartered in Tucson, Ariz. The device promised to be especially effective in the near-infrared, at wavelengths of one to five micrometers. The detector has a matrix of 58 by 62 cells etched on a crystal of indium antimonide that must be cooled to 40 K (−233° C [−387.4° F]) to function properly. Each cell independently generates an electrical charge proportional to the amount of radiation falling upon it. The charges can be read out and stored by a computer so that an image of the portion of the sky being observed can be developed. The device is 100 times as sensitive as former detectors in this spectral range and is expected to be useful in planetary studies, searches for brown dwarfs, and observations of the galactic center and of galaxies at extremely high redshifts.

Solar system. A retrospective study of data from the Solar Maximum Mission and Nimbus 7 satellites, used to measure the energy radiated by the Sun, provided a new insight into variations of the solar energy rate. Peter Foukal of Cambridge (Mass.) Research and Instrumentation, Inc., and Judith Lean of Applied Research Corp., Landover, Md., found that the Sun behaves somewhat differently from what might have been expected. Whenever a large sunspot appears on the Sun, the total energy radiated by the Sun can be diminished by as much as 0.2%. One might expect, therefore, that the Sun would brighten slightly during those times when sunspots are infrequent or absent from the solar surface. Foukal and Lean, however, found just the reverse.

By comparing common observations by the two measuring systems from 1981 to 1984, the investigators first assured themselves that any long-term trends in the satellite data were not due to a slow degradation in the instruments. They found that both satellites had recorded the same changes in brightness in the range 0.07 to 0.4%. Thus, the slow general decline in the Sun's brightness recorded by the two independent measuring systems was not an artifact of the instruments. The data indicate that the Sun is brighter on average at sunspot maximum

Mark V. Sykes, Steward Observatory, The University of Arizona

Image of Pluto and its moon, Charon, constructed from thermal radiation detected by the Infrared Astronomical Satellite, provided astronomers with data that allowed them to infer the existence on Pluto of polar ice caps made of frozen methane.

than at sunspot minimum. During the roughly four-year period over which common data were available, a time of descent from a sunspot maximum, the solar radiation declined by 0.07%.

Foukal and Lean found that the decrease in brightness due to sunspots is more than compensated by the presence of the less obvious bright regions that accompany increased sunspot activity. Thus, even as the Sun tends to brighten with the decrease in sunspots, the decrease in the accompanying bright regions is enough to diminish the net solar brightness.

From ground-based data taken before the satellites were launched, Foukal and Lean estimated that the solar radiation should have been 0.12% greater during the 1981 sunspot maximum than during the 1975 minimum. Because the Sun is now passing through a sunspot minimum, a similar brightening may be expected over the next five or six years.

Their work may provide the explanation for a period of abnormal cold recorded in Europe from the 16th into the early 19th century. During this time there occurred the so-called Maunder Minimum, from the mid-1660s to the early 1700s, when there was an almost total absence of sunspots. Foukal and Lean calculated that the protracted lack of solar sunspot activity could have been accompanied by a decrease in solar radiation of as much as 0.14%, of sufficient magnitude over the seven-decade lifetime of the Maunder Minimum to account for the change in the climate recorded in Europe.

A search of the images obtained from the Infrared Astronomical Satellite (IRAS) in 1983 turned up several measurements of Pluto. Mark V. Sykes, Roc M. Cutri, and Larry A. Lebofsky of the University of Arizona and Richard P. Binzel of the Planetary Science Institute, all in Tucson, were able to use the data to compute a model that describes polar ice caps on Pluto made of methane ice. As early as 1976 methane ice had been shown to exist on Pluto.

The IRAS data do not provide actual images of Pluto and its satellite, Charon, but instead supply a measure of their combined heat radiation. By subtracting the infrared radiation expected from Charon, it was possible to determine that produced by Pluto alone. The calculations indicated that if Pluto were completely covered by methane ice, it would be too cold to provide the radiation measured by IRAS. To match that amount of radiation, a model was devised that calls for polar ice caps of frozen methane extending to latitudes of about 45° from either pole of the planet, with a darker band free of methane ice parallel to Pluto's equator.

On the basis of that model, the investigators estimated that Pluto has an atmosphere of methane that has sublimed from the polar caps—that is, evaporated directly from solid methane—with a density only about one-thousandth that of the Earth's atmosphere. The temperature on the planet should range from about 54 K (−219° C [−362.2° F]) at the poles to about 59 K at the equator. The ice caps provide an explanation for the decrease in the brightness of Pluto over the past few decades. Previously, one of the ice caps had been presented to the Earth, making the planet appear brighter, but owing to the tilt of Pluto's rotational axis and subsequent orbital motion, more of the less reflecting equatorial band is now presented.

Stars. Two searches for other planetary systems and brown dwarfs, objects larger than planetary size but not large enough to undergo nuclear fusion and shine like a normal star, were described by a Canadian team and a U.S. team of astronomers.

The Canadian astronomers, Bruce Campbell of the Dominion Astrophysical Observatory, Victoria, B.C., and Gordon Walker and Stephenson Yang of the University of British Columbia, used a spectroscopic technique to conduct their search. If a planet or a brown dwarf were in orbit about a star, the star should reflect the motion of that object though greatly reduced in magnitude. The Doppler shifts expected in the spectrum of the star in such a system would be measured in tens of meters per second, well below the sensitivity of usual spectroscopic techniques. To enhance the ability to measure small Doppler shifts, the Canadian researchers passed the starlight through a container of hydrogen flouride gas in order to impress a set of very sharp absorption lines on the stellar spectrum. This permitted them to calibrate the stellar lines to a precision of about 10 m (32.8 ft) per second.

The investigators then systematically observed 16 solar-type stars close to the Sun. Two of them revealed positive evidence of reflected motion, and five of the others showed some sign of it. The magnitude of the motion detected so far led the researchers to conclude that the masses of the bodies inducing the motion fall in the range of one to ten times the mass of Jupiter and, therefore, are planetary in scale. A definitive mass determination would have to await further observations. It might be expected that the objects for which the astronomers were searching would have periods similar to the 12-year period of Jupiter. Since they had been observing for only six years, it was too early to claim with certainty that planetary bodies outside our solar system have been discovered.

The U.S. observers, Benjamin Zuckerman of the University of California at Los Angeles and Eric Becklin of the University of Hawaii, took another approach. They surveyed 40 white dwarf stars, looking for a possible excess of infrared radiation that would indicate dark cool bodies nearby. They chose white dwarfs because they are quite hot, around 10,-000 K, emitting mostly in visible light. White dwarfs are extremely small, of the order of the size of the Earth, and their small radiating surfaces result in low luminosities. Consequently, a brown dwarf in orbit about them could add enough infrared radiation to be readily detected.

Of the 40 white dwarfs observed with NASA's Infrared Telescope Facility at the Mauna Kea Observatory in Hawaii, Zuckerman and Becklin found only one star, Giclas 29–38, that showed an infrared excess. It had an infrared luminosity ten times that of the other white dwarfs, clearly abnormal for a white dwarf with a temperature of 11,500 K. By subtracting the average of the spectra observed for six of the other similar white dwarfs, the researchers derived a spectrum characteristic of a body at a temperature of 1,200 ($\pm$ 200) K, well within the temperature range expected of brown dwarfs. They investigated other possible explanations for the infrared excess (a distant background galaxy, a planetary body, another star, or a shell of dust), but none could explain the observation. There was, however, one disturbing fact

about the brown dwarf interpretation; Zuckerman and Becklin calculated the body to have a size 50% larger than the theoretical size of a brown dwarf. In any case, however, they identified the best, and only, candidate for a brown dwarf available to date.

One of the most exciting events in astronomy in 1987 was the discovery of Supernova 1987A (designated SN 1987A) by Ian Shelton of the University of Toronto at the Las Campanas Observatory in Chile on February 24. Even though the location of the supernova, the Large Magellanic Cloud, is some 160,000 light-years distant, it could be seen with the naked eye, the first such supernova in 383 years. Its apparent brightness and the fact that it was discovered so close to the instant of its outburst allowed it to be subject to study in a way never before possible for a supernova.

The progenitor star of the supernova was identified as a blue supergiant star, Sanduleak −69 202, so named because it was listed in a catalog of blue stars studied by Nicholas Sanduleak of Case Western Reserve University, Cleveland, Ohio, and published in 1969. This is in agreement with the designation of SN 1987A as a Type II supernova, one that results from the collapse of a massive, single star into a neutron star. (For an extended discussion of the supernova, *see* Feature Article: SUPERSTAR 1987.)

Galactic astronomy. An analysis of radio observations of three quasars by Ralph Fiedler, Brian Dennison, and Kenneth Johnston of the U.S. Naval Research Laboratory and Antony Hewish of the Cavendish Laboratory, Cambridge, may have added

Computer-processed image derived by the technique of speckle interferometry reveals Supernova 1987A and a companion that appeared suddenly several weeks after the first sighting of the exploding star.

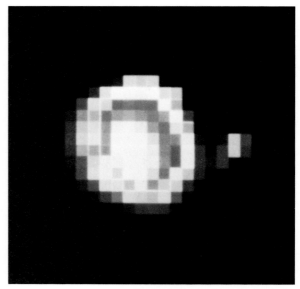

Harvard–Smithsonian Center for Astrophysics

another type of object to those already known in the Galaxy. By examining observations of 36 distant radio sources made daily over a seven-year interval at 2.7 and 8.1 GHz, they found unusual variations in the radio brightnesses of three quasars. The pattern of the variations at the lower frequency showed a slight brightening for about a week and then a rapid dimming that continued for several months. This was followed by a rapid brightening to slightly above normal and then a return to normal brightness a week or so later.

Since the brightness changes are uncharacteristic of quasars, the researchers concluded that they must be due to objects in the Galaxy occulting the sources; that is, passing in front of them. They believed the occulting bodies to be clouds of ionized gas that refract some of the radio energy out of the telescope beam when in front of the sources. As the leading and trailing edges pass by, however, some additional energy is refracted into the beam, increasing the signal modestly. In the case of one quasar, the 8.1-GHz brightness fluctuated wildly during the dim phase of the 2.7-GHz signal. This is due to a focusing effect by irregularities in the clouds but would occur only rarely, when the Earth is just at the focal point of these lenslike irregularities.

The angular speed at which the occulting bodies move across the sources can be estimated from the time it takes the source to dim and to brighten at 2.7 GHz. Assuming the sources have linear motions similar to other bodies in the galactic halo, about 200 km (125 mi) per second, they would have to be at distances of several thousand light-years and have dimensions several times the size of the Earth's orbit about the Sun. From the frequency of the occurrences and assuming the bodies have a uniform distribution in the galactic halo, the investigators estimated that there could be as many as 100 trillion such clouds present in the Galaxy, 1,000 times more numerous than stars. Even so, the low density of the ionized gas within them would imply a total combined mass of only 100 solar masses.

Peter von Ballmoos, Roland Diehl, and Volker Schönfelder of the Max Planck Institute for Extraterrestrial Physics, Garching, West Germany, observed the region of the galactic center with a gamma-ray telescope from a balloon launched in Brazil. The data returned covered the energy range from one to 14 MeV. They found only one gamma-ray line in this range, at 1.809 MeV, which arises from the radioactive decay of aluminum-26. The line had been observed before and was thought to come from aluminum-26 synthesized in novas, supernovas, Wolf-Rayet stars, and red giants that are distributed within the disk of the Galaxy. Consequently, it was proposed that the 1.809-MeV gamma rays should be present as a diffuse emission along the galactic plane. But when the West German investigators mapped the emission with the 10° resolution of their telescope, they found that the emission corresponded to a single source in the direction of the galactic center. Since they did not detect emission from decay of titanium-44, which should also be present if the aluminum-26 came from supernovas, and since it appeared unlikely that enough novas could be concentrated toward the galactic center to account for the measured intensity, they proposed that giant explosions in the center of the Galaxy within the past few million years may have supplied the aluminum-26.

Extragalactic astronomy. Two groups, Roger Lynds of Kitt Peak (Arizona) National Observatory and Vahe Petrosian of Stanford University, using the Kitt Peak 4-m telescope, and Geneviève Soucail, Bernard Fort, Y. Mellier, and Jean-Pierre Picat of Toulouse Observatory in France, using the 3.6-m Canada-France-Hawaii telescope, reported giant luminous arcs in two massive clusters of galaxies. The arcs are bizarre, being longer than 300,000 light-years but extremely thin and having luminosities of about 100 billion Suns. Both groups agreed that the arcs are caused by gravitational lensing of more distant galaxies by the mass in the clusters. The peculiar shape arises from a slight misalignment in the directions of the distant galaxies—if they were in perfect alignment, a complete ring of light would be seen. The apparent extreme brightness is caused by the concentration of extra light into the image by the gravitational lens. The lensing interpretation was confirmed when both groups independently obtained spectra of the arc seen in the cluster Abell 370. The spectrum has a redshift that is almost twice that of the cluster and shows characteristics of a galaxy. More such arcs may be discovered, and they will afford a chance to study distant objects otherwise too faint to be measured.

A huge concentration of mass in the direction of the constellation of Centaurus, which is disturbing the flow of the general expansion of the universe for our Galaxy and others in its vicinity, received additional study by one of its original discoverers, Alan Dressler of Mount Wilson and Las Campanas Observatories, Pasadena, Calif. Dressler's new information combined with the original data led him to the conclusion that our Galaxy is being pulled toward a huge collection of galaxies centered beyond the Centaurus cluster and having a combined mass of ten quadrillion Suns. Most of these galaxies, however, lie hidden from view by dust in the plane of our Galaxy. The exact geometry of the concentration therefore remained uncertain, but it may be marked by the intersection of two vast sheets of galaxies in keeping with the vast cell-like distribution of voids defined by galaxies that has been found in recent years.

R. Brent Tully, Institute for Astronomy, University of Hawaii

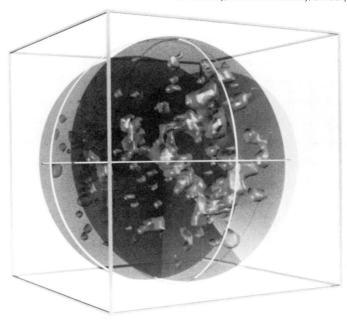

Three-dimensional computer-generated diagram reveals three supercluster complexes in the north galactic hemisphere. Each complex is estimated to contain one quintillion (10^{18}) solar masses.

The nonhomogeneity of galaxy distribution was also confirmed by the work of R. Brent Tully of the University of Hawaii, who was studying clusters of galaxies within one billion light-years of the Earth. The clusters appeared to be clumped into five distinct structures, called supercluster complexes, occupying only 0.5% of the space that he studied. He estimated that each complex contains one quintillion (10^{18}) solar masses, larger than the concentration discovered by Dressler. Both Tully's and Dressler's work caused theorists difficulties in connecting the uniformity of the microwave background radiation and the apparent nonuniformity of galaxies.

The largest quasar redshift was again exceeded. Paul Hewitt and Stephen Warren of the University of Cambridge, using the 3.9-m Anglo-Australian Telescope, discovered that Q0051-279 has a redshift of 4.43.

—W. M. Protheroe

Chemistry

In 1987, as excitement over the recent discoveries of high-temperature superconducting ceramics spread through the scientific community, chemists became increasingly involved in the synthesis and chemical characterization of the new materials. Researchers also made advances in the chemistry of fluorine; discovered novel anticancer agents and other powerful, biologically active substances; synthesized organic polymers that exhibited ferromagnetism, acting like permanent magnets; took pictures of an enzyme in action; and produced synthetic polymers that automatically assemble themselves into fibers.

Inorganic chemistry

During the past year inorganic chemists contributed their expertise to the pursuit of high-temperature superconductors, took stock of the past quarter century of noble-gas chemistry, made advances involving the carbon-fluorine bond, and synthesized new organometallic compounds having transition metals in high oxidation states.

The year 1987 would long be remembered as an exceptionally important one for the physical sciences and in particular for solid-state inorganic chemistry. It was the year in which the discovery of new oxide materials that become superconductive at liquid nitrogen temperatures generated unprecedented worldwide excitement in the scientific community and aroused general public interest in the future possibility of room-temperature superconductivity. (For comprehensive discussions of the discovery, nature, and potential applications of these materials, *see* Feature Article: THE NEW SUPERCONDUCTORS: A SCIENTIFIC BREAKTHROUGH; Year in Review: MATERIALS SCIENCES: *Ceramics.*) In the wake of this major scientific breakthrough, solid-state physicists, materials scientists, and chemists in laboratories around the world began addressing the scientific aspects and technological development of the new materials. While physicists and materials scientists concentrated largely on theory and the testing of physical properties, chemists were becoming involved primarily with syntheses.

Because these substances are inorganic compounds (mixed metal oxides), it follows that the major work of syntheses would fall to solid-state inorganic chemists. The star of the show to date, the yttrium-barium-copper oxide $YBa_2Cu_3O_{7-x}$ ($x \lesssim 0.1$), belongs to the perovskite family of compounds, with which inorganic chemists have had a long history of acquaintance. Two or three decades earlier, the compounds were extensively studied by the late Roland Ward at the University of Connecticut.

The relation of the yttrium-barium-copper oxide material (nicknamed 1–2–3 compound because of the ratio of atoms of its first three constituents) to the perovskites can be seen in (1a) and (1b). The ideal perovskite structure, represented by $CaTiO_3$, is a stoichiometric compound with no superconducting properties. By contrast, the superconductor $YBa_2Cu_3O_{7-x}$ ($x \lesssim 0.1$) is a nonstoichiometric compound, having a defect perovskite structure with too few oxygen atoms. It is this unusual defect structure that permits the solid to have superconducting properties.

Making such compounds is straightforward. For example, the preparation of 1–2–3 compound can begin with Y_2O_3, $BaCO_3$, and CuO, which are ground together and heated to 900°–1,100° C (1,650°–2,010° F). After cooling, pellets are pressed from the material, sintered at 950° C (1,740° F), then heated in O_2 at 500°–600° C (930°–1,110° F), and

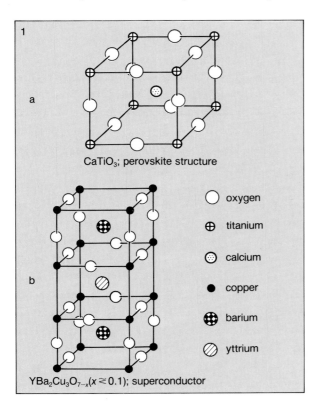

CaTiO₃; perovskite structure

○ oxygen
⊕ titanium
⊙ calcium
● copper
⊞ barium
⊘ yttrium

YBa₂Cu₃O₇₋ₓ(x ≲ 0.1); superconductor

slowly brought to room temperature to ensure the proper oxygen composition.

During the year inorganic chemists applied their extensive knowledge about the properties of the elements in the periodic table to prepare new and, it was hoped, better superconductors. Because yttrium has properties akin to a class of elements in group IIIb known as the lanthanide series (all have a common oxidation state of +3), these elements along with some of the group IIIa metals should be tested in place of Y. The same holds for barium (oxidation state +2), which could be replaced with other M^{2+} metals of group IIa and perhaps of group IIb. Since copper is present in 1–2–3 compound as Cu^{2+} and Cu^{3+}, it follows that other transition metals known to exhibit these oxidation states readily should be tried. If nothing more than these metal replacements were achieved, the large number of possible combinations would keep scientists busy for some time. Yet this is only the tip of the iceberg, for it is necessary to characterize these new materials fully by detailed studies of phase diagrams for various compositions and by X-ray and neutron diffraction studies of their structures. In spite of the worldwide effort already being invested in this research, it will take time and much investigation before anyone knows if the ultimate goal of room-temperature superconductivity is finally in sight.

Twenty-five years of noble-gas chemistry. The year 1987 is the silver anniversary of noble-gas chemistry, and it is of interest to take stock of what has been achieved in the field. Argon, the first noble gas to be found on Earth, was discovered in 1894 by the British scientists Sir William Ramsay and Lord Rayleigh. During the next four years Ramsay discovered helium (first seen spectroscopically in the Sun in 1868), neon, krypton, and xenon. Early research indicated that these elements had no chemical activity, so for more than 60 years chemists referred to the family as the inert gases. Their inertness is in accord with their having a completely satisfied valency shell of electrons and, consequently, no tendency to react with other elements. Over the years, however, some theoretical chemists predicted the formation of inert gas compounds, while some experimental inorganic chemists tried unsuccessfully to prepare them.

The first observation that this family of elements has chemical activity was made in March 1962 by Neil Bartlett of the University of British Columbia. Bartlett introduced the very powerful oxidizing reagent platinum hexafluoride (PtF_6) into gaseous xenon (Xe) and was delighted to see an instantaneous reaction take place between the two gases. Initially it was reported that the reaction merely involved an electron transfer from Xe to PtF_6 with the formation of a pure solid (2a), but later a further reaction was found to occur, resulting in the formation of a mixture of products (2b). This "simple" experiment changed overnight the nomenclature of this family of elements from inert gases to noble gases. The term noble is used as it is for "noble metals" (*e.g.*, gold, platinum, and iridium) to designate less reactivity than that of other elements. This was a dramatic discovery for chemistry and in particular for inorganic chemists worldwide.

Publication of Bartlett's discovery in the open scientific literature had the same stimulus that any important discovery has on the scientific community doing research in related areas. Chemists working on fluorine chemistry immediately turned their attention to the possible use of molecular fluorine (F_2), the most powerful oxidizing element known, for the syntheses of noble-gas fluorides. Only five months after Bartlett's discovery, inorganic chemists at Argonne National Laboratory near Chicago reported the preparation of XeF_4, and during the same year the compound XeF_2 was reported by West German chemists and XeF_6 by Yugoslav chemists. By April 1963 enough noble-gas chemistry had been done worldwide that a scientific meeting was held at Argonne National Laboratory, which culminated in a 404-page book on the subject.

How far has noble-gas chemistry progressed since then? The very name itself suggests a chemical reactivity much more limited in extent than that of more "normal" elements. Since the reactions of xenon are known to involve its formal oxidation (removal of electrons), it follows that the larger the size of the noble-gas atom, the easier oxidation should be to accomplish. Thus, compounds of radon (larger diameter than xenon) are readily prepared, whereas compounds of krypton (smaller diameter than xenon) are more difficult to obtain. Compounds have not been prepared for the still smaller elements argon, neon, and helium. Although generally the noble gases form bonds with only the most electronegative elements, fluorine and oxygen, recent success in making a xenon-nitrogen bond in compounds suggests that it may even be possible to make xenon–carbon-bonded compounds. In fact, a plasma-induced reaction of XeF_2 vapor with $CF_3 \cdot$ radicals gives a white solid, tentatively formulated as $Xe(CF_3)_2$.

Noble-gas chemistry has provided chemists with new fluorinating reagents and has introduced new classes of compounds and new species of high oxidation state. For example, compounds of ClO_4^- and of IO_4^- have been known for many years, but the first synthesis of a BrO_4^- compound was accomplished only in 1968 with use of XeF_2 as oxidizing agent: $NaBrO_3 + XeF_2 + H_2O \rightarrow NaBrO_4 + 2HF + Xe$. There is reason to be optimistic that in the next few years radon chemistry may be applied to monitoring this potentially harmful radioactive noble gas and to the removal of radon from mine atmospheres and from homes in which it appears to introduce a dangerous level of radioactivity. Twenty-five years in the scientific and technological development of an entire chemistry is still a short time, yet had it not been for Bartlett's creative approach, chemists might still be talking about the inert gases.

Making and breaking the C—F bond. Commercial applications of compounds containing carbon-fluorine (C—F) bonds are well known. For example, perfluorocarbons (compounds resembling hydrocarbons in which all the hydrogen atoms are replaced by fluorine atoms; *e.g.*, CF_3CF_3 instead of CH_3CH_3) have uses that range from nonstick coatings on frying pans and snow shovels to artificial blood. Liquid fluorocarbon emulsion succeeds as a blood supplement in humans because the fluorocarbon is a good solvent for oxygen, which it readily collects in the lungs, where the oxygen pressure is high, and releases to other parts of the body where the oxygen demand makes the oxygen pressure low. Oxygen delivery is one of the important functions performed by hemoglobin in normal blood.

Fluoroaromatics such as fluorobenzene (C_6H_5F) were prepared in the 1870s by the use of aromatic diazo compounds, and in spite of its many limitations, this methodology continues to be the most widely used today. Efforts to develop new reagents and better methods of fluorinating organic compounds have had only partial success, for the reagents either are

4

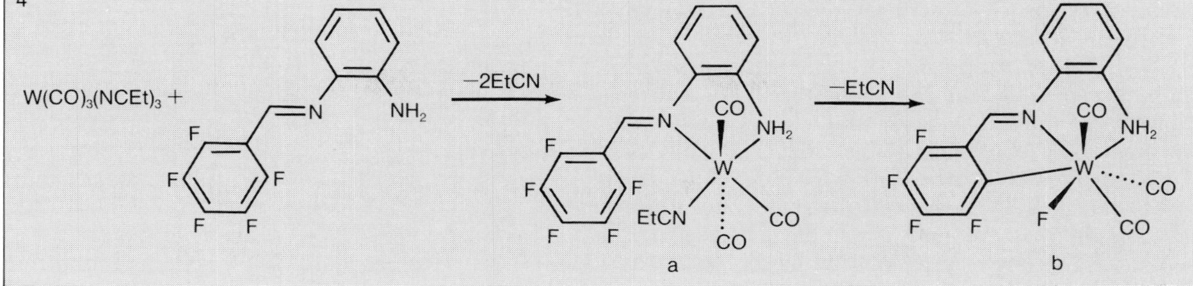

$W(CO)_3(NCEt)_3$ +
−2EtCN
−EtCN
a
b

not commercially available or, if available (*e.g.,* F_2, CF_3OF), require special equipment and experience to handle safely.

Thanks to the recent research of Darryl DesMarteau and co-workers at Clemson (S.C.) University, new, stable, easy-to-handle fluorinating reagents now exist. They are of the N-fluorosulfonimide type (3a, 3b), which are easily prepared by reaction of the desired sulfonimide with F_2 (3c). Stored in fluoropolymer plastic bottles, these fluorinating reagents are stable at room temperature. They exhibit the remarkable ability to replace hydrogen in an aromatic compound directly with fluorine at 22° C (72° F); *e.g.,* for benzene *see* (3d). The reactivity shown by these reagents is unique, but since they are just beginning to be explored, it remains to be seen how important they will become. If some become commercially available, it will certainly be much easier for chemists not experienced in fluorine chemistry to enter this area of research.

Another recent development involving C—F bonds deals not with their formation but with their breaking. It is well known that C—F bonds are much stronger than other C—X bonds (in which X represents an atom of hydrogen, chlorine, bromine, or iodine). The compound CH_3Cl readily reacts with OH^- to form CH_3OH, whereas under similar conditions no reaction takes place between CH_3F and OH^-. Furthermore, most hydrocarbons are biodegradable, while fluorocarbons are not. Therefore, chemists are interested in ways of activating C—F bonds toward chemical reaction.

During the year Thomas G. Richmond and co-workers at the University of Utah reported a facile chelate-assisted C—F bond cleavage at tungsten (0) (tungsten in a zero oxidation state). Whereas their observation that the C—F bond ruptures easily under mild conditions is good news, the bad news is that it happens under very special circumstances. First, a chelating agent is required that is bidentate (attached to the metal atom at two positions; *see* 4a) but can easily become tridentate (4b) by delivering a F^- ion to the metal. Second, tungsten is a metal known to tend to expand its coordination number from 6 (4a) to 7 (4b), which in this case allows for the formation of a strong W—F bond. The net result is the replacement of a C—F bond (4a) by C—W and W—F bonds (4b), so the energy balance favors C—F bond rupture.

High-oxidation-state metals in organometallic chemistry. The vast field of transition-metal organometallic chemistry started with the discovery of ferrocene, $Fe(C_5H_5)_2$, by two independent groups in 1951—Peter L. Pauson and a co-worker at Duquesne University, Pittsburgh, Pa., and S. A. Miller and co-workers at British Oxygen Ltd. This find was immediately followed by intense research activity in the laboratories of E. O. Fischer at the Technical University of Munich, West Germany, and of Geoffrey Wilkinson at Harvard University and later at Imperial College of Science and Technology, London, culminating in their receiving the 1973 Nobel Prize for Chemistry. During the intervening years they prepared metallocene compounds and derivatives of such compounds for all the metals in the periodic table.

The ligand π-cyclopentadienyl (π-$C_5H_5^-$) became ubiquitous in most of these metal complexes, and its stable bonding in these systems is attributed to both σ and π bonding in a manner akin to that of M—C bonding in metal carbonyls (5). Since back π bonding of electron density from M to CO makes a major contribution to the stability of metal carbonyls, it follows that the metal must be rich in electron density; *i.e.,* be in a low oxidation state. For this reason almost all of the research done in the

5

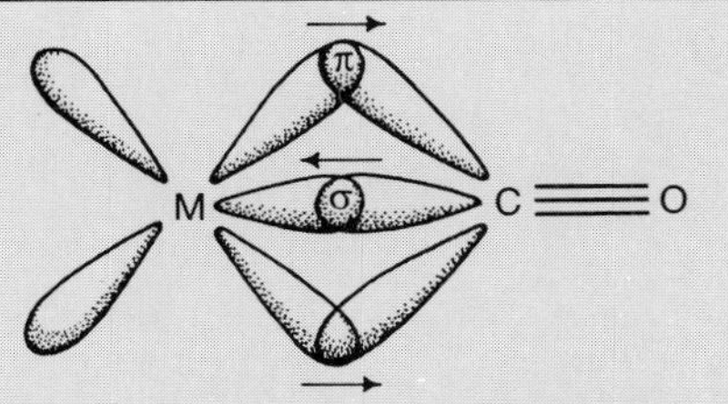

π
σ
M
C
O

One σ bond involves donation of electron pair from CO. One π bond involves back donation of electron pair from the metal to CO.

past three decades on transition-metal organometallic chemistry has dealt with compounds of metals in low oxidation states.

Nevertheless, it has long been known that many stable compounds can be formed with the transition-metal atom in a high oxidation state; *e.g.*, PtF_6, $KMnO_4$, and OsO_4, which have oxidation states of platinum(VI), manganese(VII), and osmium(VIII). In these examples the ligands F^- and O^{2-} bond to the metal atom not only by σ donation but also by π donation of electron density to the highly positively charged metal. The late Henry Gilman of Iowa State University, an outstanding organometallic chemist, tried unsuccessfully to prepare high-valent transition-metal alkyl compounds. The goal was finally achieved by Wilkinson and co-workers in 1975 when they made such stable compounds as $Zr(CH_3)_4$ and $W(CH_3)_6$. Although the metal oxidation states in these compounds are high—zirconium(IV) and tungsten(VI)—and π bonding is not involved, the metal-carbon bond is still fairly strong. Such compounds have dispelled the long-time prejudice of "inherent instability" attached to high-oxidation-state metals in organometallic compounds.

The need for inorganic chemists to pay more attention to the chemistry of such compounds was emphasized recently by the elegant research of Wolfgang A. Herrmann and co-workers at the Technical University of Munich, who were able to prepare organometallic compounds of rhenium(VII) and study their rich new chemistry. Compound (6a) contains the π-acceptor pentamethyl cyclopentadienyl ligand and three π-donor O^{2-} ligands, which may delocalize enough electron density on the rhenium

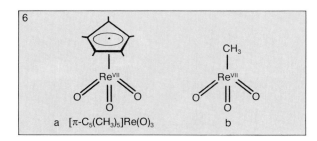

atom (Re) to stabilize its back π bonding to the ring ligand. That this is not a complete explanation, however, is shown by the stability of compound (6b), for which the fourth ligand is a σ-bonded methyl group.

Reactions of (6a), with rhenium in oxidation state VII, take place to give corresponding stable Re(V) compounds (7). In these reactions the O ligands are transferred to some reagent, and their place on Re is taken by some other ligand, such as Cl or CH_3. Eventually, should it be possible to have O ligands of such organometallic compounds transfer selectively to organic substrates in homogeneous catalytic processes, these systems would have great commercial value. For example, were ethylene ($CH_2{=}CH_2$) to react with two of the O ligands, the product could be made to release ethylene glycol and regenerate the original Re(VII) compound in a catalytic cycle (8). Because ethylene glycol is used as an antifreeze in automobile radiators, a ready market exists for the compound, and a less expensive process to manufacture the compound than is now in use would be lucrative. Industrial processes currently exploit low-valent organometallic complexes (see *1982 Yearbook of Science and the Future* Year in Review: CHEMISTRY:

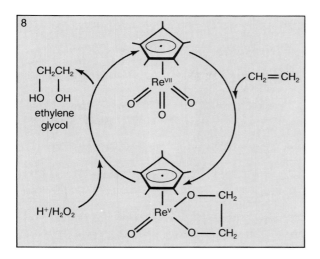

Inorganic chemistry). One day processes may make use of as yet unexplored reactions of organometallic compounds that contain metals in high oxidation states.

—Fred Basolo

Organic chemistry

In 1987 three organic chemists were honored with the Nobel Prize for Chemistry for devising cyclic (ring-containing) compounds that selectively recognize and complex small molecules or ions. The design of new conducting and superconducting materials (see *Inorganic chemistry*, above), the subject of the 1987 Nobel Prize for Physics, attracted organic chemists who were attempting to prepare wholly organic compounds that conduct electricity. Organic chemists came closer to duplicating the remarkable natural process wherein the multiple carbon rings of steroids are assembled from noncyclic precursors with precise geometric control and to understanding what happens to DNA when it is exposed to ultraviolet radiation. As in past years, research on a variety of remarkable natural and unnatural molecules continued unabated.

Host-guest chemistry. How do biologic macromolecules recognize their substrates? An insight to this fundamental question was provided over the past two decades by the research of chemists Charles J. Pedersen of Du Pont Co., Wilmington, Del.; Jean-Marie Lehn of Louis Pasteur University, Strasbourg, France, and the Collège de France, Paris; and Donald J. Cram of the University of California at Los Angeles, who shared the 1987 Nobel Prize for Chemistry. (*See* SCIENTISTS OF THE YEAR.) Pedersen invented a series of cyclic polyethers such as (1) and named them crown ethers to reflect their three-dimensional shape. These compounds, which have the ability to bind selectively to such metal ions as sodium and

to make the ions soluble in organic solvents, are of great value as catalysts and as models for biologic systems that transport ions across cell membranes. Lehn and Cram extended Pedersen's concepts to three dimensions with multicyclic compounds, containing nitrogen and other atoms, that have been termed cryptates, cryptands, cavitands, or more generally host molecules, which mimic enzymes in their ability to bind to small molecules or ions (guests).

One intriguing example reported during the year by Lehn and co-workers Beatrice Alpha and Gerard Mathis is a cryptate (2) that tightly binds europium ions, Eu^{3+}. Cryptate formation shields the ions from interaction with solvent; *e.g.*, water. Ultraviolet (UV) radiation absorbed by the organic groups of the europium cryptate is transferred (ET in the illustration) to the europium ion and reemitted as visible light. Such emission is not possible for simple aqua complexes of europium due to deactivation by solvent molecules. Light-emitting europium cryptates may find applications as labels for biologic applications; *e.g.*, in luminescence immunoassays.

Natural product chemistry. Two independent teams of pharmaceutical chemists unraveled the structures of an exceptionally potent class of anticancer agents produced by bacteria of the *Actinomycetales* order. Calichemicins, identified by May D. Lee and co-workers of Lederle Laboratories, Wayne, N.J., and esperamicins, characterized by Jerzy Golik and co-workers from Bristol-Myers Co. in Connecticut and Japan as well as from Cornell University, Ithaca, N.Y., are sugar derivatives of the same remarkable tricyclic ring system (3a) containing a pendant methyl trisulfide component (CH_3SSS-). Acting much like a molecular mouse trap, cleavage of a weak sulfur-sulfur bond is thought to trigger a chain of events culminating in formation of a phenylene diradical (3b), which removes hydrogen atoms from DNA. Effective against mouse tumors at doses of 0.1–0.5 microgram (millionth of a gram) per kilogram of body weight, this novel class of bacterial

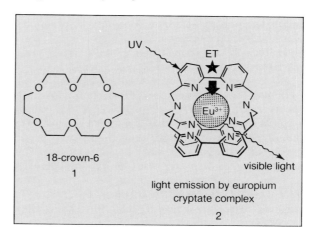

18-crown-6
1

light emission by europium
cryptate complex
2

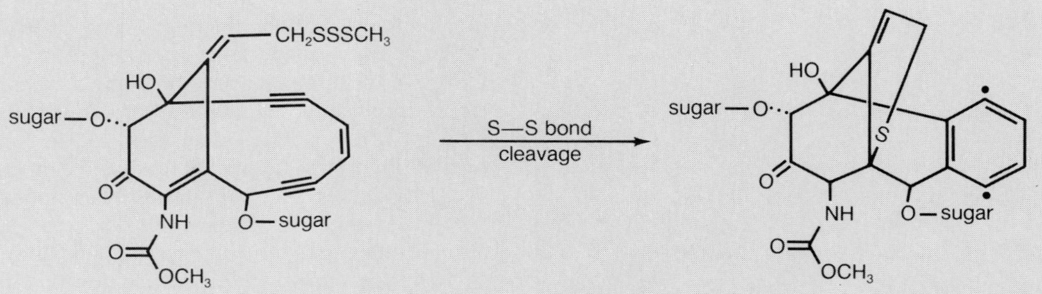

a calichemicin (esperamicin)   b phenylene diradical intermediate

fermentation products is among the most potent anticancer agents in laboratory animals ever found.

Sugar groups, such as those found in the calichemicins and esperamicins, may contain sulfur attached to the periphery of their six-membered rings, but sugars in which the oxygen atom in the ring itself has been replaced by sulfur had been unknown in nature until the past year. Chemists Robert J. Capon and John K. MacLeod of the Australian National University, Canberra, found that the orange marine sponge *Clathria pyramida* contains 5-thio-D-mannose (4), a sugar having a sulfur atom in the ring. Compounds structurally related to (4) were found to function as male contraceptives by inhibiting sperm-cell development.

Several new peptides (short proteins made of chains of amino acids) showing marked biologic activity were isolated during the year from unusual sources. George R. Pettit of Arizona State University reported the isolation and structure of the pentapeptide dolastatin 10, an exceptionally powerful cell-growth inhibitor present to the extent of one part in 100 million in an Indian Ocean sea hare. Chemist Hajime Komura of the Suntory Institute for Bioorganic Research, Osaka, Japan, and co-workers isolated and characterized andrimid, an unusual unsaturated peptide antibiotic produced by a symbiotic bacterium hosted by an insect known as the brown planthopper. Remarkably, the antibiotic shows high specific activity against the white-blight pathogen of rice plants, the favored food of the brown planthopper.

Biochemist Michael Zasloff of the National Institutes of Health, Bethesda, Md., made the curious observation that laboratory frogs that had received surgical incisions and were then returned to their microbially contaminated water-filled tanks rarely developed infections as the incisions healed. The observation led to the isolation of two antibacterial peptides, termed magainins after the Hebrew word for "shield," from the skin of the frogs. The same peptides were independently identified by Dudley H. Williams, Bradford W. Gibson, L. Poulter, and

M. G. Giovannini of the University of Cambridge.

Morphogens are signal molecules that are involved in establishing the spatial pattern of cells during development. A morphogen known as differentiation inducing factor 1 (DIF-1), which induces stalk-cell differentiation in aggregates of the slime mold *Dictyostelium discoideum,* was identified as the comparatively simple compound shown in (5) by British researchers Howard R. Morris, Graham W. Taylor, and Mark S. Masento of Imperial College, London; Keith A. Jermyn of the Imperial Cancer Research Fund's Clare Hall Laboratories; and Robert R. Kay of the MRC Laboratory of Molecular Biology, Cambridge.

Halley's Comet was found to contain polymerized formaldehyde $[-(CH_2O)_n-]$, the first polymer detected in space. Walter F. Huebner of Southwest Research Institute, San Antonio, Texas, and D. L. Mitchell of the University of California at Berkeley and co-workers identified the polymer through

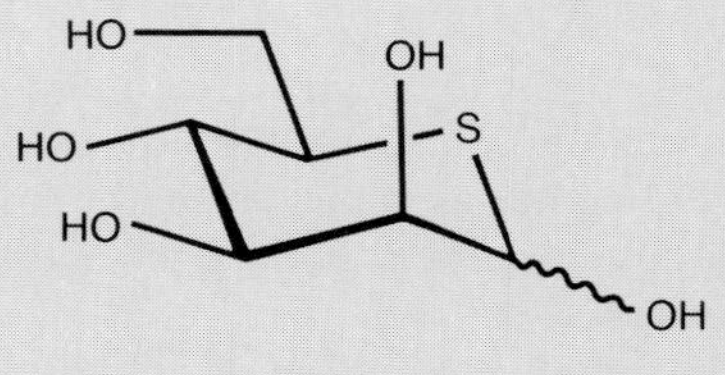

5-thio-D-mannose

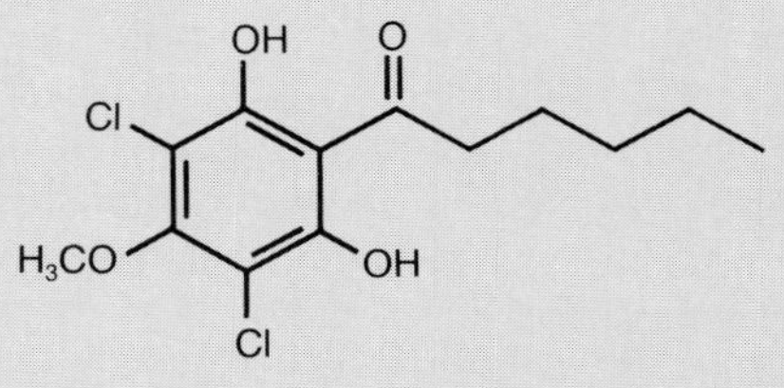

DIF-1

294

analysis of data from a heavy-ion analyzer carried by the European spacecraft Giotto as it flew past the comet in March 1986.

The remarkable formation of the four-ring carbon skeleton characteristic of steroids from 30-carbon linear polyunsaturated precursors is accomplished in nature with precise geometric control by cyclase enzymes. Efficient laboratory duplication of this feat has thus far failed owing to the difficulty of overcoming the natural tendency of a molecular chain, in the absence of an enzyme, to assume a random shape unsuitable for ring construction. William S. Johnson, Stephen J. Telfer, Soan Cheng, and Ulrich Schubert of Stanford University developed a promising biomimetic (nature-mimicking) solution to the problem that involves enhancing the laboratory cyclization process by incorporating cation-stabilizing auxiliaries (i.e., groups favoring development of a positive charge during the key ring-forming step) on an appropriate internal double bond of the acyclic precursor (see 6).

How does exposure to ultraviolet light lead to mutation and cancer? An answer to this question may result from study of the photochemistry of DNA. It has been known for some years that short-wavelength light causes molecular changes in the pyrimidinone ring of the thymidine 5'-phosphate subunit of DNA, affording reactive photoproducts. John-Stephen Taylor and Michael P. Cohrs of Washington University, St. Louis, Mo., recently identified a reversibly formed subunit photoproduct containing a highly strained Dewar pyrimidinone ring. It is suggested that this product, which has a highly reactive fused pair of four-membered rings, may play a role in DNA destruction via DNA-DNA and DNA-protein cross-linking.

Harvard University chemist E. J. Corey synthesized a number of unusual natural substances, including bilobalide (from the ginkgo tree; with co-worker Wei-guo Su) and cafestol and atractyligenin (an anti-inflammatory agent and a poisonous principle, respectively, found in coffee plants and coffee; with co-workers Gunther Weiss, Yi Bin Xiang, Raman K. Bakshi, and Ashok K. Singh). Other notable accomplishments include syntheses of the antifungal antibiotic amphotericin B by K. C. Nicolaou, T. K. Chakraborty, R. A. Daines, and Y. Ogawa of the University of Pennsylvania; avermectin A_{1a}, an antiparasite antibiotic, by Samuel J. Danishefsky, David M. Armistead, Harold G. Selnick, Randall Hungate, and Francine E. Wincott of Yale University; lauren-1-ene (7), a natural diterpene fenestrane (a molecule with a shape resembling a windowpane), by Michael T. Crimmins and Lori D. Gould of the University of North Carolina, and Tetsuto Tsunoda and co-workers of Tohoku University and Tokushima Bunri University, Japan; the quinoid antitumor agent cyanocycline A by Tohru Fukuyama, Leping Li, Alison A. Laird, and R. Keith Frank of Rice University, Texas; and aplysiatoxin, a remarkably active tumor promoter from the digestive gland of the sea hare, by Harvard chemists Yoshito Kishi, Chris A. Broka, Bruce F. Johnson, and Pyeong-uk Park.

Conducting organic polymers. The interest in the design of new electrical conductors and superconductors, highlighted by the year's Nobel Prize in physics, is shared by organic chemists who are attempting to prepare organic polymers that conduct electricity or exhibit ferromagnetism (spontaneous magnetism at room temperature). The latter property, once thought to be restricted to metals and other inorganic materials, is seen in organic polymers when the spins of unpaired electrons spontaneously orient themselves in the same direction, creating a bulk magnetic effect. Organic ferromagnets may eventually replace inorganic materials in such applications as coatings for magnetic recording tape.

A. A. Ovchinnikov, V. N. Spector, Yu. V. Korshak, and T. V. Medvedeva of the Institute of Chemical Physics of the U.S.S.R. Academy of Sciences, Moscow, and the Mendeleev Institute of Chemical Technology, Moscow, prepared a polymer (8) based on polydiacetylene, with nitroxyl biradical side groups, that remains ferromagnetic to about 150° C (300° F). Jerry B. Torrance, S. Oostra, and A. Nazzal of the IBM Almaden Research Center, San Jose, Calif., observed ferromagnetic behavior in a polymer obtained from reacting 1,3,5-triaminobenzene with

6   tetracyclization

polyene with cation-stabilizing isobutenyl group   stabilized intermediate   77% combined yield of tetracyclic products

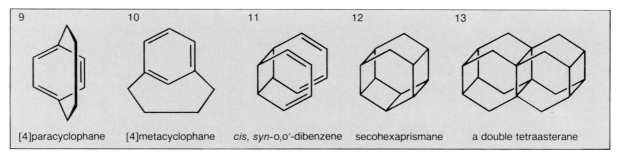

lauren-1-ene

ferromagnetic polydiacetylene

iodine. The material remains ferromagnetic to high temperatures until it decomposes near 400° C (750° F). Although the new Soviet and U.S. results were far from ideal, having poor reaction yields for the polymer syntheses and poorly characterized products, they should stimulate further efforts to prepare other organic ferromagnets. (See *Applied chemistry*, below.)

A "molecule-based" solid-state transistor was fabricated by chemists Mark S. Wrighton and Shuchi Chao of the Massachusetts Institute of Technology, who used a chip sequentially coated with polymers of 3-methylthiophene and ethylene oxide, the latter incorporating the salt lithium trifluorosulfonate. On application of voltage, the poly(3-methylthiophene) undergoes changes between a conducting and insulating form, leading to a switching between "on" and "off" states for the device. Chemists Fred Wudl, Alan J. Heeger, Abhimanyu O. Patil, and

Yoshi Ikenoue of the University of California at Santa Barbara prepared self-doped conducting polymers that are water-soluble. (Doping is the selective inclusion of impurities in a substance to give it desired electronic properties.) The novel materials, formed upon oxidation of sodium poly(3-thiophene-alkanesulfonates), display electrochromism, changing color with electric potential.

Nonnatural product chemistry. In an effort to answer the question, posed by Donald J. Cram, "How bent can a benzene be?" the chain spanning opposite ends of a benzene ring in cyclophanes (see *1987 Yearbook of Science and the Future* Year in Review: CHEMISTRY: *Organic chemistry*) was shortened by one more link. Chemists Takashi Tsuji and Shinya Nishida of Hokkaido University, Japan, and Friedrich Bickelhaupt and co-workers at Vrije University, Amsterdam, prepared [4]paracyclophane (9) and [4]metacyclophane (10), respectively, by low-temperature ultraviolet irradiation of precursors at −232° C (−386° F). The benzene hexagon can also be recognized in the framework of *cis, syn*-o,o'-dibenzene (11), prepared by Nien-chu C. Yang, Bruce J. Hrnjez, and M. Glenn Horner of the University of Chicago, and related, highly bridged structures secohexaprismane (12), synthesized by Goverdhan Mehta and S. Padma of the University of Hyderabad, India, and double tetraasterane (13), prepared by Hans Musso and Volker T. Hoffmann of the University of Karlsruhe, West Germany.

Notable among smaller reactive organic molecules prepared in the past year are thiobenzophenone S-sulfide, $Ph_2C=S=S$ (in which Ph is the phenyl group, $-C_6H_5$), produced by Rolf Huisgen and Joachen Rapp of the University of Munich, West Germany; the first stable aliphatic thioaldehyde, tris(trimethylsilyl)ethanethial, $[(CH_3)_3Si]_3CCH=S$, synthesized by Renji Okazaki, Akihiko Ishii, and Naoki Inamoto of the University of Tokyo; and vinylidene-carbene, $H_2C=C=C$:, prepared at low temperature by Gunther Maier, Hans Peter Reisenauer, and Wolfgang Schwab of Justus Liebig University, Giessen, West Germany, together with B. Andes Hess, Jr., Lawrence J. Schaad, and Petr Carsky of Vanderbilt University, Nashville, Tenn.

—Eric Block

[4]paracyclophane   [4]metacyclophane   *cis, syn*-o,o'-dibenzene   secohexaprismane   a double tetraasterane

Physical chemistry

In 1987 X-ray crystallographers succeeded in taking a three-frame "motion picture" of a protein. Their speeding of the pattern exposure technique from hours to seconds opened up a new area for investigation. Other experiments showed that a quantum mechanical effect, tunneling, plays an important role in many chemical reactions. Two recently developed bench-top devices promised to aid research in the life sciences. One, the first directly coupled enzyme electrode, should widen the scope of electron transfer studies. The other, an apparatus that can sustain oscillating chemical reactions for days, may provide a unique model of living systems.

Molecules in motion. It was X-ray crystallography that provided the evidence necessary for James Watson and Francis Crick in the early 1950s to deduce the structure of DNA, the double helix. Since then, the technique has continued to provide scientists with valuable information on molecules that are important to life, especially proteins.

Unfortunately, traditional X-ray crystallography is slow. X-ray diffraction data from a crystal of the target molecule must be gathered from many positions before an unequivocal three-dimensional image can be made, a process that can take hours or even days. At such speeds it is difficult or impossible to gather information on dynamic systems like the reaction of an enzyme with its substrate (the specific molecule on which the enzyme acts).

In 1984 J. K. Moffat and colleagues at Cornell University, Ithaca, N.Y., reported that a combination of new instrumentation and an old idea could yield enough data to make reliable pictures in seconds instead of hours. The new instrumentation is the synchrotron light source, a particle accelerator adapted to produce a beam of electromagnetic radiation from the deflection of energetic electrons in a magnetic field. The X-rays it provides are intense and can be tuned to specific wavelengths. The old idea dates back to 1912 and the work of pioneer X-ray spectroscopist Max von Laue, who found that if the target molecule is probed with a polychromatic X-ray beam, *i.e.*, a beam comprising a spectrum of wavelengths, a greater density of information about the molecule can be obtained. The synchrotron light source provides just such a variety of wavelengths at sufficient intensity that in some cases a complete data set can be obtained from a single exposure.

During the past year Janos Hajdu of the University of Oxford and co-workers applied the technique, called Laue diffraction, to a protein for the first time. Specifically, they looked at the interaction of the enzyme glycogen phosphorylase *b* with its substrate, maltoheptose, in order to get pictures before, during, and after the reaction event. Each data set, about

Courtesy, Janos Hajdu, Laboratory of Molecular Biophysics, University of Oxford

Computer-generated Laue diffraction pattern of glycogen phosphorylase b *was derived from X-ray diffraction studies of the enzyme before, during, and after reaction with its substrate. A synchrotron light source provided the intense X-rays needed for catching the reaction event in action.*

40,000 unique reflections, took only three seconds to gather and, according to the researchers, could have been gathered in milliseconds. The resulting data sets not only provided information on a fast biochemical change but also gave an individual picture that was of higher quality than that from traditional X-ray crystallography.

One requirement of the new technique is that all the crystal material be at essentially the same stage in the reaction process. This limits researchers to reactions in which the reacting molecules can be triggered as a group; for example, reactions that are light- or temperature-initiated. On the plus side, researchers expect that the technique can be applied to problems other than biochemical ones, such as questions of solid state that involve motion.

Tunneling. Most chemists can comfortably ignore quantum effects and, instead, interpret their observations within the classical framework of Newtonian mechanics. For most chemical reactions the masses involved are too high for quantum phenomena to make a significant contribution. For at least one sort of reaction, however, the hydrogen transfer, this may not be the case; recent experiments showed that tunneling, an effect not predicted by classical equations, may be a major factor.

Traditionally, if a reactant does not possess enough energy to go over an energy barrier, the chemical reaction does not occur. Water on one side of a solid dam cannot get to the other side unless it is given the necessary energy by being pumped up over the top. Tunneling defies this dictum because quantum mechanics predicts a probability of the reactant's passing, or tunneling, through the barrier rather than going over it.

Mass is a factor in tunneling; lighter particles are more likely to tunnel than heavier ones. Tunneling by the lightweight electron is a well-known phenomenon that must be accounted for by physicists. Robert J. Gordon of the University of Illinois at Chicago suspected that the lightest atom, hydrogen, also tunnels to a significant degree. He led a research effort to test this hypothesis by looking at the reactions $O(^3P) + HD \rightarrow OH + D$ and $O(^3P) + HD \rightarrow OD + H$. "$O(^3P)$" stands for an oxygen atom in its lowest, or ground, energy state, and "D" is the symbol for deuterium, an isotope of hydrogen having twice the normal mass. Theoretically, if tunneling has no significant effect, the ratio of OH to OD in the products should not be affected by temperature. If tunneling is a factor, however, the OH contribution should rise quickly as the temperature drops. When neither hydrogen isotope has sufficient energy to pass over the energy barrier and react in the conventional way, the lighter isotope's tunneling advantage should become more obvious.

In fact, the latter result is what the Illinois researchers found when they measured product ratios by the technique of laser-induced fluorescence. Moreover, their data agreed qualitatively with calculated predictions only if the tunneling correction was included. The tunneling phenomenon dominated the hydrogen transfer reaction at room temperature.

Oscillating reactions. Through most of their history, oscillating chemical reactions have been considered more a curiosity than a serious area of research. Recently, however, their value as models of periodic systems, particularly living systems, has begun to be recognized. In 1987 their potential usefulness was expanded when Zoltan Noszticzius and colleagues at the University of Texas at Austin built a device that allows investigation of spatial chemical structures, such as reaction waves, over a period of days.

One of the most familiar oscillating reactions is a classroom demonstration called the chemical clock. After the reagents are mixed in solution in a flask, the color of the solution changes from blue to colorless to yellow, back to blue, and so on at regular time intervals. This demonstration is an example of a temporal oscillation. The paradigmatic spatial oscillators are the Belousov-Zhabotinsky (BZ) reactions, named after the Soviet scientists who discovered and developed them. BZ reactions, demonstrated in petri dishes, involve the oxidation of organic compounds by acidic bromate. As a result, colorful patterns such as waves and spirals are formed.

Because both the flask and the petri dish con-

stitute closed, or batch, systems, their oscillations die out over time as equilibrium effects overwhelm them. That limitation affects the nature and quality of experiments that can be done. For years the continuous-flow stirred tank reactor has been used to provide an open system for the study of temporal oscillations like those in the flask. Essentially, the reactor continuously feeds fresh reactant into a flask while removing the product solution. Temporal oscillations can be sustained for an indefinite time, allowing detailed studies of their kinetics.

The Texas researchers put together a system that accomplishes the same thing for spatial oscillations. The key to the device, a ring of polyacrylamide gel that separates inner and outer solutions of BZ reactants, allowed the researchers to avoid two problems of previous systems—bubble formation and convective motion. By adding small amounts of reagent at one location on the ring and removing the product at another location, they sustained BZ reactions within the gel ring for four to five days. Such long-lived systems may provide improved models for the study of oscillations in living systems, such as heart arrhythmias, and elsewhere in nature, including rock formations and weather systems. (For a comprehensive discussion of oscillating chemical reactions, see *1986 Yearbook of Science and the Future* Feature Article: PENDULUMS IN THE TEST TUBE.)

Enzyme-electrode coupling. Electron transfer, the passage of electrons between components of a system, is a phenomenon that has long interested physical chemists. One limit that has been found to such electron movement is distance. The difficulty of a transfer increases exponentially with the distance between transfer sites.

Enzyme-electrode coupling is difficult because an enzyme's reaction sites are usually buried deep within an insulating glycoprotein shell (a). Chemists recently succeeded in adding electron relay molecules between the active sites and the enzyme exterior (b), effectively shortening the distance between them and allowing current to flow as the enzyme acts on its substrate.

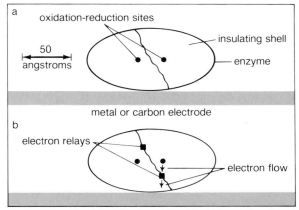

Adapted from information obtained from Adam Heller and Yinon Degani, AT&T Bell Laboratories

That dependence on distance puts tough restrictions on researchers working with enzymes, particularly those who want to use electrodes to follow the activity of oxidation-reduction enzymes (enzymes that accept electrons from a site and then donate them elsewhere). The active sites of the enzymes, where the reactions take place, tend to be buried deep within their protein structures, effectively isolated from metal electrodes. Put enzymes and their substrates in an electrochemical cell, and their activity will fail even to register with the electrode.

This lack of response is particularly frustrating for those who want to couple electrodes and enzymes to form sensors that can keep track of biologic systems, such as glucose levels in the blood of diabetics. Until recently the only way to get around the distance limit was to design and add intermediate compounds, which could carry the electrons from the interior of the enzyme out to the electrode, effectively establishing a communications link between the two. During the past year Adam Heller and Yinon Degani of AT&T Bell Laboratories, Murray Hill, N.J., found a way to "wire" the sites within the enzyme to the electrode, demonstrating the first electron transfer from an oxidation-reduction enzyme to a metal electrode.

Working with glucose oxidase, an enzyme that oxidizes glucose to gluconolactone, they first chemically exposed the electron-accepting sites. Then they reacted the interior with ferrocarboxylic acid derivatives that could act as electron relays. Finally, the enzyme was restored to its original conformation but, because of the relays, the distances between the oxidation-reduction sites within the enzyme and the electrode were effectively shortened. The result was a dramatic change in current detected upon the addition of the substrate, glucose, to the electrochemical cell.

According to the researchers, similar procedures should allow scientists to couple D-amino acid oxidase and other enzymes directly to electrodes as well. The ability could make a variety of new sensors feasible and allow physical chemists to gain a greater understanding of electron transfer in a variety of biologic systems. It also could make possible the production of electrochemical cells that could be used to drive the manufacture of useful biochemicals.

—Peter J. Andrews

Applied chemistry

During the past year research in applied chemistry led to developments in polymers, enzymes, foods, lasers, synthetic diamonds, and photographic film. The synthesis and investigation of new, high-temperature superconductors, a topic that encompasses several disciplines, including physics, ceramics, and chemistry, are treated in the Feature Article THE NEW SUPERCONDUCTORS: A SCIENTIFIC BREAKTHROUGH and the Year in Review articles *Inorganic chemistry*, above, and MATERIALS SCIENCES: *Ceramics*.

Polymers. Every year millions of kilograms of discarded shells, which contain the natural polymer chitin, pile up beside crabmeat-processing plants along Chesapeake Bay. (Polymers are high-molecular-weight substances having portions of their molecules arranged in repeating patterns.) Although chitin is a carbohydrate like cellulose, its exploitation has lagged behind that of cellulose, the main ingredient in cellophane and rayon, because until recently no methods were available for transforming it into a substance that could be processed readily by manufacturers. Retired Du Pont Co. chemist Paul Austin, age 80, adjunct professor at the College of Marine Studies, Newark, Del., discovered that a combination of lithium chloride and dimethylacetamide dissolves chitin from waste crab shells into a homogeneous sticky mass that can be processed into threads and sheets. The thread is ideal for surgical sutures because it dissolves in the body, knots more easily than synthetic materials, is nonallergenic, and seems to promote healing. Unitika Ltd., a Japanese textile- and fiber-manufacturing firm, bought the license to Austin's patents and began conducting tests of the suture thread in Japan, where it could be available for general use by 1989. Separate tests would be required before it could be offered in the U.S.

Independent research groups in the U.S.S.R. and the U.S. discovered the first organic polymers to become ferromagnetic spontaneously at ambient temperatures. Along with metallic conductivity, semiconductivity, and superconductivity, ferromagnetism is the last of the electronic properties once thought to be restricted to inorganic materials but subsequently observed in organic materials. Organic ferromagnetic compounds may someday replace metals or metallic compounds currently used for their magnetic properties; *e.g.*, chromium dioxide used to coat magnetic recording tape.

A. A. Ovchinnikov and co-workers at Moscow's Institute of Chemical Physics prepared a material, ferromagnetic at temperatures up to 150° C (300° F), by polymerizing a stable biradical monomer consisting of a cyclic nitroxyl group attached to either end of a diacetylene fragment. They were unable, however, to control the degree of polymerization or the size of the polyacetylene chains formed, and only 0.1% of the monomer was converted to ferromagnetic polymer, although this fraction could be magnetically separated from the residue. Physicist Jerry B. Torrance and co-workers at the IBM Almaden Research Center, San Jose, Calif., observed ferromagnetic behavior at temperatures as high as 400° C (750° F), the decomposition point, in a polymer

U.S. Department of Agriculture food technologist prepares clear apricot juice for viscosity testing. The juice, extracted from thick, cloudy apricot nectar by means of a new process involving enzymes and ceramic filters, may find use in fruit drinks and frozen juice bars.

produced by the reaction of 1,3,5-triaminobenzene with iodine. The yield was only 2%, and the product was not very reproducible. Both the Soviet and U.S. groups established that the ferromagnetism was not due to metallic impurities, and their work should stimulate additional efforts to synthesize other organic ferromagnetic materials. (For additional information on organic magnets, see *1988 Yearbook of Science and the Future* Year in Review: CHEMISTRY: *Applied chemistry.*)

During the mid-1970s, conducting polymers became prominent, offering many promising applications, such as cheap, lightweight plastic conductors that would be organic replacements for copper. This promise remained unfulfilled until 1987, when Herbert Naarmann and co-workers at the BASF Laboratories, Ludwigshafen, West Germany, reported that they had prepared an air-stable polyacetylene, doped with iodine, that possesses a conductivity at room temperature about a third that of copper on a volume basis, which is about twice that of copper on a weight basis. According to rumors circulating in the conducting polymer community, the BASF scientists also were said to have made a doped polyacetylene with a conductivity slightly greater than that of copper on a volume basis; *i.e.*, more than ten times as large on a weight basis. (For further information on the conductivity of doped polyacetylenes, see *1983 Yearbook of Science and the Future* Year in Review: CHEMISTRY: *Applied chemistry.*)

Wonder Co., a subsidiary of Cipel, Paris, began marketing a line of carbon-zinc dry cells in which mercury, used to protect the zinc electrode from corrosion, is replaced by a fluorinated polymer, a surfactant made by Atochem and trade named Forafec. The company claimed that the dry cells are the first

anywhere that use no mercury and therefore cannot cause environmental damage by release of mercury when the spent batteries are discarded. The cells also provide up to three times the performance life of conventional carbon-zinc cells.

Solid electrolytes made of polymer-salt complexes have strong potential for use in lightweight rechargeable batteries. Although researchers have worked on such electrolytes for more than a decade, finding a single polymer that, when dissolved with the appropriate salts, has a high level of ionic conductivity and good mechanical properties had been difficult.

Recently polymer chemist Barry Bauer and co-workers C. K. Chiang, Robert Briber, and George T. Davis of the U.S. National Bureau of Standards, Gaithersburg, Md., made polymeric electrolytes out of two interwoven polymers, one possessing high ionic conductivity and the other, strength and dimensional stability. The electrolytes comprise interpenetrating polymer networks (IPNs) in which two different polymers are intermeshed but each remains separate and continuous throughout the material. The researchers made the solid IPN electrolytes by using a cross-linked epoxy, which gives the material a rigid structure, and a viscous liquid, poly(ethylene oxide), which is a good ionic conductor. The electrolytes can be cast into thin films that have less weight and volume than other electrolytes, and they show particular promise in experimental batteries that employ lithium as the negative electrode. If early laboratory versions of the batteries can be scaled up, they could store several times the energy per unit weight of conventional lead-acid automobile batteries.

Liquid crystalline polymers that can be made to appear red, yellow, or blue (the three primary colors) were prepared by chemists Valeri Krongauz and Ivan Cabrera of the Weizmann Institute of Science, Rehovot, Israel, and Helmut Ringsdorf of the University of Mainz, West Germany. Irradiating a film of the polymer, which is made of polysiloxanes containing spiropyran groups, with visible light makes it appear pale yellow. Ultraviolet light turns the yellow film deep red if irradiation is carried out near room temperature, but blue if it is carried out at −20° C (−4° F) or below. The blue film is stable in the dark at −20° C but turns red on heating above −10° C (14° F). The red film turns yellow when irradiated with visible light. The red and blue colors are ascribed to aggregated and isolated merocyanine groups, respectively, and the yellow, to spiropyran groups. The color-changing properties of the polymers should be useful for imaging technologies.

Synthetic fibers are normally made by polymerizing material as an emulsion or suspension to form a powder, then melting or dissolving the powder, and finally extruding the liquid as a fiber through a spinneret. On the other hand, natural fibers such as collagen, cotton, and wool associate directly into fibers as they are polymerized. No synthetic polymers could be made to associate this natural way until Han Sik Yoon of the Korea Advanced Institute of Science and Technology reported a process for producing synthetic polymers—aromatic polyamides similar to the commercial fiber Kevlar—that simultaneously pack themselves into fibers without mechanical spinning. The process is similar to the self-directed ordering that occurs in the production of natural fibers. Yoon produced poly-p-phenylene-terephthalamide fibers from a gel phase containing the active oligopolymer, heterocyclic tertiary amines, alkali metal cations, and a polar solvent. When the length of the polymer chains reaches about 60 repeating units, electrostatic interactions cause them to align themselves end-to-end. A shift of half a repeating unit in the chains allows them to connect laterally by means of solvent bridges. When molecular growth is complete, the connecting bridges collapse from the center in steps. This action propagates instantly through the gel phase, resulting in aligned fibers. According to Yoon, such a mechanism "may be a universal one that applies to formation of all fibrous materials in nature."

Enzymes. Hiroyuki Aoki, Dennis Yao, Ernest Yu, and Masanaru Misawa of Allelix Inc., a small biotechnology firm in Mississauga, Ont., isolated two new enzymes (organic catalysts) that show high thermal stability and high productivity of cyclodextrins (CDs) from starch. From Ontario soil bacteria they recovered two cyclodextrin glycosyltransferases (CGTases; the names of enzymes end with the suffix -ase)—one yielding mostly α-CD and the other mostly β-CD. Information on the first enzyme is proprietary; the second enzyme contains about 680 amino acid building blocks per molecule. CDs, which are currently prepared by the action of bacterial CGTases on gelatinized starch, are used in separations, extractions, drug delivery, stabilizing agents, and other encapsulation applications in the food, pharmaceutical, and agrochemical industries. Allelix projected $50 million in annual CD sales in the U.S. within the next few years and at least twice that if food uses are approved by the U.S. Food and Drug Administration (FDA). Japan and several European countries already permit CD use in food.

Foods. As evidence accumulated that high cholesterol and fat intake are associated with coronary heart disease, Procter & Gamble Co. of Cincinnati, Ohio, spent 20 years testing a nonatherosclerotic fat substitute that is nondigestible and thus calorie-free (compared with 120 calories per teaspoon for a typical vegetable oil). Synthesized by P&G chemist Fred Mattson, known technically as sucrose polyester (SPE), and called olestra by P&G, the "fake" fat is a compound made of table sugar (sucrose) bonded with eight edible oils into a molecule too large for the digestive enzyme lipase to break down. It is organoleptic; *i.e.*, it feels the same in the mouth and tastes the same as real fat.

P&G asked the FDA for permission to use SPE as a replacement for 75% of the fat in commercial preparations of deep-frying oils and salted snacks and 35% of the fat in home cooking oils. In May 1987 the FDA agreed to review P&G's petition, but in December the Center for Science in the Public Interest (CSPI), Washington, D.C., charged that SPE causes cancer, liver damage, and even death in laboratory animals fed the substance and asked the FDA to turn down P&G's request. P&G officials denied the charges and contended that SPE is safe. If SPE is approved, it could eventually be used in making potato chips, cookies, mayonnaise, salad oils, dressings, margarines, and other high-fat foods.

Nitrites are used for curing, improving the color of, and preserving such meats as bacon, salami, hot dogs, and corned beef. When exposed to direct high-temperature heat, as in frying, however, nitrites are converted to nitrosamines, some of which are carcinogenic. Chemist Barbara Miller and coworkers at the U.S. National Center for Toxicological Research (NCTR), Jefferson, Ark., found that microwave-cooked bacon, while retaining most of its taste and pleasurable features, lacks most of the potentially cancer-causing nitrosamines. Apparently, bacon in the microwave does not reach the conversion temperature (185° C, or 365° F) long enough to cause significant conversion of nitrites to harmful nitrosamines.

Assortment of foods prepared with Procter & Gamble's fat substitute olestra is displayed by a company scientist. Known technically as sucrose polyester, olestra is nondigestible (and thus calorie-free) and contains no cholesterol.

AP/Wide World

Lasers. Using mixtures containing liquid or solid noble gases such as neon, argon, krypton, and xenon to store radiation and then emit it, chemist Vartkess A. Apkarian of the University of California at Irvine developed a novel method of producing broadly tunable lasers in the extreme ultraviolet range of the spectrum, called the vacuum UV. Existing devices, known as eximer chemical lasers, are not tunable over a wide range of wavelengths and are not very stable in the vacuum region because the molecules of the compounds used in the lasers are easily ionized by ultraviolet radiation. According to Apkarian, "The solutions are virtually indestructible, whereas the organic dyes break down rather easily. . . . The eximer laser has to work with a new dye molecule to move to a different frequency. In our case, by merely changing the temperature of the liquids, you can shift the frequency line by as many as 50 nanometers" (one nanometer equals a millionth of a millimeter, or about four hundred-millionths of an inch). In addition to its use in basic research, the laser might have microsurgical and other medical applications. For example, Apkarian said, "One could . . . selectively alter the chemistry of diseased blood by putting it through a tunable laser system with photoinitiated drugs, and then recycle it back into the patient's body."

Synthetic diamonds. Visiting professor Akira B. Sawaoka of the Tokyo Institute of Technology and co-workers at the Center for Explosives Technology Research at the New Mexico Institute of Mining & Technology, Socorro, N.M., developed a technique for fabricating synthetic diamonds that are 85% as hard as natural diamonds, a new record. They placed diamond powder in a stainless steel capsule, whereupon an explosion drove an iron plate against the capsule, producing a shock wave with a pressure of nearly one million atmospheres (14.7 million pounds per square inch) and compacting the diamond powder into a polycrystalline solid. They produced diamonds (a few millimeters in diameter) of industrial quality that could be used for machining tool bits or in electronic devices. (*See* Feature Article: CREATING WITH EXPLOSIVES.)

Superfilm. Despite the many developments in photography in the more than a century and a half since its inception, a silver iodide emulsion still constitutes the essential interface between light and film. During the past year, however, unnamed scientists at Moscow's Textile Institute developed a substitute. They discovered that crystals of the organometallic compound ferrocene, or bis(cyclopentadienyl)iron (II), became sensitive to light when combined with certain organic compounds. Although not as fast (light-sensitive) as silver-based films, the crystal emulsions are almost free of the graininess that always appears when small photographs are enlarged.

They can be used to coat other materials, such as glass or plastic, so that photographic images can be printed directly. The films may also be developed in only ten minutes without water and in normal light, thus eliminating the need for a darkroom. Photography aside, the ferrocene-based compounds could also benefit the textile industry by allowing manufacturers to use stronger dyes on fabrics, thus extending the life of the colors and of the clothes.

—George B. Kauffman

Defense research

Rapid advances in electronic and electro-optical components within the past decade had by 1988 reached the point where they were laying the technological foundation for a new generation of intelligent, autonomous weapons systems capable of spanning the entire spectrum of warfare—from the individual soldier on the battlefield to space-based antiballistic missile defenses. The "smart" weapons of the Vietnam era were evolving into "brilliant" weapons through the application of two new types of electronics: powerful miniature computers based on very high-speed integrated circuits (VHSIC) and improved sensors to be built with microwave millimeter-wave monolithic integrated circuits (MIMIC). Tying the two together are fiber-optic data links, which provide the necessary high-speed, high-volume, secure communications. VHSIC and MIMIC, sponsored by the U.S. Department of Defense at a cost of more than $1 billion, were intended to create the electronic components and subsystems that would be essential for such new military programs as the Strategic Defense Initiative (SDI); the X-30 National Aerospace Plane (NASP), which may eventually replace the space shuttle to provide low-cost access to space; and the next generation of fighter aircraft, the Air Force's Advanced Tactical Fighter (ATF) and the Navy's Advanced Tactical Aircraft (ATA).

The purpose of VHSIC was to push the performances of conventional silicon-based integrated circuits to their limits by reducing each electronic function on a semiconductor chip to the smallest size possible, thus multiplying the information processing power of each chip. By 1988 that research had been essentially completed, and it resulted in a new family of electronic components consisting of individual transistors each as small as half a micrometer (one-millionth of a meter; as a standard of comparison, the average human hair is about 100 micrometers in diameter). The first applications of VHSIC technology since the research program began in 1980 were in new airborne equipment, such as the U.S. Air Force's ALQ-131 electronic countermeasures system.

In 1988 military planners were looking for the next breakthroughs to occur in the MIMIC program, which was launched in 1987. The goal of this project was to create even more powerful devices than those based on silicon by replacing the silicon with gallium arsenide (GaAs), an advanced material capable of even greater speeds and functional densities. Just as VHSIC devices greatly increased the information processing power of new weapons systems, GaAs devices were expected to break an input bottleneck by providing comparable speeds to the front-end sensors used to detect enemy forces—in effect, serving as the eyes and ears of the weapons systems to match the VHSIC brains.

The goal was to have the new GaAs integrated circuits ready by the early 1990s. Potential applications included an ultrareliable radar for the Air Force's ATF, a shared-aperture radar for the Navy's ATA, communications terminals for the Milstar communications satellite network, fused sensors (so called because they operate across several areas of the electromagnetic spectrum) to detect enemy tanks, airborne jammers to protect U.S. aircraft by interfering with enemy electronic signals, sensors for anti-radiation missiles that home in on the electronic signals of enemy radars, and precision-guided munitions, such as the terminally guided warhead for the multiple-launch rocket system.

These applications were not direct replacements of current silicon-based devices but instead were geared to future systems in order to take advantage of the inherent advantages of GaAs. This, in turn, would dictate changes in what the military called "system architecture" by encouraging the use of distributed elements that can fail gracefully rather than a single element (a radar warning receiver, for example) that is subject to catastrophic failure.

Although GaAs technology has been under development for more than 20 years, it has always lagged behind that of silicon because of the difficulties of working with the material. In addition to requiring a deadly poison, arsenic, in the manufacturing process, GaAs is extremely brittle and thus needs special handling. Yet the material is inherently about six times faster than silicon, making it attractive for very high-speed applications measured in gigahertz, one billion cycles per second. GaAs also does not require as much electrical power as silicon-based devices.

The increased data traffic between the front-end sensors and the central processors within weapons systems created the need for a complementary technology, a need filled by fiber optics. Conventional copper cables within aircraft, ships, ground vehicles, and missiles could operate only at megahertz (one million-cycles-per-second) speeds and furthermore were heavier and more vulnerable to enemy electronic jamming than were optical fibers.

Fiber-optic cables thus were becoming popular for a new generation of military equipment. This stress on using optical fibers within weapons systems—to the point where they become integral parts of the weapon—was a departure from initial military applications. Like commercial users, the military services first began using fiber optics in relatively simple telecommunications applications as a one-for-one replacement for copper cable. The initial goal was to save weight. Enhanced performance at first was just a bonus, but it opened the eyes of systems designers to the possibilities of building entirely new systems around the fiber's unique properties.

By 1988 all three military services were moving toward more advanced applications in which fiber optics made possible new weapons that could not have been developed through the use of previous technologies. These included the Army's experiments with fly-by-light helicopter control systems under its Advanced Digital Optical Control System program and tactical missiles with pinpoint precision under the Fiber Optic Guided Missile program; Navy studies of fiber-optic undersea networks to link acoustic sensors and shore-based computers for antisubmarine warfare as part of the Ariadne program; and a growing Air Force interest in fiber optics for maintaining secure communications among the system components of the proposed SDI antiballistic missile system.

To realize the significance of fiber optics, one must understand the basic processes involved. Optical fibers are made of liquid silicon and germanium tetrachloride and then drawn into fine strands to achieve unprecedented levels of transparency. A pane of ordinary window glass 2.5 cm (one inch) thick permits half the light to pass through it, and high-quality optical glass such as the kind used for eyeglasses and microscopes can be 3 m (10 ft) thick before half the light is dispersed or absorbed. For optical fibers the comparable figure can be as great as 19 km (12 mi). This permits the extraordinary rates at which data can be transmitted.

Immunity to electromagnetic interference (EMI) is another important consideration. Signals can be transmitted through electrically noisy areas with extremely low bit error rates and with no possibility of electronic jamming. This is particularly important for the electronically noisy areas within ships, aircraft, and other weapons platforms, and it has added advantages in the operation of equipment during thunderstorms, around air bases, and even on the battlefield. Security also is enhanced with optical fibers because they radiate no telltale emissions.

Another useful property of fiber optics for military applications is their lack of electrical shock or fire hazards because of their use of photons rather than electrons in the transmission of information. This

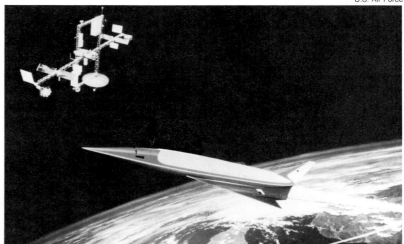

The X-30 National Aerospace Plane is shown in an artist's drawing. A joint project of the U.S. Department of Defense and the National Aeronautics and Space Administration, it is designed to be a single-stage-to-orbit manned vehicle that can cruise at speeds in excess of 6,400 kilometers per hour (4,000 miles per hour). The first test flight is expected in early 1993.

safety factor enables them to be used near ammunition storage areas and fuel tanks. Research is under way on new optical fiber materials that promise to improve system performance. Nonsilica fibers, using halide glasses, theoretically could reduce signal attenuation to the point where a single cable could span an ocean without requiring repeaters.

The new military applications, which were predicated on the use of VHSIC and MIMIC components, included upgrades to the B-1 bomber and MX (Peacekeeper) intercontinental ballistic missile (ICBM), where fiber's immunity to EMI and the effects of nuclear radiation were important considerations. Fiber optics was also being planned for the firing system of a smaller version of MX, the so-called Midgetman small ICBM. Weight was another critical factor, and it was estimated that fiber optics could replace one ton of conventional wire cabling in the B-1.

Optical fibers may also play a role in SDI. One of the key problems of such a system is concealment from detection and destruction, and in that regard fiber optics offers advantages over conventional electronic systems. Optical waveguides have extremely low power loss, thus permitting secure, undetectable communications between system components deployed far apart.

Both the ATF and X-30 program managers at the Air Force's Aeronautical Systems Division near Dayton, Ohio, said that they were confident enough about fiber optics to specify it for their programs. "Fiber optic technology has matured to a point where use for both multiplex and point-to-point data paths is considered an acceptable risk in view of fiber's advantages over older wire circuits," Col. James A. Fain, Jr., ATF system program director, said. "Both of the contractor teams for the current ATF demonstration/validation phase [Lockheed teamed with Boeing and General Dynamics, and Northrop

teamed with McDonnell Douglas] have adopted a fiber optic HSDB in their designs."

Robert R. Barthelemy, NASP program manager, added that the expected high data rates of the X-30 (more than five times greater than on the Air Force's current F-15 and F-16 fighters) would require fiber-optic data links and possibly also a new generation of optical computers using photons rather than electrons for data processing. With the selection in 1987 of the major X-30 contractors (General Dynamics, McDonnell Douglas, and Rockwell International on the airframe and Rockwell/Rocketdyne and United Technologies/Pratt & Whitney on the propulsion system), Barthelemy expected to conduct a technology readiness review by 1990 and conduct the first test flight in early 1993. Thus, he expected the technologies to be developed by 1990.

Two features of fiber optics, weight savings and immunity to EMI and nuclear radiation, will be important for the X-30, according to Barthelemy. Aerospace vehicles derived from the X-30 are expected to be used as test beds for SDI, which will require the cost of placing payloads in low-Earth orbit to be reduced by a factor of ten, according to Barthelemy, from about $4,000 per pound for today's space shuttle to $400 per pound.

Another possible application of fiber optics in a peacekeeping role emerged from studies completed in 1987 by the Max Planck Society near Munich, West Germany. There West German scientist Albrecht von Müller proposed a network of seismic sensors placed between the opposing forces in central Europe. Similar to those used to detect earthquakes, the sensors would be linked to a control center via a 5,200-sq km (2,000-sq mi) grid of optical fibers and provide an instant warning of any invasion. Another feature of Müller's plan was an "intelligent minefield" to destroy invading tanks. The fiber-optic network and sensors would cost $200 million, according to Max Planck Society planners, and the minefields would cost another $400 million. Other estimates put the total cost as high as $1.6 billion.

A new technology that in 1988 remained far from fruition might supply a solution to a major problem in designing antiballistic missile systems: sorting out the real warheads from the swarm of decoys that are likely to accompany them in any nuclear attack. In 1986 the U.S. Air Force quietly launched a research and development program calling for the expenditure of $4 million over three years for investigating the possibility of applying the rapidly emerging technology of superconductivity to a new family of extremely sensitive, space-based imaging radars. Known as the Terahertz Initiative, because the operating frequency of the radars would approach one trillion cycles per second, the program was aimed at building an entire phased-array radar on a semiconductor wafer (probably GaAs). By detecting the emissions of the wakes the reentry vehicles make as they travel through the atmosphere or even space, the new radars would provide the computers with better data for comparing these emissions against known signatures of warheads.

Radar is not the only way of spotting enemy targets, and the military services were beginning to use their newly acquired electronics technologies to create "sensor fusion." This involves the sensing of targets across a broad portion of the electromagnetic spectrum and the processing of huge amounts of threat data in real time. It was hoped that this would result in increased confidence in target identification, which enables defenders to respond more quickly. This was a change from previous weapon systems, in which each sensor provided an independent display of the sensed information and system operators had to make their own evaluations in a split second. For the next generation of weapon systems, such as the Air Force's ATF and the Navy's shipboard Advanced Combat Direction System (ACDS), fused sensor systems will integrate the data for the operator and present a single display that includes recommendations on how to respond to an enemy threat.

All the U.S. military services were moving rapidly into another area of the electromagnetic spectrum, the infrared, to develop the sensors of the future. The reason was that recent advances in electronics technology throughout the world had made radar vulnerable to detection and jamming. The solution was to complement it with electro-optical sensors that are passive and therefore immune to electronic countermeasures.

There are only three "windows" in the electromagnetic spectrum through which one can observe atmospheric propagation in order to detect targets. The most obvious (and least useful for military pur-

poses) is the visible portion, a very narrow band, covering only the region with wavelengths of 0.4–0.7 micrometer. The other two are in the infrared portion of the spectrum. The band ranging from three to five micrometers (also known as mid-infrared) is good for detecting such thermal radiation as fires and the plumes of missiles, but observers can be fooled if their adversaries shield the heat source or employ other stealth technologies. A better region is the 8–12-micrometer band (far-infrared), because there one can detect internally generated heat ranging from the body heat of individual soldiers to the heat accumulated by the skin of an aircraft as it travels through the atmosphere.

The ultimate goal of this focus on the infrared portion of the spectrum is the conversion of radiation emitted by potential targets, such as enemy missiles, into images discernible by military commanders in any kind of weather or lighting condition. Compared with conventional radar systems, these electro-optical systems of the future offer greater accuracy in tracking their targets. They are expected to find applications in systems for fire control and weapons delivery, imaging, target designation, reconnaissance and surveillance, navigation, countermeasures, and communications.

Successful application of infrared sensors also depends on advances in materials. In addition to research under way on GaAs chips, work began on producing cadmium telluride (CdTe) and mercury cadmium telluride (HgCdTe). The goal was to reduce electrical "static" so that the detectors could provide more accurate information about hostile targets.

—John Rhea

Technician examines a Lantirn (low-altitude navigation and targeting infrared system for night) navigation pod. Lantirn is expected to improve the combat effectiveness of U.S. fighter planes.

AP/Wide World

Earth sciences

Research in the Earth sciences during the past year ranged from studies of climate change to the development of theories explaining the mass extinctions of plants and animals to the devising of computer models of hydrologic systems. One of the most unusual events was the explosion of an undersea volcano directly beneath a research ship.

Atmospheric sciences

During the past year, atmospheric science advancements included work in the performance of observational field programs, the development of new weather-forecasting techniques, continued study of pollution and acid deposition, and research on climate change. International and joint governmental and private industrial agreements were signed to better coordinate cooperation in a number of these studies.

Observational field programs. Research into winter storms continued during the year. A project sponsored by the Canadian government, the U.S. Office of Naval Research, the U.S. National Aeronautics and Space Administration (NASA), and the U.S. National Science Foundation (NSF)—referred to as OCEAN STORMS—was begun in August 1987 and was scheduled to continue until June 1988. Centered in the northern Pacific Ocean near latitude 48° N and longitude 138.5° W, the study focused on ocean-atmosphere interactions during winter storm events on a scale of 5 to 250 km. (One kilometer equals 0.62 mi.) U.S. research aircraft and the Canadian ship *Parizeau* were to participate in the study. Ocean storms can raise havoc over land as well, as occurred over southern England in October, when hurricane-force winds resulted in the worst storm there in 300 years.

A joint program of the Danish Meteorological Institute, the NSF, NASA, and the U.S. Air Force Geophysical Laboratory, referred to as the Greenland-II Cooperative Observations of Polar Electrodynamics (COPE), was conducted in the upper atmosphere from February 15 to early April 1987. Ten suborbital launches from Sønde Stromfjord, Greenland, five of which were to release chemicals to create a vapor cloud at an altitude of about 250 km, were used to investigate such atmospheric features as auroral zone electrodynamics and polar ionospheric irregularities.

From May 1 to June 30, 1987, Taiwan and the U.S. completed the Taiwan Meteorological Experiment (TAMEX). Designed to improve the understanding of thunderstorm processes over mountainous terrain, it employed three Doppler radars, five conventional radars, three research ships, a U.S. National Oceanic and Atmospheric Administration (NOAA) aircraft,

Goddard Space Flight Center/NASA

On August 14 a Nike-Orion sounding rocket launched a scientific payload that will measure the concentrations and mass distributions of electrons, positive ions, and negative ions in the ionosphere.

and many other observation platforms to monitor the weather in the vicinity of Taiwan.

From October to December, the "German Front Experiment 1987" and the British and French "Mesoscale Frontal Dynamics Project" were conducted in order to develop an improved understanding of weather fronts as they propagate onto the European continent. These fronts are major contributors to rain throughout the region.

New weather-forecasting techniques. Concern for aircraft safety during takeoff and landing in the vicinity of deep cumulus clouds continued during the year. Such clouds can produce downbursts, which, when spreading out near the ground, result in rapid changes in the air speed of approaching or departing aircraft. A large change from a head wind to a tail wind can result in an airliner crash as the aircraft is slowed to below stall speed. From early August to September 4, an enhanced low-level wind shear alert system—a warning system for downbursts—was tested operationally at the Stapleton International Airport in Denver, Colo. This system used surface wind sensors to provide improved sampling of winds near runways.

Cloud-to-ground lightning caused approximately 10,000 forest fires a year between 1979 and 1982 in the U.S., burning 218,700 ha (540,000 ac) annually. Several hundred deaths per year also resulted

306

from lightning strikes. In June 1987 the U.S. National Weather Service started issuing probabilities of cloud-to-ground lightning in the western United States for six-hour periods within areas measuring about 50 km on a side. The forecasts were based on numerical weather-prediction models and on a climatology of four million lightning strikes observed by the Bureau of Land Management automated detection system from 1983 through 1985.

The U.S. National Weather Service planned to begin the installation of a 30-station microwave wind profiler network in the central U.S. in December 1988, with completion scheduled for March 1990. With a wavelength of transmission of 404 MHz, the profilers would permit high-quality hourly averages of winds from about one kilometer to eight kilometers and higher above the surface. Such information would greatly enhance the ability to monitor the vertical and horizontal structure of the atmosphere.

Pollution studies. During the first three months of 1987, the "Across North America Tracer Experiment," sponsored by NOAA and the U.S. Department of Defense, was completed. During this period every 2½ days between midnight and 3 AM Eastern Standard Time (EST) or noon and 3 PM EST, three different perofluorocarbon tracers were released from Glasgow, Mont., and St. Cloud, Minn. Ground samples for the tracers were obtained from 77 sites, mostly east of the Rocky Mountains and south of Hudson Bay. Aircraft samples were obtained

Technician adjusts a new type of wet-weather sensor. The microwave energy imaging sensor, aboard a U.S. Air Force satellite, by seeing into and through clouds will identify tropical storms earlier than conventional satellites.

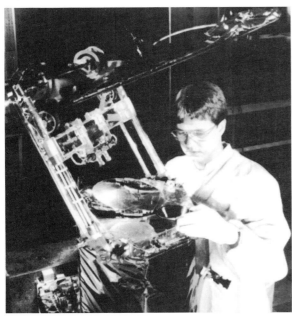

for distances of less than 500 km from each site. The purpose of the experiment was to determine how atmospheric pollutants are transported and how much dispersion occurs. Answers to such questions are critical, for example, to an understanding of the relative importance of long-range versus local sources of pollution on acid deposition.

Concern about the degradation of air quality in the National Park Service areas in the southwestern U.S. continued in 1987. In January the Subregional Cooperative Electric Utility, the Department of Defense, the National Park Service, and the Environmental Protection Agency (EPA) Study on Visibility (SCENES) released tracer material from the exhaust stack of the Navajo power plant in southwestern Utah. This material was sampled at a range of sites within several hundred kilometers of the source. At issue was the relative contribution of the power plant, as opposed to distant sources of pollution, to the degradation of visibility in the local region.

Recognition of the threat of acid deposition to the environment was achieved during the year. On March 18, 1987, U.S. Pres. Ronald Reagan announced a sharp increase in spending on the control of acid rain. A total of $2.5 billion over five years was promised for innovative demonstration projects to reduce pollution. For one week each in February, April, July, and October 1987, a NOAA twin-engine Beechcraft airplane was flown at several heights along a 1,600-km flight path parallel to and about 200 km west of the Mississippi River. Samples of sulfur dioxide, ozone, nitric acid vapor, hydrogen peroxide, and various aerosols were collected and were to be used as input to the EPA-sponsored Regional Acid Deposition Model. Currently being coordinated by Julius Chang of the State University of New York at Albany, the model is to be used to investigate the effects of different control strategies on the resultant amount of acid deposition in the eastern United States.

Climate change. U.S. and Soviet scientists agreed to work together to study trace gases in the Earth's atmosphere. During 1987 an agreement to cooperate on ozone studies in Antarctica was signed. The agreement involved close coordination between NOAA's National Climate Program Office and Air Resources Laboratory and the Soviet Union's Central Aerological Observatory. This agreement was expected to lead to joint efforts in other areas, including studies of Arctic trace gases and aerosols. Arctic haze, a winter phenomenon thought to be due to pollution from northern Europe and Asia, could have a major influence on the amount of solar radiation received at the surface in northern latitudes and, thus, directly lead to changes in climate on a global scale.

The trace gases mentioned above include methane, which is produced by decomposition as well as directly from man-made sources. The Commonwealth Scientific and Industrial Research Organization of Australia and the Oregon Graduate Center in Beaverton, using data from 23 sampling sites throughout the world, monitored a global average increase of methane of 0.78% per year. Little change was found south of the Equator, but significant increases occurred in the Northern Hemisphere. Methane is one of the "greenhouse" gases that absorb a portion of the Earth's infrared radiation and reradiate back downward, creating a warming mechanism for Earth's climate.

Land use changes also influence climate. Robert E. Dickinson of the U.S. National Center for Atmospheric Research (NCAR) used the NCAR climate-simulation model to suggest that a deforestation of the Amazon would significantly decrease evaporation over the region and cause a 3° to 5° C (5° to 9° F) increase in surface air temperatures. Researchers estimated that about one-half of the rainfall over the Amazon is returned from evapotranspiration from leafy plants. During the 1987 rainy season, from mid-March through mid-May, a joint U.S.-Brazilian research team monitored the lower near-surface atmosphere of the central Amazon by means of aircraft, satellites, and ground-based equipment. As part of the Amazon Boundary Layer Experiment, 60 researchers funded by NASA were seeking to better understand the role of the world's largest tropical rain forest in supplying trace gases and organic particles to the atmosphere. Such a supply would change as a result of deforestation in the region.

Moti Segal and associates at Colorado State University, the University of Wyoming, and NCAR, using observations from the NCAR King Air aircraft, demonstrated in July that irrigated areas adjacent to dry, natural grass areas in Colorado can have temperatures at 150 m (490 ft) above the ground as much as 3° C cooler over the wetter area during midday. Dew point temperature differences were even larger, with a variation of more than 10° C (18° F) at that height. Ground-surface temperatures varied by as much as 20° C (36° F).

Concern continued to mount regarding the observed depletion of the ozone layer over Antarctica that had occurred yearly in September–October since at least 1982. Two theories were being suggested to explain this depletion. The chemical theory proposes that chlorofluorocarbons (CFCs), which are used as refrigerants and had been used in the past as spray-can propellants, produce chlorine, which reacts with stratospheric polar clouds at the end of the polar winter, when sunlight returns, to form free chlorine ions that can destroy extremely large quantities of ozone. The dynamical theory suggests that, by October, horizontal mixing of the atmosphere is reduced because of a reduction in winter storm activity

around Antarctica. This inactivity permits areas of maximum and minimum ozone concentration to exist as distinct entities.

Ozone depletion worldwide could cause enormous, though undetermined, climatic changes. Tests on a model suggest that a 45% reduction in stratospheric ozone could decrease temperatures in the stratosphere by at least 20° C. This could permit, for instance, much more severe thunderstorm activity in the tropics and during mid-latitude summers because the storms could penetrate deeper into the atmosphere.

Russell Dickerson of the University of Maryland, using the NCAR Sabreliner jet, observed levels of carbon monoxide at the top of thunderstorm clouds as high as those found at low elevations in urban areas. Very high levels of nitric acid were also discovered. This corroborated the conclusion of Walt Lyons of R · SCAN Corp. in Minneapolis, Minn., and published in the *Journal of Climate and Applied Meteorology* in late 1986, that thunderstorm systems can vent human-generated pollutants high into the troposphere and even into the lower stratosphere. The effects of this rapid conduit of pollution on stratosphere air chemistry (which includes ozone) could contribute to major and relatively rapid changes in global atmospheric trace gas concentrations and in the global climate.

Cooperation in weather studies. An innovative memorandum of understanding was signed between NASA and the University Corporation for Atmospheric Research (UCAR) on August 3 to explore the possibility of transferring title of the NASA space shuttle giant fuel tanks to UCAR. Under the plan the fuel tanks, which now are designed to fall back to Earth, would be inserted into orbit. These tanks would then be used in the construction of space-orbiting research parks that would be financed by commercial funds.

The 19th General Assembly of the International Union of Geodesy and Geophysics (IUGG), attended by 4,000 scientists from around the world, was held in Vancouver, B.C., from August 10 to August 21. Approximately 900 of the participants attended the International Association of Meteorology and Atmospheric Physics portion of the conference. Among the major findings reported was the conclusion that the albedo of the Earth (the fraction of solar radiation that is reflected) could be increasing as a result of the presence of pollution particles in cloud droplets. Such cloud droplets appear to increase the solar reflectance from cloud tops. This effect could, by itself, eliminate any global warming due to the greenhouse effect.

An agreement was signed on May 13, 1987, between Finland and the World Meteorological Organization to strengthen meteorologic services in

Angola, Botswana, Lesotho, Malawi, Mozambique, Swaziland, Tanzania, Zambia, and Zimbabwe. These countries—members of the Southern African Development Coordination Conference (SADCC)—were to receive the equivalent of about $4 million in order to improve weather information in the region needed for agricultural operations, water management, production of solar and wind energy, and aviation activities. The year concluded with a heightened recognition that the understanding of weather and climate and societal responses to atmospheric conditions and potential changes would require close and open international cooperation.

—Roger A. Pielke

Geologic sciences

Volcanoes, earthquakes, mass extinctions of species, continental motion, and the composition of the atmosphere in ancient times were among the subjects of research in the geologic sciences during the past year. There were no major earthquakes or volcanic eruptions, but geologists hoped that their studies of the lesser events that did occur would help them to better understand the major catastrophes.

Geology and geochemistry. The decline in the search for domestic petroleum reserves in the United States, which was triggered by the precipitous drop in oil prices during 1985 and 1986, was a matter for concern not only among petroleum geologists but in the geologic community as a whole. In October 1986 the American Association of Petroleum Geologists (AAPG) reported that 25% of its members with three or more years of employment in the petroleum industry were out of work. In especially affected states such as Colorado and Oklahoma, the figure rose as high as 35%.

In the face of this critical situation, a number of industry leaders expressed guarded optimism about the immediate future. Kenneth Derr, vice-chairman and director of Chevron Corp., speaking at the convention of the AAPG held in Los Angeles in June, said that he believed that the price of crude oil had stabilized, citing the narrow fluctuation of the price of West Texas crude between $18 and $20 per barrel during the previous several months. As signs of slow recovery in the industry, Lawrence Funkhouser, the newly elected president of the association, pointed to increases in budget levels for exploration and rises in the number both of seismic crews in the field and of active drilling rigs.

Meanwhile, a number of U.S. government and industry leaders expressed apprehension that another energy "crisis" might occur, perhaps as soon as the early 1990s. It was pointed out that for the first time since 1980 there was in 1987 a rise in the importation of foreign oil into the U.S. An increasing reliance on imported oil, together with a decline in domestic exploration, could lead to an increase in the price of oil comparable to the dramatic rise in the 1970s. Debates over national energy policy can be expected to be rekindled under these circumstances.

As the shrinking of opportunities for industrial employment led to declining enrollments in geology programs in colleges and universities, geologic educators turned their attention to the question of how the geologic curriculum might be changed so as to prepare graduates to cope with the "boom and bust" cycles that had become so characteristic of their profession. The answer from thoughtful educators was to provide students with a thorough grounding in the basic sciences and in the fundamental principles of geology and, above all, to resist the temptation to graduate narrowly specialized students during periods of rapid expansion in the petroleum industry.

Hope was expressed that broader and more diversified employment opportunities would be available to geology graduates and unemployed petroleum geologists in the near future. The participants in a symposium convened at the convention of the southwest section of the AAPG, held in Dallas, Texas, in March 1987, predicted that several thousand new jobs for geologists would become available during the next two or three years in the areas of water resource and waste management and that, moreover, the scientific knowledge acquired in the practice of petroleum geology would be directly applicable in those crucial fields.

Volcanology and landslides. The attempts by geologists to meet the immediate needs of society are not limited to their search for sources of energy and economically significant minerals. Recent advances in the understanding of events that are potentially destructive to life and property were beginning to pay off in terms of the enhanced ability of geologists to predict such events.

Volcanologists meeting in New Zealand in February 1986, only three months after the disastrous eruption of Nevado del Ruiz in Colombia, called for an increase in the monitoring of potentially dangerous volcanoes throughout the world. They recommended, furthermore, that special attention be given to the training of volcanologists from less developed countries that contain high-risk volcanoes.

Since its cataclysmic eruption in 1980, Mt. St. Helens has become one of the most meticulously studied volcanic mountains in the world. Geologists, noting especially the frequency of shallow earthquakes and the behavior of the lava dome in the crater, developed a method for predicting the minor eruptions that followed the devastating explosive episode of May 1980; the accuracy of the predictions was impressive. However, Donald Swanson of the U.S. Geological Survey's Cascades Volcano Observa-

New growth of trees takes place next to areas still devastated by the eruption of Mt. St. Helens (in background) in 1980. Several varieties of fir trees have been replanted, and willows and red alders have taken root naturally.

tory, located near Mt. St. Helens, expressed doubts that knowledge of the behavior of volcanoes in general, and of this volcano in particular, had advanced to the point that the next destructive eruption could be predicted early enough to permit the evacuation of people on the mountain or very near it. Yet the U.S. Forest Service decided to open the mountain—including the crater but not the lava dome—to limited public access during the summer and unlimited access during the winter.

Bokuichiro Takano of the University of Tokyo reported that the monitoring of the chemical composition of the water in crater lakes might aid in predicting destructive eruptions. His suggestion was based upon a study of the 1982 eruption of Kusatsu-Shirane, a volcano that is located 153 km (95 mi) northwest of Tokyo. Takano found that changes in the concentration of certain chemicals in the water, especially the virtual disappearance of polythionates (complex sulfur-oxygen anions), could be related to the release of sulfur dioxide during volcanic activity on the lake bottom preceding an explosive eruption.

An 11-member team submitted a report to the U.S. Office of Foreign Disaster Assistance on the disaster at Lake Nyos in Cameroon that resulted in the death of more than 1,700 people in August 1986. According to the report, the waters below the lake's stable surface layer had become charged with gases, almost 99% of which was carbon dioxide, possibly supplied by spring waters rich in this gas that fed into the lake. The chemical composition of the water and the absence of disruptions on the

lake bottom argued against a volcanic source. Although the release of the deadly gas may have been triggered by a minor volcanic eruption beneath the lake, the fact that this release and a similar one at Lake Monoun in Cameroon in 1984 both occurred in August suggested to George Kling, a limnologist at Duke University, Durham, N.C., that such releases in Cameroon lakes may result from overturning triggered by minor events during periods of the lakes' greatest instability.

Perhaps not so dramatic as the attempt to predict volcanic eruptions and earthquakes but equally significant were recent attempts to predict the occurrence of landslides. David Keefer and his colleagues at the U.S. Geological Survey at Menlo Park, Calif., reported that they had developed a promising means of anticipating destructive, and even life-threatening, landslides in the San Francisco Bay region during and after periods of heavy rainfall. The system served as a basis for warnings issued during the storms that occurred between February 12 and 21, 1986. These warnings, the authors suggested, may have been at least partly responsible for the fact that damage and loss of life during this period was substantially less than during comparable periods in the past. The authors concluded that the system could be improved by taking into account not only rock and soil type, slope, and total precipitation but also initial soil moisture and the distribution of precipitation.

Ocean-floor and coastal research. The ocean drilling program continued in 1987 with dramatic results. During the spring the *JOIDES* (Joint Oceanographic Institutions for Deep Earth Sampling) *Resolution* on Leg 114 recovered 2,300 m (7,500 ft) of sediment from the floor of the Antarctic regions of the Atlantic Ocean under extremely adverse weather conditions. This section was believed to represent a virtually uninterrupted record of sedimentary events from Late Cretaceous to Quaternary time and promised to serve as a foundation for a substantial increase in knowledge of paleoceanographic circulation that is crucial for gaining an understanding of climatic changes during the past 100 million years. (For additional information on ocean drilling, see *Oceanography,* below.)

A paper published in the January issue of *Geology* illustrated once again how arbitrary the boundaries that separate the different historical sciences are. Yaacov Nir of the Geological Survey of Israel and Iris Eldar of the Archaeological Survey of Israel reported on their study of ancient wells along the Mediterranean coast of Israel that range in age from the Bronze Age to the time of the Crusades. Their investigations revealed that the water levels in those ancient wells nearly coincide with the present water table level in that region. The authors concluded from this evidence that the Mediterranean coast of

Israel has been tectonically stable during the past 3,000 years, a view that disagreed with conclusions reached as the result of some earlier studies.

Continental motion. The geologic evidence that the continents have moved with respect to one another throughout much of geologic history, and that they may be expected to do so in the future, has been accumulating at an increasing rate during the past 25 years. Recently more direct evidence of such motion was obtained. At the spring meeting of the American Geophysical Union held in Baltimore, Md., in May, James Ryan of the Goddard Space Flight Center in Greenbelt, Md., reported measurements of distances between points on the Earth's surface obtained by the method of very long baseline interferometry. Large radio antennas in western North America, the central Pacific, and Japan received radio signals from distant quasars. The very small difference in the arrival times of a signal at the different stations permitted a precise measurement of the distances among them. Observations over a period of only three years have led to the conclusion that the distance between a site near Fairbanks, Alaska, and one in Hawaii was decreasing at a rate of 52.3 ± 5.5 mm (2.06 ± 0.2 in) per year. Similar studies revealed that, in contrast to the relatively rapid motions recorded in the Pacific basin, Europe and North America were moving apart at a rate of only about 17 mm (0.7 in) per year.

Mass extinctions. The search for evidence of cataclysmic impacts of asteroids with the Earth and the effect that they might have had on causing mass extinction of plant and animal life continued unabated in 1987. Bruce Bohor, Don Triplehorn, Douglas Nichols, and Hugh Millard, all of the U.S. Geological Survey, reported in *Geology* that they had discovered a clay layer at the boundary of the Cretaceous and Tertiary periods, about 65 million years ago, near the top of the Late Cretaceous Lance Formation, one of the best-studied sources of vertebrate remains in North America. The layer, only one meter (3.3 ft) above a fragment of dinosaur bone and 4–7 cm (1.6–2.8 in) below the lowest lignite in the earliest Tertiary Fort Union formation, contains shock-metamorphosed minerals and the high concentration of iridium that suggest an impact on the Earth by a large extraterrestrial object. According to the authors, the Cretaceous-Tertiary boundary clay is more closely associated with dinosaur remains at the site than any previously reported.

There was, however, by no means unanimous agreement among geologists and biologists that the extinction of many species of animals that occurred at the end of the Cretaceous Period could be explained by the impact of an extraterrestrial object. Charles Officer, Anthony Hallam, Charles Drake, and Joseph Devine pointed out that the selectivity of the extinction at the end of the Cretaceous argues

against the impact of a meteorite as its cause. They noted, moreover, that the extinctions of the different kinds of organisms did not occur all at once, as might be expected if the cause had been an impact-induced dust cloud. They suggested that an increase of volcanism over a period of 10,000 years or more, which would result, among other things, in an increase in acid rain, atmospheric cooling, and a depletion of the ozone layer, provided a more plausible cause of the complexities of the extinction.

Stephen Stigler and Melissa Wagner of the University of Chicago reported on an analysis of the statistical foundations of the hypothesis, widely discussed in the paleontological literature during the past three years, that the fossil record reveals a periodicity of 26 million years for episodes of major extinctions. The authors reached the startling conclusion that for the time spans actually studied, the models applied may be expected to yield a statistically significant, but artificial, periodicity of 26 million years.

The debate about cataclysmic events and mass extinctions thus showed no signs of resolution and, in fact, appeared to be intensifying. One can expect the disagreements in this area to dominate geologic and paleontological discussion for years to come.

Ancient atmospheres. At the annual meeting of the Geological Society of America in Phoenix, Ariz., in October, two geologists reported that they had attempted to determine the concentration of oxygen in an ancient atmosphere by a rather direct method. Robert Berner of Yale University and Gary Landis of the U.S. Geological Survey measured the concentration of oxygen in air bubbles trapped in amber of late Cretaceous age. They found that the bubbles contained about 30% oxygen—50% higher than the 21% concentration in today's atmosphere. Earlier research had avoided this method because of the fear that oxygen might be diminished in the sample by reaction with the amber or that it might be diffused out of the bubbles.

Although questions about the reliability of their method remained, Berner and Landis were encouraged by the fact that their estimate of the concentration of oxygen in the atmosphere during that time was consistent with estimates obtained by other means. The possibility that oxygen had been so abundant during the late Cretaceous raised some intriguing questions, one being the effect that it may have had upon the metabolism of plants and animals, especially large reptiles, such as the dinosaurs, that were living at that time. And, inevitably, because an asteroid impact is thought to have occurred at that time, the question arose as to whether the increased oxygen concentration might have enhanced the conflagration that the impact is supposed to have caused.

Paleontology. A significant recent development in paleontology was the increasing attention being given to the very oldest fossils. A question that frequently arises in the study of organisms that lived before the appearance of hard-shelled fossils that can be observed by direct inspection is whether one is dealing with fossils at all. It may be possible to argue that an object that was recovered from sediments that were deposited more than three billion years ago is the remains of an organism because it resembles some living form. Often an object is considered to be a fossil simply because no nonorganic explanation for it can be discovered. These objects may have their status as fossils revoked if a purely physical explanation of their origin is proposed and accepted.

Although fossils of microbes and stromatolites (blue-green algae) that are older than 2.5 billion years have long been recognized, the remains of cellular microorganisms of that age have been considered to be, at best, problematic. J. William Schopf of the University of California at Los Angeles, an internationally recognized authority on very ancient fossils, and his co-worker Bonnie M. Packer reported the discovery of what appeared to be the remains of a cellular colonial microorganism from a formation of the Warrawoona Group of Western Australia that was dated at between 3.3 billion and 3.5 billion years before the present. Not only are these fossils among the oldest of any kind but the authors determined that there is good reason to conclude that they are the remains of organisms that were photosynthetic and produced oxygen. If they were, it would mean that oxygen was being contributed to the atmosphere much earlier than had previously been supposed.

In an interview published in *Geotimes*, W. Gary Ernst of the University of California at Los Angeles, the immediate past president of the Geological Society of America, expressed concern at the lack of federal funding for basic geologic research. It remains to be seen whether the vigorous and imaginative geologic research apparent during the past year can be maintained in the face of what appears to be declining financial support.

—David B. Kitts

Geophysics. Although no great earthquakes (greater than magnitude 8 on the Richter scale) or devastating volcanoes were reported in 1987, several events caused significant destruction, and several were of particular interest to researchers. Each year geophysicists intensify their efforts to understand these natural hazards, but catastrophic events are rare and still largely unpredictable. Thus, the essence of much geophysical research is to observe smaller, commoner events and then to extrapolate that knowledge to larger, rarer occurrences.

Earthquakes. Measured in human terms, the most significant earthquakes of 1987 occurred along the Ecuador-Colombia border on March 5–6. The two earthquakes, measuring 6.1 and 6.9 on the Richter scale, left 2,000 people dead, 75,000 injured, and more than 20,000 homeless. Much of the damage and loss of life was due to major landslides and flooding in the regions near the center of the earthquake (epicenter).

Seismologists also obtained important information from several U.S. earthquakes in 1987. These included a rare mid-continent earthquake and two earthquake sequences that occurred near permanent seismograph networks in southern California. These data were expected to offer researchers an unprecedented opportunity to study faulting and seismic-wave propagation. (Faulting is the fracturing of rock in the Earth's crust accompanied by a displacement of one side of the fracture with respect to the other and in a direction parallel to the fracture.)

A magnitude-4.9 earthquake struck southern Illinois on June 10. Although causing only minor damage, this moderate shock was important to seismologists. Earthquakes are relatively rare east of the Rocky Mountains, but large shocks have occurred in central and eastern North America (CENA) in historic times (for example, in 1811 at New Madrid, Mo., and in 1886 at Charleston, S.C.), and evaluation of future seismic risk in this region was identified as an important research goal even before the southern Illinois earthquake. To make quantitative seismic-risk predictions in any region, seismologists must estimate ground motions from hypothetical earthquakes: how the amplitude of ground shaking varies (scales) with the size of the earthquake and how it diminishes (attenuates) with distance from the center (focus). For this, seismologists need seismograms;

Workers clean up debris from a building in Pasadena, California, that was destroyed by an earthquake on October 1. Measuring 5.9 on the Richter scale, the quake was the worst to strike southern California since 1971.

AP/Wide World

312

thus, any well-recorded CENA earthquake receives extra attention from researchers. Few near-focus seismograms exist for large CENA earthquakes, so most CENA ground-motion estimates must be based on data from smaller shocks; these data are compared with abundant information from quakes in western North America (WNA). Research as of 1988 suggested that scaling characteristics of CENA and WNA ground motions are roughly similar but that ground motion attenuates more slowly with distance in CENA (although the attenuation difference may not be important in the distance range up to 100 km (60 mi) that is most important for the design of engineered structures). Research into other parts of the CENA seismic-risk problem, such as identifying seismically active faults and estimating the recurrence times of large earthquakes, was in its infancy.

On October 1 an earthquake that measured 5.9 on the Richter scale struck southern California near Whittier, 19 km (12 mi) east of downtown Los Angeles. Six deaths and more than $200 million in damage to more than 10,000 structures were attributed to this destructive shock. It occurred within permanent strong-motion seismograph networks operated by the U.S. Geological Survey (USGS), the California Division of Mines and Geology, and the University of Southern California; these seismographs are specially designed to record very strong ground shaking under severe conditions. Records showed that peak ground accelerations near the epicenter reached 0.45 times the acceleration of gravity (9.81 meters per second per second) and that strong high-frequency (2–10 Hz) shaking lasted roughly five seconds.

Within hours of the main shock, seismologists deployed portable seismographs at dozens of sites in the epicentral region to record aftershocks. In some cases these units were paired at the same site with strong-motion seismographs that recorded the main shock (aftershock ground motions are generally too small to trigger the strong-motion recorders). To understand why the combined main shock and aftershock datasets would be especially useful, one should consider a slightly different version of the basic ground-motion-estimation problem that was discussed above; the question is whether one can learn about details of the earthquake faulting process by modeling ground motions recorded near a large earthquake. Near-focus seismograms from large earthquakes tend to be complicated and difficult to model theoretically; they reflect complex space-time patterns of energy release during faulting and rather complex wave-propagation effects. Small-earthquake seismograms, however, are generally simpler, reflecting simple faulting. It is important to understand that seismograms from two earthquakes that have roughly the same locations will share roughly the same wave-propagation effects. Theoretically, ground motion

from a large complex fault can be built up as a summation of ground motions from simple subfaults; thus, the modeling problem can be reduced to the problem of summing seismograms from a suitable distribution of subearthquakes (such as aftershocks distributed over the main shock fault plane, which are relatively easy to record). Wave-propagation effects are included automatically in these empirical models, allowing the researcher to isolate and focus on faulting effects alone.

Another intriguing aspect of the Whittier earthquake was causing seismologists to reevaluate methods that had been used for years to predict local seismic hazards in California: it did not occur on a mapped fault. Faulting at Whittier apparently occurred at a depth of 12–14 km (7.5–8.7 mi) on a shallowly dipping fault surface, in response to a regional north–south compressive stress. This type of faulting is termed blind thrust faulting by structural geologists because it is expressed only as folding (bending of layers of rock), not faulting at the Earth's surface. The destructive earthquake near Coalinga in central California in 1983 might have reflected a similar type of faulting, which might be more common in California than had been believed.

On November 23–24 earthquakes of magnitudes 5.8 and 6.0 struck the remote Superstition Hills region of southern California, northwest of El Centro and south of the Salton Sea. Preliminary research suggested that faulting in the magnitude-6.0 event was unusually complex, consisting of at least three distinct subearthquakes separated by several seconds. These earthquakes generated extensive, complex patterns of faulting at the Earth's surface and ground failure because of liquefaction. For the first time, scientists made extensive measurements of pore-water pressure changes accompanying liquefaction in shallow sediments near Superstition Hills.

Volcanoes. Scientists monitored volcanic activity at more than 80 sites in 1987. Most activity occurred around the Pacific Ocean rim, and most reports described continuing eruptions at previously active sites, including Mt. Etna in Italy, Kilauea in Hawaii, White Island in New Zealand, and Nevado del Ruiz in Colombia, which had erupted catastrophically in 1985. Some large eruptions in remote areas were known only from sightings by airline pilots or from atmospheric smoke or ash traces on weather satellite images. At some sites where volcanoes pose a greater threat, however, observatories were created, where scientists continuously monitored the relationships between eruptions and earthquakes, volcanic tremor, and crustal deformation (tilts and strains near the volcano that represent "inflation" and "deflation" of the subsurface magma chamber).

Some interesting observations were reported by scientists aboard the geophysical research vessel

Melville, which was stationed over the MacDonald seamount in the south-central Pacific Ocean when an undersea eruption occurred. They described discolorations of the seawater and large gas bubbles that rose to the surface and shook the ship as they burst. One large bubble rose two meters (6½ ft) above the ocean surface and ejected 20 to 30 volcanic rock fragments when it burst. When *Melville* scientists dredged the top of the seamount after the eruption, they found that it was covered with fresh volcanic glass. (For additional information, see *Oceanography*, below.)

Parkfield earthquake-prediction experiment. The attention of many seismologists continued to focus on the segment of the San Andreas Fault near Parkfield in central California. On the basis of the extraordinary recurrence of magnitude-6 earthquakes at Parkfield in 1881, 1901, 1922, 1934, and 1966, scientists anticipated a similar earthquake in January 1988 ± 5.2 years. The Parkfield area was extensively instrumented in an effort to measure seismicity and crustal deformation in the earthquake source zone before, during, and after the earthquake. In particular, the USGS would try to issue an earthquake prediction minutes to days before the Parkfield event, and scientists at USGS offices in Menlo Park, Calif., were notified of significant seismicity changes at Parkfield by a real-time processor and paging system.

Global Positioning System. Designed primarily for military navigation, the Global Positioning System (GPS) was beginning to augment or replace conventional surveying methods in many geophysical applications. Like very long base-line interferometry (VLBI), GPS used radio interferometry to determine the relative positions of stations. Unlike VLBI, however, GPS equipment was compact, portable, and inexpensive. GPS used encoded signals from military satellites, but for civilian applications knowledge of the military codes was not required. Instead, the complex signal could be treated as "pseudo noise" and processed by computer like the quasar-generated noise signals in VLBI. Station separation was computed on the basis of relative signal delays determined by cross correlation. Geophysical applications might include mapping, station locating, and crustal deformation measurements, which are otherwise accomplished by relatively tedious geodetic methods.

Cooperative U.S.-U.S.S.R. seismic experiment. The establishment of future superpower treaties to limit nuclear testing is a complex scientific, as well as political, issue. In the U.S. a willingness to negotiate such agreements with the Soviet Union depends, in part, on the seismological capability to monitor and verify past, present, and future treaty compliance. Yields of Soviet test explosions must be estimated from measurements made outside the Soviet Union; seismologists must correct for the effects of wave

Joanne Silberner, courtesy of Science News

Box near Parkfield, California, holds a detector designed to measure the speed and strength of ground motion during earthquakes. Geologists predict an earthquake of magnitude 5.5–6 in the Parkfield area by 1993.

propagation and then relate the excitation of seismic waves at the source to the size of the explosion. As of 1988 the techniques used for making these estimates were largely empirical, derived from experience at the U.S. test site in Nevada.

If the physical properties of the Earth's crust and upper mantle that influence seismic excitation and attenuation are different at the Soviet test site, however, straightforward application of the Nevada relationships might lead to biased estimates of Soviet yields. Indirect seismological evidence, supported by sparse geologic data, suggests that an explosion of a given yield will generate much larger seismic waves from the Soviet test site than from the Nevada test site. If this is true, and seismic data are taken at face value, yields of Soviet tests will be overestimated.

Some of these complex questions were being addressed in a remarkable new series of experiments arranged by the Soviet Academy of Sciences and the Natural Resources Defense Council, a nonprofit U.S. environmental organization. Under the original agreement three seismic stations, operated cooperatively by U.S. and Soviet personnel, were to be installed in each country. Installation of the Soviet stations was completed in November 1986; for the first time, U.S. seismologists had access to data recorded within several hundred kilometers of the Soviet test site near Semipalatinsk in eastern Kazakhstan. Their goal was not to record Soviet tests directly; rather, the seismologists hoped to improve yield estimates through direct measurements near the Soviet test site of the propagation and attenuation of seismic waves from earthquakes, chemical explosions, and non-Soviet nuclear explosions. In a later agreement the three stations would be moved farther from the test site and two others would be built; they would be permitted to record signals from Soviet nuclear tests. By improving Soviet nuclear-test yield estimates, geophysicists hoped to resolve at least one of the controversial questions that comprise this important issue.

—Charles S. Mueller

Hydrologic sciences

Significant developments of the year in the hydrologic sciences included the first successful recovery of core from drilling on bare rock on the seafloor, the explosion of an undersea volcano directly beneath a research ship, and the discovery of a supposedly lost piece of the Earth's crust. Hydrologists continued in their efforts to use computers to develop sophisticated models of hydrologic systems.

Hydrology. In common with many of the other geophysical sciences, one of the major hydrologic events of 1987 was the International Union of Geodesy and Geophysics (IUGG) symposium in Vancouver, B.C. The hydrology sessions and workshops, organized by the International Association of Hydrological Sciences, reflected major themes in current hydrologic research, including understanding and modeling hydrologic processes (with meetings on forest hydrology, river ice, ice-sheet modeling, large-scale seasonal snow cover, and modeling catchment responses in different climatic and physiographic regions) and the variability of hydrologic processes and uncertainty of hydrologic predictions (with sessions on estimation of areal evapotranspiration, spatial variability and representativeness of hydrogeologic parameters, and the hydrologic implications of climatic change and climatic variability).

The session on climatic variability, set against a background of recurring drought in Africa, allowed an assessment of the current state of knowledge of the impacts that continuing climatic trends might have on the available water resources in different parts of the world. With the relatively short-term records that are generally available, it is difficult to distinguish long-term climatic trends from what might be complex random fluctuations in systems exhibiting long-term persistence. Recent work suggests, however, that there may be continuing trends in temperature and rainfall statistics. The causes of such trends were subjects of debate in meteorologic research, but the hydrologist had to consider their possible effects and the implications for design of water resource provision. This required the use of sophisticated computer models of hydrologic systems.

The impact of computer technology on hydrologic practice was featured in a number of the quadrennial

national reports to the IUGG. In the U.S. report, an article by Daniel Loucks and Austrian hydrologist Kurt Fedra reviewed the ways in which increased computer power at lower cost was being used in hydrology. They emphasized the direct supportive role of computing technology in water resources planning through the use of interactive modeling and graphic displays of data. They also looked forward to the time when direct links between supercomputer power and interactive graphics workstations would also allow computer-intensive models that simulate dynamic processes to play a role in such planning.

Jim Wallis of the IBM Thomas J. Watson Research Center, Armonk, N.Y., pointed out in an editorial review, however, that the use of supercomputing power in hydrology remained fragmentary and suggested that the time might be coming when hydrologists would have to become organized in new ways in order to achieve goals requiring large-scale facilities such as supercomputers. He suggested that a mechanism by which large groups of research workers could come together to work on joint problems was needed, perhaps in the form of a National Center for Hydrological Data and Research. Such organiza-

A hydraulic engineer (seated) and a soil scientist use a computer program that they developed to track the possible leaching of pesticides into groundwater in the Tifton, Georgia, area.

Agricultural Research Service, USDA

tions already existed in a number of countries and, in some cases, worked together on major projects.

One example of such cooperation is the Système Hydrologique Européen (SHE) catchment model, jointly produced by the Institute of Hydrology (U.K.), the Danish Hydraulic Institute, and Sogreah of France. The SHE model was presented in a series of papers in the *Journal of Hydrology* after some ten years of joint work. It is a model of the hydrologic behavior of catchment areas that is based as much as possible on physical descriptions of the flow processes. It makes calculations of surface and subsurface flow rates at a large number of points distributed in three dimensions to represent the structure of the topography, soil, and geology of the catchment under study. The physical characteristics of the catchment, and their variability in space, can therefore be represented by the model in some detail, provided the nature of the variability is known. The parameters of the model are intended to be physical quantities that can be measured in the field or estimated from other physical information.

Because such models are based on physical quantities, it may be possible to use them to predict the effects of changes to the system under study for which no measurements are available, such as the effects of land-use management changes or climatic changes. At present, however, this aim is limited by three factors. The first is that researchers cannot be sure that the descriptive equations used in the model are proper descriptions of the flow processes in the field. The model equations are those developed from controlled laboratory experiments and may not be appropriate to the highly heterogeneous characteristics of the soils and stream channels found in the field. Second, the resolution of the model predictions and the length of time that can be simulated are both limited by available computer power. Third, it may be difficult to estimate some of the parameters of the model with accuracy, particularly for those cases where no measurements are available.

It follows that the predictions of these highly sophisticated physically based models, such as the SHE, should also be expected to be in error and that hydrologists should therefore attempt to assess the uncertainty associated with the predictions. However, most predictive models in hydrology are nonlinear, and methods for quantifying uncertainty in nonlinear systems are not well developed. (A linear system is one in which all of the interrelationships among the quantities involved are expressed by linear equations that may be algebraic, differential, or integral.) The methods that are available tend to rely on some form of simulation in which a number of predictions are made through the use of conditions chosen randomly from a predefined set of possible model parameters and boundary conditions. As

hydrologic models become more complex, however, the computing power required for carrying out such uncertainty analyses becomes prohibitively expensive owing to the large number of computer runs required. Researchers hoped that such calculations would be greatly facilitated by the advent of parallel-processing computers.

For some quasi-linear systems (in which the relationships are substantially linear despite the presence of nonlinear elements), it is possible to reduce the computations required for assessing predictive uncertainties by using theories of stochastic differential equations (those dealing with the random disturbances occurring in an infinitesimal time interval). Considerable progress was made in this direction in modeling the flow and quality of groundwater. Groundwater systems pose particular problems to hydrologists because direct observation of underground flows is impossible except at few locations in what may be very extensive systems. It may be difficult, therefore, to characterize the nature of the flow system properly, particularly in fractured rock systems where the distribution of sizes and connectivity of the fractures may be important in controlling the flow of water and any pollutants. Understanding groundwater systems is becoming increasingly important, however, because this resource is becoming depleted as a result of overutilization and pollution. It has been estimated, for example, that in parts of the Ogallala aquifer that underlies the Great Plains of the U.S. from South Dakota to Texas, 60% of the available water may already have been removed. In the U.S. alone more than 250,000 landfill sites may be in direct hydraulic contact with groundwater systems used for water supply. By 1988 the number of wells closed down because of water-quality problems totaled more than 15,000. A number of different groups in the U.S., Canada, France, West Germany, Sweden, and the U.K. were working on the problem of water flows and pollutant transport in fractured rocks. The uncertainties associated with descriptions of such systems, however, seemed likely to be high.

—Keith Beven

Oceanography. Unusual occurrences and enhanced international cooperation marked the past year in oceanography. In October an undersea volcano near the MacDonald seamount in the Pacific Ocean, about 1,600 km (1,000 mi) southeast of Tahiti, erupted directly beneath the research ship *Melville* from the Scripps Institution of Oceanography, La Jolla, Calif. Scientists aboard the vessel described gigantic bubbles that exploded through the surface of the ocean, shooting out jets of gas and pieces of rock, some so filled with gas that they floated. When they burst in nearby waters and under the hull, the bubbles were described as making "horrendous clangs and clamors."

The Scripps expedition was aimed at collecting information on deep currents that flow near the seafloor, but it was also collecting geologic specimens from the region near the seamount. The observation of the eruption could help explain mysterious rumblings that had been observed by French seismologists in Tahiti. The rumblings had been attributed to bursting of bubbles from undersea volcanic eruptions, but the eruptions had never before been observed.

The use of bubbles for ocean studies encompasses more than just bubbles from underwater eruptions. During a recent experiment scientists from the U.K. used the motion of bubbles generated by the breaking of waves at the sea surface to measure how heat is transported downward into the ocean. With precise instrumentation the oceanographers were able to make the first direct measurement of the downward transport of warm, bubble-rich water. This information was expected to be valuable to scientists as they learned how the atmosphere affects the ocean and vice versa in the surface boundary layer.

Chernobyl fallout. The fallout from the 1986 Chernobyl nuclear power plant disaster produced an unexpected side benefit for understanding how materials are moved by the atmosphere and the ocean. The ejection of radioactive substances into the atmosphere and then into the ocean provided a dramatic demonstration of the processes by which the oceans absorb and transport material. Using sediment traps, devices attached to moorings that catch particles as they fall through the ocean, oceanographers from

Volcanic rock was recovered from an undersea volcano that erupted directly beneath the research ship Melville *on October 11 in the south-central Pacific Ocean. When first picked up from the water, the rock was too hot to handle.*

the Woods Hole (Mass.) Oceanographic Institution, the University of Hamburg, West Germany, and the Dokuz Eylul Universitesi, Izmir, Turkey, monitored the sinking rate of the particles of fallout in the North, Black, and Mediterranean seas.

The largest fluxes of radioactive material were found to be during plankton blooms, suggesting that the material is first absorbed in the upper layers of the ocean by phytoplankton (small oceanic plants) and then eaten by zooplankton (small oceanic animals). The particles that carry the fallout were believed to be aggregations of feces pellets from the zooplankton. The observations of the Chernobyl fallout provided a direct demonstration of the rate of sinking of such particles. The data were expected to help in the general understanding of how the ocean cleanses itself of contaminants.

Biological oceanography. During the summer of 1987, a mysterious brown tide of marine organisms that had previously devastated Long Island scallops reappeared. The algal bloom had killed nearly all scallop larvae by slowing their feeding during the past two years. The unusually dry summer weather in 1987 apparently reduced the salinity of the water sufficiently to make conditions favorable for algae growth. It appeared that the algae are always present in relatively low densities and increase with favorable weather conditions.

On a global scale more than 99% of the organic matter in the ocean is dissolved and dilute, yet it has important effects on ocean processes and the global carbon cycles. During the year the first detailed analysis of dissolved organic carbon in the ocean was carried out. The results revealed that the most recently formed dissolved organic material is mixed quickly into the upper ocean and then penetrates rapidly deep into the sea. Thus, the material may be a more important source of food deep in the ocean than was originally thought. The results also showed that the residence time for the material in the deep ocean was sufficient for it to interact with light and life many times as the global ocean circulation moved it around the world. It was not destroyed as fast as scientists expected, suggesting an as-yet-undiscovered process by which the sea recycles this complex mixture of organic molecules. The results could have an important impact on ideas about the global carbon cycle and the predicted warming of the atmosphere by an increase in carbon dioxide.

Interest in the use of biotechnology in ocean sciences was growing during the year. New techniques in immunology, molecular genetics, and recombinant DNA (deoxyribonucleic acid) were readily applicable to environmental and oceanographic studies and were being applied. New techniques were developed for high-yield extraction of purified DNA from mixed natural populations of planktonic microbes. This was

317

a necessary step toward the molecular biologic study of microbial communities, including the effects of "engineered" genes released into the environment.

In September the freighter *Pac Baroness* collided with another vessel off the coast of California and sank in 550 m (1,805 ft) of water near the Santa Barbara Basin. The ship carried 21,000 tons of copper ore, which could be exposed to the ocean. If it is, the dissolved copper sulfide could be used to trace currents and chemical pathways and rates of biogeochemical cycling. A group of researchers from the University of California at Santa Barbara was planning to use a low-cost, remotely operated vehicle to assess the degree of ore exposure and to begin preliminary sampling for understanding the mechanisms of biochemical transfer.

Ocean drilling. The international Ocean Drilling Program focused its attention on the Indian Ocean, investigating the geologic history of that region. A record length of core was collected by the drilling ship *JOIDES* (Joint Oceanographic Institutions for Deep Earth Sampling) *Resolution*, operated by Texas A&M University for the partnership of 17 countries that support the program. The data were being used to understand the monsoon, which dominates critical rainfall patterns of Asia and Africa, as well as regional atmospheric and oceanographic conditions. In this aspect of the program 12 sites were drilled in the northwestern Arabian Sea, yielding 4,300 m (14,108 ft) of sediment. The samples revealed evidence of changes in climate, biologic productivity, and the structure and position of the continents.

The almost five kilometers (three miles) of sediment samples retrieved on this particular segment of the Indian Ocean expedition will allow scientists to trace the initiation of the southwest Indian monsoon and its patterns of intensity during the last ten million years. Monsoonal variations over thousands of years appear to be correlated with changes in the Earth's orbit around the Sun. The variations over longer times appear to be explained only by geologic change, however—the changing elevation of the Tibetan plateau and the Himalayas. The greater the height of the Himalayas, the stronger the monsoon.

The year also marked the first successful significant recovery of core from drilling on bare rock. Earlier attempts in the Atlantic Ocean were successful only in setting a "guide base" that allowed the drill to enter on bare rock without the support of a sediment layer, but the drilling itself faltered in rubble below the surface. In the Indian Ocean, however, another attempt resulted in the recovery of almost 500 m (1,640 ft) of core. This successful attempt showed that it was now possible to drill in these areas of young crust.

The second Conference on Scientific Ocean Drilling took place in 1987 in Strasbourg, France.

Courtesy, Alfred-Wegener-Institut für Polar- und Meeresforschung

The new West German research vessel Polarstern, *operated by the Alfred Wegener Institute in Bremerhaven, performed a variety of missions in Arctic and Antarctic waters during the past year.*

The first such conference, in 1981, had led to the formation of the current Ocean Drilling Program. This 1987 meeting looked ahead to the 1990s and identified new topics of importance, ranging from studies of biologic diversity to the drilling of very deep holes for recovery of material from the Earth's mantle.

During the year marine geologists from Scripps reported the discovery of a supposedly lost piece of the Earth's crust. Geologists believed that the current existing Pacific crustal plate once had a partner that long ago was subducted (descended beneath another plate) near the Aleutian Islands. In September 1986, however, using measurements by sonar and studies of magnetic patterns, geologists in that region found a remnant of the former plate, called the "Kula" plate (Athapaskan Indian for "all gone"). The scientists hoped that the information would help them reconstruct the way in which Alaska and the Aleutian Islands were formed and to have a better idea about the distribution of petroleum and other minerals in that region. A new name for the old plate was also proposed: "Kula-Yoza," meaning "almost all gone."

Oyster shells. A good example of the application of geophysical research technology for practical benefit occurred in Pocomoke Sound, on Virginia's eastern shore. A problem for oyster breeders there had been the decline in the number of oyster shells, which are used for seeding oyster beds. Scientists from the Virginia Institute of Marine Science demonstrated that it is possible to use seismic testing techniques to make profiles of the material at and below the waterway bottom in order to reveal the presence of such shells.

The seismic method is much faster and provides a continuous record, in contrast to the older borehole technique. By early 1988 a two- to three-year supply of shells had already been discovered.

During 1987 scientists from the U.S. National Oceanic and Atmospheric Administration (NOAA) used satellite data collected during 1985 and 1986 to compare changes in tropical sea level and winds in an effort to understand the relation between fisheries and El Niño, the periodic appearance of anomalously warm water in the tropical Pacific Ocean. The satellite data were collected from the U.S. Navy altimeter satellite, Geosat (geodetic satellite), which was launched in March 1985 and which provided unprecedented temporal and spatial coverage of the changing sea level of the ocean.

The data revealed that the response of the ocean to the wind anomalies was narrowly confined to an area near the Equator and that it was dominated by month-long Kelvin waves, whose physics is related to the rotation of the Earth. This new information was expected to help oceanographers develop better models for the prediction of future El Niños.

International cooperation. The international aspect of satellite oceanography was emphasized during the year with the firming of plans for a joint U.S. (NASA) and French (CNES) satellite to measure the topography or shape of the ocean surface (TOPEX/Poseidon); the European Space Agency's plans for its Earth Resources Satellite (ERS 1); and the Japanese launch of the Marine Observations Satellite (MOS 1). The U.S. also announced plans to fly a device for measuring the color of the ocean on the next Landsat satellite, and the Japanese presented plans for an Advanced Earth Observations Satellite that would also carry an ocean color instrument. The U.S.S.R. showed interest in sharing the data collected from a number of their satellite programs.

The new West German research vessel *Polarstern*, operated by the Alfred Wegener Institute in Bremerhaven, had an active year in both Arctic and Antarctic waters. An international group of oceanographers achieved the first basin-scale full-depth section of measurements of temperature, salinity, dissolved oxygen, and a variety of chemical constituents over the Nansen Basin north of Svalbard. Information on man-made halocarbons was also collected to define the rate at which such materials are mixed into the deep ocean. Overall the data revealed a greater rate of mixing and a greater interaction with waters from

the Canada Basin and the Greenland-Norwegian Sea than had been expected.

In the Antarctic the *Polarstern* studies included observations of the hydrographic properties of waters in the Weddell Sea, both near and below the ice. A section 1,700 km (1,056 mi) long was collected from the edge of the ice to the continental margin along the Greenwich meridian. Scientists from the Lamont-Doherty Geological Observatory of Columbia University, Palisades, N.Y., used those data to reveal for the first time the characteristics of the ocean beneath the full width of the winter sea ice cover. The surface mixed layer showed significant entrainment (drawing in) of deep water into the surface layer, an entrainment that increased with location closer to the pole. It also appeared that the entrainment, which is important to understanding how the ocean transfers heat to the atmosphere in this region, continues into the spring.

A number of other studies were carried out in the Antarctic. A multi-institutional research project, Research on Antarctic Coastal Ecosystem Rates, was notable for its high-frequency, high-resolution sampling during the first three months of the year. Physical, chemical, and optical variables were sampled in an effort to understand the mechanisms that give rise to the high productivity of the coastal shelf ecosystem of the Antarctic peninsula. As of early 1988, seven distinct water masses had been revealed. Island effects appeared to be significant, producing eddies in currents that affected the distribution of phytoplankton. This information was expected to be invaluable for understanding the interaction of physics, chemistry, and biology in the region.

—D. James Baker

See also Feature Articles: ENERGY FROM THE OCEAN: A RESOURCE FOR THE FUTURE; CIRCLES OF STONE.

Electronics and information sciences

Responding to demands for the transmission of ever larger amounts of information in ever shorter periods of time, designers and engineers during the past year introduced new features that increased the power of computers. New computer architectures replaced the standard single-processor machines with models that incorporated many processors that could work on a problem simultaneously. The size of computer memories was increased, and a new technology that allowed designers to build a processor on a single silicon chip was developed. In other fields of endeavor the Soviet Union mounted an effort to sell its new Proton launch vehicles to Western nations, and work continued on the implementation of the Integrated Services Digital Network (ISDN).

Communications systems

Technological changes in telecommunications were evolutionary, not revolutionary, during the past year. Fiber optics, for example, was not new but was improved. ISDN also continued to receive attention, but it was directed toward productive applications. The central office switches being manufactured were almost totally digital, and the next generation of switches was still many years away.

Cellular radio increased in popularity, and there was talk about converting it to a digital system. Paging was becoming so sophisticated that a person could be located virtually anywhere in the country in this way. Voice mail and facsimile transmission are examples of two other technologies that were not new but were rapidly gaining in popularity.

In short, there has been great improvement in previously introduced technologies. However, there is no such thing as technology operating in a vacuum. If there is no market for a technology, or if the presentation of a technology is deemed inappropriate or even illegal, then its development is significantly affected. Such a situation was being experienced in the U.S., where a battle was going on regarding the role that the 22 Bell operating companies would play in the telecommunications arena. When those companies were divested from AT&T in 1984, they were not allowed to engage in three areas of the industry: manufacturing, long-distance telephone transmission, and information processing. In 1987 a review was held to determine whether this ruling should be changed. This was an important case because these 22 companies controlled approximately 80% of the telephone traffic in the U.S. and, therefore, about 80% of all purchases.

The presiding judge in the case decided that for the most part there should be no changes (it was only in the area of information processing that some relaxation of the rules took place). Although all seven regional holding companies were appealing the decision, it seemed unlikely that there would be significant changes in the near future.

ISDN. ISDN is a single network that will be able to transmit high-speed data, facsimile, telemetry, and slow-motion video over the same connections as voice transmission. It is not a product but an engineering concept. In order for all these services to be applicable to the same pair of wires, certain technical developments must be implemented. By 1988 such developments were under way, but just as important was the need to develop standards so that facsimile would be allowed to be transmitted over the same wire pair as slow-motion video, voice, telemetry, and high-speed data. Such standards were being developed, somewhat painfully, by various organizations under the direction and sponsorship of the

International Telegraph and Telephone Consultative Committee (CCITT), an arm of the International Telecommunications Union (ITU). When such standards are achieved and the necessary hardware is developed, great economic benefits will result. It will no longer be necessary to build corporate headquarters for communications-intensive companies with abnormally thick subfloors to hold the fiber optics, the twisted pairs of wires, and the coaxial cable. It will be possible to move work stations with relative ease, since all connections to the network will be via a minijack.

Although a few field trials of ISDN had been in operation before January 1987, nearly a dozen new trials took place during the first six months of that year. British Telecom updated its ISDN trials; in France, where nearly half of all subscribers were already connected to digital exchanges, two such trials were taking place. West Germany also had trials and expected a nationwide introduction of ISDN in 1988. Japan had trials in progress, and in the United States each of the seven regional holding companies was holding field trials.

For years it was assumed that a simple pair of wires has a limited bandwidth capacity, but this was

Researcher Han-Shing Liu examines a circuit board for an Integrated Services Digital Network (ISDN) central office module. In 1985 Liu placed the first successful ISDN telephone call, in a laboratory environment.

not true; a high-speed digital signal can in fact be transmitted over such a pair, for up to several thousands of feet. Initially, the standards dictated that each regular telephone line would be converted to a pipe for transmission of digital data and that each "basic" access line would carry two high-speed channels for voice or computer data (each at 64 kilobits per second) and one low-speed channel for data or signaling information (at 16 kilobits per second). "Primary" access lines, which were in an early stage of development, would carry 23 voice or data channels and one signaling channel. All 24 would operate at 64 kilobits per second.

There are tremendous advantages to an ISDN network, but there are also inherent problems. In order for there to be broad deployment of ISDN, there must be customers, but customers are inclined to wait until there is broad deployment. Furthermore, there are thousands of local area networks in operation; these can quite effectively carry the communications of a particular company or group of companies. The owners of those networks, and certainly the people operating them, were reluctant to become enthusiastic about ISDN, since a network would be truly a competitor for them.

Cellular radio. Once considered little more than a plaything of affluent young people, cellular radio by 1988 had grown considerably. One could see the distinctive tiny antennae on pickup trucks, campers, vans, and domestic four-door sedans. According to the Cellular Telecommunications Industry Association, there were 680,000 cellular subscribers in the U.S. at the end of 1986 and more than a million by the end of 1987. Prices dropped dramatically, from about $3,000 for a car phone in 1983 to about $1,000, installed, in 1988.

In the early days of the industry, the car phones were just that: telephones more or less permanently mounted in an automobile. By 1988, however, many of them were carried in a specially built briefcase for portability. Field trials of fixed cellular installations were also under way. They might be appropriately placed in farms that are in remote locations, vacation homes that are occupied for only a few weeks out of the year, mountainside homes, and retreats that cannot be served by telephone wires.

Many countries were using cellular radio, but they did not operate their systems in the same way and at the same frequencies. An effort was being made in Europe to adhere to the same standards, and 16 countries agreed to a single new digital system to begin operation in the early 1990s.

Fiber optics. It was just over ten years ago—1977—when the first light-wave systems carrying commercial traffic were installed in Chicago and Santa Monica, Calif. At the time the world was astounded when it was suggested that such a system—

Businessman uses a cellular mobile telephone to make a call directly from his car. By 1988 such phones had declined considerably in price and had increased greatly in popularity.

with its two strands of glass, each smaller in diameter than a human hair—could likely carry more than 8,000 conversations at a time. By 1988 a system of such capacity was taken for granted, and indeed in 1987 AT&T began commercial voice and data communications service on a light-wave system between Philadelphia and Chicago that could carry 24,000 conversations simultaneously. Also, late in 1987 Bellcore (the company owned jointly by the seven Bell regional holding companies) set a record for the amount of information transmitted over a single optical fiber. Scientists sent the equivalent of 27 billion bits of information per second over the single-mode fiber, an equivalent of 400,000 simultaneous conversations. That is enough capacity to transmit in one second the contents of 2,500 standard-size textbooks of 400 pages each.

The earliest fibers were strands of glass, covered with plastic or additional glass sheathing, about the thickness of a human hair. They were called multimode fibers because they allowed several "rays" of light to pass simultaneously. Later the single-mode fiber, with a thickness only one-tenth that of the multimode fiber, was developed.

Not only is the capacity of fiber systems increasing but so is the allowed spacing between repeaters, devices that are used to amplify the light waves. Although repeaters are often placed every 50 km (30 mi), experiments have been run with spacing of more than 370 km (230 mi).

Facsimile and voice mail. In a facsimile system one establishes a telephone connection between one facsimile machine and another and recreates at the distant end an exact copy of what is being sent from the originating end. Letters, pictures, and diagrams can all be sent in a matter of seconds or minutes.

However, if only a few people or businesses own such machines, there is little incentive for anyone to purchase one. Finally—and in this case it was during 1987—enough people began to ask, "Do you have FAX?" Businesses were persuaded that they should and, thus, the technology finally began to be utilized on a larger scale.

A second technology that began to gain widespread acceptance during the past year was voice mail, alternately called voice store and forward or voice messaging. A private branch exchange or key telephone system equipped with voice mail will answer a phone automatically and then, through a series of voice prompts, direct the caller to the desired party. A telephone with a touch-tone calling pad is necessary to permit a response to the voice prompts, but aside from that the caller simply talks on cue. For instance, the system can be programmed to answer a call after the third ring (thus permitting a live attendant two rings to pick up on the call). The recorded instructions might begin by telling the caller to dial an extension directly if it is known or to dial a single digit in order to reach a particular department. The caller might obtain assistance from the operator by remaining on the line or by pushing the special characters from a touch-tone telephone.

Chairman of Northern Telecom Ltd. in Japan talks with a U.S. government official in Washington, D.C., marking the first use of a foreign-made digital switching system by a Japanese telephone company.

AP/Wide World

As a further example, one might assume that a caller pushes "55," which he happens to know is the extension of Mr. Jones. If Mr. Jones is unavailable, a recording would tell him so and invite him to leave a message. When Mr. Jones returned to his desk, he would see a flashing light that indicated to him that a message was waiting in his voice mail box, and he could listen, relisten, erase, store, or transfer the message to someone else.

Videotex. Videotex is a system by which the telephone user (and in this case the telephone must have associated with it a television-type monitor) can call up any of hundreds of data bases and have information appear on the monitor's screen. By 1988 there were more than three million users and over 5,000 data bases in France. One of the simplest and widespread applications concerns the telephone directory. With videotex it is no longer necessary to own a directory; all one needs to do is call up the desired information on the videotex screen.

In the U.S. the Bell operating companies were not allowed to participate in information processing, and certainly videotex is just that. It had been ruled that in certain instances the companies may transmit videotex information, but they cannot be the creators or dispensors of data base information.

Future prospects. Among other technologies in telecommunications, digital carrier systems were being used at higher and higher speeds, and private party stations were gaining increased acceptance. There was also continued expansion of local area networks and of software-driven network maintenance systems.

The field of telecommunications thus continued to evolve at a rapid rate. Products were becoming highly complex; old ways of doing things were being replaced with new methods; and telecommunications continued to be one of the most exciting fields of the 1980s.

—Robert E. Stoffels

Computers and computer science

During the past year radically new computer architectures, once found only in research laboratories, emerged in commercial products. To improve the speed of conventional microprocessors, computer architects switched to machines with simpler instruction sets and began relying on smarter compilers to produce optimal sequences of the simple instructions. Finally, the year marked a significant change in personal computers as small machines began to have computational capabilities once available only on large mainframe models.

New computer architectures. Although modern computers may seem completely unlike their early predecessors, the fundamentals of computer archi-

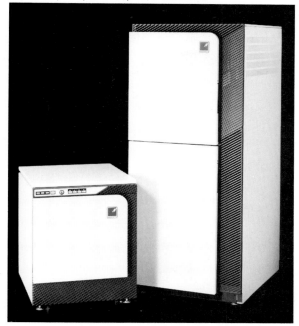

Sequent Computer Systems Inc.; photo, © Bruce Forster

Parallel computers use economical, mass-produced microprocessors, which work together to provide computing power equal to that of mainframe computers that cost many millions of dollars.

tecture have remained essentially unchanged for many decades. Most machines contain a central processing unit and a main memory. The central processing unit repeatedly fetches a single machine instruction from memory, decodes and executes that instruction, and then returns the results to memory. For example, a processor might execute an "add" operation that required it to compute a sum. Although many improvements have been made to this basic process, the biggest changes in computers have been higher speed at lower cost; capability has remained essentially constant.

Researchers have often experimented with alternatives to the single-processor model described above. However, because commercial computer companies have been slow to adopt alternative designs, few of the experiments resulted in commercial products. The past year, however, marked a change in which even the most conservative commercial computer vendors introduced several products with unusual architectures.

Perhaps the most dramatic departure from conventional architecture ever produced, the Connection Machine is a multiprocessor by Thinking Machines Inc. As the name implies, the Connection Machine offers multiple processors instead of a single one. Unlike multiprocessor machines that have two, four, or even a dozen processors, the Connection Machine has up to 65,536 (two orders of magnitude

more than any previous machine). However, each individual processor is much simpler and much less powerful than the processor found in a typical personal computer.

Thousands of processors cannot be interconnected through the single bus that is standard in most computers because the bus would not be fast enough. (A bus is a conduit in a computer through which information is transmitted from any of several sources to any of several destinations.) To solve the interconnection problem, the Connection Machine arranges processors in an "n-cube" configuration, with each processor connecting to n others. To understand an n-cube, one should envision a normal three-dimensional cube with a processor at each corner and connections along each edge. Each edge in the cube can be thought of as a wire that connects to processors. Routing a message from one processor to another requires that the message be sent along the edges of the cube, possibly through intermediate processors. In practical terms, using an n-cube interconnection means that no two processors in the Connection Machine are more than 12 wires away from each other.

What makes the Connection Machine so intriguing is its ability to use all processors operating in parallel to solve one problem. If programmers can find a way to divide the problem among processors and then route the needed data along the n-cube interconnection paths, they can reduce processing times dramatically. An example is the task of image processing. When a computer analyzes an image, it works on one small square of the image at a time, computing the average light intensity of the points that make up the square. For instance, when looking for edges in an image, the computer might choose a square with 256 points on a side and then test each point in the square to see if it is above or below a given intensity threshold. Internally, the computer represents the image as a two-dimensional array of numbers that correspond to the light intensity at each scan point. A conventional computer scans the 65,536 points in the square sequentially, taking 65,-536 steps to compare all of them to the threshold value. In contrast, the Connection Machine could assign one value to each processor and have them tested in one step.

More complex problems require clever programming to take advantage of the Connection Machine's architecture. For example, to compute the average light intensity over an entire 256 by 256 square, a conventional processor would require 65,536 steps to scan the numbers representing light intensity and compute the average. To make best use of the Connection Machine, the programmer must arrange for the processors to cooperate. To begin, each processor would be assigned one intensity value. At the first step of the computation, the processor would compute the average of its value and the value in a neighboring processor, producing 32,768 new values. At the second step the Connection Machine computes the averages of pairs of these values, and so on. Thus, in 16 steps it has computed the overall average.

Other computer vendors also began to introduce machines with novel architectures. Such companies as Sequent and Encore had made computers with between one and 16 processors for nearly two years. Unlike the Connection Machine, however, machines from those companies used more powerful processors and a bus interconnection among them. During the past year Sequent introduced a new model known as the Symmetry. Instead of having thousands of small processors, Sequent chose to keep their numbers low but to make each of them substantially more powerful than those in previous machines. To accommodate high-speed processors, Sequent had to increase the capacity of the computer's bus and the speed of its memory systems.

Like the Connection Machine, Sequent's Symmetry computer provides parallel operation, allowing all processors to work in cooperation on a single problem. Unlike the Connection Machine, however, the Symmetry machine requires the programmer to divide a problem into a few large pieces instead of many small ones. At present, it is not clear that either architecture will eventually replace the other.

Traditionally one of the most conservative manufacturers, IBM even began to include novel architectural features on its machines. Introduced during the year, its 3090 Model 600E machine used six powerful processors. More surprising, the 3090 included special-purpose circuitry that allowed it to operate on sequences of numbers, called vectors. The vector circuitry allowed the machine to solve problems for engineers and scientists quickly by operating on an entire set of values at once. Because the 3090 could perform like a conventional computer, a multiprocessor, or a vector processor, it offered users the best features of several architectures. Researchers at IBM announced that they intended to continue work on parallel architectures, hoping to produce a machine that would have 576 parallel processors.

Other manufacturers also introduced machines that combined parallel computer architectures and vector processors. For example, Alliant Computer Systems Corp. introduced the FX/8 model. Unlike the expensive IBM 3090 mainframe, the FX/8 was known as a minisupercomputer because its price was comparable to mid-range computers even though its performance on some problems was comparable to that of mainframes.

The move to architectures that support parallel computing represented a significant change in the

Sun Microsystems, Inc.

This SUN 4 engineering work station incorporates a reduced-instruction-set computer (RISC), a new processor technology that allows designers to make processors that execute tasks faster than conventional equipment can.

way computer vendors designed machines and the way programmers solved problems. The chief problem with most novel architectures is that there is no convenient way to make programs for them. With the new hardware becoming commercially available, however, computer scientists began research on new programming languages and tools. Although no startling results appeared during the past year, several new research projects were started, most using a graphic interface.

RISC technology. While some manufacturers introduced parallel and vector processing architectures, many began to incorporate a new processor technology known as the reduced-instruction-set computer (RISC). RISC does not add new functionality to a computer; it is a technology that allows designers to build processors that execute tasks substantially faster than can conventional equipment. For example, SUN Microsystems Inc. introduced a new series of engineering work stations that used RISC processors. Called the SUN 4, these machines executed the equivalent of ten million instructions per second (MIPS). The previous generation of conventional work stations, introduced in 1986, operated at approximately 4 MIPS. Thus, for most problems, the new machines were more than twice as fast as last year's models (amazingly, manufacturers have been able to double the speed of processors in each of the last four years).

RISC machines achieve high speed by having few and simple instructions. All machines include instructions for such mathematical operations as addition and subtraction. Conventional processors, known as Complex Instruction Set Computers (CISC), go far beyond the basics, however, and often include operations for such complex tasks as copying blocks of memory and searching lists of values. Internally, a clock controls the rate at which the processor executes its instructions. Vendors cite the clock speed, typically between 4 million and 25 million cycles per second (MHz), as a measure of processor performance. To achieve higher speed, a RISC machine has much faster internal clock speeds than do CISC machines. This is accomplished by restricting the set of RISC instructions only to those that can be executed in a single clock cycle, relying on software to form complex operations by composing sequences of basic instructions.

Because the RISC instruction set is simple, and because the processor uses only instructions that can be executed in a single cycle, an entire RISC processor can be implemented on a silicon chip. Shrinking a processor to a single chip eliminates the delays that occur in conventional machines when signals propagate through the circuitry that connects chips. As a result, even though the RISC machines often need several instructions in the place of a single one for a CISC model, their internal speed is so fast that they execute programs faster.

RISC machines are not limited to engineering work stations. For example, the IBM 3090 discussed above uses special-purpose RISC processors to control peripheral equipment such as high-speed disks. What was new during the past year was that chip vendors such as MIPS Inc. introduced general-purpose RISC processors that they hoped would be used in a variety of machines ranging from personal to mid-range computers. If their predictions are correct, they will eventually be able to make RISC machines perform faster than is possible with CISC machines.

Changes in personal computers. Personal computers continued to evolve. As usual, new models were taking advantage of faster microprocessors. They offered higher performance and more features than previous models for less cost. However, two major changes did occur during the year. First, vendors moved away from the simplest and cheapest home machines by offering more capability. Second, they offered a wider variety of ways to improve existing computers.

IBM, the company that set international standards with its PC models, completely revised its personal computer line by introducing the Personal System 2 (PS/2). Instead of concentrating on the home computer market, the PS/2 focused on business use by offering a complete line of machines that started with the equivalent of existing PCs and extended to much faster and more powerful models. Although some of the technology in PS/2 computers was new

for IBM, the technology was not its main selling point. Instead, IBM hoped to convince business customers that choosing the "family of compatible PS/2 computers" would guarantee them an easy growth path as their company's computing needs grew. Many vendors, including IBM, had used this strategy successfully for selling mid-range and mainframe computers, and so it might soon become widely accepted in the personal computer market.

Along with the PS/2, IBM announced that it would offer an operating system called OS/2. An operating system is a large, complex piece of software that manages system resources, controls such devices as disks, and makes it possible to run multiple programs simultaneously. In the past only large computers had operating systems. Personal computer users could execute only one program at a time. For several years, however, computer scientists have known how to build small, efficient operating systems for personal computers. They have also known that the productivity of users would increase if computers had the ability to perform simultaneous activities. A few personal computer programs even had special software built into them that allows users to print one file while using the computer for other programs. An operating system is much more general, however, because it allows users to combine arbitrary sets of programs simultaneously (and even allows multiple users to run programs simultaneously if the machine has sufficient processing power). Now that IBM had announced its operating system, other vendors of personal computers were expected to announce operating systems for their machines.

Realizing that owners will not always trade in existing personal computers for new ones, several vendors changed their marketing strategies during the past year. They introduced new technology, especially new processors, in products that plug into existing machines. For example, Imaging Technology Inc. introduced a version of its image processor in the form of a board that plugs into an IBM PC. The image processor stores an image consisting of 640 by 512 points (the resolution of a picture on a standard television set) and makes the image available to the PC for processing. The board contains a separate microprocessor, memory for storing images, and programs in read-only memory that manipulate images. Thus, the board does almost all the computation related to image processing.

Another popular set of products for personal computers introduced during the year was focused graphics. New personal computers offered more colors and higher resolution graphics than did the original models, often relying on special-purpose graphics processor chips that were available from several manufacturers. To make better graphics available on older machines, several companies introduced graphic processor boards that plug into an IBM PC.

Finally, some of the boards introduced during the year were designed to help engineers and scientists who use personal computers. Unlike business computing or games, which concentrate on information storage, retrieval, and manipulation, scientific computation relies heavily on the use of numbers with many significant digits beyond the decimal point. Known as floating point, such computation is best performed by special-purpose chips rather than by the slow processors normally found in personal computers. To make personal computers effective for engineers, several companies introduced boards for personal computers that contain the special floating point chips. If personal computers of the future have high-speed floating point hardware built in, the distinction between engineering work stations and personal computers may eventually disappear.

Some of the new boards offered conventional microcomputers more powerful than the computers to which users attached them. For example, Intel Corp., maker of the 386 microprocessor chip, introduced the Inboard 386/AT, a 386-based board that plugs into an IBM PC. The user invokes a program that shifts control from the processor in the PC to the 386 processor on the new board. The 386 executes programs two to four times faster than the PC and uses the original PC processor only for input or output operations.

—Douglas E. Comer

Electronics

During the past year it became evident that there was an increased need for transmitting greater amounts of information in ever shorter time. In response, designers, engineers, and manufacturers increased the size of computer memories and introduced a new class of chips called RISC (reduced-instruction-set computer).

The electronics industry expanded to the Pacific Rim nations of Hong Kong, South Korea, and Taiwan. They captured an ever increasing share of the world's market of electronic products. The more established electronics industries in Europe, Japan, and the U.S. attempted to maintain their positions in the marketplace by obtaining access to cheap overseas labor, by internal cooperation of the various branches of the industry, and, in the case of the U.S., by calling for a protective tariff against selected electronic products from Japan. The relationship between Japan and the U.S. demonstrated the complexities, promises, and problems of the industry.

International relations. As recently as 1980 the U.S. enjoyed a $27 billion annual trade surplus in electronic products. By 1986, however, the nation had a $2.7 billion annual deficit. Much of this deficit

resulted from the importation of Japanese electronic products into the U.S. Electronics manufacturers in the U.S. reacted against the Japanese in various ways. General Electric Co. sold its $3 billion consumer electronics business to the Thompson SA Co. owned by the French government. The Intel Corp. petitioned the U.S. Customs Service to seize microprocessor chips made in Japan by NEC Electronics Inc. because of a delay of a copyright-infringement suit that the company had filed against NEC. U.S. semiconductor manufacturers pressured Japan's Fujitsu Ltd. Corp. not to acquire the Fairchild Semiconductor Corp. Texas Instruments Co. reached an out-of-court settlement with a South Korean and eight Japanese companies that resulted in an agreement by all those firms to pay royalties to Texas Instruments.

However, the most controversial move was made by the U.S. government when on April 17, 1987, it imposed a 100% tariff on certain Japanese computers, television sets, and power tools. Various European nations pledged their support of the tariff by assuring the U.S. that they would not allow goods affected by the tariff to enter their borders. Trade figures published by the American Electronics Association showed that the U.S. electronics trade deficit declined to $5.3 billion in the first six months of

A new 32-bit microprocessor based on the principles of the reduced-instruction-set computer (RISC) can execute 17 million instructions per second, three to five times quicker than the fastest chips previously available.

Robert Holmgren

1987, down from $6.1 billion for the same period of the previous year. Concurrently, Japan's share of the world market slipped to 52% of a $2.6 billion market. In the U.S., Japan's share dropped from 14.9%, which represented about $126 million of products, to about 13%, or $120 million.

Japanese fears and reactions were predictable. Japanese officials worried that the nation's firms would suffer financial losses and a subsequent layoff of workers. The Japanese officially encouraged their citizens to buy more U.S.-made products, and U.S. electronics firms were invited to undertake joint efforts with Japanese companies. Japanese Prime Minister Yasuhiro Nakasone called on the U.S. government to rescind the tariff, and U.S. and Japanese officials began to lay the groundwork for meetings to discuss tariff issues.

U.S. reactions to the tariff were neither unanimous nor totally positive. The diversity of opinions expressed was reflective of the complexity of the tariff issue. Editorial and financial voices in the U.S. often opposed the tariff for fear of possible disturbances in the financial markets. They feared that the administration of Pres. Ronald Reagan had given up its longtime commitment to free trade. Some industry executives feared that the exclusion of Japanese chips would lead to a shortage of vital semiconductors for their products. Indeed, Motorola Inc. asked Toshiba for a shipment of chips. Such a request demonstrated the interdependence of electronics companies across national boundaries. Much of that dependency was based upon the growing complexity of chip design and manufacture.

Chips. Before the end of the century, the semiconductor industry will probably have spread throughout the world. Unlike earlier industries, which depend upon natural resources such as coal, iron, and oil, the semiconductor industry depends upon the "natural resources" of the scientific and technical competence of the people living within a region. While the former resources are a gift of nature, the latter depend upon cultural commitments and priorities. That culture becomes more important than geography is demonstrated by Japan, a nation poor in natural resources of the former kind but rich in the determination, talent, and industry of its people.

The effort to maintain a competitive edge in the semiconductor industry resulted in the adoption of various strategies. Europe, Japan, and the U.S. were all searching for cheap industrial labor for the manufacture of their products. All of them found their way to the Pacific Rim nations of Hong Kong, South Korea, Malaysia, and Taiwan. Their effort to capture the cheap labor of these nations was paralleled by an effort at national integration of their electronics industries and the formation of alliances within the industry across their national boundaries. Nev-

ertheless, however well-tested these techniques of insuring market dominance were, the unique nature of chip products and the enormous research and development efforts needed for developing them were forcing new strategies on all the major electronics producers.

In Japan the industry was seeking increased cooperation between the work force and management. The Japanese viewed the challenge of succeeding as essentially a human one. For them, cooperation of effort, sharing of information, and the adoption of the long-range view were the ingredients of success. Their approach differed from that in the U.S. While the U.S. management orientation was primarily goal-oriented, the Japanese spent more attention and time on process. For the Japanese a long-term commitment was essential; Americans generally took the short view. Commenting on the obvious success of the Japanese, Avtar Oberoi, manager of semiconductor strategies at IBM Corp., said, "Somebody besides the Japanese semiconductor industries has got to start thinking beyond the next quarter."

The U.S. semiconductor industry was known for its independence, secrecy, and jealousy. For those manufacturers, a successful chip could place them among the most profitable firms in the nation, while a chip failure could plunge them into bankruptcy. The successful methods of the Japanese, however, were forcing a rethinking of the management styles of the U.S. industry. In 1987 industry leaders decided that a cooperative effort among the various producers within the semiconductor industry and the government was needed for success. A consortium was formed between various members of the semiconductor industry and the U.S. government. The consortium, named the Semiconductor Manufacturing Technology Institute (Sematech), was initially funded at $200 million. Half of this amount came from its members, while the government paid the other half.

In the opinion of some, the success of the consortium is by no means assured. These skeptics pointed out that cooperation would be difficult to obtain, given the current climate in the industry. Furthermore, they stressed the virtue of independent research that might lead to novel configurations. Also, they claimed that the industry was not willing to put its trust into the hands of a few individuals and companies who would take responsibility for the whole of the industry.

That the cooperation of government and industry can be beneficial to the industry was illustrated by the emergence of manufacturers of computer clones throughout Asia. The government of Taiwan, in particular, decided to help its fledgling industry by undertaking the research and development efforts aimed at creating a BIOS (Basic Input/Output

System) EPROM chip. This chip makes the clones compatible with IBM's highly successful XT and AT computers. The only part within the IBM machines that was protected by copyright was the BIOS chip. The Taiwanese produced a chip that was compatible with IBM's and yet sufficiently different so that no copyright infringement could be claimed. While IBM-compatible machines share the same software, the clones are compatible with IBM in both hardware and software. Typical of the commercial success of these enterprises was Phoenix, a company that provided chips for IBM clones. The three-year-old firm supplied $3 million worth of chips in 1986. During 1987 the firm did $12 million worth of business.

Graphics. Computer-generated three-dimensional graphics were finding increasing applications in architecture, science, and engineering. As of 1988, two technologies that generate the three-dimensional graphics programs existed. The older of the two simulated a three-dimensional display on the monitor screen. The newer technique, termed stereolithography, produced a visual output and also generated a plastic model that could be physically inspected.

To generate this physical model, successive images of thin layers of the model were projected onto a vat containing molten plastic. A laser guided by the computer moved across the liquid plastic and hardened it to produce a slice of the model in conformity with the computer's image. Successive applications of this process generated the model layer by layer. The whole process took only minutes to complete.

This technique holds great promise. A designer or engineer can inspect the model to see if it conforms with expectations. Needed changes can be made with far fewer prototypes. The method can be used to make models of fractured bones, thereby allowing surgeons to study the nature of a bone fracture before surgery.

For the first time flat-panel displays that are bright, have color in their display, are crisp of image, and are affordable in price were making their appearance in the marketplace. Unlike the conventional displays of computer monitors, flat-panel displays do not rely on the impact of electrons shot from a cathode-ray tube onto a screen containing phosphorescent materials. Instead, they develop an image by the spatial orientation of crystals when subjected to electric currents. During the year Textronix Inc. exhibited bright liquid-crystal displays with high contrast and wide viewing angle. Their relatively low consumption of power made them especially suitable for computer work stations, laptop computers, and portable television sets.

Military applications. The U.S. Navy received delivery of IBM's AN-BSY-1 computer for use in its submarines. The number and complexity of its tasks could be gauged from the computer's ability to handle

TV–SAT/Aerospatiale

West Germany's TVSat 1, Europe's first high-power, direct-broadcast satellite, was launched into orbit in November. It was designed to transmit West German TV and radio programming to much of Western Europe.

77 million instructions per second. It was designed to handle all navigational tasks and the guidance and firing of all weapons.

The U.S. Air Force unveiled what it described as a "super cockpit." This system, funded at $120 million, would totally eliminate all conventional instruments. The central hardware is a helmet that will present the pilot with a three-dimensional picture of the world outside the cockpit. The pilot interacts with the system through voice and gestures. Sensors are placed within the pilot's glove that will allow touching of a switch or control. All the while, the system will monitor the pilot's performance and provide help, should the need arise.

The KH-11 spy satellite launched by the U.S. during 1987 represented a great advance over existing technology. It had powerful, yet lightweight, engines that allowed extensive orbital control of the satellite. Thus, the satellite's path and position would be more difficult to predict by a potential opponent. The satellite was constructed with materials that absorb, deflect, and misguide radar waves, thus making it largely invisible to enemy radar.

Milestones. Three-dimensional X-ray pictures were used during the year to locate deep-seated brain

328

tumors. This technology also allowed for the modeling of portions of the human skull structure that may have been damaged in a car accident. Also, the technique permitted nonintrusive observation of any possible heart defects.

NEC Electronics in Japan produced a 32-bit microprocessor that operated at 6.6 million bits per second (MIPS.). That was about 2.6 MIPS faster than the speed of its nearest competitor.

Panasonic Co. marketed a portable radio cassette recorder that allowed its user to record directly from broadcast programs. In addition, incorporated for the first time within this single unit was a condenser microphone that permitted the taping of meetings, seminars, or lectures.

Have your pi and . . . . By using the SX computer of the Nippon Electric Corp., Yasumasa Kanada of the University of Tokyo calculated to 134 million places the famous number pi, which expresses the ratio of the circumference of a circle to its diameter. Such a task is not frivolous; it tests the computer's capabilities. Writing each digit by hand, assuming that doing so would take one second per digit, would take 4.3 years.

Pi has fascinated scientists throughout the ages. Archimedes managed to get to three places and Sir Isaac Newton to 15. After Newton, the U.S. National Aeronautics and Space Administration (NASA) held the record at about one-quarter the number that Kanada achieved.

—Franz J. Monssen

Information systems and services

The body of knowledge that serves as a foundation for the storage and dissemination of information is recorded primarily in books and other printed materials. Libraries provide access to this store of information. There is, however, a serious threat to the continued survival of library materials because of chemical, atmospheric, human, and other factors that cause the paper on which the information is recorded to deteriorate. The problem is serious and worldwide, for it is estimated that roughly 25% of all research collections are at risk.

To deal with this problem, an International Conference on the Preservation of Library Materials was organized by the Conference of Directors of National Libraries with the cooperation of the International Federation of Library Associations and Unesco. Conference discussions centered on (1) determining the magnitude of the problem; (2) describing the nature and scope of library preservation activities in the world today; (3) providing specific advice for handling, storing, preserving, and converting research materials; (4) organizing preservation projects involving paper deacidification or optical-disc storage

or both; and (5) providing for the training of library preservation experts.

The Library of Congress, the largest library in the U.S. and also the one that holds the largest number of materials needing preservation, made plans for the construction of a large-scale deacidification facility to be built at Ft. Detrick, Maryland. When operational, this facility would be expected to deacidify up to one million volumes per year.

The National Archives and Records Administration is the major federal repository of U.S. government documents, some of which date back to the Revolutionary War. These archives are an irreplaceable resource that must be accessible to researchers and to the general public, but, owing to their fragile nature, handling could contribute to the destruction of these documents. Thus, the administration of the National Archives was faced with the dilemma of storing and preserving these priceless documents while encouraging their use. Soon, however, there may be a way out of this dilemma. The National Archives contracted to convert a small part of its holdings to an Optical Digital Image Storage System (ODISS). The digitized images of more than one million service records from the Civil War, pension and bounty land records, and other selected items from the 19th- and 20th-century holdings would be stored on 12-in optical discs; as many as 40,000 document images could be stored on each disc. Researchers would have access to the records stored on the discs,

Technician checks a new 35-centimeter (14-inch) optical disc that can store as much data as a 92-story stack of typewriter paper can.

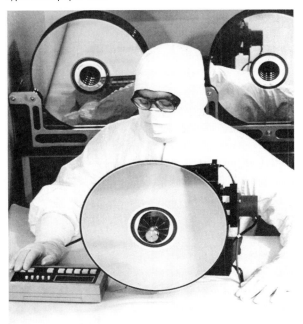

while the original documents would be preserved. Bill Hooten, the ODISS director, explained that the conversion project not only would help preserve the nation's legacy but would also enable the Archives to evaluate the permanency and the quality of the images stored on the discs.

Other U.S. government agencies began creating specialized optical-disc data bases for more efficient storage and retrieval. The Patent and Trademark Office developed a massive document storage and retrieval system that provided direct access to patents and trademarks. The Internal Revenue Service tested the feasibility of storing tax returns on optical discs for auditing. By using high-speed scanners with image-processing capabilities, tax auditors would be able to view and check the forms for accuracy exactly as they were submitted. Additionally, the Department of Defense, the Department of Agriculture, the National Center for Atmospheric Research, the Social Security Administration, and the National Security Agency all began developing storage and retrieval systems based on optical discs.

The use of discs outside the government was also increasing. Banks, perhaps the nation's largest nongovernmental user of computers, installed optical-disc systems. Insurance companies, hospitals, and educational institutions were developing automated libraries. For an expanded discussion of the problem of deteriorating books, *see* Feature Article: THE SELF-DESTRUCTING BOOK.

U.S. information services. Data base services were expanding rapidly, and the economic value of the services was expected to more than double, to perhaps $4 billion, between 1988 and 1993. The continuing success of the electronic information publishing business was due to the increased use by corporations of computer-generated information services. These services provided users with direct communication and instantaneous response from a variety of information sources accessible from terminals and personal computers, along with an ability to interact and manipulate the retrieved information.

Chemical Safety Data Guide is a data base that provides information on substances covered by the U.S. Occupational Safety and Health Administration Hazard Communication Standard and by each state's right-to-know laws. For each chemical the data include information on whether the substance causes, or is suspected of causing, cancer; physical hazards such as flammability and explosibility; long- and short-term exposure limits; spillage, leakage, and disposal procedures; and precautions for use and safe handling. This file was produced by the Bureau of National Affairs and was available through the Human Resource Information Network as an aid for safety directors and those responsible for first aid and protective equipment.

SEDBASE, produced by Elsevier Science Publishers, is a specialized data base of information on the side effects of drugs. Included are about 20,000 evaluations of all significant adverse drug reactions reported in more than 3,500 journals from 110 countries. Also included are the bibliographic citations of the original research paper on which the authors based their judgments. A unique feature of this service is that before inclusion, each report is reviewed by an expert who removes any unsubstantiated claims or speculations.

National Newspaper Data Base contains an estimated 250,000 newspaper titles published in the U.S. from 1690 to the present. The cataloging and holding information was maintained in the computer facilities of the Online Computer Library Center (OCLC) and was accessible to archivists, historians, genealogists, and other interested parties. Researchers could locate a particular newspaper by title or by searching geographically by state, county, or town. Microfilm copies of selected newspapers were obtainable through the OCLC interlibrary loan service.

Scientists, farmers, and industrialists who want to know about the latest agricultural research reports can refer to the TEKTRAN data base, provided free by the U.S. Department of Agriculture (USDA). TEKTRAN contains more than 7,000 reports, each consisting of an interpretive summary, an abstract, and the names and addresses of the authors of technical papers on such topics as genetic engineering, human nutrition, environmentally safe pest control, and soil and water conservation. The USDA provides this service in order to speed the flow of information from the laboratory to potential users in farming and industry.

The American Association of Retired Persons created the AgeLine data base of more than 22,500 documents on middle age and aging, dating from 1978 to the present. Included are abstracts of articles that contain information on family relationships, health care and costs, and policy formation on aging.

BookBrain is an interactive computer data base of children's books designed to be used by children in grades four to six. The data base contains comments on about 800 fiction books plus recommendations concerning an additional 1,200 titles. Using simple menu-driven software, children may search for books by title, author, subject, or key word. A particularly innovative feature of BookBrain is that the annotations of previous users can be displayed, and children can add their own comments to the listings. Libraries using the program could customize the data base to include only items in that library's collection.

International information systems. There are more than 90,000 libraries in Western Europe holding some 1.4 billion volumes and an untold number of journals. These represent, in both human and financial terms, an irreplaceable repository of knowledge, cultural heritage, and information. Recognizing both the value of this resource and the benefits that could be derived from cooperation, especially with respect to new information technologies, the Commission of the European Communities (EC) made plans for an EC program aimed at coordinating and harmonizing library services nationally and internationally. Harmonization would be achieved by the encouragement of internationally applicable rules and standards and the support of specific pilot/demonstration experiments based on existing achievements.

The Deutsches Bibliotheksinstitut (German Library Institute), founded in 1978, serves libraries throughout West Germany. The institute supports research and development in librarianship, and it maintains three national data bases: The German Union Catalog of Serials, the bibliographic German Union List of Conference Proceedings, and the Lower Saxonia Serials Data Base. During the past year the institute made an agreement with the U.S.-based OCLC to provide access to each other's data, software, research, and systems. In the initial phase selected libraries in each country participated in searching samples from the other country's library catalogs to determine the utility of each other's bibliographic data and to seek ways of overcoming technical barriers to such an exchange.

TASS, the Soviet Union's official news agency, entered into an agreement with Mead Data Central by which the full texts of TASS articles are transmitted to the NEXIS data base service within 48 hours of the original release. The articles cover official Soviet announcements, political and economic developments, technological advances, and everyday domestic items. Coverage dates back to Jan. 1, 1987, and is updated daily. The file provides a valuable source of information about the Soviet perspective on world events.

The Asian and Pacific Information Network on Medicinal and Aromatic Plants was formally launched with the membership of five Unesco member states (China, India, Papua New Guinea, Sri Lanka, and Thailand) and the establishment of an interim secretariat provided by the government of Thailand. Initial tasks consisted of setting up a comprehensive regional data base on medicinal and aromatic plants; a referral data base on sources of information, expertise, and research in progress; and a data base on Chinese medicines.

The British Library produced a national register of current research being carried out in universities, colleges, technical schools, and other institutions in the U.K. The data base, called Current Research in Britain, contains information on more than 65,000 projects.

The Museum Association in England prepared a Museum Data Base with more than one million items of information about British museums and art galleries. The data base contains information about collections, exhibitions, organization and management, staffing, public access, and other museum activities. The service was free to members of the Museum Association and was available on a charge basis to outside inquirers.

Information science research. Amid renewed concern for assuring that information be made public and accessible in a timely fashion, the U.S. National Science Foundation made an individual research grant to Pamela Long to conduct a critical historical analysis of the development of the idea that scientific and technical knowledge should be communicated openly and without restriction. This study was to be conducted in conjunction with an examination of the antecedents to the notion of protecting proprietary rights to ideas.

The issues of openness, secrecy, ownership, and protection are critical to both science and technology. Long's earlier research suggested that the roots of these ideas are ancient rather than being of recent derivation. Current research promises to shed light on how public policy should respond to the contradictory demands of restricting information for private profit and disseminating it openly for public benefit.

A research project of Carnegie-Mellon University, Pittsburgh, Pa., developed a model of knowledge acquisition in an environment where information is incomplete and uncertain. The model was used for examining predictions about both the social processing of information and the related shifts in social structure, information flow, and storage.

Research conducted at the University of Southern California sought to develop and implement a new method of retrieving information from data bases. Standard data base systems are searched by means of rigid formal query languages. The USC research constructed a new method that allows data base questions to be less like formal mathematics and more like normal language communication, thus making data base technology available to a much larger group of users.

Researchers at the State University of New York at Buffalo investigated linguistic devices and strategies for making inferences that need to be built into a computer system to enable it to follow stories. In order to understand a narrative fully and to answer questions about it, a system must be able to identify and track the main characters and events and follow the action of the story in space and time. The researchers were seeking to develop computer systems capable of "understanding" narratives by summarizing and answering questions about the text.

—Harold Borko

Satellite systems

Earth satellites provide a variety of services of great economic, social, and military value. Called applications satellites, the first primitive prototypes were placed in orbit more than 25 years ago. Today in each major category—communications, Earth observation, and navigation—such satellites are orders of magnitude greater than the first craft in capability, reliability, and sophistication. These satellites are designed, constructed, and operated by private industrial concerns, individual countries, and groups of nations.

Throughout 1987 the launching of new or replacement satellites was delayed because of launch vehicle failures. The U.S. space shuttle, following the tragic explosion of *Challenger* in January 1986, was undergoing redesign and testing of the solid-propellant boosters and other components. The first launch was not expected until the last half of 1988. Investigation of the failures of both the U.S. Air Force Titan 34D and Delta rockets in 1986 further delayed launch operations. By 1988 both were back in service. Two successful launches of the Titan 34D were made in October and November 1987. The Soviets suffered two failures of the Proton launcher followed by a success, and they also introduced a new superbooster, Energia. The capability of this major launch vehicle was comparable to that of the U.S. Saturn V launchers.

Throughout 1987 the Soviet Union's Glavcosmos sought commercial sales of its Proton launch vehicles to Western nations. The U.S. State Department's Office of Munitions Control, however, took a firm stand against the launching of U.S. satellites by the U.S.S.R. The regulatory policy governing export of satellites is set forth in the State Department's International Traffic in Arms Regulations. Section 126.1 states that it is U.S. national policy to deny the U.S.S.R. and a number of other countries an export license for any item on the munitions control list. A State Department official was quoted as saying, "All satellites—manned or unmanned, commercial or military—are by definition munitions list articles, their parts, components, and technologies included."

This policy caused concern by U.S. manufacturers who had contracts to build and launch satellites for other nations. In Europe British, French, and West German satellite builders were considering the choice between the European Space Agency's Ariane and the larger Soviet Proton, which was being offered at an attractive price.

The argument by private individuals who supported the use of the Proton was that it was commercially competitive and, therefore, desirable. The State Department maintained, however, that "national security and foreign policy" should control the choice.

Although the U.S.S.R. assured secure transport and protection of U.S. satellites—or those containing U.S.-made components—for the U.S. government that assurance was not enough. Even if physical security and access were controlled, considerable knowledge of technical data would be required for the interface of the satellite with the launch vehicle. Supply of such data to the Soviets was not permitted by the U.S. authorities.

Nevertheless, Glavcosmos continued an aggressive marketing effort. In November a small group of Americans visited the Baykonyr space center in Kazakhstan, where the Proton vehicle is assembled for launch. This was the first visit permitted to Americans since the Apollo-Soyuz Test Project in 1975. The quoted price of a Proton launch is $25 million–$30 million, less than one-half the estimated cost of a comparable U.S. vehicle.

Communications satellites. This category of satellites continued to be dominated by the International Telecommunications Satellite Organization (Intelsat), an international commercial cooperative of 114 member nations. Intelsat owned and operated the global communications satellite system used worldwide by countries for their international and, in many instances, their domestic communications. As of 1988 the organization had 13 satellites in operation or on standby status. Circling the world above the Equator, the operational satellites provided transoceanic telephone and television services as well as international video teleconferencing and transmission of facsimile, digital data, and telex.

In November Intelsat announced that total full-time traffic had grown to 100,000 channels, double the number carried in 1981. The growth was attributed to a greater number of Earth station antennae and to circuit multiplication gained through technical innovations such as digital modulation—a method of placing digital traffic on a microwave system by transmitting the data in the form of discrete phase or frequency states determined by the digital signal. At the end of 1987 there were 758 Earth stations accessing Intelsat, providing service through 1,600 Earth-station-to-Earth-station paths.

Ground performance tests of the large new Intelsat 6 satellite were successful. Built by Hughes Electronics Corp., it incorporated many improvements over past designs. Its anticipated lifetime in orbit, for example, was doubled to 14 years. Each satellite could carry 120,000 telephone calls and at least three television channels simultaneously. In 1987 Intelsat signed a contract with Martin Marietta Corp. to launch the first two Intelsat 6 satellites in 1989 and 1990.

In November TVSat 1, Europe's first high-power, direct-broadcast satellite, was launched by an Ariane 2 from the space center in Kourou, French Guiana.

An Astro-C satellite was launched from Japan in February 1987. It carried advanced X-ray monitoring equipment for studying black holes and neutron stars.

It was designed to provide high-quality television and radio transmissions of German programming to West Germany and much of Western Europe that would complement existing ground-based transmitters and cable networks. The satellite, weighing 2,080 kg (4,580 lb), was placed in a geostationary orbit. (A satellite in a geostationary orbit travels above the Equator at the same speed as the Earth rotates.) However, one of the two solar power panels apparently failed to unfold and extend properly. Intensive study and analysis by program engineers was under way at year's end. Failure to achieve full extension of the solar panel could greatly limit the satellite's broadcasting performance or render it useless.

At Betzdorf, Luxembourg, a ground station was built to provide tracing telemetry and command services for the Astra 16-channel television satellite. The privately financed Astra was scheduled for launch in 1988 by Ariane. The Betzdorf facility would also provide transfer orbit services for Japan's Superbird communications satellites that were scheduled for launch in 1989.

Mobile communications using satellite linkage rather than ground-based radio facilities moved closer to commercial realization. Aeronautical Radio, Inc. (Arinc), planned to initiate aviation satellite service over the Atlantic and Pacific oceans by means of International Maritime Satellite Organization (Inmarsat) spacecraft. Arinc would lease Inmarsat channels via the Communications Satellite Corp. (Comsat), the U.S. member of Inmarsat (as well as of Intelsat).

An international consortium of 50 member countries, Inmarsat was similar in organization to Intelsat. It operated a system of satellite communications services to ships and offshore drilling rigs.

The first trials of telephone service by airline passengers began in October. This was a joint venture between the U.S. and Japan, utilizing an airborne antenna aboard a Japan Air Lines 747 operating weekly between Los Angeles and Tokyo. Similarly, Comsat installed pay telephones aboard several ocean cruise liners. Such telephones provided not only voice communication but also facsimile transmission, teleconferencing, and computer linkages.

Earth observation satellites. This category of applications satellites consists of three major types: weather (meteorologic), Earth resources, and military reconnaissance.

Weather satellites. Continuous global weather observations were obtained from U.S., European Space Agency (ESA), Soviet, and Japanese satellites that had been placed in geostationary orbits above the Equator. Supplementing this capability were two U.S. satellites in polar orbits.

The U.S. normally has two Geostationary Operational Environmental Satellites (GOES) stationed at longitude 75° W and longitude 135° W to provide eastern and western coverage of the Western Hemisphere. They continuously tracked the movement of clouds, weather fronts, and storms and transmitted a new image each half hour. Because of a failure in operation of GOES-East in 1984, the GOES-West satellite was moved to the east above the Equator to longitude 108° W. From that point the U.S. landmass could be satisfactorily covered. In February 1987 a new GOES-East satellite was launched successfully, and GOES-West was returned to its usual position.

Japan launched Momo, or MOS-1, a maritime observation satellite, in February. Three spectral frequencies (thermal infrared, visible, and microwave) are used in observing and transmitting images of landmasses, ocean color and temperature, and the distribution of water vapor, snow, and ice.

Earth resources and reconnaissance satellites. Photographs of the Earth were rapidly becoming more distinct and also more available to the public. The U.S. Landsat 4 and 5 images, which record in seven spectral frequencies, can resolve features on the Earth as small in diameter as 30 m. (One meter = 3.28 feet.) The ESA satellite SPOT (Satellite pour l'Observation de la Terre), launched in 1986, transmits images that have a resolution of ten meters. The difference in clarity of images is quite startling.

Houses, boats, and sometimes even airplanes can be discerned.

In the fall of 1987 the Soviet Union began to market photographs of the Earth's surface with a resolution of five meters. The U.S.S.R. State Scientific Center for Nature established Soyuz Karta, which processed and sold Earth images made with the military space camera KFA-1000. This camera was flown on both the manned Mir spacecraft and the unmanned Cosmos satellites. The images were captured on film rather than light-sensitive digital electronics.

Military reconnaissance satellites have long been the province of the U.S. and the Soviet Union. Ground resolutions of less than one meter are believed to be routine, although their actual capabilities were highly classified. During the year there were signs that this U.S.-Soviet monopoly was about to be broken. China reportedly had developed a satellite with a resolution of five meters and expected to launch it in 1988. In addition, Japan, Canada, and ESA all had the capability and, perhaps, industrial interest to produce Earth images of high resolution.

During congressional hearings on the future of the Landsat program, it was stated that commercial demand for sophisticated multispectral Landsat images had not developed. The Earth Observation Satellite Co. (Eosat), which had been chosen by the U.S. government to exploit Landsat imagery commercially, announced that it wished to launch a sensor with a resolution of five meters. Images would be marketed primarily to the news media.

A law that went into effect in August required the owner of a space-based surveillance device to obtain a license from the U.S. Department of Commerce before launch. The Department of Defense and Department of State maintained veto power over the application. In addition, the owner would have to agree to "operate the system in such a manner as to preserve and promote the national security of the United States." A fine of $10,000 per day was specified for noncompliance. At year's end it was clear that there were strongly conflicting views as to the requirement for stringent secrecy of Earth images versus an "open skies" policy.

In October a Titan 34D launched a U.S. Air Force satellite believed to be a KH-11 reconnaissance satellite. This was the first Titan launch in more than a year. On-board propulsion systems were designed to overcome atmospheric drag and alter orbital angles.

A second Titan 34D was launched in November. It carried an early-warning satellite. Two of these satellites, each carrying an infrared telescope approximately four meters long, were placed in geostationary orbit over the Eastern Hemisphere. Their purpose was to detect the launch of Soviet and Chinese ballistic missiles on the basis of heat emitted

U.S. Air Force

A Titan 34D rocket launched a U.S. Air Force KH-11 imaging reconnaissance satellite from Vandenberg Air Force Base in California in October. It was the first successful launch of a heavy booster in more than a year.

by rocket exhaust. The latest design of these heat-detection satellites carried a device capable of discriminating between rocket launches and forest fires. Laser communications transmit data from one satellite to the other and to a ground station in Australia.

A different type of reconnaissance satellite was launched by the U.S. Navy. Designated "White Cloud," this class of satellites used special radar techniques to track ships at sea.

Navigation satellites. September 1987 marked the fifth anniversary of the multinational Search and Rescue Satellite-Aided Tracking (Sarsat) program. Sponsored initially by the U.S., Canada, France, and the Soviet Union, it used U.S. and Soviet satellites to relay emergency beacons carried on aircraft and vessels. The U.K., Norway, Finland, Denmark, and Bulgaria later joined the project. With four such satellites in operation, a distress signal from anywhere on the Earth would be received and its position determined (by Doppler shift) within about two hours.

By 1988 the Sarsat/Cospas system had proved successful. Despite a high percentage of false alarms (over 90%), more than 1,000 persons in distress had been rescued through this program. Many would have died if rescue had been delayed.

—F. C. Durant III

Energy

As the 1980s were coming to a close, the energy situation throughout the world differed radically from that prevailing ten years earlier. Much greater serenity prevailed. Sudden rises in prices had given way to efforts to keep prices stable at levels well below the heights reached in the early 1980s. This actually was a return to normal. Energy shortages historically have been more of a perceived than an actual problem. The threat posed by the Organization of Petroleum Exporting Countries (OPEC) proved less severe and persistent than extreme predictions had indicated.

Both before and after the oil price rises of the 1970s, energy market conditions differed considerably among countries. Each of at least the 25 or so countries for which reasonably detailed data are readily available had unique features in its situation before the oil price rise and also had different opportunities for, and attitudes toward, adjusting to the rise. Thus, a wide range of responses to higher energy prices occurred throughout the world. No

Solar energy researcher examines a solar mirror being tested at the Sandia National Laboratories in New Mexico. The heliostat is made of a highly reflective steel membrane that is much lighter and cheaper than a glass mirror.

Sandia National Laboratories

single solution was universally adopted. Each potential alternative, however, made contributions in some places.

At least five solutions had been enthusiastically advocated. These included the development of supplies of coal, of oil from various non-OPEC sources, of natural gas, and of nuclear power. Other solutions stressed conservation in at least two senses. The first was that both high prices and technical progress would produce voluntary market actions (whether generated spontaneously or as a conscious reaction to the prices) to reduce energy use. The alternative view was that such conservation should be imposed by government regulation.

Neither form of conservation necessarily excluded the other. Many analysts argued that market solutions could fruitfully be supplemented by government regulations. However, a wide range of views prevailed on what each approach could and should do. At one extreme, those who strongly preferred voluntary market actions over government intervention believed that the best approach was simply to free all energy prices from regulation. At the other extreme, it was argued that only stringent government regulation would have any material effect.

For present purposes, a full resolution of this debate is neither feasible nor essential. The evidence does suggest that substantial market response did occur and that few of the government-decreed consumption changes were effective. Questions remain about which programs did help and whether, with better effort, government could have made a greater contribution.

In addition to the changes widely advocated when energy prices rose, various other, less widely anticipated responses occurred. Among the most critical were the restructuring of the world energy business, the development of new procedures for conducting business, and, when necessary, the modification, if not abandonment, of existing arrangements.

Energy experience. One convenient division of the world is into three sectors: (1) the members of the Organization for Economic Cooperation and Development (OECD; most of the advanced industrial countries of the non-Communist world); (2) the rest of the non-Communist world; and (3) the Communist bloc. The three areas differ greatly in their overall situations, and additional differences prevail among the regions and countries of each group. Moreover, because the OECD provides extensive data on its members' energy situation, it can be analyzed more thoroughly.

Total 1986 world energy consumption was only 28% above that of 1973 and only 9% above 1979 (*see* Table). This is the weighted average of quite different trends in each of three groups of countries described above. At one extreme, the OECD countries had an overall increase of energy use from 1973 to 1986 of about 4%. At the other extreme, the rest of the non-Communist world, which supposedly faced the greatest difficulty in securing energy, had the highest rate of increase—about 85%. The Communist countries increased energy consumption by 60%. This rise, however, occurred mainly in the two giants of the bloc; China roughly matched the non-OECD non-Communist countries with an 85% increase, while the Soviet Union's rise was 62%. The increase for other Communist countries was only 35%.

The most universal characteristic of these consumption changes was a move toward reduced dependence on oil. Oil use declined in OECD countries and elsewhere grew less rapidly than did the use of other fuels.

Substantial international differences prevailed in regard to gains of alternative fuels. Overall, the largest relative and absolute increases in fuel use in OECD countries were in nuclear power. The rate of nuclear consumption growth exceeded that of any other fuel in all three subareas of the OECD—North America, the Pacific, and Western Europe. Only in North America was the absolute increase in coal use greater than the rise in nuclear power. In Western Europe the relative and absolute use of gas rose more than that of coal. Differences also took place at the country level. In North America, for example, the U.S. increased coal consumption more than that of nuclear power; the reverse was true for Canada. In the Pacific region, Japan was the only OECD country with nuclear power.

Coal use for the OECD as a whole grew at less than 2% per year. North American growth was about 2.7%, and Pacific growth was close to the overall OECD rate. The European rise, however, was only about 0.5% per year.

Overall, OECD Europe coal use increased for electricity generation but fell for other uses. Coal use on balance grew little because increases in other countries were offset by curtailments in France, the United Kingdom, and West Germany. In all three countries, difficulties facing the steel industry reduced the use of coal. The large French nuclear program led to lower coal use in French electricity generation, and the same situation occurred in West Germany. Total British fuel use for generation of electricity in 1986 was below 1973 levels.

The gross increases in U.S. energy use were predominantly in coal and nuclear power; gas use fell more than that of oil. In absolute as well as relative terms, Japanese increases were in nuclear, gas, and coal, in that order.

In the non-Communist countries outside the OECD, oil use rose 53%. The higher percentage rises in coal and gas use were applied to a much smaller base and thus produced smaller absolute rises (of 124 million and 109 million metric tons of oil equivalent, respectively) than the rise in oil use (202 million metric tons). The biggest absolute gains in the Soviet Union were in natural gas; the natural gas increase in the rest of the Communist world was within one million metric tons of oil equivalent of the coal increase.

OPEC revisited. The biggest and one of the most misunderstood events of 1987 was the second phase of the Saudi Arabian campaign to produce a world oil situation that it would consider satisfactory. A key characteristic of the mid-1980s was the tendency of other OPEC countries to rely heavily on Saudi Ara-

World Energy Consumption by Region and Fuel
(Million metric tons of oil equivalent)

Country or region	Total 1973	Total 1986	Oil 1973	Oil 1986	Gas 1973	Gas 1986	Coal 1973	Coal 1986	Nuclear 1973	Nuclear 1986
United States	1,813	1,801	818	747	562	417	335	437	22	113
Canada	191	231	84	67	42	43	16	35	4	17
West Germany	265	269	150	120	27	40	82	77	3	27
United Kingdom	225	207	113	77	26	49	78	67	6	13
France	186	193	127	86	16	23	29	19	3	52
Italy	138	142	104	87	14	28	9	14	1	2
Rest of Western Europe	397	456	242	217	45	52	43	73	4	45
Japan	348	372	269	204	5	36	54	70	2	41
Australasia	65	100	33	31	4	18	23	41	0	0
Total OECD	3,627	3,771	1,939	1,635	742	706	669	832	44	310
Rest of non-Communist world	620	1,150	379	581	75	184	117	241	1	16
Total non-Communist world	4,247	4,920	2,318	2,216	817	890	787	1,073	45	326
Soviet Union	874	1,414	326	445	199	505	315	376	3	35
China	363	671	54	99	6	12	292	531	0	0
Other centrally planned economies	431	584	100	121	46	100	273	328	1	12
Total centrally planned economies	1,668	2,669	479	665	251	617	881	1,236	4	47
World	5,915	7,589	2,798	2,881	1,068	1,507	1,667	2,309	49	373

Note: Hydroelectric is not shown separately but is included in the total.
Source: *BP Statistical Yearbook Review of World Energy.*

Distillation plant near Ingolstadt, West Germany, produces unleaded gasoline. As West Germans have become more conscious of protecting the environment, the number who have switched to unleaded fuel has increased.

bia to maintain world oil prices. The Saudis allowed output to drop steadily in an attempt to stabilize the market, and by mid-1985 Saudi output was about half of its permitted amount.

The failure to reach a negotiated settlement with other OPEC countries led the Saudis to increase output. This, in turn, caused a fall of oil prices from $28 to $8 a barrel. The Saudis thus inspired the other OPEC countries to be more cognizant of Saudi interests. As of 1988 an uneasy truce continued, with oil prices fluctuating around $18 a barrel.

Unlike earlier Middle East upheavals, the Iran-Iraq war has tended on balance to lower rather than to raise oil prices. Initially, the war led to increased prices because of substantially decreased production. The financial problems of both countries, however, made them anxious to raise output to recover revenues. Through the first eight months of 1987, Iran was producing at levels well above those prevailing since 1980. Iraq too increased its production above the levels of the early 1980s.

While the political ramifications of the war undoubtedly aggravated the situation, economic considerations alone suggested that Saudi Arabia would be displeased by these developments. Oil traders remained uncertain about what would happen. Oil prices on the London and New York commodity exchanges have fluctuated around a fairly flat trend.

Predictions that prices surely must resume their rise sometime in the 1990s still abounded, but, nonetheless, there was little effort to develop alter-

native supply sources. Another view was that the Iran-Iraq war could not last forever and that its end would produce increased difficulties in maintaining OPEC cooperation.

Energy recontracting. Given the continued strained cooperation of OPEC countries, energy actions elsewhere remained modest. The renegotiation of deals undertaken during the height of energy concerns was increasingly important. Consumers who had contracted for resources at prices that by 1988 were higher than those readily available from other suppliers were seeking to renegotiate those contracts. Such activity was taking place in every fuel.

The most thoroughgoing changes seemed to have occurred in oil and uranium. The large private international oil companies no longer served as marketers of OPEC crude oil. The producing countries assumed that role. Long-term deals for supplies became unattractive, and oil was being traded on commodity exchanges.

Whatever might still remain mysterious about oil, it was no longer the manner in which transactions were conducted. Commercial dealings became as open, short-term, and simple as those of other traded commodities. One particularly graphic element of the process was the termination of the long-standing special arrangements between Saudi Arabia and the Aramco partners (Exxon, Chevron, Texaco, and Mobil). What long had been perceived by Aramco as an attractive way to assure supplies had become a burden to abandon.

Although open markets had not developed for uranium, slower-than-anticipated growth and ample uranium supplies led to a substantial realignment of purchasing arrangements. In particular, U.S. electric utilities shifted heavily from U.S. to foreign suppliers.

Less radical readjustments took place in coal and natural gas. Those U.S. electric utilities with unsatisfactory experiences in operating their own coal mines—such as American Electric Power, Duke Power, and Pennsylvania Power and Light—reduced their involvement in that activity. Many contracts for coal remained the subjects of contention as buyers sought many forms of redress. Many cases had arisen because the coal proved difficult to burn in the buyers' boilers. Renegotiation also was becoming important with natural gas, particularly in the U.S.

International trade in gas and coal. Important also was the development of a European natural-gas market. Increased production of natural gas in the Soviet Union and in the Norwegian and British North Sea fields provided the major impetus. Both the Soviet Union and Norway found it profitable to develop export markets for gas. In other parts of the world, the U.S. lessened but did not completely offset the impact of the decline of domestic gas output by importing from Canada and Mexico.

Through 1986 the U.S. continued to lose ground in coal exports, while Australia and South Africa gained. U.S. exports continued to fall from the peaks in 1981. Australia remained the world's leading coal exporting country, exporting the majority of its production. Colombia planned to join Australia in exporting more than it consumed domestically.

By far the largest component of the U.S. decline was reduced sales to the Japanese steel industry. Total Japanese steel industry coal use was stagnant in the 1980s. Purchases from the U.S. were cut from 22 million to 11 million metric tons, with offsetting increases divided between Canada and South Africa.

Another major U.S. market decrease was in steam coal sales to Western Europe. Total Western European steam coal imports in 1986 were about ten million metric tons above 1981, but purchases from the U.S. were down about six million. The biggest gain was by Australia—ten million metric tons.

Nuclear prospects. On the nuclear policy front, the main concern was the impact of the Chernobyl power-plant disaster in the Soviet Union. The reactions appeared to be modest, suggesting that previously developed attitudes had not been greatly altered. However, these attitudes were already quite antagonistic to nuclear power. France and Japan continued to be the only major energy-consuming countries that were unequivocally devoted to substantial new ventures into nuclear power. The reaction of the Italian public following the accident at Chernobyl confirmed that they did not share the desires of that nation's electric power industry to undertake a nuclear expansion program.

OECD forecasts indicated that, given the U.S. lead in nuclear power and the plants ordered in the early 1970s that were still under construction, the U.S. would continue to be the largest producer of nuclear-generated electricity. The largest growth was expected in Japan, which was predicted to take over second place with about 90 million metric tons of oil-equivalent in nuclear power, just ahead of France. It was estimated that West Germany would remain fourth, with perhaps half the French level.

The spread of objections to new plants continued, particularly in the U.S. New orders were nearly nonexistent; postponements continued; and efforts were increasingly exerted to develop low-cost energy alternatives.

Policy stagnation. Generally, there were few energy policy initiatives during the past year. The U.S. Department of Energy issued a policy review that failed to reconcile the conflicting views within the U.S. government. Continuation of existing policies was advocated, with some acknowledgement of the need for more import controls.

The U.S. Congress continued to be unwilling to make many changes in energy laws. For example,

efforts to remove the ban on bidding for any new federal mineral leases by a holder of any federal coal lease that remained undeveloped after ten years were unsuccessful. The Department of the Interior finished an exhaustive overhaul of coal-leasing procedures. Two manuals giving detailed instructions for conducting leases and evaluating the coal were issued to meet the requests of the Commission on Fair Market Value for Federal Coal Leasing. Interest in leasing, however, had diminished to the point that the department had no plans for reinstituting major lease sales and would limit itself to responding to individual requests for leasing. However, a new system of leasing onshore oil and gas was created.

In Great Britain Prime Minister Margaret Thatcher continued efforts to reduce the amount of government-owned industry. The gas-distribution company had already been privatized, and the government had sold more of its holdings in British Petroleum. A sale of the more recently created and once totally government-owned Britoil was under way. The government was even considering denationalizing the coal industry—historically considered the most critical nationalized industry.

—Richard L. Gordon

See also Feature Article: ENERGY FROM THE OCEAN: A RESOURCE FOR THE FUTURE.

Environment

The most important environmental phenomenon during the past year was a major change in the distribution of heat on the Earth's surface. Two aspects of the phenomenon were particularly noteworthy: the startling contrasts between the climatic changes in different regions and the discrepancy between observed conditions and the predictions from the widely publicized "greenhouse effect" warming theory.

In regard to the first aspect, a summer heat wave in southern Europe coincided with unusually cold weather in northwestern Europe. On the face of it, this appeared to be a meteorologic rather than an environmental phenomenon. As with so many environmental problems, however, the situation could be understood only through exploration of the connections between apparently unrelated events and processes. During the year a large body of documentation became available concerning the links in a chain of evidence pointing to an environmental phenomenon, deforestation, as the root cause of this climate change.

Plants, carbon dioxide, and climate. For some years climate modelers have been concerned about the effect on climate of the worldwide increase in the concentration of carbon dioxide in the atmosphere. Using admittedly oversimplified computer models, which, for example, did not deal realistically with the effects of clouds, the researchers determined that a doubling of the carbon dioxide concentration in the global atmosphere would raise the average air temperature about 2° C (3.6° F) in a belt between 10° N and 10° S. At 80° N or S the projected temperature increase was about 7° C (12.6° F). For the last two years, however, instead of a very slight temperature increase at low latitudes and a larger increase at high latitudes, there has been a startling temperature increase at many low-latitude locations and an equally startling temperature decrease at high latitudes. The changes bore no simple relationship to latitude, however; position with respect to ocean and wind currents was also clearly involved. Thus, some rather low-latitude regions experienced unusually cold weather; they included northern Florida and southeastern Australia.

The magnitude and consistency of the changes can be demonstrated most simply through the examples of four widely separated cities that represent different types of climatic regimes. Oslo, at a latitude of about 60° N, is representative of a large number of northern European high-latitude cities that were unusually cold in 1987. If the warm ocean currents flowing from south to north in the northern Atlantic Ocean were functioning normally, all such cities

Researchers at the Lawrence Berkeley Laboratory in California conduct an experiment with a fog chamber that was developed for the study of the physics and chemistry of acid rain and other aspects of air pollution.

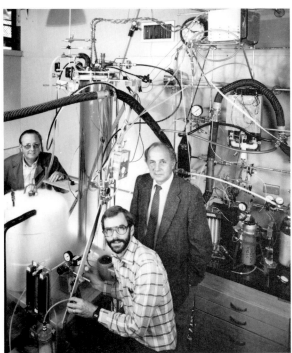

Lawrence Berkeley Laboratory, University of California/Authenticated News International

should be about 5.5° C (10° F) warmer than one would expect, given their latitude. Thus, unusually low temperatures in those cities may imply some alteration of North Atlantic ocean currents. Vancouver, B.C., at about 49° N, normally has a cool marine environment with remarkably little annual temperature change for any particular time of year. This evenness results from its location as a coastal city with a climate moderated both by ocean currents and by prevailing westerly winds that have blown over a vast expanse of ocean. Water, because of its high specific heat, tends to moderate the temperature of winds that blow over it. Sydney, Australia, an oceanside city at a latitude of about 35° S, would, from one year to another, also be expected to have a relatively even temperature for a particular time of year. Riyadh, Saudi Arabia, at 24° N, is typical of a latitudinal belt of subtropical cities that recently were unusually hot.

During 1987 Oslo varied from 4.4° to 8.9° C (8° to 16° F) below normal on many days of the year. Vancouver and Sydney were consistently much cooler than usual throughout much of the year, Vancouver by as much as 6.1° C (11° F) and Sydney by as much as 7.2° C (13° F). Riyadh, on the other hand, was as much as 5.6° C (10° F) above normal on many days of the year. These differences give no sense of the environmental consequences unless one bears in mind that the depressed temperatures occurred in cities that are normally cool and the elevated temperatures in hot cities that are typically close to the limit of conditions human beings can endure. For example, on July 25 Riyadh reached 48° C (118° F), instead of the 42° C (108° F) normal high for that date; Tunis, Tunisia, was 42° C instead of 32° C (90° F); and New Delhi, India, was 39° C (102° F) instead of 35° C (95° F).

Northern India in 1987 suffered its worst drought in decades; the yearly monsoon failed to appear. Without rain, large areas of fertile farmland crumbled into dust. In the hardest hit areas farmers did not bother to plant crops, and farm animals lay dead along the roadsides. By December hundreds of people had died in areas severely affected by drought, probably because of contaminated water and food. In October winds gusting up to 177 km/h (110 mph) swept across England and blew down 15 million trees, one-fifth of the timber in several counties. The storm was the worst in centuries. There were record low temperatures in April in the eastern and southern U.S.; a vast forest fire swept through northeastern China in May for nearly a month; and in the fall there were enormous losses of young lambs to cold weather in southeastern Australia.

Such numerous and large discrepancies between recent and normal conditions raised questions about how heat is distributed on the Earth's surface and about possible changes occurring in those mechanisms. Much new information became available on those topics during the year. When the various bits of new information are connected, a plausible theory to account for the climate change can be constructed. The elements in the causal chain are forests, cloud cover, ocean currents, and the concentration of carbon dioxide in the global atmosphere.

Perhaps as many as 2.6 billion tons of carbon are being released to the atmosphere each year because of the conversion of forested land to agriculture, principally in the tropics. This, along with global energy consumption that was increasing at about 0.9% per year, resulted in a steady annual increase in the concentration of carbon dioxide in the global atmosphere. Massive deforestation not only results in a one-time injection of carbon into the atmosphere if part of the wood is burned but also decreases the global volume of plant tissue available for converting carbon dioxide to oxygen through photosynthesis.

During the year Rosanne D'Arrigo, Gordon C. Jacoby, and Inez Y. Fung found that the seasonal growth of the combined high-latitude forests of North America and Eurasia accounted for about 30% of the mean annual fluctuation of carbon dioxide concentration at the Mauna Loa monitoring station in Hawaii. They also found that for the period 1971 to 1982 the amount of seasonal decrease in the carbon dioxide concentration in the air as measured at Point Barrow, Alaska, increased with the rate of growth of tree rings in trees from northern Canada. Such observations strengthened the argument for an inverse relationship between the total volume of tree biomass in the world and the concentration of carbon dioxide in the atmosphere.

It seemed plausible, therefore, to argue that massive deforestation in the tropics contributes to the increase in the global atmospheric concentration of carbon dioxide. That, in turn, decreases the extent to which infrared (heat) radiation from the Earth's surface can penetrate the atmosphere and radiate outward into the sky. Such an effect would be expected to cause gradual heating of the Earth's surface, at least at low latitudes, and that heating has been observed.

It is also plausible to assume that heating at low latitudes would increase the evaporation from the ocean surface, thereby increasing cloud cover; under the influence of prevailing wind systems, this cloud cover would gradually increase at high latitudes. During the year William L. Seaver and James E. Lee reported that for 44 out of 45 U.S. cities, there were fewer cloud-free days from 1950 to 1986 than there had been from 1900 to 1936. Also, a team in Hamburg, West Germany, using a computer climate model that simulated the role of cloud optical properties, found that increased carbon dioxide concentrations produced a net cooling effect at the Earth's surface. The reason is that increased cloud cover caused more of the incoming solar radiation to be reflected back into space before reaching the Earth's surface; this effect dominated the greenhouse warming effect. Because of the apparent importance of clouds in modifying the Earth's climate, an International Satellite Cloud Climatology Project was under way.

Because there has been an increase in high-latitude cloud cover in this century, one would expect to find increased high-latitude precipitation. A team headed by R. S. Bradley discovered a gradual increase in precipitation from 1850 to the present in areas between 35° and 70° N latitude and a marked recent decrease in precipitation in regions between 5° and 35° N latitude. Thus, the widely publicized recent increase in desertification in low-latitude countries and the increase in glacial cover at high latitudes could be viewed as part of a historical trend that has been in operation for about 140 years.

The argument to this point suggests that one can postulate a causal pathway from deforestation to carbon dioxide concentration and from that to cloud cover. It is possible that cloud cover is somehow connected to the next link in the argument, a major planetary ocean current explained during the year by Wallace S. Broecker. There is a global oceanic circulation pattern, in which warm, shallow currents from the northern Pacific and Indian oceans combine southeast of Africa and then move up the west coasts of Africa and Europe to a region south of Iceland. In this part of the northern Atlantic, the warm surface current gives off its heat to the westerly winds that have passed over northern Canada and become very cool. The heat exchange from the warm water to the cold winds has two effects. The heat that the westerlies pick up from the ocean makes European cities as warm as northeastern United States cities that are located at latitudes 10° farther south. Also, because the ocean current loses its heat, the water becomes denser and sinks. It then becomes a deep, cold current, which moves south in the Atlantic Ocean and east south of Africa, where it splits into two. One branch goes up the east coast of Africa to India; the other flows south of Australia and north in the Pacific Ocean toward the Bering Sea. The cold water is then heated in both the northern Indian and Pacific oceans, after which it rises and becomes the warm surface current flowing in the opposite direction, back toward the Atlantic Ocean and Iceland.

As Broecker pointed out, one reason for the present curiosity about this current is that recent research has revealed that major changes in temperature in past eras were accompanied by large changes in the global atmospheric carbon dioxide concentration. Furthermore, the changes in carbon dioxide concentration, as revealed through measurements of air trapped in the ice in deep borings made in southern Greenland, occurred in times as short as a few hundred years. This confirmed previous findings from paleoecologists studying pollen samples in borings down into the Earth, which indicated that the shift from interglacial to glacial periods in the planet's history occurred rapidly, with some estimates as low as 50 years.

When this information is put together, it appears that the concentration of carbon dioxide in the atmosphere is implicated in some type of little-understood planetary regulatory mechanism that functions as a fast-acting switch to shift the system into either of two states: glacial or interglacial. Further, based on knowledge of the temperature history of the Earth, scientists know that this mechanism acts to determine the distribution of heat between the U.S. and Europe; glacial periods are characterized by a sudden, localized cooling of the waters of northern Canada and of northern Europe. It appears that this situation results from a sudden stop of, or decreased effectiveness in, the great oceanic heat conveyor belt just described. It is possible that the marked changes in planetary heat distribution in 1987 were related to a weakening of this global ocean current system. The position of the affected cities with respect to ocean currents and the direction of the changes in temperature are consistent with that notion.

One important argument implicates forests rather than the combustion of fossil fuels as the key determinants of carbon dioxide concentration and thus as the ultimate regulators of the planetary climatic switch mechanism. There have been repeated interglacial-to-glacial cycles in planetary history, long before there was any known civilization to burn fossil fuels. Therefore, it seems plausible to postulate that the real root cause for the glacial-to-interglacial-to-glacial cycle is the nutrient state of high-latitude forests. As thousands of years pass after the last glacial period, there is a gradual leaching out of the soil mineral nutrients by rainfall and thus a gradual decline in the nutrition level of high-latitude trees; as a consequence of this, the trees are less effective in removing carbon dioxide from the atmosphere. The long-run decline in high-latitude soil fertility during interglacial periods has been documented by soil ecologists. In general, then, it is the global volume of healthy plant tissue that acts as the key determinant of the planetary atmospheric carbon dioxide concentration. This global volume can be decreased either by deforestation or by a decrease in the nutritional status of the standing vegetation.

The preceding discussion offers an alternative explanation for the mass mortality and reduced growth rate of high-latitude trees that many people have explained in terms of acid rain. Given the great eco-

nomic implications of the deforestation on the scale now occurring, one would expect considerable controversy to surround these alternative explanations. A number of recent studies by teams of scientists raised questions about the severity of the impact of acid rain and pointed out that part or all of the observed effects may have other explanations. For example, a U.S. federal task force interim report, representing five years' work of a ten-year study on the causes and effects of acid rain, concluded that relatively few lakes have been damaged by such rain and that further harm is unlikely to occur over the next few decades. It also determined that damage to human health, crops, and forests by acid rain has yet to be proved. The report received sharp criticism from some, however. They argued that the criteria used in defining acid lakes were inadequate and that data were used selectively.

Researchers also found that acid rain painted on tree seedlings in soil with inadequate nutrients actually has a beneficial effect on growth. Many studies determined that year-to-year changes in tree growth were correlated not with changes in acid rain but instead with year-to-year changes in climate.

During the year there was a curious environmental phenomenon that may be linked to the changes in ocean currents discussed above. Several hundred bottle-nosed dolphins died along the coasts of several Middle Atlantic states. Also, from June to early August there were 300 documented cases of people suffering from infections after swimming in New Jersey coastal waters. The immediate cause of these occurrences may have been discovered in December. Nine humpback whales that died at that time along Cape Cod beaches were found to have in their stomachs mackerel that contained a paralytic shellfish toxin that originates in red tide. This red discoloration of ocean water is caused by large numbers of red algae. Scientists doubted that the poison originated in the immediate area because shellfish along the New England coast had not shown signs of the toxin. This suggests that the toxin may have had its ultimate cause in some altered oceanographic conditions in the Atlantic, perhaps associated with the changed global heat distribution pattern.

AIDS. AIDS (acquired immune deficiency syndrome) has a number of curious epidemiological characteristics, which in combination make this disease an almost unprecedented threat to humanity. Also, these characteristics, when examined together with certain statistical properties of the human population, suggest that the disease may become an important factor in the balance between global population and resources. The number of diagnosed AIDS patients has a high compound growth rate; in the United States and the United Kingdom, the number of cases is almost doubling annually.

Billboard in Delaware warns against AIDS (acquired immune deficiency syndrome). The disease could become an important factor in the balance between the Earth's population and its resources.

Several factors were conspiring to veil the true severity of the epidemic. Governments and families often responded to the stigma associated with the disease by being secretive. Also, AIDS increases the number of cases of a wide variety of other diseases, such as tuberculosis, thus creating the possibility of misdiagnosis of cause of death.

A subject of great concern among scientists in 1987 was the accurate determination of the incubation period of the disease—the time interval from infection to diagnosis. By late August G. F. Medley, R. M. Anderson, D. R. Cox, and Lynne Billard had reported that the incubation time of AIDS depended on age and sex. The average incubation period was about two years for children under five years old at time of infection, 8.2 years for people from 5 to 59 years of age, and 5.5 years for those 60 and older; for females of all ages it was 8.8 years, and for males 5.6 years.

The implication of these facts is that for the public at large the perception of the severity of the epidemic at any time is a response to the risk that AIDS actually had represented about seven years earlier. Therefore, for each demographic group that becomes infected, the response to date has been grossly inadequate, given the actual severity of the threat. Furthermore, surveys have made it clear that the teenage and post-teenage groups within the general, heterosexual population underestimate the severity of the potential threat and that their present sexual behavior patterns make them vulnerable to the disease.

Two behaviors increase the likelihood of succumbing to AIDS, all other factors being equal: the number of sexual partners and the failure to use either birth control devices or spermicidal ointments. It is reasonable to expect, therefore, that should the infection become widely spread throughout the heterosexual population, the likelihood that any given individual would become infected would be statistically related to the probability that that person would be involved in the conception of a child in a given year.

The significance of these remarks becomes clear when birthrates and death rates within different demographic groups are examined. The U.S. National Center for Health Statistics uses a single statistic, the intrinsic rate of natural increase, which combines the information from birthrate and death rate data. It describes the population growth rate that would eventually result if present birthrates and death rates for each year of life were to continue indefinitely. Surprisingly, that rate has been negative for the overall U.S. population since 1972. However, the rate is very different in different demographic groups. For example, the intrinsic rate of natural increase is still positive but has a declining trend for nonwhites.

Within each demographic group, the average birthrates are a composite of a large proportion of that group with low birthrates and a small proportion with very high birthrates. Thus, among whites, about 69% of all women intend to have two or fewer births in their lifetimes; 9% expect to have four or more. Clearly, the average birthrate for the entire group is being disproportionately affected by a small proportion of the total number of women. Therefore, the appearance of vigorous population growth in large demographic groups may be illusory, resulting from the averaging of statistics for a majority subgroup that is actually declining with a small minority group that is rapidly increasing in numbers.

Any phenomenon that decreases the population growth rates of demographic subgroups differentially, such that the intensity of the decrease is proportional to the current population growth rate, would soon have a dramatic impact on the absolute and relative population growth rates of nations. AIDS is clearly such a phenomenon. Given the likely prognosis for the disease, imminent population decline will probably be a major concern before the end of the century.

Agroecology and farming systems research. Few topics receive so little discussion, relative to their importance, as does the present situation in world agriculture. Two problems in this area were becoming very serious. In some developed countries, such as the U.S., agriculture, as presently conducted, was becoming permanently unprofitable. In other countries, such as Bangladesh, agricultural productivity was running into a variety of limits as population increase gradually overwhelmed both the number of hectares of land suitable for agriculture and the inherent productivity of each hectare of soil.

The most immediate problem confronting many farmers at present is avoiding bankruptcy; this suggests the notion of evaluating agricultural success relative to the amount of money required each year just to pay the interest on old debt and avoid foreclosure. Accordingly, a useful measure of agricultural profitability is the net income of farm operators from farming, expressed as a proportion or multiple of the annual interest on debt. After World War II, when U.S. agriculture was very profitable, that ratio was about 42 for the entire national agricultural sector. By 1983 the ratio was 0.607. That is, for the entire U.S. agricultural sector in 1983, net income was only 61% of the amount required for paying the interest on old farm debt. This rather astonishing finding suggests that the present view of the appropriate way to do farming in the U.S. is erroneous.

In a monograph published by the World Resources Institute, Washington, D.C., the authors noted that future historians of agriculture would perceive the last half of the 20th century as a curious developmental detour, characterized by sizable energy subsidies, resource-depleting practices, and a constricted research focus. The measure of performance was limited to short-term increases in crop output, overlooking net economic gain as a goal. Productivity had commonly come to be thought of as crop yield per hectare rather than as output per unit input. In fact, according to the analysis, profitability could be increased enormously by reducing inputs of energy and chemicals purchased off the farm and by increasing the "information content" of agroecosystems: the variety of species being grown, the ways in which the crops are distributed geographically, and the sophistication of farm-management strategies.

A few examples from the documents published during the year help explain these somewhat abstract concepts. One approach to increasing the information content in agriculture is polyculture—mixing crop and animal production units in complex, interrelated systems. Exemplifying this are the Javanese home gardens of Indonesia. These plots resemble natural forests; one survey of 351 gardens discovered 607 plant species, organized vertically as well as horizontally to take advantage of all available sunlight.

Such mixtures perform best when different species complement one another as to growth rhythms, rooting depths, and the use of nutrients and light. In Java the gardens are organized so that there are four distinct canopy layers, which together intercept as much as 99.75% of the sunlight, leave almost none of the soil uncovered, and therefore almost eliminate soil erosion. One way of comparing the relative effectiveness of different agricultural strategies is the land-equivalent ratio, which is the relative amount of land planted to a monoculture that would be required for achieving the same yield as a mixture. S. R. Gliessman and his colleagues discovered, for example, that 1.73 ha of land would have to be planted in corn to produce as much food as one hectare planted with a mixture of corn, beans, and squash. (One hectare equals approximately 2.5 ac.)

The idea of multicropping can be extended to systems in which trees are interspersed with crop plants. Where rows of tree windbreaks protect crops, grain yield per kilogram of water used is more than 40% higher than in open areas. By planting belts of trees around hillsides, alternating with hillside-encircling strips of crop plants, farmers can minimize the effect of soil erosion on steep slopes.

New agroecological research was pointing toward a more systemic approach to agriculture, in which upland and lowland management practices are viewed as interdependent system components. In many areas of the world, lowland agriculture depends heavily on the washing of nutrients from uplands for its fertility. Over the long term this situation would undermine both systems; the uplands would degrade so that ultimately they could no longer retain water or soil, and the consequence for the lowlands would be flooding and the siltation of irrigation systems. Also, contamination of drinking water by pest-control agricultural chemicals was incompatible with the health of people supposedly benefiting from the pest control.

This systemic view of agriculture and agricultural research was exposing some odd phenomena. For example, it can cost up to twice as much to transport fertilizer from an African port to the interior of that continent as it does to ship the material from the U.S. to Africa. Thus, the cost and uncertainty of supply of external inputs, as well as ecological considerations, favor using local biologic sources of nutrients and pest-control agents.

The present crisis in world agriculture has come

about for two basic reasons. First, for the past half century almost all agriculture and agricultural research has been focused on increasingly energy-intensive and high-input strategies. Those strategies have recently been carried to the less developed world as well. Second, government has provided various forms of encouragement to farmers to adopt those strategies, including subsidizing the prices of chemical fertilizers and pesticides. The problem is that government policy has distorted the true long-run economic costs and benefits of various alternate strategies and made it excessively difficult to discern the true long-run optimal economic strategy. Now that the economic consequences of following the policy encouraged by government are becoming evident, government is leaving the farmers to absorb the costs themselves. The result is that in many places, and for many crops, the average farmer is operating at a loss in a typical year.

There is, however, a strategy that results in profitable farming. This is to produce all inputs on the farm that can be made most economically there, even including electricity.

—Kenneth E. F. Watt

Food and agriculture

The plight of the U.S. farmer, characterized during the middle third of the 1980s by substantial numbers of farm bankruptcies, had been significantly ameliorated by 1988 through stabilized commodity prices, as well as by serious international negotiations among the major international traders of agricultural and forest commodities. Key among these were the European Communities, the U.S.S.R., Australia, New Zealand, Japan, Canada, Brazil, and Argentina.

Field experiments in biotechnology were begun in 1987 and showed considerable economic promise. They also caused concern, especially among citizens with limited knowledge of the potential, risks, and scientific security measures normally associated with such experiments. There was evidence that people in their 20s, although more knowledgeable than their predecessors about diet and health issues, do not tend to change their eating habits accordingly, preferring to postpone such concerns until later in their lives.

Agriculture

The 1988 agricultural outlook was for smaller crop harvests worldwide but with increased availability of animal products and with somewhat increased demand. Adverse weather in a number of areas, plus reduced plantings, cut production of several crops in 1987–88, notably corn, rice, wheat, and cotton.

As a result, crop prices were expected to rise while the price for animal products, in general, decreased. U.S. farmers would see increased receipts from crops but lower receipts from livestock and poultry. Farm income would continue to be supported by government programs, although in 1987 crop subsidies, amounting to $23 billion, were more than $3 billion below the record support values of 1986. Cash farm receipts in 1987 totaled a record $57 billion, but a small reduction was expected in 1988. Farmers' debt burdens were lower and their asset values were more stabilized than in recent years.

Because of lower meat and poultry prices, retail prices for food were expected to climb more slowly in 1988—only 2–4%. Total beef production probably would decline 4–5% in 1988, continuing the trend begun in 1987. However, supplies of competing meats were expected to boost total meat production to yet another record level; the U.S. Department of Agriculture (USDA) predicted that the increase would probably be the largest since 1975–76. Part of this increase would be from pork production, causing hog prices to average around $40 per hundredweight. The egg and poultry industries could be facing hard times because of large total meat supplies. The broiler industry would be particularly hard hit because it was in a heavy expansion phase.

With smaller world crop supplies and increased consumption, global trade in farm products was expanding, and the U.S. share was increasing. The value of U.S. farm exports in fiscal 1988 was expected to be about $4 billion above the 1987 total of $28 billion. However, this was still substantially below the record $44 billion of 1981. In volume terms, world trade in wheat and flour would probably rise by 25%, coarse grains by 10%, and cotton by about 12%. Corn acreages and production were down, but higher yields for wheat and soybeans offset acreage reductions.

From test tube to table. Research scientists continued to search for techniques that would enable producers to give consumers not only what they want but what they need to maintain good health. At the University of Wisconsin at Madison, researchers were using a method called supercritical fluid extraction to remove cholesterol from foods. Carbon dioxide is compressed to the point where it behaves somewhat like a cross between a gas and a liquid. A freeze-dried or spray-dried food is then heated to a specified temperature, and the compressed carbon dioxide is run through the vessel, dissolving most of the cholesterol. At Iowa State University researchers were working on an enzyme that could be sprinkled on foods to reduce the cholesterol level. Workers at several universities, in cooperation with the USDA's Agricultural Research Service, produced a "super-carrot" that looks and tastes like an ordinary carrot

A plant physiologist attaches a temperature sensor to an orange blossom inside a cold chamber as part of a study to determine at what temperature plant tissue freezes in relation to surrounding air temperatures.

but contains 50% more beta carotene, used by the body to produce vitamin A.

Workers at the University of Georgia were developing new products from the peanut, including a highly nutritious noodle made from peanut flour combined with wheat and cowpea flour and a tofu-like spread that has no cholesterol, is high in protein, and comes in a variety of flavors. Also being developed was a fermented peanut product that looks, tastes, and smells like yogurt and can be used as a substitute for dairy products.

Low-input agriculture. One of the most promising areas of agricultural research is variously called low-input or sustainable agriculture. The techniques involved are closely allied to those of small-scale agriculture and what has been called organic farming. The common denominator among them is an effort to reduce the cost of inputs; *e.g.*, chemical fertilizers and pesticides. The Food Security Act of 1985 allowed the USDA to launch a program focusing on low-input agriculture and related fields, and the 1988 Appropriations Act provided money for conducting research in these areas. Many agricultural experiment stations, such as the one at the University of Nebraska, have conducted related programs for a number of years, and the University of California

began a new program in 1986 addressing sustainable agriculture. For several years the Rodale Institute, a privately funded research effort in Pennsylvania, has dedicated its activities to these important areas. The Agricultural Research Service has had a resident scientist at the Rodale farm for some time. Using nature is the key to success in low-input agriculture. Integrated pest management, in which the use of chemicals is minimized in favor of natural predators and other biological controls, appropriate and well-timed cultural practices, and careful selection of seed stocks are all part of a systems approach to agriculture in which costs are decreased.

After decades of emphasis on increasing the size of agricultural units to gain economies of scale, one of the notable phenomena of the 1980s was a substantial rise in the number of small farm units. Small farms were proliferating at a much faster rate than large farms, and there was a concomitant decrease in the number of medium-sized farms. A related development was the return of home gardens and hobby gardens as prominent features of American life. (Their popularity had never really declined in the rest of the world.) The net result was that environmentalists and agriculturalists were meeting on common ground. A new scientific publication, *American Journal of Alternative Agriculture*, was one outgrowth of the increased interest in this area.

Alternative crops. Another effect of the Food Security Act of 1985 was the spurring of the search for alternative crops in the United States. There had been a major reversal in the trend, prominent in the 1960s, and '70s, toward concentration on a small number of agricultural products in any given part of the U.S. In 1987–88 major demonstration projects, jointly supported by industry, the state agricultural experiment stations, and the USDA, involved several commodities.

Kenaf, a bamboo-like product, can be used to produce a high-quality paper that takes up less ink than paper made from wood pulp and requires one-third the amount of acid to break down the lignin in the paper-making process. Kenaf was used to produce the paper for a full run of the *Bakersfield Californian* newspaper. It can be grown in tropical or semitropical environments and is ideally suited for the southern tier of the U.S. Utilization of kenaf could lower U.S. imports of wood pulp.

Commercial production of guayule, a natural rubber product used in World War II to produce some tires for the war effort, was under way on the Gila River Indian Community Reservation in Arizona. A plant facility had been constructed jointly by the U.S. Department of Defense, the USDA, and the Firestone Tire and Rubber Co. High-quality tires produced in this plant would be used for planes on U.S. aircraft carriers. Crambe, a low-growing broadleaf plant, and winter rapeseed are sources of erucic acid, a chemical used in the manufacture of plastics. A demonstration project being conducted in Iowa was funded by the USDA and carried out in cooperation with Iowa State University, Kansas State University, and the University of Missouri.

The striped bass, native to the estuaries of the U.S. East Coast, are dying out, and fishing for them has been restricted by law. However, a cross between the striped bass and the white bass provides a hybrid that does well in fresh, brackish, or salt water and can be raised in ponds or estuaries. A demonstration project conducted at Chesapeake Bay on Maryland's Eastern Shore was being funded by the USDA and involved the Maryland Agricultural Experiment Station and the Campbell Soup Co. The project would demonstrate how farmers can use farm ponds and other water areas to raise the fish for market.

Revolution in biology. In 1987 the Smithsonian Institution's National Museum of American History in Washington, D.C., opened a new exhibit, scheduled to be made permanent, entitled "The Search for Life." Focusing on the effect of science on agriculture and health, the exhibit, designed by Peter Wexler of New York, commemorated the centennials of the state agricultural experiment stations and the National Institutes of Health (NIH). It depicted the work of Thomas Hunt Morgan in proving that genes were real; of Linus Pauling, George Beadle, and Edward Tatum on the relationship of genes to protein formation; of James Watson and Francis Crick on the architecture of DNA (deoxyribonucleic acid); of Marshall Nienberg, Gobind Khorana, and Robert Holley in deciphering the genetic codes; and of Paul Berg, Stanley Cohen, and Herbert Boyer in developing recombinant DNA technology.

The exhibit also told the story of the social controversy that accompanied the revolution in the biologic sciences, from the eugenics movement of the early 20th century to recent debates over altering human inheritance. It emphasized new genetic technologies in agriculture that make it possible to bypass natural sexual reproduction and cross the barriers between species. Biotechnology contains keys to understanding herbicide resistance, nitrogen fixation, and the mechanism of photosynthesis in plants. Altering crop characteristics, improving the nutrient content of common foods, improving plant and animal fertility, and creating new life forms are within reach of agricultural science.

The exhibit came at a significant time, when U.S. citizens were asking whether scientific safeguards on biotechnological research were adequate. In 1987 the National Research Council of the National Academy of Sciences published *Agricultural Biotechnology: Strategies for National Competitiveness,* which identified the concerns raised by the

Agricultural Research Service, USDA

Nitrogen-rich roots of Nitro alfalfa (right) are significantly larger than those of a conventional alfalfa variety. Nitro, an annual, fixes almost twice as much nitrogen from the atmosphere in the soil as do other alfalfas.

new techniques and proposed ways to alleviate them while, at the same time, achieving the commercial successes those techniques promised.

Meanwhile, research conducted by Advanced Genetic Sciences in cooperation with the University of California on the so-called ice minus bacteria, *Pseudomonas syringae* with gene deletion, was subjected to a series of vandal attacks by a group calling itself the Mindless Thugs Against Genetic Engineering. The purpose of the experiments was to duplicate under field conditions what had been demonstrated in the greenhouse, namely, that fruit and vegetable crops can survive at temperatures well below freezing if the naturally occurring *Pseudomonas syringae* is replaced with the genetically altered variety. The altered variety does not withstand other environmental stresses as well as the natural form, does not carry over well into a second year, and does nothing to precipitate pathogenecity; thus, its safety is assured. Nevertheless, the issues raised by biotechnology will be prominent for years to come. Governments, particularly those in developed countries, have been working to coordinate plans for overseeing these new scientific developments.

—John Patrick Jordan

See also Feature Article: "MICROLIVESTOCK"— WHEN SMALLER IS BETTER.

Nutrition

Since the 1940s the "ideal" body for women has become significantly thinner. Pressure on women to diet has been intensified by a tendency of some women to overestimate their own size and to underestimate the body size of others. Misperceptions of this kind, especially among young women, play a role in such eating disorders as anorexia nervosa, in which the victim will not eat, and bulimia nervosa, characterized by food binges followed by induced vomiting or evacuation. This pathological concern over body shape and image stems from a culturally and socially defined standard of beauty, which may have little relation to function and health. Both men and women, by holding to an ideal of the opposite sex that does not accord with function and health, may encourage eating disorders. However, women comprise 90% of persons with eating disorders, and most firmly believe that their aberrant dietary practices will lead to beauty and success.

Dietary guidelines for Americans. The 1985 Dietary Guidelines for Americans endorsed by the American Heart Association and other health-oriented organizations recommended the avoidance of "too much fat, saturated fat and cholesterol." The explanation states that calories from fat should be reduced to no more than 30% of total caloric intake, with less than one-third of those calories coming from saturated fat. Cholesterol intake should not exceed 300 mg per day. By contrast, in the Lipid Research Clinics Prevalence Study carried out in 1972 and 1975, fat actually accounted for 38–40% of calories consumed by the participants.

People who eat out daily must be careful to avoid a high saturated fat intake. A knowledgeable diner should choose foods with a low fat content and avoid commercially fried foods, rich pastries, and frozen desserts such as rich, nutty ice creams. Among frozen desserts, sherbet contains 1 to 2% fat, ice milk 2 to 7%, ice cream 8 to 12%, and "gourmet" ice cream 16%. Half a cup of gourmet ice cream has 309 calories, 53% of which are from fat. Such foods should be eaten only rarely and in small quantities.

Chicken and fish are recommended as low-fat substitutes for red meat, and some fast-food restaurants have added chicken and fish dishes to their menus, at least partly in an effort to attract health-conscious diners. In these dishes, however, the chicken and fish are commonly coated with a fat-absorbent breading and fried in deep fat composed of beef tallow, palm and coconut oils, and other fats that do not smoke or deteriorate at high cooking temperatures. To determine the fat content of these foods, *Science Digest* commissioned Frank Sacks of the Harvard Medical School to analyze chicken, fish, and French fries served at four popular fast-food outlets—McDonald's, Burger King, Howard Johnson's, and Kentucky Fried Chicken.

Sacks concluded that the "fatty acid profile" of the food from all four restaurants was more like that of beef than chicken or fish. The advantage of chicken and fish over red meat was lost in the cook-ing process. Beef tallow was the cooking medium for McDonald's Chicken McNuggets and Filet-O-Fish as well as for Burger King's Chicken Sandwich and Whaler. Neither Howard Johnson's nor Kentucky Fried Chicken used beef tallow, but they did use palm oil and a highly saturated vegetable oil. *Science Digest* quoted a McDonald's representative who defended the cooking medium used "because it produces the highest quality finished product and the best-tasting one." In November 1987 the Center for Science in the Public Interest urged restaurants to stop using beef fat for frying or at least to list it as an ingredient.

Normally food requires from four to six hours for digestion, a fact that influences the pattern of daily meals in our culture. The time required for digesting a meal varies somewhat depending on the amount of fiber, the carbohydrate, protein, and fat content, and the total amount of food eaten. Carbohydrates, including starches and sugars, are digested most rapidly, but when fat is added, the time for digestion is increased. The same is true for protein foods such as meat and eggs, which take longer to digest when they are cooked in fat. High-melting-point fats that contain saturated fatty acids digest very slowly, especially when combined with protein as in a fried steak. This may account for a lack of appetite in children who have eaten a fried hamburger, French fries, ice cream, or fried pie for lunch. Providing the correct proportions of carbohydrate, protein, and fat in each meal is essential.

Eating the day's food requirements at three or four conveniently spaced meals contributes to a healthful pattern of living. Skipping meals or eating highly disproportionate amounts at irregularly spaced meals can interfere with adequate nutrition as well as general health—"starve and stuff" can damage health and performance. A wise dietary guide is "Enough of a good thing is enough." Too much of one food, however healthful, can result in the omission of another essential type of food.

Cholesterol, fat, and heart care. The *Journal of the American Medical Association* (*JAMA*) reported that U.S. mortality rates from cardiovascular disease had declined about 30% in the past 25 years. This was attributed to "decreases in blood pressure, fewer smokers, and improvements in medical care." Since the early 1960s it had been known that elevated serum cholesterol levels lead to coronary heart disease, and in 1984 a lowered serum cholesterol level was shown to correlate with lowered cardiovascular disease mortality and morbidity (*JAMA* 253:2087, 1985). Three nationwide surveys of the U.S. population taken between 1960 and 1980 showed that mean serum cholesterol levels had declined over that period. Analysts suggested that changes in dietary and life-style factors could be responsible. An estimated decrease of 1% in blood cholesterol level corresponds to a 2% reduction in the incidence of coronary heart disease. Clinical guidelines from the NIH support the concept that lowered serum cholesterol levels, even in patients who are at moderate risk (those with levels of 200 to 240 mg per deciliter [mg/dl]), will reduce the risk of heart attack.

Cholesterol levels have become a public concern because "millions of Americans are at risk." Assuming that cholesterol at 200–239 mg/dl is borderline, an estimated 40 million Americans aged 20 to 74 have moderate to high cholesterol levels. Health groups such as the National Heart, Lung and Blood Institute and the American Heart Association have urged doctors to be aggressive in prescribing diets as the first line of control for high cholesterol levels. In some people, however, therapeutic diets that reduce fat and cholesterol intake may need to be supplemented with cholesterol-lowering drugs. After an 18-month study, a 22-member panel recommended that people be tested to determine the type of diet they require and whether drug therapy should be considered. Patients with high cholesterol levels should allow from three to six months on a controlled diet for blood levels to become normal. If improvement is not sufficient, drug therapy should probably be started. (Of course, these are general guidelines, and each person must be treated individually.)

Guidelines for healthful eating include the following: (1) attain and maintain normal weight (controlling calorie intake to balance a planned activity schedule); (2) reduce fat in the diet to no more than 30% of the total calories (fat has 9 cal per gram or 100 cal per level tablespoonful; many foods are almost pure fat, *e.g.*, margarine, butter, mayonnaise, and gravy); (3) decrease intake of saturated fats (all animal fats, hydrogenated shortenings, and margarines as well as palm and coconut oils); (4) lower cholesterol intake to less than 300 mg per day.

Nondigestible dietary components. In the last ten years the number of publications dealing with nondigestible components in the diet has increased 40-fold. The general conclusion is that nondigestible residues may be important for normal healthy functioning of the gastrointestinal tract. As a result, dietary fiber has become a popular topic for investigation, and a whole new assortment of dietary and health products that emphasize fiber content have appeared on the market.

Nondigestible components include such substances as cellulose, hemicellulose, pectins, and lignin, which contribute no calories or other nutrients. Nonetheless, they are important to health. One function of fiber is to attract water in the digestive tract and thus keep the mass of material soft for excretion as fecal matter. Fiber also helps to exercise the muscles in the walls of the intestines so they remain toned and

"No, you're not too late. Cathy's just beginning to put calcium into perspective."

active and resistant to disease. Food residues must move rapidly and efficiently through the gastrointestinal tract to avoid irritation of the intestinal wall.

At the University of Kentucky, James Anderson was able to reduce the insulin requirements of diabetic patients by increasing their dietary fiber intake. The American Dietetic Association stressed the inclusion of fiber in the diet by including information about it in the Diabetic Exchange Lists. Soluble fiber, found in oats, beans, and many vegetables and fruits, has been found effective in lowering both cholesterol and triglyceride levels in the blood, thereby reducing the risk of heart disease. All types of fiber are helpful in weight control since foods with fiber require more chewing, thus taking longer to eat, and increase the volume of food with noncaloric material. Studies at Michigan State University and Hunter College in New York City found that dieters who ate a high-fiber bread lost more weight than a control group that ate ordinary bread.

Most foods that are high in fiber also contain a good supply of starch rather than sugar. Pasta, especially when it has been enriched with iron and multiple B-vitamins, was emerging as a recommended health food. It contains plenty of starch, some protein, and no cholesterol, saturated fat, or sodium. Pasta varieties incorporating vegetables such as spinach, carrots, or tomatoes or made with whole wheat flour have been introduced. New methods of cooking are recommended using limited water to produce tender but firm pasta with no rinsing or leftover cooking water.

Mineral elements and health. Minerals—the so-called trace elements—comprise less than one-hundreth of 1% of the total body weight of an adult, but they are indispensable to life. Required amounts for five—iron, zinc, iodine, phosphorus, and magnesium—are included, along with calcium, in the Recommended Dietary Allowances. Six elements had estimated "safe and adequate ranges" in the diet as of 1980, and the other five to seven were known to be essential, but no amount had been established. The inclusion of all 14 to 16 elements in the daily food intake is assured if the diet includes an assortment of foods that retain their "natural composition" and have not been refined or purified.

A mineral deficiency problem that was receiving wide attention involved calcium, which is required throughout life, especially by women. Lack of calcium has been implicated in osteoporosis, or softening of the bones, in postmenopausal women. Calcium intakes of 1 to 1.5 g per day are required. A wide variety of calcium compounds was being marketed, but the solubility and absorption of calcium taken in this manner was uncertain, and it was believed that calcium obtained from food was absorbed more readily. Milk products are the major food sources of calcium, with smaller amounts obtainable from assorted other foods. Exercise and calcium were considered to be major factors in the maintenance of strong bones.

—Mina W. Lamb

Life sciences

Among the most significant developments in the life sciences during the past year were new findings concerning the relationship between plants and atmospheric conditions, a discovery that shed new light on human evolution, the use of recombinant DNA technology to clone a gene that codes for a cellular receptor of the AIDS (acquired immune deficiency syndrome) virus, and the discovery that sulfur-oxidizing bacteria play an important role in recycling sulfur in the marine environment.

Botany

Among the many interesting events in botany during the year were the development of additional ways to engineer plant DNA (deoxyribonucleic acid), elucidation of the structure of the photosynthetic action center, consideration of the feedback that plants may have on atmospheric conditions, and the inclusion of new natural areas into federal systems.

Forests. Additions to both the U.S. National Park and National Forest systems were made during the past three years. Great Basin National Park was dedicated Aug. 15, 1987, as the 49th national park. The only national park in Nevada and the first new one in the 48 coterminous states in the past 15 years, Great Basin included three stands of the bristlecone pine *Pinus aristata*. These were among the oldest living things; some were thought to be 4,500 years old. Because of their age, bristlecones are invaluable

for tree-ring studies that provide important information for climatology and archaelogical dating.

The newest national forest had a much different history. Finger Lakes National Forest in north central New York state comprised 5,200 ha (13,000 ac) that had been under multiple-use management since the Revolutionary War. It was part of the larger area of the Finger Lakes region that was settled by Revolutionary War veterans and had been farmed nearly continuously until large parts were abandoned in the early 1900s. The portion destined to become the national forest was assembled between 1938 and 1941 by a federal resettlement agency and was administered by various governmental bodies until its new status was conferred in 1985. Its distinction might not be only in its return to natural area status with multiple use under U.S. Forest Service policy; it might also be one of the last national forests created in the U.S.

Most people are aware of the devastation brought to forests and other ecosystems by uncontrolled burning, yet relatively few are aware of the wide-ranging effects of drought. The figures for the "Great Drought of 1986" became available during 1987. Particularly for the southeastern part of the U.S., the results were devastating. The 1986 drought extended from Mississippi through all of the southeastern states and north to Delaware. A prolonged period of limited rainfall was followed by record-high summer temperatures and a continued lack of rain. As much as 50.8 to 76.2 cm (20 to 30 in) below normal were experienced in some areas.

The effect of the drought on trees was great. The most devastated were first-year seedlings, planted by the millions during the planting season of December 1985–April 1986. Authorities estimated that 227 million seedlings on private nonindustrial lands died, 27% of the drought area's annual planting. Industrial forests fared somewhat better because they were managed, yet an estimated 20% of the 700 million seedlings were lost there. On a state-by-state basis Kentucky and Tennessee lost the largest percentage of seedlings (50%), Alabama lost the greatest number of plants (67.2 million), and Georgia will have the highest replanting cost ($8,125,000).

In regard to established trees the kinds of damage to be expected were decreased Christmas tree crops, decreased growth in mature lumber trees with delayed harvesting, increased vulnerability to disease and insects, increased vulnerability to air-pollution stress, and thinner stands with decreased yield. All of these were expected to result in increased costs of forest products as many as 40 years into the future.

Plant biochemistry. Ozone is an important gas in the atmosphere, where it resides in a large layer and absorbs harmful external radiation. Recent depletion of this layer over Antarctica and, potentially, over other areas led to concern among scientists about the causes and effects of such a depletion. Some called for worldwide action to attempt correction.

Less obvious attention was being given to the effects of ozone near the Earth's surface, although it was pointed out that ozone can be detrimental to living things. That it is harmful to plants had been known for some time, but as of 1988 no one had yet analyzed in detail the type and extent of damage that might be sustained. For instance, some plants are more susceptible to sporadic ozone fluctuations than to regular exposure. Horst Mehlhorn and Alan Wellburn of the University of Lancaster, England, suggested that the plant itself may make the difference. They found that pea seedlings release ethylene and suffer damage upon one exposure to ozone after being raised in clean air. Also, they found that similar seedlings, exposed every day to ozone, produce little ethylene and suffer little leaf injury. When plants were sprayed with an ethylene inhibitor and then exposed to ozone, they suffered far less injury than if they had not been sprayed. The investigators could not determine the exact causal relationship of ethylene to ozone, but they suggested that ozone reacts with ethylene to cause the plant injury.

The complex process of photosynthesis involves membrane-ordered photosystems of molecules capable of converting the light of the Sun into chemical energy. The substances acting as raw materials and products of this complex process enter and leave the membrane or at least relate to its surface. Operating in tandem within the membranes of green plants are two kinds of photosystem that are arranged efficiently for the production of ATP (adenosine triphosphate) and NADPH (nicotine adenine dinucleotide phosphate). These high-energy molecules provide the driving power for the part of photosynthesis that incorporates carbon dioxide and produces the chemical building blocks for other, more complex, biologic molecules.

It has been accepted for some time that each photosystem has within it specially constructed molecules of chlorophyll that can be made highly reactive, thus collecting energy from the remainder of the bulk chlorophyll that has absorbed the light. These reaction centers, as they are called, provide energetic electrons that flow through a chain of compounds within the photosystem. At strategic points in the pathway, some of the energy is used to produce the ATP and NADPH.

Of particular interest during the past year was the isolation of the reaction center, up to that time quite resistant to description. Many researchers had worked on the problem, but it remained for two Japanese investigators to report their techniques for visualizing the complex. At the International Congress of Photosynthesis Research held in Prov-

idence, R.I., in 1986, Osamu Namba and Kimiyuki Satoh of Okayama University presented evidence that they had isolated a molecular complex that produces electrons in the same way that all reaction centers do. Further work by these and other researchers was reported at a meeting at Okazaki, Japan, in the spring of 1987. It has been generally accepted that the reaction center is a complex of very specific proteins and a cytochrome. (A cytochrome is an enzyme that functions as a transporter of electrons to molecular oxygen by undergoing alternate oxidation and reduction.)

How do some plants grow at low temperatures when most plants cannot? Plant physiologists suggest that in the low-temperature varieties there is a higher lipid content and degree of unsaturation of fatty acids (more double bonding in the hydrocarbon chains), which may relate to the necessity of greater fluidity of membranes at colder temperatures. Albert-Jean Dorne and his associates from the University of Grenoble, France, studied a chilling-resistant plant to determine whether such a pattern would be found. They located this plant on an island of the Kerguelen Archipelago in the southern Indian Ocean where the flora is unique. It is now accepted from pollen studies that certain species survived glaciation of the Pleistocene Epoch and have been isolated in this subantarctic location for a long time. Most of the species have not survived until the present, but at least one, the Kerguelen cabbage (*Pringlea antiscorbutica*), is believed to be a true relic and a good candidate for having chilling-resistant characteristics.

The researchers studied the Kerguelen cabbage to determine whether it fit the usually accepted model for plants growing at low temperatures. To their surprise it did not. The polar-lipid composition and the fatty-acid pattern of the leaves are nearly the same as those found in plants growing in much higher temperatures. Therefore, it appeared that the criteria of higher lipid content and greater degree of unsaturation in fatty acids are not necessary for acclimation of all plants to growing at low temperatures.

Plants and the atmosphere. Well-documented increases in atmospheric levels of carbon dioxide challenged scientific prophets to predict what will happen to climate and thus to plants. The accepted annual increase was about 1.5 parts per million (ppm) from a base level of 348 ppm. Botanists expected that the increase in carbon dioxide should have some effect on plant growth. An investigator from the University of Cambridge reported that the density of stomata (minute openings through which gaseous interchange takes place) of leaves of several tree species had been decreasing for two centuries, the same period during which carbon dioxide concentrations were increasing. F. I. Woodward studied herbarium specimens of eight temperate woody species and noted a 40% reduction in stomatal density. Because stomata also control water loss from leaves, Woodward concluded that there had also been a trend toward efficiency in the use of water in plants. In this way not only would the growth rate of plants be increased but the atmosphere could be affected by the change in water-use efficiency as well as by the increase in carbon dioxide.

It is possible that plants influence atmospheric conditions much more than was thought. Robert Charlson and Stephen Warren (University of Washington), James Lovelock (Coombe Mill Experimental Station, Launceston, England) and Meinrat Andreae (Florida State University) concluded that plants may influence cloud formation high over the ocean. Certain marine algae are known to excrete dimethyl sulfide, which is oxidized in the atmosphere. Some of the products of this oxidation are tiny particles of sulfate salts that provide seed particles necessary for forming cloud droplets. Clouds reflect radiation from the Sun back into space, and so these algae may be responsible for moderating global temperatures. These researchers believe that the algae may have helped keep climate changes moderate at certain times in the history of the Earth during which the Sun is believed to have increased in brightness. Even the kinds of algae involved support this theory; they are the ones that inhabit warm, salty, and brightly illuminated water. When the water becomes warmer, the algae produce more particles to help form more clouds to shield out more sunlight.

Plant genetics. One of the most exciting areas of research during recent years has been the genetic engineering of plants. However, an engineering barrier seems to exist between monocotyledonous and dicotyledonous plants. (A cotyledon is the first leaf or one of the first pair or whorl of leaves developed by the embryo of a seed plant.) The most success was experienced with dicots by the use of cellular fusion, where plant cells without cell walls are combined, or through the transfer of genes by an infectious agent such as *Agrobacterium tumefaciens,* the bacterial cause of crown gall disease. These techniques were successful with dicots but not with monocots or across the monocot-dicot boundary. This continued to be of concern because major grain crops are monocots, and significant genetic improvements might be made with them if techniques successful with dicots could be used. As of 1988 regeneration of the nucleus, cytoplasm, and plasma membrane of a rice cell was the only successful use of those techniques in monocots.

Two outstanding pieces of work took different approaches and met with some success in breaking barriers. Three workers at the Max Planck Institute for Breeding Research in Cologne, West Germany, were able to inject DNA directly into rye plants in

order to produce genetic transformations. Alicia de la Pena and her associates prepared plasmids (small circular DNA molecules) carrying a dominant gene for resistance to kanamycin, an antibiotic lethal to plants, and other marker genes. From previous work these researchers had learned that cells, destined to undergo meiosis (cell division), might have incorporated materials injected into their floral structure at about 14 days before the onset of meiosis. They injected the newly prepared plasmids, waited for the floral structure to develop, crossed the plants, and attempted to germinate resulting seeds on a kanamycin-containing medium. Out of more than 3,000 seeds, seven seedlings survived, thus indicating kanamycin resistance, and two of these proved to have integrated the foreign DNA into plant DNA. The authors believed that the results demonstrated the possibility of introducing new genetic information into germ cells of cereal grains and then producing from resultant seeds normal plants with foreign genes.

One outstanding example of engineering involving *Agrobacterium tumefaciens* utilized corn (*Zea mays*) and maize streak virus (MSV). Some important elements known about these organisms are: (1) *Agrobacterium* is not a usual infector of monocots; (2) MSV is transmitted by a leafhopper, and so the DNA of the MSV is never introduced to its host plant as naked DNA; and (3) MSV infection produces stunting and yellow streaking in corn leaves. Four European investigators were challenged to put these elements together to show that *Agrobacterium* can be used to transform corn plants with MSV DNA so as to produce yellow streaking.

Nigel Grimsley, Thomas Hohn, and Barbara Hohn of the Friedrich Miescher Institut in Basel, Switz., and Jeffrey Davies of the John Innes Institute in Norwich, England, prepared a series of tumor-inducing (Ti) plasmids of *Agrobacterium* into which they inserted copies of the MSV DNA in a section of the plasmid designated T-DNA. It seems that the *Agrobacterium* Ti plasmid transfers its T-DNA into the host cell and that part of that T-DNA is then integrated into the host nuclear DNA. If any MSV DNA is integrated into corn nuclear DNA in this manner, the production of yellow-streaked leaves should serve as indication that this has occurred. Although the researchers did not know what determines the transfer of MSV DNA from the T-DNA to host DNA or why MSV DNA alone is not infectious, they were able to produce yellow-streaked corn. This result demonstrated that both *Agrobacterium* infection and the transfer of certain viral genes are possible in some cereal grains where previously there had been a barrier to genetic manipulation.

Roots. Ordinarily, tree roots grow downward and sometimes outward in the soil; substantial research

From "Signaling for Growth Orientation and Cell Differentiation by Surface Topography in *Uromyces*," H. C. Hoch *et al.*, *Science*, vol. 235, no. 4796, pp. 1659–62, March 27, 1987, © 1987 AAAS

was under way to determine how and why this is usually the case. Robert Sanford, Jr., of North Carolina State University found at least 12 species of trees in the Amazon forest of Venezuela that have some roots that actually grow upward. He called them apogeotropic roots and proposed that they were responding to a nutrient gradient caused by precipitation flowing down the stem of the tree (stem flow) to the nutrient-poor forest. As is found elsewhere in the tropics, the root mat in the soil is denser near the tree stem, indicating an increased ability there to absorb nutrients that perhaps are washed down by stem flow. In his study area Sanford found roots growing up from such root mats on the bark of all tree stems. The average measurement for the root growing the highest on each of the stems was 152 cm (59.8 in). Artificial tree stems made of plastic pipe 16 cm (6.3 in) in diameter were used for investigations of new apogeotropic root growth. Various nutrient sources were tied to the upright pipes 50 cm (19.7 in) above the soil surface. Within four months climbing roots had appeared on all eight of the artificial stems bearing cow manure and on two bearing forest floor litter; none was found on empty stems (the controls). Later, even empty stems bore some climbing roots, but these roots did not grow as rapidly or as far as they had on treated stems. Other researchers showed that mineral enrichment (particularly calcium) may provide the gradient that encourages this growth.

Fungi. Fungi continued to be a focus of research because of their important pathogenic, ecological, and economic functions. A group of researchers from Cornell University, Ithaca, N.Y., reported that at least one fungus is able to find the stomata of bean leaves by touch. This bean rust fungus, *Uromyces appendiculatus*, is transmitted to bean leaves in the spore form; from these spores, hyphae, the typical threads of most fungal growth, germinate and grow over the surface of the leaf.

Harvey Hoch and his associates questioned why these hyphae seemed to know where they were going; wherever they started, they always grew toward the stomata, where they produced their characteristic infection bulbs. From these the interior invasion of the leaf is effected. Hoch and his associates found that the fungus explores the surface of the leaf until it comes to the stomatal guard cells, which have ridges about 0.5 micrometer (millionths of a meter) higher than the surrounding surface. This difference in height seems to trigger the infection bulb stage.

Confirmation of Hoch's findings came from experiments in which fungi were cultured on molded silicon wafers with ridges of varying height and spacing. Approximately 70% of the time, infection structures formed over ridges that were 0.5 micrometer high, and they never formed over the ridges lower

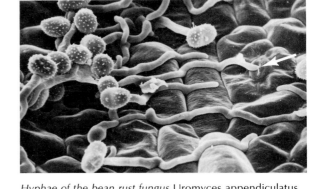

Hyphae of the bean rust fungus Uromyces appendiculatus grow toward a stomate (arrow) on a bean leaf, apparently because the stomatal guard cells rise slightly above the surface of the leaf.

than 0.1 micrometer or higher than one micrometer. Spacing seemed to be important for channeling the fungal growth over the complex terrain of the leaf surface. This situation, in which a fungus uses tactile clues to facilitate infection, could be exploited by developing beans with stomatal cells that are higher or lower than those preferred by the fungus.

From the University of California at Davis came a report that some plants may actually be aided when they are attacked by two different pathogens. Richard Karban and his associates found that exposure of cotton plants *Gossypium hirsutum* to spider mites *Tetranchus urticae* seems to decrease the appearance of symptoms when the cotton plants are later exposed to the fungus causing verticillium wilt even if the mites are no longer present. Karban did not suggest how the relationship works, but this form of "immunity" might prove to be more important as a way to promote disease resistance in some crop plants.

Algae. Some algae, or at least parts of them, may continue to function long after they are eaten, according to Diane Stoecker and two of her associates at Woods Hole (Mass.) Oceanographic Institution. Plankton are the tiny plantlike and animallike organisms that inhabit waters over the whole Earth, particularly the upper layers of nutrient-rich areas. Since the animallike plankton (often protozoan ciliates) eat the plantlike ones (algae), an important link in food chains is found at this level. The tiny algae are said to be producers because they use sunlight to carry out photosynthesis. The protozoa are called herbivores, and they can be eaten by larger carnivores.

The most interesting finding of these researchers is that many of the ciliates have active chloroplasts in them. The source of these must have been the algae that they had eaten. It was found that up to 42% of the ciliates have chloroplasts during the spring and summer months and at least 10% during the fall and winter. Other researchers discovered a genus of ciliates that may even multiply chloroplasts.

Miscellany. Donald T. Krizek and his associates at the Plant Stress Laboratory of the U.S. Department of Agriculture (USDA) in Maryland found that growing plants in smaller pots may achieve higher yields. After growing tomatoes in pots measuring 8.75 cm (3.5 in) and 27.5 cm (11 in) in diameter, they noted that about three times as many plants could be grown in the same space if they were placed in small pots. The size of tomatoes may be greater in large pots, but yield is nearly doubled in small pots if attention is given to adequate water and nutrients.

A possible substitute for wood in some kinds of papermaking is a plant called kenaf (*Cannabinus hibiscus*). It was described by Daniel E. Kugler of the USDA as resembling a giant hollyhock. It may grow to a height of 3.7–4.6 m (12–15 ft) in five months and makes suitable pulp for newsprint. Charles Taylor of Kenaf International in Texas planned a commercial kenaf mill that he believed might help ease the great demand on pulpwood resources. Perhaps as important, kenaf would provide an alternative crop for depressed areas in the cotton belt.

It is known that some plants heat up considerably by the time of pollination. This process may send out chemicals that indicate readiness for pollination. Certain members of the philodendron and calla-lily family evidence this mechanism. As an example, Ilya Raskin of E. I. du Pont de Nemours and Co., Inc., and her associates studied the voodoo lily *Sauromatum guttatum Schott* and found that temperatures of its reproductive parts rose as much as 14° C (25° F) above those of the surroundings. They found that salicylic acid is the trigger for this action.

The question of how to investigate plant functions without destroying them often taxes the imagination of botanists. During the past year researchers from the Georgia Experiment Station at Griffin used computed tomography (CT) to study root systems, plant pesticide distribution, and water absorption patterns. Brahm Verma reported that CT scanning, usually associated with highly detailed studies of human beings, had already helped determine how pesticides move in soil in respect to plants and insects, detect bruises on fruit before visual evidence was there, and analyze water uptake by roots.

—Albert J. Smith

Microbiology

Microbiologists in laboratories from many countries were continuing their efforts to harness the metabolic processes of microorganisms in order to degrade chemical pollutants that had found their way into the environment. Many encouraging results were

obtained. More and more microorganisms that are able to degrade various polluting chemicals were being isolated. Some of these organisms had never previously been isolated, and so their identities remained unknown.

A case in point was the discovery by a microbiologist at Michigan State University of an entirely new anaerobic (one that does not use oxygen) bacterium that can remove chlorine from aromatic compounds. The removal of chlorine is a key step, and one that until recently had been considered unlikely, in the microbial degradation of such important pollutants as polychlorinated biphenyls (PCBs), dioxins, and chlorinated phenols and benzenes. The organism in question appeared to be unlike any other previously studied.

It was becoming increasingly apparent that "teamwork" between more than one species of microorganism is necessary for the complete degradation of certain chemical pollutants. In some cases one microorganism is able to degrade a chemical agent only partially. Other species of microorganisms are then needed for completing the process by metabolizing the degradation products that were produced by the first organism. For example, the unidentified anaerobic organism described in the preceding paragraph can remove chlorine from aromatic compounds but cannot further degrade the resulting dechlorinated compounds (such as benzoic acid). Instead, a second organism must take over and degrade the benzoic acid to acetic acid, hydrogen, and carbon dioxide. Finally, a methane-producing bacterium is then able to convert those products to methane. It should be pointed out that most microbiologists have had little experience in working with mixed cultures of more than one microbial species, as opposed to working with a single species.

Another approach is to clone degradative genes from other species into a single bacterial species that would then be able to degrade the chemical pollutant completely to harmless products. Researchers from West Germany and Switzerland cloned genes for enzymes in five different degradative pathways from three distinct bacteria into a single bacterium. The objective was to construct a bacterium with an "all-inclusive" degradative pathway that could degrade and grow on mixtures of chloro- and methylaromatic compounds. Unlike the parent bacterial species, the newly constructed bacterium could grow well on and degrade those toxic compounds. Microbiologists believed that similar research approaches might be developed for producing various types of genetically constructed bacteria that could degrade many different types of environmental chemical pollutants.

Fungi. Workers from the U.S. Department of Agriculture, the Environmental Protection Agency, and North Carolina State University began testing the ability of a wood-rotting fungus to degrade chlorinated aromatic compounds. The organism is a white-rot fungus that degrades lignin, a complex aromatic substance that, together with cellulose, forms the woody cell walls of plants. Thus far, the organism has shown the ability to degrade chlorinated lignin by-products of pulp and paper mills and also to degrade TNT (2,4,6-trinitrotoluene) in wastewater from an explosive-manufacturing plant.

Mycorrhizal fungi are those that are associated with the roots of vascular plants. The fungi benefit the plants by increasing the efficiency of the uptake of nitrogen, phosphorus, and other substances. Recently scientists have found fossil mycorrhizal fungi associated with plant roots in Antarctica dating from the Triassic Period (about 190 million to 225 million years ago). This finding supports earlier ideas that the appearance of vascular plants was aided by the evolution of symbiotic mycorrhizal fungi.

Bacteria. Microfossils dating back as far as 3.3 billion to 3.5 billion years ago were also found in Western Australia. The cell types in the fossil material appeared to be those of oxygen-producing, photosynthetic cyanobacteria. If this proves to be correct, then a photosynthetically produced, oxygen-containing environment must have occurred over a longer period during Precambrian times than had previously been thought.

Scientists from West Germany recently described a new group of archaebacteria that they isolated from marine hydrothermal systems off the coast of Italy. Archaebacteria are thought to have existed since the earliest (Archean) times in the history of the Earth. The isolates grew at extremely high temperatures, the temperature for their optimal growth being 83° C (181° F). These organisms were sulfate reducers. While the Archean oceans are thought to have contained little sulfate, it is probable that these organisms could have existed since Archean times in hydrothermal systems. Organisms such as these that can grow at high temperatures and can reduce sulfate to hydrogen sulfide could possibly account for the hydrogen-sulfide-rich "sour oil" found in geothermally heated oil wells.

Another group of workers from Georgia studied sediments from high-temperature deep-sea vents in the Gulf of California. They detected "fingerprint" compounds found only in archaebacteria. This discovery suggested that these ancient bacteria both existed and presently exist in association with the deep-sea hydrothermal-vent communities.

Bacteria that produce methane also belong to the archaebacteria group. Methane-producing bacteria use molecular hydrogen (H_2) and carbon dioxide (CO_2) to produce methane (CH_4) in the absence of oxygen. Scientists recently described a new group of methane-producing bacteria that uses electrons from iron to reduce hydrogen ions (H^+) from water in order to produce molecular hydrogen. Since either elemental iron or iron from steel can be used for this reaction, the data suggest that these methane-producing bacteria may play an important role in the corrosion of iron-containing materials in environments that lack oxygen.

Synechococcus is a genus of marine cyanobacteria that is unusual in that it can swim even though it lacks flagella, the usual organelles of locomotion for bacteria. Microbiologists recently found that its swimming is sodium-dependent. The organism apparently forms an electrochemical gradient of sodium ions across its cell membrane. The differences on opposite sides of the membrane in the concentration of sodium ions and in electrical charge provide energy for swimming. The exact mechanism that propels the bacterium, however, remained unknown.

Canadian and West German workers showed that sulfur-oxidizing bacteria play an important role in recycling sulfur in the marine environment. Especially important are sulfur-oxidizing bacteria that grow in mats in shallow coastal waters. The mats are formed from sediments, sand, and flocculent materials held together by sticky, mucous material produced by organisms. The bacteria—mainly colorless *Beggiatoa*—oxidize sulfides to sulfur and sulfates, thus biologically "fixing" the latter compounds in the mats. Gastropods and other organisms graze on the mats. The researchers also found that the resuspension and disruption of the mats by waves, tides, and currents was also an important means of sulfur flux in the coastal waters because it horizontally dispersed sulfur-based nutrients into the water.

Acid rain. Acid rain continued to be a topic of much debate and concern. The view generally held was that acidifying sulfur enters the atmosphere as a result of such human activities as the use of coal-burning power plants. It is also recognized, however, that sulfur compounds arise from the ocean because of biologic reactions there. Recently Australian and Canadian scientists reported that up to 30% of the acidifying sulfur burden in the atmosphere in remote areas of Canada arose from microbial activities in wetlands, bogs, and marshes. This evidence of a previously unsuspected source of the sulfur was a matter of considerable interest and one that needed further study.

Certain types of bacteria can oxidize sulfur compounds, while other types can reduce sulfur compounds. This suggests that microorganisms might play a helpful role in the control of acidification of lakes by acid rain. Indeed, such has now been shown to be the case. It is, however, a complex situation in which microbial activities are both beneficial and harmful. On the one hand, some microorganisms located in the mud in the bottom of lakes are able

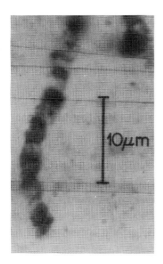

Photomicrograph reveals fossil microorganisms found in Western Australia. The fossils are estimated to be between 3.3 billion and 3.5 billion years old, indicating that a photosynthetically produced oxygen-containing environment must have occurred over a longer period in Precambrian times than had previously been thought.

From ''Early Archean (3.3-Billion to 3.5-Billion-Year-Old) Microfossils from Warrawoona Group, Australia,'' J. W. Schopf and B. M. Packer, *Science,* vol. 237, no. 4810, pp. 70–72, July 3, 1987, © 1987 AAAS

to minimize or limit the effects of acid rain by consuming sulfuric and nitric acids. These microorganisms can remove 50–70% of the acids in lakes where water that flows into the lake remains there for a long time. Little acid, however, is removed from lakes that are flushed quickly by flowing water. On the other hand, bacteria in acidic lakes were found to convert the extremely small amounts of mercury that are naturally present in the lakes to the highly toxic compound methylmercury. Once formed, methylmercury can accumulate in fish to levels as much as 100,000 times greater than the concentration found in water.

Soil research. Scientists recently discovered abundant and diverse microbial populations in core samples of soil from depths of 300 m (985 ft). This was surprising in that until recently scientists believed that living organisms existed beneath the Earth's surface only at relatively shallow depths. This idea will now have to be reconsidered.

Investigators from Idaho found that microorganisms may be useful in moderating selenium toxicity in soil by reducing selenate and selenite to metallic selenium. This is important because in some parts of the world the two forms of this toxic metal, selenate and selenite, may be leached from seleniferous soil and accumulate in water or soil. In particular this is the case where water used in the irrigation of soil accumulates. It is believed that increased concentrations of selenate and selenite may be responsible for death and deformities of water fowl and fish. These results suggest that the use of microorganisms shows promise for the treatment of waters and soils containing selenate and selenite.

Health-related microbiology. Most bacteria fall into one of two physiological classes on the basis of staining reactions, either gram-negative or gram-positive. The difference in staining reactions is due

to the nature of the structure and composition of the cell walls of the two classes of bacteria. An important difference is that gram-negative bacteria possess an outer membrane in their cell walls, whereas gram-positive bacteria do not. Lipopolysaccharide (LPS) is a necessary component of the outer membrane of gram-negative bacteria, which, in turn, is essential for the survival of such bacteria. Consequently, microbiologists recognized that an agent that could inhibit the synthesis of LPS would be a valuable chemotherapeutic agent in the treatment of infections caused by gram-negative bacteria.

A computer-based analysis of the structure and substrate specificity of a purified enzyme that is necessary for the incorporation of an essential compound into LPS was undertaken by scientists in a U.S. pharmaceutical company. They were able to synthesize a chemical analogue of KDO (3-deoxy-D-*manno*-octulosonic acid), an essential component of LPS. This analogue, though chemically and structurally similar to KDO, inhibits the enzyme that normally activates KDO prior to the insertion of KDO into LPS during LPS synthesis. Consequently, the analogue inhibited gram-negative bacterial growth and rendered the bacteria susceptible to other chemotherapeutic agents and to the immune defenses of human blood serum. Whether this new agent would prove useful outside of the laboratory in the treatment of patients had yet to be determined. The important aspect of the research, however, was that it provided an example of the rational development of a new chemotherapeutic agent.

Recently scientists in the U.S., Sweden, and West Germany, in unrelated work, reported that certain cationic peptides (those that react as bases) of low molecular weight had antimicrobial properties. Some insects, for example, were shown to protect themselves from bacterial infection by producing such peptides. In another case, it was found that the skin of an African clawed frog contained two unusual cationic peptides—each comprising 23 amino acids—that could kill both gram-negative and gram-positive bacteria. Finally, researchers discovered bacteria that produce cationic peptides that are inhibitory to other bacteria. In some cases the peptides acted by inhibiting the synthesis of bacterial cell walls. These findings held promise that similar cationic peptides might ultimately prove useful in the treatment of bacterial infections.

The notion has long been held, but has not been conclusively proved, that syphilis originated in the Americas and that it was transported to Europe by persons sailing with Christopher Columbus. Lending credence to this concept were recent observations of lesions characteristic of a syphilis-like infection in the bones of a Pleistocene bear that lived in the Western Hemisphere 11,500 years ago. Similar lesions had previously been seen in bones of Inca, Aztec, and North American Indians dated 1,000–3,000 years ago. Pre-Columbian bone evidence for syphilis has never been found outside of the Americas.

—Robert G. Eagon

Molecular biology

So many accomplishments in molecular biology took place during the past year that selecting the best topics for review must be somewhat arbitrary. Advances in the practical uses of recombinant DNA were particularly dramatic, but they occurred in the midst of political phenomena that persisted in spite of compelling arguments for removing DNA from the political arena. Another noteworthy set of discoveries concerns the newly found properties of RNA, previously thought to be rather inert chemically but now shown to have catalytic activity.

The first experiments in which a fragment of DNA from an animal was cloned into a plasmid and propagated in the common intestinal bacterium *Escherichia coli* were reported in the mid-1970s. Since then, a small group of scientists and a slightly larger group of lay persons concerned with "protecting the environment" have attempted to block experimentation on recombinant DNA. Their early efforts focused on experiments in *E. coli,* but extensive review of potential hazards by various agencies resulted in the conclusion that modest adherence to good laboratory practice would suffice to protect the public from any conceivable hazard.

The reasonableness of this view has been supported by recent history. There has not been a single example of illness or untoward consequence resulting from the construction of recombinant organisms anywhere in the world. On the other hand, the benefits of the new technology are being felt over a wide range of human activity. The most obvious examples are in the field of medicine, where new pharmaceutical products—for example, human growth hormone, human insulin, the interferons, and tissue plasminogen activator (which helps blood clots dissolve)—have already made significant contributions. The molecular biology of the virus that causes acquired immune deficiency syndrome (AIDS) has been extensively studied, and recombinant DNA methods were used recently to clone a gene that codes for a cellular receptor of the virus. The receptor is a protein that binds to the coat protein of the virus—the first step by which the virus penetrates a target cell. The recombinant DNA-produced receptor protein has been found to have a blocking effect on virus-cell binding, thus offering a start on a possible treatment or preventative for AIDS.

In agricultural research recombinant DNA methods were used to generate tomato plants that carry a novel gene for a bacterial toxin that is lethal to a narrow range of insect larvae. Although the transgenic plants are normal in most respects, the larvae of such major pests as the tobacco hornworm do not eat their leaves. Ordinary tomato plants are stripped bare by the hornworm.

DNA fingerprinting. The most unexpected recent application of recombinant DNA technology is in forensic medicine. New methods for "fingerprinting" DNA make it possible to establish the relatedness of two individuals, as in questions of paternity, or to establish the identity of two tissue samples, as in the case of one taken from the scene of a crime and another from a suspect. The new methods are based on restriction endonucleases and restriction fragment length polymorphisms (RFLPs).

Restriction endonucleases are bacterial enzymes that recognize short sequences of nucleotides in the DNA double helix, bind to them, and cleave both strands of the DNA at specific sites. (It should be recalled that a strand of DNA consists of a linear sequence of the nucleotides adenine, cytosine, guanine, and thymine, abbreviated A, C, G, and T. Specific hydrogen bonds between A and T and between C and G, in a process called base pairing, holds two DNA strands together to form the double helix.) To date over 100 different restriction enzymes have been described, each recognizing a different nucleotide sequence. (See *1988 Yearbook of Science and the Future* Year in Review: LIFE SCIENCES: *Molecular biology.*)

The target site for cleavage by a given restriction endonuclease is a sequence of four, five, or six nucleotides that features a certain kind of symmetry: the complementary sequence with which it pairs up to form the DNA double strand is identical to itself but oriented in the reverse order, since the two strands of the DNA molecule have opposite chemical polarity. For example, the enzyme called *Eco*RI recognizes the paired sequences

```
————————GAATTC————————
————————CTTAAG————————
```

wherever it occurs in DNA and cleaves between the G and A on each strand. It should be noted that the sequence of the site on one strand is identical to that on the other strand, although opposite in orientation. This requirement is a reflection of the structure and mechanism of cleavage by restriction enzymes, which are dimeric proteins (built of two identical protein subunits).

In a random sequence of nucleotides, the sequence GAATTC will occur by chance about once every 5,000 nucleotides. In a real DNA molecule, such as a chromosome, the frequency and distribution of such sites is determined by the order of genes in the chromosome and the detailed sequence of the nucleotides that encode the amino acid sequence of proteins. If the protein-coding potential of the *Eco*RI site is considered, the DNA sequence GAATTC could be interpreted several different ways in RNA: as GAA/UUC, which corresponds to the amino acid sequence glutamic acid/phenylalanine; or as G/AAU/UC ·, which corresponds to the amino acid sequence asparagine/serine; or as · GA/AUU/C · ·, which would translate as arginine or glycine followed by isoleucine. (In RNA the nucleotide uracil, abbreviated U, takes the place of thymine.) Each of these cases constitutes a separate "reading frame" in which consecutive groups of three nucleotides code for consecutive amino acids.

If the nucleotide sequence were changed as a consequence of mutation, such that the DNA sequence became GAGTTC (GAGUUC in RNA), the amino acid sequence—depending on the context of the protein reading frame—would either be unchanged (because GAG also codes for glutamic acid) or become serine/serine or arginine(or glycine)/valine. In the latter two cases the protein, although it now contains a different amino acid, might function in a way that is indistinguishable from the one encoded by GAATTC. Put more broadly, there are many ways in which a nucleotide sequence can be changed without a deleterious or even noticeable change in the function of the protein product.

Such variations in fact commonly exist in many parts of the chromosomes of plants, insects, and mammals. If the DNA from two apparently identical individuals is cut with a restriction enzyme, it should be possible to detect differences in the lengths of fragments that contain a sequence corresponding to a particular gene, the differences being due to mutations of the kind described. On the other hand, such mutations are relatively rare, so that two individuals who share a parent, or two tissue samples from the same individual, will have recognizable patterns of fragment lengths (owing to the distribution of restriction sites) that can be revealed by hybridization with DNA probes that identify particular genes.

The variation in the distribution of restriction sites gives rise to individual variation in the lengths of DNA fragments corresponding to a region of a chromosome; this variation is termed restriction fragment length polymorphism. Since, as mentioned above, mutation is infrequent and genetic recombination (breakage and reunion of chromosomes during the maturation of germ cells) is infrequent, RFLPs are inherited in much the same way as conventional genetic traits, such as eye color in humans, leaf shape in plants, and wing structure in insects. Because RFLPs can be detected in DNA samples taken from very young individuals, they are potentially of immense use to breeders. In the plant business, for example, if a desirable trait can be linked to a particular RFLP, the RFLP can be determined in DNA

extracted from hundreds of seedlings and only those with the correct RFLP grown to maturity.

The results of RFLP analysis have to be expressed in terms of probability. If two DNA samples show the same distribution of fragment lengths for a given probe, what is the likelihood that the identity would have been obtained by chance? It is clear that the more enzymes that are used to cut the DNA, or the more fragments that are identified by a given probe, the more certain is the conclusion to be drawn. Since the DNA sample is often the limiting material in forensic applications, it is useful to use probes that have a number of complementary sequences in the chromosome, so that many (but not too many) fragments can be identified in a single experiment. Alec Jeffreys of the University of Leicester, England, recently developed a set of probes based on DNA elements found in human chromosomes in a number of locations. Because each of the sequences complementary to the probes exists in a different genetic context in the chromosome, cutting with a single enzyme gives rise to a large number of different-sized fragments revealed by hybridization.

How is this technology applied to questions of paternity? Except for the sex chromosome, an individual receives half of his or her DNA from each parent. DNA prepared from blood cells of a child will display a characteristic RFLP pattern. DNA from the mother will make it possible to assign roughly half of the fragments as "maternal." The other half will be "paternal." Their origin can be proved or disproved with a DNA sample from the presumptive father. If he is not available or cooperative, his RFLP pattern can be determined from a child he is certain to have fathered or from a combination of other blood relatives.

Other forensic applications are more straightforward. For instance, enough DNA can be obtained from semen to make positive identification of a rapist possible, no matter how many witnesses swear that he was with them at the time of the crime.

Enzymatic RNA. The astonishing ability of certain RNA molecules to cut and splice themselves was described in the *1984 Yearbook of Science and the Future* Year in Review: LIFE SCIENCES: *Molecular biology*. Continuing those studies, Thomas Cech and his colleagues at the University of Colorado made a further stunning discovery: certain RNA molecules can catalyze the splicing of RNA molecules other than themselves. In other words, they can act as enzymes in the true sense, catalyzing chemical reactions from which they emerge unchanged. This discovery opens an entirely new window on molecular biology. For some biochemical reactions whose mechanisms have been hard to explain in terms of the properties of conventional protein enzymes, it may be necessary to look for involvement of RNA in the mechanism.

The implications for biochemical evolution are also significant. If RNA can both carry information (in its nucleotide sequence) and function as a catalyst, it may well have preceded both DNA and protein in the origin of life.

The enzymatic property of RNA was observed in the course of experiments intended to reveal the way in which introns are removed from RNA. Introns, or intervening sequences, were first seen in the late 1970s when the methods for determining the sequence of nucleotides in genes were introduced. It was found that the genes in some animal viruses and the genes encoding the protein parts of hemoglobin and antibody molecules have extra stretches of DNA in their interiors. That is, the genes are split into sections that code for protein and sections that code for nothing recognizable. Genes function by being transcribed into RNA; the enzyme RNA polymerase makes an RNA molecule containing the nucleotides A, G, C and U (uracil) in a sequence that faithfully reflects the sequence of A, G, C, and T in the DNA. Thus, the RNA transcript of a "gene in pieces" contains extra RNA that must be removed before the RNA sequence can be translated by the cell's protein synthesis machinery, the ribosomes and transfer RNA, to link the correct amino acids in sequence to make the protein product of the gene.

The cutting and splicing of RNA to remove introns takes place in the cell nucleus for those genes carried on the nuclear chromosomes and translated on ribosomes in the cytoplasm. This cutting and splicing usually requires the participation of enzymatic machinery consisting of particles that contain both protein and RNA. The precise role of each component of this splicing machine is still unknown. Until recently it had been thought that the RNA component directs the machine to the site at which cutting and splicing is needed, while the protein part catalyzes the breakage and rejoining of the RNA targets. This view may have to change as a result of Cech's new discovery.

Introns are found outside the nucleus as well. Both mitochondria and chloroplasts contain DNA, which is transcribed into RNA within the organelles themselves and translated there into protein. Roughly 10% of the proteins of each organelle are encoded, transcribed, and translated within; the remainder are encoded in the nucleus, translated in the cytoplasm, and transported into the organelle by virtue of "transit" sequences in the proteins that target them to their appropriate locations inside. Some of the protein-coding genes in mitochondria and chloroplasts contain introns. These introns must be spliced out of the RNA within the organelle. Is the splicing machinery made in the organelle? Or is it encoded in the nucleus and transported into the organelle? Or is it needed at all? The answer is not the same for all organellar introns, but for several introns in fungal mitochondria no protein is required.

The catalog of RNA molecules capable of self-splicing is impressive. The first and best studied example is the ribosomal RNA made in the nucleus of the protozoan *Tetrahymena* studied by Cech and his colleagues. This RNA contains the sequences shown to have true enzymic activity as well. Other examples of self-splicing (proved rigorously by synthesis of the precursor RNA in vitro through the use of bacterial components) include a mitochondrial intron from the fungus *Neurospora*, studied by Alan Lambowitz and colleagues at St. Louis (Mo.) University; several yeast mitochondrial introns studied by Henk Tabak and colleagues at the University of Amsterdam; and, most incredible of all, several introns in genes of the bacterial virus (bacteriophage) T4, studied by Marlene Belfort and her colleagues at the New York State Department of Health in Albany.

In all of these cases, the nucleotide sequences of the introns were found to be related to each other in terms of the three-dimensional structure into which the sequence can be folded and held together by base pairing. These structural features were noticed independently by François Michel and Bernard Dujon of the Center for Molecular Genetics, Gif-sur-

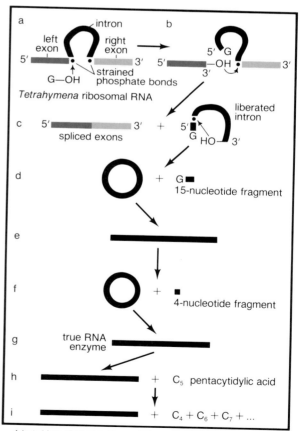

Yvette, France, and by R. Wayne Davies of the Victoria University of Manchester, England. Evidence has been accumulating that the three-dimensional structures suggested by these workers in the early 1980s are correct and required for self-splicing. The most telling experiments are genetic; mutations in the form of single-nucleotide replacements that disrupt the base-paired regions of the proposed structures result in loss of self-splicing activity, while additional nucleotide replacements that restore base pairing also restore self-splicing activity.

The discovery of self-splicing introns in bacteriophage T4 should allow rapid progress in elucidating further details of the splicing mechanism because of the ease and speed with which mutants of the bacteriophage can be isolated. In the 1950s Seymour Benzer used the rII gene of bacteriophage T4 to show that the smallest unit of mutation is the nucleotide pair, the smallest unit of recombination is the nucleotide pair, and the unit of function is the gene, defined as the stretch of nucleotides encoding one polypeptide chain. Virtually identical genetic methods, supplemented by nucleotide sequencing, were used by Belfort and her colleagues to define the regions of the T4 introns that are necessary for self-splicing and those that are dispensable.

Although the nucleotide sequences of the self-splicing introns differ considerably, it is possible to fold the sequences into a structure that is similar for all, based on stable base-paired loops. It is this structure that provides the key to the catalytic activity of the RNA and also to the enzymic activity noticed by Cech. Each self-splicing intron (see Figure, step a) contains, near its 5' end, a short sequence rich in the nucleotides A and G. (Opposite ends of a nucleotide sequence are called the 3' end and the 5' end.) This sequence pairs with a complementary C,U sequence at the 3' end of the coding region (exon) adjacent to the intron. The pairing strains the internucleotide phosphate bond that joins the exon and the intron. That bond is attacked by water or, more efficiently, by guanosine (G—OH in the Figure), which breaks the bond, liberating a free hydroxyl (—OH) group at the 3' end of the exon (step b). The structure, however, positions this group to attack the phosphate bond at the other intron-exon boundary, liberating the linear intron (lengthened by a G at its 5' end) and leaving the perfectly spliced exons (step c).

The liberated intron retains its active structure. An A,G sequence near its 5' end finds another C,U sequence, base pairing forms another loop and induces strain in a phosphate bond, and attack by the —OH group at the 3' end of the intron itself liberates a short RNA from the 5' end while circularizing the rest of the intron (step d). The circular molecule then opens (step e) and repeats the cycle of folding, cyclization, and removal of nucleotides from the 5'

end (step f). After these two rounds of cyclization and cleavage, the structure can no longer position C,U sequences against A,G sequences appropriately, and further cleavage does not occur.

This final cleavage product, a linear molecule, is the true RNA enzyme (step g). It retains a binding site for C,U sequences, consisting of the A,G region mentioned above. If pentacytidylic acid (a short nucleotide sequence consisting of five cytidines, abbreviated C_5) is added to a solution containing the fully cleaved intron (step h), the C_5 molecule is both cleaved (e.g., to $C_4 + C$) and lengthened (to C_6, C_7, etc.; step i). Although RNA molecules made entirely of cytidine are not very interesting, the result demonstrates that RNA can catalyze the synthesis of more RNA. One of the prerequisites for biochemical evolution has been met.

—Robert Haselkorn

Zoology

Paleobiology. Aspects of evolutionary biology were prominent during the past year. In particular, the controversy concerning the causes of major extinctions of species was widely debated, and new information concerning primate evolution appeared. In 1980 Luis Alvarez, Walter Alvarez, Frank Asaro, and Helen Michel of the University of California at Berkeley had published their theory that the mass extinctions of animals some 65 million years ago at the end of the Cretaceous Period was due to the collision of a massive meteor or asteroid with the Earth. They proposed that this collision threw up enormous amounts of dust into the atmosphere, cutting off sunlight and dropping temperatures. This so upset the Earth's ecology that a great number of species perished. This concept immediately triggered an intensive search for evidence, pro and con, which in 1988 was still continuing.

Compelling evidence for the meteor hypothesis was the presence of unusually large concentrations of iridium and shocked quartz grains in the Cretaceous-Tertiary (K-T) boundary deposits in many places around the world. Contrary views were presented by Anthony Hallam of the University of Birmingham, England, in the Nov. 27, 1987, issue of *Science* magazine, in which he summarized the evidence for volcanic activity, climatic changes, and falling sea level and suggested that these were the major causes of the extinctions. He attributed both the iridium layer and the shocked quartz grains to extensive volcanic emissions. Opponents argued that the quantity of iridium currently found in volcanic emissions appears to be much less than could account for the amount found in the K-T deposits and, as pointed out by Bruce Bohor of the U.S. Geological Survey, the small quantity of shocked quartz that has been discovered to be associated with volcanoes does not have the multiple shock planes found in the grains produced by a meteor impact.

Perhaps the most intriguing evidence in favor of volcanic activity was the presence of extremely large lava flows at about the time of the K-T boundary. V. E. Courtillot, of the Institut de Physique du Globe in Paris, believes that the age of the Deccan Traps lava has been established at 66 million years. The Deccan Traps, a remainder of the largest known volcanic eruptions, is a massive lava flow that covers an area of about 650,000 sq km (251,000 sq mi) in west-central India. Courtillot suggested that the outgassing of the lava produced great quantities of acid rain as well as darkness and cooling over much of the Earth.

The Triassic-Jurassic transition was another period of mass extinctions but, because it occurred about 200 million years ago and boundary deposits are sparse, it has been difficult to determine if the extinctions were gradual or sudden. Paul E. Olsen of Columbia University, New York City, Neil H. Shubin of Harvard University, and Mark H. Anders of the University of California at Berkeley described a rich fauna from the early Jurassic from well-developed deposits along the Bay of Fundy, Nova Scotia. They found that there was an absence there of quadruped animals from the Triassic Period, indicating an abrupt extinction at the end of the Triassic. They suggested that a catastrophic event, such as a meteor fall, may have occurred then.

A much more recent mass extinction took place about 11,000 years ago at the end of the Pleistocene ice age. At that time the Earth was populated with a large variety of mammals, including such giant forms as the mammoth, giant beaver, ground sloth, glyptodont, dire wolf, saber-toothed tiger, and giant bear. Why these impressive creatures all disappeared suddenly is unknown. Two theories have been put forward. Unlike what occurred during the K-T and Triassic-Jurassic extinctions described above, small animals were little affected in the Pleistocene, and so a major catastrophic event is unlikely to have happened. It has usually been assumed that climatic change was the cause, but Paul S. Martin of the University of Arizona advanced the idea that humans were the agents. In areas such as the Americas, large animals were unaccustomed to humans and became easy prey to tribes that crossed the Bering Strait land bridge and spread over North America.

Killing the large herbivores would have had a great ecological impact, as pointed out by Norman Owen-Smith of the University of the Witwatersrand, Johannesburg, South Africa. Very large plant eaters, such as the elephant and several of the extinct forms, eat large plants and thus prevent woodlands from overrunning savanna areas. In their absence the savanna would become forest or tall grassland and be unsuitable for many smaller herbivores, greatly decreasing their numbers.

The earliest record of animal life on dry land was pushed back by more than 50 million years by the discovery of small burrows in 450 million-year-old late Ordovician deposits near Potters Mills, Pa. G. J. Retallack and C. R. Feakes of the University of Oregon interpreted the features of the burrows as indicating that they were produced by a millipede-like arthropod. The presence of these creatures in a dry soil habitat led researchers to the conclusion that there necessarily must also have been a well-developed terrestrial ecology.

An interesting observation on mosasaur fossils suggested that those large marine reptiles, which appear to have been well adapted to the seas of the Cretaceous Period, may have lacked adequate adaptations for prolonged deep diving. Bruce Rothschild of the Museum of Natural History, Lawrence, Kan., and Larry D. Martin of the University of Kansas examined the vertebrae of three genera of mosasaurs and found internal damage frequently present in the vertebrae of two of the three genera. This avascular necrosis (lesions inside the bone) appeared to be due to damage caused by nitrogen bubbles that formed in the blood when the animal returned to the surface after a long, deep dive. This condition was found in *Platecarpus* and *Tylosaurus* but not in *Clidastes*. Rothschild and Martin interpreted this to mean that *Clidastes* did not dive deeply and that mosasaurs lacked the adaptations that deep-diving mammals have that protect them from such damage.

Though usually associated with steamy tropical environments, dinosaurs actually lived in a variety of habitats. An extreme case was presented by Elisabeth M. Brouwers, Thomas A. Agar, L. David Carter, and William V. Sliter of the U.S. Geological Survey; William A. Clemens of the University of California at Berkeley; and Robert A. Spicer of Goldsmiths' College, London. They examined the extensive remains of several dinosaur groups along the Colville River near the north shore of Alaska. The fossils are of late Cretaceous age and contain numerous examples of both adult and young duckbill hadrosaurid dinosaurs. Other remains indicate that the climate was cold to moderate, with the temperature averaging about 2° C (36° F) in the winter and 12° C (54° F) in the summer. At that time Alaska was farther north than it is today, and the area would have been above latitude 70° N. During the winter, months of darkness would have occurred. Whether the dinosaurs migrated or endured the darkness is unknown. The investigators suggested that the presence of immature individuals favors the latter.

Among many other reports of interest was the finding of fossil remains of the largest known seabird.

AP/Wide World

The thin-spined porcupine, Chaetomys subspinosus, last seen in 1952 and thought to be extinct, was photographed during the past year by the Brazilian biologist Ilmar Bastos Santos in the eastern tropical forests of Brazil.

Storrs L. Olson of the Smithsonian Institution, Washington, D.C., and members of the Charleston (S.C.) Museum described the 5 million–50 million-year-old bony-toothed pseudodontorn as having a wingspan of 5.5 m (18 ft), almost twice that of an albatross. The pseudodontorns had bony outgrowths along their beaks that may have served as teeth. These extinct birds, related to the modern pelicans, apparently fed on marine fish and squid.

Primate evolution. The past year was an especially interesting one in the study of human evolution. Among a number of advances, two events stood out. An exciting find occurred at Olduvai Gorge in Tanzania. A team led by Donald Johanson of the Institute of Human Origins and Tim White of the University of California at Berkeley found a fossilized skull and limb bones of an adult female *Homo habilis*. Remains of this species of hominid were scarce, and previously only skull bones had been recovered. Labeled Olduvai Hominid (OH) 62, this first find of *H. habilis* limb bones showed the female to be only a little over 1 m (3½ ft) tall, much smaller than previously assumed, and to have had much more apelike proportions than expected. The size and proportions are similar to those of the "Lucy" specimens of *Australopithecus afarensis*. Many paleoanthropologists believe that *A. afarensis* is ancestral to *H. habilis*, which in turn gave rise to *Homo erectus*. The latter species is much larger than the other two and lacks the marked difference in size between the sexes that apparently characterized the former two. If this evolutionary sequence is correct, a rapid and abrupt evolutionary change took place between 1.8 million

and 1.6 million years ago to give rise to *H. erectus*.

Molecular comparisons continued to play an ever greater role in unraveling biologic relationships. Rebecca Cann of the University of Hawaii and Mark Stoneking and Allan Wilson of the University of California at Berkeley used mitochondrial DNA (mtDNA) comparisons of different living human populations to estimate the source and time of origin of modern humans. Their results indicated that modern human populations originated in Africa approximately 100,000–200,000 years ago and then spread over the Earth, displacing other hominid species in the process. Some investigators questioned these results on the grounds that the rate of change of mtDNA through time was still uncertain. Another problem, as Wilson himself pointed out, was that the mtDNA data cannot distinguish whether the time of origin is a true beginning of modern humans or represents only a genetic "bottleneck" where an already human species was reduced to small numbers and then recovered and became the ancestors of modern populations.

Ecology. The thin-spined porcupine, *Chaetomys subspinosus*, feared to be extinct, was photographed and reported during the year by Brazilian biologist Ilmar Bastos Santos in the eastern tropics of that country. It was possible that this little-known mammal, despite its name, might turn out to be related to the spiny rat family.

The last known wild California condor was captured on April 19, 1987, by members of the California Condor Research Center. It was taken to join other surviving members of its species in the San Diego (Calif.) Wild Animal Park, where it was hoped that they would take part in the breeding program that someday might allow these condors to be reintroduced into the wild. This huge bird once ranged over much of the southwestern United States and Florida but by 1988 had been reduced to 27 living individuals. That number rose to 28 in May 1988 when the first condor to be born in captivity was hatched at the Wild Animal Park. S. D. Emslie of the University of Florida dated fossil remains of condors from the Grand Canyon and found that they disappeared from there about 9,500 years ago. This coincided with the extinction of many large herbivores. Emslie suggested that the condor was dependent upon the carcasses of those animals for food and that its current restricted range and precarious existence were due to their disappearance.

Researchers discovered that a major ecological disaster was taking place in the northern Caribbean Sea. From the Yucatán Peninsula to Florida and to the Virgin Islands and The Bahamas, reef corals were "bleaching." Reef corals are characterized by the presence of symbiotic algae that live in their tissues and contribute to their nutrition. Without

The last known wild California condor was captured on April 19, 1987, and taken to join other members of its species in the San Diego (California) Wild Animal Park. Only 28 of these birds remained alive in early 1988.

the algae the corals live poorly and often die. For unknown reasons, masses of corals were expelling their algae and, consequently, turning a pasty white. A similar event occurred in the eastern Pacific off the coast of South America in 1983. Most of those corals died and, according to Peter Glynn of the University of Miami, that coral community has shown little recovery since then. The loss of algae in coral typically follows stressful environmental conditions. Scientists speculated that in the Caribbean situation higher than normal water temperatures might have been a cause, but this idea was advanced only because no other cause could be found.

Also on an unhappy note, the list of endangered species in the U.S. increased by 37 during the year, to a total of 449. One extinction was recorded when the last living dusky seaside sparrow died in Florida in June 1987.

Behavior. For most nonbiologists, an all-female species of vertebrates would be regarded as rather strange. Actually, a number of species of fish and reptiles exist in this condition and reproduce parthenogenetically—by the development of unfertilized eggs. However, David Crews, a professor of zoology at the University of Texas at Austin, was surprised to see courtship and pseudocopulatory behavior between individuals of an all-female species of whiptail lizards, *Cnemidophorus uniparens*. Suspecting that this behavior plays a role in reproduction, Crews and a number of co-workers conducted a series of studies that supported this thesis. Without courtship, the size of the resulting nests of eggs declined to less than one-third of normal. They found that female lizards in the first stage of repro-

duction—when eggs were developing in the ovary and estrogen hormone levels were high—behaved as females. Following ovulation, when estrogen levels dropped and progesterone levels rose, the female behaved as a male and would initiate courtship with females who were in the ovulatory stage. The courtship ritual, presumably stimulated by the brain and hormones, promoted egg development. Crews and his colleagues also found evidence that strongly suggested that progesterone stimulates the area of the brain that controls mounting and copulation in males of species closely related to *C. uniparens*. Normally, male sex hormones, androgens, stimulate this brain center. There was interest in seeing if courtship behavior occurs and plays a similar role in other parthenogenetic vertebrates and invertebrates. These studies also suggested that perhaps the difference between male and female might not be as great as had been assumed.

The bolas spiders of the genus *Mastophora* hang from a simple "trapeze line" and capture prey by throwing a line with a sticky droplet on its end. Curiously, they almost exclusively catch male moths. Following the lead suggested by this observation, Mark K. Stowe of Harvard University and James H. Tumlinson and Robert R. Heath of the Agricultural Research Service, U.S. Department of Agriculture, found that specimens of *M. cornigera* emit scents identical to components of the sex pheromones of certain female moths. Since individual spiders may capture several species of male moths, the investigators proposed that the spiders may be able to vary the proportions of the chemicals that make up the scent so as to mimic the scents of various species of female moths.

In two simultaneously reported but independent studies, Monica H. Mather and Bernard D. Roitberg of Simon Fraser University, Burnaby, B.C., and Erick Greene of Princeton University, Larry J. Orsak of the University of Georgia, and Douglas W. Whitman of the U.S. Department of Agriculture showed that certain tephritid fruit flies mimic a spider predator to frighten it away. When approached by a jumping spider, these flies stick their wings out from their bodies, wave them up and down, and move about with little jerky motions. The wings have stripes that make them resemble a spider's legs, and spots on each side of the flies' abdomens resemble eyes. The appearance and movements seem to be interpreted by the spider as aggressive movements by another jumping spider into whose territory it has encroached. In most cases the spider retreats or allows the fly to back away and fly off. This appears to be the first known case of an animal protecting itself by mimicking its predator.

Physiology. Scattered among the nerve cells of the central nervous system of vertebrates are a number

362

of other cell types. One of these, the astrocyte, received considerable attention during the year. Astrocytes are so called because of their star-like shape, with the points of the star extending like irregular fingers from the central region of the cell. Robert C. Janzer and Martin C. Raff of University College, London, found evidence that a secretion of these cells promotes the formation of "tight junctions" between the endothelial cells that make up the walls of the blood capillaries in the brain. These junctions greatly reduce the kinds of materials that may pass from the blood to the brain cells and are thought to be an important aspect of this blood-brain barrier.

Olaf B. Paulson of the State University Hospital, Copenhagen, and Eric A. Newman of the Eye Research Institute of Retina Foundation, Boston, also found that astrocytes appear to be important in regulating blood flow to the brain. When nerve cells increase in activity, the astrocytes release potassium ions near small arterioles (small terminal twigs of arteries). This relaxes the muscles in the blood vessel walls so that the diameters of the vessels increase, thereby also increasing blood flow.

Another function of astrocytes was demonstrated by Francis J. Liuzzi and Raymond J. Lasek of Eastern Virginia Medical School. They found that astrocytes apparently secrete a material that causes nerve cell extensions, the axons, to stop growing. This discovery revealed that the presence of astrocytes in the brain and spinal cord is an important reason why axon regeneration after injury is usually not successful in those areas. The authors speculated that the normal function of the astrocytes' ability to prevent elongation of the axons may be to prevent axons from growing away from their proper connections in the brain and spinal cord.

For many years zoologists had speculated that there are substances—"morphogens"—that concentrate in developing tissues and that induce structural

A tephritid fruit fly (left) has stripes on its wings and a wing-waving display that together mimic a jumping spider, its predator. The spider at the right stopped stalking the fly when the fly waved its wings.

AP/Wide World

differentiation that varies depending upon the level of concentration. During the past year it appeared that one of those substances had been identified. Christina Thaller and Gregor Eichele of Harvard Medical School demonstrated that there are varying levels of concentration of retinoic acid in the developing limb bud of the chicken. They extracted 5,500 different regions of the limb buds of chicken embryos and found retinoic acid, a chemical similar to vitamin A, to be most concentrated in the back margin of the bud and least in the front margin. Previously it had been demonstrated that the application of retinoic acid to limb buds would cause them to differentiate, but whether this occurred without such application had not been known. The measured concentrations of retinoic acid in the chicks were similar to those that caused developmental effects when applied artificially. It seemed likely that similar mechanisms controlling development are universal among animals.

Sociobiology. As with all science, biology was becoming a more prominent aspect of everyday life and was frequently in the news. During the year several important events took place in the legal courts rather than in the laboratory or field. Prominent among these was the U.S. Supreme Court's 7–2 decision ruling that a Louisiana law requiring "creation science" to be given equal time in the classroom with the theory of evolution was unconstitutional.

In what many hoped would be a trend-setting procedure, Bolivia canceled a small part of its national debt in return for expanding the Beni Biosphere Reserve in its northern tropical region. Acting as intermediary, Washington, D.C.-based Conservation International arranged an exchange in which debtors accepted $100,000 to cancel $650,000 of loans to Bolivia. As part of the deal, Bolivia agreed to set up and protect nature reserves. It was hoped that this kind of arrangement could be made with many less developed nations with similar large debts.

Grube Messel, an old oil-shale mine in West Germany's Rhein Main, is perhaps the best fossil site in the world of the Eocene Epoch (about 54 million–38 million years ago). It has provided hundreds of fossils, many unique, of animals ranging from insects to mammals. The pit is located in a highly industrialized region, and over the years a fight has been waged to keep it from being used as a dumping site for garbage. Again during the past year the site was designated as a dump. Fortunately, as a result of lobbying by scientists from many countries, a December court ruling blocked the use of the site for that purpose.

—J. R. Redmond

See also Feature Articles: SCIENCE AND THE THOROUGHBRED HORSE; "MICROLIVESTOCK"—WHEN SMALLER IS BETTER.

Materials sciences

A major breakthrough—the discovery of high-temperature ceramic superconductors—took place in the materials sciences during the past year. Other notable activity included work on developing a more efficient means of extracting lead from its ores and efforts to produce alloys that combine high strength, low density, and resistance to high temperatures.

Ceramics

While progress was made in a number of areas during the past year, the single most significant advance was the discovery of high-temperature ceramic superconductors. The original discovery of superconductivity was closely tied to cryogenic (very low-temperature) research. In 1877 oxygen was liquefied by being cooled below its boiling point, and hydrogen was liquefied in 1898. Then Heike Kamerlingh Onnes, a Dutch physicist, liquefied helium in 1908. It was the most difficult gas of all to liquefy because it had to be cooled to just 4.2 K above 0 K, absolute zero (−273.15° C [−459.67° F], the temperature at which there is no heat).

In 1911, while studying the properties of various materials at these very low temperatures, Onnes and one of his students discovered that mercury loses all of its electrical resistance and thus becomes a superconductor as its temperature approaches 4.2 K. Onnes was awarded the Nobel Prize for Physics in 1913.

The existence of superconductivity immediately suggested tremendous advantages for the construction of electrical equipment, especially electromagnets. Unfortunately, working at liquid-helium temperatures was both inconvenient and expensive. Also, early attempts to make superconducting magnets were stymied by the discovery that the superconducting state disappears not only above some critical temperature, T_c, but also above specific critical current and magnetic field levels, and those critical levels in all of the elements that were found to be superconducting were too low for practical applications. (A critical current is the current in a superconductive material above which the material is normal and below which it is a superconductor, at a specified temperature and in the absence of external magnetic fields.)

The first major step toward a theoretical explanation of superconductors took place in 1933, when it was shown that they have virtually no magnetic susceptibility. Because of this property, superconductors exclude any applied magnetic field. This is called the Meissner effect, and it is one of the major tests for the existence of true superconductivity.

The theory of low-temperature superconductivity,

now known as the BCS theory, appeared in 1957. It was named for its authors—John Bardeen, Leon Cooper, and John Schrieffer—who won the 1972 Nobel Prize for Physics for its discovery. It is based on the transition of the material to a state in which electrons form bound pairs (Cooper pairs) that move through the material in an orderly, unimpeded fashion without interacting with the vibrations of the atomic lattice. This contrasts sharply with the normal situation, in which electron-lattice interactions cause scattering of the electrons, energy absorption, and conventional levels of electrical resistance.

Unfortunately, while the BCS theory explained most aspects of superconductivity, it could not predict which new materials might have higher critical temperatures and magnetic fields, and further progress was agonizingly slow. In 1953 a compound of vanadium and silicon (V_3Si) was found to be superconducting at 17.5 K, and then Bernd Matthias found a niobium-tin compound (Nb_3Sn) to be superconducting at 18 K. By 1973 the search had led to niobium-germanium (Nb_3Ge) with a T_c of 23.2 K, and then the search stalled completely. Pessimists, in fact, suggested that on the basis of the BCS theory,

Technician inserts a projectile into a gas-powered "gun" at Sandia National Laboratories. The device tests materials by hurling projectiles at them at speeds of about 5,800 kilometers per hour (3,600 miles per hour).

superconductivity might not even be possible above about 30 K.

The niobium-tin materials had the advantage of higher critical magnetic fields and, as ways were found to make them into wires, large superconducting magnets were finally built. They still had to be cooled by liquid helium, however, and their use was therefore very limited.

Within this framework of stalled progress, Karl Müller and Johannes Bednorz at the IBM Zürich (Switz.) Research Laboratory made a truly amazing discovery. Although all previous empirical approaches to the search for higher T_c superconductors had suggested that ceramics were unlikely candidates, in 1983 Müller and Bednorz began looking at hundreds of different combinations of metal oxides. In December 1985 they found a barium lanthanum copper oxide whose resistance dropped sharply at 35 K. They published their findings a few months later, but most researchers paid little attention because Müller and Bednorz had not tested for the Meissner effect.

Some researchers did pay attention, however, and soon a few in Japan, China, and the U.S. had obtained similar results. When Japanese researchers announced at a Materials Research Society meeting in December 1986 that they had in fact seen the Meissner effect in Müller and Bednorz's material, interest in ceramic superconductors took off at a dizzying pace.

AT&T Bell Laboratories put a team of scientists to work in the area and soon reached 38 K. Paul Chu and co-workers at the Universities of Houston (Texas) and Alabama reached 40 K, and Zhao Zhongxian's group at Beijing (Peking) University reached 46 K in closely related materials, all by the end of 1986.

Then, in January 1987, Chu's group found that through application of pressure to barium lanthanum copper oxide, the T_c could be raised to 52.5 K. With headlines around the world announcing advances almost daily, Chu's group made the most astonishing announcement of all. Maw-Kuen Wu, head of the team's University of Alabama group, had substituted yttrium for the lanthanum in their material and found a T_c of about 93 K. By the end of January, he and Chu had prepared an yttrium barium copper oxide with a T_c of about 97 K. A superconductor with the long-sought ability to operate above the boiling point of inexpensive liquid nitrogen (77 K) had finally been found.

By March the attention of the physics community was focused on these new ceramic superconductors, and thousands of physicists jammed the ballroom at the American Physical Society's annual meeting to hear the first rush of reports by scientists from around the world. Though papers were limited to

Scientists at an AT&T laboratory make ceramic tape out of the recently discovered high-temperature superconductors. One of the steps in the process is to grind various elements by hand (foreground).

five minutes each, the session went on into the early hours of the morning.

The enthusiasm of the scientists was matched by the eagerness of many companies to position themselves to enter what may be a revolutionary new commercial market. Spurred by the possibility of inexpensive operation above liquid nitrogen temperatures and perhaps even at room temperature someday, these firms quickly generated long lists of potential applications. Ceramic superconductors could be used to make not only magnets with incredibly high magnetic fields but also highly efficient electrical generators, power-transmission lines, and energy-storage devices. They could be used to levitate high-speed trains, but they could also be used in the form of compact, powerful motors on the wheels of efficient electric cars.

Applications in the form of superconducting ceramic thin films could probably be among the first to be commercialized. Superconducting quantum interference devices (SQUIDS) that can detect minute magnetic fields had been fabricated by the beginning of 1988. They were expected to be used in a variety of applications, ranging from the detection of brain impulses for medical diagnostics to the detection of underground or underwater objects for geologic and defense purposes. In the form of devices that would eliminate the problems of heat buildup, thin-film ceramic superconductors could make possible a new

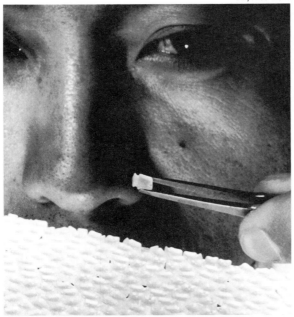

Technician inspects an orthodontic brace made of a durable and stain-resistant ceramic material. The ceramic blends with the natural color of teeth and straightens them as effectively as traditional metal braces do.

generation of much more compact and much more powerful computers.

Thin-film ceramic superconductors might also revolutionize data-transmission systems. Researchers at Cornell University, Ithaca, N.Y., and the University of Rochester, N.Y., showed that in the superconducting state, yttrium barium copper oxide films can conduct electrical pulses of 10–15 picoseconds without absorption or distortion. Building on this, they proposed a superconducting data-transmission line that could carry one trillion bits of information per second, a rate 100 times faster than fiber-optic cables.

The economic implications of these and a host of other possible applications set large corporations throughout the world to work at a feverish pace to establish patent positions and find early commercialization opportunities. Large Japanese companies, such as Hitachi, Toshiba, Sumitomo Electric, and Mitsubishi Electric, sped ahead without waiting for government initiatives, though a Japanese Ministry of International Trade and Industry planning study was quickly begun. In July in Washington, D.C., U.S. Pres. Ronald Reagan addressed a federal conference on commercial applications of superconductors and announced a government-supported initiative to foster U.S. leadership in the area.

While experimentalists pressed on with their search for better materials, theorists readily admitted that the BCS theory did not, and probably could not,

account for the high T_c behavior of the new ceramic superconductors. Bardeen, for example, suggested that entirely new mechanisms might be at work.

What was known was that all of the ceramics that had been found to exhibit high T_c levels had the perovskite crystal structure, in which planes of copper and oxygen atoms are separated at regular intervals by planes containing the alkaline-earth and rare-earth atoms. In the composition that Chu's team found, the yttrium barium copper oxide, the ratio of the elements and the oxygen content is critical. The best results were obtained with the so-called 1-2-3 compound, $YBa_2Cu_3O_{7-x}$, where x is typically about 0.02. Most researchers found that control of the oxygen content during fabrication was especially important. Much of the research centered on trying to understand the role of these structural factors in the formation of Cooper pairs and the superconducting state in these materials.

In the meantime, most of the experimental work in the area was focused in three major directions. These were improvements in critical current density, the development of practical fabrication processes, and the search for still higher T_cs.

Many practical applications for bulk superconductors require current densities, J_cs, of the order of one million amperes per square centimeter (A/cm^2), and even many of the thin-film applications require J_cs much higher than the 10–1,000 A/cm^2 found in the polycrystalline high-T_c ceramic superconductors fabricated early in the year. In May, however, IBM researchers produced small single crystals of these materials and found J_c values above 100,000 A/cm^2, suggesting that the low values observed are not an inherent property of these materials. Indeed, polycrystalline materials produced since that time, with increased attention to grain orientation and grain boundary quality, demonstrated promising improvements in J_c.

Ceramic superconductors also need to be fabricated into usable shapes. This is not particularly difficult for thin-film devices that can be deposited on substrates by a variety of familiar techniques. Many bulk forms will be much more difficult to fabricate, however, because, like conventional ceramics, the ceramic superconductors are inherently brittle. What can be done easily in the fabrication of a ductile metal, such as the manufacture of wire, can be a major problem for a ceramic superconductor. During the year a number of companies sought ways to resolve this problem. For example, AT&T studied tape casting, while Argonne National Laboratories and Toshiba each pursued wire extrusion, and IBM focused on plasma spraying.

With superconductivity at 97 K well accepted, the search began for still higher T_c values, and a number of researchers reported intriguing observations.

Many different groups had seen a resistance drop in their materials at about 240 K, which some believed might represent the presence of a new superconducting phase with a higher T_c. Some witnessed tantalizing hints of even higher T_cs, including observations near 290 K.

—Norman M. Tallan

For an extended discussion of superconductivity, *see* Feature Article: THE NEW SUPERCONDUCTORS: A SCIENTIFIC BREAKTHROUGH.

Metallurgy

Production of lead. Construction of metallurgical plants that employ revolutionary new technology for the production of lead began during the past year. The conventional process for making lead, which has been in use for more than 100 years, is a batch process involving separate reduction and oxidation steps. In the first step, air is blown through a moving bed of concentrated lead sulfide ore to produce a lead oxide sinter (coherent mass) and sulfur dioxide gas. This oxidation reaction is extremely exothermic (generates considerable heat), and control of the temperature during sintering requires that the feed material contain twice as much recycled sintered oxide as new ore concentrate. The sintered material is then fed, along with slag-making fluxes and metallurgical coke, to the second stage of the process; this comprises reduction in a blast furnace to produce a slag containing the zinc and the iron present in the ore and an impure metallic lead bullion that is taken on for refining.

Operators of this conventional process are finding it increasingly difficult to keep the emissions of lead from the sinter plant and of sulfur dioxide from the blast furnace below the increasingly stringent levels mandated by air-pollution regulations. Also, the cost of raw materials is forcing operators to seek a fuel and reductant that is less expensive than metallurgical coke.

A major goal throughout the nonferrous metals extraction industry has been the development of a continuous process conducted within a single reaction vessel. In the envisioned process, the reactor would continuously produce from a continuous feed of concentrated ore, slag-making flux, and fuel a reasonably pure metal, a slag that could be discarded, and a small volume of gas containing a high concentration of sulfur dioxide. The challenge was thus to invent and develop a technology in which both the required chemical oxidation and reduction reactions could be conducted within a single reactor that would be tight enough to eliminate air pollution.

The revolutionary new technology that achieved those goals is embodied in the QSL process, which is named for the initials of its U.S. inventors, P. E.

Queneau and R. Schuhmann, Jr., and the German firm, Lurgi. After 12 years of development work, QSL plants capable of producing 52,000 metric tons and 120,000 metric tons per year were being constructed, respectively, in Gansu (Kansu), China, and in British Columbia.

The QSL process uses a long cylindrical reactor that is inclined slightly to the horizontal and is capable of being rotated 90° about its axis. It operates on a countercurrent-flow principle in which an upper layer of slag flows from the entry end toward the discharge end and a lower layer of liquid lead flows in the opposite direction. It is a chemically staged reactor in which oxidizing conditions, maintained near the entry end, are gradually changed to reducing conditions at the discharge end. The oxidation and reduction zones are separated by a weir over which the slag flows and under which the lead flows. During operation a moist pelletized mixture of ore concentrate, fluxes, recycled flue dust, and coal is continuously fed to the slag layer at the entry end; also at that end oxygen is blown into the melts through gas-cooled nozzles in the bottom of the reactor.

The exothermic reactions that occur in the QSL process produce sulfur dioxide gas, a slag containing 30–35% lead, and metallic lead, which sinks to the layer of metal beneath the slag. The heat released by the reactions maintains a temperature of 1,000°–1,100° C (1,830°–2,010°F). The slag flows over the weir into the reducing zone, in which powdered coal and oxygen or air are blown into the melts through nozzles in the bottom of the vessel. The nozzles are spaced at intervals in order to produce a mixer-settler configuration in which moderately turbulent reaction pools are separated by calmer settling pools. This causes reduction of the lead oxide in the slag to metallic lead, which then joins the metal layer. The layer of metallic lead continuously flows toward the entry end of the vessel, where it is removed via a siphon, and the slag continuously leaves the vessel via an overflow at the discharge end. Depending on the nature of the charge materials, the recovery rate of lead can be as high as 98%.

It has been estimated that the sulfur dioxide emissions, lead emissions, and the total energy costs of the QSL process are, respectively, 5, 25, and 40% of those occurring in the conventional process. Also, in comparison with the conventional process, the use of oxygen for the oxidation reactions produces a relatively small volume of product gas that can contain up to 25% by volume of sulfur dioxide (which is more easily removed than is a small percentage from a large volume of gas). In addition, the problems associated with materials handling are decreased, and inexpensive coal fines are used instead of metallurgical coke.

Alloys. The decision to build the National Aerospace Plane (the X-30 aircraft) intensified research on alloys that combine high strength, low density, and resistance to high temperature. Separate research programs were being conducted on nickel-based superalloys and aluminum alloys.

A significant increase in the operating temperature of the nickel-based superalloy blades used in gas turbines was achieved by means of improved processing technology and alloy design. The first improvement was achieved by the introduction of directional solidification of the blades during casting. In this process solidification was controlled in such a manner that the grain boundaries in the casting were aligned parallel to the direction of the principal stress exerted on the blade during service. This permitted high-strength alloys of limited ductility to be used. A further significant improvement was achieved by the casting of the turbine blades as single crystals. It was found that the incipient melting temperature of the single-crystal blades was 80°–110° C (150°–200° F) higher than that of the columnar-grained blades produced by directional solidification. In the latter the incipient melting temperature was determined by the presence, at the grain boundaries, of boron, carbon, and zirconium, which had been added to strengthen the grain boundaries.

The increase in the incipient melting temperature, which was due to the elimination of the grain boundaries, permitted the single-crystal blades to be heat-treated at temperatures high enough to dissolve completely the coarse gamma prime phase that had formed as a result of the slow cooling during casting. (The gamma prime phase is an intermetallic compound of general formula $Ni_3(Al,Ti)$. (Ni is nickel, Al is aluminum, and Ti is titanium.) The consequent control of the gamma prime precipitation during subsequent cooling permitted improvements to be made in the resistance of the blades to creep strength and thermal fatigue. (Creep strength is the stress that, at a given temperature, will result in a creep rate of 1% deformation in 100,000 hours.)

Further alloy design using such elements as Al, Ti, and W (tungsten) permitted control of the volume percentage of the gamma prime precipitates, and the addition of Co (cobalt) allowed manipulation of the temperature range over which the gamma prime phase precipitates. The use of fewer alloying elements in the single-crystal design also permitted additional increases in the maximum allowable heat-treatment temperatures, and the inclusion of Al increased the resistance to oxidation.

Aluminum alloys were being developed for aerospace service at lower temperatures (177°–343° C [350°–650° F]), and interest was focused on rapid solidification processing (RSP) and metal matrix composites (MMCs) based on aluminum, both

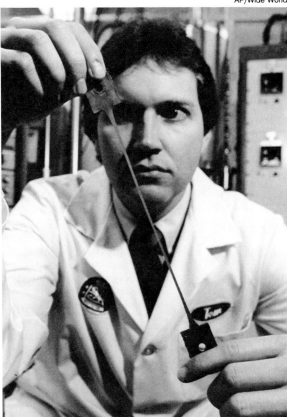

AP/Wide World

Research scientist examines a specially formed sample of a new lithium-aluminum alloy that can be stretched to more than ten times its original length when heated and is expected to have applications in the aerospace industry.

of which increased the stiffness of the alloy. RSP facilitated control of the microstructure by refining the grain size, increasing the solubilities of solute elements, and eliminating or minimizing the precipitation of undesirable intermetallic compounds. RSP thus permitted increased structural refinement, although MMCs, in which conventional aluminum alloys are reinforced with boron and silicon carbide fibers, whiskers, or particles, are stiffer.

Lithium-aluminum alloys were also being considered for applications in which weight is critical. The addition of each percentage of lithium to the total weight of the alloy increases its stiffness by 6% and decreases the density by 3%. However, with the use of conventional casting techniques, a maximum of only 4.2% of lithium can be retained in solid solution in aluminum. A higher lithium content could be obtained through the use of RSP and, therefore, a significant increase in stiffness could be obtained, but such alloys have poorer resistance to fracture than do those that are conventionally cast.

—David R. Gaskell

Mathematics

After the many exciting achievements of the past several years, mathematics in 1987 experienced no major research breakthroughs. Mathematicians instead turned their attention to celebration, as the American Mathematical Society prepared for its centenary in 1988, and also to taking stock of mathematics education.

Two events precipitated intense discussion among mathematics educators at all levels, from grade school to college. The first was the release of results from the International Assessment of Educational Progress. This comparison of the level of mathematics achievement of 13- and 17-year-olds in a score of countries revealed that U.S. students lagged behind students in virtually all other countries—and far behind students in Japan. Many potential explanations for this embarrassing result, such as differences in class size, elite foreign students being compared with average U.S. students, and differences in amount of class time spent studying mathematics, were found not to be the case. Attitudinal surveys revealed that U.S. students tended to regard mathematics as unnecessary and too hard for them to learn, while Japanese students believed that mathematics was difficult but that anyone could succeed at it by working hard enough. At the same time, U.S. parents seemed satisfied with the low level of achievement of their children in mathematics, while Japanese parents wanted their students to learn even more mathematics in school.

The international comparisons added fuel to a fire that had been building for some years: a sense among U.S. educators, intellectuals, and government leaders that future U.S. leadership in science and mathematics was seriously at risk because of the poor state of mathematics education. In 1987 for the first time, foreign-born students received more than 50% of the Ph.D.'s in mathematics awarded by U.S. institutions. The increasingly enormous foreign debt of the U.S. forced leaders to consider that a loss of scientific intellectual leadership might well have economic consequences as well.

Calculus. While the above concerns were directed primarily to elementary and secondary education, the second major focus of discussion was on the teaching of calculus, usually taken at the college level in the U.S. Calculus is the quantitative study of continuous change. The mainline calculus course for science students generally is two to three semesters in length, though abbreviated versions are offered to students in other disciplines.

Success in mastering calculus depends on not just acquaintance with but mastery of virtually all of the topics of high-school mathematics. At colleges throughout the U.S., shockingly low proportions of

students—often as low as 50%—succeed in their first calculus course; the others drop out or receive grades of D or F. This dismally low success rate has been unchanged for many years, and research shows that many variables of instructional style (such as class size) have little effect.

As more U.S. college students have majored in business (25% of the total in 1980, compared with 12% in 1970) and as the quantity of students has declined, the number of students going on to careers in science and engineering—for which calculus is a requirement—has fallen by about 50% since 1970. To meet the needs of the nation, however, calculus must become, in the words of Robert White, president of the National Academy of Engineering, "a pump, not a filter."

Calculus, in fact, is a prerequisite for more than half of the major fields of study in college, and enrollments in the subject have not declined. About 750,000 U.S. students study calculus each year, and courses in both calculus and precalculus are among the top five in enrollment. As student preparation and motivation in mathematics have declined over the past 15 years, however, calculus courses have evolved away from their former emphasis on proof and rigor to testing students mainly on mechanical and calculational problems.

Two internal influences have caused mathematicians to reexamine calculus. The first is the drive by computer scientists in the past four years, spearheaded by Anthony Ralston of the State University of New York at Buffalo, to include discrete mathematics in place of some of the calculus studied in the first year of college. Discrete mathematics includes topics more relevant to computer science, such as difference equations, recurrence relations, finite probability distributions, graphs, trees, and proof by mathematical induction.

Such an accommodation may be long past due by 1990, when twice as many students may graduate in computer science as in mathematics, statistics, physics, and chemistry combined. Mathematicians, many of whom also teach computer science, have proved receptive to considering such change and have been closely scrutinizing the calculus syllabus. The degree of change and the specifics of what part of calculus is to be left out or postponed still needed to be worked out and agreed upon.

The second and concurrent influence leading to a reexamination of calculus has been technology. At the January 1988 banquet celebrating the 100th birthday of the American Mathematical Society, 1,500 of the approximately 2,000 mathematicians present purchased (at a 75% discount) a Hewlett-Packard calculator that could perform almost all of the arithmetic and symbolic calculations of calculus as well as graphing multiple equations on its display

Calculator introduced during the past year can perform almost all of the arithmetic and symbolic calculations of calculus and can graph multiple equations on its display screen. It also can display mathematical matrices in the same form as they are written on paper.

screen. Just as the appearance a dozen years ago of the inexpensive calculator for ordinary arithmetic raised the question as to whether students should spend eight years learning arithmetic, the new calculator forced the analogous issue for calculus.

Mathematicians in 1988 were hard at work on devising and implementing a "lean and lively" calculus, and the National Science Foundation was providing $2 million in funding initiatives for experiments in formulating a new calculus course. There was concern, however, that the new calculus might prove more difficult for students than the old; with the computations taken care of by calculator, both teaching and testing could and had to concentrate on thinking and concept development, and students were substantially weaker in those areas (*e.g.,* interpreting and setting up word problems) than in calculation.

Milestones. Television became a major medium for communication of mathematics with the debut of two extended series of half-hour programs on public television. "Square One," a series of 75 programs for 8- to 12-year-olds from the Children's Television Workshop (creators of "Sesame Street," "The Electric Company," and "3-2-1 Contact"), began in early 1987. A series of 26 programs on contemporary applied mathematics, titled "For All Practical Purposes" and targeted at adults, began being aired in early 1988. This series (and its accompanying book of the same title) originated with the observation that most college students take only a single course in mathematics, and its content represented the responses of leading mathematicians concerning the topics of basic mathematical importance that

play a critical role in a person's economic, political, and personal life.

The members of the Mathematical Association of America, expressing faith in the research of a number of its members, decided in 1987 to elect their president and vice-president by a procedure called approval voting. Approval voting allows each elector to vote for as many candidates as he or she wishes, with one vote for each. This voting method, which has been carefully analyzed by mathematicians, does not suffer from some of the potential anomalies of other common systems, nor is it as complicated as other proposed alternatives. (Voting methods, including approval voting, were the subject of one of the programs of "For All Practical Purposes.")

—Paul J. Campbell

Medical sciences

An important discovery concerning muscular dystrophy, the development of electronic anesthesia in dentistry, the introduction of a new cancer therapy, the detection of a new virus that affects cats, and continued research on AIDS (acquired immune deficiency syndrome) were among the highlights of the year in the medical sciences.

General medicine

Once again AIDS dominated the medical news headlines, but scientists also recorded progress in other areas. They identified the protein whose absence causes muscular dystrophy and worked on surgical and dietary interventions for Parkinson's disease and on surgical and drug treatments for heart disease. Scientists developed new vaccines and treatments for cancer. Genes responsible for several diseases were discovered, and more was learned about the common cold.

Muscular dystrophy. Scientists made major inroads into the mystery of Duchenne muscular dystrophy (DMD), the most common form of the muscle-wasting disease. Having identified the genetic basis for DMD in 1986, the researchers worked backward from the gene and quickly figured out the key protein. It was an obvious follow-up, but the discovery generated a great deal of excitement because it greatly expanded the understanding of the disease.

DMD is inherited via the X chromosome. Females have two X chromosomes and, therefore, two chances that one of them is normal, so they very rarely suffer from this form of muscular dystrophy. If a male's single X chromosome is defective, however, he has no backup, and roughly one in 3,500 male births results in DMD. The victims begin to show signs of muscle problems around the age of 3, lose the ability to walk by about 11, and generally die by the age of 20 after the muscles that work their lungs weaken.

Researchers led by Louis M. Kunkel at Harvard University found the gene by comparing a normal X chromosome with an X chromosome from a boy with DMD. In the boy's chromosome they found a gene similar to one in mice that have an inherited muscle defect that in some ways resembles DMD. Proteins constructed by pieces of the mouse and human genes when injected into animals caused the animals to make antibodies to the protein segments. The antibodies were then isolated and used as probes to look for the normal protein in muscle cells; Kunkel and his colleagues discovered that the probe found the protein in normal muscle cells but failed to do so in cells from two boys with DMD.

The protein, which the researchers named dystrophin, is extremely rare, comprising only 0.002% of a muscle cell's protein. As of early 1988, its function was not known but, once it was understood, scientists hoped to be able to figure out a way to place it in people with DMD. A second potential benefit from the work may be earlier diagnosis. Currently it is difficult to distinguish between DMD and another, more benign, form of muscular dystrophy. Developing a test for dystrophin would enable physicians to differentiate between the two diseases earlier.

In the meantime, another discovery may help DMD patients in the short run. Researchers at Johns Hopkins University, Baltimore, Md., announced that the drug prednisone can delay the devastating effects of the disease by two years or more. In their study untreated boys had to use wheelchairs by age 10, but the drug kept 16 boys from that fate until the age of 12.

Parkinson's disease. Scientists were throwing everything they could at Parkinson's disease, a progressively crippling condition that generally strikes people over 60 years of age. The disease causes degeneration of brain cells, resulting in shaking and tremors. While the drug L-dopa provides temporary relief by replacing dopamine, a chemical lost as a result of the brain degeneration, side effects limit its long-term use. As the search for more effective drugs continued, two strikingly different approaches—diet and surgery—showed promise.

The diet approach was under investigation at Yale University, where preliminary studies showed that patients with Parkinson's disease who eat little or no protein during the day can use less L-dopa. Studies revealed that the daily ups and downs in symptoms seen in long-term patients are not due to changes in the body's sensitivity to the drug. Instead, changes in the body's ability to absorb the drug seem to be part of the problem, and these changes, scientists hypothesized, could be due to what the patient eats during the day, especially because the drug uses the same transport system as do protein components to move from the gut to the blood and from the blood to the brain. Thus, one possible explanation for the daily changes is that less of the drug gets through to the brain if there is a large amount of protein in the patient's digestive system.

On the basis of the hypothesis described above, the Yale University researchers decided to try a low-protein approach. When they switched seven patients between very low- and high-protein diets, they discovered that the patients' symptoms remained minor and consistent on the low-protein diet but were more severe and changeable on the high-protein regimen. However, at the National Institute of Neurological and Communicative Disorders and Stroke, a part of the U.S. National Institutes of Health (NIH), researchers tested the effect of high protein on six patients and found that while extra-high levels reduced the effectiveness of L-dopa, normal protein consumption did not affect blood levels of the drug. The two studies might not be contradictory—the Yale team used a much lower level of protein—but the NIH researchers nevertheless concluded that because the levels of the drug and the symptoms of the disease seemed unrelated to meals with an average level of protein, low levels of protein probably would not be helpful.

The use of brain implants with fetal tissue to counteract Parkinson's was also considered a promising treatment. Because it used fetal tissue, the surgery proved to be controversial.

The surgical technique was pioneered by Ignacio Madrazo of Mexico City. Madrazo and his colleagues

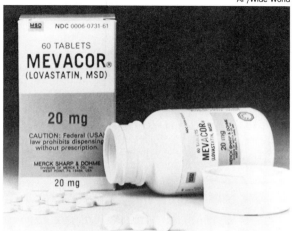
< align="left">

AP/Wide World

Lovastatin, a new drug to be marketed under the name Mevacor, blocks cholesterol-producing enzymes in the liver and, according to the U.S. Food and Drug Administration, reduces total cholesterol levels by 18 to 34%.

had previously performed operations using the patients' own adrenal glands because these glands, like the section of the brain that degenerates in Parkinson's patients, produces dopamine. Fetal tissue, they suspected, would grow better and also would be immunologically neutral. In September Madrazo took tissue from the brain and adrenal gland of a 13-week-old fetus that had been spontaneously aborted and used it for two patients. While the adrenal gland procedure provided some relief, no judgment could yet be made on the effectiveness of the fetal surgery.

Heart disease. In the never-ending effort to limit the Western world's greatest killer—heart disease— researchers have tried everything from artificial hearts to blasting out clogged arteries with lasers. Among the treatments considered during the past year were new drugs and "scaffolding" to shore up heart arteries.

The heart scaffolding, called a stent, was first used by Swiss and French researchers to solve a problem that arose as a result of a solution. The initial solution is called percutaneous transluminal coronary angioplasty (PTCA), which solves the problem of clogging in the heart's own arteries—the arteries that serve up fresh blood to the heart muscle. PTCA is a procedure in which a balloon is snaked into the constricted artery and inflated, pushing back the walls.

In one-third of the cases, however, the arteries quickly close up. Therefore, scientists, led by Swiss researcher Ulrich Sigwart, developed the stent, a flexible coil that can hold the artery open. They first used it in humans in 1986 and continued developing it through 1987. By the time they described it at the 1987 meeting of the American Heart Association, several U.S. groups had also developed stents.

The U.S. joined several other nations during the year in another approach to cardiology, drug treatment after a heart attack. The other countries had already approved the use of t-PA, a drug that breaks up the artery-blocking clots that cause heart attacks. Other clot-busters were already available, but the genetically engineered t-PA was believed by many researchers to work more quickly. However, only in the early stages of a heart attack is the drug effective.

The U.S. also approved another new drug, called lovastatin. Rather than treating heart attacks, though, lovastatin is aimed at preventing them by reducing blood cholesterol levels. The drug inhibits the action of an enzyme that is necessary for the production of cholesterol. With a decreased ability to manufacture its own cholesterol, the body scavenges it from the blood.

The U.S. inaugurated a massive public education program in an attempt to stave off heart attacks before they occur. The hope was to make the entire nation aware of the problem of high blood cholesterol and also the ability to reverse the condition with diet or, in severe cases, with drugs. According to the National Heart, Lung, and Blood Institute, which was spearheading the program, anyone with a cholesterol level over 240 milligrams per deciliter should try to reduce it, and even levels between 200 and 240 warrant further investigation. The program faced an uphill battle if it was to succeed; it had to reach and convince millions of people—as many as a quarter of all U.S. adults—to make some changes in their life-styles.

Some physicians remained skeptical about the importance of cholesterol, and they received support from a study by William Taylor of Harvard University and his colleagues. They analyzed data from a long-term study of the residents of Framingham, Mass., and determined that lowering the level of cholesterol increases life expectancy only three days to three months for people with no other risk factors. People who are at the highest risk—who smoke and have high blood pressure and high cholesterol levels—can extend their lives by an average of 12 months, they estimated. The initial collectors of the Framingham data disagreed with Taylor's analysis, however

One study proved convincing to many investigators—a careful look at the coronary arteries of men on cholesterol-lowering drugs. University of Southern California researchers found that clogged arteries became less clogged when blood cholesterol dropped, indicating that lowering cholesterol not only will stop the progression of disease but in some cases will actually reverse it.

Vaccines. Vaccines by 1988 had relegated smallpox to the annals of history and had nearly eliminated other formerly devastating infectious diseases in much of the developed world. There were still

372

many diseases for which there was no effective vaccine, however, among them malaria, chicken pox, and a form of meningitis that can lead to deafness or retardation in infants.

The Hib vaccine, developed in Finland, proved to be especially thorny. It was aimed at *Haemophilus influenzae b,* a bacterium that can cause meningitis (an inflammation of the covering of the brain and spinal cord) and several other conditions. While the vaccine was 90% effective in Finland, it did not do nearly as well in the U.S. after it was approved for use in 1985. In the state of Minnesota, in fact, more vaccinated than unvaccinated children got the disease. One possible reason for this was the genetic variation in the U.S. population. Several companies were working on a new vaccine that may stimulate the immune system better. They were attempting to accomplish this by hooking a portion of the *Haemophilus* bacterium to part of the toxin produced by the diphtheria bacterium, which is a powerful stimulator of the immune system. One such vaccine was approved by the U.S. Food and Drug Administration in December.

U.S. trials with a chicken-pox vaccine neared completion, in the midst of debate about its effectiveness. The vaccine was developed in Japan in the early 1970s and has been used on more than 100,000 children there, but U.S. experts were hesitant. Chicken pox is a serious condition for pregnant women and children whose immunity is hampered by disease, drugs, or cancer, but for most children chicken pox is not life-threatening. In addition, no one knew if the protection given by the vaccine would be permanent; if it wears off, as many vaccines do, it could leave adults unprotected, and the disease is much worse in adults.

Researchers were coming closer to developing a vaccine for malaria. The microbe temporarily stymied investigators because of its life-style—the parasite is only "naked" in the bloodstream and thus is vulnerable to a vaccine for a short part of its life. Swedish researchers during the year described the development of a vaccine that attacks the parasite before it burrows into red blood cells. NIH researchers were also working on a vaccine that creates antibodies to the stage of the parasite that infects liver cells.

Cancer. A new cancer therapy came to light in 1987. Called photopheresis, the process involves giving a patient a drug activated by light, then draining off the blood, running it past the light, and reinfusing it into the patient. Researchers from Yale University and several U.S. and European institutions reported success in using the approach on patients with cutaneous T-cell lymphoma, a cancer of the white blood cells that can be deadly. The drug cleared the signs of disease in 27 of 37 people, evidently by a vaccination effect—cancer cells had picked up the drug, and when the drug was activated by light it damaged the cells. When those cells went back into the body, the immune system sensed them as different and began attacking not only the treated cancer cells but also the untreated cancer cells in the body.

Having already implicated a fatty diet as a cause of breast cancer, scientists moved on to alcohol. Studies at the National Institutes of Health and Harvard University indicated that a moderate amount of alcohol—as little as one to three drinks a week—

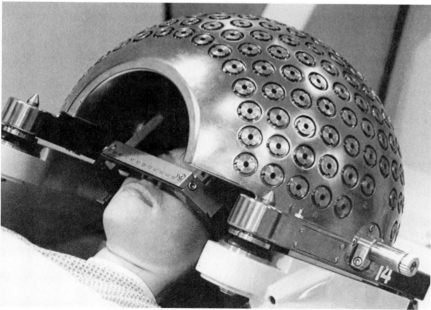

Gamma Knife focuses more than 200 individually harmless gamma rays through a hair-drier-shaped helmet to converge on deep-seated brain tumors and intracranial vascular abnormalities that are beyond the reach of a surgeon's scalpel.

increases a woman's likelihood of developing breast cancer by 40%. The relationship is stronger with heavier drinking. Three or more drinks a week doubles the risk, they found. Other nondietary risk factors include age, early menstruation, late menopause, late childbirth or no children, and a mother or sister with the disease.

In August British researchers added colorectal cancer to the list of cancers caused by the absence of genetic material, and in October scientists from several U.S. institutions added small-cell lung cancer to the same list. The British work, done by scientists of the Imperial Cancer Research Fund, London, found that many people with colorectal cancer are missing a small segment of chromosome 5.

Genetics. Although the first human gene transplant had yet to be accomplished, geneticists had much to keep them busy during the past year. U.S. politicians and geneticists spent much of the year arguing about the project to determine the exact location and molecular construction of all the human genes. The Department of Energy, National Science Foundation, and the National Institutes of Health were all vying for the project, expected to cost $1 billion or more. By the end of the year, there was no solution to the question of which government agency would fund and supervise the effort and whose genes would be sequenced. Japanese researchers were considering an effort of their own.

A Massachusetts company announced in October that it had mapped 400 genetic markers, thus providing signposts on each chromosome by which to gauge the position of other genes. While the 400 markers were helpful, they were a far cry from a complete map—there are roughly 100,000 genes on the 46 human chromosomes.

Some of the impetus was removed from the effort to achieve gene transplants by the announcement of a treatment for a rare immunodeficiency disease called ADA deficiency. This often-fatal disease had been targeted by NIH researchers as a prime candidate for gene transplantation, and much of their effort had gone in that direction. By shielding ADA with a protective chemical, however, researchers at Duke University, Durham, N.C., were able to supply it to several infants with ADA deficiency. With a treatment already available, many scientists doubted that the risky gene-transplant approach would ever be used on this disease.

Several groups of scientists appeared to be homing in on the gene for manic-depressive psychosis. An investigation of a genetically isolated Amish community by researchers from several U.S. institutions revealed that those who inherited a certain gene segment were much more likely to have a mood disorder. While the researchers had not yet pinpointed the gene or genes, they did discover their general

location—the tip of chromosome 11. There may be more than one gene that can cause problems. A U.S. and Israeli team studying families in Jerusalem also found a potential culprit on the X chromosome.

Scientists developed a new weapon for getting genes into cells. A researcher at Cornell University, Ithaca, N.Y., used a "shotgun" to propel gene-coated tungsten pellets into onion cells and found that afterward the genes remained functional. Also, two laboratory advances may speed the development of human gene therapy. Researchers at Baylor College of Medicine, Houston, Texas, managed to use viruses to carry foreign genetic material into liver cells. The inserted genes produced an enzyme that prevents phenylketonuria, an inborn inability to digest a protein component. The roughly one in 12,000 infants born without the enzyme must eat a restricted diet. Liver cells as targets were a new approach for gene therapy; most work had been done with bone-marrow cells.

With many genetic diseases, defects must be present on both of a pair of chromosomes for problems to arise. A person who has only one faulty gene is a carrier. Sickle-cell anemia, a condition that afflicts blacks, is one such disease, but a study during the year indicated that the carrier condition might not be so benign. Researchers from the Walter Reed Army Institute of Research, Washington, D.C., found that it might also be hazardous; in a study of military recruits, they found that sickle-cell carriers were at 40 times the risk of suddenly dying during exertion.

Alzheimer's disease. Alzheimer's disease research had its ups and downs during the year. Scientists initially announced that the same gene that manufactures a protein that clogs the brains of Alzheimer's victims actually causes the disease. Studies in Belgium and at Harvard University, however, indicated that the gene that causes Alzheimer's, while located near that gene, is not the same.

There were also setbacks in the area of treatment. THA, a drug intended to slow the breakdown of a key neurotransmitter, had shown memory-improving effects in a small group of Alzheimer's disease patients. The trials were called off, however, when the recipients began showing signs of liver damage.

Colds. Medical researchers continued to chase their long-time nemesis, the common cold. Though they were learning more about it, there still was no cure in sight.

University of Virginia and Johns Hopkins University scientists identified the agent that causes symptoms. Called kinins, these chemicals appear when symptoms do and go away when symptoms go away. Any of the myriad viruses that cause colds cause kinins to appear in the blood. An antikinin, the researchers suggest, may be able to stop the symptoms of a cold from developing.

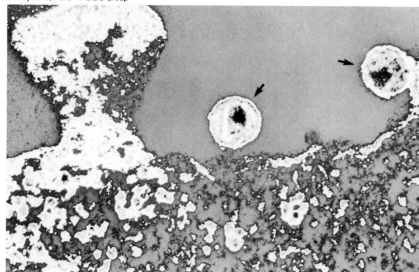

Virus (arrows) related to HIV-1, the virus that causes AIDS (acquired immune deficiency syndrome), was discovered in the blood of sick West Africans. Named HIV-2, it appears to be much rarer than HIV-1 and by 1988 had been seen only in West Africans and in Europeans who had been in that area or had had sexual relations with people from that area.

Austrian researchers made progress on a cold vaccine. X-ray pictures of the cold virus made several years ago highlighted a problem for vaccines—the segment of the outer coat that is constant from virus to virus and thus a good vaccine candidate is located deep in a "canyon" on the surface of the virus particles. The Austrians injected just the proteins in those canyons into rabbits, and the rabbits in turn generated antibodies to nearly two-thirds of the cold viruses tested. Other scientists, however, were concerned that the antibodies would never be able to "see" into the narrow canyon to identify the virus.

Even the way in which colds spread was a matter of debate. University of Virginia researchers believed that it spreads by hand, when the virus gets from someone's mucous membranes onto his or her hand, and that person touches someone who then touches his or her nose or eyes. However, University of Wisconsin scientists concluded that colds are spread when the viruses become dispersed in the air and an unwitting victim inhales them. As evidence, the Wisconsin researchers pointed to their studies of poker players. They infected student volunteers with cold viruses and had them play cards with healthy people. Some of the healthy volunteers were constrained from touching their faces after handling the cards and chips already used by the infected students, while other volunteers were not prevented from doing this. The two healthy groups got sick in approximately equal numbers. In another experiment, healthy men were given poker chips and cards that had been used by cold sufferers, and none of them caught cold.

AIDS. The past year brought tests of potential vaccines, more widespread use of a drug that can delay death from AIDS, and the suggestion and subsequent debunking of a genetic connection, but there still was no cure in sight. The genetic connection was suggested by British researchers, who were studying why only some people infected by the AIDS virus develop the disease within a few years. They found that among white infected men in London, the ones who tended to come down with AIDS were the ones who had a specific protein on the surface of their white blood cells. A Berkeley study failed to find the same relationship, however, and by year's end the genetic connection had fallen into disfavor.

Meanwhile, a new virus related to HIV-1, the virus that causes AIDS, remained a mystery. A group from the Pasteur Institute in Paris found the virus in the blood of sick West Africans. While a Harvard University researcher and his colleagues also found the virus in healthy West Africans, most researchers concluded that the new virus causes disease. Rarer by far than HIV-1, HIV-2 had by 1988 been seen only in West Africans and in Europeans who had been to that area or had had sexual relations with people from that area.

Another controversy arose about peptide T, a protein discovered by researchers at the National Institute of Mental Health. This protein, they thought, blocked AIDS virus infection by binding to the same cells as does the virus, and small-scale trials began in Sweden. Other researchers were unable to duplicate the laboratory studies of the drug, however.

Dozens of drugs were under investigation, and one was approved for widespread use in temporarily staving off death. Nevertheless, while AZT (renamed zidovudine) became the standard against which other drugs were measured, it was not a cure. Another suggested approach was to use synthetic AIDS virus targets to divert the virus from the targets that exist on white blood cells.

Several vaccines were under development. The first to be used on humans was developed by Daniel Zagury of the Pierre and Marie Curie Hospital in Paris, who injected himself and several others with a vaccine. In the U.S. the National Institute of Allergy and Infectious Diseases and MicroGeneSys Inc. began human trials with a genetically engineered protein from the outer coat of the virus.

Some ancient AIDS history was unearthed as well. Missouri doctors, who had been unable to explain the 1969 death of a 15-year-old boy, took a look at some of his stored tissue and confirmed the presence of the AIDS virus. Thus, the disease may have lurked quietly for more than a decade before becoming an epidemic. The discovery sent researchers back to their freezers to check for other AIDS-tainted tissue.

—Joanne Silberner

Dentistry

Dentistry during the past year focused on the growing need for closer cooperation among the worldwide scientific community. A special fact-finding committee was appointed by the American Dental Association (ADA) to assess the role of U.S. dentistry and the ADA in the world dental community. "If we can eliminate tooth decay in a third of U.S. children, certainly we have an obligation to share that knowledge with other nations, particularly the emerging countries of the world," said James A. Saddoris of Tulsa, Okla., ADA president. By consulting with other dental organizations throughout the world, including the World Health Organization (WHO), the committee planned to study world dental affairs and make recommendations to the ADA leadership.

Electronic anesthesia. A new option for pain-free dental treatment involves electricity rather than the injection of a drug. Research into the safety and success rate of "electronic dental anesthesia" (EDA) revealed that it is a viable alternative to injections in many cases, according to Stanley F. Malamed, professor of anesthesia and medicine at the University of Southern California School of Dentistry. The technique uses electrodes that are carefully positioned in the area of the mouth to be treated. The patient controls the amount of current through a hand device and thus finds the desired comfort level. Although it is not fully understood how this process works, it is believed that the electrical impulse blocks the transmission of pain signals from the nerves to the brain and therefore blocks perception of pain by the patient.

EDA was used successfully in "85 to 90%" of controlled test cases, which included crown and bridge work, nonsurgical periodontal (gum) treatment, and fillings. "I don't expect that EDA will replace local anesthesia, but it will be an adjunct. The best and primary anesthesia technique remains local anesthesia," Malamed concluded.

Another approach to neutralizing dental fear might be combining linguistics (the study of human speech) and psychology to communicate with a patient through his or her "favorite sensory reception." Carl Jepsen of San Diego, Calif., founder and president of the Institute for Behavioral Research in Health Care, successfully tested a technique called neurolinguistic programming (NLP) that stresses clear communication between patient and dentist. The technique is based on the premise that people communicate in either visual, auditory, or kinesthetic (touch or feel) terms.

Divided into phases, the NLP process begins by establishing a rapport with the patient and then merging that with the patient's negative feelings about dental treatment. The second phase involves "anchoring and then merging" the fearful feelings with a pleasant feeling. The patient is lightly touched on the shoulder or arm to "anchor" the negative feeling to the spot touched, associating the feeling with the touch. The patient is then instructed to visualize something pleasant, and the dentist gently squeezes the patient's shoulder or arm to "anchor" the positive feeling. The negative and positive feelings are then merged when the patient again visualizes the negative experience. Both body points are touched simultaneously, bringing together the two feelings to create a third that is neutral and free of anxiety. When the fear is neutralized by the conversion of the two feelings, the patient becomes more comfortable and confident and treatment can begin, Jepsen said. During NLP's final phase, a stop sign is established so that the patient can interrupt treatment at any time to reinforce a sense of control.

Radiology and TMJ diagnosis. Advances in the use of computer imaging techniques led to a success rate of about 95% in diagnosing certain internal disorders of the jaw (temporomandibular) joint (TMJ) and its surrounding tissues. The use of computer imaging as a diagnostic tool progressed from techniques involving an incision, such as arthrography, in which an opaque dye is injected in the jaw joint space to highlight the TMJ disk, to computed tomography (CT) scans, which enable observation without injection. Magnetic resonance imaging (MRI) also emerged as an effective diagnostic method because it provides much greater detail of the jaw joint disk and requires no ionizing radiation, according to Richard W. Katzberg, director of the Magnetic Resonance Center at the University of Rochester (N.Y.) Medical Center. Disorders detectable by means of MRI include displacement and perforation of the jaw joint disk and such deformities as holes in the soft tissue surrounding the disk.

The MRI scanner pinpoints differences in tissue

proton (water) density in the body through sound waves. Processed by computer, the sound waves are converted to density pattern images. Variations of normal water-density patterns lead to TMJ disorder diagnosis. The natural progression of TMJ disorders "is for disk damage to occur first, leading to mechanical dysfunction and subsequent degenerative arthritis of the hard tissue," said Katzberg. Early diagnosis can lead to more conservative treatment. Of the ten million people in the U.S. afflicted with TMJ disorders, 5% have a significant problem that might require treatment that could range from the use of a splint (fitted mouthpiece used to reposition the jaw or to stop clenching or grinding of the teeth) to surgical correction.

Computers and tooth repair. A device with the sophistication of a computer and the precise cutting ability of a milling machine can design and form crowns, fillings, or dentures in a fraction of the time required by current methods. Conceived and developed by François Duret, at Le Grande Lemps, France, the CAD/CAM (computer-aided design/computer-aided manufacture) system could eliminate the need for tooth impressions, limit the patient to one office visit in some cases, and decrease production time for making replacement teeth by eliminating the need for the dental laboratory. The system includes an optical probe (a laser/scanner camera), an image-processing system, a digital controller, and a micromilling machine, all of which are attached to a centralized computer system.

The process to fabricate a single crown begins with use of the optical probe to take computerized, three-dimensional measurements of the tooth; these are stored in the computer's memory. The tooth is then prepared by the dentist in the traditional manner for placement of the crown. A second set of measurements is taken of the prepared tooth and is also stored in the computer's memory. The computer, with instructions from the dentist, begins to design the individualized crown by comparing the two sets of tooth measurements with the computer's preprogrammed image of an "ideal" tooth. This image is then altered by the dentist, who manually adjusts the computer system so that the crown will be designed to fit a particular patient's tooth. The processing system then calculates the dimensions needed for making the crown. These dimensions, which can be modified by the dentist if necessary, are sent to the milling machine via the digital controller. Operating through the computer, the digital controller directs the milling machine's saw to fashion the crown. Final polishing is done by the dentist.

Laser knife. Soft-tissue lesions in the mouth can be successfully biopsied or removed on an outpatient basis with a pulsing carbon-dioxide laser beam, according to a State University of New York at Buffalo (SUNY-Buffalo) dental researcher. Charles Liebow told the Society of Optical and Quantum Electronics that the technique had been used successfully on 15 patients. The pulsing, rather than continuous, laser beam has distinct advantages in the oral cavity. The continuous beam can produce inflammation in healthy tissue that is adjacent to the diseased tissue. "Patients who underwent treatment with pulsing laser experienced no postoperative bleeding and little, if any discomfort compared to what would be expected using traditional surgical procedures," Liebow said.

Because the laser can deliver a pulsing beam in 0.00001 sec in a circle as small as 0.1 mm radius, small amounts of tissue can be treated. Deep lesions can be lased in layers, and the laser can be used to cut around and under tissue in a pie-shaped wedge so that biopsy samples can be removed intact. Laser treatment did not appear to be useful for oral surgery involving bone. SUNY-Buffalo researchers did, however, use a carbon-dioxide laser to treat one case of periodontal disease, with good results.

Tooth implants. New endosteal dental implants (those placed directly into bone) have a 95% chance of success, largely owing to the use of advanced "bioactive" materials that chemically bond the bone and implant, according to Louisiana State University Dental School researchers. Most endosteal implants are made of a biocompatible metal such as titanium or titanium alloy. The implant is mechanically held in place by means of slots, holes, and grooves in the bone. Newer implants are coated with a component of natural bone, hydroxylapatite; this creates a chemical bond with the bone. While both systems have been successful, the chemical bonding with a bioactive system has proved most effective. "I have been working with implants since 1972, and of 400-plus hydroxylapatite-coated implants inserted, only four have been lost in the past five years," said Roland Meffert, a professor of periodontics in New Orleans, La. He agreed that implants are not appropriate for everyone, citing such factors as bruxism (teeth grinding) and systemic illness (diabetes) as reasons why a patient may not be a suitable candidate for one. On the other hand, "approximately 25% of all toothless patients can have implants," in place of full dentures, Meffert estimated.

Gum disease. Traditional gum-disease treatment usually involves the removal of plaque from teeth and also pus from the pockets between the teeth and the gum. If the pockets do not shrink, they are surgically removed. The patient is then asked to follow a strict regimen of brushing and flossing. The recurrence rate is between 5 and 10% and, if not properly treated, bleeding along the gums, which is gum disease's first sign, may not be the only concern; teeth may loosen and eventually fall out. Researchers at

377

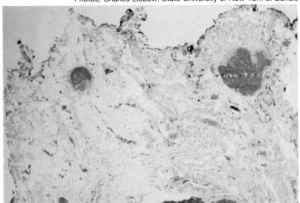

Site of a benign tumor on the lip (left) is seen immediately after the tumor was excised with a pulsing carbon-dioxide laser beam. There was no bleeding during or after surgery. A microscopic view of the excised tumor (right) reveals a narrow, darkly stained line at the top; this represents heat damage caused by the laser beam cutting the tissue.

SUNY-Buffalo found a way to cut the recurrence to less than 1 to 2%, said Robert J. B. Genco. "Instead of treating the signs and symptoms, we now can treat the infection itself."

Genco's research team and other investigators identified three specific forms of bacteria that account for 85% of advanced periodontal disease. If they know the specific strain of bacteria, dentists can use appropriate antibiotic therapy. With two of the strains, *Bacteroides gingivalis* and *Bacteroides intermedius,* a local antibiotic is used because they penetrate only the gum's outer surface. With *Actinobacillus actinomycetemcomitans,* however, a general antibiotic is used because the bacteria penetrate deep into the gum. Conventional treatment also is used, and both inflammation and the bacteria are monitored, Genco explained. These bacteria are not found naturally in humans. Possible sources might be dogs and cats, which harbor two types of the bacteria, and soil, which has not yet been studied.

Eating disorders. Dental professionals were becoming increasingly involved in identifying patients who might be susceptible to eating disorders and providing appropriate referrals to physicians. Such eating disorders as anorexia nervosa and bulimia had previously been believed to be problems of young women. However, such disorders were being seen in other individuals, according to Jesley G. Ruff at St. Mary's Hill Hospital in Milwaukee, Wis.

Anorexia nervosa, a condition in which a person is at least 25% below his or her recommended weight, often is accompanied by another potentially life-threatening disorder called bulimia. Individuals with bulimia rapidly eat large amounts of high-calorie food and then purge their bodies of the food by self-induced vomiting or through the use of laxatives. A recent poll estimated that about two million U.S. women between the ages of 19 and 39 show symptoms of bulimia or anorexia nervosa. The binge-purge cycle of bulimics can result in numerous health disorders, including damage to the esophagus and stomach, swollen salivary glands, gum recession, tooth erosion, and cracks at the corners of the mouth. This dangerous practice, usually done in secrecy, is often difficult to diagnose. Because dentists see a broad spectrum of the population on a regular basis, they are in a pivotal position to identify the general symptoms and tissue changes in the mouth that may indicate the presence of an eating disorder.

—Lou Joseph

See also Feature Article: The Changing Practice of Dentistry.

Veterinary medicine

"Veterinarians for Society in the 21st Century" was the theme of the ninth Symposium on Veterinary Medical Education, which was held during the past year at the University of California at Davis. Symposium discussion groups examined a variety of topics, including American Veterinary Medical Association (AVMA) accreditation of veterinary schools and colleges, National Board examinations, licensing requirements, faculty research, the explosion of scientific information, specialization, goals of veterinary education, admission requirements, cost of veterinary education, and nonpractice careers. Many of the issues were too complex to be easily targeted for definitive changes in the near future. However, several key areas were identified with recommendations for specific changes.

Education. Heading the list of these areas was the explosion of scientific and medical knowledge and how it should be applied to veterinary medicine. It was recommended that veterinary medical educational institutions place more emphasis on develop-

378

ing such student skills as information management, problem solving, and effective communication and place less emphasis on "stuffing" the student with endless details about every species.

The level of teaching skills of veterinary educators was a second area identified for change. These educators are often also expected to have active research and service programs, which leave them little time for perfecting teaching skills. It was determined that better opportunities for "educating the educators" are needed in veterinary institutions. Another recommendation noted the need to place increased emphasis on introducing students to alternatives to standard private practice and on selecting students with interests in nontraditional veterinary careers.

Special assistance in charting new pathways and strengthening current ones for veterinary medical education should result from a $5.5 million grant from the Pew Charitable Trusts of Philadelphia. The proposed four-year program, termed the Pew National Veterinary Education Program, will be managed by Duke University's Institute of Policy Sciences and Public Affairs, Durham, N.C. The grant by the Pew Charitable Trusts arose from the recognition that veterinary medicine, by assuring the safety of foods of animal origin and by expanding knowledge of medical science through research, contributes directly to human health by controlling those diseases in animals that can be communicated to humans. Twenty-seven U.S. and four Canadian veterinary schools planned to participate in the program, which was to include a study of the status of veterinary medicine, leadership training seminars for faculty members and veterinary school administrators, and an institution educational grants program.

Total enrollment in veterinary medical colleges in the U.S. for the 1986–87 school year was 8,887, of whom 47% were males and 53% females. This represented a 0.3% increase in total enrollment over the preceding year. Total enrollment in veterinary medical colleges in Canada during the 1986–87 school year was 1,031, with 40% being males and 60% females. A new U.S. veterinary school achieved a significant milestone when the charter class of 76 students was graduated from the University of Wisconsin School of Veterinary Medicine. The school was established by the Wisconsin legislature in 1979, and construction of facilities began in 1981.

A new veterinary school was recently established in Rehovot, Israel. Known as the Koret School of Veterinary Medicine, it was the first veterinary school in Israel and was expected to play a vital role in the health care of the animal population in the Middle East. As of 1988 there were 286 veterinary colleges or faculties in 72 countries. The National Veterinary School in Toulouse, France, established in 1762, was the oldest active school.

In May 1987 the 200th anniversary of veterinary education in Hungary was celebrated by that country's veterinary association and the World Veterinary Association. After World War II the Hungarian livestock industry was faced with disease problems not present in that country prior to the war; these problems necessitated the reorganization of veterinary services. Since 1953 veterinary services for the livestock industry have been provided free of charge.

The Virginia-Maryland Regional College of Veterinary Medicine was officially dedicated on May 15, 1987. Associated with the ceremony was the opening of the new veterinary teaching hospital, library, college center, and administrative areas. Nearly half of the investment in the college's physical plant came from private sources. A ground-breaking ceremony was held at Adelphi, Md., for the $12.5 million Avrum Gudelsky Veterinary Center, the first building to be constructed in Maryland as a component of the college. The center was to provide office, classroom, and research space for the regional college's Maryland campus and would also house the animal health section of the Maryland Department of Agriculture.

New facilities. A new $2.7 million facility for the care of laboratory animals was completed at the University of Illinois College of Veterinary Medicine. The new facility not only provided more space for efficient, high-quality laboratory animal care but also enabled improved monitoring for adherence to federal laboratory animal care standards. Research conducted at the new facility was to be directed primarily toward diseases of food animals and companion animals.

The horse industry was growing in the U.S. A 1988 estimate of the economically productive horse population (excluding wild horses) was 5,250,000, with estimated annual expenditures by owners and breeders totaling $13.2 billion. This investment led to increased interest in the quality and technological level of health care provided to horses as well as leading to increased support for facilities for equine health care and research. Consequently, a new equine neonate unit was established at the New York State College of Veterinary Medicine. A specially designed suite of stalls enabled around-the-clock care for critically ill foals. The suite was equipped with heavily padded cribs and with a heated water bed to prevent bedsores in foals unable to move. Digitalized and computerized volumetric fluid pumps controlled delivery of precise amounts of fluids intravenously to sick foals. Vital signs such as blood pressure and respiration could be monitored.

The $2,250,000 Connelly Equine Intensive Care Unit (ICU) and Graham French Neonatal Section were established during the year at the University of Pennsylvania College of Veterinary Medicine to provide care primarily for critically ill horses and

Director of the new facility for the care of laboratory animals at the University of Illinois College of Veterinary Medicine views one of the rooms especially designed for mice.

foals. The facility was also to be used for the critical care of other species of large animals. The John W. Galbreath family pledged $1.5 million toward the construction of an equine trauma, intensive care, and research center at the Ohio State University College of Veterinary Medicine. The center was scheduled for completion in 1991. The $9 million Maxwell H. Gluck Equine Research Center was dedicated at the University of Kentucky on June 5. It was designed to provide for the expansion of the equine research program of the university's veterinary science department as well as to enable exploration of such new areas as nutritional pathology as related to disease problems in young, growing horses. Much of the funding for support of the center was provided by the horse industry.

Veterinary societies and organizations. A number of new veterinary societies and organizations began operation in 1987. This in many instances reflected an increase in specialization in veterinary medicine. Growth in veterinary interest in animal dentistry led to the organization of the Academy of Veterinary Dentistry, which admitted 25 charter fellows on the basis of their credentials, and the successful completion of the academy's first qualification examination. The academy was seeking AVMA recognition as a specialty organization. This required the establishment of residency programs in dentistry to provide special training in that field to interested veterinarians. Veterinary dentistry involves such special procedures as endodontics (root canals), periodontics (gum surgery), orthodontics (straightening of teeth), and restorative dentistry, which includes bonding and the insertion of porcelain jacket crowns.

An organizing committee was appointed to identify and certify charter diplomates in the specialty of animal behavior. A process of board certification

was being established, and AVMA recognition of the specialty was being sought. Preliminary efforts were under way to establish an international veterinary ear, nose, and throat association.

Veterinarians who operate mobile veterinary clinics were in the process of establishing the American Mobile Veterinary Association. About 600 veterinarians in the U.S. operate mobile veterinary clinics. It is probable that in the future many standard practices will offer mobile practices as satellite clinics. The American Association of Retired Veterinarians began its first full year of operation and held its annual meeting in Chicago in 1987 in conjunction with the annual meeting of the American Veterinary Medical Association. The goal of the association was to promote continued involvement of its members in the veterinary profession, to exchange ideas for enriching one another's lives, and to provide community service.

In 1987 the Mexican Association for the History of Veterinary Medicine and Zootechnics was founded in Mexico City. Mexico in 1853 was the location of the first school of veterinary medicine on the North American continent.

A statewide program regarding hearing dogs for the deaf was being cosponsored by the California Veterinary Medical Association and the San Francisco Society for the Prevention of Cruelty to Animals. In addition to promoting public awareness of the value of hearing dogs, the program was providing information about how stray and abandoned animals from shelters can be specially trained to alert deaf persons to such important sounds as the ring of a telephone and the trill of a smoke detector. Training of service or helping dogs was being encouraged by the AVMA Committee on the Human/Animal Bond. These dogs can assist owners confined to wheelchairs in such

380

tasks as overcoming physical barriers, picking up dropped items, pushing elevator buttons, and turning light switches.

Animal disease problems. Marlo Brown, a veterinary assistant with special interest in homeless cats, observed a condition in those animals that had similarities to human AIDS (acquired immune deficiency syndrome) patients. Neils C. Pedersen at the University of California at Davis College of Veterinary Medicine and his colleagues conducted studies on those cats that led to the discovery of a new feline retrovirus that can produce a severe AIDS-like disease in cats. The new virus, termed feline T-lymphotropic lentivirus (FTLV), is not the same virus as the feline leukemia virus (FLV). Persons associated with cats infected with FTLV have not contracted the disease, which supports the belief that the cat virus is not infectious to humans. Pedersen's studies were kept secret initially to minimize controversy and to avoid the unnecessary sacrifice of pet cat lives because of owners' fears of contracting the disease.

The U.S. Department of Agriculture (USDA) approved a new genetically engineered vaccine for the prevention of pseudorabies in swine. This was the second live genetically engineered vaccine to be li-

A dog that had been abandoned has been trained to alert its new hearing-impaired owner to such often-missed sounds as the ring of a doorbell and the buzz of an alarm clock. Some of these dogs have saved the lives of their owners.

The San Francisco Society for the Prevention of Cruelty to Animals
Hearing Dog Program

censed by the USDA since January 1986. The name pseudorabies was devised because animals with the disease have symptoms similar to those of rabies, but the diseases are not related. In the new vaccine the virus used was modified by recombinant DNA technology, which resulted in the deletion of two genes. By contrast, the virus used in the other vaccine had only one gene deleted. The additional gene deletion provided a vaccine that produces a modified immune response that is capable of protecting the animal from natural infection but differs from the response associated with natural infection, thereby enabling differentiation between vaccinated animals and those naturally infected with a field strain of the virus.

A 70% increase in reported cases of equine infectious anemia (EIA) was reported in Michigan. The infection may be fatal, and horses that recover are carriers of the virus. The disease is spread by the transfer of infected blood by horseflies and mosquitoes. Unfortunately, no effective treatment was yet available, and infected horses had to be destroyed. Vaccines for the prevention of the disease were being tested experimentally.

Potomac horse fever, now termed equine monocytic erlichiosis (EME), was a problem in at least 24 states of the U.S. and in Canada. Approximately one-third of infected horses die during acute outbreaks. The mode of transmission of this disease remained a mystery. Ticks that carry other rickettsial organisms do not carry this one. The fact that an equine veterinarian contracted the disease indicated the potential for its transmission to humans. Fortunately, new breakthroughs in the development of vaccines and diagnostic tests were expected to aid in the prevention, control, and diagnosis of the disease. The vaccine was considered a breakthrough because it had been difficult to prepare effective rickettsial vaccines. Researchers at the University of Illinois College of Veterinary Medicine found that it confers complete protection on 66 to 86% of treated horses, with the remainder having only a mild form of the disease. The new diagnostic test, termed the plate latex agglutination test (PLAT), was considered a breakthrough because it can be performed at the horse's side and the results can be known within five minutes. Some controversy existed regarding the accuracy of the test, but it was generally agreed that it is a valuable screening tool during acute outbreaks. EME could not be diagnosed by clinical signs alone.

Ultrasound techniques for examining the interior of an animal's eyes painlessly were being tested at the University of Florida Veterinary Medical Teaching Hospital. The technique was helping ophthalmologists diagnose tumors and detached retinas in animals when cloudiness of the eye precluded visual examination with an ophthalmoscope. Also, veterinary researchers at the University of Florida used a technique for removing kidney stones from dogs that had originally been developed for application in humans. The technique, percutaneous nephrostomy, involves making a small incision in the side of an anesthetized dog and inserting a basket-like trap through the incision to catch and remove the stones. Recovery from the operation is rapid. Lithotripsy, which involves shock-wave treatment, has been used to break up kidney stones successfully without surgery in people, but it could not be used in dogs because of the different anatomical arrangement of dog kidneys.

An ophthalmic surgeon and a veterinary ophthalmologist at the University of Illinois successfully ruptured two cysts in the eye of a horse by means of a newly developed portable (suitcase-size) laser unit that can operate off a car battery. The horse was expected to regain full vision in the eye. Lasers were used as a fast, noninvasive method of alleviating a variety of eye problems in human medicine, and new applications were rapidly being found in veterinary ophthalmology. The portable laser unit was originally designed for offering eye therapy in remote areas, especially in less developed nations.

During the past 50 years, the life expectancy of

A veterinarian examines a dog. Because of improved care by veterinarians and owners, the life expectancy of pets in the United States has more than doubled during the past 50 years.

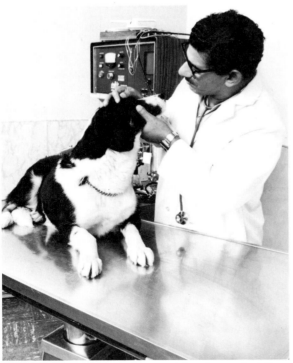

© Frank Siteman—Stock, Boston

pets in the U.S. has more than doubled. Veterinarians have played a prominent role in enabling pets to live longer, along with the willingness by pet owners to make available to their pets the latest technologies in medical care. Older pets are more susceptible than young ones to disease and physical disabilities. Thus, geriatric veterinary medicine introduced new dimensions to such veterinary specialties as ophthalmology, dermatology, dentistry, immunology, emergency care, osteoarthritis, and cardiology. Improved nutrition for aged pets also contributed much to their continued good health.

—John M. Bowen

Optical engineering

The field of optical engineering continued to advance in 1987. Some important new laser sources became available because of innovations in the fabrication and construction of such devices. There was an expansion in the use of optics in industrial processes, and laser applications continued to grow in such routine mechanical shop activities as cutting and welding. The development of new markets in optical memories did not progress as well as had been expected, and the development of the completely optical digital computer appeared to have slowed relative to the expectations of the past few years.

The 35-mm camera continued to regain popularity, with many new models offering fully automatic operation, including focusing. Production of conventional optics continued to be healthy, especially from sources in Singapore, Taiwan, and South Korea. Attempts were made to strengthen the U.S. precision optical industry through the mechanism of a restrictive clause in government purchase regulations, but this appeared to have no appreciable impact in 1987.

Consumer acceptance of compact audio discs continued to increase. The obvious application of this technology to the delivery of information in addition to entertainment appeared to be beginning, but slowly. A single data disc, referred to as CD-ROM (compact disc-read only memory), could hold information equivalent to about 140,000 pages of text and be produced in quantity at the cost of an audio disc. With the use of this approach, there are obvious economies in the dissemination of data bases, investment information catalogs, and reference materials. A major innovation announced by General Electric and RCA was the ability to include lengthy portions of compressed video on a compact disc. This provided the possibility of a combined text and interactive video presentation on the same disc.

The implications of this new communication technology upon education, marketing, and information dissemination were significant, but there was a lag in the development of computer software capable of handling these immense data bases in a manner acceptable to the average user. The lack of widespread availability of computer-compatible drives for these discs has also limited sales so far. Because the new compressed video format is competitive with an already proposed CD-I, or interactive format, some time will probably pass before manufacturers will commit themselves to a single acceptable standard for encoding data on the disc. Until that occurs, it is likely that the acceptance of optical data storage devices will lag in the marketplace.

The application of optical-disc technology to on-line information storage also showed growth with the introduction of a number of "write-once-read-many" (WORM) optical-disc storage systems. Systems delivered in 1987 ranged from 12.5-cm (5-in)-diameter optical-disc drives for personal computers that could hold 200 megabytes of data to large "jukebox" systems using several 25-cm (10-in) discs that could hold on line more than one trillion words of permanently stored data. The cost of such storage was reasonable, and the permanence of the stored record was attractive. However, the inability to erase and rewrite records on these storage devices impeded their acceptance by computer users.

The development of erasable optical storage continued, but it remained in the laboratory stage. The principal problems appeared to be with the reliability and stability of the rare-earth materials required for the recording medium in these applications.

A major growth of interest in holographic optics, especially for use with optical-disc devices, took place during the past year. Several laboratories began investigating the possibility of a totally integrated optical head for disc devices. In this concept the laser source, signal detectors, imaging components, beam splitters, and polarizers would be fabricated on a single silicon or gallium arsenide chip. These diverse elements must be integrated into a single structure. During 1987 some hybrid devices were demonstrated, but full integration was not achieved.

Other applications of optics to computers increased during the past year. Optical page scanners, both for input to computers and as telecopy terminals, became almost as common as office copiers. At the end of 1987 the cost of an optical scanner dropped to about $1,000, making it possible for almost every office to have direct access to such terminals.

Computation using fully optical techniques was a strong area of research. However, digital computation using optical means had not yet emerged from the laboratory. Switching speeds of a fraction of a nanosecond with room-temperature optical devices were demonstrated, but the energy required for such operations and the cost of fabricating these components remained much greater than in integrated electronic systems. The emphasis in the future would probably shift from the development of computer components to the investigation of computer designs that exploit optical computing devices having characteristics close to those of existing components.

One potential advantage of all optical computing is that parallel access between arrays of computing elements is possible by imaging arrays of gates upon each other. (A gate is a device that outputs a signal when specific input conditions are met.) Exploiting this capability would allow many computational

A new 35-mm camera, the S900, was introduced by Eastman Kodak Co. in 1987. Fully automatic and employing electronic exposure control, the camera has two all-glass lenses and a mirror system that allows the user to switch instantly from wide-angle to telephoto lenses after viewing the scene in either mode.

AP/Wide World

operations to be done simultaneously, providing extremely high computation speeds. Thus far, digital computation has been demonstrated only on simple systems using four or five active components.

Other applications of optics and lasers in computers were growing. The ability to carry out operations between two images in order to compare or select portions of an imaged scene had been practical for several years. Such a device would permit rapid comparison between a stored image or map and an image being recorded by a sensor such as a television camera. During the past year engineers devised optical assemblies that permitted practical application of these correlators in missile-guidance systems. Potentially, these techniques would lead to the development of "smart" sensors in which optical images would be examined simultaneously at all parts of each image in order to make decisions about pointing, tracking, or accessing particular portions of the space surrounding the sensor. In this sense optical analog computers could carry out certain operations such as correlation much faster than any electronic computer. One eventual application for these devices was in manufacturing, as a machine-vision adjunct to industrial robots.

New fabrication techniques led to improvements in the reliability and efficiency of several types of laser systems during the past year. One of the most interesting was the YAG microlaser. YAG lasers were traditionally constructed from yttrium-aluminum-garnet crystals pumped (exposed to radiation) by a flash lamp surrounding the crystal. Moderate-length pulses of quite high power could be produced by this technique, and YAG lasers found wide use in materials processing and medicine. The new microlaser, however, employed an array of laser diodes to pump the laser crystal in place of the flash lamp. The improved efficiency and simplicity of this all-solid-state laser permitted new, very compact forms of lasers to be produced with greater economy and longer operational lifetime.

Even the traditional red helium-neon gas laser was developed into a more versatile light source. Several companies succeeded in producing helium-neon lasers that could operate on as many as 18 different wavelengths. Powers of 10–20 Mw were possible on several of these lines, making this simplest and cheapest gas laser available for a large number of applications in scanning, image display, and measurement.

Diode lasers continued to increase in reliability and power output during the year. Several new forms of these lasers with power output approaching a full watt became available, and shorter wavelengths of operation were frequently being reported. The combination of high power and a selection of wavelengths continued to make these lasers ever more practical for use in machining and materials processing.

Another important development took place in the area of stable and reliable metal vapor lasers. Copper vapor lasers had been available for a long time, but newer models permitted the production of ten or more watts of pulsed green light that was suitable for communications applications; these models were also reliable and long-lived. Gold vapor lasers that produced several watts of power at spectral lines in the yellow or red particularly suitable for medical and surgical applications became available. These lasers promised to be useful in the selective treatment of malignant tumors.

In the arena of large optical systems for astronomy, work continued on the fabrication of the 36 segments for the primary mirror of the Keck telescope, which was to have an aperture 10 m (400 in) in diameter. This project was planned to be in operation on Mauna Kea in Hawaii about 1992, and the housing for the telescope was under construction. A less optimistic decision was made by the U.S. National Optical Astronomy Observatory and the National Science Foundation to defer indefinitely the construction of the National New Technology Telescope. With restrictions in funding, it appeared that the development of very large telescopes in the U.S. had slowed considerably. The European Southern Observatory did succeed in finding backing to begin planning and construction of a large array telescope using four eight-meter-diameter mirrors, to be located in the Southern Hemisphere.

The Strategic Defense Initiative program continued to provide challenges to optical engineers. One of the programs incorporated the development of a several-megawatt free electron laser. This type of laser is based upon a high-energy electron accelerator that contains a lengthy path within which the accelerated electrons are forced by a varying magnetic field to oscillate and produce coherent light. There was a plan to couple this laser, if it could be built, to a ground-based beam director that has an aperture about four meters in diameter. Experiments to determine its feasibility of tracking and projecting to a space-based relay mirror were expected to be carried out in the mid-1990s.

The space laser program appeared to be almost extinct but did receive a new mandate near the end of 1987. A 4-m (157-in)-diameter segmented primary mirror appropriate for a space-based laser beam director was completed by the Itek division of Litton Industries. Work also continued on a 2-Mw gas dynamic laser fueled by hydrogen flouride at TRW Corp. Near the end of the year, it was announced that an experiment that would mate those two developments for a test in a space-borne laser beam weapon in about 1995 had been planned.

—Robert R. Shannon

Physics

The recent discoveries of ceramic metal oxides that become superconducting at record high temperatures generated worldwide excitement in the scientific community in 1987, as physicists joined with chemists, materials scientists, and engineers in interdisciplinary studies of the new materials. In other investigations physicists detected the rarest natural nuclear decay process ever observed in the laboratory, continued to pursue a variety of tantalizing hints for the existence of additional fundamental forces, and looked forward to conducting new colliding-particle-beam experiments to support and extend their theoretical picture of matter. The detection on Earth of neutrinos from a distant supernova supported astrophysical descriptions of the death of massive stars and added to a scientific understanding of the mysterious neutrino itself.

General developments

In 1987 advances continued in the "anti" sciences—antigravity and antimatter. Physicists also looked back 100 years to 1887 and the Michelson-Morley experiment, which established the constant velocity of light in all reference frames, ushering in the concept of relativity and the era of modern physics.

Looking for an "antigravity" force. For many years Frank Stacey and co-workers at the University of Queensland, Australia, had been measuring the gravity of the Earth in towers and in mine shafts. (See *1988 Yearbook of Science and the Future* Year in Review: PHYSICS: *General developments*.) After taking into account known effects, they found that their measured value of the gravitational attraction of the surface layers of the Earth was about 1% lower than the calculated value, suggesting a short-range repulsive force.

Theorist Ephraim Fischbach of Purdue University, West Lafayette, Ind., proposed that the effect was caused by a so-called fifth force, termed hyperforce (in addition to the known strong, weak, electromagnetic, and gravitational forces), that is proportional to the number of nucleons (protons plus neutrons) in a body. The hyperforce would be larger for a kilogram of lead than a kilogram of feathers. Fischbach and co-workers reexamined gravity data taken between 1889 and 1908 by Hungarian scientist Roland Eötvös and his Budapest colleagues and found additional evidence for hyperforce effects. Other theorists developed alternative theories in which a repulsive fifth force, an attractive sixth force, or both would depend on such other properties as the spin of the nucleus or the difference between the number of protons and neutrons in the nucleus. These experiments and theories inspired a number of new experiments in

1987 to search for further evidence of anomalous, short-range gravity-like forces.

Peter Thieberger of Brookhaven National Laboratory, Upton, N.Y., floated a carefully balanced 5-kg (11-lb) hollow copper sphere in a tank of distilled water. The copper sphere displaced an equal weight of water, creating a copper-water differential balance, one mass being copper and the other being a "hole" in water. If a large mass were put on one side of this differential balance and Newtonian gravity was the only coupling force, the gravitational pull on the copper ball and the water around the ball would be the same, and the copper ball would not move. However, when Thieberger put his apparatus near the top edge of a cliff, where there was granite on one side of the apparatus and air on the other side, he found that the copper sphere drifted away from the cliff, indicating a short-range, substance-dependent force that is more repulsive for copper than for water.

A similar "cliff-edge" experiment was carried out by Paul Boynton, David Crosby, Phillip Ekstrom, and Anthony Szumilo at the base of a granite wall 130 m (427 ft) high in the Cascade Range near Index, Wash. Their differential balance was a metal ring, 9 cm (3.5 in) in diameter and weighing 11 g (0.39 oz), suspended from a tungsten wire. One-half of the ring was made of beryllium; the other half was made of aluminum with holes drilled in it to make the mass of both halves equal. When the ring was twisted a few degrees and let go, it slowly oscillated back and forth on the wire suspension with a period of 975 seconds.

If the two halves of the ring have exactly the same mass and the only force acting on them is Newtonian gravity, then the oscillation period should remain constant despite the presence of nearby massive objects. When the experimenters put the instrument near the edge of the granite cliff, however, they found a significant change in the period that depended on the orientation of the two halves of the ring to the granite cliff. Part of the change was due to a slight tilt in the mass distribution of the two halves of the ring interacting with the gravity gradients of the cliff, but that effect was canceled by the judicious juxtaposition of some 272 kg (600 lb) of lead. After the cancellation there still existed a significant residual effect that was four times the background interference level. To complicate the life of the theorists, the sign of the effect indicated that the coupling is proportional to the difference between the number of neutrons and protons, not to their sum.

A 600-m (2,000-ft) television tower in North Carolina was the site of gravity experiments that complimented the Australian measurements. Andrew Lazarewicz, Christopher Jekeli, Anestis Romaides,

Hexagonal frame of fine wire forms part of a Muppats detector, a device developed by physicists at Argonne (Illinois) National Laboratory in order to reveal the exact three-dimensional arrangement of atoms in small molecules. Muppats may assist in studies of subjects as diverse as acid rain and interstellar dust.

Roger W. Sands, and Donald Eckhardt of the U.S. Air Force Geophysical Laboratory, Hanscom Air Force Base, Massachusetts, raised a gravity meter up the tower. Their measurements indicated deviations from the expected diminishing of Newtonian gravity with distance. Although the variations were small, they were ten times greater than the detection sensitivity of their gravity meter. The experimenters found evidence for both a short-range, repulsive fifth force and an intermediate-range, attractive sixth force. By early 1988 more experiments in search of gravity-like forces were being planned or in progress around the world.

The "Antimatter Underground." A recent experiment that demonstrated the first capture and storage of a particle of antimatter subsequently awakened a large community of scientists, engineers, and medical researchers to the realization that antimatter science and technology is no longer science fiction. In 1986 Gerald Gabrielse, now at Harvard University, led an international team that included scientists from the University of Washington, Fermi National Accelerator Laboratory (Fermilab), Batavia, Ill., and the University of Mainz, West Germany, in a visit to the Low Energy Antiproton Ring (LEAR) at CERN in Switzerland. (See *1988 Yearbook of Science and the Future* Year in Review: PHYSICS: *General developments.*) There they set up their antiproton trap and succeeded in capturing hundreds of antiprotons (negatively charged antimatter counterparts to protons) at a time, holding on to them for many minutes. Shortly after this experiment the CERN antiproton source was shut down for a year for a planned upgrade. It was reactivated in late 1987 with an antiproton production rate ten times larger than the earlier rate. Since LEAR was the only source of low-energy antiprotons in the world, no antimatter experiments were possible in 1987, but many meetings were held to make plans for the future.

The major antimatter meeting in 1987 was the IV LEAR Workshop sponsored by CERN and held in the Swiss Alps south of Geneva. More than 200 scientists attended to discuss the results of the previous two years' work using low-energy antiprotons from the LEAR machine and to plan future experiments on the upgraded machine. One of the approved future experiments is that of Gabrielse and co-workers to capture a single antiproton in a trap and compare the inertial mass of an antiproton with that of a proton to one part in a billion or better. There should be no difference, but if there is, significant new physics should result. A second approved experiment will also start with antiprotons in a trap, but these particles will be "tossed" up a long vacuum tube and their trajectory timed to see if the Earth's gravity pulls on antiprotons with the same force as on protons. Because any existing hyperforce effect of the antiproton would be negative while that of the proton would be positive, a gravity-like hyperforce should certainly show up in these experiments.

In January 1987 a group of atomic scientists from the U.S. gathered to formulate plans for making antihydrogen out of antiprotons and positrons (positively charged antimatter electrons), then growing "cluster ions" of antihydrogen atoms surrounding a central antiproton. Since the cluster ion would be charged, it can be kept in the same types of traps used to capture antiprotons. In November European scientists held a second meeting on the formation of antimatter atoms in Karlsruhe, West Germany, at which there was even discussion of concepts for making atoms of antideuterium and antitritium (antimatter heavy isotopes of hydrogen) and antihelium.

In April 1987 and again in October, U.S. scientists, engineers, and medical researchers held workshops on antiproton science and technology in Santa Monica, Calif. Their primary goal was to define a low-energy antiproton facility for use in the U.S.

Although antiprotons are made daily at Fermilab for use in the Tevatron proton-antiproton collider machine, they are kept in their storage ring at high energy and are unavailable for trapping or other experiments; thus, a new low-energy antiproton facility is needed. A surprise result of the workshop was the realization that the existing machines at Brookhaven National Laboratory could be easily reconfigured to produce large quantities of low-energy antiprotons at low cost.

Studies were under way in 1988 to determine if Brookhaven or Fermilab should be the site of the first low-energy antiproton facility. Once this facility is available, other researchers who have designed and built transportable, battery-powered traps and low-energy storage rings can take them to the antiproton "filling station," take on a load of a few hundred billion antiprotons, and carry the particles back to a university physics laboratory, an industrial testing facility, or a cancer-treatment hospital.

Medical researchers at the workshop learned that even small numbers of antiprotons (a few hours' production with the use of existing machines) could be shot, one antiproton at a time, into patients to produce a computed tomography (CT) scan that would be of better quality than CT scans done with X-rays and at $1/15$ the radiation dose. Then, if a tumor were found, the same antiproton beam could be used to kill the tumor with minimal damage to surrounding tissue.

In more ambitious sessions, machine designers who had been involved in the building of past particle accelerators confidently discussed machine designs that could produce milligrams (thousandths of a gram) of antimatter per year, compared with the nanograms (billionths of a gram) presently produced at CERN and Fermilab. Propulsion engineers discussed designs for antimatter-powered rocket engines that could use those milligrams of antimatter to move tons of payload rapidly and efficiently in space. Thus, in just two years concepts for the practical uses of antimatter have gone from science fiction to scientific proposals.

Michelson-Morley experiment centennial. It was in 1887 that German-born Albert A. Michelson, a young physicist at the Case School of Applied Science in Cleveland, Ohio, and Edward Morley, a physical chemist at neighboring Western Reserve University (they since have merged into Case Western Reserve University), announced the results of an experiment to measure the velocity of the Earth through the "ether."

In the 1800s it was thought that all waves required a medium to propagate in. A wave was not a separate entity but just the collective motion of the particles in the medium. The ether was invented by theorists as the medium in which light waves traveled. In 1886

Recognition was paid during the year to perhaps the most significant "failed" experiment in physics—the attempt a century ago by A. A. Michelson (above) and Edward Morley to measure the motion of the Earth through the "ether."

Michelson and Morley had measured the velocity of light within a stream of flowing water and compared it with the velocity of light in still water or water flowing in the opposite direction. From these experiments they concluded "that the luminiferous ether is entirely unaffected by the motion of the matter which it permeates."

If this was true, then the Earth should also move through the ether and not drag the ether along with it. Thus, by measuring the velocity of a light beam through the ether at right angles to the motion of the Earth and comparing it with the measurement of the velocity of a light beam through the ether in the direction of motion, they should be able to measure the absolute motion of the Earth through the stationary ether. Their apparatus was accurate to 0.04 wavelength of light and should have shown a difference of 0.4 wavelength in the path lengths of the two beams, but no effect was seen. Michelson always considered the experiment a failure.

The Michelson-Morley experiment showed that there was no ether. Light behaved like a wave, but the wave was not the motion of particles in some medium. Light waves were self-contained waves that needed no medium. In addition, any measurement of the velocity of light in a vacuum always gave the same result, currently accepted as 299,792,501 meters per second (approximately 186,000 miles per second), even if the light source or the velocity-measuring apparatus was moving. This constant-velocity behavior of light waves that was independent of the observers was drastically different from the behavior of other types of waves known to physicists. Einstein's theory of mechanics at high velocities, the theory of special relativity, was able to explain this behavior, and as a result physics was revolutionized—all because of an experiment that "failed."

—Robert L. Forward

High-energy physics

Interesting experimental and theoretical developments occurred in high-energy physics during the past year, but most of the excitement in the field was focused on new accelerators. Some accelerators were just coming into operation, including the SLC electron-positron collider at the Stanford Linear Accelerator Center in California. SLC uses a novel technology to produce collisions between oppositely moving beams of electrons and positrons (antimatter counterparts of electrons), each with an energy of about 50 billion electron volts (GeV). To maximize the probability of collisions, each beam is focused to a size no larger than a human cell. Tristan, an electron-positron collider producing particles of similar energy but using more conventional techniques, began operation in late 1986 at the KEK Laboratory in Japan. Other accelerators, such as the large electron-positron (LEP) collider at CERN near Geneva, were nearing completion. When finished in 1989, LEP will fill a tunnel whose circumference is about 27 km (17 mi), measured to a tolerance of 2½ cm (1 in). The particles in its beams will each carry about 100 GeV of energy when the final stage is completed.

In the U.S. much attention was being given to the proposal to build a giant proton-proton collider, the Superconducting Super Collider (SSC). The SSC would use superconducting magnets and fill a tunnel more than 80 km (50 mi) in circumference. The particles accelerated by the SSC would each carry about 20,000 GeV of energy. Many states entered proposals to build the SSC, and a decision on a site was expected early in 1989, with completion projected for the late 1990s. Meanwhile, experiments were beginning in the U.S. at Fermi National Accelerator Laboratory (Fermilab), Batavia, Ill., using a proton-antiproton collider called the Tevatron with particle energies of about 900 GeV in each beam.

Cleaning up the standard model. Why are physicists building these accelerators, and what do they hope to learn from them? To understand this, one should recall that the so-called standard model of subatomic particles and their interactions, developed

Particles of Subatomic Physics

quarks	u quark	c quark	t quark (?)
	d quark	s quark	b quark
leptons	electron neutrino	mu neutrino	tau neutrino
	electron	muon	tauon
bosons	photon	Z boson	gluon
		W boson	
hypothetical particles	Higgs boson (?)		
	graviton (?)		

Particles in the same row have the same electric charge, while those in each category in the same column are associated in weak interactions. Each quark and lepton, as well as the W boson, has an associated antiparticle. Each quark comes in three varieties known as colors. Particles shown with question marks have not yet been observed.

between 1960 and 1980, accurately describes most of the experimental information currently available to particle physicists. The standard model is based on three types of particles: the quarks, the leptons, and the bosons (see Table). It explains such observations as the result of two particles colliding at high energy and the spectrum of energy levels seen among hadrons (such as the proton), which are bound systems of quarks held together by the exchange of gluons.

As a basic physical theory, however, the standard model is complicated. In its most common version it assumes the existence of 24 types of quarks and leptons but does not account for why this specific number of particles exists. Furthermore, each of the particles must be assigned a rest mass, and these masses are not predicted by the theory. Various additional assumptions have been suggested to account for particle rest masses, and one of the main reasons for building new high-energy accelerators is to see whether the assumptions are correct.

The most popular such assumption is based on the idea known as spontaneous symmetry breaking. It assumes that in completely empty space, all quark and lepton masses would be zero. It is thought, however, that the actual space inhabited by the subatomic particles is not empty. It is filled with the energy of a specific type of field, known as the Higgs field after Peter Higgs, the British physicist who first studied it. The presence of the Higgs field changes some of the properties of particles immersed in it, causing most of their masses to become different from zero. Although this model still does not determine the actual values of the masses, it relates them to other observable quantities. In the Higgs model there exists an additional type of particle, the Higgs boson, which is another manifestation of the Higgs field that pervades space. The strengths of interaction of this as yet unobserved Higgs particle with the various quarks and leptons are related to their masses. Therefore, if physicists could observe the Higgs particle and measure the interaction strengths, they could test whether the Higgs model for the origin of masses is correct.

The Higgs model does not predict the mass of the Higgs boson itself. Nevertheless, indirect arguments have convinced many physicists that if the particle exists, its mass corresponds to a rest energy of about 1,000 GeV. This energy is too high for the particle to have been produced in present accelerators; hence the need for new machines of higher energy. With the energies that would be available in the proposed SSC, it is believed that the Higgs particle would be produced in collisions between some of the gluons contained in the colliding protons. The Higgs particle would then decay rapidly, most often into Z or W bosons, which in turn would decay into more familiar particles such as electrons and muons. The detection of several pairs of such particles, with the proper energies to have emerged from the described sequence of decays, would signal the production of a Higgs particle. From observations of the rate at which this sequence of events happens, the interactions of the Higgs particle could be inferred, and from the energies of the observed particles, its mass could be determined. Further measurements could then reveal the interactions of Higgs particles with quarks and leptons.

There are, however, other models for explaining the way in which the masses of quarks and leptons arise. Some models are extensions of the successful idea that such particles as protons are tightly bound systems of quarks. In one model it is assumed that quarks—and also leptons—are themselves composites, made up of still simpler particles that have been called preons by Abdus Salam and Jogish Pati. In another, sometimes referred to as the hypercolor model, it is the Higgs particles that are composite, consisting of tightly bound combinations of very heavy quarklike objects, held together by a new type of gluon. The hypercolor model predicts that many such bound states will be observed in the form of new particles having rest energies of several thousand GeV, analogous to the many hadrons observed with energies of a few GeV. This possibility of a rich new spectrum of particles is one reason that high-energy physicists are so eager to begin exploring the thousand GeV energy range.

Such energies are not accessible to the electron-positron colliders, such as SLC, presently coming into operation. Nevertheless, there are important questions that these machines will help answer. One is whether there are yet unknown types of the essentially massless neutral particles known as neutrinos. At present, three types of neutrinos are known, as-

Dashed lines superposed on a photo of the SLAC Linear Collider (SLC) trace the paths of separate beams of electrons and positrons, which emerge from a linear accelerator and are bent in opposite directions to collide head-on.

sociated with the three known charged leptons (see Table). In most circumstances these neutrinos are produced when heavier particles decay; that is, transform into lighter particles. In such decays a neutrino is usually emitted together with its charged lepton partner. It is conceivable that there exist other neutrinos associated with much heavier charged leptons. There are arguments, based on the analysis of the way light elements were synthesized during the early universe, that suggest that no other neutrino types exist, but the arguments are inconclusive. Neutrinos associated with very heavy charged leptons would not have been observed in the decays of known particles because those particles have insufficient rest energy to decay into a heavy charged lepton and the new neutrino. However, there are reasons to believe that the Z particle can sometimes decay into a pair of any type of neutrino, without any charged leptons. Every such decay will affect the width of the Z particle; that is, the spread in energy over which particles emerge from any Z decay. An accurate measurement of this width, which can be made through observations of decays of Z particles into charged particles, could determine whether there are extra neutrinos, or any other kind of unknown particle appearing in Z decays, without the need for direct observation of those particles.

In order for such a measurement to be made, a large sample of decaying Z's is needed. The Z has many possible decay modes other than neutrinos, and its actual decay width is several GeV, while the contribution to this width of an extra neutrino would

389

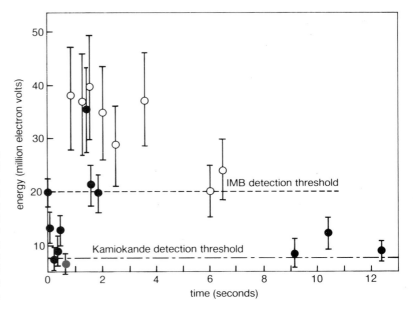

Neutrinos from Supernova 1987A were observed over an interval of several seconds at two underground detectors, the Kamiokande detector in Japan (filled circles) and the IMB detector in Ohio (open circles). One detection at Kamiokande was of such low energy (shaded circle) that it might have been background rather than a true neutrino signal. The T-shaped bars above and below each data point indicate the range of error for the measured neutrino energy.

be only about 0.15 GeV; thus, measurement of the width to an accuracy of 1% or so is necessary for a definitive answer to the number of neutrinos that exist. Just to eliminate statistical fluctuations in the data, many thousands of decaying Z's would be required, far more than have ever been observed. At the SLC it is expected that thousands of Z particles will be produced and detected during each day of operation. It should therefore be possible to carry out an accurate measurement of the Z width there and settle the question of whether there are any unknown neutrinos in nature.

The standard model assumes a close correspondence among the number of neutrinos, the number of charged leptons, and the number of quarks. Although theoretical physicists have invented variations of the standard model without these correspondences, the discovery of extra neutrino types would strongly suggest that unknown, very heavy charged leptons and heavy quarks also exist. Such a discovery would then spur an intense search for those new particles. These searches could be carried out at SLC and LEP for particles whose rest energies are less than the energies of the particles in each of the colliding beams of those accelerators. Searches for particles of still higher rest energy would require the use of either higher energy proton-proton colliders, such as the SSC, or much higher energy electron-positron colliders. It has been proposed in the U.S., in Western Europe, and in the Soviet Union that electron-positron colliders having beam energies of 1,000 GeV or more be built. For such colliders to function, the beams would have to be focused down to the size of a virus or smaller—a formidable technological challenge.

Neutrinos from a supernova. Interesting information about neutrinos arrived from a novel source, an exploding star, in February 1987. Neutrinos from a supernova that took place in the Large Magellanic Cloud reached the Earth at that time, and a small number were observed in two underground detectors, the IMB detector in the U.S. and the Kamiokande detector in Japan. These detectors were originally set up to search for rare decays of protons that had been predicted by some theoretical physicists in the 1970s, but no such decays were observed. However, the large mass of the detectors and their position deep underground, which shields them from the effects of most outside charged particles, make them useful for detecting high-energy neutrinos from astronomical bodies.

Even before the detection of neutrinos from the 1987 supernova, astrophysicists were convinced that supernovas involved the collapse of a massive star into a neutron star, with the concurrent emission of large amounts of energy. They expected that much more energy would be released in the first few seconds as neutrinos and antineutrinos than as electromagnetic radiation. The typical neutrino would have an energy of a few million electron volts. The stellar collapse would produce an immense flood of neutrinos, which, for the 1987 supernova, would travel 160,000 light-years to reach Earth. Some hundred million billion (10^{17}) neutrinos hit each detector in a period of a few seconds, but because of the low probability of interaction between neutrinos and matter, only a few of this number were detected.

The number of neutrinos observed was in line with that expected on the basis of theoretical models of a supernova. All the neutrinos detected were of the type associated with electrons. The other neutrino types were also thought to be present, but the detectors were insufficiently sensitive to record them. Furthermore, important information about a possible small mass for neutrinos could be inferred from the data. If the neutrino mass is zero—the conventional view—then all neutrinos would travel at the same speed, the speed of light. By contrast, if neutrinos had a rest mass, then neutrinos of different energy would travel at different speeds below that of light. Since all of the neutrinos coming from the supernova were thought to have been produced in a period of a few seconds, the variation in speed would show up as a variation of arrival time with neutrino energy. No definite effect of this type was observed, implying that the neutrino mass, if it exists at all, is less than about a ten-thousandth (10^{-4}) that of an electron. This result shows, among other things, that electron-type neutrinos alone do not contribute enough to the total mass of the universe to slow and eventually reverse its present expansion, as some cosmologists had suspected. Because even tiny neutrino masses can make major contributions to the fate of the universe, however, it would be interesting to have information about possible rest masses for the other neutrino types. Obtaining such information from observation of astronomical neutrinos will require more sensitive detectors, which should be in place by the time that the next relatively close supernova goes off. (See *Nuclear physics,* below, and Feature Article: SUPERSTAR 1987.)

—Gerald Feinberg

"NEUTRINOS, QUARKS, MESONS — ALL THOSE CONFOUNDED PARTICLES YOU CAN'T SEE. THAT'S WHAT DROVE ME TO DRINK. BUT NOW I CAN SEE THEM."

Sidney Harris

Nuclear physics

During the past year, nuclear physicists succeeded in predicting the appearance of phase transitions in atomic nuclei at high temperatures, detected the rarest natural nuclear decay process ever observed in the laboratory, and gathered more information in the quest to establish the mass of the neutrino. Possibly the most dramatic results in the field came from studies of high-energy heavy-ion collisions carried out in laboratories in the U.S. and Europe.

Hot nuclei. During the past 75 years, since the discovery of the atomic nucleus by Ernest Rutherford, almost all studies on it have been restricted to very low temperatures, to nuclei near their quantum ground states. During the past year, impressive progress was made in moving into higher temperature regimes in which the nucleus gives access to a hot quantum system. Applying Landau theory (a thermodynamic theory based on the absolute minimum number of parameters required to reproduce the phenomena under study) to this system, John Manoyan and Yoram Alhassid at Yale University succeeded in predicting the appearance of phase transitions at energies between 2 and 3 MeV (million electron volts; equivalent to temperatures of 24 billion to 36 billion K) as well as a triple critical point where first- and second-order phase transitions come together. The signature of the phase transitions is predicted to be a rapid change in the nuclear shape—from spherical to oblate (doorknob-shaped) and from oblate to prolate (football-shaped).

Fortunately, Kurt Snover and his colleagues at the University of Washington, in their study of giant dipole resonances in nuclei, found it possible to observe these signatures and what appeared to be the first example of the predicted phase transitions. This giant resonance corresponds to an oscillation of all the protons in the nucleus against all the neutrons as though the two were interpenetrating fluids. If the nucleus is spherical, the frequency of these vibrations and, therefore, the energy of the photons that remove energy from (deexcite) the nucleus are all of the same value and are independent of the orientation of the oscillation within the nucleus. On the other hand, if the nucleus is football-shaped, having one long axis and two short ones, two-thirds of the oscillations (in crude approximation) should have a high frequency and one-third a lower frequency; therefore, the distribution of photons deexciting this giant resonance would be expected to show two peaks, with the higher energy peak having twice the intensity of the lower energy one. If, however, the nucleus is doorknob-shaped, having two long axes and one short one, the photon distribution (to the same crude approximation) would again split into two peaks, but the lower energy one would have twice the intensity of the higher energy one. These are precisely the kinds of photon distributions that Snover was able to measure for nuclei in the rare-earth region of the periodic table—distributions whose detailed shapes Landau theory thus far appears able to reproduce in quantitative fashion. The success of this theory has implications for many other quantum systems that are just beginning to be explored.

Double-beta decay. When a nucleus undergoes normal beta decay, under the action of the weak nuclear force, one of its neutrons changes into a slightly less massive proton and ejects an electron and an electron antineutrino in the process. Although the atomic weight of the nucleus remains unchanged, the atomic number increases by one; for example, when carbon-14 (six protons, eight neutrons) transforms by beta decay into nitrogen-14 (seven protons, seven neutrons). Because of pairing effects in the nucleus, however, it turns out that in many cases such a simple process is forbidden by conservation of energy; *i.e.*, the nucleus that would result after the emission of the electron and antineutrino is more massive than the original one. In such circumstances, as was recognized by Eugene Wigner of Princeton University in the 1930s, it is possible to imagine a process that would simultaneously change two of the nuclear neutrons into protons and simultaneously eject two electrons and two antineutrinos, leading to a final nucleus significantly less massive than the original. In 1939 Wendell Furry at Harvard University recognized that if the neutrino and its antineutrino counterpart were in fact identical (*i.e.*, the neutrino was its own antiparticle), it is possible to imagine that the conversion of two neutrons into two protons within the nucleus would involve the emission of only two electrons that share the fixed energy determined by the initial and final nuclear masses. This concept has come to be called zero-neutrino double-beta decay, by contrast with Wigner's suggestion of two-neutrino double-beta decay. There were obvious reasons to expect that the zero-neutrino mode would be many orders of magnitude more probable than the double-neutrino one. Moreover, because in the zero-neutrino mode the electrons shared a fixed energy with none being lost to neutrinos, this mode was expected to be much easier to detect.

Despite continuing study over the past 50 years, and despite indirect evidence from geochemical studies suggesting that double-beta decay processes do occur, it was not until the past year that double-beta decay was detected directly in the laboratory—the rarest natural decay process ever to be so observed. Michael Moe and his collaborators at the University of California at Irvine succeeded after a decade of work in detecting, strangely enough, the two-neutrino (rather than the zero-neutrino) double-beta decay of selenium-82 to krypton-82 and in determin-

ing a half-life of 1.1×10^{20} years for the process. Because such two-neutrino decay is expected within the framework of the so-called standard model of fundamental interactions, the new result provides a remarkably stringent test of the nuclear models used to calculate the nuclear wave functions for ^{82}Se and ^{82}Kr and thus the theoretical value of the half-life.

Detection of the zero-neutrino decay mode would have much more far-reaching consequences. It would signal a breakdown of the fundamentally observed, but not fully understood, law of lepton conservation as is predicted by some of the current grand unified theories (GUTs) of the forces of nature. It would also imply a nonzero mass for the electron neutrino. Because of this fundamental interest, extensive searches for the zero-neutrino decay mode are under way in laboratories around the world.

Prominent among the groups engaged in this work has been that formerly led by V. A. Lyubimov at the Institute for Theoretical and Experimental Physics (ITEP) in Moscow, which in 1981 first suggested a nonzero neutrino mass. In 1988 this group, led by A. A. Vasenko, was searching for double-beta decay of germanium-76 and was reporting lower limits on the half-life for the zero-neutrino decay of 1.5×10^{23} years and for the two-neutrino decay of 3×10^{20} years. Furthermore, there was a slight indication in their latest data, based on 652 hours of counting, that they may be on the verge of detecting the zero-neutrino process.

Neutrino mass. In parallel with these double-beta decay studies, a number of attempts at direct determination of the mass of the electron neutrino, which traditionally has been considered to have zero mass, were completed during the year. The ITEP group in Moscow, after repeating and refining its 1981 measurement based on the beta spectrum from the decay of tritium (hydrogen-3) in a valine molecule, quoted the most probable neutrino mass as 30.3 eV; from their measurements on the mass difference between the isotope of helium of mass 3 (*i.e.*, the helion) and tritium, they report that the neutrino mass is greater than 17 eV and less than 40 eV. The major uncertainty in these measurements relates to the binding of the parent tritium atom in the valine molecule. To avoid this difficulty, J. F. Wilkerson and his collaborators at the Los Alamos (N.M.) National Laboratory carried out parallel studies on free molecular tritium and reported an upper limit of only 27 eV for the neutrino mass.

In February 1987 the detection of neutrinos from Supernova 1987A simultaneously in Japan and the U.S. provided a quite different focus on the question of neutrino mass. Since photons take just over five trillion seconds to reach the Earth from the supernova, if the neutrinos have even a very small mass, they cannot travel quite at the speed of light and so would reach the Earth slightly later than would the photons; moreover, higher energy neutrinos with mass would be expected to arrive before lower energy ones. Sidney Kahana and his collaborators from Brookhaven National Laboratory, Upton, N.Y., and the Steward Observatory at the University of Arizona reviewed all available data and analyses and concluded that these astronomical data establish an upper limit on the neutrino mass of about 15 eV. (See *High-energy physics*, above, and Feature Article: SUPERSTAR 1987.)

Because of their fundamental importance to physics, measurements on the neutrino and on neutrino-related interactions will continue to play a very important role in nuclear physics. It bears emphasis that all of these fundamental measurements are representative of that part of the science that is not dependent on large accelerators, massive detectors, or large group efforts.

Electron-positron pairs from heavy nuclear collisions. Several years ago groups led by Jack Greenberg of Yale University and by Paul Kienle of the Gesellschaft für Schwerionenforschung (GSI), Darmstadt, West Germany, using the UNILAC heavy-ion accelerator in the latter laboratory, reported the surprising experimental result that monoenergetic positrons (positrons, or antimatter electrons, of a precise energy) were emitted from collisions of heavy nuclei (*e.g.*, uranium-uranium or uranium-thorium). More recently Greenberg's group succeeded in demonstrating that these monoenergetic positrons were being produced with monoenergetic electrons of the same energy and that the electron-positron pair appeared to be emitted from a long-lived particle-like entity at rest with respect to the center of mass of the collision. During the past year, refinement of these measurements demonstrated that there are, in fact, four quite separate pairs of monoenergetic electrons and positrons in the energy range of 1–2 MeV. In addition, a group at the Lawrence Berkeley (Calif.) Laboratory led by Walter Meyerhof of Stanford University also reported observing back-to-back emission of monoenergetic photons associated with these heavy nuclear collisions, possibly corresponding to a fifth and lowest energy member of the sequence discovered at the UNILAC.

These experimental results have generated enormous theoretical interest in both the nuclear- and the particle-physics communities, but as of early 1988 there was no satisfactory explanation for them. Early speculations that the electron-positron pair originated in the decay of the long-sought axion or of some other previously unknown fundamental boson appear to be untenable in the light of a wide range of other precision measurements on the electron-positron system. In view of this major puzzle, preparations were being made at a number of other laboratories with newly available beams of heavy nuclear projectiles to extend the measurements and continue the search for the origin of the monoenergetic leptons. Parallel measurements were being made on the scattering of accelerated positrons from electrons in the hope of finding evidence of this mysterious entity through its appearance as a sharp resonance in the scattering cross section. Clearly, new nuclear or atomic physics or both are involved.

Relativistic heavy nuclear collisions. Perhaps the most dramatic new results in nuclear physics during the past year were those from relativistic heavy-ion collisions carried out both at the European Laboratory for Particle Physics (CERN) in Geneva and at Brookhaven National Laboratory. At CERN projectile beams of oxygen-16 and sulfur-32 ions were accelerated to energies of 215 GeV (billion electron volts) per nucleon (per each nuclear proton or neutron), while at Brookhaven these same beams as well as those of silicon-28 were accelerated to 15 GeV per nucleon. Although in both cases the measurements were considered very preliminary, a number of im-

Interaction of a gold target with a beam of oxygen-16 ions (coming from the left) accelerated to 200 GeV per nucleon appears in a computer reconstruction of a streamer chamber photograph taken at CERN. In such collisions physicists are seeking to create quark-gluon plasma, an extremely energetic state of matter thought to have existed in the early moments of the universe.

Courtesy of the NA-35 Research Group and William Willis of CERN

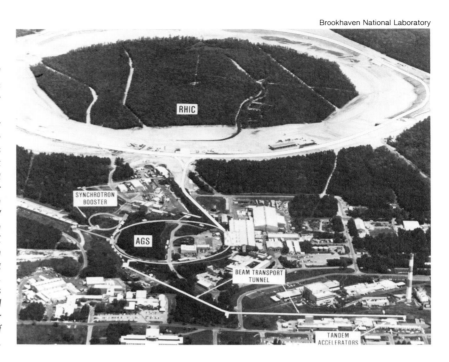

Aerial view of Brookhaven National Laboratory shows the components of the proposed Relativistic Heavy Ion Collider (RHIC) project. Pulsed beams of ions as heavy as gold will be produced in the twin MP tandem accelerators and taken via the beam transport tunnel to the existing Alternating Gradient Synchrotron (AGS) for acceleration, with assistance from the synchrotron booster, to 15 GeV per nucleon. The beams will then be injected into the large RHIC ring in opposite directions to form counterrotating ion beams having an energy of 100 GeV per nucleon. Collisions between the two beams will take place at six points around the ring, yielding 200 GeV per nucleon at the center of mass of each collision.

portant new results already emerged. Perhaps most significant was the discovery at Brookhaven that, at 15 GeV per nucleon, the projectiles were entirely stopped by heavy target nuclei instead of, as some had feared, passing through the targets as though they were transparent; at the higher energies at CERN, there already was evidence of partial transparency. Using a variant of an interferometry-based technique that was developed originally to measure the diameter of the star Sirius, investigators made measurements on the positively charged particles emerging from these heavy-ion collisions and determined that the particles were being emitted from a superhot volume substantially smaller than that of the target nuclei, suggesting that the relativistic projectiles were superheating a relatively small region of the target nuclei while leaving the remaining part to function effectively as a "spectator."

Clear evidence was also found at CERN for the production of charmed quarks in these collisions through clear observation of the now famous J/ψ particle, which is the lowest energy state of charmonium—an entity that comprises a bound charmed and anticharmed quark pair. (Quarks, the constituents of protons, neutrons, and related particles, are believed to come in six types, the charmed quark among them.) This observation, although of great interest in its own right, demonstrated clearly that under the conditions of the experiments of the past year, which involved comparatively light projectiles, no true quark-gluon plasma was being formed, since in such a plasma charmonium would not be expected to appear.

The quark-gluon plasma represents an entirely new state of matter wherein nucleons have effectively melted into their constituent quarks and the gluons that mediate the force binding the quarks together in the nucleons. Its creation is a major goal of relativistic heavy-ion research, but the experiments to date have not yielded high enough energy densities to create it in a clear and unambiguous state. Definitive experiments will necessitate the proposed Relativistic Heavy Ion Collider (RHIC) at Brookhaven, which will provide beams of projectiles as heavy as gold with effective energies ten times greater than any presently attainable at either Brookhaven or CERN. Relativistic heavy-ion research is rapidly becoming one of the most active fields in nuclear physics.

—D. Allan Bromley

Condensed-matter physics

The awarding of the 1987 Nobel Prize for Physics to J. Georg Bednorz and K. Alexander Müller of the IBM Zürich (Switz.) Research Laboratory (*see* SCIENTISTS OF THE YEAR) came as a culmination of their dramatic discovery of so-called high-temperature superconductors in 1986 (see *1988 Yearbook of Science and the Future* Year in Review: PHYSICS: *Condensed-matter physics*). Although the original discovery increased the superconducting transition temperature from 23 K (−250° C [−418° F]) to "only" about 30 K (−243° C [−406° F]), it pointed the way to a completely new class of materials for superconductivity. On this basis the Swedish Academy of Sciences honored the two physicists with the prize despite subsequent revolutionary work, primarily by Paul Chu of the University of Houston, Texas, and co-workers, that raised the transition temperature by more than a factor of three to the vicinity of 100 K (−173° C [−280° F]).

The dream of a material that superconducts at room temperature has fueled the race to find new materials with ever higher transition temperatures. The original material was composed of atoms of barium (Ba), lanthanum (La), copper (Cu), and oxygen (O), arranged in a so-called layered perovskite structure. Although by early 1988 the basic mechanism was still not understood, it was clear that the copper-oxygen layers are the crucial part of the structure that determines the unique electrical properties of these materials. By substitution of lanthanum with the element yttrium (Y), the transition temperature was raised to about 100 K. The latter material crystallizes in a structure that also contains corrugated layers and linear chains of copper and oxygen atoms. Substitution of the copper atoms lowers the transition temperature dramatically, while substitution of the heavier metals barium and yttrium causes an increase in the transition temperature. For example, scientists at the IBM Almaden Research Center, San Jose, Calif., recently reported achievement of a transition temperature of 125 K (−148° C [−235° F]) by the use of thallium, calcium, and barium atoms to separate the Cu-O network.

Despite advances in increasing the transition temperature, other factors may turn out to limit the engineering applications of these materials. One such factor is the critical current density. Even if the electrical resistance for a superconductor is zero, it cannot carry an infinite amount of current. At a certain maximum current the superconducting material reverts to a normal electrical conductor. The current density is measured in amperes per square centimeters (A/sq cm). In order for the new superconducting materials to carry the heavy currents encountered in energy-transmission and storage devices, the current density must be of the order of 100,000–1,000,000 A/sq cm. Although such values were achieved for the new materials when they were grown as a very thin layer on top of a single crystal, the values achieved for the materials in the more useful bulk shapes of wires and sheets were still not high enough to make them practical. (For comprehensive discussions of high-temperature superconductors, *see* Feature Article: THE NEW SUPERCONDUCTORS: A SCIENTIFIC BREAKTHROUGH; Year in Review: MATERIALS SCIENCES: *Ceramics*.)

Diamond thin films. The discovery of high-temperature superconductors and the subsequent exploratory work to understand their behavior and to develop them into engineering materials for technical applications have highlighted the importance of advanced materials and materials research. It has become increasingly common in applications research for condensed-matter physicists to work closely with investigators from such other disciplines as chemistry, materials sciences, and engineering. Another example of cross-disciplinary work is the search for an exotic material at the opposite end of electrical conductivity; namely, the "ideal" electrical insulator. Spectacular progress in this search was made recently with the development of methods of making diamond thin films.

Since ancient times gold and diamond have been the "shining stars" of materials and therefore the key materials of the jewelry industry. Gold resists tarnishing and therefore retains its pleasing yellow color indefinitely. Diamond has the highest optical refractive index, which is responsible for its fiery sparkle. The alchemist's dream of being able to convert cheap materials into gold has a counterpart in the dream of being able to convert simple coal into diamond, since diamond consists entirely of carbon atoms. Although nuclear physicists have transmuted tiny amounts of other elements into gold, the technique has no commercial value since it is too expensive and complicated. On the other hand, the dream of making diamond has partially come true—not for producing gemstones but for making diamond in the form of thin films having practical applications.

Carbon is among the most important elements in the periodic table. The biologic systems of all life on Earth are built on carbon chemistry. The diversity and variety of its chemistry have elevated it to a separate and distinguishable branch called organic chemistry. Nevertheless, the inorganic forms of carbon are significant and scientifically interesting. Pure carbon exists in three solid forms: amorphous carbon, graphite, and diamond. A carbon atom has a total of six electrons, of which four are so-called valence electrons. These four electrons are available to form chemical bonds with other atoms. Each of them would like to pair up with another electron to give a total electron configuration of eight electrons, which is quantum mechanically a very stable configuration. One can imagine the four electrons sticking out from the carbon atom in four different directions in three-dimensional space, each at the same angle to the others. If carbon atoms bond to each other in these four directions, a tetrahedral structure of carbon atoms is built up. This tight-knit framework, shown in Figure 1, is the diamond structure.

In amorphous carbon the structure is very distorted, with some bonds missing neighboring atoms. A technical form of amorphous carbon, called carbon black, is obtained, for example, when carbon-containing material is incompletely burned to make soot. The black ink on this printed page illustrates a principal application of carbon black. In the graphite

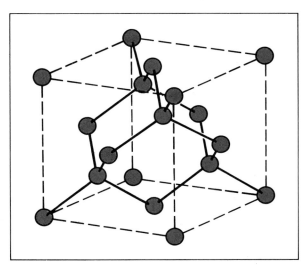

Figure 1. In the crystal structure of diamond, each carbon atom is linked to neighboring atoms by four chemical bonds, each bond at the same angle to the others. This tetrahedral structure is shared by silicon and germanium.

form of carbon, the atoms are arranged in planar, ring-shaped structures in two dimensions. This configuration gives graphite a layered structure. Since mechanical friction is very small when these layers glide over each other, graphite makes a good lubricant. Its soft, slippery properties and dark color also account for its application in pencil lead.

To a physicist the most interesting form of carbon is diamond. Diamond is the hardest known material and is therefore used as the standard against which the hardness of other materials is measured. This hardness sharply contrasts with the softness of graphite. The difference in this mechanical property of two materials made from the same kind of atoms is a good illustration of the importance of a material's atomic structure in determining physical properties. The extreme hardness of diamond makes it ideal for abrasive applications and for wear protection.

Thermodynamically the most stable form of carbon is graphite. At extremely high pressure and high temperature, however, graphite can be converted into diamond. Natural diamonds were produced under such extreme conditions in the Earth's crust and remained in this metastable form when the crust cooled. The industrial use of diamonds for cutting tools and abrasive applications was the driving force in trying to emulate the natural conditions of high pressure and temperature for making diamonds in the laboratory. This work was pioneered in the U.S. in the 1950s by the General Electric Co. Currently a few tons of artificial diamonds, commonly called industrial diamonds, are made annually.

Diamond is also a very brittle material that cleaves easily along exact planes, a property exploited by

diamond cutters of the jewelry industry. The same brittleness, however, is a nuisance when diamonds are used in grinding and cutting tools. Industrial diamonds are therefore embedded in a matrix of softer materials. It would be a great advantage if one could find ways of making diamonds in any desired shape.

In addition to its interesting mechanical properties, diamond also has unusual electrical and thermal properties. It belongs to the same family of elements as the semiconductor materials silicon and germanium. In the periodic table these three elements appear in row IVa, indicating that all of them have four valence electrons. They have the same tetrahedral crystal structure shown in Figure 1. A semiconductor is characterized by its band gap, which is an energy gap between the bound valence electrons and the energy region in which the electrons can move through the crystal and conduct electricity. The larger the band gap, the higher the electrical resistance of the material. Diamond has a band gap of 5.45 eV (electron volts), compared with 1.1 eV for silicon, and thus is one of the best electrical insulators.

High electrical conductivity is usually associated with high thermal conductivity. For example, copper metal is a good conductor of both heat and electricity. Diamond is the truly outstanding exception to this rule. Despite being a very good electrical insulator, it is the best heat conductor—five times better than copper. Furthermore, the optical properties of diamond are unique. It is transparent to electromagnetic radiation over a very wide range of wavelengths. Because it is a light element, it is also transparent to soft X-rays (X-rays of comparatively low energy near the ultraviolet region of the spectrum).

All these special properties would make diamond an ideal material for many applications. The constraining factor has been the difficulty of making it in the laboratory. During the last decade, however, new synthesis methods have been developed that allow fabrication of diamonds in the shape of thin films by means of plasma decomposition of hydrocarbon gases, primarily methane, mixed with hydrogen gas.

When a gas is exposed to a high electric field, for example, by applying a potential of a few thousand volts between two electrodes in a gas chamber or by exciting the gas with microwaves, it can be transformed into a mixture of electrons, ions, and neutral but energetically excited atoms. This material, called a plasma, is sometimes referred to as the fourth state of aggregated matter, after the gas, liquid, and solid forms. In their excited state the constituents of a plasma can react to form a material that is otherwise difficult to obtain. If a suitable substrate is present in the reaction chamber, it can become coated with a thin film of the new material. Plasma methods have become increasingly important in materials applications both for the synthesis of new materials and for

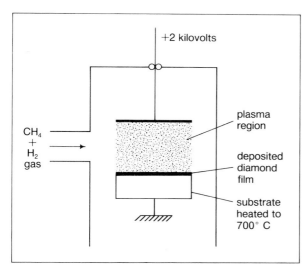

Figure 2. A plasma—a mixture of ions, electrons, and excited neutral atoms—can be created by exposing a gas to a high electric field set up across electrodes in a chamber. If the gas is a mixture of methane and hydrogen, a thin layer of diamond can be induced to deposit on a substrate.

materials etching. Figure 2 illustrates the principle of creating a plasma in a chamber.

If a gaseous mixture of methane and hydrogen is passed through a plasma chamber, it is possible to obtain a deposit of diamonds on a substrate, which can be a metal, an insulator, or a semiconductor. The resulting diamond film may be made very thin, perhaps only a few atomic layers thick, or as thick as several thousandths of a millimeter (a millimeter is about 0.04 in).

The plasma-deposition process was pioneered in the Soviet Union in the 1970s. It is said to have grown out of a program to make cheap diamonds for personal nuclear radiation detectors, since a diamond can measure the dose of such radiation. It later attracted the attention of Japanese researchers and is now of worldwide interest because of the progress that has been made in the past year or two.

It is not well understood how diamond can form under the conditions within a plasma chamber at such low pressures and modest temperatures. The temperature of the substrate is between 500° and 1,000° C (930° and 1,830° F). It is clear that atomic hydrogen in the plasma plays the most crucial role. One theory is that hydrogen atoms etch away other forms of carbon, such as amorphous carbon or graphite, that are being formed on the substrate while leaving the diamond intact or etching it at a much lower rate. There are several competing theories, however, to explain the observed growth of diamond.

A number of small companies have been formed with the sole purpose of making diamond films, and many large industrial laboratories have become involved in this field. The major obstacle for the widespread application of the technique is the fact that growth rate is very low; it may take several days to grow a diamond film thick enough for a practical application. As scientists better understand the basic process of diamond formation, they should be able to increase the growth rate to make the process industrially viable. Figure 3 shows single-crystal diamonds grown from the decomposition of methane, as observed through a microscope.

Possible uses of diamond films are numerous. Diamond-coated tools, for example, may have exceptional cutting ability and resistance to wear. If scientists could make a solid-state laser of diamond, because of the large band gap the emitted light would be blue. Diamond's electrical insulating properties and high heat conductivity make it the ideal substrate for electronic circuits and electronic power devices. Furthermore, since diamond has the same crystal structure as silicon, the addition of suitable impurities may make it a useful semiconductor as well.

—Stig B. Hagstrom

See also Feature Articles: CERN—THE EUROPEAN LABORATORY FOR PARTICLE PHYSICS; CREATING WITH EXPLOSIVES; A NEW UNDERSTANDING OF OUR SUN; PROBING THE SUBATOMIC WORLD: THE FERMI NATIONAL ACCELERATOR LABORATORY.

Figure 3. Scanning electron micrograph of a plasma-deposited diamond film reveals it to be formed of an unbroken mass of individual single crystals having well-defined crystal facets. The ball-shaped particles are also diamond material.

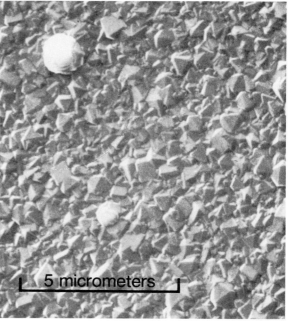

5 micrometers

Courtesy, K. V. Ravi, Crystallume Corp.

Psychology

An especially comprehensive perspective on the international status of psychology was presented by Fatoli M. Moghaddam of McGill University, Montreal, in an article in the October 1987 issue of the *American Psychologist*. He distinguished "three worlds" in which psychologists perform research and practice. The first world was the United States, which is the dominant force in contemporary psychology. The second world consisted of the other developed nations, and the third was the less developed countries.

Some idea of the predominant position of the United States can be seen in just one measure, the number of psychologists with academic appointments. There are 13,600 of them in the U.S., compared with 602 in the United Kingdom and 58 in Nigeria, which was representative of the third world.

In spite of the clearly dominant position of U.S. psychology, its views were being challenged, particularly in the area of sociocultural affairs. The present dissatisfaction with U.S. social psychology was one indication of such challenge, to some extent a result of an emerging European social psychology as well as the basic discontent within U.S. social psychology itself. More important, perhaps, was the fact that the growing signs of truly indigenous third world psychologies give promise of an increased tendency to import those ideas into U.S. psychology.

A different kind of "world view" was the surprisingly vigorous emergence of peace activism within U.S. psychology. Concern with nuclear disarmament had grown to such an extent that submission of articles on that topic to the *American Psychologist* had accelerated to the point that the editor was prompted to comment that "with so many submissions the *American Psychologist* could have become a journal dedicated to that issue alone."

Memory. Research on memory continued to be an active concern of experimental psychology. One of the most popular subtopics was the relationship between memory and aging. In a large-scale study (involving nearly 1,500 participants) of the accuracy of memory in the answering of survey questions, psychologists Willard L. Rodgers and A. Regula Herzog of the University of Michigan asked persons in three age groups questions about readily verifiable facts (for example, questions on the make and age of owned automobiles, voting records, and distances to such neighborhood facilities as drugstores and hospitals). They found that persons 60 to 69 years old and those over 70 years were equally proficient on most of those measures and were actually superior to persons under 60 years. Persons over 70 did tend to overestimate, and persons under 60 tended to underestimate the distance to the nearest drugstore. Persons over 70 were somewhat less accurate in

estimating the value of their homes, but those 60 to 69 were more accurate in doing this than were the younger persons.

In another study of age and memory, psychologist Hilary Horn Ratner of Wayne State University, Detroit, compared 24 college women, 16 noncollege women of college age (all of them high-school graduates), and 24 older, retired adults (mean age of 69 years) on their ability to recall information after reading 14-sentence prose passages. The college women recalled more information than did the elderly women, as expected on the basis of earlier research, and they also recalled more than the noncollege young women. The researcher found that the college students organized their reading and memorization effectively and suggested that "without the demands to memorize that education requires, the old and perhaps any out-of-school group may lose the ability to remember as effectively as possible" and that "many differences between old and young may have been overattributed . . . to the natural aging process."

Cognition. Among the many types of experimentation on cognitive processes, increased attention was being paid to the manner in which propositions are presented as a determinant of their acceptability. Two recent studies were representative. (*See also* the discussion of acceptance of occult phenomena, below.)

Psychologist Irwin P. Levin of the University of Iowa demonstrated the effectiveness of a relatively simple variable, positive versus negative "framing." He found more favorable responses to the purchase of beef, for example, when it was described as "percent lean" (positive framing) rather than "percent fat" (negative).

In a somewhat similar vein, Linda Behr and Jody L. Wagner of the University of Maryland found that statements that were presented in main clauses were evaluated more positively than those presented in subordinate clauses. In a second experiment false information was detected more readily when it was presented as logically subordinate rather than as central.

Developmental psychology. Some stimulating new research on the problem of the ways in which young children develop notions of causality was reported by psychologist Rochel Gelman, noted for her demonstration of previously unsuspected quantitative skills in preschool children. Intrigued by the apparent ability of three- and four-year-old children to discriminate between objects that can and cannot move by themselves—contrary to Jean Piaget's theoretical position—Gelman and her associate, Christine Massey at the University of Pennsylvania, questioned children of that age level very closely. They concluded that children use high-level abstract principles as frameworks within which various bits and pieces of new information are organized. For the problem of discrimination of movement potential, the researchers concluded that children had formulated the so-called "innards" principle, according to which self-starting objects like animals are seen as initiating movement by means of some kind of internal mechanism. The operation of such a high-level abstraction was supported by the frequency with which the preschoolers mentioned the internal contents of self-moving objects—food, bones, blood, and the like.

Neurophysiological support for Piaget's "stage" theory of cognitive development was reported from two laboratories. William Hudspeth of the University of Northern Colorado, using published EEGs (electroencephalograms) from 561 children and adolescents (one to 21 years of age), studied the growth of four functional areas of the brain. With just one exception, growth spurts were found at each of the ages that Piaget pinpointed.

Robert Thatcher of the University of Maryland-Eastern Shore also found five dominant growth periods, more or less in accord with Piagetan stage theory. In addition, he found differential growth curves in the left and right hemispheres of the brain. The left hemisphere reaches 90% of adult growth by age five, but somewhat discontinuously, whereas the right hemisphere, with a more uniform rate of growth, reaches the 90% mark at nine years.

More encouraging news for parents of some children with apparent mental retardation appeared. Before the mid-1960s children with Down's syndrome had been believed to be hopelessly retarded and therefore had been routinely institutionalized. Since that time it has been proved that most of these children are clearly educable. Research demonstrated a high degree of variation among children with Down's syndrome. Some of them were found to have the potential to achieve proficiency levels, in one or another skill including cognitive, not formerly believed possible.

The key to an improved educational prognosis for those children seemed to be early parental intervention by means of child-parent interaction in communication lessons beginning when the child is about 30 months of age. Adequate subsequent formal education was also believed to be crucial for the intellectual development of such children. Psychologist John Rynders of the University of Minnesota recently reported that about three-fourths of the children in his long-term study were reading at the second-grade level and that they had more years of effective education for further cognitive achievement.

An active issue in this area concerned the use of plastic surgery to eliminate the characteristic slant-eyed facial expression of children with Down's syn-drome. The argument in support of this operation was that the slant-eyed facial feature has been responsible for much of the automatic labeling of these children and the consequent failure to give them adequate individual attention, so that many are never permitted to realize their educational potential. Improved social acceptance is another alleged benefit of the operation. Critics argued that the operation does not really transform the child's Down's syndrome appearance sufficiently and that it is merely another form of social rejection.

Controversy also continued to surround the question of day care for children, a problem that has assumed great dimensions because there are so many single-parent households and families where both parents have full-time jobs. Studies reported by psychologist Margaret Burchinal of the University of North Carolina at Chapel Hill indicated that some day-care programs had beneficial effects on intellectual development. Burchinal and her colleagues also found that very young (one-year-old) children in day-care programs were no more likely to resist their mothers—in a special test administered after a brief separation and an encounter with a stranger—than were those kept at home. Also, they seemed to show less insecurity after the separation experience.

Applications. In 1984 the U.S. Army, apparently concerned that its personnel "be all that you can be" in accordance with the widely circulated recruiting advertisements, commissioned the National Research Council (NRC) to examine a large number of allegedly beneficial training procedures. The interesting results of the $475,000 study were announced by committee chairman John Swets, a member of the Massachusetts consulting firm of Bolt, Beranek, and Newman.

The special techniques that the committee was able to report on positively were mainly concerned with the improvement of motor skills. For example, so-called mental practice, the use of imagined performance, was found to have some beneficial effects, especially when combined with actual practice. The relationship of this kind of training to motor skills important in military service, such as marksmanship, was noted.

There were some surprises in the report. "Sleep learning," the oral presentation of materials to a sleeping subject, had seemed to have been largely discredited by earlier, carefully controlled experimentation but was found by the committee to be worth further study. Also, "speed learning," the accelerated learning widely promoted in some commercial programs, was found to contain certain innovative and potentially effective elements.

Most of the techniques examined, however, were found to be ineffective. The committee could find only negative or, at best, ambiguous evidence in support of neurolinguistic programming, the attempt to improve learning by concentrating on supposed "mental modes," such as images or feelings, used in processing information. A more definitely negative conclusion was reached by the committee in regard to the theories of extrasensory perception and psychokinesis (the movement of physical objects by the mind without the use of physical means): "The claimed phenomena and applications range from the incredible to the outrageously incredible."

An unfortunate by-product of such theories was noted by the NRC committee: their acceptance by some decision makers in the military. This observation reflected the disturbingly high level of acceptance of occult beliefs in the general population in the U.S. as periodically documented by public-opinion surveys. Two recent studies dealt with this problem. Psychologists Mark Snyder and Peter Glick at Lawrence University, Appleton, Wis., compared believers in astrology and skeptics. They found that both tended to ask the kind of questions that solicited positive information, such as evidence of extroversion after being told that an individual was rated as "highly extroverted" in an experimentally arranged horoscope. Such information strengthened the faith of the believers and weakened the skepticism of the nonbelievers. Although the reported acceptance level of the skeptics was found to be clearly dependent upon the kind of questions that were asked, the acceptance level reported by the believers seemed to be unaffected in this respect.

Israeli psychologist Gershon Ben-Shakhar and colleagues had three professional graphologists rate handwriting samples from 52 bank employees and make predictions about their personal interrelationships and their work efficiency. These predictions were poorer than those made on the basis of standardized personality tests. A similar result occurred in a second experiment, in which five graphologists did no better than chance in identifying the occupations of 40 professional men who supplied handwriting samples. Ben-Shakhar and his colleagues concluded that the acceptance by so many people of graphology was based largely on the generality of the predictions, the difficulties in checking them, and the underlying desire to believe in some such simple system. The results were especially unsettling in light of the fact that surveys revealed that more than 85% of European firms and at least 3,000 companies in the U.S. used some form of graphology as part of the selection procedure in hiring employees.

Clinical psychology. Psychologists, among others, were becoming increasingly concerned by the disproportionately small number of mental health professionals available to handle the accelerating number of persons in need of treatment. The American Psychological Association established a task force on prevention of mental illness to find programs and models worthy of emulation. Chaired by Richard H. Price, director of the University of Michigan Prevention Research Center, the task force contacted more than 900 mental health workers throughout the U.S. Nearly 300 prevention programs were thereby identified and studied. Although these programs were so varied as to defy any simple overall description, the chairman of the task force was encouraged to conclude that there was much support for the notion that mental illness and related problems could be prevented.

Howard S. Friedman and Stephanie Booth-Kewley of the University of California at Riverside simultaneously compared several emotional measures of personality with respect to the strength of their links to five diseases with alleged psychosomatic components: arthritis, asthma, coronary heart disease, headaches, and ulcers. They found good statistical support for the linkage of such emotional factors as depression, anger-hostility, and anxiety with heart disease and less clear but suggestive support for relationships with the other diseases studied. They concluded that there is good reason to recommend further research on the ways in which psychological factors can contribute to the prevention as well as the treatment of disease.

Rare indeed is the parent who at one time or another has not yearned for an effective way of handling a child's perverse behavior. During the year just such a technique was widely advocated by some psychotherapists. "Paradoxical therapy" is perhaps best described with an example. In dealing with a child who is throwing a temper tantrum, conventional practice and, presumably, conventional wisdom are blatantly adversarial; the parent attempts to stop the tantrum by "reasoning" or by threatened or actual punishment. Paradoxical therapy, on the contrary, encourages such unwanted behavior—but within definitely circumscribed limits. Thus, the child is told that tantrums are acceptable but only in a "tantrum place" or at a "tantrum time." Ultimately, without the motivation to persist that is so often provided by parental opposition, the tantrum tends to dissipate and more socially desirable behavior gradually appears. This strategy has been employed in formal therapy sessions.

If viewed historically, paradoxical therapy is not new; it was first advanced more than 50 years ago by Viennese psychiatrist Victor Frankl. However, if considered in terms of its relatively recent popularity and the widely varied types of problems to which it is being seriously applied, it can be regarded as a new approach. Interesting examples are provided in *Making Things Better by Making Them Worse* by psychiatrist Allen Faye.

—Melvin H. Marx

International developments. In September 1988 psychologists from all parts of the world will congregate in Sydney, Australia, for the 24th International Congress of Psychology. The congress is held every four years under the auspices of the International Union of Psychological Science. Responsibility for organizing this major international event for scientific exchange within the discipline falls to the national psychological society of the host country. The latest national society to be elected into membership of the International Union of Psychological Science was the Egyptian Association for Psychological Studies, bringing the number of national member states represented to 47 by the end of 1987.

The International Union of Psychological Science has established international research networks in many areas of psychology. One of these, the International Network of Cognitive Science, Artificial Intelligence and Neuroscience, published an overview of current research in those areas. Also, the first workshop of the International Network of Centres of Research in Psychology in the Third World was held as part of the International Congress of Cross-Cultural Psychology in Istanbul.

During the year psychologists were invited to participate in a world summit of health ministers concerned with the spread and control of AIDS (acquired immune deficiency syndrome). The spread of this disease can be slowed down by the adoption of appropriate behavior. Psychological knowledge can, however, be applied to the remediation of practical problems only if professional psychologists have been properly trained in psychology. In many countries acceptance of this principle has led to the licensing of properly qualified practitioners. Laws have been passed to permit only those practitioners who have completed a recognized education in psychology to use the title "psychologist."

A different nonstatutory form of regulation was introduced within the United Kingdom in December 1987. The government conferred on the British Psychological Society authority to maintain a voluntary register of "chartered psychologists." Only those members of the society who had at least six years of education, training, and experience of psychology and had agreed to abide by a code of conduct could be entered on the register. Following registration, which remains a voluntary process, a registered psychologist is permitted to use the title "chartered psychologist," a special privilege conferred by the Queen through the royal charter under which the British Psychological Society is incorporated. Thereafter, members of the public would know that if they wish to consult or employ a properly qualified practitioner, they should approach only a chartered psychologist.

—Colin V. Newman

Space exploration

The Soviet Union continued to forge ahead in space during the past year with its first launch of the world's most powerful booster rocket and expanded operations aboard the Mir space station. U.S. preparations for the next launch of the space shuttle continued, and the space station program moved slowly under the threat of budget cuts.

Manned flight

During the year the Soviet Union set new records for spaceflight endurance and displayed steadily maturing technical capabilities, while the U.S. continued its painful recovery from the *Challenger* shuttle disaster of January 1986 amid controversy and political infighting. By early 1988 many observers of the U.S. program were concerned less with the technical problems facing the space shuttle program than with the political landscape, littered by memories of the *Challenger*'s demise. Meanwhile, events in Europe, Japan, and the Soviet Union signaled growing competition and led to concern in the U.S. over its eroding position as the world's preeminent spacefaring power.

U.S. manned flight. There were no U.S. manned flights in 1987 for the first time in six years. The year began with an ironic and telling confluence of events. On January 8, almost 15 years to the day after U.S. Pres. Richard Nixon formally approved the space shuttle program, the U.S. began burying

The AX-5 all-metal space suit, developed at NASA's Ames Research Center, has joints that permit movement at the shoulder, elbow, hip, knee, and ankle. The large helmet permits a wide field of view.

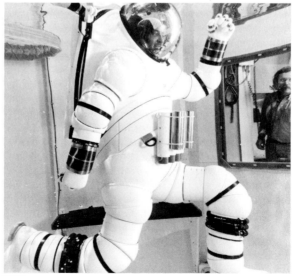

NASA

the more than 97,500 kg (215,000 lb) of shuttle debris recovered from the Atlantic Ocean in the long weeks that followed the *Challenger* disaster. Only three days before the burial of *Challenger*—a spacecraft whose destruction was due in part to the effects of cold weather—the Soviet Union launched its 15th Meteor-2 weather satellite. The successful launch took place in subzero temperatures.

That irony seemed to sum up the U.S. year in space, a year in which retrenchment was a hallmark of the space program. For the National Aeronautics and Space Administration (NASA), action took place not in orbit but in the decision-making arenas of government and in laboratories, conference rooms, and proving grounds. Efforts to return the space shuttle to flight remained a top priority at NASA and concentrated largely on the redesign of the solid-fuel rocket boosters that had caused the *Challenger* accident and on the development of a crew escape system and new quality-control procedures.

Two major policy revisions, in combination with a well-publicized NASA internal study, set the tone for future space endeavors. All three were outgrowths of the political climate that developed after *Challenger*.

In April the government announced that designs for the proposed U.S. space station would be reduced in scope. Henceforth, the facility would be built in two phases, and NASA's designs for an extensive trusswork on which to mount the living and working quarters for astronauts, as well as other scientific equipment, were effectively abandoned until Phase II, after the year 2000. This action, due in large part to spiraling cost estimates, cut the size of the "dual keel" space station plans by more than half and left NASA designers working on core elements only. These elements included a laboratory module, a habitation module and connecting structures, power generation systems, and mechanisms by which to mount the entire assembly on a large central truss.

Even with these economical measures, NASA's own estimates of total space station cost exceeded $14 billion. Original cost estimates when the program began in 1984 had been $8 billion, and the U.S. National Research Council said in July that its experts doubted that the facility could be built for less than $27.5 billion.

In May details of an internal NASA study headed by astronaut Sally Ride began to emerge. The study, intended to identify weaknesses in the U.S. space effort and suggest goals for the future, was widely read and discussed by government leaders throughout the summer months but was not formally released to the public until August. "Leadership and America's Future in Space," known popularly as the "Ride Report," said that the U.S. could ill afford to rest on past laurels and recommended four goals to give focus and direction to the faltering NASA program.

These included an intensive study of the Earth from orbit, unmanned missions to explore the solar system, establishment of a manned base on the Moon, and manned missions to Mars. One outgrowth of the study, even before it was officially released, was NASA's establishment of an Office of Exploration to explore and coordinate these goals.

The second major space policy revision of the past year was foreshadowed in late July when the government announced a complete review of the U.S. program, to be completed in time for the fiscal year 1989 budget requests, which were due in January 1988. The interagency study involved NASA, the National Security Council, the White House Office of Science and Technology Policy, and the Departments of Commerce and Transportation. After five months U.S. Pres. Ronald Reagan endorsed a new space policy in broad terms on Jan. 5, 1988, a year after burial of the *Challenger* debris. It encompassed a broad redefinition of U.S. policy, including the declaration that space leadership, a stated goal, "does not require United States preeminence in all areas and disciplines of space enterprise."

The policy also continued the Reagan administration's efforts to commercialize space exploration. One aspect of that effort was the decision that the U.S. government would encourage development of a manned commercial space platform by becoming an "anchor tenant" and guaranteeing 70% occupancy.

The new national space policy, "Space Policy and Commercial Space Initiative," made public in February 1988 along with an $11.5 billion NASA budget request for fiscal year 1989, lacked a certain potency, coming as it did from an administration with only slightly more than 11 months left in office. While NASA's 1989 budget request seemed to bolster the space community, observers pointed out that the fiscal 1988 request for $10.5 billion was cut $1,650,000,000 by Congress in December 1987, resulting in a one-year delay in deployment of the U.S. space station. The associate administrator for the space station, Andrew Stofan, who resigned early in 1988, said that further cuts in future appropriations for the space station could mean no space station at all. Research by the Library of Congress showed that the entire U.S. space expenditure in 1987—including NASA, the Department of Defense, the National Oceanic and Atmospheric Administration, and other bodies—totaled $26 billion. During the same period, the research showed, the Soviet Union was believed to have spent the equivalent in rubles of $39 billion.

Meanwhile, hardware continued to be processed for the resumption of shuttle missions as flight crews were formed and tests were conducted on the redesigned solid rocket boosters. In January NASA named a crew for the first flight after *Challenger*, originally scheduled for February 1988 but later

The redesigned booster rocket for the U.S. space shuttle undergoes a successful test firing in August near Brigham City, Utah.

moved to August. The crew consisted of five veteran space travelers and was headed by Capt. Frederick H. Hauck. At the time of the announcement, Hauck was serving as deputy associate administrator for external communications at NASA, one result of the Rogers commission recommendation that astronauts be given more say in the management of the agency. Lieut. Col. Richard Covey, who served as capsule communicator in Mission Control during *Challenger*'s ill-fated launch, was named second-in-command. The mission specialists, whose primary responsibility would be the deployment of a second Tracking and Data Relay Satellite, were George Nelson, John Lounge, and Maj. David Hilmers.

In August and December full-scale test firings of the redesigned booster rocket were conducted in Utah. Although the first test was considered a success, the December firing pointed to problems not in the rebuilt joint connecting the booster segments but in the nozzle of the rocket. The nozzle, also a concern for several years, had also been redesigned after the *Challenger* accident. When the problem surfaced in December 1987, NASA said that the next mission would be delayed by six to ten weeks and then instituted an improved nozzle design. A third major test in April 1988 was judged a complete success.

Training for the flight crews and ground controllers resumed at the Johnson Space Center in Houston, Texas, during 1987, and in August workers at Florida's Kennedy Space Center powered up the orbiter *Discovery*. Although the pressure to fly was cited by the Rogers commission as an underlying factor in the *Challenger* accident, NASA imposed tight launch schedules on the Florida work force and on other teams around the U.S.

Soviet manned flight. In January 1987 the Soviets launched the first of seven unmanned Progress supply ships, which were designed to carry provisions to the Mir space station. This was followed three weeks later by the launch of Yury Romanenko and Aleksandr Laveikin aboard Soyuz TM-2, bound for the Mir station. The TM series, an upgraded version of the workhorse Soyuz capsule, was first launched unmanned in 1986. The Soviets hailed the mission as the beginning of a permanent manned presence in space and promised the setting of new endurance records.

In March 1987 the Soviets launched the first of several large specialized modules intended to add living and working room to the Mir complex. Known as Kvant ("Quantum"), the module was designed primarily for work in astrophysics. It weighed more

A model of Kvant (right), a specialized Soviet space module, is shown attached to a model of the Mir space station. In March 1987 the Soviets launched Kvant, designed primarily for work in astrophysics, to dock with Mir; the docking was achieved on the second attempt.

than 20 tons, was almost as large as the Mir, and in itself almost doubled the habitable volume of the space station. On April 5, however, the planned docking of Mir and Kvant failed owing to problems in the science module's onboard guidance and automatic rendezvous systems. The two 20-ton spacecraft passed within about 183 m (600 ft) of one another during the aborted attempt, and U.S. observers speculated that at such close ranges the failure must have posed a significant collision hazard.

Four days later the Soviets were ready to try again. After Kvant's guidance system was reprogrammed, a second attempt brought the two modules together in what engineers described as a "soft dock," meaning airtight integrity between the two vehicles was not achieved. For some reason a "hard dock" was not possible. On April 12 Romanenko and Laveikin floated in space to Mir's docking hub to survey the problem. On inspection they discovered what was described as "an extraneous object" preventing a hard dock. In an extraordinary display of the utility of humans in space, Romanenko reached into a scant gap separating more than 40 tons of orbiting metal and pulled out a plastic bag, inadvertently left there by ground technicians, which had been fouling the docking mechanism. The two cosmonauts then floated nearby as the hard docking was completed.

Kvant went into operation and with its specialized equipment became a valuable tool in the study of one of the great cosmic events of 1987, the eruption of a massive supernova in the Large Magellanic Cloud, a companion to the Milky Way Galaxy. The supernova became the biggest astrophysics story of the year, and the Soviet Union was the only country with a manned astrophysics observatory in orbit (*see* Feature Article: SUPERSTAR 1987).

To U.S. observers the drama of the Kvant linkup to Mir pointed to a growing confidence and boldness in the Soviet program. Launches were being carried live, just as in the U.S.; news conferences were being held at the mission control center; and cosmonauts were performing heroic feats in orbit.

On May 15, for the first time since the launch of Skylab in 1973 aboard the last Saturn V rocket, the ground shook beneath the rumble of a heavy-lift, liquid-fueled launch vehicle capable of placing more than 220,000 tons in low-Earth orbit. The vehicle was called Energia, and with its launch it became by far the largest operational rocket in the world. While the first flight of the rocket itself was successful, its attached payload was prematurely jettisoned and reentered the atmosphere over the Pacific Ocean rather than going into orbit. That, however, was considered minor by comparison with the success of Energia, a vehicle that in the future could launch both manned and unmanned cargos, including a Soviet space shuttle.

A week after the Energia launch, United Press International observed that this development "highlights current budget woes and a lack of political commitment that threaten to make the United States a second-rate space power. The towering Energia rocket . . . gives the Soviet Union a capability that will be unmatched in the West for up to a decade."

In June attention shifted from Energia back to the Soviet manned program. In their second walk in space, Romanenko and Laveikin began installation of a third solar array in an attempt to solve an acute power shortage aboard Mir that had resulted from Kvant's additional electrical demands. On June 16 installation of the array was completed. When fully extended, it was approximately 10 m (35 ft) long and had a sunlight-collection surface of 22.5 sq m (242 sq ft).

On July 22 Soyuz TM-3 was launched. It carried two Soviet cosmonauts, Aleksandr Viktorenko and Aleksandr Aleksandrov, and a Syrian guest cosmonaut, Lieut. Col. Muhammad Faris. Faris was the first Syrian to travel in space. After the spacecraft linked up with Mir on July 24, the Soviet deputy flight director, Viktor Blagov, announced that there were concerns with recent electrocardiograph readings from Laveikin. With a fresh crew and capsule in place, the Soviets elected to bring him home with two of the TM-3 crew members on July 30, leaving Aleksandrov at Mir in his place.

Energia, a new Soviet liquid-fueled launch vehicle, is capable of placing more than 220,000 tons in low-Earth orbit and in 1988 was the largest operational rocket in the world.

Tass/Sovfoto

Soviet cosmonaut Yury Romanenko is interviewed upon his return to Earth in December 1987 after having set a new endurance record of 326 days in space.

For most of the remainder of 1987, Romanenko and Aleksandrov stayed aloft in Mir. On September 30 Romanenko equaled the endurance record of 237 days that was set in 1984 by a Soviet crew in the Salyut 7 space station. In December Romanenko and Aleksandrov were replaced by another flight crew, Romanenko having set a new endurance record of 326 days in space. In reflecting on the heady Soviet year in space, the *Washington Times* quoted Vladimir Kotelnikov, vice-president of the Soviet Academy of Sciences, as saying, "In the number and length of space missions, we have the advantage over the U.S. But in the space shuttle field, they are ahead of us." He left little doubt, however, that competition would increase in that arena as well.

—Brian Welch

Space probes

No missions into deep space were launched during the past year, although the U.S. planetary program appeared to be getting back on track, with two launches being scheduled for the space shuttle. The Soviet Union made final preparations to launch two spacecraft to Mars in 1988, and the U.S. was close behind with plans for a Venus mapper in 1989.

In the U.S. the National Aeronautics and Space Administration (NASA) in October 1987 scheduled four planetary missions to be launched from the space shuttle. While the redesign of the shuttle continued to suffer nagging delays, the planetary missions did not seem threatened since NASA normally gave highest priority to flights with specific planetary "windows"; the first planetary launch was scheduled to take place on the fifth shuttle mission. Planning for most other planetary missions, though, indicated that they would fly on expendable launchers as NASA tried to devote its reduced shuttle flights to missions truly needing manned involvement. The Soviet Union announced tentative plans for a number of probes that would range in destinations from the fiery edge of the Sun to the cold of Jupiter. Although the U.S. and Soviet programs continued to be viewed as competitive, the two nations in 1987

fine-tuned a five-year agreement for cooperation in several scientific fields, including coordinating Mars missions and exchanging data.

Ride Report. "Leadership and America's Future in Space" was criticized in a report by that title. A task group chaired by former astronaut Sally Ride found that the place of the U.S. in space was eroding in all areas: "The United States has clearly lost leadership in [planetary and manned] areas, and is in danger of being surpassed in many others during the next several years." Partly in response to those criticisms, NASA established an office of exploration to be devoted to fostering human missions through the solar system. The Ride Report suggested that the U.S. space program be reshaped along four leadership initiatives. All planetary in nature, they included a manned space station in Earth orbit, unmanned exploration of the solar system, an outpost on the Moon, and humans to Mars.

Three missions highlighted the solar system exploration initiative; they would "study representatives of the three distinct classes of solar system bodies in exquisite detail." The first mission on the list, already rejected by the Reagan administration as a part of the fiscal 1989 NASA budget, is the Comet Rendezvous/Asteroid Flyby, for which science teams and instruments were selected in 1987. During the year scientists tested and proved the design for a probe 1.5 m (one meter = about 3.3 ft) in length that could plunge into rock-hard ice at almost any angle. Such a probe would carry gamma-ray spectrometers to assay the chemistry of the comet nucleus. Had this mission been approved, it would have been launched in 1993, flown past the asteroid Hestia, and then spent several months flying in formation with Comet Tempel 2.

The second mission described in the Ride Report was Cassini, a spacecraft that would orbit Saturn. It would contain an atmospheric probe and semisoft lander for Titan, a methane-shrouded moon of Saturn, and an atmospheric probe for Saturn itself. It would be launched in 1998 and arrive at Saturn in 2005. This was being studied by NASA and the European Space Agency (ESA) as a possible joint mission.

The most ambitious mission on the list was a series of three flights to Mars to return samples of the planet's surface, an undertaking that had been advocated since before landers from the Viking spacecraft set down on Mars in 1976. The first two missions would be launched in 1996 and return in 1999, and the third would be sent off in 1998. The manned space station in Earth orbit might be used as a quarantine laboratory for the returning samples. During the year NASA awarded four contracts to aerospace firms for studies of Mars rovers and landers. Significant advances would be needed in automation and robotics in order to assure success of the rovers.

Inner solar system. No probes to the innermost planet, Mercury, were planned, although a sounding rocket flight in 1988 was proposed to observe its tenuous sodium-vapor atmosphere with ultraviolet instruments. The Magellan spacecraft that was scheduled to peer through the cloudy veil of Venus with high-resolution mapping radar was to be delivered to the Kennedy Space Center in Florida in November 1988 for final integration with its upper stage. A structural test model of Magellan was assembled using a Voyager mock-up borrowed from the U.S. National Air and Space Museum. Launch was scheduled for April 1989. Comet McNaught, apparently a new comet, was observed by the Pioneer Venus Orbiter during November 19–24 as the spacecraft continued its studies of Venus.

Europe's Ulysses solar polar mission was scheduled for an October 1990 launch aboard the space shuttle and a solid-rocket upper stage. Ulysses, once a dual U.S.-European spacecraft, would use Jupiter's intense gravitational field to make a hairpin turn and fly out of the plane of ecliptic (the plane of the Earth's orbit extended to meet the celestial sphere) and over the Sun's poles at a distance from the Sun of about 150 million km (one kilometer = 0.62 mi). The Soviets announced plans for a more demanding mission, to be launched in 1995, that would fly within 3.5 million to 5 million km of the Sun's surface.

Small bodies. The return of unmanned Soviet craft to the Moon was scheduled to begin in 1993 with a lunar polar orbiter to provide comprehensive global maps of the Earth's only natural satellite. In 1996 there was to be an ambitious retrieval of samples from the surface of the far side of the Moon. Finally, in the year 2000, the Soviets planned to send to the Moon an unmanned lunar laboratory and lander that would conduct extensive analyses of the surface. These missions were expected to rely heavily on technologies being developed for the Mars missions.

NASA, meanwhile, had a Lunar Geoscience Observer under study as the next planetary observer after Mars. It would map the global, regional, and local composition of the Moon's surface, including remote sensing of possible resources for lunar bases. NASA had not undertaken a lunar polar mission since the Apollo program ended in 1972.

Analysis of data from an ion composition instrument on Europe's Giotto spacecraft yielded the discovery of polymeric formaldehyde, the first polymer seen in space; apparently it was formed by the linking of simple formaldehyde. Long, whiskerlike polymers attaching themselves to the carbon and silica grains in the nucleus of Halley's Comet could account for the extreme darkness of the nucleus as seen by Giotto during its March 1986 flyby.

A long-lived interplanetary explorer, meanwhile, was given up for dead. Pioneer 9, launched into solar orbit on Nov. 8, 1968, had not been heard from since May 13, 1983. A final attempt with 80 different radio commands and sensitive receivers was made on March 3, 1987. The other Pioneers, 6 through 12, continued to operate in good health.

The Soviets announced that they were discussing with the European Space Agency and France an asteroid probe named Vesta to be launched in 1994. It would use Mars or Venus and Mars for a gravity assist to place it in the asteroid belt, land on one of the asteroids, and possibly return with samples.

Mars. Support for Mars exploration grew stronger during the year, mostly from the Soviet Union as that nation disclosed an ambitious strategy to explore the planet. Spearheading the Soviet missions was Phobos, announced in 1985. A pair of spacecraft were to be launched in July 1988 to circle Mars and to make slow flyby inspections of Phobos and Deimos, Mars's two asteroid-like moons. The spacecraft were to close to within 50 m of the moons as they passed by at a speed of 2–5 m per second; at that time they would deploy "hopper" landing craft that would use springs to hop around the surface of these low-gravity worlds. A laser on the main spacecraft would vaporize small samples of surface material for analyses in a mass spectrometer.

The first pair of new Soviet missions, called Columbus and scheduled for launch in 1992 or 1994, would place landers on the surface of Mars. These would then deploy French-built balloon-borne atmospheric packages to sail through the Martian atmosphere. The French supplied balloon packages that earlier Soviet spacecraft carried to Venus. The Columbus orbiters would carry mapping radar for detailed surveys of the surface and its soil characteristics and moisture content. Tentative agreement was reached with NASA to equip the U.S. Mars Observer with a radio relay that would pick up faint transmissions from the French package. The landers would also have rovers equipped with drilling equipment to obtain samples from several meters beneath the surface of Mars.

Missions to return samples from Mars to the Earth would be attempted by the Soviets in 1996 and 1998. These would require long-lived, accurate guidance systems and a rocket stage that would have enough energy to boost a sample capsule back to Earth. Such a spacecraft probably would carry a small rover so that samples could be collected away from the landing site, which would be contaminated by rocket exhaust.

Finally, a Mars long-term rover would be launched in 2002. The rover would be designed to roam the surface of Mars, never returning to its lander, under remote control from the Earth. This would require advances in the understanding and development of robotics, artificial intelligence, and teleoperations.

AP/Wide World

A British Skylark research rocket is launched from Australia in August 1987 by a team of West German scientists to study Supernova 1987, the first supernova to be seen distinctly with the naked eye in almost 400 years.

Meanwhile, the only approved Mars mission of the U.S., the Mars Geoscience Observer, suffered a setback when its launch was delayed from 1990 to 1992, largely to conserve funds. The science community appealed the delay and asked NASA to shift the Observer from the space shuttle to an expendable Titan booster; however, lacking direction from the government, NASA stuck with the shuttle. In building the Mars Observer, engineers planned to use designs from the Satcom communications satellite and from military weather satellites to develop a low-cost craft. The Observer's instruments were to include a high-resolution mapping camera and a visible-infrared mapping spectrometer.

Outer planets. The Galileo program moved ahead as final tests were performed in preparation for storage until launch. The project was almost derailed by the *Challenger* accident in 1986 and had to find an alternate upper stage when the high-energy Centaur was barred from being used on the space shuttle. Galileo, atop an inertial upper stage, was to be launched by the shuttle on Oct. 8, 1989, not to Jupiter but to Venus.

Because the upper stage lacked the power of the Centaur, a unique trajectory using three "gravity slingshots" was to be flown. Galileo would fly past Venus on Feb. 9, 1990, the Earth on Dec. 8, 1990, and the Earth again on Dec. 8, 1992, on a trajectory known as Venus-Earth-Earth Gravity Assist. Each encounter would leave the spacecraft's speed unchanged but would retarget it farther away from the Sun. Asteroid flybys were scheduled on Oct. 29, 1991, and Aug. 28, 1993.

In July 1995 Galileo would release a probe that would plunge into the atmosphere of Jupiter on Dec. 7, 1995, the same day that the mother spacecraft would be inserted into orbit around the planet. The probe was expected to transmit data down to a depth where the pressure would be equal to 100 times that at sea level on the Earth before it was crushed. From December 1995 to October 1997, Galileo would take a grand tour of the moons of Jupiter, a miniature planetary system in its own right.

Although exploration of Jupiter would be the primary objective, the Galileo mission would also provide the first measurements of interplanetary space over a wide range of the solar system. Because of the long delays in the program, however, a number of components had to be rebuilt, solar shields added for the excursion to the inner solar system, and heaters changed to ease demand on the power output that was declining because of aging radioactive power sources.

The Soviets also announced their first plans for missions to the outer planets. The first, in 1995, would be similar to the Ulysses solar polar mission, using Jupiter to make a hairpin turn for a close flyby of the Sun. A year later the Soviets would launch a Jupiter/Saturn flyby mission that also would drop a probe into the atmosphere of Titan, the largest moon of Saturn.

In March Voyager 2 fired its rocket engine to arrive at Neptune 12 hours earlier than planned, on Aug. 24, 1989, so that a better arrangement of Earth-based tracking stations would be available. Voyager, which had flown past Jupiter, Saturn, and Uranus, was to pass within 5,000 km of the cloud tops of Neptune's north pole and then within 40,000 km of its moon Triton.

Observations by Voyagers 1 and 2 provided a better assay of cosmic radiation flowing in from interstellar space. Scientists reported detecting carbon and argon for the first time in 1985–86, along with hydrogen, helium, nitrogen, oxygen, and neon. The lack of carbon had earlier puzzled scientists until they realized that it was ionized and deflected by the solar wind before it could penetrate deep into the solar system. Images taken by Voyager 2 during its Uranus encounter, as well as elevation data derived by geologists, were processed by a special computer program to generate a one-minute presentation depicting a flight around its moon Miranda at a height of 14.5 km.

—Dave Dooling

Transportation

From a traffic standpoint, 1987 was a good year for most U.S. freight and passenger modes, although continued rate/fare discounting in a largely deregulated and highly competitive environment held earnings down and thus put a damper on some major research and development projects. Pressures to hold down costs in order to reduce the federal budget deficit also forced delays in developing and installing advanced technology concepts.

Despite the financial problems many innovations were introduced during the year as a means of holding down costs, ensuring safer operations, and expediting movements of goods and people. Prominent among these was the rapidly expanding use of electronic data processing.

Even fully computerized rate making—a long-sought goal in freight transport that had been held back by statutory restraints, concern about discrimination between large and small carriers and shippers (now eased by the availability of minicomputers), and the complexity of trying to program billions of continuously changing rates affecting thousands of different commodities—took a forward step as the Interstate Commerce Commission formally endorsed such innovations as electronic calculation of miles (a major component of rate making). Also, greater standardization of commodity classifications and carrier identification moved forward as other key steps toward automated rate making.

Air transport. Rapid growth in numbers of airline flights and in both passenger and freight traffic encountered increasing constraints as many airports and the airways traffic control system neared full-capacity operations. The oft-delayed $12 billion National Airspace System Plan of the U.S. Federal Aviation Administration (FAA) did, however, take a major step toward implementation. It began installation of 20 Host computer centers with new IBM mainframe computers capable of accommodating traffic levels projected for the 1990s, processing instructions ten times faster than the old computers, and taking up only one-third the space. Real gains in controlling expected increases in airline traffic, however, require new software that will meter automatically the traffic flow en route and alert controllers of pending traffic conflicts.

A major roadblock to the FAA plan was the reluctance of airlines to install on their aircraft on-board receivers for the FAA's microwave landing system (MLS). Most airline pilots continued to favor the instrument landing system in use for over 40 years and now modernized by the use of solid-state technology. Military aircraft began using satellite navigation systems for achieving precision location, although the FAA claimed that they could not provide the level of accuracy available with MLS.

Early introduction of the high-tech commercial aircraft, the B-7J7, was dashed when the Boeing Co. announced that it was shelving the project and reassigning most of those persons working on it. Boeing cited as reasons the high cost of the many technological advances to be applied to the 150-seat, twin-engine aircraft and the concern about damage to the unique but exposed contrarotating propeller engines by birds in flight or debris on the ground. Another problem was a potential loss in marketability since domestic U.S. carriers wanted the 150-seat version, while international and foreign carriers wanted the plane to carry at least 200 passengers. Despite extensive and reportedly successful tests of the new prop engines by several manufacturers, Boeing doubted that they could power the larger models.

Boeing believed, however, that many of the technologically advanced developments for the B-7J7 could be applied to other aircraft. These developments included electronic control of wing and tail surfaces, advanced displays of cockpit instrument readings, and the ability to utilize composite plastics more fully because of the development of a long-polymer thermoplastic that can be reheated and re-shaped if casting is imperfect.

It was not known what effect the B-7J7 action would have on research and testing of prop engines by other groups, including General Electric Co. (the builder), McDonnell Douglas Corp. (which planned to use such engines on models of its MD-80 aircraft), and the U.S. National Aeronautics and Space Administration (NASA; a major sponsor). Rolls-Royce said that the limited thrust range of such engines made it unlikely that they could be used in commercial service until at least the mid-1990s.

While no major technological breakthroughs were announced, extensive research in development of a high-speed commercial transport (HSCT) in the hypersonic range (five or more times the speed of sound in air) continued to be sponsored by the U.S. Department of Defense, NASA, and the FAA. Three U.S. aircraft frame and two engine manufacturers were awarded multiyear research contracts by NASA/U.S. Department of Defense, worth $225 million, to design such advanced aircraft and to analyze various options to fit the potential market. McDonnell Douglas, one of the firms, foresaw a 300-passenger aircraft operating at a speed of four to six times the speed of sound, as compared with the 100-passenger Concorde, which flew at twice the speed of sound.

A major roadblock to the development of an HSCT, according to a Boeing Co. spokesman, was its need for very high-cost cryogenic fuels, such as liquid methane or hydrogen. These require installation of expensive and space-consuming storage, distribution, and delivery systems at already congested airports.

In an effort to revitalize lagging sales of business aircraft, two long-established builders introduced advanced-technology planes similar in that both were powered by twin turboprop engines with pusher propellers located at the trailing edges of the main wing. The larger aircraft also featured a small variable wing with controllable flaps at the front of the fuselage; according to the builders, this wing would

Starship 1, introduced during the past year by Beech Aircraft Corp., is an advanced-technology plane designed for business use. Powered by twin turboprop engines with pusher propellers located at the trailing edges of the main wing, the plane is made mostly of composite materials in order to achieve better aerodynamic shaping.

virtually eliminate the possibility of a stall in the takeoff or landing configuration since it would stall first and cause the plane's nose to drop before the main wing could stall. Both planes could operate up to an altitude of 12,500 m (41,000 ft) and were powered by Pratt & Whitney Canada engines.

The larger aircraft, built by Beech Aircraft Corp. and named Starship 1, had a gross weight of 6,360 kg (14,000 lb) and was built almost entirely with composite materials for better aerodynamic shaping and ease of manufacturing. The builder noted that its main wing had four different airfoil configurations to provide the most efficient airflow for varying flight conditions.

The smaller aircraft, built by Rinaldo Piaggio SpA, a privately owned firm of Genoa, Italy, and named P. 180 Avanti, had a gross weight of less than 5,675 kg (12,500 lb) and was built largely of light metallic materials. Its wing skin was machined from a single piece of metal and made with integral ribs and stiffeners that eliminated the need for external rivets.

The huge Australian freight transport group TNT, which operated 19,000 trucks and 68 ships in 105 countries, signed a $1.5 billion contract in 1987 to purchase 72 British Aerospace BAe 146 Quiet Trader cargo aircraft over the next five years. The four-engine jet had a cargo capacity of 10,000 kg (22,000 lb) and was called "the quietest airliner in the world." The latter feature was a key factor in the purchase, with TNT claiming that it would be able to deliver parcels faster than competitors because the plane would not be subject to noise restrictions on nighttime flights at many European and U.S. airports.

Highway transport. The controversy over the reliability of truck brake antilock devices continued in the U.S. throughout 1987 despite their extensive use in Europe. For many years drivers of large trucks in the U.S. had been allowed to disengage front brakes because of fear—based on past experiences—of

their locking and causing loss of steering control and jackknifing. The U.S. Congress subsequently passed a law, effective Feb. 26, 1987, closing this loophole and requiring all commercial trucks and buses of more than 4,500 kg (10,000 lb) gross vehicle weight and manufactured after July 24, 1980, to contain brakes on all wheels. A one-year retrofit period was authorized for trucks built after July 24, 1980, and before Oct. 27, 1986.

To allay continued concerns by drivers, the U.S. Department of Transportation contracted with the University of Michigan Transportation Research Institute to perform tests to resolve the safety issue. They found that front brakes on heavy trucks help in safe stopping under virtually all conditions. U.S. truckers then were given until late February 1988 to comply with the new front-brake regulation.

The antilock devices had been steadily improved during the past several years, but as of early 1988 the Department of Transportation did not require their use in the U.S. They supplemented conventional braking systems by employing sensors that electronically controlled the pressure on each wheel's brake in order to ensure even distribution of pressure and thus directional control. The need for front-brake limiter valves to adjust pressures automatically had been called a must by U.S. truck owners, yet some truckers contended that road debris or ice could block the sensors and make them inoperative. This, in turn, resulted in the manufacturers of antilock brakes making so-called soft systems that did not interfere with conventional braking systems in case the antilock sensors failed.

Continuous tracking of trucks via satellite communications took another step forward in 1987 as Geostar Corp. of Princeton, N.J., announced the successful implementation of the first phase of its planned system—to permit Mayflower Transit of Indianapolis, Ind., to track its household moving vans, each of which contained low-power transmitters that communicated via satellite to Geostar's Washington, D.C., computer facility. The second phase, to start in 1988, would increase messages from vans from four times a day to an hourly basis through the use of Geostar's own satellite. The third phase, to start in 1989, would allow two-way communications.

Advanced technology was being used during the year to maximize motor-vehicle traffic flow on congested city freeways. In Chicago a computer linked to electronic sensors that measured traffic volume and speed along 177 km (110 mi) of freeway controlled lights that, in turn, adjusted traffic flow. In Detroit cameras and sensors along the major highways provided data for automated traffic lights at 51 access ramps that controlled the entry of vehicles. In Los Angeles remotely controlled television cameras mounted every mile over a portion of the Santa Monica Freeway sent pictures to a computerized traffic-control station.

Pressure by highway safety organizations forced the U.S. Congress to consider requiring large trucks to install on-board computers to monitor operations and hours of service by drivers. The organizations contended that handwritten driver logs could easily be altered in order to bypass truck safety laws. Many other high-tech devices—for such purposes as automated engine and brake control, advanced communications, and tracking—could add almost 50 gauges, switches, and controls on the driver's dashboard. Unfortunately, the devices would be located on dashboards that were far from standardized, creating a problem that truck builders and maintenance spokespersons warned would have to be solved if the devices were to be utilized efficiently without creating a safety hazard on the nation's highways.

Seeking to attract self-move business from young, highly mobile singles and couples, U-Haul Rental System ordered 2,500 new 8.2-m (27-ft)-long moving vans from Navistar International Transportation Corp. The vans featured a rear air-suspension system that could lower the floor to 61 cm (24 in) above ground level for easy loading and unloading. This eliminated the need for a rear lift gate and minimized the use of a rear ramp. The van's diesel engine, according to Navistar, would save up to 50% in fuel costs compared with gasoline engines.

Congressional actions demanding the use of spray-reducing flaps and side skirts on the wheels of large trucks were labeled unproductive by the U.S. Department of Transportation following extensive operational tests. The department found that neither device was able to solve the problem, called by safety advocates "the driving public's most frequently cited problem with big trucks." The department thus did not plan to implement the congressional directive, which would cost the trucking industry an estimated $60 million, unless some new technology had been found by April 1988.

Pipelines. The highly automated and computerized oil pipeline industry, which handled nearly 50% of all intercity transport of crude oil and refined products consumed in the U.S., continued to seek better ways of ensuring safe operations. This goal was made difficult by the fact that such lines were built mostly below the ground and were progressively more susceptible to damage because of urban and industrial spread.

The Office of Pipeline Safety of the U.S. Department of Transportation required pipeline corrosion testing four times a year along with other steps to pre-

U-Haul Rental System's "Super Mover" is a moving van with a rear air-suspension system that can lower the deck to just 61 centimeters (24 inches) above the ground for easy loading and unloading; the standard deck height for such a van is 122 centimeters (48 inches).

Navistar International Transportation Corp.

vent leaks and breakages that could cause spillages dangerous to the public. Most of the quarterly tests were conducted by means of analyzing low-level electrical current flows through the pipeline; there were also both ground and aerial inspections.

More sophisticated corrosion and leakage tests were also made periodically by the use of so-called smart pigs, articulated sections of sophisticated instruments and sensors with circular ends to fit into the pipeline interior. One operator, the Southern Pacific Pipe Lines, used such devices to inspect about 565 km (350 mi) of pipeline yearly.

The pig, once placed into the pipeline, disappears from sight as it is propelled by the product moving through it. The data collected—from sensors on one of the pig sections that examines the pipeline wall for corrosion and leaks—are transferred to and recorded in the instrument section. After the pig has completed its journey and has been removed, a test examiner can determine the locations of any major problems from odometer readings on its instrument panel.

Using similar smart pigs, British Gas of England offered a complete pipeline inspection service for crude-oil, natural-gas, and refined-petroleum-products pipelines. Its pigs were fully self-contained, using powerful on-board magnets and sensors to identify defects on both the inside and the outside walls of the pipeline. The company said that miniaturization of the inspection elements permitted their use in pipelines ranging from 20 to 122 cm (8 to 48 in) in diameter. British Gas not only performed the inspections but also provided a detailed written report on any corrosion, leaks, or damage found in the line—including their locations to within 1.5 m (5 ft).

A full-time, continuous leak-detection system was installed by Williams Pipe Line, which delivered about 185 million bbl a year throughout a 12-state area in the U.S. over a 13,000-km (8,000-mi) liquid-petroleum-products pipeline system. It moved this huge volume of petroleum to 47 delivery terminals by using 117 pump stations—more than 90% of which were controlled by a centralized station in Tulsa, Okla.

The highly computerized leak-detection system was based on data received from meters throughout the pipeline that measured volume, pressure, flow deviation, and temperature at every delivery and discharge point, at the suction and discharge side of intermediate pump stations, and along each eight-kilometer (five-mile) segment of the line. The computers could analyze this information and convert it into easy-to-read display screens for operators.

Because Williams Pipe Line's system moved a variety of products in batches, the computer model displayed each of the seven different product ranges (as classified by the American Petroleum Institute) in a different color. Also, the screen designated the batch name, volume, and estimated time of arrival at the next (identified) downstream meter. With the data continuously entering the leak-detection system, early analysis of changes could thus be made to determine the size of the leak and its location.

Rail transport. Progress continued in efforts of U.S. and Canadian railroads to develop electronic train-control systems. The Union Pacific Railroad, in conjunction with Tandem Computers Inc. of Cupertino, Calif., and SEL Canada of Don Mills, Ont., tested parts of such a system on 325 km (200 mi) of track in Nebraska. Its ultimate goal was to control all its trains on 34,600 km (21,500 mi) of track from a central dispatch center.

The Union Pacific system featured on-board computers that collected and relayed a variety of data on train operations: freight car pickups and discharges, train tracking through use of transponders embedded in the tracks, fuel efficiency, and safety through speed control. The Burlington Northern Railroad and Rockwell International Corp. joined to develop a similar system.

CSX Transportation claimed during the year that when its new central dispatch facility was completed by late 1988 at its West Jacksonville, Fla., yard, it would be the first major railroad to dispatch all of its trains from one location. Expected to cost $12.5 million, it would require relocation of dispatchers previously scattered in 33 locations across the U.S.

As a safety measure the U.S. Department of Transportation ordered all operators of freight and passenger trains in the Northeast Corridor (Boston to Washington, D.C.,) to be fitted with automatic train control (ATC) devices that would automatically stop a train if an engineer failed to obey signals ordering the train to slow or stop. All trains would have to be in compliance by July 1, 1990. The department's Federal Railroad Administration (FRA) also was to explore the need to extend the order to other corridors connecting with the Northeast.

The FRA rejected arguments that ATC could not be safely utilized on rail freight systems, pointing out its successful use in actual operations and computer simulations. According to the Association of American Railroads, ATC made use of two hardware elements: a single transmission system located in the rail, and a receiver unit in each locomotive and power unit. A change in a signal calling for a speed reduction was relayed to the engineer in the locomotive; if he or she did not respond properly within a specified time (eight seconds), the train was automatically slowed and stopped.

Major U.S. railroads agreed to undertake a new program to enable all to communicate with one another via electronic data interchange (EDI). An industry spokesman called this a "major breakthrough" that should be of benefit to both carriers and their shipper customers. The computer software was expected to be ready by June 1988. It was to be designed to utilize personal computer systems and would be furnished free of charge to shippers. Thus, it should encourage additional shippers to use EDI.

After many years of development and promotion, the RoadRailer (a semitrailer with both rail and highway rear wheels that could be interchanged for movements by rail as integrated units or by highway as single units) began to prove itself. Two major roads—Norfolk Southern and CSX—were using them successfully, and the Union Pacific ordered a sizable number.

Two factors helped stimulate operations and orders. One was agreement by unions to allow integrated RoadRailer trains to operate with two-person crews. Another was the introduction of so-called Mark V RoadRailers, which could detach the heavy equipment needed for operation on rails and thus operate on the highways at a far less unloaded weight.

Changes in the way automobiles were hauled in rail freight trains continued to be made. General Motors Corp. asked railroads to retrofit their trilevel auto-rack cars so that a new wedge system for securing the vehicles during transport could be used in place of the current chain tie-down system.

A product of Thrall Car Manufacturing Co., the wedge system consisted of two metal wedge-shaped chocks pushed under each tire on one side of the automobile and locked onto the metal track holding it. A harness was then strapped around the wheel. This allowed the auto's own suspension system to absorb about 80% of the shock of rail transport. By contrast, the chain tie-down system pulled the automobile down so far that it disengaged its suspension system—thus forcing the "overbuilding" of the

auto's frame to endure the shock of transport. The holes in the frame used to hook the chain no longer were needed with the chocks.

Renewed interest in high-speed rail passenger service in the Boston–New York corridor was demonstrated by a study for the Coalition of Northeastern Governors. It called for "tilt-body" cars that could operate at high speeds on existing tracks and for the installation of high-powered turbopropelled locomotives able to run independently and on the electrified lines in the corridor. The goal was to reduce the present minimum travel time of 4½ hours between the two cities to 3 hours, thus making rail transport competitive with air travel.

Canadian National Railway, whose tracks were used extensively by many high-speed passenger trains operated by the government-owned Via Rail, began building a high-tech inspection car for measuring the effect of such trains on its tracks. It would be the third version of such a car, the others being used for the same purpose for slower, but much heavier, freight trains. Calling the technology employed "the most sophisticated of its kind in the world," the railway estimated that the 26-m (85-ft) car would cost $1.2 million. Lasers, infrared sensors, video cameras, and computers would enable the car to check the rail's alignment, condition, and fastenings, as well as the crossties and the holding capability of the ground beneath. A computer would collect measurements from the sensors, convert them into digital form, and then reprocess them into report form.

Water transport. Kloster Shipping A/S of Oslo began negotiating with shipbuilding firms to build the world's largest passenger cruise ship. To cost almost $1 billion, it would weigh 250,000 gross tons, with a length of 380 m (1,250 ft) and beam of 75 m (250 ft). Able to carry 5,200 passengers, primarily on

Express train of Japan Railways passes through the Seikan Tunnel, the world's longest undersea tunnel. Connecting the Japanese islands of Hokkaido and Honshu, the Seikan is 53.9 kilometers (33.4 miles) long.

AP/Wide World

Caribbean cruises, it was scheduled for its maiden voyage in mid-1991.

A consortium of three large Japanese shipyards was favored to win the contract. Each would build one of three parts: bow, stern, and midsection. To be called the *Phoenix*, the huge ship would be propelled and serviced by eight 70,000-kw diesel engines and employ new technology that, for the first time, would link the rudder to the ship's stabilizers via a computer that could calculate the strength of waves for adjusting the stabilizers automatically. As a result only one set of stabilizers would be needed, compared with the three sets normally required.

Another feature of the ship was to be the placing of bulkheads lengthwise, rather than across the width, in order to strengthen the hull. The three watertight bulkheads would contain special escape routes to the ship's 20 huge lifeboats—each able to carry 400 persons belted down in seats. The lifeboats would be built to be unsinkable. Also featured would be an on-board marina accommodating four 30-knot cruising vessels, each able to carry 400 passengers for sightseeing trips and for moving passengers to and from harbors unable to berth the *Phoenix*.

A study for the U.S. Maritime Administration of an automated around-the-clock fuel-monitoring and operating system predicted that it would reduce fuel consumption by more than 10%. The system, called MEMEX, would be capable of duplicating the know-how of a full-time expert marine engineering service on a 24-hours-a-day, 7-days-a-week basis.

A subsidiary of Babcock and Wilcox Co. of New Orleans, La., announced the manufacture of a new computer system called Network 90 that linked several shipboard operations systems, such as the control of the engine room and damage control, along with an emergency shutdown. The builder claimed that the system, when installed on new ships, would cost only 40% as much as single-function systems now in use, weigh half as much, and save 50% in space.

Mitsui O.S.K. Lines Ltd. of Japan announced the development of a quiet, energy-saving ship propeller. When used on a freighter or tanker, it could save up to 7% in fuel consumption, the firm claimed. Through the use on each propeller blade of a fin that made the propeller less dependent on the hull form through better control of the prop wash, engine horsepower efficiency was expected to be increased from 3 to 7% and propeller efficiency by 4%. The reduction in propeller noise made the innovation especially valuable for submarines, as had already been experienced by the use of such technology by Soviet submarines as a means of avoiding detection devices.

The Norfolk, Va., International Terminal began using new dual-hoist cranes designed to move two containers at a time and, eventually, up to 50 an hour. The port of Gulfport, Miss., was using a new container crane, costing $3.4 million, that operated at twice the speed of older cranes. It could discharge 30 containers an hour.

—Frank A. Smith

U.S. science policy

The gloom cast upon the previous year by the twin disasters of the *Challenger* space shuttle explosion and the Chernobyl nuclear reactor explosion was almost magically lifted in 1987—first by a smudge on a photographic plate on a Chilean peak and then by an unusual fusion of elements in a Zürich, Switz., laboratory.

The smudge was Supernova 1987A, discovered by a resident astronomer at Las Campanas Observatory when at 3 AM on February 24 an exposed photographic plate of the Large Magellanic Cloud appeared different from one he had taken the previous evening. When he compared the two, he discovered the most exciting astronomical event in the past four centuries. As one astronomer proclaimed at one of a dozen or more press conferences in succeeding months, "There is simply no way to convey the excitement of having an opportunity in your own professional career to test the speculations of a lifetime." (*See* Feature Article: SUPERSTAR 1987.)

The seminal event in the IBM research laboratory in Zürich actually took place in January 1986, when two scientists, K. Alexander Müller and J. Georg Bednorz, discovered that a ceramic material composed of barium, lanthanum, oxygen, and copper became superconducting at 30° above absolute zero ($-273.15°$ C [$-459.67°$ F]). Superconductivity—the capability of transmitting electricity without resistance—has been one of the most eagerly sought scientific secrets since it was first noted in 1911. It was not until 1987, however, that the extraordinary scientific significance of the discovery in Zürich (discussed elsewhere in this volume) penetrated first the internationally competitive technical community, then the news media, and finally the political arena. The potential ability to transmit electricity essentially without cost was the 20th-century equivalent of the medieval alchemist's dream of converting base metals into gold. When, in March 1987, the American Physical Society scheduled a symposium on the subject in a New York City hotel, 1,800 physicists pushed and crowded into an auditorium designed for 1,100 and listened to research reports until 3:15 AM. (*See* Feature Article: THE NEW SUPERCONDUCTORS: A SCIENTIFIC BREAKTHROUGH.)

Super collider. All in all, it was a good year for physicists. An idea hatched in a 1962 summer workshop of the American Physical Society moved

U.S. Pres. Ronald Reagan watches as Alan Schriesheim, director of the Argonne (Illinois) National Laboratory, uses liquid nitrogen to cool one of the newly discovered high-temperature superconductors. Reagan announced a federal program to help U.S. businesses develop marketable technologies based on the superconductors.

onto center stage on Jan. 30, 1987, when U.S. Pres. Ronald Reagan announced that he was going to ask Congress to provide funding for the world's largest and most expensive experimental device, a Superconducting Super Collider (SSC); its ultimate cost began with an estimated $4.4 billion and rapidly began to climb. By mid-February its administration proponents were admitting that inflation alone would raise the cost to $5.3 billion. Since its successful construction would also depend on devices not yet invented, much less designed, almost any final figure could be argued.

The powerful zealotry of the high-energy physics community, combined with the strong force of international scientific competition, had persuaded the budget-sensitive Reagan administration to accept an extraordinary proposal. It was to build a subterranean racetrack 84 km (52 mi) in circumference that would employ 10,000 helium-cooled superconducting magnets to hurl atomic particles on a collision course that would yield impacts of 40 trillion electron volts, 20 times the energy of any existing accelerator.

The question soon arose as to how this project would be financed. Congress had been demonstrating increasing reluctance to fund scientific research at the enthusiastic levels proposed by the Office of Management and Budget. For instance, although President Reagan's asking budget for fiscal 1989 treated science generously, many believed that Congress would never approve it. Under the terms of a previous agreement, nondefense discretionary spending must be held to a 2% increase each year. Increases above that level in one area can be offset by decreases elsewhere, but no one believed that Congress would give a 20% increase to the National Science Foundation (NSF) by cutting, for example,

health benefits for war veterans. To compound the problem, the NSF undertook new commitments in 1987 in anticipation of a big increase in its funding for fiscal 1988. The increase did not materialize and, as a result, everyone's grant from the NSF was cut 12.5%. Without new revenues science will have to fight hard just to get another 3% increase in fiscal 1989—and there usually are no new revenues in election years.

Even within the science budget itself, questions were being raised about the propriety of allocating massive funding for the SSC. In a September editorial the *Washington Post* noted that although the Reagan administration gave its blessing to the SSC, its funding would have to come from another administration. Furthermore, the *Post* warned, the SSC should be funded only if Congress is willing to protect present support for other exciting fields in physics, especially those in university laboratories, which have the added benefit of training the next generation of scientific workers.

Another piece of evidence that estimating costs of proposed "big-science" projects is a practice more driven by political considerations than by scrupulous auditing principles appeared in the Feb. 27, 1987, issue of *Science* magazine. It disclosed that an internal study by the U.S. National Aeronautics and Space Administration (NASA) of the ultimate cost of the proposed space station had yielded cost estimates of more than $14 billion—almost twice the figure quoted when the project was approved in 1984.

Election campaign. One of the oddities of the policy year was that although science and technology were coming to play an increasingly significant role in the national welfare, they were almost never discussed in the primary campaigns of either major political party. This was "astonishing" to Frank Press, who had been reelected to a second six-year term as president of the National Academy of Sciences. "For the most part," he complained, "science and technology have been left out in the cold during the winter months of the campaign, rarely raised as issues important to the nation's future."

Since Press had learned the political game as science adviser to Pres. Jimmy Carter, he recognized that few of these issues contained political appeal to large voting blocs. Yet, he argued, one should consider the important issues that will confront the next administration:

● Which nation will be first to bring superconductivity to the drawing boards and reap the enormous financial benefits in terms of jobs and balance of payments?

● What can be done about a space program that has worsened since the *Challenger* disaster? Some of our brightest young scientists are now avoiding the field, Press pointed out, in part because there is no national consensus for long-term support of reasonable goals in space.

● How will the nation deal with such situations as the growing evidence of global ozone depletion, the beginning of a new industrial revolution based on the electronic chip, and biotechnology and its attendant social issues? The list is almost endless, he said.

There is almost no end of scientific questions that are crucial to our future as a nation and a planet, Press said. "Any candidate with vision should be telling us how he will lead us there."

Advising the president. The quality of science advice to the president again drew attention from the scientific leadership. The absence of a visible representation of distinguished scientists among presidential advisers had been galling to the leadership since the virtual dismantling of the apparatus by Pres. Richard Nixon. President Reagan's former principal science adviser, George A. Keyworth, had been a source of puzzlement to scientists. On the one hand, Keyworth antagonized many by ignoring well-publicized scientific objections and vigorously supporting the president's determination to proceed with the Strategic Defense Initiative (SDI; "Star Wars"); on the other hand, the president had been generous in his proposed budget for the support of scientific research, even though most of it was sluiced through military channels.

Keyworth resigned in late 1985, however, to be replaced by William Graham. Graham also made it clear during 1987 that he had no interest in publicizing the work of his office or, for that matter, revealing the names of his professional staff. *Science and Government Report*, a newsletter published in Washington, D.C., complained that it had been unable to obtain a list of Graham's principal staff until it dispatched legal representation to the White House with a demand based on the Freedom of Information Act.

As an almost invisible voting bloc, the scientific community has few avenues available through which it can register effective political protest. Therefore, it most frequently deals with dissatisfaction by scheduling discussions by the recently dispossessed and volunteering warnings to friendly congressional committees.

The latest discussion took place at a full-day session at the annual meeting of the American Association for the Advancement of Science in Boston in February 1988. Proposed cures for the ailing White House Science Office ranged from creation of a secretary of science and technology, with no department, to a return to the president's Science Advisory Council. The exception was William Graham, who said things were just about perfect now. Lewis Branscomb, a former director of the National Bureau of Standards and chief scientist at IBM, now a Harvard University professor, favored amending the Federal Advisory Act to permit greater privacy for groups advising the president, while his Harvard colleague Ashton Carter argued for greater reliance on advisory institutions that openly publish their analyses for all interested consumers. A few days later, oversight hearings on presidential science advice were conducted by the House of Representatives Subcommittee on Science Research and Technology. The unsurprising consensus was that no advisory structure would help a president who did not want advice.

Financial support. A decline in spending increases on the part of both government and industry led the National Science Foundation to predict that overall growth of research and development (R & D) expenditures would drop in 1988 to its lowest rate since 1977. Total national R & D investment was predicted to reach about $132 billion, representing a 3% real increase after inflation was taken into account, according to a report by the Foundation's Division of Science Resources Studies. Of the total the U.S. was expected to spend $15 billion on basic research, $27 billion on applied research, and $90 billion on development. Investments by government and industry accounted for roughly equal shares.

In contrast, the real growth rate in R & D was 4 to 5% per year from 1978 to 1982 and 6 to 8% from 1982 to 1985 before dropping back to 4% during 1986 and 1987. As a proportion of the gross national product, R & D expenditures rose steadily from 2.1% in 1978 to 2.7% in 1985, where it remained.

On the other hand, the Division of Policy Research and Analysis of the NSF looked into its economic crystal ball and predicted that the financial needs of academic research would increase by 250% in constant dollars over the next decade merely to maintain virtually the present level of activities. The increase would be accounted for primarily by rising costs for facilities and increasingly sophisticated equipment, plus salary competition for a demographically shrinking pool of scientists and engineers. The NSF did not predict where the money would come from.

Strategic Defense Initiative. Disputes about the efficacy of President Reagan's dream of a hair-trigger defense against incoming ballistic nuclear missiles continued to preoccupy a considerable portion of the scientific community. In "The Science and Technology of Directed Energy Weapons," released in April, a study group organized by the American Physical Society (APS) concluded that the development of an effective ballistic missile defense utilizing directed energy weapons (DEW) would require performance levels that vastly exceeded current capabilities. The study group estimated that "even in the best of circumstances, a decade or more of intensive research would be required just to provide the technical knowledge needed for an informed decision about the potential effectiveness and survivability of directed energy weapon systems." Meanwhile, the report pointed out, the Soviet Union could be expected to use the time to make their missiles less vulnerable to such weapons and to develop the means to attack the defensive system.

A week later the APS governing council chose not only to embrace the report of its study group but also to enlarge its implications and impart a political spin. The council expressed the belief that "it has a public responsibility to express concerns about the Strategic Defense Initiative that go beyond the issues of DEW covered in the Study" and concluded that "in view of the large gap between current technology and the advanced levels required for an effective missile defense . . . it is the judgment of the Council of the American Physical Society that there should be no early commitment to the deployment of an SDI system."

Both reports received extensive media coverage and, consequently, political responses. For example, the administration's Strategic Defense Initiative Organization (SDIO) replied: "Although the chapters in the report . . . represent an objective independent appraisal of various technologies, we find the conclusions to be subjective and unduly pessimistic. . . . We would not have made several of the assumptions they made in defining the technical requirements."

SDIO added, "The report has the additional problem of being a snapshot in time that dates to the preparation of the report." (Whereupon the APS privately complained that this was a rather cheeky reaction to a report that SDIO had bottled up for nearly seven months and also that progress made since the study had not invalidated any conclusions of the report.)

While the APS council was defending its panel's report against the administration, however, 14 out of 17 members of the panel protested the use of their report as a basis for the council's opposition to the overall SDI policy of the Reagan administration. In a letter published in *Physics Today*, they declared, "We object to being included in the council's statements on matters neither we nor they studied."

The APS study on directed-energy weapons was also hotly challenged by a group of SDI supporters led by Frederick Seitz, a distinguished former president not only of the National Academy of Sciences but of the APS itself. He declared in a briefing on Capitol Hill that the DEW report is "not worthy of serious consideration."

The academic attack on the Strategic Defense Initiative was later enlarged to a two-flank operation; while many physicists argued that SDI was "Mission Impossible," another smaller group warned that the very devices proposed to provide the ultimate national defense would actually be capable of ultimate destruction. "SDI will not produce weapons which only destroy other weapons. They will also serve as strategic arms, almost perfectly suited to strikes against population centers, or as instruments of coercion and destruction," declared Peter Zimmerman of the Carnegie Endowment for International Peace at the 1988 meeting of the American Association for the Advancement of Science.

Genetic engineering. The debate about the safety of gene-splicing techniques in the creation of new organisms continued to occupy both the scientific community and energetic advocacy groups who feared the introduction of suddenly virulent strains into the environment. In Bozeman, Mont., Gary Strobel, a plant physiologist at Montana State University, wept as he destroyed 14 elm saplings with which he was testing the use of a genetically altered bacterium intended to protect the trees against the ravages of Dutch elm disease. Although preliminary results had been promising, the test itself had been performed in advance of final approval from the Environmental Protection Agency. Strobel had chosen to commit the act of "civil disobedience" to avoid losing a year of research. When it appeared that both he and possibly his faculty colleagues faced possible retaliation in the federal granting procedures, Strobel ended the experiment with a chain saw.

Nevertheless, it seemed likely that Strobel had developed something that was good for the elms. He had injected all 14 young trees with a genetically altered bacterium that had the capacity to increase the production of an antibody to Dutch elm disease. Eight of the 14 had also been injected with the disease fungus. Six additional trees had been injected only with the fungus. According to Strobel, the six trees that had received only the fungus died within weeks, but all the infected trees that had also received the

Gary Strobel, a plant physiologist at Montana State University, destroys an elm sapling on which he was testing a genetically altered bacterium intended to protect the tree against Dutch elm disease (see text).

altered bacteria, as well as all the trees that had received only the bacteria, had survived. Strobel had planned to monitor the survival of the survivors over the winter before announcing his results.

Scientists differed in their reactions to the episode. One industrial researcher called it an "unfortunate circus" and predicted that the treatment would likely be patented by competitors in The Netherlands. Others thought that, unfortunate as the episode had been for Strobel's work, the rules had to be followed to protect the public and agricultural workers.

Reassuring words came from the Council of the National Academy of Sciences. While appreciating the legitimate need for regulation of genetically modified organisms proposed for large-scale environmental or agricultural uses, the scientific elders opposed "strict and rigid" controls on all genetically engineered organisms simply because of the techniques involved. In a widely publicized report it said, "There is no evidence that unique hazards exist either in the use of R-DNA techniques or in the movement of genes between unrelated organisms."

Integrity of research papers. Fraudulent research did not suddenly spring upon the scene in the 1980s, but it was routinely dismissed by the scientific leadership as almost insignificant in quantity. There were bound to be a certain percentage of frauds in any large community, it was argued, but science was almost completely protected from damaging fraud by the very process of research in which research results were routinely submitted to review not only

before publication but afterward as well. Thus, any significant research was bound to be subjected to confirmatory repetition by colleagues in the field.

That defense appeared to be more convincing in the case of laboratory research under controlled conditions than in human experimentation, in which the number of varying parameters was almost endless. In any event, by the end of 1987 the argument that the scientific process provides automatic assurances against scientific frauds seemed in itself to be a highly questionable hypothesis.

Early in the year the author of several influential studies on the use of psychoactive drugs with the mentally retarded was accused of perpetrating a massive scientific fraud in an investigation conducted for the National Institute of Mental Health (NIMH). The investigative panel was unanimous in finding that Stephen E. Breuning "knowingly, willfully, and repeatedly engaged in misleading and deceptive research . . . that he did not carry out the described research, and that only a few of the experimental subjects described in publications and progress reports were ever studied, and that the complex designs were not employed." The sponsoring agency not only accepted the panel's report but also referred the case to the U.S. Department of Justice with the unprecedented recommendation that criminal prosecution be considered. Although that decision had not been made as of early 1988, the University of Pittsburgh, Pa., paid $163,604 to NIMH as restitution of the institute's grants to Breuning.

The later repudiation by the National Institutes of Health of a study of children and cholesterol that had been published in a major scientific journal raised new questions about the efficacy of peer review, the bastion of scientific publishing. The NIH termed the work performed at the University of Cincinnati, Ohio, College of Medicine as "serious scientific misconduct" and misrepresentation of data.

The central problem, as examined by Lawrence K. Altman, a physicist-reporter for the *New York Times*, was the efficacy of the refereeing system central to the publication of scientific literature in influential journals. According to Altman, the system was beginning to show its inadequacies. In the case of the cholesterol study, for instance, the journal reviewers never saw the raw data on which the published paper was based, yet it had been an examination of the raw experimental data by a university committee of inquiry that led to the NIH censure. According to the committee, "Had this present inquiry not taken place, the material would have entered the scientific literature without further comment and, inappropriately, would have had profound implications for the treatment of children with elevated cholesterol levels" in their blood.

—Howard J. Lewis

Scientists of the Year

Honors and awards

The following article discusses recent awards and prizes in science and technology. In the first section the Nobel Prizes for 1987 and the Britannica Awards for 1988 are described in detail. The second section is a selective list of other honors.

Nobel Prize for Chemistry

The 1987 Nobel Prize for Chemistry was shared by three scientists—Donald James Cram and Charles John Pedersen of the U.S. and Jean-Marie Lehn of France—for their contributions to the study of molecular recognition, now known as "host-guest" chemistry. Working independently, the three laureates succeeded in synthesizing molecules that mimic the chemical and biologic behavior typical of molecules found in living systems—that is, the synthetic molecules selectively recognize and react with other molecules. Pedersen was credited with laying the groundwork for the prizewinning research in the 1960s, while he was a research chemist for E. I. du Pont de Nemours & Co. He has since retired. Cram and Lehn were recognized for their roles in extending his work and furthering the understand-

The Nobel Foundation, Stockholm

Jean-Marie Lehn

ing of the mechanism whereby reacting molecules recognize one another. Cram is an organic chemist and a professor in the chemistry department of the University of California at Los Angeles, where he has taught since 1948. Lehn has been a professor at the Collège de France in Paris since 1979.

While he was with Du Pont, Pedersen synthesized an unusual class of two-dimensional, ring-shaped compounds as an unintentional by-product of a chemical reaction. The new molecules were composed of a loose, flexible ring of carbon atoms punctuated at regular intervals with oxygen atoms. Pedersen discovered that these molecules could bind, in their centers, with certain, normally highly reactive alkali metal ions—specifically lithium, sodium, potassium, rubidium, and cesium. The product of such a reaction was an organized, less reactive molecule. It was more rigid than the original ring-shaped compound and had a characteristic crown-like shape. Thus, Pedersen named the new ring-shaped molecules "crown ethers" for their structure. By varying the structure of the crown ethers, he was able to tailor the molecules to combine with metal ions of certain sizes. His results, published in 1967, demonstrated that it was possible to synthesize molecules that would selectively react with other atoms and compounds much as do molecules found in living organisms.

Pedersen's discoveries were expanded independently by Lehn and Cram, who won their share of the prize for synthesizing a group of three-dimensional organic compounds with a chemistry and behavior similar to Pedersen's crown ethers. In 1969 Lehn, by substituting nitrogen atoms for two oxygen atoms in the original crown ether molecule, was able to

Donald J. Cram

University of California, Los Angeles; photo, Terry O'Donnell

Charles J. Pedersen

stack two rings, one on top of the other. The resulting three-dimensional bicyclic compounds were more rigid than the two-dimensional crown ethers. Furthermore, they could combine more selectively with a greater variety of metal cations to form more stable compounds.

As Lehn worked, he developed a terminology that thereafter became an accepted part of organic chemistry nomenclature. He named the bicyclic compounds cryptands because they contained molecular cavities, or what he called crypts, in which the substrates were bound. He named their complexes cryptates.

Meanwhile, Cram worked to achieve a long-standing goal in organic chemistry—the synthesis of a molecule that behaves as enzymes in the body do. His research was aimed at altering crown ethers in such a way that they could distinguish between chiral molecules—molecules that are mirror images of each other but that are identical in every other way. By 1973 he had succeeded in creating crown ethers that could distinguish between chiral amino acids. Cram coined the term host-guest chemistry for the emerging field of molecular recognition, viewing crown ethers and their descendants as hosts and their substrates as guests. In the following years Cram and his colleagues synthesized numerous hosts and used them to study the process of molecular recognition.

The achievements of Lehn and Cram represent a crucial step toward the synthesis of fully functional mimics of natural molecules because natural molecules that interact selectively are known to have complementary three-dimensional structures. According to the accepted "key-lock" model of molecular selectivity, molecules that do not have

complementary shapes will not fit together properly and therefore will not react. Enzymes, for example, which are indispensable to life and which regulate nearly all chemical reactions that take place in living things, owe much of their characteristic behavior to their three-dimensional structure. Each enzyme acts on only one kind of substrate and catalyzes only one kind of reaction. Scientists believe that the enzyme's shape, at least in part, permits only molecules of a particular substrate to fit into the enzyme's active site.

The work of the three laureates may have far-reaching consequences in biology, medicine, and industry. Scientists foresee such developments as the synthesis of artificial enzymes that possess greater stability and selectivity than their natural counterparts. Lehn was cited in particular for synthesizing a host molecule that specifically recognizes the neurotransmitter acetylcholine, a chemical transmitter of nerve signals in the human brain and nervous system. Cram has synthesized molecules that resemble hollow hemispheres. Binding two of these hemispheres together at the rims makes it possible to "trap" a compound inside the resulting sphere. Cram believes such spheres can someday be used to deliver timed-release drugs or pesticides.

In addition, the products of host-guest reactions are easier to detect and separate from solution than are the original guest molecules. Thus, host molecules may be able to bind with and neutralize or remove certain guest molecules. Synthetic molecules have already been used in experiments to partially detoxify rats poisoned with lead or radioactive strontium. Similarly, drug molecules could be designed to recognize and bind to cancer cells and other specific targets in the body. Other possibilities include the application of highly sensitive compounds to remove contaminants from the environment and to extract gold and other valuable materials from low-grade ores or even seawater.

Cram was born on April 22, 1919, in Chester, Vt. He received a bachelor's degree from Rollins College, Winter Park, Fla., in 1941 and a master's degree from the University of Nebraska in 1942. For the next three years he worked as a research chemist at Merck & Company, Inc., in New Jersey, studying the antibiotics penicillin and streptomycin. He entered Harvard University in 1945 and received his Ph.D. in organic chemistry two years later. He became assistant professor in the chemistry department of the University of California at Los Angeles in 1948 and full professor in 1956.

Lehn was born on Sept. 30, 1939, in Rosheim, France. He received a Ph.D. in chemistry from the University of Strasbourg in 1963. In 1970 he became a professor of chemistry at the Louis Pasteur University in Strasbourg, where he remained until

1979, when he took a professorship at the Collège de France in Paris.

Pedersen was born on Oct. 3, 1904, in Pusan, Korea. In the 1920s he moved to the U.S. to study chemical engineering at the University of Dayton, Ohio, where he received his bachelor's degree. He earned a master's degree in organic chemistry from the Massachusetts Institute of Technology. Rather than pursue a doctorate, Pedersen chose to launch his career as a research chemist for Du Pont, where he remained until his retirement in 1969.

Nobel Prize for Physics

The 1987 Nobel Prize for Physics was shared by Johannes Georg Bednorz of West Germany and Karl Alexander Müller of Switzerland for their discovery of high-temperature superconductivity in oxide ceramic materials. Before their discovery, superconductivity was thought to occur only at extremely low temperatures—hundreds of degrees below 0° C (32° F). Their work has already led to the discovery of superconductivity at significantly higher temperatures, raising the possibility that superconductivity may someday be possible at room temperatures and so may finally lend itself to practical applications. Müller is a fellow at the IBM Zürich Research Laboratory, where he has worked in solid-state physics since 1963. Bednorz joined the IBM laboratory in 1982 and was quickly recruited by Müller into the study of superconductivity.

A material is superconducting if it abruptly loses all electrical resistance when cooled below a characteristic temperature, called the transition temperature. The Dutch physicist Heike Kamerlingh Onnes first discovered superconductivity in 1911 in the element mercury; he won the 1913 Nobel Prize for Physics for his research. In the years following Onnes's discovery, superconducting behavior was found in approximately 25 other chemical elements and in thousands of alloys and chemical compounds.

In 1957 the U.S. physicists John Bardeen, Leon N. Cooper, and John R. Schrieffer developed a comprehensive theory to explain the behavior of superconductors. The theory (named the BCS theory after the scientists' surname initials) won them the Nobel Prize for Physics in 1972. In a solid, vibrations of the atoms that form the solid structure, or lattice, result in waves similar to sound waves that travel through the solid. These waves are called phonons. According to the BCS theory, at very low temperatures the free electrons in a superconductor, which would normally repel one another, interact with one another by using phonons as intermediaries. These electron-phonon interactions serve to attract the electrons to each other, and the electrons bind weakly together into pairs called Cooper pairs. The application of an electrical voltage to a superconductor causes all of its Cooper pairs to move, constituting a current. These electrons travel through the lattice without any opposition—that is, without any electrical resistance.

The BCS theory predicts that the transition temperature of a superconductor increases with the strength of the electron pairing interaction. This interaction, in turn, depends directly on the degree of electron-phonon interaction and on the density of electrons in the superconducting material. Thus, as scientists experimented with different materials in hopes of raising the transition temperatures, they restricted their search primarily to metals and alloys with high electron densities. Nevertheless, the highest transition temperature found in these "classic" superconductors was 23.3 K (kelvins; 23.3 K is equal to −249.7° C, or about −417.5° F). This record temperature was observed in 1973, and by the late 1970s many researchers had abandoned the search for higher-temperature superconductors.

In 1983 Bednorz and Müller began a systematic search for superconductivity in an entirely different class of materials—ceramic metal oxides. These materials have a significantly lower electron density than the traditional metallic materials, but Müller, a specialist in oxides, had found that the electron-phonon interaction was stronger in many of the oxides. He and Bednorz reasoned that they could raise the transition temperature of oxides by increasing their electron densities to levels comparable to those in good metals. The scientists searched for oxides with specific metallic properties and then altered samples to improve those properties. By the spring of 1986 Bednorz and Müller had succeeded in raising the transition temperature of a barium lanthanum copper oxide sample to 35 K (about −238° C, or −396° F)—about 12° above the previous record high temperature.

Johannes Georg Bednorz

Since the announcement of the laureates' work, new research has revealed related ceramic materials that become superconductors at still higher temperatures—nearly 100 K (about $-173°$ C, or $-279.4°$ F). Scientists believe that the mechanism of high-temperature superconductivity may be fundamentally different from that proposed by the BCS theory. In fact, there is some speculation that the mechanism involved in the 35 K superconductors may even be different from that responsible for the most recent high-temperature superconductors, because some theorists believe that phonon-mediated electron pairing cannot result in transition temperatures as high as 100 K.

Transition temperatures of about 100 K are high enough to be achieved with refrigeration using liquid nitrogen, which is cheaper and easier to use than the liquid helium needed to cool conventional superconductors. Thus, for the first time, these new superconductors have a strong potential for practical applications, including the manufacture of generators and power lines of unprecedented efficiency, tiny supercomputers, and high-speed trains that ride on a magnetic cushion.

Bednorz was born in West Germany on May 16, 1950. He graduated from the University of Münster in 1976 and received his Ph.D. from the Swiss Federal Institute of Technology in Zürich in 1982. He then joined the IBM Zürich laboratory, where he met Müller and joined him in his superconductivity research.

Müller was born on April 20, 1927, in Basel, Switz., and received his Ph.D. in physics from the Swiss Federal Institute of Technology in 1958. He spent five years as a project manager with Battelle Institute in Geneva before joining the IBM Zürich laboratory in 1963, where he worked in solid-state physics. In 1973 he was named manager of the

Karl Alexander Müller

The Nobel Foundation, Stockholm

laboratory's physics department. He was appointed an IBM fellow in 1982 and soon afterward met and recruited Bednorz.

Nobel Prize for Physiology or Medicine

The Japanese molecular biologist Susumu Tonegawa was awarded the 1987 Nobel Prize for Physiology or Medicine for his discovery of the mechanism by which as few as 1,000 gene segments can produce as many as one billion different, specialized antibodies in the human immune system. Tonegawa's work may help scientists improve the effectiveness of vaccines, understand the process of cancer formation, and develop a means of inhibiting such immune disorders as AIDS (acquired immune deficiency syndrome) and rheumatoid arthritis. Tonegawa began his research on the production of antibodies at the Basel (Switz.) Institute for Immunology. He has been a professor at the Massachusetts Institute of Technology (MIT) since 1981.

The mechanism by which antibodies protect the human body from antigens (foreign particles or microbes) has long been understood. Each antibody is designed to bind to and neutralize only one specific antigen. The exact manner in which antibodies are able to bind with specific antigens was explained by biochemists Gerald Maurice Edelman and Rodney Porter, whose work won them the 1972 Nobel Prize for Physiology or Medicine. Edelman and Porter found that an antibody is composed of two pairs of amino acid chains that form a flexible shape resembling the letter Y. The sequence of amino acids in the base of the Y is relatively constant for all antibodies of a particular type. However, the amino acid sequence in the arms of the Y varies from one antibody to another. Edelman and Porter identified these arms as the exact sites on the antibody molecule where antigen binding occurs. The variation in the structure, or coding, of these sites explains why a given antibody can fit and bind to only one particular antigen.

The process by which these antigen-specific antibodies are produced within the body, however, remained unclear. When Tonegawa began his research in the early 1970s, it was already known that antibodies are produced by the white blood cells known as B lymphocytes, or B cells. Scientists had also established that antibody production is governed by genes within the B cells. It was not understood, however, how the variation in the amino-acid sequences of antibodies is effected—that is, how a single B cell can produce such a large variety of antibodies. A number of scientists had suggested that a separate gene in the B cell might be responsible for coding each type of antibody. According to this theory, there would have to be an extremely large number of genes

421

Susumu Tonegawa

available in order to account for the wide diversity of antibodies. This was not the case, however—the number of antibody types in the immune system can exceed by hundreds of thousands the total number of genes in the B cells. Thus, scientists were forced to abandon this model.

In 1965 William Dreyer and Claude Bennett of the California Institute of Technology proposed a different theory. They postulated that the base and arms of the antibody molecule were encoded by separate genes that were later combined as the B cell matured. In this way one "base" gene could combine with a number of "arm" genes, and B cells could produce a large number of antibody molecules from a relatively small number of genes. In 1976 Tonegawa and his colleague Nobumichi Hozumi obtained experimental evidence in support of this theory by studying the arrangement of genes encoding the different parts of a single antibody molecule. They found that the genes were placed closer together in a mature antibody-producing B cell than they were in an embryonic cell—proof that the genes had been rearranged. Over the next few years Tonegawa and other researchers continued to unravel the mystery of antibody diversity. Their work showed that not only do antibody genes combine at random, they also mutate. It is this combination of genetic shuffling and mutation that gives rise to the millions of specialized antibodies responsible for the exquisite selectivity of the body's immune system.

422

Tonegawa was born on Sept. 5, 1939, in Nagoya, Japan. He received a bachelor's degree in chemistry from Kyoto University in 1963 and a Ph.D. in biology from the University of California at San Diego in 1969. He remained in San Diego to do postgraduate work at the University of California and later at the Salk Institute. In 1971 Tonegawa moved to Switzerland and began his antibody research at the Basel Institute for Immunology. In 1981 he returned to the U.S. as a full professor at MIT. In 1987 Tonegawa shared the Albert Lasker Basic Medical Research Award; he also won the Bristol-Myers award for distinguished achievement in cancer research. Tonegawa is the first Japanese scientist to receive the Nobel Prize for Physiology or Medicine and only the third person since 1961 to be the sole laureate in that category.

—Carolyn D. Newton

Britannica Awards

Britannica Awards for 1988, honoring exceptional excellence in the dissemination of learning, were presented to five persons. Two of them, a Chinese social anthropologist and a U.S. writer on urban sociology, were engaged in scientific research.

Although many medals and prizes mark original contributions to the world's sum of knowledge, the Britannica Awards, presented for the first time in 1986, celebrate both exceptional skills in imparting learning to others and a passion for its dissemination. Candidates for the awards are nominated by members of Britannica's Board of Editors and its Editorial Advisory Committees drawn from the faculties of great universities in the United States, Canada, Japan, Australia, the United Kingdom, and continental Europe.

Fei Xiaotong

Fei Xiaotong. Fighting his way back from the obscurity to which the Cultural Revolution condemned him, Fei Xiaotong (Fei Hsiao-t'ung), China's foremost social anthropologist, has revived the scientific study of village life in China. Born Nov. 2, 1910, in Wujiang (Wu-chiang) District, Jiangsu (Kiangsu) Province, Fei was graduated in 1933 from Yanjing (Yen-ching) University in Beijing (Peking) and did graduate work at Quinghua (Chi'ing-hua) University in Beijing, the London School of Economics, and the University of London. He became professor of anthropology at Quinghua in 1945 and deputy dean there in 1949. His star appeared to be rising until he made the mistake of taking Mao Zedong's (Mao Tsetung's) Hundred Flowers movement too literally. He rebounded from these troubles but fell victim to the Cultural Revolution in 1967. Fei reappeared, fully rehabilitated, in 1972 and is now professor and director of the Institute of Sociology of Beijing University and chairman of the Chinese Democratic League.

In addition to his writings, Fei's effectiveness in communicating knowledge in recent years has resided in his scholarly contacts with Western colleagues. Among his books originally written in English are *Peasant Life in China* (1939), *China's Gentry* (1953), *Chinese Village Close-up* (1983), and *Small Towns in China* (1986).

Jacobs, Jane. An acute observer of urban life and problems, Jane Jacobs has brought to the study of city planning a distinctive vision that made her widely celebrated even while it infuriated those whose oxen were being gored. Born Jane Butzner on May 4, 1916, in Scranton, Pa., the daughter of a physician, she obtained a job after graduation from high school as a reporter on the *Scranton Tribune*. About a year later she went to New York City, where she built a reputation as a competent and versatile free-lance writer.

In 1944 she married Robert Hyde Jacobs, Jr., an architect. Already keenly interested in city neigh-

Thomas Studios

Jane Jacobs

borhoods and their vitality, both as writer and—increasingly—as community activist, she explored urban design and planning at length with her husband. In 1952 she became an associate editor of *Architectural Forum*, where she worked for a decade. Near the end of her tenure there she contributed a chapter, "Downtown Is for People," to a book produced by the editors of *Fortune* magazine, *The Exploding Metropolis* (1958), and three years later published her first full-length book, *The Death and Life of Great American Cities*, a brash and passionate reinterpretation of the actual needs of modern urban places. Translated into Japanese and several European languages, it established her as a force to be reckoned with by planners and economists.

In 1969 she moved to Canada with her husband and later took Canadian citizenship. Her *The Economy of Cities* was published in 1969 and *Cities and the Wealth of Nations* in 1984.

AWARD	WINNER	AFFILIATION
ANTHROPOLOGY		
MacArthur Prize Fellow Award	Richard W. Wrangham	University of Michigan, Ann Arbor
ARCHITECTURE		
Frank P. Brown Medal	Paul Weidlinger	Weidlinger Associates, New York, N.Y.
National Medal of Science	H. Bolton Seed	University of California, Berkeley
Prix de Rome	John Shnier	Toronto
ASTRONOMY		
Beatrice M. Tinsley Prize	S. Jocelyn Bell Burnell	Edinburgh Royal Observatory, Scotland
Catherine Wolfe Bruce Medal	Edwin E. Salpeter	Cornell University, Ithaca, N.Y.
George P. Merrill Award	G. W. Lugmair	Scripps Institution of Oceanography, University of California, San Diego
John Adam Fleming Medal	Sir David R. Bates (Emeritus)	Queen's University of Belfast, Northern Ireland
National Medal of Science	James A. Van Allen (Emeritus)	University of Iowa, Iowa City
Paul Dirac Medal and Prize	Stephen Hawking	University of Cambridge, England
Paul Dirac Medal and Prize	Yakov Borisovich Zeldovich	Space Research Center, Moscow
Robert J. Trumpler Award	Stephen E. Schneider	University of Virginia, Charlottesville
Simon Newcomb Award	Conrad Dahn	U.S. Naval Observatory, Flagstaff, Ariz.
Van der Pol Gold Medal	Tor Hagfors	Cornell University, Ithaca, N.Y.
William Procter Prize for Scientific Achievement	James A. Van Allen (Emeritus)	University of Iowa, Iowa City
Wolf Prize	Herbert Friedman (Emeritus)	Naval Research Laboratory, Washington, D.C.
Wolf Prize	Riccardo Giacconi	Space Telescope Science Institute, Baltimore, Md.
Wolf Prize	Bruno B. Rossi (Emeritus)	Massachusetts Institute of Technology, Cambridge
CHEMISTRY		
Arthur C. Cope Award	Kenneth B. Wiberg	Yale University, New Haven, Conn.
Auburn-G. M. Kosolapoff Award	Herbert C. Brown (Emeritus)	Purdue University, West Lafayette, Ind.
Charles E. Pettinos Award	Terry Baker	Auburn University, Ala.
Chemical Pioneer Award	Herbert S. Eleuterio	E. I. du Pont de Nemours
Coblentz Society Award	Alan Campion	University of Texas, Austin
C. V. Boys Prize	Malcolm R. Mackley	University of Cambridge, England
Ellis R. Lippincott Award	C. Bradley Moore	University of California, Berkeley; Lawrence Berkeley Laboratory
Fernly H. Banbury Award	R. Warren Wise	Monsanto Co.
Garvan Medal	Marye Anne Fox	University of Texas, Austin
Gunnar Nicholson Gold Medal Award	Barrett K. Green (Retired)	National Cash Register Corp.

AWARD	WINNER	AFFILIATION
Gustavus John Esselen Award for Chemistry in the Public Interest	Alfred P. Wolf	Brookhaven National Laboratory, Upton, N.Y.
Gustavus John Esselen Award for Chemistry in the Public Interest	Joanna S. Fowler	Brookhaven National Laboratory, Upton, N.Y.
G. W. Wheland Medal	Frank Westheimer (Emeritus)	Harvard University, Cambridge, Mass.
Jacob F. Schoellkopf Medal	Stanley Bruckenstein	State University of New York, Buffalo
James Flack Norris Award	Glenn Crosby	Washington State University, Pullman
Korean Science Award	Suh Jung Hun	Seoul National University, Rep. of Korea
Leo Hendrik Baekeland Award	Ben S. Freiser	Purdue University, West Lafayette, Ind.
Michelson-Morley Award	George A. Olah	University of Southern California, Los Angeles
National Medal of Science	R. Byron Bird	University of Wisconsin, Madison
National Medal of Science	Walter H. Stockmayer (Emeritus)	Dartmouth College, Hanover, N.H.
National Medal of Science	William Johnson (Emeritus)	Stanford University, Calif.
Nichols Award	Kurt Mislow	Princeton University, N.J.
Parsons Award	Norman Hackerman (Retired, president)	Rice University, Houston, Texas
Pauling Award	Harden McConnell	Stanford University, Calif.
Perkin Medal	Robert L. Banks	Phillips Petroleum Co.
Perkin Medal	J. Paul Hogan	Phillips Petroleum Co.
Priestley Medal	Frank H. Westheimer (Emeritus)	Harvard University, Cambridge, Mass.
Robert A. Welch Award in Chemistry	Harry G. Drickamer	University of Illinois, Urbana
Stein and Moore Award	Emil Smith (Emeritus)	University of California, Los Angeles
William Bowie Medal	Robert N. Clayton	University of Chicago, Ill.
Willard Gibbs Medal	Allen J. Bard	University of Texas, Austin; *Journal of the American Chemical Society*
Wolf Prize	David M. Blow	Imperial College of Science and Technology, London
Wolf Prize	Joshua Jortner	Tel Aviv University, Israel
Wolf Prize	Ralphael D. Levine	Hebrew University, Jerusalem
Wolf Prize	Sir David C. Phillips	University of Oxford, England

EARTH SCIENCES

Arthur L. Day Medal	Don L. Anderson	California Institute of Technology, Pasadena
William Bowie Medal	James C. I. Dooge (Retired)	University College, Dublin, Ireland
Charles A. Whitten Medal	William M. Kaula	University of California, Los Angeles
Charles Chree Medal and Prize	Brian J. Hoskins	University of Reading, England
Esselen Award for Chemistry in the Public Interest	Mario Molina	Jet Propulsion Laboratory, Pasadena, Calif.
Esselen Award for Chemistry in the Public Interest	F. Sherwood Rowland	University of California, Irving

AWARD	WINNER	AFFILIATION
Ewing Award	John Imbrie	Brown University, Providence, R.I.
Fleming Medal	George E. Backus	Scripps Institution of Ocenography, University of California, San Diego
John and Alice Tyler Ecology-Energy Prize	Gilbert F. White	University of Colorado, Boulder
Penrose Medal	Marland P. Billings (Emeritus)	Harvard University, Cambridge, Mass.
Smith Award	Thomas F. Malone	Butler University, Indianapolis, Ind.
Vetlesen Prize	Wallace S. Broecker	Lamont-Doherty Geological Observatory of Columbia University, Palisades, N.Y.
Vetlesen Prize	Harmon Craig	Scripps Institution of Oceanography, University of California, San Diego

ELECTRONICS AND INFORMATION SCIENCES

AWARD	WINNER	AFFILIATION
Albert A. Michelson Medal	Rodolfo Bonifacio	University of Milan, Italy
Albert A. Michelson Medal	Luigi A. Lugiato	Polytechnic Institute of Turin, Italy
Arthur M. Bueche Award	William O. Baker	AT&T Bell Laboratories
David Richardson Medal	Janusz S. Wilczynski	IBM T. J. Watson Research Laboratory
Founders Award of the National Academy of Engineering	John R. Whinnery	University of California, Berkeley
Industrial Research Institute Medal	Ian M. Ross	AT&T Bell Laboratories
Inventor of the Year Award	Amar G. Bose	Massachusetts Institute of Technology, Cambridge; Bose Corp., Framingham, Mass.
Inventor of the Year Award	William R. Short	Bose Corp., Framingham, Mass.
Italgas Prize	Raffaele Meo	Polytechnic Institute of Turin, Italy
John Price Wetherill Medal	Dennis Klatt	Massachusetts Institute of Technology, Cambridge
John Scott Award	Eugene Garfield	The Institute for Scientific Information; *The Scientist*
Marconi International Fellowship Award	Robert W. Lucky	AT&T Bell Laboratories
Marconi Young Scientist Award	Michael A. Isnardi	David Sarnoff Research Center
National Medal of Science	Ernst Weber (Emeritus)	Polytechnic Institute of New York
National Medal of Technology	Joseph Charyk (Retired)	Communications Satellite Corp., Washington, D.C.
National Medal of Technology	Robert N. Noyce	Intel Corp., Santa Clara, Calif.
Vannevar Bush Award	David Packard	Hewlett-Packard Co., Palo Alto, Calif.
Wilkes Award	Harold Thimbleby	University of York, England

ENERGY

AWARD	WINNER	AFFILIATION
Ernest Orlando Lawrence Memorial Award	James Gordon	Los Alamos National Laboratory, N.M.
Ernest Orlando Lawrence Memorial Award	Miklos Gyulassy	Lawrence Berkeley Laboratory, Calif.

AWARD	WINNER	AFFILIATION
Ernest Orlando Lawrence Memorial Award	Sung-Hou Kim	Lawrence Berkeley Laboratory and University of California, Berkeley
Ernest Orlando Lawrence Memorial Award	James Kinsey	Massachusetts Institute of Technology, Cambridge
Ernest Orlando Lawrence Memorial Award	J. Robert Merriman	Oak Ridge National Laboratory, Tenn.
Ernest Orlando Lawrence Memorial Award	David Moncton	Argonne National Laboratory, Ill.
Enrico Fermi Award	Gerald F. Tape	Brookhaven National Laboratory, Upton, N.Y.
Meritorious Service Award of the U.S. Department of Energy	Daniel H. Wilken	U.S. Department of Energy
Robert E. Wilson Award	Alfred Schneider	Georgia Institute of Technology, Atlanta

ENVIRONMENT

Award of Merit of the Japanese Institute of Electrostatics	Edmund Potter	Australian Commonwealth Scientific and Industrial Research Organization
Crafoord Prize in Biosciences	Howard T. Odum	University of Florida, Gainesville
Crafoord Prize in Biosciences	Eugene P. Odum (Emeritus)	University of Georgia, Athens
Distinguished Achievement Award	Theodore T. Kozlowski	University of Wisconsin, Madison
George Westinghouse Award	John H. Seinfeld	California Institute of Technology, Pasadena
Honda Prize	Jean Dausset	Collège de France, Paris
Horton Medal	Abel Wolman (Emeritus)	Johns Hopkins University, Baltimore, Md.
John and Alice Tyler Ecology-Energy Prize	Richard E. Schultes (Retired)	Botanical Museum, Harvard University, Cambridge, Mass.
John and Alice Tyler Ecology-Energy Prize	Gilbert F. White (Emeritus)	University of Colorado, Boulder
J. Paul Getty Wildlife Conservation Prize	Hermanta R. Mishra	King Mahendra Trust for Nature Conservation, Nepal
MacArthur Prize Fellow Award	Jon Seger	University of Utah, Salt Lake City
Wallenberg Award	Derek Barnes	MacMillan Bloedel Ltd., Canada

FOOD AND AGRICULTURE

Bio-Serv Award in Experimental Animal Nutrition	Richard Weindruch	National Institutes of Health, Bethesda, Md.
Borden Award in Nutrition	Paul M. Newberne	Boston University, Mass.
General Foods World Food Prize	M. S. Swaminathan	International Rice Research Institute, Manila
Kenneth A. Spencer Award	John M. Bremner	Iowa State University, Ames
Lederle Award in Human Nutrition	Raymond F. Burk, Jr.	Vanderbilt University, Nashville, Tenn.
Mead Johnson Award for Research in Nutrition	Rune Blomhoff	University of Oslo, Norway
National Medal of Science	Theodor O. Diener	U.S. Department of Agriculture
National Medal of Technology	John Franz	Monsanto Crop.
Sterling B. Hendricks Award	Ralph W. F. Hardy (Retired)	E. I. du Pont de Nemours Co.
Wolf Prize	Theodor O. Diener	U.S. Department of Agriculture

Scientists of the Year

AWARD	WINNER	AFFILIATION
LIFE SCIENCES		
Artois-Baillet Latour Health Prize	Tomas Hokfelt	Karolinska Institutet, Stockholm, Sweden
Artois-Baillet Latour Health Prize	Viktor Mutt	Karolinska Institutet, Stockholm, Sweden
Charles Doolittle Walcott Medal	Andrew H. Knoll	Harvard University, Cambridge, Mass.
Edgar D. Tillyer Award	Russell Devalois	University of California, Berkeley
Edgar D. Tillyer Award	Donald H. Kelly	SRI International, Menlo Park, Calif.
Eli Lilly Award in Biological Chemistry	Peter Walter	University of California, San Francisco
Eli Lilly Research Award	Randy W. Schekman	University of California, Berkeley
Franklin Medal	Stanley Cohen	Vanderbilt University, Nashville, Tenn.
Gairdner Foundation International Award	Walter J. Gehring	University of Basel, Switzerland
Gairdner Foundation International Award	Edward B. Lewis	California Institute of Technology, Pasadena
Gairdner Foundation International Award	Eric R. Kandel	Columbia University, New York, N.Y.
International Prize for Biology	John B. Gurdon	University of Cambridge, England
King Faisal International Prize	Pierre Chambon	University of Strasbourg, France
King Faisal International Prize	Ricardo Miledi	University of California, Irvine
Korean Science Award	Park Sang Dal	Seoul National University, Republic of Korea
Louisa Gross Horwitz Prize	Günter Blobel	Columbia University, New York, N.Y.
Louis Jeantet Award for Medicine	Bert Sakmann	Max Planck Institute for Biophysical Chemistry, Göttingen, West Germany
MacArthur Prize Fellow Award	Ira Herskowitz	University of California, San Francisco
MacArthur Prize Fellow Award	Stuart A. Kauffman	University of Pennsylvania, Philadelphia
MacArthur Prize Fellow Award	Robert M. Sapolsky	Stanford University, Calif.
Marvin J. Johnson Award	Michael L. Shuler	Cornell University, Ithaca, N.Y.
National Academy of Sciences Award for Initiatives in Research	Jeremy Nathans	Stanford University, Calif.
National Medal of Science	Har Gobind Khorana	Massachusetts Institute of Technology, Cambridge
National Medal of Science	Rita Levi-Montalcini	Laboratory of Cell Biology, Rome
Richard and Hinda Rosenthal Foundation Award	Brian E. Henderson	University of Southern California, Los Angeles
Scholar Award in Neuroscience	Aaron Fox	University of Chicago, Ill.
Scholar Award in Neuroscience	F. Rob Jackson	Worcester Foundation for Experimental Biology, Shrewsbury, Mass.
Scholar Award in Neuroscience	Tim Tully	Brandeis University, Waltham, Mass.
Scholar Award in Neuroscience	Patricia Walicke	University of California, San Diego

AWARD	WINNER	AFFILIATION
MATERIALS SCIENCES		
Henry Clifton Sorby Award	Gareth Thomas	Lawrence Berkeley Laboratory, Calif.
Hewlett-Packard Europhysics Prize	Igor Yanson	Ukrainian Academy of Sciences, U.S.S.R.
IBM Europe Science and Technology Prize	Elisabeth Bauser	Max Planck Institute, Stuttgart, West Germany
IBM Europe Science and Technology Prize	Manijeh Razeghi	Thomson CSF Research Laboratory, France
IBM Europe Science and Technology Prize	Bruce Joyce	Philips Research Laboratories, Redhill, Surrey, England
Medal for Achievement in Physics	Anthony S. Arrott	Simon Fraser University, Burnaby, B.C., Canada
MATHEMATICS		
Dannie Heineman Prize for Mathematical Physics	Rodney J. Baxter	Australian National University, Canberra
George David Birkhoff Prize	Elliott Lieb	Princeton University, N.J.
Korean Science Award	Ki U Hang	Kyungpook National University, Taegu, Republic of Korea
Korean Science Award	Park Yong Moon	Yonsei University, Seoul, Republic of Korea
Leroy P. Steele Prize	Samuel Eilenberg	Columbia University, New York, N.Y.
Leroy P. Steele Prize	Martin Gardner	Woods End, Inc.; *Scientific American*
Leroy P. Steele Prize	Herbert Federer	Brown University, Providence, R.I.
Leroy P. Steele Prize	Wendell H. Fleming	Brown University, Providence, R.I.
MacArthur Prize Fellow Award	Robert F. Coleman	University of California, Berkeley
MacArthur Prize Fellow Award	David Mumford	Harvard University, Cambridge, Mass.
National Medal of Science	Raoul Bott	Harvard University, Cambridge, Mass.
National Medal of Science	Michael Freedman	University of California, San Diego
National Medal of Technology	W. Edwards Deming	Private consultant
Wolf Prize	Kiyoshi Ito	Kyoto University, Japan
Wolf Prize	Peter D. Lax	New York University, N.Y.
MEDICAL SCIENCES		
A. Cressy Morrison Award	James F. Gusella	Harvard University, Cambridge, Mass.
Albert Lasker Basic Medical Research Award	Leroy Hood	California Institute of Technology, Pasadena
Albert Lasker Basic Medical Research Award	Philip Leder	Harvard University, Cambridge, Mass.
Albert Lasker Basic Medical Research Award	Susumu Tonegawa	Massachusetts Institute of Technology, Cambridge
Albert Lasker Clinical Medical Research Award	Mogens Schou	University of Århus, Denmark
Alfred P. Sloan Prize	Robert A. Weinberg	Massachusetts Institute of Technology, Cambridge

Scientists of the Year

AWARD	WINNER	AFFILIATION
Bolton L. Corson Medal	Theodore M. Bayless	Johns Hopkins University, Baltimore, Md.
Charles F. Kettering Prize	Basil I. Hirschowitz	University of Alabama, Birmingham
Charles S. Mott Prize	R. Palmer Beasley	University of California, San Francisco; University of Washington Medical Research Unit, Taiwan
Charles S. Mott Prize	Jesse W. Summers	Institute for Cancer Research, Philadelphia, Pa.
Distinguished Senior Scientist Award	Lois K. Cohen	National Institutes of Health, Bethesda, Md.
Fidia-Georgetown Award in Neuroscience	Viktor A. Hamburger (Emeritus)	Washington University, St. Louis, Mo.
Fiuggi International Prize	Paul C. Lauterbur	University of Illinois, Urbana
Franklin Medal	Stanley Cohen	Vanderbilt University, Nashville, Tenn.
Gairdner Foundation International Award	René G. Favaloro	Clinica Guemes, Buenos Aires, Argentina
Gairdner Foundation International Award	Robert C. Gallo	National Institutes of Health, Bethesda, Md.
Gairdner Foundation International Award	Luc Montagnier	Institut Pasteur, Paris
Gairdner Foundation International Award	Michael Rossmann	Purdue University, West Lafayette, Ind.
Hammer Prize	Bernard Fisher	University of Pittsburgh, Pa.
Hammer Prize	Donald Metcalf	Walter and Eliza Hall Institute of Medical Research, Melbourne, Australia
Hammer Prize	Malcolm Moore	Memorial Sloan-Kettering Cancer Center, New York, N.Y.
H. R. Lissner Award	Van C. Mow	Columbia University, New York, N.Y.
John Scott Award	David W. Fraser	Swarthmore College, Pa.
King Faisal International Prize	Janet Rowley	University of Chicago, Ill.
Louis Jeantet Award for Medicine	Rolf Zinkernagel	University of Zürich, Switzerland
Louis Jeantet Award for Medicine	John Skehel	National Institute for Medical Research, Mill Hill, London
National Medal of Science	Michael DeBakey	Baylor University, Waco, Texas
National Medal of Science	Harry Eagle	Yeshiva University, New York, N.Y.
National Medal of Science	Paul C. Lauterbur	University of Illinois, Urbana
Senior U.S. Scientist Award	Arnost Fronek	University of California, San Diego
Wolf Prize	Pedro Cuatrecasas	Glaxo, Inc., Research Triangle Park, N.C.
Wolf Prize	Riccardo Giacconi	Space Telescope Science Institute, Baltimore, Md.
Wolf Prize	Bruno B. Rossi	Massachusetts Institute of Technology, Cambridge
Wolf Prize	Meir Wilchek	Weizmann Institute, Rehovot, Israel

AWARD	WINNER	AFFILIATION
OPTICAL ENGINEERING		
Frederic Ives Medal	Anthony J. Demaria	United Technologies Research Center, East Hartford, Conn.
John Tyndall Award	Michael K. Barnoski	PCO Inc., Chatsworth, Calif.
R. W. Wood Prize	Joseph A. Giordmaine	AT&T Bell Laboratories
R. W. Wood Prize	Robert C. Miller	AT&T Bell Laboratories
PHYSICS		
Adolph Lomb Medal	Janis A. Valdmanis	AT&T Bell Laboratories
Alan T. Waterman Award	Edward Witten	Princeton University, N.J.
Albert A. Michelson Medal	Rodolfo Bonifacio	University of Milan, Italy
Albert A. Michelson Medal	Luigi Lugiato	Polytechnic Institute of Turin, Italy
Andrew Gemant Award	Philip Morrison	Massachusetts Institute of Technology, Cambridge
Beams Award	Paul H. Stelson	Oak Ridge National Laboratory, Tenn.
Charles Hard Townes Award	Arthur Ashkin	AT&T Bell Laboratories
Edward Longstreth Medal	Joseph L. Smith	Massachusetts Institute of Technology, Cambridge
Elliott Cresson Medal	Gerd Binnig	IBM Research Laboratory, Zürich
Elliott Cresson Medal	Heinrich Rohrer	IBM Research Laboratory, Zürich
Ewald Prize	John M. Cowley	Arizona State University, Tempe
Ewald Prize	Alexander F. Moodie	Commonwealth Scientific and Industrial Research Organization, Australia
E. W. R. Steacie Prize	Nathan Isgur	University of Toronto, Ont.
Frank H. Spedding Award	Hans Bjerrum Møller	Risø National Laboratory, Denmark
Frank H. Spedding Award	Allan R. Mackintosh	University of Copenhagen; Nordic Institute for Theoretical Physics, Copenhagen, Denmark
Frederic Ives Medal	Amnon Yariv	California Institute of Technology, Pasadena
Guthrie Medal and Prize	Sir Sam Edwards	Cavendish Laboratory, University of Cambridge, England
Herzberg Medal	André-Marie Tremblay	Université de Sherbrooke, Quebec
Holweck Medal and Prize	Edouard Fabre	École Polytechnique, Palaiseau, France
Korean Science Award	Ok Hang Nam	Yonsei University, Seoul, Republic of Korea
Korean Science Award, Grand Prix	Kim Jihn E	Seoul National University, Republic of Korea
Langevin Theoretical Physics Prize	Bernard Julia	École Normale Supérieure, Paris
Leibnitz Prize	Julius Wess	Transuranium Elements Institute, Karlsruhe, West Germany
MacArthur Prize Fellow Award	John Schwarz	California Institute of Technology, Pasadena
MacArthur Prize Fellow Award	David Gross	Princeton University, N.J.
MacArthur Prize Fellow Award	Daniel H. Friedan	University of Chicago, Ill.
MacArthur Prize Fellow Award	Stephen Shenker	University of Chicago, Ill.

AWARD	WINNER	AFFILIATION
Maria Goeppert-Mayer Award	Louise Dolan	Rockefeller University, New York, N.Y.
Max Born Award	Girish S. Agarwal	University of Hyderabad, India
Max Born Medal and Prize	Cyril Hilsum	University of Durham, England
Max Planck Medal	Julius Wess	Transuranium Elements Institute, Karlsruhe, West Germany
Maxwell Medal and Prize	Michael B. Green	Queen Mary College, London
Michelson-Morley Award	Robert H. Dicke (Emeritus)	Princeton University, N.J.
National Medal of Science	Walter Elsasser	Johns Hopkins University, Baltimore, Md.
Paul A. M. Dirac Medal	Bryce S. Dewitt	University of Texas, Austin
Paul A. M. Dirac Medal	Bruno Zumino	University of California, Berkeley
Robert R. Wilson Prize	Ernest Courant	Brookhaven National Laboratory, Upton, N.Y.
R. W. Wood Prize	Daniel S. Chemla	AT&T Bell Laboratories
R. W. Wood Prize	David A. B. Miller	AT&T Bell Laboratories
Senior U.S. Scientist Award	Norman H. Tolk	Vanderbilt University, Nashville, Tenn.
Shanti Swaroop Bhatnagar Award	Girish S. Agarwal	University of Hyderabad, India
William F. Meggers Award	W. Carl Lineberger	University of Colorado, Boulder
Wolf Prize	Herbert Friedman	Naval Research Laboratory, Washington, D.C.

PSYCHOLOGY

AWARD	WINNER	AFFILIATION
American Association for the Advancement of Science Behavioral Science Research Prize	Robert Altemeyer	University of Manitoba, Winnipeg
MacArthur Prize Fellow Award	David Rumelhart	University of California, San Diego
National Medal of Science	Anne Anastasi (Emeritus)	Fordham University, New York, N.Y.

TRANSPORTATION

AWARD	WINNER	AFFILIATION
I. B. Laskowitz Award	Robert Fischell	Johns Hopkins University, Baltimore, Md.
Nelson P. Jackson Aerospace Award	Richard P. Laeser	Jet Propulsion Laboratory, Pasadena, Calif.
Robert J. Collier Trophy	NASA Lewis Research Center and NASA/Industry Advanced Turboprop Team	Cleveland, Ohio
Wright Brothers Memorial Trophy	Allen E. Paulson	Gulfstream Aerospace Corp., Savannah, Ga.

SCIENCE JOURNALISM

AWARD	WINNER	AFFILIATION
American Institute of Physics Writing Award	Shannon Brownlee	*Discover*
American Institute of Physics Writing Award	Allan Chen	*Discover*
American Institute of Physics Writing Award	Clifford M. Will	Washington University, St. Louis, Mo.
James T. Grady-James H. Stack Award for Interpreting Chemistry for the Public	Arthur Fisher	*Popular Science*

AWARD	WINNER	AFFILIATION
MacArthur Prize Fellow Award	Horace F. Judson	Johns Hopkins University, Baltimore, Md..
Michael Daley Award	Bob Beale	*Sydney Morning Herald*

MISCELLANEOUS

Delmer S. Fahrney Medal	William Nierenberg (Retired)	Scripps Institution of Oceanography, University of California, San Diego
Enrico Fermi Award	Luis W. Alvarez (Emeritus)	University of California, Berkeley; Lawrence Berkeley Laboratory
Glazebrook Medal and Prize	Brian H. Flowers	University of London
MacArthur Prize Fellow Award	Eric S. Lander	Harvard University, Cambridge, Mass.
MacArthur Prize Fellow Award	Michael C. Malin	Arizona State University, Tempe
National Academy of Sciences Public Welfare Medal	Dale R. Corson (Emeritus)	Cornell University, Ithaca, N.Y.
National Medal of Science	Philip H. Abelson	*Science Magazine*
National Medal of Science	George Pake	Xerox Corp.
National Medal of Science	George J. Stigler (Emeritus)	University of Chicago, Ill.
National Medal of Science	Max Tishler (Emeritus)	Wesleyan University, Middletown, Conn.
Scientific Freedom and Responsibility Award	Francisco J. Ayala	University of California, Davis
Scientific Freedom and Responsibility Award	Roger M. Boisjoly	Willard, Utah
Scientific Freedom and Responsibility Award	Richard Garwin	International Business Machines Corp.
Scientific Freedom and Responsibility Award	Norman D. Newell (Emeritus)	American Museum of Natural History, New York, N.Y.
Scientific Freedom and Responsibility Award	Stanley L. Weinberg	National Center for Science Education
Vannevar Bush Award	I. I. Rabi	Columbia University, New York, N.Y.
Westinghouse Science Talent Search	1. Chetan Nayak	Stuyvesant High School, New York, N.Y.
	2. Janet Tseng	Stuyvesant High School, New York, N.Y.
	3. Benjamin S. Abella	University of Chicago Laboratory Schools High School, Ill.
	4. Vijay S. Pande	Langley High School, McLean, Va.
	5. Brian D. Conrad	Centereach High School, Centereach, N.Y.
	6. Weiva Y. Sieh	Bronx High School of Science, New York, N.Y.
	7. Stacey E. Beaulieu	Palm Beach Gardens High School, Palm Beach Gardens, Fla.
	8. Kurt M. Cuffey	State College Area Senior High School, State College, Pa.
	9. Brian C. Hooker	Benjamin E. Mays High School, Atlanta, Ga.
	10. Meredith A. Albrecht	Evanston Township High School, Ill.

Obituaries

Aaronson, Marc Arnold (Aug. 24, 1950—April 30, 1987), U.S. astronomer, with Jeremy R. Mould discovered an error in Hubble's constant, used to determine the distance between objects in space, and was thus able to recompute the age of the universe, determining that it is actually 12 billion, rather than 20 billion, years old, as scientists had previously believed. For their findings, the two were honored in 1984 as recipients of the Newton Lacy Pierce Prize of the American Astronomical Society, which is awarded to astronomers under the age of 36 for outstanding achievement in observational astronomical research. Aaronson earned his B.A. at the California Institute of Technology in 1972 and went on to receive his M.A. (1974) and Ph.D. (1977) from Harvard University. As a research assistant at Harvard, he helped conduct studies on the infrared properties of spiral galaxies. In 1977 Aaronson joined the University of Arizona as associate professor of astronomy, and he was an associate astronomer at the university's Steward Observatory. Another significant finding was the importance of using the infrared Tully-Fisher relation in measuring redshift-independent relative distances of galaxies, and he suggested the observation of carbon stars that determined that, in the stages of stellar evolution, they were a characteristic of intermediate-age stellar populations. Aaronson was killed when he was crushed between a door and a 150-ton revolving telescope dome at Kitt Peak (Ariz.) National Observatory.

Ali, Salim (Nov. 12, 1896—June 20, 1987), Indian ornithologist, was an internationally acclaimed expert on the birds of India and a leading conservationist. His lifelong interest in birds was pursued with great dedication, and he was able to spend most of his working life in his chosen field. He started out, however, as a clerk before studying accounting in Bombay and taking a course in zoology at the same time. Eventually he went to Germany to study ornithology. On his return he undertook surveys for the Bombay Natural History Society and wrote his first studies on Indian bird life. His greatest work, written with S. Dillon Ripley, was the authoritative ten-volume *Handbook of the Birds of India and Pakistan* (1968–74), which was under revision for a second edition at the time of his death. In 1976 Ali was appointed a member of the upper house of the Indian Parliament. His work for conservation brought him many honors in India and abroad. He was the first non-British scientist to receive the medal of the British Ornithologists' Union, and he was awarded the John C. Phillips Medal of the International Union for Conservation of Nature and Natural Resources, The Netherlands Order of the Golden Ark, and the J. P. Getty International Prize for Wildlife Conserva-

tion. From 1954 Ali was a member of the permanent executive committee of the International Ornithological Congress. His autobiography, *The Fall of a Sparrow,* was published in 1985.

Allen, Clabon Walter (Dec. 28, 1904—Dec. 11, 1987), Australian astronomer, was assistant (1926–51) at the Commonwealth Observatory, Canberra, and first Perren professor of astronomy (1951–72) at University College, London. His major contributions to astronomy, detailed in his textbook *Astrophysical Quantities* (1955), were based upon careful collation of data obtained through various methods of work: spectroscopy, eclipse studies, and laboratory atomic physics. His chosen subject was the temperature, magnetic fields, and atmosphere of the Sun. Allen expanded knowledge of the effects of both continuous and spasmodic (sunspot and flare) solar emissions on the Earth's atmosphere and on terrestrial radio communications. During World War II he helped the Allies by predicting periods of radio disruption. He took part in eclipse expeditions to Japan (1936), South Africa (1940), Sweden (1954), Ceylon (1955), and the Canary Islands (1959). He was responsible for establishing, at University College, the first undergraduate degree course in astronomy available to students in England and Wales.

Baker, Peter Frederick (March 11, 1939—March 10, 1987), British physiologist, was head of the department of physiology at King's College, London, and the author of important research into the mechanism of secretions from the adrenal medullary cell, a breakthrough that paved the way for the understanding of all cell secretions. Educated at Emmanuel College, Cambridge, he worked for the physiology department at Cambridge and for the Marine Biological Laboratory in Plymouth. At Cambridge, together with Trevor Shaw and Sir Alan Hodgkin, he published the results of research into the ionic theory of nerve conduction. From 1966 to 1974 Baker was a lecturer at Cambridge, and in the following year he became Halliburton professor of physiology at King's College. In 1976 he was elected a fellow of the Royal Society. In addition to his research into cell secretion, he built his department into a recognized center for research and teaching. He served as a member of committees of the Medical Research Council and the Royal Society and was on the editorial board of *The Journal of Physiology.* Baker was coauthor of *Calcium Movement in Excitable Cells* (1975) and wrote *The Squid Axon* (1984), as well as numerous scientific papers. He was awarded the Scientific Medal of the Zoological Society of London in 1975 and the Wander Prize in 1981.

Brattain, Walter Houser (Feb. 10, 1902—Oct. 13, 1987), U.S. scientist, shared the 1956 Nobel Prize for Physics with John Bardeen and William Shockley for their investigations into the properties of

Walter Houser Brattain
AP/Wide World

semiconductors; this led to the development of the transistor, which they invented on Dec. 23, 1947, at the American Telephone and Telegraph Co.'s Bell Laboratories in Murray Hill, N.J. Though Brattain was born in China, where his father was teaching, he was raised in Spokane, Wash. After earning a B.A. (1924) from Whitman College in Walla Walla, Wash., he earned an M.A. from the University of Oregon and a Ph.D. from the University of Minnesota. In 1929 he joined Bell Telephone Laboratories, where he conducted research on semiconductors, the materials that are used in transistors. The transistor replaced the bulkier vacuum tube and provided the technology for miniaturizing electronic equipment, a development that was needed for the construction of computers. After leaving Bell Laboratories in 1967, Brattain served as adjunct professor at his alma mater, Whitman College, until 1972. He was also elected to the National Inventors Hall of Fame.

Broglie, Louis-Victor-Pierre-Raymond, 7th duc de (Aug. 15, 1892—March 19, 1987), French physicist, was awarded the 1929 Nobel Prize for Physics for his discovery of the wave nature of electrons. His discovery, outlined in his doctoral thesis, *Recherches sur la théorie des quanta* (1924), was that elementary particles of matter possess the properties of waves as well as those of particles and that these properties were not contradictory but linked. Broglie, who advanced the work of Albert Einstein and Max Planck, made a fundamental contribution to the development of quantum theory. In 1927 Clinton Davisson and Lester Germer in the U.S. and George Thomson in Scotland found the first experimental evidence of the electron's wave nature. Broglie turned to physics only after obtaining a university degree in history. He earned (1924) a Ph.D. in physics from the Sorbonne and became professor of theoretical physics at the Henri Poincaré Institute (1928). Broglie taught there until his retirement in 1962. He was permanent secretary of the French Academy of Sciences (1942–75), and he was elected to the Académie Française in 1944. In 1952 he was awarded the United Nations Kalinga Prize in recognition of his science writings, which were geared to the general

public and explored the philosophical implications of modern physics. Broglie was the author of more than 20 books; some of his popular writings appeared in English translations, including *The Revolution in Physics* (1953) and *Physics and Microphysics* (1960). He succeeded his brother as duc de Broglie in 1960.

Carr, Archie Fairly, Jr. (June 16, 1909—May 21, 1987), U.S. zoologist, conducted extensive studies on the habitat, migration patterns, and breeding habits of giant sea turtles and with his scholarly writings and conservation efforts helped save those reptiles from extinction. Carr, who earned both his undergraduate (B.S., 1933) and graduate (M.S., 1934, and Ph.D., 1937) degrees from the University of Florida, spent his entire professional career at his alma mater as a professor of biology. By using funding from the U.S. Navy and implementing laborious tagging techniques, he was able to track the exceptional navigational abilities of green turtles, which sometimes journey as many as 2,000 km (1,200 mi) each way from the beaches of Ascension Island, where they hatch, to the east coast of South America, where they mature, and then, in five or six years, back to Ascension, where they lay their eggs. After decades of research Carr eventually discovered in 1984 the migration patterns of green turtle babies after they hatched. He found that the hatchlings, weighing only a few ounces, slip onto rafts of floating seaweed called sargassum, where they feed on small shrimp, crabs, and jellyfish that also live in the rafts. He also concluded that ocean pollution posed a particular hazard to the undiscriminating babies, who sometimes chomp on fragments of Styrofoam, droplets of heavy oil, or globs of tar, which consequently glue their jaws shut, causing them to perish. With the Navy's help, Carr was able to reestablish the giant turtle population along the shores of Mexico, Colombia, Florida, and the Caribbean islands, where human predators had decimated their number. His award-winning books included: *Handbook of Turtles* (1952), *High Jungles and Low* (1953), and *The Windward Road* (1956).

Cox, Allan V(erne) (Dec. 17, 1926—Jan. 27, 1987), U.S. geophysicist, conducted important studies in remanent magnetism (also called paleomagnetism), the permanent magnetism in rocks resulting from the orientation of the Earth's magnetic field at the time of rock formation in a past geologic age. Cox, who earned (1959) a Ph.D. at the University of California at Berkeley, was a member of the U.S. Geological Survey from 1950. In 1959 on the basis of a theory, put forth by S. K. Runcorn, that the Earth's magnetic field had episodically reversed its polarity, Cox persuaded the Geological Survey to pursue an investigation of this phenomenon and, together with Richard Doell, he began working on the project. In 1971 Cox, Runcorn, and Doell were awarded the

Vetlesen Prize for their work, which helped resolve issues relating to the Earth and past movements of its continents. In 1967 Cox became a professor at Stanford University, and in 1979 he was named dean of earth sciences there. He was the principal architect in 1968 of the first sophisticated magnetic-reversal time scale, one of the cornerstones of plate tectonics. In 1983 he and his colleagues published a new geologic time scale that has become a standard guide used by geologists to correlate their findings. In 1984 Cox was the recipient of the Arthur Day Prize of the National Academy of Sciences. He died as a result of injuries sustained in a bicycle accident.

Draper, Charles Stark (Oct. 2, 1901—July 25, 1987), U.S. aeronautical engineer, was dubbed the "father of inertial navigation," an electronic guidance system that continuously monitors the position and acceleration of aircraft, ships, submarines, missiles, satellites, and space vehicles independently of a base station or other external sources. In order to develop his system Draper used gyroscopes, which provide fixed reference direction; accelerometers, which measure changes in the velocity of the system; and a computer, which processes information on changes in direction and acceleration of the vehicle and feeds its results to the vehicle's navigation system. Though he earned a B.A. degree in psychology from Stanford University in 1922, Draper became fascinated with aeronautics and enrolled in the Massachusetts Institute of Technology (MIT), where he earned a B.S. (1926) in electrochemical engineering and an Sc.D. (1938) in physics. The following year he became a full professor at MIT and founded its Instrumentation Laboratory, where he developed the Mark 14 gyroscopic gunsight, which was used on most U.S. naval vessels during World War II and enabled gunners to shoot down more than 30 Japanese kamikazes. As a professor he was known as Doc Draper and was renowned for piloting terrifying airplane missions to demonstrate a principle on aerodynamics to his colleagues. His laboratory also devised the guidance systems for jet fighter planes and for Polaris, Poseidon, and Trident submarines and missiles; in 1961 he began working on the lunar

Charles Stark Draper
The Charles Stark Draper Laboratory, Inc.

navigation system for the spacecraft of the Apollo Project. After the Moon landing in 1969, Draper resigned his post as director of the Instrumentation Laboratory when protests erupted over the laboratory's role in defense work. In 1973 the laboratory became independent of MIT and was christened the Charles Stark Draper Laboratory. In 1965 Draper received the National Medal of Science.

Grzimek, Bernhard (April 24, 1909—March 13, 1987), German zoologist and conservationist, as the longtime director (1945–74) of the Zoological Garden of Frankfurt, West Germany, rebuilt the war-torn zoo into one of the world's most renowned zoological gardens and a major center for wildlife reproduction. Grzimek, who earned a Ph.D. (1932) in veterinary medicine from the University of Berlin, saved the burned ruins of the Frankfurt Zoo from extinction by persuading officials to allow him to assume responsibility for the 12 remaining half-starved animals. He used fund-raisers to keep the zoo operational and on one occasion was able to enhance the animal population by hijacking a truckload of animals out of the Leipzig zoo shortly before the Soviet occupation forces entered that city. Some of his innovative techniques, including displaying animals with a minimum amount of cages and fences, providing them with a balanced diet, and making their habitats as natural as possible, fostered the successful breeding of several animal species that ordinarily failed to reproduce in captivity.

A familiar television personality, Grzimek was known for the hedgehog tiepin he sported as host of a wildlife television series that he launched in 1956. His dedication to conservation took him on several expeditions to western, central, and eastern Africa; to North and South America; and to the Soviet Union, Japan, Australia, and New Guinea. In 1957 Grzimek and his son Michael began making a documentary film dealing with the wildlife and ecology of Serengeti National Park in Tanganyika (now Tanzania). Just prior to the completion of the survey, Michael was killed (1959) in a plane crash. The film, *Serengeti Shall Not Die*, won the Academy Award in 1960 for the best documentary of the year.

Grzimek was also a prominent figure in government circles, serving as environmental ombudsman (1969–77), until he resigned to protest inadequate efforts to protect wildlife. In later years the internationally known author of such books as *No Room for Wild Animals* (1956), *Such Agreeable Friends* (1964), *He and I and the Elephants* (1966), and the 13-volume *Grzimek's Animal Life Encyclopedia* (1974) divided his time between raising Arabian thoroughbreds on a farm in Franconia and traveling in Tanzania.

Hanson, Wesley Turnell, Jr. (May 28, 1912—May 20, 1987), U.S. chemist, as a research chemist at the Eastman Kodak Co., was instrumental in refining (1943) the color quality of Kodacolor film, which had been introduced a year earlier. By using a process known as the color coupler masking system, Hanson produced clearer photographic prints with purer colors. Hanson, who in 1934, at the age of 21, earned his Ph.D. from the University of California at Berkeley, joined Kodak in the same year. His process, which was incorporated into Kodacolor film in 1945, ushered in the era of modern photography and also helped improve the quality of color motion-picture film. In 1943 Hanson was recruited to the U.S. Manhattan Project in Oak Ridge, Tenn. There he helped develop enriched uranium for use in the first atomic bomb, which was dropped on Hiroshima in 1945. He then returned to Kodak, where he spent the rest of his professional career in a number of management posts. He served as assistant director of research in 1961 and was made director in 1972. He retired from the company in 1977 as a vice-president. Hanson published *Principles of Color Photography* in 1953. He was also the recipient in 1956 of the Herbert T. Kalmus Medal from the Society of Motion Picture and Television Engineers, and in 1966 he was awarded the society's Progress Medal.

Henle, Werner (Aug. 27, 1910—July 6, 1987), German-born virologist, was credited, together with his wife, Gertrude, with a breakthrough during the late 1960s that established a link between the Epstein-Barr virus, infectious mononucleosis, and Burkitt's lymphoma, a cancer common in areas of Africa. For this pioneering work, the couple was honored in 1979 with the prestigious Bristol-Myers Award for distinguished achievement in cancer research. After earning his M.D. (1934) at the University of Heidelberg, Henle joined (1936) the staff of the University of Pennsylvania; three years later he became a staff member of the university's Children's Hospital in Philadelphia. Together with his wife, he was associated with the University of Pennsylvania School of Medicine for more than 45 years. The two demonstrated the effectiveness of influenza inoculations and devised a test for the early diagnosis of mumps as well as an evaluation of a vaccine to combat that viral disease. They also collaborated with Joseph Stokes, Jr., in the original work that exhibited the effectiveness of gamma globulin against infectious hepatitis. In 1982 the husband-wife research team retired from the university faculty, but they continued to conduct research until shortly before Henle's death. They wrote more than 385 articles for scientific journals, dealing with topics on virology, immunology, and viral oncology.

Kolmogorov, Andrey Nikolayevich (April 25 [April 12, old style], 1903—Oct. 20, 1987), Soviet mathematician, wrote *Grundbegriffe der Wahrscheinlichkeitsrechnung* (1933; *Foundations of the Theory*

Andrey Nikolayevich Kolmogorov
Novosti/Sovfoto

of Probability [1950]), a seminal work in modern mathematics. Together with his subsequent contributions to probability theory, the ideas developed in this work had wide applications in mathematics, physics, astronomy, and other fields. Kolmogorov's elegant treatment of probability, built up rigorously from fundamental principles in a way that was compared to the methods of the Greek mathematician Euclid, was crucial to contemporary descriptions of randomness and predictability in physical processes. Kolmogorov later extended his basic theories to such diverse physical systems as the motion of the planets and the turbulent behavior of air in the jet stream of aircraft. In 1941 he published two papers on turbulence that had extensive implications, and in 1954 he developed his work on dynamic systems in relation to planetary motion, demonstrating the crucial role of probability theory in physics. His broad range of interests led him to pursue such topics as form and structure in the poetry of Pushkin and to devote much attention, particularly in his later years, to the mathematical training of Soviet schoolchildren. Kolmogorov graduated from Moscow State University in 1925 and subsequently taught there as instructor and, from 1931, as professor. In 1939 he was elected to the Soviet Academy of Sciences at the early age of 36, and he subsequently was made a foreign member of learned societies in the U.S. and the U.K., among others. He received the Lenin Prize (1965) and the Order of Lenin on six occasions.

Leloir, Luis Federico (Sept. 6, 1906—Dec 2?, 1987), Argentine chemist, was awarded the 1970 Nobel Prize for Chemistry for the discovery of sugar nucleotides and their role in the biosynthesis of carbohydrates. After earning his M.D. at the University of Buenos Aires in 1932, he worked at the university's Institute of Physiology for two years before studying in England for a year under Gowland Hopkins at the Biochemical Laboratory of the University of Cambridge. In 1937 he returned to the Institute of Physiology, where he undertook investigations of the oxidation of fatty acids. In 1943 political pressures caused Leloir to resign his post and move to the U.S. There he worked at Washington University,

Luis Federico Leloir
AP/Wide World

St. Louis, Mo., and at the College of Physicians and Surgeons, Columbia University, New York City. He returned to Argentina in 1946 and the following year secured financial support for his own laboratory, the Instituto de Investigaciones Bioquímicas, Buenos Aires. Leloir assembled a dedicated group of scientists and conducted research on the formation and breakdown of lactose, or milk sugar, in the body. This work led to the discovery of sugar nucleotides and their vital role in carbohydrate metabolism.

Levine, Philip (Aug. 10, 1900—Oct. 18, 1987), U.S. research scientist, discovered in 1939 (with R. E. Stetson), the Rh blood-group system, a means for classifying blood according to the presence or absence of the Rh antigen, often called the Rh factor, in the cell membranes of the red blood cells. After earning his M.D. at Cornell University Medical School, Ithaca, N.Y., Levine spent seven years at the Rockefeller Institute, New York City, conducting research with Karl Landsteiner on blood disorders. In 1927 the two discovered the MN and P blood-group systems. For his pioneering research on the Rh factor, Levine received numerous awards. His discovery led to safer blood transfusions and the identification of the Rh hemolytic disease in pregnancies in which the father's and infant's blood is Rh positive and the mother's blood is Rh negative. The mother's antibodies destroy the fetus's red blood cells, and the fetus can spontaneously abort or a newborn can die unless a blood transfusion is administered immediately. Levine also discovered that the blood serum of some cancer patients can become toxic to their cancer cells and destroy them; this finding explained why remission occurs in some types of cancer. From 1932 until 1935 he was an instructor in bacteriology at the University of Wisconsin Medical School, and from 1935 to 1944 he served as a bacteriologist and immunologist at Beth Israel Hospital in Newark, N.J., before becoming (1944) director of the biologic division of the Ortho Research Foundation in Raritan, N.J., a post he held until his retirement in 1965.

Li Choh Hao (April 21, 1913—Nov. 28, 1987), Chinese-born biochemist, conducted pioneering research in the study of the chemistry and biology of anterior pituitary hormones. In 1971 he isolated and synthesized the human pituitary growth hormone, a feat that was hailed as an immense scientific breakthrough with far-reaching applications in various branches of medical research. After graduating from Nanjing (Nanking) University in China, he immigrated to the U.S. in 1935 and earned a Ph.D. (1938) from the University of California at Berkeley, where he founded the Hormone Research Laboratory in 1950. Together with his colleagues, Li identified, isolated, and purified six of the eight known hormones secreted by the anterior pituitary. In 1967 he moved with his laboratory to the university's San Francisco campus, where he became director (1983) of the newly named Laboratory of Molecular Endocrinology. Li and his associates also discovered (1978) beta-endorphin, a substance produced in the brain that acts as a natural painkiller; this finding paved the way for assessing a new series of compounds and their effects on pain. Li was the first to synthesize insulin-like growth factor 1, which acts on bones to promote growth of cartilage cells. Li, who garnered numerous awards for his research, including the prestigious Lasker Award for Basic Medical Research (1962) and the Nichols Medal of the American Chemical Society (1979), was also editor in chief of the *International Journal of Peptide and Protein Research* and co-executive editor of the *Archives of Biochemistry and Biophysics.*

Marvel, Carl Shipp (Sept. 11, 1894—Jan. 4, 1988), U.S. chemist, during the 1930s conducted research on the nature of polymers, substances with very large chainlike or network molecules. Marvel, who earned both an M.A. (1916) and a Ph.D. (1920) in organic chemistry from the University of Illinois, spent 41 years (1920–61) there as a teacher before moving to the University of Arizona, where he taught until his death and conducted research in his laboratory until the summer of 1987. He laid much of the groundwork for plastics technology and made such important contributions as the development of polybenzimidazoles, which could withstand heat up to 871° C (1,600° F) and could therefore be used in space rocketry. During World War II he headed a top-secret project at his alma mater that led to the development of synthetic rubber. His research also encompassed hydrogen bonding and the synthesis of polymers, especially those with thermal stability. He published some 200 papers dealing with amino acids, polyunsaturates, organometallics, organic free radicals, and the optical activity of vinyl polymers. He was inducted into the Plastics Hall of Fame, and in 1986 he received the National Medal of Science from U.S. Pres. Ronald Reagan. Marvel also served as the president of the American Chemical Society from 1945 to 1947.

Medawar, Sir Peter Brian (Feb. 28, 1915—Oct. 2, 1987), British physician, was co-winner with the Australian physician Sir Macfarlane Burnet of the 1960 Nobel Prize for Physiology or Medicine for the discovery of acquired immunologic tolerance. He was a dedicated biologist whose work made possible many advances in the grafting of skin and the transplantation of organs. Educated at Marlborough College and at Magdalen College, Oxford, Medawar served as Mason professor of zoology at Birmingham University (1947–51), Jodrell professor of zoology and comparative anatomy at University College, London (1951–62), and director of the U.K. National Institute for Medical Research (1962–71). Although he suffered the first of a series of increasingly incapacitating strokes in 1969, he worked with the Medical Research Council's external scientific staff (1971–84) and at the Clinical Research Centre (1984–86). Medawar's work developed from studying the problems of skin-graft rejection in those suffering burns during World War II; he demonstrated that an organism's immune system is not innate but develops during embryonic life and that foreign cells introduced at that stage are not rejected. This discovery laid the foundation for contemporary research into autoimmune disease. A brilliant communicator, Medawar wrote a number of books, including *The Uniqueness of the Individual* (1957) and *Memoir of a Thinking Radish* (1986). He was knighted in 1965.

Northrop, John Howard (July 5, 1891—May 27, 1987), U.S. biochemist, shared with James B. Sumner and Wendell M. Stanley the 1946 Nobel Prize for Chemistry for their work on the purification and crystallization of enzymes, which revealed how proteins aid in digestion, respiration, and general life processes. Their discoveries also later helped in the diagnosis of certain kinds of cancer and heart disease and in the manufacture of antibiotics and detergents. Northrop, who earned a Ph.D. (1915) from Columbia University, New York City, served as a captain in the U.S. Army's Chemical Warfare Service during World War I. In this post he conducted research on fermentation processes that would make possible the industrial production of acetone and ethyl alcohol. In 1930 Northrop crystallized pepsin, a digestive enzyme present in gastric juice, thus ending the controversy about the chemical nature of enzymes by proving that pepsin is a protein. He later isolated (1938) the first bacterial virus. Northrop, who joined the Rockefeller Institute for Medical Research in New York City as an assistant in 1916, later was a member there until his retirement in 1962, when he became professor emeritus. He also served as a visiting professor at the University of California at Berkeley (1949–58) and as a resident biophysicist at the Donner Laboratory there (1958–59). He was the author of *Crystalline Enzymes*.

Isidor Isaac Rabi
UPI/Bettmann Newsphotos

Rabi, Isidor Isaac (July 29, 1898—Jan. 11, 1988), U.S. physicist, was awarded the 1944 Nobel Prize for Physics for the invention (1937) of the atomic and molecular beam magnetic resonance method for registration of magnetic properties of atomic nuclei. This important discovery enabled precise measurements, which were needed for the development of the atomic clock, the laser, and diagnostic scanning of the human body by nuclear magnetic resonance. Rabi immigrated to the U.S. with his parents when he was an infant. He studied chemistry before finding his niche in physics. After earning (1927) a Ph.D. in physics at Columbia University, New York City, he joined the faculty of his alma mater in 1929 and became professor of physics in 1937. During World War II, while working at the Radiation Laboratory of the Massachusetts Institute of Technology, he helped develop radar. He also helped arrange international conferences on the peaceful uses of atomic energy that were held in 1955, 1958, and 1964. As a U.S. representative to the United Nations Educational, Scientific, and Cultural Organization (Unesco), he was instrumental in promoting the establishment of CERN—the European Organization for Nuclear Research—an international laboratory for high-energy physics. In the U.S. he was a founder of the Brookhaven National Laboratory, Upton, N.Y. Besides serving as a member of the General Advisory Committee of the Atomic Energy Commission from 1946 to 1956 and as its chairman from 1952 to 1956, he was also a science adviser to Pres. Dwight D. Eisenhower.

Severny, Andrey Borisovich (1913—April 4, 1987), Soviet astronomer, was an expert on the physics of the Sun and the stars and specialized in the study of solar flares, sudden intense outbursts of energy from a small part of the Sun's chromosphere. Severny sought to relate solar flares to the existence of magnetic fields on the Sun, and in 1952 he was awarded the Stalin prize for his work. After graduating from Moscow University in 1935, he became an associate of the Crimean Astrophysical Observatory. He became director of the observatory in 1952 and was instrumental in establishing astronomical observations on artificial satellites that were orbiting the Earth. In 1968 he was named a full member of the Soviet Academy of Sciences, and from 1964 to 1970 he served as a vice-president in the International Astronomical Union. In 1973 he was awarded the title Hero of Socialist Labor, the country's highest civilian award. Some of his writings included *A Study of the Development of Chromospheric Flares on the Sun* (1954), *Solar Physics* (1957), *A Study of the Fine Radiation Structure of Active Formations and Nonstable Processes on the Sun* (1957), and *Nuclear Processes in Chromospheric Flares* (1963).

Strömgren, Bengt Georg Daniel (Jan. 21, 1908—July 4, 1987), Danish astrophysicist, was recognized internationally as an expert on interstellar matter and was the first to explain the properties and activities of the spherical clouds of gas surrounding hot stars; these ionized areas, each heated by a hot central star, were named Strömgren spheres. As the son of the renowned Swedish-born Danish astronomer Svante Elis Strömgren, director of the Royal Copenhagen Observatory, he became fascinated with astronomy and at the age of 21 earned his Ph.D. from the University of Copenhagen. Strömgren served as an assistant and then associate professor at the University of Chicago from 1936 to 1938 before succeeding his father as director of the Royal Copenhagen Observatory in 1940. After World War II he returned to his professorship at the University of Chicago, and in 1951 he became director of both the Yerkes Observatory, Williams Bay, Wis., and McDonald Observatory, Fort Davis, Texas. In 1957 he became a member of the Institute for Advanced Study in Princeton, N.J., but in 1967 he returned to the University of Copenhagen as professor of astrophysics. Strömgren also conducted studies on the internal constitution of stars and contributed to the understanding of the solar atmosphere. He did pioneering work on the classification of stellar spectra by using photoelectric techniques to measure them. He served as president of the International Astronomical Union from 1970 to 1973 and remained in Copenhagen teaching and writing scientific papers until his death.

Wilson, Sir Graham Selby (Sept. 10, 1895—April 5, 1987), British microbiologist, was the joint author, with W. W. C. Topley, of *Principles of Bacteriology and Immunity*, first published in 1929 and recognized as a classic of medical literature. The two-volume opus was reprinted seven times. From 1941 to 1963 Wilson gained an international reputation as director of the Public Health Laboratory Service. Educated at King's College, London, and at Charing Cross Hospital, he served with the Royal Army Medical Corps during World War I before lecturing at the University of London and the Victoria University of Manchester. Wilson was reader in bacteriology and

then professor at the London School of Hygiene and Tropical Medicine, where his studies on the bacteriology of milk lent strong support to a policy of pasteurization. During World War II he helped organize a national emergency service to cope with epidemics that might follow mass bombing and then urged the establishment of the Public Health Laboratory Service to deal with more routine infections. By 1948 the service boasted 36 laboratories, and it continued to grow under Wilson's highly personal style of administration. Wilson, who continued his research into microbiology into his retirement, was knighted in 1962 and elected a fellow of the Royal Society in 1978. He served as a consultant to the British Council and to the World Health Organization in Poland, the U.S.S.R., and such Middle Eastern countries as Egypt, Iran, and Iraq. Wilson was also honorary physician to King George VI and an honorary fellow of the American Public Health Association.

Wittig, Georg (June 16, 1897—Aug. 26, 1987), West German chemist, shared the 1979 Nobel Prize for Chemistry with Herbert C. Brown of Purdue University, West Lafayette, Ind., for the development of a technique that uses phosphorus compounds in the synthesis of natural substances through the regrouping of carbon atoms in the molecules. The "Wittig reaction," which he discovered in 1953, opened the way to the economical production of substances such as Vitamin A on an industrial scale. A gifted pianist, he had at one time considered a musical career. Wittig studied at the University of Tübingen, served in World War I, and graduated from the University of Marburg (1923), where he earned a Ph.D. in 1926. He taught at Marburg (1926–32), at the Braunschweig Technical College (1932–37), and at the universities of Braunschweig and Freiburg (1937–44) before returning to Tübingen, where he taught for 12 years. In 1956 he became professor and director of the Institute of Organic Chemistry at the University of Heidelberg, where he stayed for the remainder of his academic career. Wittig retired as professor emeritus in 1965 but continued to conduct research. His publications included a *Textbook of Stereochemistry* (1930).

Georg Wittig
UPI/Bettmann Newsphotos

Contributors to the Science Year in Review

Peter J. Andrews *Chemistry: Physical chemistry.* Science writer, Rockville, Md. Winner in 1984 of the National Award of Excellence of the Society for Technical Communications.

D. James Baker *Earth sciences: Oceanography.* President, Joint Oceanographic Institutions Inc., Washington, D.C.

Fred Basolo *Chemistry: Inorganic chemistry.* Morrison Professor of Chemistry, Northwestern University, Evanston, Ill.

Keith Beven *Earth sciences: Hydrology.* Hydrologist, Department of Environmental Science, University of Lancaster, Lancaster, England.

Eric Block *Chemistry: Organic chemistry.* Chairman and Professor, Department of Chemistry, State University of New York at Albany.

Harold Borko *Electronics and information sciences: Information systems and services.* Professor, Graduate School of Library and Information Science, University of California, Los Angeles.

John M. Bowen *Medical sciences: Veterinary medicine.* Associate Dean for Research and Graduate Affairs and Professor of Pharmacology and Toxicology, College of Veterinary Medicine, University of Georgia, Athens.

D. Allan Bromley *Physics: Nuclear physics.* Henry Ford II Professor of Physics, Yale University, New Haven, Conn.

Paul J. Campbell *Mathematics.* Associate Professor of Mathematics and Computer Science, and Director of Academic Computing, Beloit College, Beloit, Wis.

Douglas E. Comer *Electronics and information sciences: Computers and computer science.* Professor of Computer Science, Purdue University, West Lafayette, Ind.

Dave Dooling *Space exploration: Space probes.* Program Developer, U.S. Space Academy, Space & Rocket Center, Huntsville, Ala.

F. C. Durant III *Electronics and information sciences: Satellite systems.* Aerospace Historian and Consultant, Chevy Chase, Md.

Robert G. Eagon *Life sciences: Microbiology.* Franklin Professor of Microbiology, University of Georgia, Athens.

Gerald Feinberg *Physics: High-energy physics.* Professor of Physics, Columbia University, New York, N.Y.

Robert L. Forward *Physics: General developments.* Science consultant, Forward Unlimited, Malibu, Calif.

David R. Gaskell *Materials sciences: Metallurgy.* Professor of Metallurgical Engineering, Purdue University, West Lafayette, Ind.

Richard L. Gordon *Energy.* Professor of Mineral Economics, Pennsylvania State University, University Park.

Stig B. Hagstrom *Physics: Condensed-matter physics.* Professor and Chairman of the Department of Materials Science and Engineering, Stanford University, Stanford, Calif.

Robert Haselkorn *Life sciences: Molecular biology.* F. L. Pritzker Distinguished Service Professor, Department of Molecular Genetics and Cell Biology, University of Chicago, Ill.

John Patrick Jordan *Food and agriculture: Agriculture.* Administrator, Cooperative State Research Service, U.S. Department of Agriculture, Washington, D.C.

Lou Joseph *Medical sciences: Dentistry.* Senior Science Writer, Hill and Knowlton, Inc., Chicago.

George B. Kauffman *Chemistry: Applied chemistry.* Professor of Chemistry, California State University, Fresno.

Badru M. Kiggundu *Architecture and civil engineering.* Program Manager, National Center for Asphalt Technology, Department of Civil Engineering, Auburn University, Auburn, Ala.

David B. Kitts *Earth sciences: Geology and geochemistry.* Professor of the History of Science, University of Oklahoma, Norman.

Mina W. Lamb *Food and agriculture: Nutrition.* Professor Emeritus, Department of Food and Nutrition, Texas Tech University, Lubbock.

Howard J. Lewis *U.S. science policy.* Managing Editor, National Association of Science Writers, Bethesda, Md.

Melvin H. Marx *Psychology* (in part). Professor Emeritus of Psychology, University of Missouri, Columbia, and Senior Research Scientist, Department of Psychology, Georgia State University, Atlanta.

Charles W. McNett, Jr. *Anthropology.* Professor of Anthropology, American University, Washington, D.C.

Franz J. Monssen *Electronics and information sciences: Electronics.* Instructor, Department of Electronic and Computer Engineering Technology, Queensborough Community College, New York, N.Y.

Charles S. Mueller *Earth sciences: Geophysics.* Geophysicist, U.S. Geological Survey, Menlo Park, Calif.

Colin V. Newman *Psychology* (in part). Executive Secretary, British Psychological Society, Leicester, England.

Carolyn D. Newton *Scientists of the Year: Nobel prizes.* Assistant Science Editor, *Compton's Encyclopedia,* Chicago, Ill.

Roger A. Pielke *Earth sciences: Atmospheric sciences.* Professor of Atmospheric Science, Colorado State University, Fort Collins.

W. M. Protheroe *Astronomy.* Professor of Astronomy, Ohio State University, Columbus.

J. R. Redmond *Life sciences: Zoology.* Professor of Zoology, Iowa State University, Ames.

John Rhea *Defense research.* Free-lance Science Writer, Woodstock, Va.

Robert R. Shannon *Optical engineering.* Professor and Director, Optical Sciences Center, University of Arizona, Tucson.

Joanne Silberner *Medical sciences: General medicine.* Associate Editor, Health, *U.S. News and World Report,* Washington, D.C.

Albert J. Smith *Life sciences: Botany.* Professor of Biology, Wheaton College, Wheaton, Ill.

Frank A. Smith *Transportation.* Senior Associate, Transportation Policy Associates, Washington, D.C.

Robert E. Stoffels *Electronics and information sciences: Communications systems.* Editor, *Telephone Engineer & Management* magazine, Geneva, Ill.

Norman M. Tallan *Materials sciences: Ceramics.* Chief, Metals and Ceramics Division, Materials Laboratory, Wright-Patterson Air Force Base, Ohio.

Kenneth E. F. Watt *Environment.* Professor of Zoology, University of California, Davis.

Brian Welch *Space exploration: Manned flight.* Public Information Specialist, NASA Johnson Space Center, Houston, Texas.

James D. Wilde *Archaeology.* Codirector, Office of Public Archaeology, Brigham Young University, Provo, Utah.

Contributors to the Encyclopædia Britannica Science Update

Barbara B. Decker *Volcanism* (in part). Coauthor of *Volcanoes* (1981).

Robert W. Decker *Volcanism* (in part). Professor of Geophysics, Dartmouth College, Hanover, N.H., and Coauthor of *Volcanoes* (1981).

Christine Sutton *Subatomic Particles.* Physics Consultant to *New Scientist* magazine and Free-lance Science Writer, West Hagbourne, England.

A

Science

Classic

Sir Isaac Newton

Mathematical Principles of Natural Philosophy

Three hundred years after it was first published, Sir Isaac Newton's *Philosophiae Naturalis Principia Mathematica* (*Mathematical Principles of Natural Philosophy*) remains one of the greatest scientific works of all time, a ground-breaking investigation into the nature of the universe. In this volume of the *Yearbook of Science and the Future* two introductory sections of the book, The Definitions and the Axioms, or Laws of Motion, are reprinted. The entire *Principia* has been published by Encyclopædia Britannica, Inc., as one of the *Great Books of the Western World*.

Definitions

Definition I

The quantity of matter is the measure of the same, arising from its density and bulk conjointly.

Thus air of a double density, in a double space, is quadruple in quantity; in a triple space, sextuple in quantity. The same thing is to be understood of snow, and fine dust or powders, that are condensed by compression or liquefaction, and of all bodies that are by any causes whatever differently condensed. I have no regard in this place to a medium, if any such there is, that freely pervades the interstices between the parts of bodies. It is this quantity that I mean hereafter everywhere under the name of body or mass. And the same is known by the weight of each body, for it is proportional to the weight, as I have found by experiments on pendulums, very accurately made, which shall be shown hereafter.

Definition II

The quantity of motion is the measure of the same, arising from the velocity and quantity of matter conjointly.

The motion of the whole is the sum of the motions of all the parts; and therefore in a body double in quantity, with equal velocity, the motion is double; with twice the velocity, it is quadruple.

Definition III

The vis insita, *or innate force of matter, is a power of resisting, by which every body, as much as in it lies, continues in its present state, whether it be of rest, or of moving uniformly forwards in a right line.*

This force is always proportional to the body whose force it is and differs nothing from the inactivity of the mass, but in our manner of conceiving it. A body, from the inert nature of matter, is not without difficulty put out of its state of rest or motion. Upon which account, this *vis insita* may, by a most significant name, be called inertia (*vis inertiae*) or force of inactivity. But a body only exerts this force when another force, impressed upon it, endeavors to change its condition; and the exercise of this force may be considered as both resistance and impulse; it is resistance so far as the body, for maintaining its present state, opposes the force impressed; it is impulse so far as the body, by not easily giving way to the impressed force of another, endeavors to change the state of that other. Resistance is usually ascribed to bodies at rest, and impulse to those in motion; but motion and rest, as commonly conceived, are only relatively distinguished; nor are those bodies always truly at rest, which commonly are taken to be so.

Definition IV

An impressed force is an action exerted upon a body, in order to change its state, either of rest, or of uniform motion in a right line.

Sir Isaac Newton
By courtesy of the National Portrait Gallery, London

This force consists in the action only, and remains no longer in the body when the action is over. For a body maintains every new state it acquires, by its inertia only. But impressed forces are of different origins, as from percussion, from pressure, from centripetal force.

Definition V

A centripetal force is that by which bodies are drawn or impelled, or any way tend, towards a point as to a centre.

Of this sort is gravity, by which bodies tend to the centre of the earth; magnetism, by which iron tends to the loadstone; and that force, whatever it is, by which the planets are continually drawn aside from the rectilinear motions, which otherwise they would pursue, and made to revolve in curvilinear orbits. A stone, whirled about in a sling, endeavors to recede from the hand that turns it; and by that endeavor, distends the sling, and that with so much the greater force, as it is revolved with the greater velocity, and as soon as it is let go, flies away. That force which opposes itself to this endeavor, and by which the sling continually draws back the stone towards the hand, and retains it in its orbit, because it is directed to the hand as the centre of the orbit, I call the centripetal force. And the same thing is to be understood of all bodies, revolved in any orbits. They all endeavor to recede from the centres of their orbits; and were it not for the opposition of a contrary force which restrains them to, and detains them in their orbits, which I therefore call centripetal, would fly off in right lines, with an uniform motion. A pro-jectile, if it was not for the force of gravity, would not deviate towards the earth, but would go off from it in a right line, and that with an uniform motion, if the resistance of the air was taken away. It is by its gravity that it is drawn aside continually from its rectilinear course, and made to deviate towards the earth, more or less, according to the force of its gravity, and the velocity of its motion. The less its gravity is, or the quantity of its matter, or the greater the velocity with which it is projected, the less will it deviate from a rectilinear course, and the farther it will go. If a leaden ball, projected from the top of a mountain by the force of gunpowder, with a given velocity, and in a direction parallel to the horizon, is carried in a curved line to the distance of two miles before it falls to the ground; the same, if the resistance of the air were taken away, with a double or decuple velocity, would fly twice or ten times as far. And by increasing the velocity, we may at pleasure increase the distance to which it might be projected, and diminish the curvature of the line which it might describe, till at last it should fall at the distance of 10, 30, or 90 degrees, or even might go quite round the whole earth before it falls; or lastly, so that it might never fall to the earth, but go forwards into the celestial spaces, and proceed in its motion *in infinitum*. And after the same manner that a projectile, by the force of gravity, may be made to revolve in an orbit, and go round the whole earth, the moon also, either by the force of gravity, if it is endued with gravity, or by any other force, that impels it towards the earth, may be continually drawn aside towards the earth, out of the rectilinear way which by its innate force it would pursue; and would be made to revolve in the orbit which it now describes; nor could the moon without some such force be retained in its orbit. If this force was too small, it would not sufficiently turn the moon out of a rectilinear course; if it was too great, it would turn it too much, and draw down the moon from its orbit towards the earth. It is necessary that the force be of a just quantity, and it belongs to the mathematicians to find the force that may serve exactly to retain a body in a given orbit with a given velocity; and *vice versa*, to determine the curvilinear way into which a body projected from a given place, with a given velocity, may be made to deviate from its natural rectilinear way, by means of a given force.

The quantity of any centripetal force may be considered as of three kinds: absolute, accelerative, and motive.

Definition VI

The absolute quantity of a centripetal force is the measure of the same, proportional to the efficacy of the cause that propagates it from the centre, through the spaces round about.

Thus the magnetic force is greater in one load-stone and less in another, according to their sizes and strength of intensity.

Definition VII

The accelerative quantity of a centripetal force is the measure of the same, proportional to the velocity which it generates in a given time.

Thus the force of the same loadstone is greater at a less distance, and less at a greater: also the force of gravity is greater in valleys, less on tops of exceeding high mountains; and yet less (as shall hereafter be shown), at greater distances from the body of the earth; but at equal distances, it is the same everywhere; because (taking away, or allowing for, the resistance of the air), it equally accelerates all falling bodies, whether heavy or light, great or small.

Definition VIII

The motive quantity of a centripetal force is the measure of the same, proportional to the motion which it generates in a given time.

Thus the weight is greater in a greater body, less in a less body; and, in the same body, it is greater near to the earth, and less at remoter distances. This sort of quantity is the centripetency, or propension of the whole body towards the centre, or, as I may say, its weight; and it is always known by the quantity of an equal and contrary force just sufficient to hinder the descent of the body.

These quantities of forces, we may, for the sake of brevity, call by the names of motive, accelerative, and absolute forces; and, for the sake of distinction, consider them with respect to the bodies that tend to the centre, to the places of those bodies, and to the centre of force towards which they tend; that is to say, I refer the motive force to the body as an endeavor and propensity of the whole towards a centre, arising from the propensities of the several parts taken together; the accelerative force to the place of the body, as a certain power diffused from the centre to all places around to move the bodies that are in them; and the absolute force to the centre, as endued with some cause, without which those motive forces would not be propagated through the spaces round about; whether that cause be some central body (such as is the magnet in the centre of the magnetic force, or the earth in the centre of the gravitating force), or anything else that does not yet appear. For I here design only to give a mathematical notion of those forces, without considering their physical causes and seats.

Wherefore the accelerative force will stand in the same relation to the motive, as celerity does to motion. For the quantity of motion arises from the celerity multiplied by the quantity of matter; and the motive force arises from the accelerative force mul-tiplied by the same quantity of matter. For the sum of the actions of the accelerative force, upon the several particles of the body, is the motive force of the whole. Hence it is, that near the surface of the earth, where the accelerative gravity, or force productive of gravity, in all bodies is the same, the motive gravity or the weight is as the body; but if we should ascend to higher regions, where the accelerative gravity is less, the weight would be equally diminished, and would always be as the product of the body, by the accelerative gravity. So in those regions, where the accelerative gravity is diminished into one-half, the weight of a body two or three times less, will be four or six times less.

I likewise call attractions and impulses, in the same sense, accelerative, and motive; and use the words attraction, impulse, or propensity of any sort towards a centre, promiscuously, and indifferently, one for another; considering those forces not physically, but mathematically: wherefore the reader is not to imagine that by those words I anywhere take upon me to define the kind, or the manner of any action, the causes or the physical reason thereof, or that I attribute forces, in a true and physical sense, to certain centres (which are only mathematical points); when at any time I happen to speak of centres as attracting, or as endued with attractive powers.

Scholium

Hitherto I have laid down the definitions of such words as are less known, and explained the sense in which I would have them to be understood in the following discourse. I do not define time, space, place, and motion, as being well known to all. Only I must observe, that the common people conceive those quantities under no other notions but from the relation they bear to sensible objects. And thence arise certain prejudices, for the removing of which it will be convenient to distinguish them into absolute and relative, true and apparent, mathematical and common.

I. Absolute, true, and mathematical time, of itself, and from its own nature, flows equably without relation to anything external, and by another name is called duration: relative, apparent, and common time, is some sensible and external (whether accurate or unequable) measure of duration by the means of motion, which is commonly used instead of true time; such as an hour, a day, a month, a year.

II. Absolute space, in its own nature, without relation to anything external, remains always similar and immovable. Relative space is some movable dimension or measure of the absolute spaces; which our senses determine by its position to bodies; and which is commonly taken for immovable space; such is the dimension of a subterraneous, an aerial, or celestial space, determined by its position in respect of the earth. Absolute and relative space are the same in figure and magnitude; but they do not remain always numerically the same. For if the earth, for instance, moves, a space of our air, which relatively and in respect of the earth remains always the same, will at one time be one part of the absolute space into which the air passes; at another time it will be another part of the same, and so, absolutely understood, it will be continually changed.

III. Place is a part of space which a body takes up, and is according to the space, either absolute or relative. I say, a part of space; not the situation, nor the external surface of the body. For the places of equal solids are always equal; but their surfaces, by reason of their dissimilar figures, are often unequal. Positions properly have no quantity, nor are they so much the places themselves, as the properties of places. The motion of the whole is the same with the sum of the motions of the parts; that is, the translation of the whole, out of its place, is the same thing with the sum of the translations of the parts out of their places; and therefore the place of the whole is the same as the sum of the places of the parts, and for that reason, it is internal, and in the whole body.

IV. Absolute motion is the translation of a body from one absolute place into another; and relative motion, the translation from one relative place into another. Thus in a ship under sail, the relative place of a body is that part of the ship which the body possesses; or that part of the cavity which the body fills, and which therefore moves together with the ship: and relative rest is the continuance of the body in the same part of the ship, or of its cavity. But real, absolute rest, is the continuance of the body in the same part of that immovable space, in which the ship itself, its cavity, and all that it contains, is moved. Wherefore, if the earth is really at rest, the body, which relatively rests in the ship, will really and absolutely move with the same velocity which the ship has on the earth. But if the earth also moves, the true and absolute motion of the body will arise, partly from the true motion of the earth, in immovable space, partly from the relative motion of the ship on the earth; and if the body moves also relatively in the ship, its true motion will arise, partly from the true motion of the earth, in immovable space, and partly from the relative motions as well of the ship on the earth, as of the body in the ship; and from these relative motions will arise the relative motion of the body on the earth. As if that part of the earth, where the ship is, was truly moved towards the east, with a velocity of 10,010 parts; while the ship itself, with a fresh gale, and full sails, is carried towards the west, with a velocity expressed by 10 of those parts; but a sailor walks in the ship towards the east, with 1 part of the said velocity; then the sailor will be moved truly in immovable space towards the east, with a velocity of 10,001 parts, and relatively on the earth towards the west, with a velocity of 9 of those parts.

Absolute time, in astronomy, is distinguished from relative, by the equation of correction of the apparent time. For the natural days are truly unequal, though they are commonly considered as equal, and used for a measure of time; astronomers correct this inequality that they may measure the celestial motions by a more accurate time. It may be, that there is no such thing as an equable motion, whereby time may be accurately measured. All motions may be accelerated and retarded, but the flowing of absolute time is not liable to any change. The duration of perseverance of the existence of things remains the same, whether the motions are swift or slow, or none at all: and therefore this duration ought to be distinguished from what are only sensible measures thereof; and from which we deduce it, by means of the astronomical equation. The necessity of this equation, for determining the times of a phenomenon, is evinced as well from the experiments of the pendulum clock, as by eclipses of the satellites of Jupiter.

As the order of the parts of time is immutable, so also is the order of the parts of space. Suppose those parts to be moved out of their places, and they will be moved (if the expression may be allowed) out of themselves. For times and spaces are, as it were, the places as well of themselves as of all other things. All things are placed in time as to order of succession; and in space as to order of situation. It is from their essence or nature that they are places; and that the primary places of things should be movable, is absurd. These are therefore the absolute places; and translations out of those places, are the only absolute motions.

But because the parts of space cannot be seen, or distinguished from one another by our senses, therefore in their stead we use sensible measures of them. For from the positions and distances of things from any body considered as immovable, we define all places; and then with respect to such places, we estimate all motions, considering bodies as transferred from some of those places into others. And so, instead of absolute places and motions, we use relative ones; and that without any inconvenience in common affairs; but in philosophical disquisitions, we ought to abstract from our senses, and consider things themselves, distinct from what are only sensible measures of them. For it may be that there is no body really at rest, to which the places and motions of others may be referred.

But we may distinguish rest and motion, absolute and relative, one from the other by their properties, causes, and effects. It is a property of rest, that bodies really at rest do rest in respect to one another. And therefore as it is possible, that in the remote regions of the fixed stars, or perhaps far beyond them, there may be some body absolutely at rest; but impossible to know, from the position of bodies to one another in our regions, whether any of these do keep the same position to that remote body, it follows that absolute rest cannot be determined from the position of bodies in our regions.

It is a property of motion, that the parts, which retain given positions to their wholes, do partake of the motions of those wholes. For all the parts of revolving bodies endeavor to recede from the axis of motion; and the impetus of bodies moving forwards arises from the joint impetus of all the parts. Therefore, if surrounding bodies are moved, those that are relatively at rest within them will partake of their motion. Upon which account, the true and absolute motion of a body cannot be determined by the translation of it from those which only seem to rest; for the external bodies ought not only to appear at rest, but to be really at rest. For otherwise, all included bodies, besides their translation from near the surrounding ones, partake likewise of their true motions; and though that translation were not made, they would not be really at rest, but only seem to be so. For the surrounding bodies stand in the like relation to the surrounded as the exterior part of a whole does to the interior, or as the shell does to the kernel; but if the shell moves, the kernel will also move, as being part of the whole, without any removal from near the shell.

A property, near akin to the preceding, is this, that if a place is moved, whatever is placed therein moves along with it; and therefore a body, which is moved from a place in motion, partakes also of the motion of its place. Upon which account, all motions, from places in motion, are no other than parts of entire and absolute motions; and every entire motion is composed of the motion of the body out of its first place, and the motion of this place out of its place; and so on, until we come to some immovable place, as in the before-mentioned example of the sailor. Wherefore, entire and absolute motions can be no otherwise determined than by immovable places; and for that reason I did before refer those absolute motions to immovable places, but relative ones to movable places. Now no other places are immovable but those that, from infinity to infinity, do all retain the same given position one to another; and upon this account must ever remain unmoved; and do thereby constitute immovable space.

The causes by which true and relative motions are distinguished, one from the other, are the forces impressed upon bodies to generate motion. True motion is neither generated nor altered, but by some force impressed upon the body moved; but relative motion may be generated or altered without any force impressed upon the body. For it is sufficient only to impress some force on other bodies with

which the former is compared, that by their giving way, that relation may be changed, in which the relative rest or motion of this other body did consist. Again, true motion suffers always some change from any force impressed upon the moving body; but relative motion does not necessarily undergo any change by such forces. For if the same forces are likewise impressed on those other bodies, with which the comparison is made, that the relative position may be preserved, then that condition will be preserved in which the relative motion consists. And therefore any relative motion may be changed when the true motion remains unaltered, and the relative may be preserved when the true suffers some change. Thus, true motion by no means consists in such relations.

The effects which distinguish absolute from relative motion are, the forces of receding from the axis of circular motion. For there are no such forces in a circular motion purely relative, but in a true and absolute circular motion, they are greater or less, according to the quantity of the motion. If a vessel, hung by a long cord, is so often turned about that the cord is strongly twisted, then filled with water, and held at rest together with the water; thereupon, by the sudden action of another force, it is whirled about the contrary way, and while the cord is untwisting itself, the vessel continues for some time in this motion; the surface of the water will at first be plain, as before the vessel began to move; but after that, the vessel, by gradually communicating its motion to the water, will make it begin sensibly to revolve, and recede by little and little from the middle, and ascend to the sides of the vessel, forming itself into a concave figure (as I have experienced), and the swifter the motion becomes, the higher will the water rise, till at last, performing its revolutions in the same times with the vessel, it becomes relatively at rest in it. This ascent of the water shows its endeavor to recede from the axis of its motion; and the true and absolute circular motion of the water, which is here directly contrary to the relative, becomes known, and may be measured by this endeavor. At first, when the relative motion of the water in the vessel was greatest, it produced no endeavor to recede from the axis; the water showed no tendency to the circumference, nor any ascent towards the sides of the vessel, but remained of a plain surface, and therefore its true circular motion had not yet begun. But afterwards, when the relative motion of the water had decreased, the ascent thereof towards the sides of the vessel proved its endeavor to recede from the axis; and this endeavor showed the real circular motion of the water continually increasing, till it had acquired its greatest quantity, when the water rested relatively in the vessel. And therefore this endeavor does not depend upon any translation of the water in respect of the ambient bodies, nor can true circular motion be defined by such translation. There is only one real circular motion of any one revolving body, corresponding to only one power of endeavoring to recede from its axis of motion, as its proper and adequate effect; but relative motions, in one and the same body, are innumerable, according to the various relations it bears to external bodies, and, like other relations, are altogether destitute of any real effect, any otherwise than they may perhaps partake of that one only true motion. And therefore in their system who suppose that our heavens, revolving below the sphere of the fixed stars, carry the planets along with them; the several parts of those heavens, and the planets, which are indeed relatively at rest in their heavens, do yet really move. For they change their position one to another (which never happens to bodies truly at rest), and being carried together with their heavens, partake of their motions, and as parts of revolving wholes, endeavor to recede from the axis of their motions.

Wherefore relative quantities are not the quantities themselves, whose names they bear, but those sensible measures of them (either accurate or inaccurate), which are commonly used instead of the measured quantities themselves. And if the meaning of words is to be determined by their use, then by the names time, space, place, and motion, their [sensible] measures are properly to be understood; and the expression will be unusual, and purely mathematical, if the measured quantities themselves are meant. On this account, those violate the accuracy of language, which ought to be kept precise, who interpret these words for the measured quantities. Nor do those less defile the purity of mathematical and philosophical truths, who confound real quantities with their relations and sensible measures.

It is indeed a matter of great difficulty to discover, and effectually to distinguish, the true motions of particular bodies from the apparent; because the parts of that immovable space, in which those motions are performed, do by no means come under the observation of our senses. Yet the thing is not altogether desperate; for we have some arguments to guide us, partly from the apparent motions, which are the differences of the true motions; partly from the forces, which are the causes and effects of the true motions. For instance, if two globes, kept at a given distance one from the other by means of a cord that connects them, were revolved about their common centre of gravity, we might, from the tension of the cord, discover the endeavor of the globes to recede from the axis of their motion, and from thence we might compute the quantity of their circular motions. And then if any equal forces should be impressed at once on the alternate faces of the globes to augment or diminish their circular motions, from the increase or decrease of the tension of the

cord, we might infer the increment or decrement of their motions; and thence would be found on what faces those forces ought to be impressed, that the motions of the globes might be most augmented; that is, we might discover their hindmost faces, or those which, in the circular motion, do follow. But the faces which follow being known, and consequently the opposite ones that precede, we should likewise know the determination of their motions. And thus we might find both the quantity and the determination of this circular motion, even in an immense vacuum, where there was nothing external or sensible with which the globes could be compared. But now, if in that space some remote bodies were placed that kept always a given position one to another, as the fixed stars do in our regions, we could not indeed determine from the relative translation of the globes among those bodies, whether the motion did belong to the globes or to the bodies. But if we observed the cord, and found that its tension was that very tension which the motions of the globes required, we might conclude the motion to be in the globes, and the bodies to be at rest; and then, lastly, from the translation of the globes among the bodies, we should find the determination of their motions. But how we are to obtain the true motions from their causes, effects, and apparent differences, and the converse, shall be explained more at large in the following treatise. For to this end it was that I composed it.

Axioms, or laws of motion

Law I

Every body continues in its state of rest, or of uniform motion in a right line, unless it is compelled to change that state by forces impressed upon it.

Projectiles continue in their motions, so far as they are not retarded by the resistance of the air, or impelled downwards by the force of gravity. A top, whose parts by their cohesion are continually drawn aside from rectilinear motions, does not cease its rotation, otherwise than as it is retarded by the air. The greater bodies of the planets and comets, meeting with less resistance in freer spaces, preserve their motions both progressive and circular for a much longer time.

Law II

The change of motion is proportional to the motive force impressed; and is made in the direction of the right line in which that force is impressed.

If any force generates a motion, a double force will generate double the motion, a triple force triple the motion, whether that force be impressed altogether and at once, or gradually and successively. And this motion (being always directed the same way with the generating force), if the body moved before, is added to or subtracted from the former motion, according as they directly conspire with or are directly contrary to each other; or obliquely joined, when they are oblique, so as to produce a new motion compounded from the determination of both.

Law III

To every action there is always opposed an equal reaction: or, the mutual actions of two bodies upon each other are always equal, and directed to contrary parts.

Whatever draws or presses another is as much drawn or pressed by that other. If you press a stone with your finger, the finger is also pressed by the stone. If a horse draws a stone tied to a rope, the horse (if I may so say) will be equally drawn back towards the stone; for the distended rope, by the same endeavor to relax or unbend itself, will draw the horse as much towards the stone as it does the stone towards the horse, and will obstruct the progress of the one as much as it advances that of the other. If a body impinge upon another, and by its force change the motion of the other, that body also (because of the equality of the mutual pressure) will undergo an equal change, in its own motion, towards the contrary part. The changes made by these actions are equal, not in the velocities but in the motions of bodies; that is to say, if the bodies are not hindered by any other impediments. For, because the motions are equally changed, the changes of the velocities made towards contrary parts are inversely proportional to the bodies. This law takes place also in attractions, as will be proved in the next Scholium.

Corollary I

A body, acted on by two forces simultaneously, will describe the diagonal of a parallelogram in the same time as it would describe the sides by those forces separately.

If a body in a given time, by the force M impressed apart in the place A, should with an uniform motion be carried from A to B, and by the force N impressed

apart in the same place, should be carried from A to C, let the parallelogram ABCD be completed, and, by both forces acting together, it will in the same time be carried in the diagonal from A to D. For since the force N acts in the direction of the line AC, parallel to BD, this force (by the second Law) will not at all alter the velocity generated by the other force M, by which the body is carried towards the line BD. The body therefore will arrive at the line BD in the same time, whether the force N be impressed or not; and therefore at the end of that time it will be found somewhere in the line BD. By the same argument, at the end of the same time it will be found somewhere in the line CD. Therefore it will be found in the point D, where both lines meet. But it will move in a right line from A to D, by Law I.

Corollary II

And hence is explained the composition of any one direct force AD, out of any two oblique forces AC and CD; and, on the contrary, the resolution of any one direct force AD into two oblique forces AC and CD: which composition and resolution are abundantly confirmed from mechanics.

As if the unequal radii OM and ON drawn from the centre O of any wheel, should sustain the weights A and P by the cords MA and NP; and the forces of those weights to move the wheel were required. Through the centre O draw the right line KOL, meeting the cords perpendicularly in K and L; and from the centre O, with OL the greater of the distances OK and OL, describe a circle, meeting the cord MA in D; and drawing OD, make AC parallel and DC perpendicular thereto. Now, it being indifferent whether the points K, L, D, of the cords be fixed to the plane of the wheel or not, the weights will have the same effect whether they are suspended from the points K and L, or from D and L. Let the whole force of the weight A be represented by the line AD, and let it be resolved into the forces AC and CD, of which the force AC, drawing the radius OD directly from the centre, will have no effect to move the wheel; but the other force DC, drawing the radius DO perpendicularly, will have the same effect as if it drew perpendicularly the radius OL equal to OD; that is, it will have the same effect as the weight P, if P : A = DC : DA, but because the triangles ADC and DOK are similar, DC : DA = OK : OD = OK : OL. Therefore, P : A = radius OK : radius OL. As these radii lie in the same right line they will be equipollent, and so remain in equilibrium; which is the well-known property of the balance, the lever, and the wheel. If either weight is greater than in this ratio, its force to move the wheel will be so much greater.

If the weight $p = P$, is partly suspended by the cord Np, partly sustained by the oblique plane pG; draw pH, NH, the former perpendicular to the hori-

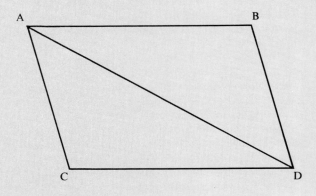

zon, the latter to the plane pG; and if the force of the weight p tending downwards is represented by the line pH, it may be resolved into the forces pN, HN. If there was any plane pQ, perpendicular to the cord pN, cutting the other plane pG in a line parallel to the horizon, and the weight p was supported only by those planes pQ, pG, it would press those planes perpendicularly with the forces pN, HN; to wit, the plane pQ with the force pN, and the plane pG with the force HN. And therefore if the plane pQ was taken away, so that the weight might stretch the cord, because the cord, now sustaining the weight, supplied the place of the plane that was removed, it would be strained by the same force pN which pressed upon the plane before. Therefore, the tension of pN : tension of PN = line pN : line pH. Therefore, if p is to A in a ratio which is the product of the inverse ratio of the least distances of their cords pN and AM from the centre of the wheel, and of the ratio pH to pN, then the weights p and A will have the same effect towards moving the wheel, and will, therefore, sustain each other; as anyone may find by experiment.

But the weight p pressing upon those two oblique planes, may be considered as a wedge between the two internal surfaces of a body split by it; and hence the forces of the wedge and the mallet may be determined: because the force with which the weight p presses the plane pQ is to the force with which the same, whether by its own gravity, or by the blow

of a mallet, is impelled in the direction of the line pH towards both the planes, as pN : pH; and to the force with which it presses the other plane pG, as pN : NH. And thus the force of the screw may be deduced from a like resolution of forces; it being no other than a wedge impelled with the force of a lever. Therefore the use of this Corollary spreads far and wide, and by that diffusive extent the truth thereof is further confirmed. For on what has been said depends the whole doctrine of mechanics variously demonstrated by different authors. For from hence are easily deduced the forces of machines, which are compounded of wheels, pullies, levers, cords, and weights, ascending directly or obliquely, and other mechanical powers; as also the force of the tendons to move the bones of animals.

Corollary III

The quantity of motion, which is obtained by taking the sum of the motions directed towards the same parts, and the difference of those that are directed to contrary parts, suffers no change from the action of bodies among themselves.

For action and its opposite reaction are equal, by Law III, and therefore, by Law II, they produce in the motions equal changes towards opposite parts. Therefore if the motions are directed towards the same parts, whatever is added to the motion of the preceding body will be subtracted from the motion of that which follows; so that the sum will be the same

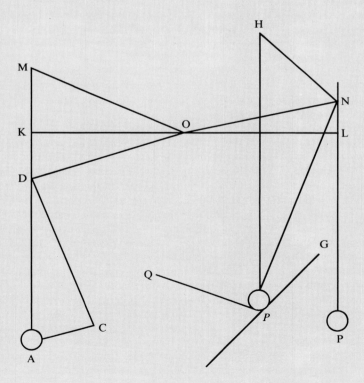

as before. If the bodies meet, with contrary motions, there will be an equal deduction from the motions of both; and therefore the difference of the motions directed towards opposite parts will remain the same.

Thus, if a spherical body A is 3 times greater than the spherical body B, and has a velocity $= 2$, and B follows in the same direction with a velocity $= 10$, then the motion of A : motion of B $= 6 : 10$. Suppose, then, their motions to be of 6 parts and of 10 parts, and the sum will be 16 parts. Therefore, upon the meeting of the bodies, if A acquire 3, 4, or 5 parts of motion, B will lose as many; and therefore after reflection A will proceed with 9, 10, or 11 parts, and B with 7, 6, or 5 parts; the sum remaining always of 16 parts as before. If the body A acquire 9, 10, 11, or 12 parts of motion, and therefore after meeting proceed with 15, 16, 17, or 18 parts, the body B, losing so many parts as A has got, will either proceed with 1 part, having lost 9, or stop and remain at rest, as having lost its whole progressive motion of 10 parts; or it will go back with 1 part, having not only lost its whole motion, but (if I may so say) one part more; or it will go back with 2 parts, because a progressive motion of 12 parts is taken off. And so the sums of the conspiring motions, $15 + 1$ or $16 + 0$, and the differences of the contrary motions, $17 - 1$ and $18 - 2$, will always be equal to 16 parts, as they were before the meeting and reflection of the bodies. But the motions being known with which the bodies proceed after reflection, the velocity of either will be also known, by taking the velocity after to the velocity before reflection, as the motion after is to the motion before. As in the last case, where the motion of A before reflection (6) : motion of A after (18) $=$ velocity of A before (2) : velocity of A after (x); that is, $6 : 18 = 2 : x$, $x = 6$.

But if the bodies are either not spherical, or, moving in different right lines, impinge obliquely one upon the other, and their motions after reflection are required, in those cases we are first to determine the position of the plane that touches the bodies in the point of impact, then the motion of each body (by Cor. II) is to be resolved into two, one perpendicular to that plane, and the other parallel to it. This done, because the bodies act upon each other in the direction of a line perpendicular to this plane, the parallel motions are to be retained the same after reflection as before; and to the perpendicular motions we are to assign equal changes towards the contrary parts; in such manner that the sum of the conspiring and the difference of the contrary motions may remain the same as before. From such kind of reflections sometimes arise also the circular motions of bodies about their own centres. But these are cases which I do not consider in what follows; and it would be too tedious to demonstrate every particular case that relates to this subject.

Corollary IV

The common centre of gravity of two or more bodies does not alter its state of motion or rest by the actions of the bodies among themselves; and therefore the common centre of gravity of all bodies acting upon each other (excluding external actions and impediments) is either at rest, or moves uniformly in a right line.

For if two points proceed with an uniform motion in right lines, and their distance be divided in a given ratio, the dividing point will be either at rest, or proceed uniformly in a right line. This is demonstrated hereafter in Lem. 23 and Corollary, when the points are moved in the same plane; and by a like way of arguing, it may be demonstrated when the points are not moved in the same plane. Therefore if any number of bodies move uniformly in right lines, the common centre of gravity of any two of them is either at rest, or proceeds uniformly in a right line; because the line which connects the centres of those two bodies so moving is divided at that common centre in a given ratio. In like manner the common centre of those two and that of a third body will be either at rest or moving uniformly in a right line; because at that centre the distance between the common centre of the two bodies, and the centre of this last, is divided in a given ratio. In like manner the common centre of these three, and of a fourth body, is either at rest, or moves uniformly in a right line; because the distance between the common centre of the three bodies, and the centre of the fourth, is there also divided in a given ratio, and so on *in infinitum*. Therefore, in a system of bodies where there is neither any mutual action among themselves, nor any foreign force impressed upon them from without, and which consequently move uniformly in right lines, the common centre of gravity of them all is either at rest or moves uniformly forwards in a right line.

Moreover, in a system of two bodies acting upon each other, since the distances between their centres and the common centre of gravity of both are reciprocally as the bodies, the relative motions of those bodies, whether of approaching to or of receding from that centre, will be equal among themselves. Therefore since the changes which happen to motions are equal and directed to contrary parts, the common centre of those bodies, by their mutual action between themselves, is neither accelerated nor retarded, nor suffers any change as to its state of motion or rest. But in a system of several bodies, because the common centre of gravity of any two acting upon each other suffers no change in its state by that action; and much less the common centre of gravity of the others with which that action does not intervene; but the distance between those two centres is divided by the common centre of gravity of all the bodies into parts inversely proportional to the total sums of those bodies whose centres they are; and therefore while those two centres retain their state of motion or rest, the common centre of all does also retain its state: it is manifest that the common centre of all never suffers any change in the state of its motion or rest from the actions of any two bodies between themselves. But in such a system all the actions of the bodies among themselves either happen between two bodies, or are composed of actions interchanged between some two bodies; and therefore they do never produce any alteration in the common centre of all as to its state of motion or rest. Wherefore since that centre, when the bodies do not act one upon another, either is at rest or moves uniformly forwards in some right line, it will, notwithstanding the mutual actions of the bodies among themselves, always continue in its state, either of rest, or of proceeding uniformly in a right line, unless it is forced out of this state by the action of some power impressed from without upon the whole system. And therefore the same law takes place in a system consisting of many bodies as in one single body, with regard to their persevering in their state of motion or of rest. For the progressive motion, whether of one single body, or of a whole system of bodies, is always to be estimated from the motion of the centre of gravity.

Corollary V

The motions of bodies included in a given space are the same among themselves, whether that space is at rest, or moves uniformly forwards in a right line without any circular motion.

For the differences of the motions tending towards the same parts, and the sums of those that tend towards contrary parts, are, at first (by supposition), in both cases the same; and it is from those sums and differences that the collisions and impulses do arise with which the bodies impinge one upon another. Wherefore (by Law 2), the effects of those collisions will be equal in both cases; and therefore the mutual motions of the bodies among themselves in the one case will remain equal to the motions of the bodies among themselves in the other. A clear proof of this we have from the experiment of a ship; where all motions happen after the same manner, whether the ship is at rest, or is carried uniformly forwards in a right line.

Corollary VI

If bodies, moved in any manner among themselves, are urged in the direction of parallel lines by equal accelerative forces, they will all continue to move among themselves, after the same manner as if they had not been urged by those forces.

For these forces acting equally (with respect to the quantities of the bodies to be moved), and in the direction of parallel lines, will (by Law 2) move all the bodies equally (as to velocity), and therefore will never produce any change in the positions or motions of the bodies among themselves.

Scholium

Hitherto I have laid down such principles as have been received by mathematicians, and are confirmed by abundance of experiments. By the first two Laws and the first two Corollaries, Galileo discovered that the descent of bodies varied as the square of the time (*in duplicata ratione temporis*) and that the motion of projectiles was in the curve of a parabola; experience agreeing with both, unless so far as these motions are a little retarded by the resistance of the air. When a body is falling, the uniform force of its gravity acting equally, impresses, in equal intervals of time, equal forces upon that body, and therefore generates equal velocities; and in the whole time impresses a whole force, and generates a whole velocity proportional to the time. And the spaces described in proportional times are as the product of the velocities and the times; that is, as the squares of the times. And when a body is thrown upwards, its uniform gravity impresses forces and reduces velocities proportional to the times; and the times of ascending to the greatest heights are as the velocities to be taken away, and those heights are as the product of the velocities and the times, or as the squares of the velocities. And if a body be projected in any direction, the motion arising from its projection is compounded with the motion arising from its gravity. Thus, if the body A by its motion of projection alone could describe in a given time the right line AB, and with its motion of falling alone could describe in the same time the altitude AC; complete the parallelogram ABCD, and

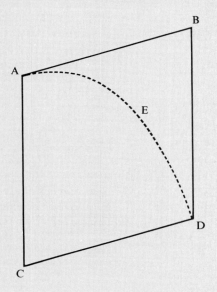

the body by that compounded motion will at the end of the time be found in the place D; and the curved line AED, which that body describes, will be a parabola, to which the right line AB will be a tangent at A; and whose ordinate BD will be as the square of the line AB. On the same Laws and Corollaries depend those things which have been demonstrated concerning the times of the vibration of pendulums, and are confirmed by the daily experiments of pendulum clocks. By the same, together with Law 3, Sir Christopher Wren, Dr. Wallis, and Mr. Huygens, the greatest geometers of our times, did severally determine the rules of the impact and reflection of hard bodies, and about the same time communicated their discoveries to the Royal Society, exactly agreeing among themselves as to those rules. Dr. Wallis, indeed, was somewhat earlier in the publication; then followed Sir Christopher Wren, and, lastly, Mr. Huygens. But Sir Christopher Wren confirmed the truth of the thing before the Royal Society by the experiments on pendulums, which M. Mariotte soon after thought fit to explain in a treatise entirely upon that subject. But to bring this experiment to an accurate agreement with the theory, we are to have due regard as well to the resistance of the air as to the elastic force of the concurring bodies. Let the spherical bodies A, B be suspended by the parallel and equal strings AC, BD, from the centres C, D. About these centres, with those lengths as radii, describe the semicircles EAF, GBH, bisected respectively by the radii CA, DB. Bring the body A to any point R of the arc EAF, and (withdrawing the body B) let it go from thence, and after one oscillation suppose it to return to the point V: then RV will be the retardation arising from the resistance of the air. Of this RV let ST be a fourth part, situated in the middle, namely, so that RS = TV, and RS : ST = 3 : 2, then will ST represent very nearly the retardation during the descent from S to A. Restore the body B to its place: and, supposing the body A to be let fall from the

point S, the velocity thereof in the place of reflection A, without sensible error, will be the same as if it had descended *in vacuo* from the point T. Upon which account this velocity may be represented by the chord of the arc TA. For it is a proposition well known to geometers, that the velocity of a pendulous body in the lowest point is as the chord of the arc which it has described in its descent. After reflection, suppose the body A comes to the place *s*, and the body B to the place *k*. Withdraw the body B, and find the place *v*, from which if the body A, being let go, should after one oscillation return to the place *r*, *st* may be a fourth part of *rv*, so placed in the middle thereof as to leave *rs* equal to *tv*, and let the chord of the arc *t*A represent the velocity which the body A had in the place A immediately after reflection. For *t* will be the true and correct place to which the body A should have ascended, if the resistance of the air had been taken off. In the same way we are to correct the place *k* to which the body B ascends, by finding the place *l* to which it should have ascended *in vacuo*. And thus everything may be subjected to experiment, in the same manner as if we were really placed *in vacuo*. These things being done, we are to take the product (if I may so say) of the body A, by the chord of the arc TA (which represents its velocity), that we may have its motion in the place A immediately before reflection; and then by the chord of the arc *t*A, that we may have its motion in the place A immediately after reflection. And so we are to take the product of the body B by the chord of the arc B*l*, that we may have the motion of the same immediately after reflection. And in like manner, when two bodies are let go together from different places, we are to find the motion of each, as well before as after reflection; and then we may compare the motions between themselves, and collect the effects of the reflection. Thus trying the thing with pendulums of 10 feet, in unequal as well as equal bodies, and making the bodies to concur after a descent through

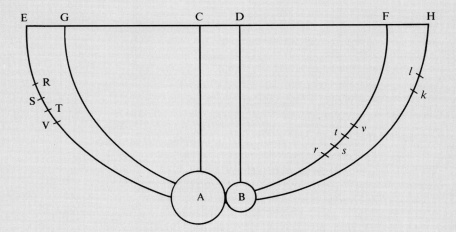

large spaces, as of 8, 12, or 16 feet, I found always, without an error of 3 inches, that when the bodies concurred together directly, equal changes towards the contrary parts were produced in their motions, and, of consequence, that the action and reaction were always equal. As if the body A impinged upon the body B at rest with 9 parts of motion, and losing 7, proceeded after reflection with 2, the body B was carried backwards with those 7 parts. If the bodies concurred with contrary motions, A with 12 parts of motion, and B with 6, then if A receded with 2, B receded with 8; namely, with a deduction of 14 parts of motion on each side. For from the motion of A subtracting 12 parts, nothing will remain; but subtracting 2 parts more, a motion will be generated of 2 parts towards the contrary way; and so, from the motion of the body B of 6 parts, subtracting 14 parts, a motion is generated of 8 parts towards the contrary way. But if the bodies were made both to move towards the same way, A, the swifter, with 14 parts of motion, B, the slower, with 5, and after reflection A went on with 5, B likewise went on with 14 parts; 9 parts being transferred from A to B. And so in other cases. By the meeting and collision of bodies, the quantity of motion, obtained from the sum of the motions directed towards the same way, or from the difference of those that were directed towards contrary ways, was never changed. For the error of an inch or two in measures may be easily ascribed to the difficulty of executing everything with accuracy. It was not easy to let go the two pendulums so exactly together that the bodies should impinge one upon the other in the lowermost place AB; nor to mark the places s, and k, to which the bodies ascended after impact. Nay, and some errors, too, might have happened from the unequal density of the parts of the pendulous bodies themselves, and from the irregularity of the texture proceeding from other causes.

But to prevent an objection that may perhaps be alleged against the rule, for the proof of which this experiment was made, as if this rule did suppose that the bodies were either absolutely hard, or at least perfectly elastic (whereas no such bodies are to be found in Nature), I must add, that the experiments we have been describing, by no means depending upon that quality of hardness, do succeed as well in soft as in hard bodies. For if the rule is to be tried in bodies not perfectly hard, we are only to diminish the reflection in such a certain proportion as the quantity of the elastic force requires. By the theory of Wren and Huygens, bodies absolutely hard return one from another with the same velocity with which they meet. But this may be affirmed with more certainty of bodies perfectly elastic. In bodies imperfectly elastic the velocity of the return is to be diminished together with the elastic force; because that

force (except when the parts of bodies are bruised by their impact, or suffer some such extension as happens under the strokes of a hammer) is (as far as I can perceive) certain and determined, and makes the bodies to return one from the other with a relative velocity, which is in a given ratio to that relative velocity with which they met. This I tried in balls of wool, made up tightly, and strongly compressed. For, first, by letting go the pendulous bodies, and measuring their reflection, I determined the quantity of their elastic force; and then, according to this force, estimated the reflections that ought to happen in other cases of impact. And with this computation other experiments made afterwards did accordingly agree; the balls always receding one from the other with a relative velocity, which was to the relative velocity with which they met as about 5 to 9. Balls of steel returned with almost the same velocity; those of cork with a velocity something less; but in balls of glass the proportion was as about 15 to 16. And thus the third Law, so far as it regards percussions and reflections, is proved by a theory exactly agreeing with experience.

In attractions, I briefly demonstrate the thing after this manner. Suppose an obstacle is interposed to hinder the meeting of any two bodies A, B, attracting one the other: then if either body, as A, is more attracted towards the other body B, than that other body B is towards the first body A, the obstacle will be more strongly urged by the pressure of the body A than by the pressure of the body B, and therefore will not remain in equilibrium: but the stronger pressure will prevail, and will make the system of the two bodies, together with the obstacle, to move directly towards the parts on which B lies; and in free spaces, to go forwards *in infinitum* with a motion continually accelerated; which is absurd and contrary to the first Law. For, by the first Law, the system ought to continue in its state of rest, or of moving uniformly forwards in a right line; and therefore the bodies must equally press the obstacle, and be equally attracted one by the other. I made the experiment on the loadstone and iron. If these, placed apart in proper vessels, are made to float by one another in standing water, neither of them will propel the other; but, by being equally attracted, they will sustain each other's pressure, and rest at last in an equilibrium.

So the gravitation between the earth and its parts is mutual. Let the earth FI be cut by any plane EG into two parts EGF and EGI, and their weights one towards the other will be mutually equal. For if by another plane HK, parallel to the former EG, the greater part EGI is cut into two parts EGKH and HKI, whereof HKI is equal to the part EFG, first cut off, it is evident that the middle part EGKH will have no propension by its proper weight towards either side, but will hang as it were, and rest in an equilibrium between both. But the one extreme part HKI will with its whole weight bear upon and press the middle part towards the other extreme part EGF; and therefore the force with which EGI, the sum of the parts HKI and EGKH, tends towards the third part EGF, is equal to the weight of the part HKI, that is, to the weight of the third part EGF. And therefore the weights of the two parts EGI and EGF, one towards the other, are equal, as I was to prove. And indeed if those weights were not equal, the whole earth floating in the nonresisting ether would give way to the greater weight, and, retiring from it, would be carried off *in infinitum*.

And as those bodies are equipollent in the impact and reflection, whose velocities are inversely as their innate forces, so in the use of mechanic instruments those agents are equipollent, and mutually sustain each the contrary pressure of the other, whose velocities, estimated according to the determination of the forces, are inversely as the forces.

So those weights are of equal force to move the arms of a balance, which during the play of the balance are inversely as their velocities upwards and downwards; that is, if the ascent or descent is direct, those weights are of equal force, which are inversely as the distances of the points at which they are suspended from the axis of the balance; but if they are turned aside by the interposition of oblique planes, or other obstacles, and made to ascend or descend obliquely, those bodies will be equipollent, which are inversely as the heights of their ascent and descent taken according to the perpendicular; and that on account of the determination of gravity downwards.

And in like manner in the pulley, or in a combination of pulleys, the force of a hand drawing the rope directly, which is to the weight, whether ascending directly or obliquely, as the velocity of the perpendicular ascent of the weight to the velocity of the hand that draws the rope, will sustain the weight.

In clocks and such like instruments, made up from a combination of wheels, the contrary forces that promote and impede the motion of the wheels, if they are inversely as the velocities of the parts of the wheel on which they are impressed, will mutually sustain each other.

The force of the screw to press a body is to the force of the hand that turns the handles by which it is moved as the circular velocity of the handle in that part where it is impelled by the hand is to the progressive velocity of the screw towards the pressed body.

The forces by which the wedge presses or drives the two parts of the wood it cleaves are to the force of the mallet upon the wedge as the progress of the wedge in the direction of the force impressed upon it by the mallet is to the velocity with which the parts of the wood yield to the wedge, in the direction of lines perpendicular to the sides of the wedge. And the like account is to be given of all machines.

The power and use of machines consist only in this, that by diminishing the velocity we may augment the force, and the contrary; from whence, in all sorts of proper machines, we have the solution of this problem: *To move a given weight with a given power,* or with a given force to overcome any other given resistance. For if machines are so contrived that the velocities of the agent and resistant are inversely as their forces, the agent will just sustain the resistant, but with a greater disparity of velocity will overcome it. So that if the disparity of velocities is so great as to overcome all that resistance which commonly arises either from the friction of contiguous bodies as they slide by one another, or from the cohesion of continuous bodies that are to be separated, or from the weights of bodies to be raised, the excess of the force remaining, after all those resistances are overcome, will produce an acceleration of motion proportional thereto, as well in the parts of the machine as in the resisting body. But to treat of mechanics is not my present business. I was aiming only to show by those examples the great extent and certainty of the third Law of Motion. For if we estimate the action of the agent from the product of its force and velocity, and likewise the reaction of the impediment from the product of the velocities of its several parts, and the forces of resistance arising from the friction, cohesion, weight, and acceleration of those parts, the action and reaction in the use of all sorts of machines will be found always equal to one another. And so far as the action is propagated by the intervening instruments, and at last impressed upon the resisting body, the ultimate action will be always contrary to the reaction.

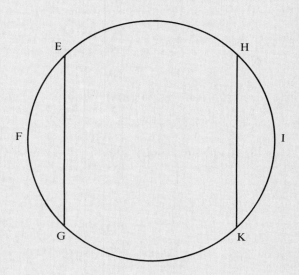

Institutions
of
Science

by Harald H. Bungarten

From a small and modest beginning in 1954, CERN has grown into the largest laboratory for fundamental scientific research in Europe.

Through the ages humans have reflected on the nature of matter and the laws governing the universe. In ancient times philosophers and scientists were already wondering what the world was made of. For centuries it was common belief that everything in material existence was composed of only air, earth, fire, and water. As long ago as 400 BC the pre-Socratic philosophers presented a materialist explanation of nature, which reached its definite form in the atomic theory of Leucippus and Democritus. This theory determined that matter had to be composed of an unlimited number of atoms differing only in size and shape. The rest of the universe was empty space.

At the end of the 19th century, atoms were still considered to be the fundamental constituents of matter, and physics no longer appeared to be an interesting field of research. Since then, however, scientists have learned much more. Atoms are composed of even smaller particles, such as electrons, protons, and neutrons, and the latter two in turn consist of quarks and gluons. Electrons and quarks now seem to be elementary particles; that is, they have no further inner structure. Gluons are "field particles" or "gauge bosons," transmitting the fundamental force between the quarks in the same way that photons make electrons orbit around an atomic nucleus.

Particle physics emerged in the 1930s and 1940s from the confluence of three research traditions: nuclear physics, cosmic-ray physics, and quantum field theory. Most of the experimental contribution came from cosmic-ray physics, which had its heyday from the late 1920s to the early 1950s, when a new generation of high-energy particle accelerators came into operation. Cosmic rays are high-energy particles that reach the Earth from outer space. The detection of their interactions as they pass through the atmosphere and the study of their characteristics were limited both by unforeseeable natural conditions

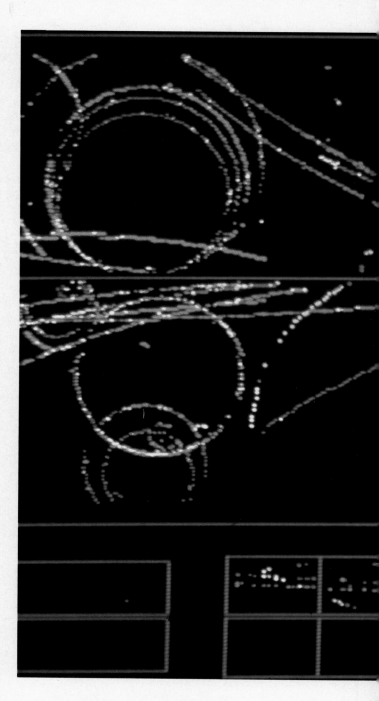

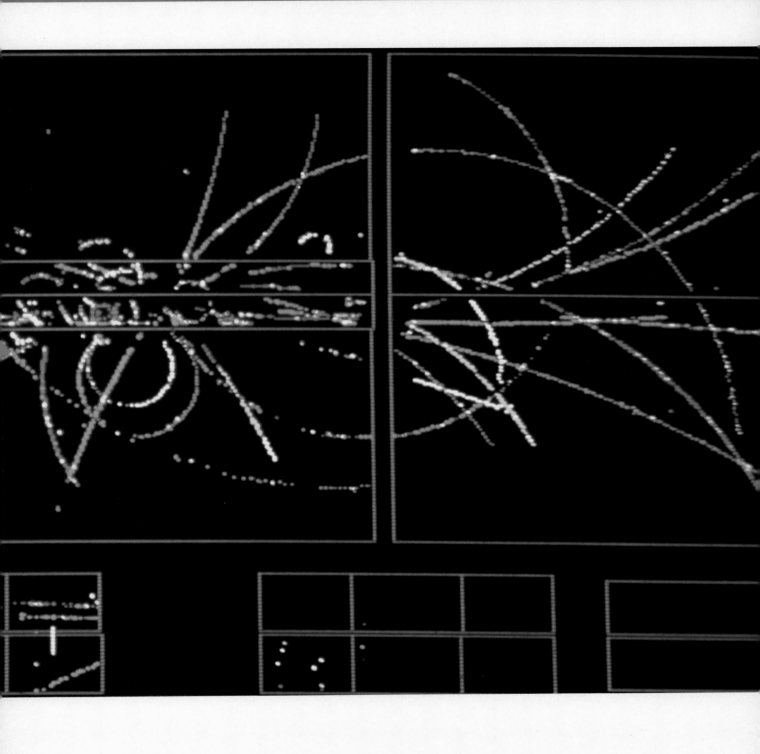

HARALD H. BUNGARTEN is Head of the Media Section at CERN, the European Organization for Nuclear Research, at Geneva, Switzerland.

(Overleaf) Computer-reconstructed image of a proton-antiproton collision that took place in CERN's Super Proton Synchrotron.

Photographs courtesy of CERN

and by their absorption in the atmosphere. Physicists had no control over the quantity or composition of particles in cosmic rays, but accelerators could provide them with beams of particles in large, regular quantities and under optimal, selected conditions. They did this essentially by imparting high velocities and kinetic energies to particles. (For an extended discussion of the basic work of particle accelerators, *see* Feature Article: PROBING THE SUBATOMIC WORLD: THE FERMI NATIONAL ACCELERATOR LABORATORY.)

In the 1930s proton and electron accelerators already existed, but they could not endow the particles with energies high enough to produce new matter—that is, unknown particles—from their collisions. It was not until the late 1940s that accelerators attained the energies required for such production (the pi-meson in 1948, the strange particles in 1954, and the electron decay of the pion in 1957). In essence, particle accelerators came to be for elementary particle physicists what the telescope is for astronomers and the microscope for biologists—the main tool for their research.

The Making of CERN

In 1945 Europe emerged from six years of war weakened and impoverished. Because individual countries lacked the financial resources to build the costly installations required for modern scientific research, a large number of physicists immigrated to the United States, thus continuing the exodus of European scientists from Germany and Italy that had begun during the 1930s. As a consequence, the intellectual center of gravity of particle physics shifted from Europe to the United States. It is in this light that one should look at the early steps toward the creation of CERN.

The participants at the meeting that created the "provisional organization" of CERN sent a letter to Nobel Prize winner Isidor Isaac Rabi, who was one of the first to suggest such an undertaking (below). Villa de Cointrin (below right), near the Geneva airport, was the preliminary headquarters of the laboratory. (Opposite page) The main entrance to CERN is lined with the flags of the member nations.

2

The first public discussion of the idea to create a European science laboratory took place at the European Cultural Conference in Lausanne, Switzerland, in December 1949. In June 1950, at the fifth General Conference of Unesco in Florence, Italy, Nobel Prize winner Isidor Isaac Rabi put forward a resolution, which was unanimously passed, authorizing the director-general of Unesco "to assist and encourage the formation of regional centers and laboratories in order to increase and make more fruitful the international collaboration of scientists in the search for new knowledge in fields where the effort of any one country in the region is insufficient for the task." During the next few years two main groups of scientists worked to advance the European laboratory project: first, physicists, such as Edoardo Amaldi, who were concerned about doing pure science at a "big science" level comparable to that of the United States; and second, science administrators who believed in the idea of European unity and hoped to foster this idea by nurturing a project that was too large for one or even a few nations to manage by themselves.

In December 1951 Unesco organized a meeting of official government delegates, and three months later a similar meeting with representatives from 11 European countries created the "provisional organization"—the Conseil Européen pour la Recherche Nucléaire (CERN), translated into English as the European Organization for Nuclear Research. A letter was sent from the participants at the meeting to Rabi, saying, "We have just signed the Agreement which constitutes the official birth of the project you fathered in Florence. Mother and child are doing well, and the doctors send their greetings."

Two important problems remained to be solved: the site of the laboratory and the design for the first accelerator to be built there. After long discussions Geneva was chosen, mainly for its central position between

Members of CERN and Their Financial Contributions		
	Austria	2.43
	Belgium	3.23
	Denmark	2.02
	France	19.25
	Germany, West	24.42
	Greece	0.40
	Italy	14.11
	Netherlands, The	5.26
	Norway	1.96
	Portugal	0.15
	Spain	2.15
	Sweden	3.59
	Switzerland	4.22
	United Kingdom	16.81

Member nation — 1988 contribution as % of the total budget

461

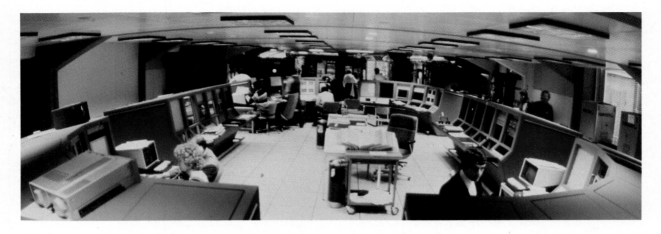

the capitals of member countries but also because of its tradition of being host to international organizations, the neutrality of Switzerland, the good rail and air connections, and, last but not least, the natural beauty of the environment. In a referendum in 1953 the Canton of Geneva accepted the creation of the laboratory by a two-to-one majority.

By the end of September 1954, nine European countries had ratified the CERN Convention, thus establishing CERN as a European organization. By February 1955 CERN already had 12 members: Belgium, Denmark, France, West Germany, Greece, Italy, The Netherlands, Norway, Sweden, Switzerland, the United Kingdom, and Yugoslavia. Austria and Spain joined in 1959 and 1961, respectively; Yugoslavia ceased to be a member in 1961; and Portugal joined in 1985, bringing the membership in 1988 to 14 European nations. According to Article 2 of the CERN Convention, the organization was created to "provide for collaboration among European States in nuclear research of a pure scientific and fundamental character, and in research essentially related thereto. The

In the control room (above), scientists operate the Proton Synchrotron (right). When it first went into operation in 1959, the Proton Synchrotron was the world's most powerful accelerator. It has a ring 200 meters (656 feet) in diameter around which are placed 100 magnets that hold protons in their orbits within a narrow vacuum tube as they are accelerated to high energies. Originally designed to supply protons directly to experiments, the Proton Synchrotron now provides the protons and antiprotons for the Super Proton Synchrotron.

Organization shall have no concern with work for military requirements and the results of its experimental and theoretical work shall be published or otherwise made generally available.''

Since its modest beginnings in barracks, hangars, and a villa near the airport, CERN has grown into the largest European laboratory for fundamental research. Its scientific facilities are the most powerful and versatile of their kind in the world. The site now covers more than 100 hectares (250 acres) in Switzerland and, since its extension over the border in 1965, more than 450 hectares (1,125 acres) in neighboring France. In 1988 the annual budget was 793 million Swiss francs, shared among the member nations in proportion to their net national revenue.

Soon after the 600-MeV synchrocyclotron began operating in 1957, physicists at CERN were the first to observe the decay of a pion into an electron and a neutrino—an important breakthrough in developing the theory of weak interactions. (One MeV = one million electron volts, an electron volt being a unit of energy equal to the energy gained by an electron in passing from one point of potential to a point one volt higher.) In 1959 the Proton Synchrotron went into operation as the first accelerator using the ''strong focusing'' technique; it was the most powerful machine in the world. In 1963 experiments with neutrino beams were started, a field of research that eventually became a specialty of CERN's physics program.

New machines, new discoveries

In 1971 the Intersecting Storage Rings (ISR) started operation, the first and, as of the end of 1987, the only machine in the world that provided head-on collisions between protons and protons. The facility was closed down in 1984 to free funds for the construction of the Large Electron-Positron collider. The ISR consisted of two rings, each with a circumference of about one kilometer (about 0.62 mile), in which protons were

When the intersecting storage rings (ISR) facility became operational in 1971, it was the first machine in the world to provide head-on collisions between protons. The ISR, closed in 1984, consisted of two rings, each about one kilometer (0.62 mile) in circumference, in which protons were accelerated and guided to collisions at eight intersecting points.

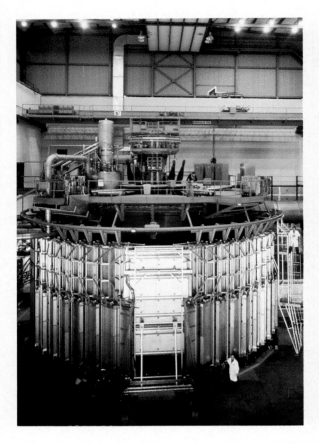

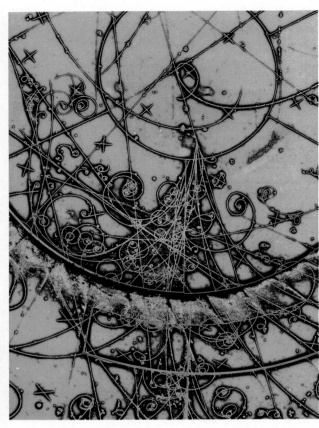

The 3.7-meter (12.1-foot) hydrogen bubble chamber (above), operational from 1973 to 1984, was equipped with the largest superconducting magnet in the world. During its lifetime the bubble chamber produced about 6.3 million photographs of particle interactions and their trajectories, some of which had considerable aesthetic appeal (above right).

accelerated and brought to head-on collisions at eight intersecting points. This machine led to breakthroughs in several regards. For example, vacuum technology took a leap forward as the accelerator produced a vacuum 10,000 times higher than had ever before been reached on a comparable industrial scale; it was identical to that existing on the Moon. This proved to be important for the lifetime of the proton beams, which could circulate within the rings at a high current with a lifetime of weeks. Also, Simon van der Meer and other CERN scientists developed a technique called stochastic cooling, which allowed the proton beams to be concentrated to intensities never before reached. At the same time, detector technology progressed with the transition from bubble chambers to electronic detectors and with the improvement of the trigger technique. Both developments were decisive for the detection of new particles.

The year 1973 was an extraordinary one for CERN; one of its greatest physics discoveries was made in the French-built Gargamelle bubble chamber at the Proton Synchrotron when it was found that neutrinos could interact with another particle without changing into muons. This behavior is known as the "neutral current interaction" and was the discovery that opened the door to what some physicists now call "the new physics." It had great implications for the theoretical ideas about the fundamental forces of physics. In particular, it gave strong support to the theory that attempted to unite the understanding of the weak force (governing such phenomena as radioactivity) with the familiar electromagnetic force.

During the same year, the construction of a 3.7-meter (12.1-foot) hydrogen bubble chamber equipped with the largest superconducting magnet in the world was completed. During its working life until 1984 the bubble chamber took about 6.3 million photographs of particle interactions, pictures not only of great scientific interest but also of a particular aesthetic appeal, very much resembling abstract art.

CERN's next big accelerator, the Super Proton Synchrotron, with a seven-kilometer circumference, went into operation in 1976. Built 50 meters (164 feet) underground, it was conceived as a fixed-target machine with an energy as great as 450 billion electron volts (GeV). By using van der Meer's stochastic cooling technique, the Italian physicist Carlo Rubbia saw the possibility of creating head-on collisions of protons and antiprotons in a single accelerator. To accumulate sufficient numbers of antiprotons in concentrated beams, van der Meer developed the Antiproton Accumulator Ring. In 1981 the Super Proton Synchrotron was converted into a proton-antiproton collider and since that time has operated in both collision and fixed-target experiments. The first collisions between protons and antiprotons at an energy of 270 GeV per beam took place in July 1981 in two underground experimental areas. In January and May 1983 these collaborations discovered the $W^{\pm}$ bosons and the Z^0 boson, the carriers of the weak nuclear force, thus confirming the theory of electroweak interactions that unifies the weak and electromagnetic forces. For their contribution to this extraordinary discovery, Rubbia and van der Meer were awarded the Nobel Prize for Physics in 1984.

Large Electron-Positron Collider

Also in 1983 construction began on the Large Electron-Positron Collider (LEP), which was scheduled to be completed in 1989. It will then be

Located in a tunnel 50 meters (164 feet) underground, the 450-GeV (billion electron volt) Super Proton Synchrotron is used for collisions between protons and antiprotons and for fixed-target experiments. It has 1,000 magnets positioned in a ring that is 2.2 kilometers (1.4 miles) in diameter.

the largest ring collider in the world. A tunnel with a circumference of almost 27 kilometers (17 miles) was drilled at a depth of 50–170 meters (164–558 feet) beneath the surface; its internal diameter is 3.8 meters (12.5 feet). The ring passes under both Swiss and French territory. Eighteen access shafts connect the tunnel with the surface buildings at eight different points around the circumference. Four huge underground experimental halls were excavated to house the large detectors.

Because all preparations for LEP were running on schedule in early 1988, physics experiments that collide electrons with their antiparticles, positrons, were expected to begin in 1989 with an initial energy of about 60 GeV per beam. After its inauguration LEP will be extended in phases, taking several years to reach the design energy of 200 GeV.

The LEP ring is not a perfect circle but consists of eight curved sectors, each 2,800 meters (9,184 feet) long, interlinked by eight straight sections that are each 500 meters (1,640 feet) long. The particles are guided in the curved sectors by 3,400 bending magnets, and the particle beams are focused by 760 quadrupole and 512 sextupole magnets. Electrons travel clockwise and positrons circulate counterclockwise. The particles are accelerated each time they pass through the straight sections. Their collisions are observed by four large detectors installed in the experimental halls. Each of these experiments is carried out by an international team, comprising 300–350 scientists from more than 30 universities and research institutes. The cost of the experiments was being shared equally among CERN, its member nations, and the participating nonmember nations from virtually all over the world.

The capital outlay for LEP amounted to about 1.3 billion Swiss francs at 1988 prices. (As of February 1988, 1.40 Swiss francs equaled $1). In real terms, this was about the same amount that was spent on its immediate predecessor, the Super Proton Synchrotron. Although other research

The Antiproton Accumulator Ring (above) is used to concentrate and store antiprotons for use in the Super Proton Synchrotron. At the right is the detector of the UA2 experiment for studying the proton-antiproton collisions. It consists of 240 cells of electronic instrumentation that provide independent detection of the different types of particles emerging from the collisions.

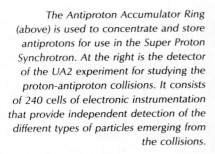

institutes have been granted special resources for the completion of projects of this size, CERN was financing LEP out of its ordinary operating budget. One of the conditions for the approval of LEP in 1981 was, in fact, that the project had to be completed at a constant CERN budget—that is, without extra funds or staff. This was accomplished only by shutting down older installations and pruning the CERN research program. Consequently, about 1,000 CERN employees had to take on changed and sometimes completely new tasks. This flexibility on the part of the staff has been seen as a sign of the continuing vitality of the institute.

When the LEP project was proposed in 1981 by the director-general, Herwig Schopper, various options were foreseen for the future with an eye to making the most cost-effective use of the high capital investment that was required. Thus, the LEP tunnel was designed to provide enough room above the LEP magnets for the installation of superconducting magnets for a large proton collider, the Large Hadron Collider. It would be able to operate in an energy range of eight trillion–nine trillion electron volts (TeV), some ten times greater than the highest energies so far available anywhere in the world. With only minor modifications, the existing CERN accelerators could be used as preaccelerators for such a machine.

In the search for a new state of matter, the "quark-gluon plasma," CERN's accelerator complex surpassed itself at the end of 1987. Sulfur ions (atomic nuclei of sulfur) were added to the long list of particles already handled at CERN and were being accelerated to an energy of 6.4 TeV, the highest energy ever reached in a laboratory. At the other end of the energy range, the availability of intense beams of antimatter opened the way for a promising new experimental program; antiprotons at low energy from the Low-Energy Antiproton Ring might lead to a better understanding of the behavior and properties of antimatter.

A political success story

Thus, CERN proved that it could provide physicists with the scientific equipment and working conditions they needed in Europe to stop the so-called brain drain. By 1988 more than 4,000 research workers and engineers from all over the world were cooperating successfully on CERN experiments as external users (*i.e.*, the majority were paid by their home universities). Some 3,500 CERN staff were in charge of the construction and operation of the extensive research facilities. In its scientific program CERN expanded far beyond the confines of Europe. It has formal cooperation agreements with the Soviet Union and China and less formal but strong traditional collaborative ties with the U.S. Department of Energy, with many U.S. universities and research institutes, and with Brazil, Canada, Finland, Hungary, India, Israel, Japan, and Poland.

What were—and are—the reasons for this success? First, CERN has an enviable technical record of building powerful and versatile research tools, both accelerators and detectors. The second, more political, reason for success was born out of the necessity of pooling the large resources needed for building these machines. The member nations realized that a

Simon van der Meer of The Netherlands (left) and Carlo Rubbia of Italy, physicists on the staff at CERN, shared the 1984 Nobel Prize for Physics for planning and executing the experiments that in 1983 demonstrated the existence of elementary particles called intermediate vector bosons. Rubbia proposed that the Super Proton Synchrotron be modified so that colliding-beam experiments could be undertaken, and van der Meer developed the method of controlling the antimatter so that it could be adapted to the requirements of the experiment.

467

A full-face boring machine (right) was used to drill the main tunnel and other galleries of the Large Electron-Positron Collider (LEP). When completed in 1989, the main tunnel, at depths ranging from 50 to 170 meters (164 to 558 feet) below the surface, will have a circumference of almost 27 kilometers (17 miles) and an internal diameter of 3.8 meters (12.5 feet); LEP will be the largest ring collider in the world. A spherical "low-loss" radiofrequency cavity is mounted on top of accelerator cavities (below) as a possible means of reducing the energy burden of the LEP ring.

laboratory of the size and performance of CERN would not be possible on a national basis.

There is also an economic reason for CERN's success. It stems from the experience industry has had in working with the institute. Though there is no policy of "just returns" from national contributions, European industry has benefited from its contracts with CERN. The institute has always followed a policy of promoting the dissemination of technological knowledge and, therefore, has never taken out patents but has always made available to industry the knowledge gained during the development of its equipment. The advantages for the participating firms have been considerable; a recent study revealed that over a period of ten years the economic advantage from producing for CERN has surpassed the contract value by several times.

The fourth, and probably most significant, reason for CERN's achievements, however, is based on what Rubbia calls "quantum jumps due to intellectual breakthroughs," attainable only through the pooling under one roof of many of the best research workers from all over the world. Considering its success as an international research laboratory, it is not surprising that other European research organizations have patterned themselves after CERN. These include the European Southern Observatory in Munich, West Germany, and the European Molecular Biology Organization in Heidelberg, West Germany.

And the search goes on . . .

Despite CERN's success a large number of questions remain to be solved. The driving force behind CERN's ambitious scientific activities will continue to be the intellectual curiosity of its users. One major effort will be to try to understand what happened during the first moments of the "big

bang" some 15 billion years ago, when the universe was but a speck, nothing but an incredible concentration of energy. A fraction of a second after the big bang, the universe started to expand; symmetries broke, and energy "condensed" or "crystallized" into matter. The once-united fundamental force split into the four forces that are observed today.

The electromagnetic force governs the behavior of atoms and causes the negatively charged electrons to orbit around the nucleus of the atom. The carrier of this force is the massless photon. The weak force gives rise to radioactivity. Its carriers, the heavy W and Z bosons, were discovered at CERN in 1983. The third force, the most powerful of all and therefore called the strong force, is mediated by gauge bosons called gluons, detected in 1978 at the West German high-energy physics research center. The gluons grip the quarks within neutrons and protons and hold the nucleus of an atom together. The fourth force, gravitation, acts over great distances and holds the planets in their orbits and people on the ground. Though its action was described in the 17th century by Sir Isaac Newton, scientists do not know yet how it works, nor do they know anything about its carrier particle, the so-called graviton. A search for gravity waves was being carried out at CERN, but as of 1988 it had not produced positive results.

As Victor F. Weisskopf, a former director-general of CERN, once said, scientific knowledge is like an island in the ocean of the unknown. Researchers have found that elementary particles, fundamental building blocks of matter that have no inner structure, consist of six kinds of leptons, the best known of them being the electron, and six kinds of quarks. They make up all the matter that is presently known. Scientists, however, do not know why there are just six of them, whether there might be more, or whether they really are fundamental. Another basic

White lines added to an aerial photograph of CERN reveal the locations and comparative sizes of the Super Proton Synchrotron and the Large Electron-Positron Collider. The SPS is the smaller ring that is almost totally enclosed within the still uncompleted LEP.

question also remains to be answered: why most of the particles have a mass, and why these masses are so different. Theorists, therefore, predict the existence of another particle responsible for creating mass, the Higgs boson, which will be sought for on the LEP.

In the search for answers to these questions, physicists use ever stronger "microscopes," the accelerators and detectors. The fact that these tools of research are so large and expensive has two consequences. First, it leads to concentration of research. Nowadays only a few major particle-physics laboratories with high-energy accelerators are left throughout the world; aside from CERN, they include three in the United States and one each in the Soviet Union, Japan, and West Germany. They have developed close working links involving the exchanges of scientists, but the only truly international center is CERN.

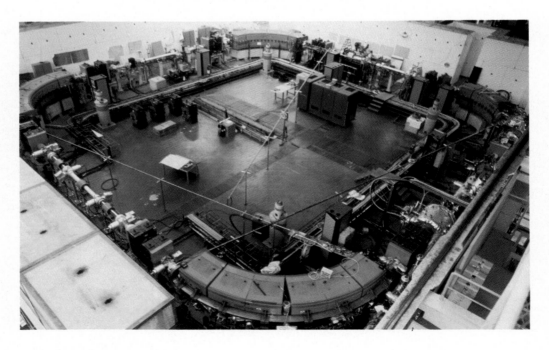

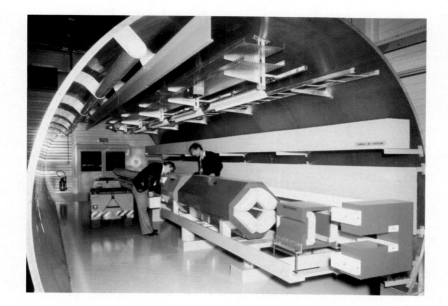

A mock-up reveals a portion of the completed tunnel of LEP. The head-on collisions in the tunnel of electrons and their antimatter counterparts, positrons, are expected to produce new and exotic particles.

The second consequence, specialization, can be seen in the plans for future accelerators. The Soviet Union is building a proton fixed-target accelerator with an energy of 3,000 GeV at Serpukhov; West Germany plans to commission in 1990 an accelerator in Hamburg, where electrons accelerated to 30 GeV will hit protons accelerated to 820 GeV; and the U.S. is planning a large proton-proton collider, the Superconducting Super Collider. (*See* Feature Article: PROBING THE SUBATOMIC WORLD: THE FERMI NATIONAL ACCELERATOR LABORATORY.)

At CERN a proton-proton collider built in the same tunnel as that used by the LEP could reach 8–9 TeV per beam. This would cover an energy range where, according to present knowledge, interesting new phenomena should appear. Owing to the everlasting curiosity of human beings to learn about their origins and to unveil the secrets of the infinitely small and the infinitely large, the struggle goes on to try to decode the blueprints of life and galaxies, to understand the laws of matter and of forces that govern the universe from its unknown beginning to its equally unknown future.

FOR ADDITIONAL READING

Laurie M. Brown and Lillian Hoddeson, eds., *The Birth of Particle Physics* (Cambridge University Press, 1983).

Frank Close, Michael Marten, and Christine Sutton, *The Particle Explosion* (Oxford University Press, 1987).

Frank Close, *The Cosmic Onion* (Heinemann, 1983).

A. Hermann, J. Krige, U. Mersits, and D. Pestre, *The History of CERN* (North-Holland, 1987).

Philip and Phylis Morrison, *Powers of Ten* (Scientific American Library, 1982).

Steven Weinberg, *The First Three Minutes* (Basic Books, 1977).

Victor F. Weisskopf, *Knowledge and Wonder* (Doubleday, 1963).

Probing the Subatomic World:
The Fermi National Accelerator Laboratory

by Leon M. Lederman

In the 20 years since it was established, the Fermi National
Accelerator Laboratory has become one of the world's
major centers of research in high-energy physics.

In 1987 the Fermi National Accelerator Laboratory (Fermilab) commissioned a particle accelerator that had the highest energy in the world. Although this was reason enough for rejoicing on the part of the scientists who use such accelerators for their research, the focus of attention was instead upon the concept of an accelerator 20 times larger. It was called the Superconducting Super Collider (SSC), and plans called for its completion by 1997.

Also during the year the nations of Western Europe, in a consortium known as CERN (European Organization for Nuclear Research), were constructing a large electron-positron collider in a 27-kilometer (17-mile) tunnel straddling Switzerland and France just east of Geneva. Similar large accelerators were under construction in Japan, West Germany, and the Soviet Union. (*See* Feature Article: CERN—THE EUROPEAN LABORATORY FOR PARTICLE PHYSICS.)

The objective of these huge investments is simply stated. It is to continue a 2,500-year-old quest to answer one question: "How does the universe work?" The strategy that has been evolved is to find the basic building blocks of all matter and to discover the laws or the forces that cause these particles to cluster and interact in order to form the more substantial ingredients of the world. This "atomistic" philosophy has had enormous success, especially during the past 100 years, and has revolutionized all of science and all of technology. The history of this epoch is also a history of the invention of instruments of increasing power, able to observe and measure at ever smaller domains. These "microscopes" have successively gathered data about molecules, atoms, atomic nuclei, and the subnuclear domain of neutrons, protons, quarks, and leptons.

In the 1930s the first generation of particle accelerators was invented. These were based upon the well-understood principles of electricity and magnetism. The first machines were simply high-voltage electrostatic devices. In them an electrically charged particle emerges from a slit and

LEON M. LEDERMAN is Director of the Fermi National Accelerator Laboratory, Batavia, Illinois.

(Opposite page) Photograph © Dan McCoy—Rainbow

472

In the Cockcroft-Walton generator (right) hydrogen gas is ionized and the ions are accelerated to 750,000 electron volts. They are then passed on to the linear accelerator (below), where they travel through a series of cavities and gain energy at each one until after about 145 meters they reach 200 million electron volts. From the linear accelerator the ions move to a circular " booster" accelerator, where the electrons are stripped off and the remaining protons are increased in energy to 8 billion electron volts. The protons are then transferred to the main ring (opposite page). There they are joined by other proton beams and accelerated either throgh the upper ring of red and blue magnets to 400 billion electron volts or through the the lower ring of yellow and red superconducting magnets to almost one trillion electron volts.

experimenter teams require the primary protons for their research. Others require beams of secondary particles produced from the collision of primary protons with a target. A useful secondary particle is one that is produced in adequate quantity and has a comparatively long lifetime. Typically, one can select useful beams of pions, kaons, and hyperons among the charged particle debris, and one can also find photons, neutrons, neutral kaons, and hyperons in the electrically neutral beams. More finicky experimenters may want tertiary particles; that is, particles generated as decay products of the secondaries. For example, pions of 100 GeV will have a more than 10% probability of decaying into muons and neutrinos after traversing a kilometer of free space. Thus, intense beams of neutrinos and muons are also available.

The experimental program

In fashioning a laboratory, the design of the machine is only part of the task. Thought had to be given to the experimental program, including its organization and scale. To that end the Laboratory appointed a Program Advisory Committee (PAC) consisting of a dozen experts from throughout the United States.

Proposals for the first series of experiments were called for in 1968. In that year the Laboratory was host to a workshop in Aspen, Colorado, so that the capabilities of the accelerator and the scientific problems could be thoroughly reviewed. It was recognized that the size of the machine, ten times larger than any previous accelerator, would make it complicated to use but also would present tremendous scientific potential.

Table II. Population Distribution of Fermilab Users (1987)		
	Fixed-Target Program	Collider Program
U.S. Ph.D.s	427	310
U.S. graduate students	207	66
Foreign Ph.D.s	249	92
Foreign graduate students	52	22

Note   There are an estimated 1,500 experimental physicists in the U.S. devoted to high-energy physics. More than half are Fermilab users. Western Europe and Japan have approximately 3,000 experimentalists, and about 15% are Fermilab users.

Above, researcher connects cables to a beam station to study the production and decay of short-lived particles. Aerial view of Fermilab (below) shows the main ring and three experimental lines extending at tangents from it from a base at Wilson Hall. Beams of protons are directed through these lines toward target areas.

The procedure that was eventually permanently adopted was for the PAC to review all proposals and to recommend to the director those deemed of greatest scientific merit. Other considerations included technical feasibility, the competence of the group of scientists making the proposal, and overall costs. The origin of the proposal—from which university, or, in fact, from which country—was not a relevant consideration. The approved proposals would then obtain resources from the Laboratory and have a strong argument for gaining support from the funding agencies. Typically, consortia of scientists and students from several universities would combine to make proposals. As the complexity of experimental research increased, the average group size grew from as few as 5–10 members to as many as 40–60 scientists and students. The time between proposal and completion of the research increased from about one year to as long as four to five years. The number of collaborating institutions grew from one or two to as many as ten or more. About 30% of the users were from foreign countries. These included the nations of Western Europe, the Soviet Union, Japan, China, Taiwan, Mexico, and Brazil (Table III).

In March 1972 the first particles were accelerated to 200 GeV, and the physics program began soon afterward. The accelerator magnets were actually much more powerful than were specified for a 200-GeV machine. Robert Wilson, a magnet expert, had taken several shortcuts in the magnet design, and in so doing he had made a magnet that could guide particles of more than twice the design energy. In 1974 the accelerator went to 400 GeV and even made a brief excursion to 500 GeV. This pushed the limits of conventional iron-copper magnets, which normally show poor performance at magnetic field values over 20 kilogauss. At 500 GeV the Wilson magnets were operating at 22.5 kilogauss. At this time 14 lines of beams were being used in the research program, whereas the design called for only 10. What shocked the federal bureaucrats far beyond the accomplishment of exceeding specifications, however, was the fact that the Laboratory still had more than $10 million of the original appropriation left over.

The philosophy that guided the choice of experiments during the early period of Fermilab was diversity. The Laboratory had achieved a new domain of energy, and the expected new results could be in any of an extensive frontier of possible experiments. Relatively simple experiments across this broad frontier were encouraged as the best way to spend the limited resources. The idea was that as an understanding of the physics in the new domain was gained, more powerful (and hence more expensive) research efforts could be constructed.

By 1979 some 100 publications per year were based on the completion of approximately 25 experiments annually. A few of their titles are suggestive:

Observations of Structure in Elastic p-p Scattering at 100 GeV and 200 GeV.

A Precise Measurement of the Lambda Magnetic Moment

Neutron-Nuclear Total Cross-Sections Between 30 GeV and 300 GeV

Measurement of Neutrino and Anti-neutrino Cross Sections at High Energies

The Search for New Families of Elementary Particles

Observation of a Dimuon Resonance at 9.5 GeV in 400-GeV Proton-Nucleus Collisions.

The experimental program studied the strong, weak, and electromagnetic forces; provided a mass of data on the interactions of known particles and precision measurements of their properties; probed the quark structures of protons, neutrons, and pions; and discovered a new quark (the bottom quark, b) and new regularities in a class of collisions that was indicative of quark structures. By 1982 some 300 experiments had been completed, and 30 were under way.

The Tevatron

In 1976 CERN activated its 400-GeV proton synchrotron, and the competition between the laboratories became as brisk as their collaboration.

481

Also, in the early 1970s the oil crisis caused a painful increase in the cost of electrical power that was exacerbated by the fact that between 1973 and 1978 total power usage at Fermilab doubled and the power cost per kilowatt-hour also doubled. The Laboratory consumed some 60 megawatts of power just to run the accelerators. The Laboratory in the early 1970s had begun a small research and development program on a new magnetic technology. This involved superconductivity, the property of certain metals and alloys to conduct electricity without any losses of power due to resistance. Since essentially all of the 60 megawatts of electrical energy were expended in warming the copper windings of the main ring magnets, any extension of the accelerator complex would almost surely require a new breed of conductor that would offer much less resistivity and thereby save power and operating funds. The Laboratory selected as the most promising material a niobium-titanium alloy that becomes superconducting below 10 K ($-263°$ C [$-441.4°$ F]).

Another virtue of superconducting magnets is their ability to produce much more powerful magnetic fields than can the conventional iron-copper magnets. Superconducting magnets had been constructed, but not for accelerator applications, in which the field had to be rapidly increased in precise synchronization with particle acceleration. In 1977 the Laboratory formally proposed to build a superconducting magnet ring. The reason for doing this was to solve the problems of European competition and escalating power costs by adding such a ring to the cascade of accelerators. The main ring would become part of the preaccelerator injection system and would now accelerate particles only to 150 GeV and then transfer them promptly to the new superconducting ring; this could bring the particles up to as high as 1,000 GeV. The estimated power savings were about 40 megawatts, which could easily save $10 million per year at 1980 power costs. Those making the proposal realized that

482

the 1,000 GeV would also be a new energy domain and would be needed because Fermilab and CERN had been exploiting the 400-GeV domain for many years.

The Laboratory worked in close association with many commercial vendors from 1973 to 1978 and made numerous prototype magnets. In 1977 Robert Wilson recognized that mass production was a crucial feature of making a superconducting accelerator. Some 1,000 superconducting magnets, dipoles, and quadrupoles were needed to make a new ring in the same tunnel as the old main ring. The process of assembling these magnets was carried out in a magnet-assembly facility that was directed by Richard Lundy. Stringent quality control and some 20 hours of measurements for each magnet assured a product of acceptable quality. Space for the new ring was found below the old machine.

In 1978 Wilson retired from the directorship of Fermilab, and Leon M. Lederman was designated to replace him. At this time the Laboratory reviewed its options with the U.S. Department of Energy for the exploitation of the new technology. As was traditional, the Laboratory consulted its university-based user community, its PAC, and the URA management organization. What emerged was a three-tiered plant that was collectively called the Tevatron.

In the first phase of the plan, the superconducting ring was constructed. Begun in July 1979, it required the production of 774 dipole magnets (plus about 130 spares), 216 quadrupole magnets, a new radio-frequency acceleration system, and all of the computer-activated controls, utilities, and safety devices that would make it a reliable accelerator. The managers of this program were physicists J. Ritchie Orr and Helen Edwards.

A refrigeration plant was needed for producing liquid helium to keep the 6.3-kilometer (3.9-mile) length of superconducting magnets at a temperature of 4.5 K. This required liquid helium in previously unimaginable

In the tunnel of the antiproton source the magnets at the right comprise the "debuncher ring," where antiprotons produced by bombarding a small, dense target with protons are compacted. The antiprotons are then transferred to the accumulator ring at the left, where they are collected until there are enough to be injected into the main ring in order to collide with protons traveling in the opposite direction.

Fermi National Accelerator Laboratory

quantities. Such a plant was assembled by William Fowler and eventually proved to be extremely reliable. The accelerator was variously referred to as the Energy Saver or Energy Doubler since it was designed to do both.

The second phase was based on the preexisting program of beams of energized particles striking fixed targets. The task was to rebuild all the beam lines and experimental areas so that they could handle the expected energy of nearly 1,000 GeV. All experiments approved after 1980 were required to have capabilities of 1,000 GeV. Construction of this part of the Tevatron program began in 1982. It was managed by Tom Kirk.

The third phase exploited the power of the superconducting machine and a subtle discovery made at CERN. It was called the proton-antiproton collider. The motivation for this discovery is that head-on collisions of high-energy particles are far more violent and, therefore, more interesting than the conventional kind, in which protons hit a nucleus at rest. Antiprotons, the negative twin of protons, could circulate in the superconducting ring in the opposite direction of protons and, if both beams could coexist simultaneously, head-on collisions would take place and be observed.

The challenge centered on the scarcity of antiprotons. These can be produced in high-energy reactions at the level of about one in every 100,000 collisions. Some tens of billions of antiprotons would have to be accumulated for there to be enough to inject into the accelerator complex and accelerate to high energy.

If the required number of antiprotons could be obtained, the experiment would start with two beams of particles, protons and antiprotons, counterrotating in the same vacuum pipe of the Energy Saver. These could be accelerated simultaneously to almost 1,000 GeV and then caused to collide. The Energy Saver would remain at maximum energy for many hours (it takes no power to keep superconducting magnets at high field strength) until the number of collisions per second would deteriorate. The collider with its antiproton source was designed in the 1981–83 period, and actual construction began in 1983. In July 1983 the Energy Saver, phase one of Tevatron, operated successfully. By 1985 phase two, the conventional fixed-target program, was in full operation at 800 GeV. In 1987 the collider, phase three, operated successfully, with 900-GeV protons striking 900-GeV antiprotons. This provided 1,800 GeV, allowing the study of an entirely new domain of physics, more than three times higher than any other accelerator in the world.

To obtain the antiproton source, 120-GeV protons were extracted from the main ring. They then hit a small, dense target from which negative particles, emitted at an energy of almost 8 GeV, were collected. The negative particles were transported to two concentric magnetic rings. Now mostly antiprotons, they were injected into the "debuncher ring," where they were compressed in the space they occupied while circulating rapidly around the ring. The antiprotons were then crowded together and transferred to an accumulator ring, where further compression and accumulation took place. Several million antiprotons were so stored every three or four seconds. After several hours enough antiprotons had

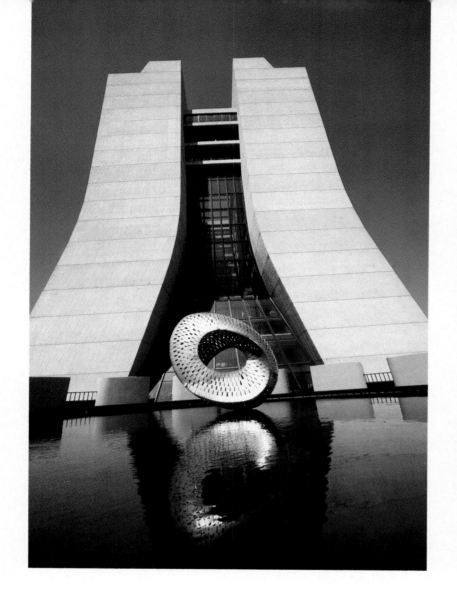

Herd of bison on the grounds of Fermilab (top) spends most of the winter near a barn. Along with a project to restore the native prairie grasses of the area (above), the bison remind visitors of the original appearance of this part of the Middle West.

Photos, Cameramann International, Ltd.

been accumulated that they could be extracted from the accumulator and injected into the main ring, where their direction of revolution was opposite that of protons because of the negative electric charge. In the main ring antiprotons were accelerated from 8 GeV to 150 GeV and transferred to the Energy Saver, where protons had been patiently coasting. Both groups were then accelerated to 900 GeV, after which powerful quadrupole magnets were turned on to squeeze both groups to small, dense bundles. This process greatly increased the probability of a collision as the dense bunches crossed through one another. From January to May 1987 some two billion collisions took place.

Art and ecology

The founding director was not only a skilled accelerator designer but also a professional sculptor with an eclectic taste in art and architecture. Before accepting his appointment, he obtained agreement from the AEC to use a small percentage of the construction funds for aesthetics. The result is a spectacular arrangement of buildings and facilities that form a coherent architectural unity. Water management, required for cooling the magnets, was organized into streams and lakes. A circular waterway delineated the accelerator tunnel, and ponds were constructed that reflect a unique, high-rise central laboratory building. This spectacular structure is patterned on the Beauvais Cathedral in France but was constructed at bargain prices to form a central focus for all the activities spread out over the 2,800-hectare laboratory.

Over the years and with the concurrence of the federal agency that succeeded the AEC, the U.S. Department of Energy, the Laboratory has enhanced its attractiveness and added many ecological features: a bison herd reminds visitors of the original state of this Midwest area, as do a large prairie restoration; flocks of Canada geese, swans, and ducks; and deer and coyotes. In the high rise a changing art show enlightens

486

the staff. An auditorium series, open to the public, brings music, dance, theater, and lectures to the Fermilab audience and its neighbors.

All of this had the purpose of enhancing the attractiveness of the Laboratory for recruitment of scientists and engineers, but it also demonstrated to citizens what a government laboratory associated with "atomic" research can do. An additional feature is the openness of the Laboratory to the general public. Visitors are encouraged; the Laboratory is crisscrossed with bicycle paths, walking trails, and self-guided tours. Many programs are organized to show the work of the Laboratory, and some 30,000 visitors a year come in to see for themselves and also to show their children, the next generation of scientists, what a basic research laboratory looks like.

Outreach activities

Fermilab's mission is to advance knowledge in the area of high-energy physics. Nevertheless, a laboratory that appreciates the deep connections between artistic and scientific creativity can be expected to use its resources for other activities. What follows is an outline of voluntary activities undertaken by the Laboratory and its staff with the help of a private organization, Friends of Fermilab, Inc., and with the cooperation of the Department of Energy:

1. Precollege Science Education. Since 1980 the Laboratory has been host to approximately 300 high-school students per year. Saturday Morning Physics takes 100 students from some 80 high schools in the Chicago suburbs and gives them three hours of lectures and tours on Saturday mornings. The ten-week course is repeated three times during the school year. The structure is informal; the theme: science is fun, science is interesting. Saturday Morning Physics led to Summer Institute for Science Teachers, a four-week program to upgrade the skills of science teachers. The Laboratory then also moved into junior-high programs, videotapes for high-school libraries, and programs for minority high-school students in Chicago.

2. Technology Transfer. The vast and interdisciplinary array of professional talent required for an accelerator laboratory lends itself to the invention of devices that may have commercial use. Fermilab has physicists and resident professionals representing every engineering discipline. Computing science is a ubiquitous laboratory activity. The Fermilab Industrial Affiliates is a group of about 40 companies that keep in touch with developments in the Laboratory, exchange engineers, and attend an annual symposium on technology-transfer topics.

3. Cancer Treatment. The linear accelerator that injects protons into the booster is also used to furnish a beam of 60-MeV neutrons that since 1975 has been used to treat tumors. In 1987 the Laboratory undertook to build a 250-MeV proton synchrotron as a prototype for a hospital-based medical treatment device.

4. Aid to Less Developed Countries. The Laboratory maintains close contacts with professional colleagues in many less developed countries in Latin America. Fermilab in 1987 cosponsored the third Pan American

In a simulation a patient in the neutron therapy facility is prepared for irradiation of the head area. Among Fermilab's voluntary outreach activities is the use of the linear accelerator to furnish beams of neutrons that since 1975 have been used to treat tumors.

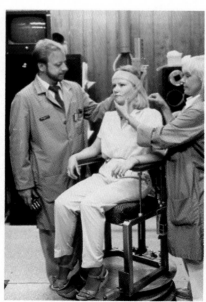

Fermi National Accelerator Laboratory

Symposium on Collaboration in Physics. The objective is to make Fermilab's extensive technical expertise available for the training of Latin-American scientists and engineers. By 1987 some 100 scientists and engineers had availed themselves of this opportunity.

The future

In 1987 the Laboratory possessed the world's highest-energy collider, 1,800 GeV, and the highest-energy fixed-target program, 800 GeV. The Laboratory expected these to increase to close to 2,000 GeV and 1,000 GeV, respectively, by 1990. That situation should then last for the next eight to ten years, and it represents an opportunity and a responsibility.

The collider presents the principal challenge. In order to make more incisive measurements of this new energy domain, it is necessary to examine a very large number of collisions. This is because the probability of producing collisions of great interest is rare. For example, one can calculate that only one collision in a hundred million will produce a W-particle.

If the collider produces 100,000 collisions per second, a W appears every 1,000 seconds. Not all W's are caught and recognized, however, and so only about ten are recorded per hour. An experiment that might require 10,000 W's would, therefore, take most of a year. A not-yet-discovered particle of higher mass may yield only one event in a year's (3,000 hours) worth of data taking. If, however, the collision rate can be improved to one million collisions per second, the collider acquires a new thrust far deeper into the unexplored domain. Thus, Fermilab must work to improve the rate of collisions, that is, the "luminosity," of the collider. An ambitious project was under study in 1987 to improve the luminosity by about 50-fold over the original design. It was estimated that this would take five years. With this new luminosity the Tevatron should be able to examine the point nature of quarks and leptons to a new level of precision and discover whether these are composites of something simpler. The 2,000-GeV collisions of protons and antiprotons would be a powerful searchlight on the microworld.

The fixed-target program will also evolve over the next five years as the physics issues sharpen. Great emphasis is expected to be placed on the bottom quark, the heaviest one so far identified. High-energy collisions produce, in small numbers, a particle (meson) that consists of a bottom quark bound to an "up" quark. The measurement of a large number of these rare and exotic objects would reveal much about the nature of quarks and the strong forces between them.

Finally, this article began with a mention of the SSC. It would be a proton-proton collider with a total energy of 40,000 GeV and has a proposed completion date of the late 1990s. Its technical specifications were inspired by Fermilab's superconducting and colliding experience. Much of the research and development required for the SSC was carried out at Fermilab. By the end of the century the quest for an understanding of the physical universe will have been passed on to the SSC. This is indeed a satisfying future to contemplate.

488

Index

This is a three-year cumulative index. Index entries for review articles in this and previous editions of the *Yearbook of Science and the Future* are set in boldface type, *e.g.,* **Archaeology.** Feature articles appear under the article title and are identified as such. Entries to other subjects are set in lightface type, *e.g.,* radiation. Additional information on any of these subjects is identified with a subheading and indented under the entry heading. Subheadings in quotes refer to feature articles on that topic. The numbers following headings and subheadings indicate the year (boldface) of the edition and the page number (lightface) on which the information appears. The abbreviation "*il.*" indicates an illustration.

> **Archaeology 89**-278; **88**-321; **87**-325
> field research **89**-278
> honors **88**-478
> "New Light on the Maya" **88**-204

All entry headings are alphabetized word by word. Hyphenated words and words separated by dashes or slashes are treated as two words. When one word differs from another only by the presence of additional characters at the end, the shorter precedes the longer. In inverted names, the words following the comma are considered only after the preceding part of the name has been alphabetized. Names beginning with "Mc" and "Mac" are alphabetized as "Mac"; "St." is alphabetized as "Saint." Examples:

> Lake
> Lake, Simon
> Lake Placid
> Lakeland

a

A helix
  fiber diffraction pattern **88**-406
A320
  air transport **87**-457
AACR2: *see* Anglo American Cataloging Rules
AAPG: *see* American Association of Petroleum Geologists
Aaronson, Marc Arnold **89**-434
abalone shell **88**-339
Abell 400 *il.* **87**-330
aberration
  Bradley's discovery **87**-250
ABM: *see* antiballistic missile
abscess
  antiseptic treatment **88**-506
absolute effect
  synesthesia studies **88**-225
Abu Hureyra, Tell (Syr.)
  excavations **89**-279
AC Josephson effect: *see* alternating current Josephson effect
acacia
  environmental concerns **88**-391
accelerator, particle: *see* particle accelerator
accelerator mass spectrometry, *or* AMS
  Old Crow Basin finds **88**-315
accident and safety
  aircraft **89**-306
  automobile brakes **87**-371
  explosives **88**-29
  freight vehicles **89**-409
  wind-change warning **87**-349
  see also disaster
accretion disk
  black hole **87**-19
ACDS: *see* Advanced Combat Direction System
acetylene
  toy chemistry **88**-174
Acheulean industry
  Toth's interpretation **89**-279
achira *il.* **87**-50
acid
  paper deterioration **89**-216, *il.* 220
acid rain
  atmospheric sciences **89**-307; **87**-350
  bacterial control **89**-354
  climatic cooling **88**-388
  deforestation studies **89**-341
acquired immune deficiency syndrome: *see* AIDS
ACRIM, *or* active cavity radiometer irradiance monitor
  solar constant monitoring **89**-76, *il.*
Across North America Tracer Experiment
  atmospheric pollution study **89**-307
Actinomycetales
  anticancer drugs **89**-293
active cavity radiometer irradiance monitor: *see* ACRIM

Active Magnetobarium Particle Tracer Explorers, *or* AMPTE
  artificial comet creation **87**-453
ADA: *see* American Dental Association
ADA deficiency
  treatment **89**-374
Adams, Pat
  painting **89**-25, *ils.* 26
Addra gazelle *il.* **88**-265
adenine **88**-406; **87**-311
adenosine diphosphate, *or* ADP
  Thoroughbred horse physiology **89**-183
adenosine triphosphate, *or* ATP
  animal metabolism **89**-183, *il.* 184
  plant research **88**-399
adiabatics
  truck-engine technology **87**-459
Adler, Alan **87**-434
ADP: *see* adenosine diphosphate
Advanced Combat Direction System, *or* ACDS **89**-305
Advanced Land 1 **88**-24
Advanced Orbital Test System, *or* AOTS **88**-26
Advanced Tactical Aircraft, *or* ATA **89**-302
Advanced Tactical Fighter, *or* ATF **89**-302; **88**-345; **87**-344, *il.* 345
Advanced Technology Bomber, *or* ATB **87**-346
Advanced Train Control System: *see* automatic train control
Advanced Turboprop transport, *or* ATP **87**-459
Advanced Very High Resolution Radiometer, *or* AVHRR **87**-362
AEC: *see* Atomic Energy Commission
aeolian process
  planetary gradation **88**-70
aerobie
  aerodynamic principles **87**-435, *il.* 434
aerodynamics
  flying disks **87**-434
  kite research **87**-143
Aerosat
  European space program **88**-10
aerosol
  greenhouse effect **88**-348; **87**-352
aerospace plane
  defense research **88**-342, *il.*
  speed and takeoff *il.* **87**-457
African swine fever **88**-430
Afrotarsius: *see* tarsier
AFT (Ire.): *see* National Agricultural Research Institute
Agar, Thomas A.
  dinosaur research **89**-360
Ageline (data base)
  information services **89**-330
Ageotropum
  hydrotropism studies **87**-400
aging
  interstellar travel **88**-513
  memory research **89**-398
  psychological studies **87**-445
  see also senior citizen

"Agricultural Biotechnology: Strategies for National Competitiveness" (sci. pub.) **89**-346
agricultural experiment station system (U.S.) **88**-393
agriculture: *see* Food and agriculture
Agriculture, U.S. Department of, *or* USDA
  crop-price lowering **87**-392
  information services **88**-375
  meat prices **89**-344
  research data base **89**-330
  veterinary medicine **89**-381; **88**-428
"Agritechnology: Building a Better Plant" (feature article) **88**-101
Agrivideotel **88**-376
Agrobacterium tumefaciens **89**-351; **88**-399
AGS: *see* Alternating Gradient Synchrotron
AHA: *see* American Heart Association
AHA: *see* applied historical astronomy
AI: *see* artificial intelligence
AIDS, *or* acquired immune deficiency syndrome
  dental diagnosis **89**-167
  feline retrovirus similarities **89**-381
  global population influence **89**-341
  medical research **89**-375; **88**-422; **87**-423
  oral lesion linkage **87**-426
  prevention efforts **89**-401
  recombinant DNA research **89**-356
AIDS-associated retrovirus, *or* ARV **87**-426
Aika, Ken-ichi **88**-337
Aimes, Andrew **88**-375
air conditioning
  OTEC source possibilities **89**-110
Air Force (U.S.)
  computerized cockpit **89**-328
  defense research **89**-302; **88**-342; **87**-344
  electronic systems **88**-374
  military transport **87**-457
air pollution: *see* pollution
air shower **87**-432
air transport, *or* aircraft: *see* aviation
airfoil sail **87**-146
Airy, Sir George Biddell **87**-253
albedo **89**-308
alcohol **88**-329
  breast cancer link **89**-373
aldicarb **87**-89
aldosterone **87**-411
Aldridge, Bill G. **88**-468
alegría (food mix) **87**-49
Aleksandrov, Aleksandr
  space travel **89**-404
Aleut-Eskimo languages **88**-314
Alfvén wave
  solar corona **89**-79
algae
  bacteria consumption **88**-405
  botanical research **89**-351, 352
  hazardous-waste elimination **87**-341
  oceanographic botany **87**-401
  scallop devastation **89**-317
  see also individual genera and species by name
Ali, Salim **89**-434
Ali ibn Ridwan **87**-36
alkaloid
  bitter taste **88**-74
alkene
  catalytic hydration **88**-329
Allen, Clabon Walter **89**-434
Alliant Computer Systems Corp.
  FX/8 model computer **89**-324
alloy **89**-368
"Almagest," *or* "He mathematike syntaxis" (Ptolemy) **87**-31
alpha-2 interferon **88**-421
alpha-A interferon **88**-421
Alpha Centauri, *or* Rigil Kent **88**-511
alpine region
  stone circles **89**-88
alternating current Josephson effect, *or* AC Josephson effect
  instrumentation **89**-140
Alternating Gradient Synchrotron, *or* AGS **89**-439
  Fermilab comparisons **89**-476
Altman, Lawrence K.
  U.S. science policy **89**-417
alum, *or* aluminum potassium sulfate
  papermaking **89**-216
aluminum
  alloy development **89**-368
  explosives manipulation **89**-118, 124
  lake pollution treatment **87**-387
  ocean thermal energy conversion **89**-106
  tenfold symmetry **87**-443
  zeolite composition **87**-210
aluminum-26
  gamma-ray line **89**-287
aluminum phosphate **87**-223
aluminum potassium sulfate: *see* alum
aluminum sulfate: *see* papermaker's alum

Alvarez, Luis **88**-350
  mass extinction theory **89**-359
Alvarez, Walter **89**-359
"Alvin" (submersible) *il.* **88**-361
Alzheimer's disease **89**-374
amaranth **87**-48, *il.* 51
Amazon Boundary Layer Experiment
  atmospheric research **89**-308
Amazon River region (S.Am.)
  deforestation problems **89**-346; *il.* **87**-389
  forest system studies **89**-308
  health program **89**-235
Amblyseus fallacis *il.* **87**-96
"Ambroise Vollard" (paint.)
  Cubism *il.* **89**-21
American Association of Petroleum Geologists, *or* AAPG **89**-309
American Association of Retired Persons **89**-330
American Association of Retired Veterinarians **89**-380
American Association of Zoological Parks and Aquariums **89**-244
American Cyanamid **88**-108
American Dental Association, *or* ADA **89**-376
American Heart Association, *or* AHA
  dietary recommendations **89**-347; **88**-397
  medical advances **88**-422
American Indian, *or* Native American
  "Lost Crops of the Incas" **87**-42
  microlivestock raising **89**-200
  Nash's applied anthropology **89**-276
  "New Light on the Maya" **88**-204
  Tierra del Fuego field research **89**-238
"American Landscape" (paint.)
  Precisionism *il.* **89**-22
American Mobile Veterinary Association **89**-380
American Physical Society, *or* APS
  U.S. science policy **89**-416
American Psychological Association **89**-400
"American Psychologist" (journ.) **89**-398
American Telephone & Telegraph (Co., U.S.): *see* AT&T
American Veterinary Medical Association, *or* AVMA **89**-378; **88**-428; **87**-426
Americas **88**-313
Amerind languages **88**-314
Amiga microcomputer *il.* **87**-368
amino acid
  dissociation with lasers **87**-182
  electron transfer research **88**-335
  molecular biology **88**-407; **87**-405
ammonia
  electride salt synthesis **88**-329
  nitrogen fixation **88**-337; **87**-341
amorphous carbon **89**-395
amphibian
  urban adaptation **87**-76
Amphipithecus mogaungensis **87**-409
AMPTE: *see* Active Magnetobarium Particle Tracer Explorers
AMS: *see* accelerator mass spectrometry
An Foras Talúntais (Ire.): *see* National Agricultural Research Institute
Anabaena **87**-405, *il.* 406
anaerobic bacteria **88**-39
Anchorage International Airport (Alsk., U.S.) **88**-354
Anders, Mark H.
  dinosaur research **89**-360
andrimid
  isolation **89**-294
Andromeda Galaxy, *or* M31 **87**-22
anesthesia
  dentistry **89**-168, 376
ANF: *see* atrial natriuretic factor
ANFO
  rock blasting **89**-120
  tunneling **88**-142
anger
  heart disease linkage **88**-449
angiogenin **87**-410
angle of attack
  kite flying **87**-146
Anglo American Cataloging Rules, *or* AACR2 **88**-377
angular momentum **88**-440; **87**-440
angular resolution **87**-266
Anik
  space shuttle launch **87**-448
animal: *see* zoology
animal art
  Upper Paleolithic **89**-40, *ils.* 42, 45, 46
animal behavior **89**-362
  captive environment breeding **88**-255
  Lincoln Park Zoo **88**-260
  primate societies **87**-59
  volunteer fieldwork **89**-232
animal breeding, *or* animal husbandry
  San Diego Zoo **88**-244
animal communication
  cliff swallows **88**-410
  primates **87**-64

Acknowledgments

68, 73, 75 Illustrations by Anne Hoyer Becker

101 (Bottom) Adapted from information obtained from the U.S. Department of Energy

103 Illustrations by John Draves

144–145, 149 Illustrations by Marta Lyall

242 Courtesy, CERN

297 From "Millisecond X-ray Diffraction and the First Electron Density Map from Laue Photographs of a Protein Crystal," J. Hajdu, P. A. Machin, J. W. Campbell, T. J. Greenhough, I. J. Clifton, S. Zurek, S. Gover, L. N. Johnson, and M. Elder, reprinted by permission of *Nature*, vol. 329, no. 6135, September 10, 1987, cover, copyright © Macmillan Magazines Limited

422 (Bottom) Xinhua News Agency

Now there's a way to identify all your fine books with flair and style. As part of our continuing service to you, Britannica Home Library Service, Inc. is proud to be able to offer you the fine quality item shown on the next page.

Booklovers will love the heavy-duty personalized embosser. Now you can personalize all your fine books with the mark of distinction, just the way all the fine libraries of the world do.

To order this item, please type or print your name, address and zip code on a plain sheet of paper. (Note special instructions for ordering the embosser). Please send a check or money order only (your money will be refunded in full if you are not delighted) for the full amount of purchase, including postage and handling, to:

Britannica Home Library Service, Inc.
Attn: Yearbook Department
Post Office Box 6137
Chicago, Illinois 60680

(Please make remittance payable to: Britannica Home Library Service, Inc.)

IN THE BRITANNICA TRADITION OF QUALITY...

PERSONAL EMBOSSER

A mark of distinction for your fine books. A book embosser just like the ones used in libraries. The 1½″ seal imprints "Library of _____" (with the name of your choice) and up to three centered initials. Please type or print clearly BOTH full name (up to 26 letters including spaces between names) and up to three initials.
Please allow six weeks for delivery.

Just **$20.00**

plus $2.00 shipping and handling

This offer available only in the United States.
Illinois residents please add sales tax

 Britannica Home Library Service, Inc.